MEANING AND SALVATION
IN
RELIGIOUS STUDIES

STUDIES

IN THE HISTORY OF RELIGIONS

(SUPPLEMENTS TO *NUMEN*)

EDITED BY

M. HEERMA VAN VOSS • E. J. SHARPE • R. J. Z. WERBLOWSKY

XLVI

MEANING AND SALVATION
IN
RELIGIOUS STUDIES

LEIDEN
E. J. BRILL
1984

MEANING AND SALVATION
IN
RELIGIOUS STUDIES

BY

DOUGLAS JAMES DAVIES

LEIDEN
E. J. BRILL
1984

ISBN 90 04 07053 2

PRINTED IN THE NETHERLANDS BY E. J. BRILL

CONTENTS

ACKNOWLEDGEMENTS

Whilst it is but a small token of gratitude to mention those who have contributed to the research lying behind this book such acknowledgement does offer the reader a glimpse of those influences which have affected its author.

A Social Science Research Council Studentship held at the Oxford Institute of Social Anthropology enabled me to engage in a study of Mormon religion. Dr. Bryan Wilson of All Souls supervised that work in an exemplary way which resulted in more than a mere study of sects. Among former teachers in both anthropology and theology at Durham Professor Eric Sunderland read an early draft of this manuscript, while Professor John Rogerson's interdisciplinary work has been an encouragement to my own. I would also thank Professor R. J. Zwi Werbloswky for critical comments and E. J. Brill for accepting this book for publication in the NUMEN monograph series.

Nottingham University has been generous in helping to finance this publication as well as accepting an earlier version of it for a doctor's degree. The University also granted me sabbatical leave in India where I was welcomed by the members of the Punjabi University Religious Studies Department. The British Academy also aided that period of study.

The Theology Department at Nottingham University has provided opportunity for varied teaching within an atmosphere of research and discussion. In particular Sister Charles Murray's support has been constant and her theological appreciation of anthropological issues constructively critical. To Professor John Heywood Thomas I owe more than can be expressed in a passing comment, both as a former teacher and as a colleague. From him and Mair Heywood Thomas has come the joy of friendship and the advice of sound judgement: dim meddyg fel cyfaill.

I would finally thank my mother and father for their perpetual trust and encouragement through the years of study marked by this volume which was largely completed by 1982 and which I dedicate to them.

D. J. DAVIES

INTRODUCTION

How does the human drive for meaning come to express itself as a need of salvation? In an attempt to answer this question two rather different kinds of data have been incorporated into the following chapters. The one is historical and looks at the way theories have developed and changed within the broad field of religious studies. In particular we trace the rise and fall of evolutionary ideas and the subsequent emergence of what we might call the model of meaning. This theoretical study tries to show how many varied disciplines concerned with man have tended towards a relatively unified perspective in the second half of the twentieth century, and suggests a definition of salvation which would possess a wide application and which is not dependent upon any one specific religious ideology. The other data drawn upon deal with actual religious events and ideas in the life of particular cultures. Here we relate phenomena belonging to preliterate societies to those drawn from the culture of Sikh and Mormon populations. One major reason for linking these groups lies in the theoretical assumption that salvation processes are as universal as the drive for meaning, and that the traditional distinction drawn between so called primitive and advanced religions was misleading being grounded in the presuppositions of evolutionism.

While it is as impossible as it is undesirable to separate theoretical discussion and practical description of religious things we have sought to clarify the argument of the book by dividing it into two major parts. The first five chapters constitute an analysis of theoretical developments in the anthropology, sociology, history, and phenomenology of religion, while chapters six to eight offer more concrete examples of religious life and salvation processes. In the conclusion we move to a possible solution of that question of meaning and salvation with which we begin our explorations.

But we begin with the fact that the nineteenth century was one in which religion was much discussed, adopted and abandoned and taken up anew by a variety of thinkers. The critical study of religion as a major aspect of life quickly assumed a priority among intellectuals which it had scarcely ever been given before, for all of a sudden the theory of evolution seemed to provide both a key to open the mysteries of religion and a motivation to engage in their unlocking. Theologians had been hard at work on the bible and some of them, especially the Germans, had cast serious doubt on the traditional stories of creation and of Adam and Eve in the divine garden. If the theologians were in the process of losing certainty about religious origins others were just catching a vision of how to gain insight into the beginnings of man's spiritual endeavours. It was as though exciting discoveries about man had passed from the theologians to this new group of scholars stimulated by that philosophical ideal of progress recharged and redirected by the pragmatic discoveries of biology. This company of historians, philologists, philosophers and classical scholars set about unearthing the stages through which mankind had passed in its supposed rise from insignificance to a lofty maturity at the pinnacle of cosmic development. Though many of the findings of these men have been shown to be worthless they at least mark out unfruitful paths and suggest to us the power of theory in the task of interpreting immense amounts of material belonging to the religious world of mankind. Indeed E. J. Sharpe in his excellent history of comparative religion neatly suggests that the whole field is precisely an accumulation of material in search of a method.[1]

In the following chapters we will look at some of the conclusions arrived at by that generation of scholars, as enshrined in terms like totemism and animism which have become part of the general vocabulary of western thought. But despite the immense and apparent progress made in the study of religion in the last third of the nineteenth century there soon set in a loss of impetus and interest as the idea of evolution lost power as part of an all embracing explanation of things in the early years of the twentieth century. Some indeed see the Boer War as having initiated the decline in evolutionary optimism in the philosophical world. One of the great British Victorians, Bishop Charles Gore, is reported as having preached on the last day of the nineteenth century 'a most despondent sermon on the hollowness of modern progress'.[2] While evolutionary thought obviously remained of critical importance for the natural sciences: psychologists, anthropologists, philosophers and linguists all tended to wander into their own increasingly distinctive methods and theories. This is one important reason why books about religion written after the second world war spend some considerable time in spelling out various approaches to religion.

In this book we argue that the period between about 1910 and 1960, with a margin of say a decade around these somewhat arbitrary dates, was one lacking any unified theory by which to approach religious phenomena. But that the latter part of the twentieth century resembles the latter part of the nineteenth inasmuch as there has emerged a general concept powerful enough to match that of evolution which, in a sense, it now replaces.

This approach focuses upon the concept of meaning as that which best identifies the nature of human activity within the world. Starting with a general view of man as an animal engaged in creating significant realms of communication with his fellows we are enabled to pass from the domain of ordinary behaviour to that distinctive aspect of life deemed to be religous. An immediate benefit deriving from this perspective is that the problem of defining religion besomes less acute, for if we are genuinely helped to see how mundane concerns are related to so called religious activity which often bears an other-worldly component then the pursuit of pure essences becomes less pressing. The model of meaning places mundane and supernatural concerns on a continuum of significance as far as the student of religion is concerned. Actual religious believers will invest different levels of explanation and significance with qualitatively varied status, but as far as the theoretical assumptions of this book are concerned all explanations partake in a basically similar motivation and drive. So the question 'what must I do to be saved?', which lies at the heart of the so called world religions, is presumed to be present although unvoiced in these terms in every culture. Accordingly we will find ourselves pursuing

---

[1] Sharpe, E. J., 1975: 2.
[2] Elliot-Binns, L. E., 1946: 357.

the theme of man's dissatisfaction with the world as he finds it and the corresponding human attempt at transforming that world. In other words the problem of evil and the process of salvation are interpreted by means of the concept of meaning and the human drive for meaning.

It will be immediately apparent that this is not a theological approach. It does not start from certain assumptions about God nor are words given theological significance. In fact the very term salvation is invested with a meaning that is derived from a phenomenological background. The importance of doing this lies in the need for neutral terms in the task of comparative religious study. To say this is not to deride any particular kind of theology, indeed it may even serve the purpose of engaging in a preparatory exercise opening the way for theological explorations of soteriology. For it is the case that both theologians and, for example, anthropologists are concerned with epistemology, a concern which manifests itself in a distinctively different way in the two traditions and which may be characterized by the processes of revelation and projection. Both terms point to the question of knowledge and access to knowledge, they also raise the issue of validity of whatever knowledge has been acquired.

This divergent view is not without representation in the field of religious studies as such and has been typified by J. A. Saliba as the contrast between the 'descending' approach of the historian of religion and theologian and the 'ascending' approach of the anthropologist and sociologist.[3] Most views can be placed in one or other type depending on whether divine impulses are thought to originate in God or in man. But too simple an ascription of ideas to one or other of these realms could be harmful in theology and would not always be beneficial in the non-theological study of religion as the more phenomenologically orientated scholars attest.

It is somewhat ironic that one of the clearest exponents of projection was the nineteenth century German philosopher-theologian Ludwig Feuerbach who thought that theology should be replaced by a philosophical anthropology because the essence of theology was simply a projected idea about man. By means of some mechanism which he never explained Feuerbach believed the mystery of religion to consist in the fact that 'man projects his being into objectivity and then again makes himself an object to this projected image of himself thus converted into a subject'.[4] On the basis of this he believed that 'religion is man's earliest and most indirect form of self-knowledge', while the apparent object of knowledge, the divine being, is in fact 'nothing less than the human being freed from the limits of the individual, made objective'.[5] This philosophical argument resembles the explanation of human thought offered by the French sociologist Emile Durkheim for whom it was the whole society and not simply the self that is projected as the notion of God. So too evil beings are 'nothing other than collective states objectified: they are society itself seen under one of its aspects'.[6] Not only in his book *The Elementary Forms of the Religious Life* published in 1915, but in an earlier work written with Marcel Mauss entitled *Primitive Classification* he sought to show how

---

[3] Saliba, J. A., 1976: 41.
[4] Feuerbach, L., 1957: 29.
[5] Ibid., p. 14.
[6] Durkheim, E., 1976: 412.

man's classifying of things in the world was influenced by social experience.[7]

It is interesting to note as a contrasting methodological approach that Max Weber's sociology of religion which dates from the nineteen twenties hardly concerns itself at all with the idea of projection. Instead he emphasizes the process of analogy in the human anthropomorphizing of deities, and even when he does fleetingly refer to projection it is more part of his descriptive endeavour in the construction of ideal types than in any explanatory move.[8]

Another book of 1913 advanced a theory of projection which was to be of longstanding influence. This was *Totem and Taboo* written as a psychological study by Sigmund Freud. Freud used the term projection in two ways, a general sense suggested that man 'turns his emotional cathexes into persons, he peoples the world with them and meets his internal mental processes again outside himself.'[9] This view of exteriorization sees man as reckoning to talk about God whilst all the while he really speaks of himself. The more technical use of projection in Freud supposes that an individual transposes to another person hostility he feels towards himself or to some aspect of his personal thought or action. In another book, *The Future of an Illusion*, Freud went on to argue that the idea of God is itself an externalized personification of human wish-fulfilment.[10] So just as Feuerbach questioned the validity of theological statements Freud too believed that assertions about God were essentially statements about man.

It is quite easy to brush aside these theories as purely reductionist explanations which turn the highest truths of mankind into nothing but the products of an over-worked or pathological mind. It would be quite unwise to adopt an ill-conceived methodological superiority on this issue as can easily be done by theologians and some historians of religion, for behind the exaggerated claims of projectionist explanation lies a sound point concerning human thought. We will have to return to this issue again when discussing symbolism towards the end of the book, but some preliminary remarks must be made now.

The key point is that speech itself is a type of projection. It is an externalization of thought such that ideas come to expression instead of remaining dormant and perhaps ill-formed in the mind. This is not the place to engage in the philosophical and linguistic debate over the relation of thought and speech but the point must be made that whatever doctrine is held it must be agreed that speech is intrinsically related to thought and can be seen as the manifestation of thought in a different plane. This line of argument is as old as the Stoics and their notion of logos or wisdom immanent in God and as externalized in creation.[11]

In terms of the model of meaning we can view man as possessing a drive to express himself and to assert something that has appeared to him to be true. Analogies, stories, parables and so on all continue the process of externalizing individual insight and mark human creativity in forming endless variations of ideas through the recombination of learned units of language. Projection cannot be denied as an

[7] Durkheim, E. and Marcel Mauss, 1963.
[8] Weber, Max, 1922.
[9] Freud, Sigmund, 1960: 92.
[10] Freud, Sigmund, 1928.
[11] The distinction between λογος ἐνδιαθετος and λογος προφορικός.

aspect of thought and speech, but that is not to say that all human utterances are solely about mankind. Once external objects or events are used in the process of thought formation and expression in language we have to inquire into the influence exerted upon ideas by those very objects. In one non-theological sense it is possible to speak of revelation as the inherent restraints of an external source incorporated into thought by human beings. Once seen in this way it becomes clearer that projection and revelation are not as unrelated as might at first be thought. This is also to make a positive contribution to the debate between theology and the social sciences over the question of the nature of knowledge. It is not insignificant to note that the expression 'saving knowledge' which can be interpreted theologically in terms of soteriology, is also quite intelligible in the domain of the sociology of knowledge as we shall argue in a moment.[12] Both the disciplines of theology and sociology know that their real concern is with the question of meaning even if their respective frames of reference differ. But as we will show later in this book the model of meaning is able to provide a higher order reference than is available to specific disciplines and by means of this can afford a basis for genuine intercourse between them.

Of course it is the case that the very word 'meaning' is not without its own problems of clarity. No clearer statement about this can be found than in C. K. Ogden and I. A. Richards' book on *The Meaning of Meaning* which took up the theme of meaning in the varied realms of philosophy, psychology and linguistics. Their conclusion was that the word should be abandoned for the time being precisely because of its diverse significance and potentially confusing effect. But Ogden and Richards wrote in the nineteen twenties and perhaps it is now quite possible to return to the question of meaning in a distinctively new way which will increase clarity and further interdisciplinary work. This is what we are attempting throughout the book and will bring to an explicit formulation at its close.

Our emphasis on meaning may be seen as an example of what Thomas Kuhn called a paradigm, or a basic model directing the way we think about and approach particular academic problems. In his influential work on the structure of scientific revolutions Kuhn shows how scholars become increasingly orthodox until a series of theoretical questions arise and bring about a shift from that conservative interpretation to a radically different one. In the second edition of his book Kuhn clarified the idea of paradigm so as to distinguish between a general intellectual consensus about problems on the one hand, and particular theories or principles adopted as the basis of this consensus on the other.[13] In the following pages our recourse to a general theory of communication will be the equivalent of the broad intellectual perspective or paradigm, this is the paradigm of meaning, while the more specific element is what will be called plausibility theory. It is this theory of plausibility which will be utilized in the central discussion on salvation as a human phenomenon.

Although we have argued so far that the difference between the nineteenth and twentieth century approach to religious studies is considerably different this is not

---

[12] Cf. David Martin et al., 1980 on the alliance and conflict between sociology and theology.
[13] Kuhn, T. S., 1970.

to say that vital developments did not originate in the earlier period. Indeed it would be impossible for us to proceed any further without taking up the original work of Wilhelm Dilthey who from about 1880 until 1910 devoted himself to expounding the need for a true science of human culture as distinct from the science of natural phenomena. His preoccupation with meaning (bedeutung) is reflected in our later discussion while his interest in the task of interpretative understanding of phenomena underlies the sections devoted to hermeneutics.[14] Our goal is to extend one particular aspect of Dilthey's argument, for whereas he is quite clear on the point that 'meaning is the comprehensive category through which life can be understood'[15] we go on to analyse the way in which systems of meaning come to be invested with religious attributes. The concern lies with a phenomenology of the attributes of idea or meaning systems and in particular with those attributes believed to possess saving power.

The question is whether there is any distinctive difference between what might be called order and super-order, that is, between meaning and salvation? At what point and under what circumstances does an order of meaning attain the significance of an order of salvation? The same question might be posed negatively in asking why established forms of explanation come to be seen as unsatisfactory? Of course these are issues of the highest magnitude and we can only hope to go a little way towards offering some adequate treatment. Yet it is our belief that something positive can be said in this direction under the direction of the paradigm of meaning.

In answering these very questions it would be easy to adopt a simple sociological explanation and talk of changed circumstances and altered needs. But this will not do, for the very fact that one answer to life's hardships comes to be replaced by another leads to a definite historical awareness which sets potential and former answers in a series of solutions to human ills. As one ideology, myth or theology replaces former creeds it itself becomes potentially redundant. As human horizons expand so does the need of salvation sought. To borrow a comment from Aldous Huxley it could be said that 'when there is a change in the being of the knower there is a corresponding change in the nature and amount of knowing'.[16] In other words both historical and theological elements must be given full weight in any sociological analysis. It is doubtless true that altered social conditions bring about changes which call for a higher level of salvation than had hitherto obtained, but this thought should not be used as the basis for a further reductionist argument.[17] In a real sense there is a cumulative demand for explanation capable of explaining the failure of its predecessors and the power of its own claim to supremacy. There are orders of salvation in terms of a hierarchy of explanation with ethnic and preliterate religions affording a relatively low degree and the world religions a relatively high degree of explanatory power. Care must be taken in interpreting this assertion because we are not lapsing into the evolutionist assumption that low levels of thought exist amongst the primitives and high levels amongst the advanced

---

[14] Dilthey, Wilhelm, 1883, 1894, 1905, 1911.
[15] Rickman, H. P., 1976: 235. Cf. Rickman 1979 for a sound appreciation of Dilthey and the notion of Geisteswissenschaften.
[16] Huxley, Aldous, 1947: 1.
[17] Wach, Joachim, 1944 cap. V.

members of imperial societies. Rather we are making a much more pragmatic and obvious point, namely that the religions which exist in one small and relatively isolated community will not possess the same ability in providing explanations for very many human and cultural features as found in those traditions which have encountered many cultures and peoples in the past. This is almost a truism but it does stress the importance of the explicit historical dimension.

As cultures meet and interact questions of salvation come to be questions about competing explanatory systems. But whether resulting from such competitive explanations or from the creative insights of religious virtuosi salvation is experienced as a scheme offering the highest available validation of life and thought, and as something able to confer a strong sense of identity.

The concept of identity is theoretically important because it serves as a restraint upon a too strict sociological analysis. Once identity as a psychological feature is admitted into the discussion the individual also enters the picture and limits the fall into an extreme sociological reductionism. Identity also contributes a dynamic and emotional element to the sense of meaning and is an inevitable dimension to soteriological discourse. The sociology of knowledge itself tends to overemphasize rational components of meaning so benefits from an inclusion of the concept of identity which roots meaning in the individual. Although identity has only recently gained any popular attention in religious studies its essential aspects occupy a central place in Dilthey's approach to the study of human and cultural material or *Geisteswissenschaft*.

When Dilthey says that 'meaning is related to the totality of the knowing subject' he is virtually equating the totality of the individual with the notion of identity.[18] Indeed he criticizes the idealized individuals lying at the heart of Locke, Hume, and Kant's philosophies. There is no red blood in their veins for it has been withdrawn and replaced by the diluted juice of reason. Such actors will not serve the human part as far as Dilthey is concerned, he requires the dimension of personal individuality alongside interpersonal relations and the sense of an eternal world. Man's sense of meaning comes to him as one possessing a body in relation to other bodies, and as one driven by the constant flux of external change to seek an inner strength.

Dilthey did not develop this particular notion of strength but we will pursue it here so as to provide a basis for the notion of identity and also as one manifestation of the concept of power to which we return in a moment. The inner strength of an individual is, we may suppose, closely related to his identity as a religious being and therefore to his state of salvation. Such an individual must remain a clear focus of discussion in religious studies and should not be allowed to vanish beneath other emphases upon the social level of life. There is a perpetual dialectic between individual and society and in one area this reaches significant proportions in the present context, namely in the conflict between the pressure arising within individuals as a result of their fear of death and extinction on the one hand, and the socially approved and provided comforts in the face of decease on the other. At least both Dilthey and Peter Berger take death as a major force acting upon the construction of religious belief, for the former it is the fact of death that drives man to seek to

---

[18] Rickman, H. P., 1976: 233.

make both death and life comprehensible, for life itself possesses a grief resulting from a sense of its own finitude. As we will see in the study of Mormonism the dynamics of death can be handled in such a way as to make it much less an existentially awesome phenomenon than seems to be the case in the hypotheses of the more traditional existential philosophers and theologians. Although Dilthey did not of course use the terminology of systems theory which was to emerge some fifty years later his attention is similarly focused upon the relation between self and society and those factors working towards the integrity and dissolution of the individual.[19] Indeed integrity of self is but another way of referring to salvation as we will define it later. Dilthey's model of man is grounded in what could be called the expansion and contraction of the self under personal or social pressures. There exists a perpetual qualitative change in the state of the self as some relationships increase its sense of existence and happiness and others work towards a decrease. He refers to his power being heightened or drained by the varied encounters of life. Whatever the actual dynamics of the self and personality are in relation to these influences it is the social dimension that will be emphasized throughout the following chapters. Salvation does indeed possess resonances within individual minds otherwise it would hardly be worthy of attention but in any comparative study it must necessarily be the group formulation that takes priority. While doctrines remain the result of consensus it cannot be assumed that they are adopted by individuals in any univocal sense.

Here then Dilthey provides one intriguing suggestion as to how salvation ideas come to be held firm by religious devotees, who themselves have to discriminate between options of explanation available to the flux-confronted self. In some societies there will be but little option as traditional modes pass from age to age, but in others there will be something of an open market for ideologies.[20] Once choice becomes available then it is quite reasonable to talk of the adaptive significance of beliefs and religious communities. For the separation of religious institutions from the other institutions of a society as has taken place in very many economically advanced societies means that persons or groups can seek a faith which suits them. The adaptive significance of a religion can thus be distinguished from the adaptive capacity of an entire social complex of institutions.

In terms of identity, salvation can therefore be discussed as a form of self-perception involving a maximization of meaning in a world of competing explanatory schemes. And along with the maximization of meaning will be found an increase of inner strength or integrity. Dilthey in fact came close to the heart of what we presume to be an essential human phenomenon, one that does not possess the advantage of an established name but which can be clearly seen in van der Leeuw's phenomenology of religion and in the desire for contact with power. Van der Leeuw's major stress lies on power as the essence of religion as man encounters it, it is a word of many meanings or manifestations. His entire study spells out this variation and it is unnecessary to itemize the spheres of power again, but it will be

---

[19] Wansbrough, J., 1978: 132. Focuses on Islamic salvation history in terms of the relation of individual and epistemology.

[20] B. R. Wilson, 1976, deals indirectly with this under the expression of new missions to old believers.

beneficial to look at apparently non-religious examples of the same thing. We can but indicate the broad field here and say that power exists, phenomenologically speaking, on a continuum. The particular social structure and cosmology will to a large degree influence the mode of its appearance. Power may be vested in a political figure, a monarch, a religious leader or in some form of corporation like a parliament, army, university, church or family. Taking van der Leeuw's dictum that 'everything can be a power bearer' we apply it to apparently non-religious aspects of life.[21] We say 'apparently' because as already indicated there is a continuum from the profane pole to the opposite one of the holy and the precise point at which the sacred ascription is given to an experience will vary.

Status is to be gained by the individual as a result of access to or association with these power points, and this can increase his sense of identity. Similarly, if his desired approach to the loci of power is thwarted he will fall in his own esteem and possibly in that of his peers. The religious experience of salvation involves a parallel idea of access to that power which increases the individual's sense of significance and worth. Whether the experience involves a profound emotional element or whether a ritual alteration of status as in a rite of passage lies at the heart of the change, the important fact is the recognition of a changed identity. In any event status and affect will inevitably feedback upon each other.

While particular cultural systems will afford models of power which religious movements can adopt at will, and while specific anthropomorphisms will usually reflect social ideals, it is quite possible for the religious imagination to invert such images or otherwise transform them into quite diverse patterns, or to move into a diametrically opposed scheme of thought. If contradiction emerges there may well be a direct competition between religious and state ideologies as in many movements of religious protest. A somewhat similar point is made by Max Weber in his sociology of religion where he refers to the 'awareness of the perfection of life pattern' and to the 'underived, ultimate and qualitatively distinctive being' found among elite nobilities.[22] Religious imagination is thus wedded to cultural forms but in a way that allows their transcendence through recombination of units to produce novelty. Almost by analogy with biological combination of genetic material one might add that new ideas need not be viable, and it is the harsh realities of the life-world which aid their survival or demise.

Perhaps it would be appropriate to explain at this point why Max Weber's excellent study of salvation in different social groups is only discussed to a limited extent in the following chapters. Primarily it is a question of method and pre-supposition, for while Weber is much devoted to the idea of meaning and intelligibility in human thought and action, largely under the influence of Dilthey, his basic soteriological presupposition is that 'every need for salvation is an expression of some distress', whether it is that of economic oppression of the disprivileged or the psychological reassurance of legitimacy needed by privileged classes.[23] Throughout this book we follow a less evaluative path, talking less of need in distress than of the apparently natural drive for appropriate forms of meaning and

---

[21] Van der Leeuw, G., 1967 section 3: 2.
[22] Weber, Max, 1963: 106.
[23] Ibid., p. 107.

power. This very point resembles Weber in his specific treatment of intellectualism, for he believed that intellectuals possessed 'an inner need to understand the world as a meaningful cosmos'.[24] What he restricted to intellectuals we would broaden and apply to all groups, with the provision that 'understanding' also embraces the affective dimension of life.

Thus the sense of religious salvation is theoretically related to the prestige, status and pleasure gained by persons in the non-religious world. Rudolph Otto's notion of the sense of the numinous is not far removed from the experience within the everyday life-world of an Englishwoman meeting her Queen, an American the President or a teenager his favourite football or pop-star. Such encounters not only involve transcendence of the mundane level of life but also confer some permanent or transitory change in self-evaluation and well-being. It is interesting to note that while Otto stressed the distinct and irreducible nature of the numinous, making it a mental state which is completely *sui generis*, he also argued or at least thought it a necessary possibility to mention that the means by which 'the religious impulse works are very frequently at first of an unspiritual, earthly nature'.[25] Though he appears reluctant to admit that all world religions share in something of a basic nature and process he does make the direct point that an 'impulsion to redemption' seems to lie behind the growth of religious doctrine and experience. In fact he is saying much the same thing as has been argued throughout this introduction, namely that a drive for meaning can exist at lowly and exalted levels of life. Otto talks of the unresting activity and continual urgency of an impulsion to salvation, an impulse manifest in diverse religions and aspects of life.[26] The key to his argument lies in seeing the numinous as a category of value used to describe a particular level of mental awareness, one that emerges only at an advanced stage of religious development. That is to say, the numinous is a qualitative state of mind arising from an underlying impulse in the direction of advanced and higher sensation. There remains an evolutionary trend in Otto's thought which we would eliminate whilst retaining his often ignored concept of the impulse for redemption. The experience of power can occur in practically any context even though its definition as an experience of the holy may be defined differently by any specific theology.

On the negative side an individual or group may experience a diminution in its store of power if access to a power source is withdrawn leaving him or them in a state of potential destruction or damnation. Again we would relate both secular and explicitly religious units of behaviour in this form of deprivation. At one level a sense of homesickness in a traveller resulting from the absence of family and familiar environment affords an example of power loss while at another level the religious person cut off from the means of grace by excommunication, or a group sent into exile away from its cherished sacred space, both manifest similar responses.

The whole sphere of religious ritual and ethics seeks to maintain adequate access to a power source for religious devotees and we shall explore cases of this later with the help of Peter Berger's discussion of plausibility maintaining devices. But it should be noted that the idea of power can itself be expressed quite starkly

---

[24] Ibid., p. 117.
[25] Otto, Rudolph, 1924: 171, 7.
[26] Ibid., p. 23.

as physically perceived energy as in the yogic concept of *tapas* or the Christian Charismatic belief in the outpouring of the Holy Spirit in glossolalia, or again it may adopt a more implicit form as in sacramental doctrines of transubstantiation in classic Roman Catholicism.[27] This power-model facilitates a discussion of competing explanatory or soteriological schemes since the advent of a new system easily leads devotees of former movements to opt for the more compelling or all-embracing system. The appeal will lie in an offer of greater access to power or control of the environment as we will see in the case of cargo-cults. The dynamics of power systems involves the human drive for status and prestige which is assumed to be common to man as Leach once argued in his study of Burmese political systems.[28] The idea of a continuum of power can cope particularly well with the phenomenon of transcendence in its two distinct meanings.

Traditionally transcendence was defined as a quality of the divine, an attribute of the supernatural being, as presupposed in Otto's scheme of religious experience and in Karl Barth's dialectical theology. We shall see a similar case in our chapter on Sikh identity. But another and substantially different approach identifies transcendence with a quality of human life. The teaching of the Buddha is a good example of access to saving power which derives from the individual apart from any supernatural entity. Here transcendence of self is dependent upon a personal spontaneity of insight and not upon any supernaturally revealed truth. Durkheim affords a sociological and Harvey Cox a more theological example of this kind of existentialism.[29] But whether transcendence is defined by those involved as an attribute of God or of the atheist consciousness its essence lies in that perceived access to power which makes for a new self-identity and a sense of power or salvation in life. It is this perception that makes power and salvation necessary correlates in religious studies. It is interesting to see the broad concept of power being utilized once more in these studies as in the case of the anthropologist John Beattie's scheme for interpreting sacrifice. He argues that power can be conceived as individualized and personal or as diffuse and impersonal, while men themselves either seek contact with it or set about avoiding it by ritual means.[30]

As might be expected the one area which has witnessed a fairly constant interest in power has been that of language. The power of words is well represented in van der Leeuw's phenomenology of the preacher and teacher.[31] In anthropology the magical and ritual power of words has a long tradition especially in Malinowski's early work and the later study of S. J. Tambiah. While theologians have been much preoccupied with the entire question of meaning, hermeneutics and semantics, on a scale which cannot be treated simply in passing,[32] it must suffice to say that theology shows its kinship with other intellectual fields of the later twentieth century in acknowledging that it cannot ignore the question of language itself. Once language gains attention as a proper focus of study it is obvious that man

---

[27] Werner, Karel, 1977: 28.
[28] Leach, E. R., 1954.
[29] Cox, Harvey, 1969, 1974.
[30] Beattie, John, in M. C. F. Bourdillon and Meyer Fortes 1980. Cf. D. J. Davies 1982.
[31] Van der Leeuw, G., 1967, 28: I.
[32] Tambiah, S. J., 1968. Ebeling, Gerhard, 1973. Grabner-Haider, Anton, 1973.

himself has attained a state of self-analysis. This is a critical moment for in it man either ceases to be distanced from his mental products or else is enabled to understand them more clearly. The degree of sophistication attained in handling the products of human thought is thus of crucial significance and naturally leads to methodological questions of reductionism. While it might initially be possible to agree with the eighteenth century expression of David Hume that mankind possessed a universal tendency to conceive all beings like themselves and to transfer to every object those qualities with which they are themselves so familiarly aquainted, such a complete notion of anthropomorphic projection would not do justice to the more subtle insights of theology. In the concluding chapter we will return to this question of human creativity.

But now we must ask a direct question which will summarize much of what we have already said and which will clarify some of the assumptions upon which the following chapters rest. The question is whether there is any justification for distinguishing between salvation-religions and other religions? This question can be answered in the affirmative and in the negative, and each of those replies characterizes basic methodological presuppositions. Throughout this book the answer given is that there is no ultimate justification in distinguishing between salvation and non-salvation religions. This requires a word of explanation which will also repeat what has already been said about the status and role of theology vis-à-vis religious studies.

Those who would clearly differentiate between salvation and other forms of religion are likely to do so for one of two reasons. Firstly because they are theologically committed to their own religion and regard other schemes as not affording access to ultimate truth and bliss. This is a theological and devotional reason. Secondly there are those academic students of religion who take the explicit teachings of a religion as the basis for their own classification. Accordingly Christianity, and Hinduism afford clear examples of salvation ideas in most of their sub-traditions, while for example Theravada Buddhism and Confucianism are open to dispute on points of whether they are philosophical, ethical, or religious schemes. And so on from religion to religion and school to school. A good example of this view is found in a collection of studies published as *Man and His Salvation* in 1973.[33] There eminent historians and phenomenologists of religion considered the explicit soteriological motifs of a wide number of religions. Jewish, Iranian, Egyptian, Buddhist, Islamic, and Christian ideas all came in for analysis as the texts, history, and doctrine of respective faiths were scrutinized.

It cannot be denied that the construction of classifications for religions should entertain the explicit doctrinal schemes of the faiths concerned. Indeed this kind of study is vital for any real knowledge of the subtle distinctions made by theologians within their own doctrinal world, let alone for a sound knowledge of the differences between religions. But the task of this book is rather different. It involves the presupposition that implicit factors and motivations underlying theological construction cannot be ignored. Accordingly we assume that all religious phenomena are associated with the process of salvation when that term is interpreted by means of the sociology of knowledge and not in terms of any one specific theology.

---

[33] E. J. Sharpe, and J. R. Hinnells, 1973.

So we answer the leading question by saying that no justification exists for establishing an ultimate divide between religions of salvation and other religions. This presupposition is grounded in the judgement that a social scientific approach to religions cannot be ignored as the starting point for the comparative study of religions. And within that approach it argues that the older evolutionist stance should fully give way to that of sociological phenomenology. In other words we are concerned with the very processes of religious groups and traditions rather than with the specific content of their theologies. And those processes are believed to show a marked similarity in terms of the perception of negative aspects of life and their resolution.

In avoiding the evolutionist preoccupations we sidestep those issues which loomed large in the early debates on salvation as they touched on the status of primitive religions. The typical nineteenth century stance took salvation ideas to be the outcome of long periods of evolution and resulting in the so called higher or world religions. Evolution had affected belief as much as any other human feature, and the majority opinion did not expect to find doctrines of salvation or monotheism in the primitive realm. When Andrew Lang began to argue for the idea of primitive monotheism in 1898 he was in a small minority, but was soon joined by the Americanist Paul Ehrenreich, and a little later by K. T. Preuss.[34] Among other things these were interested in the saviour figures and culture heroes of the North American Indians in their relation to the ultimate deity himself. In a most illuminating passing comment Wilhelm Schmidt, who perhaps became the most ardent supporter of the primitive high god theme, argued that this discussion of soteriology in connection with tribal groups of Indians sprung up because evolutionism was 'shaken off earlier and more emphatically in America than elsewhere'.[35]

We too eschew the evolutionary stance whilst also relegating the avowed content of each religious tradition to a secondary position as far as establishing the notion of salvation is concerned. For when the dominant teaching is taken as the classificatory label of the tradition then we arrive at religions of ancestor worship, of sacrifice for moral transgression, of witchcraft accusation and of trance for the elimination of social friction and psychological malaise. In fact this was the way early anthropologists and nineteenth century students of religions organized their schemes of religious development, taking the dominant concern of the rites and relating them to the equally apparent interests of the higher forms of world religion. But in this book we wish to adopt a different view, one that moves from the apparent and explicit doctrines and expectations of religious behaviour to the implicit function of religious actions. As we show in the detailed consideration of the sociology of knowledge and in the paradigm of meaning, the idea of salvation may be given a significance and content beyond that afforded by the practitioners themselves. If once the definition of salvation put forward is accepted it becomes possible to argue that all religions are salvation religions. This distinction also carries with it a methodological issue for it shows how the phenomenological approach grounded in the sociology of knowledge can focus on essential aspects

---

[34] Lang, A., 1900. Ehrenreich, P., 1906.
[35] Schmidt, W., 1935: 197.

of religious life irrespective of cultural difference between societies, while also emphasizing that the historical, philological, textual, and philosophical dimension of study is of vital significance for any full grasp of the specific content of any one religious tradition. In other words we argue for an interrelating of those beliefs deemed important by a religion in its self-understanding with the more abstract issues of the scholar as he interprets the significance of those beliefs in the overall process of human life. The study of religion involves the construction of categories by which the multitudinous data can be organized and understood, but a major difficulty encountered in arriving at appropriate categories lies in the concepts provided by the religions themselves. As a neutral academic discipline it ill behoves the student of religion to utilize any one theological idea as the basis of classifying other religions. R. C. Zaehner, as but one example, referred to the misleading nature of the word salvation when used of the Hindu concept of *moksha*.[36] It is only at a higher level of analysis than that of juggling with indigenously provided terms that the scholar of religion can attain any truly comparative analysis of religious processes. In this book we argue at a metalevel that all religions are salvation religions including those of tribal and preliterate society. This does not, however, obviate the necessity of drawing on the particular meaning of religious ideas within specific traditions for the purpose of giving an accurate sense of what kind of salvation-religion each one constitutes. There will be salvation-religions which call themselves salvation-religions and which may even go further and label all other religions as leading to damnation, while there will be other forms of religiosity which never ever entertained the idea that salvation was a possibility. Some general theoretical framework will inevitably be used by scholars to relate various religions and to account for their degree of clarity over soteriological issues and religious preoccupations and it is as well to be clear as to the basis of one's own approach. A major concern in this book is to show how the nineteenth century evolutionist scheme did in fact influence the way the so called higher and lower, world and tribal, religions were related to each other. That approach is abandoned in favour of another one grounded in plausibility theory and the sociology of knowledge.

The great emphasis given in subsequent chapters to this idea of plausibility and to the concept of meaning is intended to shift conceptual categories away from those provided by religious traditions themselves, to those made available by the tradition of the social sciences. This is an attempt to respond to Willard Oxtoby's astute observations on the increased use of salvation-religion and saviour figures as categories within the study of religion. He argued that it was the use of terms drawn from committed theological traditions that made for a potential lack of integrity in religious studies. He was drawing attention to the fact that scholars sometimes use words in a neutral way and sometimes in a confessional way, especially in the instance of salvation. His appeal was for a sophisticated and careful use of any word that already bore rich theological connotations. This is certainly the case with salvation. He also underlined the fact that while comparative religion no longer dealt with all religions as being false, nor with only one religion as being

---

[36] Zaehner, R. C., 1963: 218. In S. G. F. Brandon (Ed), 1963.

true, it still needed to decide whether 'all religions are in some sense true'.[37] This book does not answer that final question, for it assumes that questions of truth can only be answered in a confessional way. But what we do seek to assert is that all religions necessarily consist in processes that are universally the same. This is the higher order thesis that man is a meaning maker and utilizes religious processes for the construction of ultimately secure spheres of certainty. On this basis salvation processes are natural to man who is both a meaning maker and a morality former. These are questions of philosophical anthropology.

The precise content of each religious tradition and the potentially true or false status of it is a question that cannot be treated in a work of a non-confessional kind. What we do assume is that the ideas about man and his religious and social worlds which emerge from this study must inevitably be taken up by theologians when they set about evaluating truth claims. Indeed it will be no easy task for them once the complex relation between the form of meaning construction and particular content elements is seen to embrace the universal tendency of man to desire a meaningful world. Which is to say that the status of particular explanations must be viewed in a different light once it is accepted that all particular contents are motivated by the same underlying force of meaning construction. At one level this is quite obvious but in a historical and hermeneutical sense this knowledge of man which has been clarified and brought to clear focus through the phenomenology and sociology of religion and knowledge raises a question of a higher logical order than had hitherto been the case.

It is the very concept of meaning construction as an attribute of man which requires theological explanation, and which needs to be related to the varied cultural and historical contexts within which doctrines have come to birth. Werblowsky has argued cogently for the distinction between that study of religion carried out academically from 'an archimedic point outside religion', and that committed study from within religious groups.[38] And this distinction needs to be made clear for the purpose of critical evaluation of the motivation of authors and their works. Furthermore it is only by knowing where the distinction lies that creative theological thought will be enabled to proceed in its task of generating a theological anthropology. The fact that in this book we adopt a definition of salvation derived from the sociology of knowledge rather than from theology ought not to lead to those intractable debates about definition and the propriety of using a theological term with a transformed significance, rather it should advance the debate to the point at which the theologian questions the significance of this human drive in relation to the assumed divine initiative of redemption. That at least is the author's intention as far as theologians are concerned.

It is with such methodological issues before us that we now turn to an examination of hermeneutical problems involved in the perception of evil and its removal. Again we retain the use of this theologically overtoned word and seek to explore its varied phenomenological significance. First in sociological and anthropological fields and then in the history and phenomenology of religion we attempt to relate

---

37 Oxtoby, W. G., 1973: 37. In E. J. Sharpe, and J. R. Hinnels, 1972.
38 Werblowsky, R. J. Zwi, 1976.

theoretical development and ethnographic data. The goal of the study is to show
how the theological notion of salvation can be understood in a non-theological way,
a way in which the drive for meaning embraces a moral tendency as the individual
comes to a fuller knowledge of himself within a particular culture and society. To
this end we have chosen a variety of religious groups for purposes of exemplification
of our central thesis. Some explanation of this choice might be useful to the reader
and will go some way in revealing the implicit assumptions and predilections of the
author.

In the first part of the book several tribal groups are discussed in connection
with the theme of evil and witchcraft, and these have been adopted because of
their classic status in anthropological literature. This covers the Azande and Nuer
material, while the Mbuti are included as a case which serves to extend the debate
on questions of evil as perceived implausibility. In the second part of the book the
examples of the Sikh and Mormon religions are drawn upon to show how the
difference between western and eastern cultures pales into relative insignificance
once theoretical issues are adopted as of prime concern. This choice of two apparently
diverse movements also indicates my own research interests in the past, having
worked on aspects of religious development in groups of Latter Day Saints and
Sikhs. The material drawn from the literature on Australian Aborigines is added
because of the historical significance of Aborigines in the development of the
Durkheimian tradition of interpreting religion. What is obvious from this is the fact
that ethnographic examples have been adopted for illustrative purposes rather than
as elements entering into the construction of some extensive comparative analysis
of religious phenomena. One has had to be particularly selective in choosing authors
who typify those positions singled out for criticism. Such is the case with Spiro's
discussion of the relation between the great world traditions of religion and their
manifestation at the local level, for while it is not the purpose of this book to engage
in a broadscale debate on this theoretical point, it is our intention to show how
scholarly and other presuppositions can easily influence entire trends of thought.
In other words our goal is to identify and discuss certain typical perspectives
rather than to be encyclopaedic. It is with this intention of reducing several major
disciplines to a common set of interests that we now turn to an examination of
hermeneutical problems associated with the perception of evil and with its resolution.

PART ONE

CHAPTER ONE

THE SOCIOLOGY OF KNOWLEDGE

The debate about the problem of knowledge which has actively engaged the attention of sociologists and anthropologists in the twentieth century is of particular importance to historians and phenomenologists of religion because it raises the whole question of salvation and the function of religions. In this chapter we trace the emergence of social scientific concern with religions as systems of meaning, and we provide a working definition of the term salvation. This is done at a fairly high level of generalization and it is couched in terms of what we will call plausibility theory. In later chapters we then take this generalization and see how it may be applied to concrete religious situations, both as far as preliterate societies and developed societies are concerned.

Epistemology, or the theory of how we come to know and to be certain of our ideas, has always been a central concern of philosophers and theologians. In the later nineteenth century anthropologists also took up the problem as they became fascinated by the question of how the thought processes of primitive peoples resembled or differed from those of western and civilized man. Even when it became no longer fashionable to talk about primitive tribes as belonging to a different order of mankind the question still remained as to the distinctive quality of the mental operations of exotic groups. Instead of the issue of primitive mentality there arose the notion of distinctive rationalities, for the obvious diversities in culture, which nineteenth century exploration brought to light and which twentieth century anthropology documented with ever increasing precision, led inevitably to the question as to whether all men thought in the same kind of way.[1]

Under the influence of evolutionary principles it was presumed by many, and Lucien Lévy-Bruhl is usually singled out as the advocate of this position, that primitive man possessed a 'pre-logical mentality'.[2] Primitives were rather like the children of civilized societies, they lacked a clear understanding of how cause and effect operated in the world around them. Instead of employing clearly defined categories of analysis the primitive operated more by means of an immediate and felt response to things, he was more caught up in a sense of the participation of one object with another in his world of sense. The same was true of his social experience when as an individual the primitive felt part of a greater whole that was his social group. In all such discussions it was presumed that the goal of life for the primitive differed from that of the civilized european. It was not until the opening decades of the twentieth century that the actual working of a primitive society was analysed in any satisfactory way. Bronislaw Malinowski and E. R. Radcliffe Brown went a long way to establish what has been called the functionalist school of anthropology which based its interpretation of primitive life on the experience of actual fieldwork

---

[1] Wilson, B. R., 1970a.
[2] Lévy-Bruhl, L., 1923.

among specific tribes. But even this approach did not focus upon the question of meaning, it emphasized the importance of present day activity of tribal peoples rather than harping back to historical conjecture on the supposed development of human societies. What is more the individual as such almost vanished from consideration as the emphasis was placed more and more on the social group itself.

The transition from this functionalist perspective to what may be called a weak form of structuralism took place in Britain through the work of E. E. Evans-Pritchard and grew out of his Sudanese fieldwork. His interest in the French anthropologists must not be overlooked especially when it is recalled that both Emile Durkheim and Marcel Mauss had already published significant work on the structure of human thought and of conceptual categories. The change in emphasis in Evans-Pritchard's work was away from the function of institutions to the significance and meaning of actions for actual people set amidst their particular system of values and beliefs.

In the second of his major studies, *The Nuer*, published in 1940 some three years after *Witchcraft, Oracles and Magic among the Azande* which we will consider in chapter three, Evans-Pritchard described Nuer society in terms of their own linguistic usage. This study he saw as an 'exploration of ideas' and as a descriptive interpretation of Nuer ideas and practices, a methodology which he made more explicit and which was directed towards religious issues in *Nuer Religion* published in 1956. In this book he is not content merely to compare certain Nuer words and ideas with apparently equivalent western ideas, rather he offers a full reconstruction of the Nuer world-view as a totality and as a means of expressing the Nuer conception of *kwoth* or spirit. If we wanted to describe this book in academic terms we might say that it was the first anthropological study that could reasonably be called phenomenological. Of course Evans-Pritchard was not a phenomenologist in any philosophical sense of that word, but the method which he employed led to a product which would be the goal of any phenomenologist studying the religious life of a nation. It is one that explains the essential structure of the life and thought of the people concerned, and does so without imposing alien concepts and categories upon the basic data.

Despite this very real contribution to the problem of knowledge the anthropologist who is generally credited with having established the fact of man's mental relation with his social and natural environments as a primary field of study is Claude Lévi-Strauss. In his earlier work on kinship and marriage, *The Elementary Structures of Kinship*, in which he considered the value of kinship structures as systems of communication, and in the later volumes on mythology, his prime task is to show the interrelationship that exists between man's mind and the structure of his society.[3]

This approach came to be known as structuralism and was much influenced by the work of linguists. It marks the great influence that language itself has had on twentieth century scholarship. In philosophy the study of language came to be the over-riding concern of most post-war scholars, it is as though the very idea of language came to serve as the inspiration of intellectual endeavours. In this it

---

3 Lévi-Strauss, C., 1949; 1955; 1963; 1964.

replaced the nineteenth century fascination with the organic change in physical bodies. The word took over from the animal as a basis for thought. Structuralist thought presupposed a theory of mind involving a binary analysis of phenomena, and has been utilized by many including Edmund Leach, Mary Douglas and Rodney Needham in Britain whose work bears directly upon the field of religion and which we consider later in this book.[4] Yet it must be said that despite this intellectual interest in structuralism, with its implicit theme of human creativity in the construction of cultural systems of meaning, something of a dichotomy based to a certain extent upon academic insularity has been maintained between anthropological and sociological concerns with the problem of meaning. The former have tended to restrict their study to specific cultural groups whereas the latter have focused more upon western man within the same cultural tradition as the scholar. This inevitably meant that the problem of meaning was understood differently by both and means of analysing areas of interest were chosen accordingly. Added to this is the fact that British anthropology, largely influenced by Durkheimian assumptions, emphasized the significance of group activity in ritual and religion, while sociologists either focused on individual activity or else engaged in rather high level theorizing with respect to religious sects and wider society and the like.

Durkheim, who has already been mentioned as a significant influence on Evans-Pritchard, is particularly worthy of comment inasmuch as his theory of religion is inextricably associated with the notion of human nature and with the systems of knowledge generated by man from his social experience. In the opening section of 'The Elementary Forms of the Religious Life' he discusses what he calls the theory of knowledge arguing that the very categories of thought originate not in some innate human understanding but are derived from social experience itself. For Durkheim, and here his position is fundamentally different from that of the nineteenth century intellectualists like E. B. Tylor, J. G. Frazer and Andrew Lang, religion was 'a permanent aspect of humanity' essential to the very nature of man.[5] It was no mere passing phase and it was not grounded in errors of judgement or logic. While Durkheim did not argue any thesis which emphasized meaning as an explicit drive in man (for in his day this way of expressing the problem had not emerged) yet his fundamental interest lies in how man comes to understand and express the forces and apparent realities impingeing upon his life. A major distinction introduced by Durkheim was that the reasons given by the faithful and the actual state of affairs discovered by the scientist for religious phenomena were often very different. This indicates the two levels of meaning which are involved in religion for Durkheim and which might still be argued in the paradigm of meaning; for while the faithful may act towards the ultimate expression of truth as to a divinity the analyst might assert that such a deification of validating systems is merely a natural human process, or as Durkheim would have expressed it a social one. This dichotomy will be raised again in the context of presuppositions appropriate to scholars of religion respecting ultimate entities. The fact that Durkheim makes his method quite clear is instructive with respect to other and subsequent scholars and the way

---

4 Douglas, M., 1966; 1970. Leach, E., 1968; 1976. Needham, R., 1973; 1972.
5 Durkheim, E., 1976: 2.

the tradition of scholarship has developed, especially in the anthropological dimension, and specifically in terms of projection processes.

Within the specifically sociological tradition the question of meaning had, even before Durkheim, been of paramount importance in the manner in which it was advocated by Karl Marx. Yet his view that man's perception of life was inextricably associated with and derived from his precise social location, in terms of social class and involvement with the mechanisms of production, was of minor significance to the development of the study of religion in Britain. This was due perhaps to the political implications of his theory of dialectical materialism. In any event, his level of analysis was not sufficiently rigorous with respect to its own presuppositions to appreciate the problem of meaning implicit in religious phenomena.

In terms of the sociology of knowledge it was Karl Mannheim who helped make such issues clear and developed theoretical and more philosophical arguments for this purpose. Mannheim did not think that Marx had achieved a satisfactory sociology of knowledge despite his keen awareness of the relation existing between members of capitalist society and the mechanisms of its operation in respect of structure of consciousness. For Mannheim the Marxist failure in theory lay in its inability to see that its own ideology was also related to specific social factors as though there was an unconscious reluctance to admit the relativity of all ideas. He was committed to the importance of acquiring a sense of historical and social perspective as a precondition for the sociology of knowledge, yet he did not direct his attention solely into a form of historical or social relativity. By contrast he urged a form of relational perspective which did not assert any 'static ideal of eternal unperspectivistic truths independent of the subjective experience of the observer'.[6] The role of the individual thinker in relation to styles of thought and objects of thought he had learned from Husserl and Scheler. Even so Mannheim's work, as to a certain extent is also true for Karl Popper's answering argument, has remained at a fairly high level of generalization with little relevance to the more pragmatic studies of religion in sociology and anthropology.[7]

A similar point can be made, with reservations, concerning Max Weber's sociological work on the relation between idea systems and the resulting action engaged in by religious believers. His concern does embrace the meaning of a religion for a practitioner but more in the sense of a motive for action than as a reason for living. But a qualification is necessary here; for, as will be shown later, his discussion of types of salvation does indicate an awareness of the variety of meanings sought by different categories of persons. Yet his intention is rather different from that of Alfred Schutz, for example, whose work facilitated an application of Husserlian phenomenology to sociology. This can be seen more clearly if we consider Schutz's achievement.

The work of Alfred Schutz was enormously important in the development of the study of religion. In the first place, he was one of Berger's intellectual mentors and Berger in his turn has been so very influential over the broad field of religious studies. Secondly, and this is more important, Schutz offers a distinctive

---

6 Mannheim, K., 1952: 271.
7 Popper, K., 1966.

perspective upon the question of meaning as such. This view of meaning has to do with the level of self-awareness manifested by a subject and this, we might argue, is different for the phenomenologist and for the person he observes. Nevertheless this distinction should not be allowed to obscure an underlying similarity between the meaning construction which is fundamental to all human activity, and that which is deployed at the level of phenomenological analysis. It is precisely these two levels, both of which involve processes of meaning construction, which require clarification before the paradigm of meaning can be seen in its full heuristic strength in the study of religion.

The ordinary person inhabiting his life-world participates naively in many finite universes of meaning, and little self-reflection need be involved in this. Schutz discusses what he calls the 'in order to', and the 'because motives', maintained by ordinary subjects as part of the routine of social interaction, though they too need not involve any self-reflective attitude. There is, then, a fundamental distinction to be drawn between the 'wide awake' state in which *attention de la vie* is at its most intense and the subject most active in the world, and the reflective attitude of the phenomenologist set a distance from the behaviour of others.

The phenomenologist sets himself apart from those he observes, in Schutz's terms his *actio* or action in progress, is directed towards the *actum* or the performed act of his subject.[8] Meaning for Schutz results from the phenomenologist's *actio* as it seeks to understand both the nature of the interior activity and the inter-subjective action of subjects set within the life-world. The operational structures of the life-world are accepted as normative for philosophical analysis but with the proviso of an addition of self-reflection at a high level of abstraction. One significant aspect of the difference between the ordinary inhabitant of the life-world and its critical analyst lies in the fact argued by Schutz that 'I can look at my own self only *modo praeterito* and then grasp merely a partial aspect of this my past self, myself as a performer of a role'.[9] What this means for the methodological difference between Schutz and Berger is that the non-reflective actor lives permanently within an entirely plausible system, which Berger documents at length, while the phenomenological analyst, and he is the concern of Schutz, engages in an act essentially different from any performed in the ordinary life-world. Being aware of these issues Schutz represents the stance of the ordinary man in terms of the 'epoche of the natural attitude' in which no doubt is thrown upon the reality of the structure of everyday life. By contrast, the phenomenologist utilizes the notion of epoche in a formal and self-conscious way.[10]

The significance of this difference ought not be to undervalued for it relates directly to the important concept of 'meaning' in Schutz's work and also underlies much of the argument contained in the following chapters. The basis of the difference consists in what might be called the locus of meaning which varies from phenomenologist to layman, and will become clearer if we expand upon Schutz's use of the term 'meaning'.

Schutz abandons William James's use of the concept sub-universe of reality

---

8 Schutz, A., 1973: 214.
9 Ibid., p. 221.
10 Ibid., p. 229.

because it implied an ontological reality, or we might say an external locus of meaning, which confronts an individual in the process of perception. He prefers the term 'finite province of meaning' in order to reflect the subjective locus of reality, 'because it is the meaning of our experiences and not the ontological structure of objects which constitutes reality'.[11] So meaning in the sense of 'how man, in the natural attitude of daily life and common sense, can understand another's action at all', is the primary concern for Schutz and he analyses it in terms of structures of self knowledge and its relation to others as generated in the inter-subjectivity of social life. Meaning is thus a term descriptive of the taken for granted outlook present to and gained within everyday life.

While the activity of the phenomenologist is different from that of the layman, as indicated in the terminology of *actio* and *actum*, there remains an underlying similarity, a point which Schutz stresses when he discusses the theoretical justification of the social sciences. For he argues that despite the disparity in levels of self-awareness between layman and phenomenologist, both are concerned with meaning structures and it is because of this that 'the empirical social sciences will find their true foundation not in transcendental phenomenology but in the constitutive phenomenology of the natural attitude'.[12] This means that the phenomenologist realizes that he is engaged in the same enterprise as the ordinary person, but that he is aware of his activity. So while the task of phenomenological analysis of behaviour can be seen to resemble the phenomenon itself the fact of self-conscious awareness and reflection at a higher level of abstraction serves to differentiate between a man naively engaged in the *epoche* of the life-world and one formally adopting the outlook of *epoche* as a methodological procedure.

To speak of a paradigm of meaning is thus to identify an aspect of social reality which lies absolutely central to the phenomenological enterprise. The following chapters seek to show how religious phenomena also exemplify the process of meaning construction and care is taken to establish the two levels at which the notion of meaning may be seen to operate, on the one hand as a given aspect or characteristic of human life, and on the other as a specific method of analysis. The paradigm of meaning might thus be viewed as a discussion of meta-meanings, as a study in the meaning of meaning in religious phenomena.

Peter Berger

In collaboration with Thomas Luckmann, Berger developed Schutz's phenomenology in a study entitled *The Social Construction of Reality*, which was conceived as a contribution to the sociology of knowledge.[13] It sought to explain how individuals and groups attained a sense of meaning and security by analysing the processes which lead to the establishment of objective and subjective systems of identity. Central to the argument was the notion of legitimation defined as a kind of second-order objectivation of meaning. It is a function of religious and perhaps also philosophical paramount universes of meaning and serves to 'integrate meanings

---

11 Ibid., p. 230.
12 Ibid., p. 149.
13 Berger, P. L. and Thomas Luckmann 1967.

already attached to disparate institutional processes'.[14] Such legitimation processes which produce a sense of certainty and plausibility about how things are and should be in the world, vary from the implicit legitimations effected by the very languages used by a group, through the level of folk-beliefs, proverbs and general maxims to more explicit propositions of a scientific and philosophical kind which finally are embraced by theological or other ultimate kinds of philosophical schemes. Berger and Luckmann see the entirety of human existence as involving a search for meaning and set about identifying the social processes which constitute the mechanics of the endeavour. In so doing they provide an application of Schutz's phenomenology of everyday life, which centres upon the notion of legitimation. The ordered sense of reality emerging from legitimation processes they identify as the 'nomic function' and this may be said to represent and express the central use of the term 'meaning' in Berger and Luckmann's sociology of knowledge.[15]

Berger continued this general form of argument in *The Social Reality of Religion* which developed one aspect of the earlier joint work away from Luckmann's perspective. While Berger views religious phenomena as similar but not identical to the general human activity of meaning construction, Luckmann argued that religion is but one aspect of the ordinary human enterprise of transcending biological nature through cultural systems. Berger can be seen to follow the more traditional perspective of *Religionswissenschaft* in identifying the sacred, a category embracing ultimate explanatory systems by referring to a supernatural dimension, as the category which enables religious phenomena to be differentiated from other systems of meaning. One reason for his adopting this category as a distinctive feature lies in the fact that Berger sees Luckmann's identification of religious systems and other systems as involving the loss of any heuristic power in specific explanatory categories.

Following Rudolph Otto, and to a certain extent Mircea Eliade, Berger interprets the sacred as 'a quality of mysterious and awesome power other than man and yet related to him, which is believed to reside in certain objects or experience'.[16] It is the perception of this quality of experience as associated with schemes of legitimation which invests legitimation with 'an ultimately valid ontological status', as can be seen in the eastern notions of *Tao* and *rita* to which might be added the western notion of *creatio ex nihilo*.[17] One of the major contributions of religion to the mental development of man, according to Berger, was the way it facilitated the process of symbol construction. The ability to form mental constructs and abstractions was thus part of the development of religious thinking and, as far as Berger is concerned, was also a necessary step in all thought processes. This rather evolutionary argument, which is similar to some of the points already raised in discussing projection, is but conjectural; since it does not bear significantly upon the rest of his argument its particular weakness may be ignored for present purposes.

Throughout *The Social Reality of Religion* Berger presented a heavily sociological analysis of the nature and function of religion combining the Durkheimian emphasis

---

[14] Ibid., p. 110.
[15] Ibid., p. 115.
[16] Berger, P. L., 1969: 34.
[17] Ibid., p. 43.

upon the social structure and its determination of conceptual categories, with the
phenomenological understanding of socialization and world building derived from
Husserl and Schutz. The resulting picture of man seemed to leave no possibility
of human freedom in religious activity. So sociologically dogmatic was its tone
that Berger was impelled to write *A Rumour of Angels* as a complementary volume
to offset the possible 'counsel of despair for religion in the modern world' which
the earlier book seemed to imply if not actually to advocate.[18] Far from being a
mere recitation of caveats this later volume, which he subtitles 'modern society and
the rediscovery of the supernatural', is a creative attempt at relating sociological
and theological enterprises. The major theme of *Rumour of Angels* is that of
transcendence, a notion which may be singled out as one which most clearly
identifies the inherent contradiction between the ideas of projection and revelation
which themselves indicate a major methodological and ideological distinction
between social scientific and theological disciplines. It might be said that Berger
engages in a kind of natural theology originating in the notion of transcendence. He
offers five arguments as suggestive of the actual existence of a transcendental
realm beyond that of human life, but which originate in the every day life world.
These arguments are reminiscent of the classical arguments for the existence of God
but are themselves the result of the phenomenological method, they bring together
several descriptions of human nature provided by the various human sciences in
recent decades. These arguments are particularly relevant to this book because the
first one is called the 'argument from ordering'.[19] What we have called the paradigm
of meaning is directly applicable to this basic theme and, indeed, to the very
language Berger uses to describe what he calls 'signals of transcendence'. The core
of his argument is that 'in the observable human propensity to order reality there is
an intrinsic impulse to give cosmic scope to this order, an impulse which implies
not only that human order in some way corresponds to an order that transcends it,
but that this order is of such a character that man can trust himself and his destiny
to it'.[20]

Alongside this argument from ordering are those from play, hope, damnation
and humour, which together provide the basis for an inductive faith which fully
appreciates the historical and sociological issues of relativity, yet which seeks to do
full justice to the human nature of man as it appears in phenomenological analysis.
Berger is careful in his suggestions for theological study because he is well aware
of the fundamental difference existing between sociological and theological frames
of reference. While he does assert the importance of 'what appears as human
projection' in sociological studies – as exemplified in *The Social Reality of Religion* –
he also wants theologians to recognise the fact that the same phenomena may also
be identified 'as a reflection of divine realities. The logic of the first perspective
does not preclude the possibility of the latter', and this explains the rationale behind
his writing *A Rumour of Angels*, which is to encourage theologians to utilize the
perspective of the sociology of knowledge within their theological exercises. This
intention reasserts the importance of the projection model of analysis in religious

---

[18] Berger, P. L., 1971.
[19] Ibid., p. 72.
[20] Ibid, p. 75.

studies but goes further in suggesting a relation between human projections and 'reality as such'. His suggestion is that 'what is projected is itself a reflection, an imitation of ultimate reality. Religion, then, is not only (from the point of view of empirical reason) a projection of the human order, but (from the view of what might be called inductive faith) the ultimately true vindication of human order'. [21] Such an assertion is not, of course, necessarily true and involves an *a priori* assumption about the nature of reality. Yet it offers a distinctive method of study and one which has already been taken up by John Bowker in his Wilde Lectures.

What this suggestion does imply, however, is that the objective existence of certain phenomena be taken into account when discussing the process of projection. This itself involves a change in the way projection is understood and introduces another theoretical perspective which, in its turn, leads to the establishment of a distinctive model which could be called the cybernetic or communication theory model. Reference to this model will be made throughout the following chapters before a final assessment is made of it in the concluding chapter. Mention of it here has been necessary in order to justify the more philosophical stance adopted in some of the cases studied below. The basic issue in this model is that there exist systems of various kinds which interact with each other, constraining each other and causing responses which might not otherwise have occurred. Human systems of religion are thus seen as resulting from an interrelation between man's endeavour to achieve meaning and those phenomena which demand explanation or which frustrate the processes of meaning construction.

It is in this context that Bowker criticizes Berger's use of the idea of legitimation in his sociology of knowledge. For while Berger argues that the process of meaning construction involves a dialectical relation between individuals and the world he overstresses that part of the relation which he describes as man pouring meaning onto the world, and at the same time underestimates the fact that external stimuli may actually cause man to react in one way or another. This pinpoints Bowker's central argument that there are 'cues of meaning' provided for man by the world and which enable him to make sense of it. [22] In many respects both writers hold rather similar positions and differ more on where they place the emphasis than on matters of substance. This is clear from the key expressions they use to focus their arguments, for while Berger's signals of transcendence indicate the human source of meaning construction, Bowker's cues of meaning assert the importance of *extra-human* factors feeding into the human process of making sense of things.

The important theoretical questions involved in the interrelation of meaning systems will be discussed and resolved in the Conclusion of this book. But first we must take up the more pragmatic aspects of man and society and how both relate to the world of nature, at least as far as religious phenomena are concerned. So far we have established the significance of the paradigm of meaning as a potential unifying perspective in religious studies, following the fragmented state of the field after the demise of evolutionary theories in the human sciences. The relevance of this notion of meaning has also been seen by Robert Bellah and Zwi Werblowsky to

---

[21] Idem.
[22] Bowker, J., 1973: 45.

mention only two scholars, the one representing the sociological and the other the more explicitly history of religions tradition.[23]

Let us now look at the implications of the paradigm of meaning for the problem of evil and its opposite, the process of salvation. We approach these traditional domains of theology by the route we have already suggested as a rather neutral but helpful one, namely that of plausibility theory. This will enable us to gain a theoretical perspective which we will then be able to apply to the more concrete cases of African witchcraft in chapter three, and to the Sikhs and Mormons in subsequent chapters.

---

23 Bellah, R. N., 1970: 9, and R. J. Z. Werblowsky, 1976: 108.

CHAPTER TWO

EVIL AND PLAUSIBILITY

From what has already been said about the phenomenology of the everyday
life world, Berger and Luckmann's assertion that a 'plausibility structure is the
social base for the particular suspension of doubt without which the definition of
reality in question cannot be maintained in consciousness' is quite intelligible.[1]
This particular quotation can serve as a useful definition of plausibility theory
inasmuch as it refers to three major phenomenological ideas which require further
comment and which imply a fourth idea, that of 'evil', which itself is taken as the
central argument and theme of this chapter.

In the definition of plausibility the first significant point is raised by the phrase
'social base'. Its precise significance for the present argument lies in the fact that
both cognitive and affective factors are fundamental constituents or aspects of
social institutions, whether they are family; economic; political; leisure or religious
in kind. Plausibility theory, when applied to religious phenomena, does not only
concern itself with doctrinal schemes or philosophical systems of abstract forms,
but also pays due regard to the emotional elements entering into religious conceptions
and to the manner in which people hold to and maintain their beliefs. The fact
that western scholarship tends to eliminate affective aspects of life in their use of
the notion of reason is to be regretted, as the discussion of Tillich's comment to
this effect which is taken up in the Conclusion will show, meanwhile the importance
of affective aspects of social bases will be presumed and incorporated in studies of
particular religious groups.

The phrase 'suspension of doubt' indicates the second phenomenologically
important notion, that of the natural *epoche* in which most men live most of the
time. The entire process of socialization conduces to this state, yet as will be shown
below this condition is not beyond question for it involves a certain fragility which
is also to be interpreted in terms of the notion of evil. The suspension of doubt is
possible, however, because of the power exerted by processes of legitimation
which, in terms of the third phrase, provide a 'definition of reality' for people.
Despite the fact that within a social group people find it possible to suspend doubt
in the light of given interpretations of reality there are moments when crises of the
given plausibility take place.

The precise way in which the relation between plausibility structures and processes
which militate against them is discussed is instructive with respect to the status
given by a writer to both phenomena. Berger tends to reify what he calls 'intrusion
of the anomic phenomena of suffering, evil and above all of death', he also talks of
the 'forces of chaos' which 'threaten' humanly constructed worlds of meaning.[2]
Perhaps such reification is inevitable when discussing a phenomenon which is so

---

[1] 1967; 175.
[2] Berger, P. L., 1969: 61.

inextricably part of the human, and thereby personal, awareness of the world. What is certainly the case is that Berger establishes 'the problem of theodicy' as a central aspect of the maintenance of religious plausibility; in the use of the well established theological notion of theodicy Berger is careful to say that his specific meaning varies from that adopted and customary in theology. For him theodicy focuses upon the human task of legitimation rather than upon any questioning of the purpose of an almighty and beneficent deity in the light of evil occurrences. It sometimes appears that Berger espouses and voices a form of existentialism which sees the world as essentially fragile and tending more to dissolution than to a robust perpetuation. 'The worlds that man constructs are forever threatened by the forces of chaos, finally by the inevitable fact of death'.[3]

A much less personified conception of negative features in religious structures is offered by John Bowker in his Wilde Lectures; these argue in some depth a theory of religion which, while similar to Berger's is by no means identical. Religions are taken to be 'route finding activities, as homeostatic and conservative life-ways, through which *as a whole* human lives are made significant, and in which the meaning of their lives and of the universe is able to discerned'.[4] The similarity to Berger's position and the significance of Bowker's thesis for the present argument lies in the emphasis upon that 'meaning' and 'significance' which religions are said to confer. Yet Bowker's perspective is more powerful than Berger's because it is, essentially, more analytical and operates at a higher level of theoretical abstraction. While the importance of this will be taken up at the end of this book it must be mentioned here that what Bowker is asserting is that religions are one kind of communication system set amidst other systems. In other words he does not follow Berger in accentuating the autonomy of human thought in processes of meaning construction. While man does impose significance upon external reality, as Berger powerfully argues in his notion of exteriorization, there are also sources external to man which influence his conceptions. Now Berger does admit the fact that external phenomena exert an influence on man and he handles this idea by means of the socialization processes of internalization, but, and this is where the two scholars differ, the external influences were themselves creations of society. For Berger it is external social reality which exists in a dialectical relation with succeeding generations; for Bowker there are important external sources of influence which are not of social or human origin. One caveat might, perhaps, be introduced into such a criticism of Berger inasmuch as society may itself be conceived as a natural phenomenon as it was by the Durkheimian tradition of French sociology. Even allowing for this there remains a basic difference of approach, and in the following chapters the outlook of Bowker which presupposes the existence and significance of non-human and non-social sources of influence is adopted.

One issue which is not directly stated in Bowker's quotation on religions as route finding activities but which is important for his argument as a whole, and which shows the closeness of his thought to that of Berger, is the question of negative factors in experience. Berger's notion of theodicy is represented in Bowker

---

[3] Ibid., p. 87.
[4] Bowker, J., 1973: 82.

through the expression 'compound of limitation' which denotes precisely those factors which hinder legitimation processes. The emphasis in Bowker is upon the positive aspect of meaning construction, on the fact that human society tends more in the direction of a firm cosmos than it does towards chaotic states. One reason for this lies in his belief that what he calls 'cues of meaning' are not all socially derived, as is the case with Berger. Religions are rather like evolutionary systems which have survived because they have discovered or merely adopted patterns of behaviour which facilitate life which is, itself, associated with problems and hazards. Religions are thus routes through the difficulties but they are supported in their work by factors emerging from the very external world which is at the same time the source of difficulties, or as Bowker expresses it, 'there are enough cues in the universe to support the plausibility of an eventual way through'.[5] The world is not as fragile and tenuous a structure for Bowker as for Berger.

The problem which has been identified in this brief comment on two scholars will recur throughout the following chapters and will be detailed in terms apposite to the academic tradition of those whose work has yet to be considered. For the present this problem of evil may be further described in terms of the phenomenological concepts already mentioned and which relate to the basic model of meaning.

The maintenance of a plausible world view may be seen to depend on two different kinds of mental perspectives. The first is that of the natural *epoche* which involves the suspension of doubt about the given legitimating structures provided by both society and universe, and here we may combine Berger's and Bowker's position to include both realities. So much we have already considered and may now describe as a naive structure of consciousness which may be differentiated, at least for the purposes of the present argument, from the second or fully conscious and directed state of mind which is aware of the particular problems posed by aspects of the world. The difference between these states is one of explicitness and of level of articulation of the perception of negativities found in particular groups. The significant phenomenological point is that there emerge conditions in which the normal suspension of doubt becomes impossible. Those circumstances which lead to questions of theodicy are precisely those in which doubt cannot be suspended. We may then say that the problem of evil, phenomenologically speaking, is a question of identifying those areas or aspects of life which call the natural *epoche* itself into question.

The following studies in particular religious movements will exemplify the kinds of factors which serve such negative functions, what is true for them all is that man operates rather differently under what might be called routine challenges to *epoche* on the one hand and under critical challenges on the other. The first kind is met with the naive, non-directed style of *epoche*, while the second involves a far more specific and explicit kind of legitimation. These differences are of degree rather than of kind so that the basic processes operating in the everyday life world are also observable, albeit at a more intensive level of operation, in periods of crisis. Berger

---

[5] Ibid., p. 78.

argues in this kind of way in seeing theodicy proper as but an application of a
general human attribute.[6]

So it is that meaning assertion as the characteristic activity of man is no neutral
activity but takes place in a context of perceived implausibility. It is this perception
of implausibility or of what might be called an inadequacy of meaning in the
world that constitutes the starting point, logically at least, for the study of specific
rellgous movements. The advantage of adopting a paradigm of meaning in respect
of implausibility lies in the fact that if such a paradigm is set within the context of
a communication-type theory, then the issue of whether the sense of evil precedes
the salvation response or merely results from the message of salvation is made
redundant. Such a cause and effect rationale is replaced by the notion of interrelated
systems involving mutual changes and no immediately given priority either to the
anomic or to the legitimating processes.

Phenomenologically speaking this means that the notion of salvation, like that
of evil, is grounded in human perception of the particular context of life in which a
person finds himself. Both contexts and perceptions of life change and as they do
so the relative significance and meaning of salvation and evil alter in relation the
one to the other. If this is the case then it is possible to suggest a working definition
of salvation which focuses more upon the mechanics of plausibility processes than
upon any specific doctrinal schemes of belief in gods or the like.

Salvation as Plausibility

The present writer has already argued elsewhere that it is desirable to adopt a
working definition of salvation in religious studies which is not the direct product
of any religious tradition, and that the sociology of knowledge is precisely the kind
of theoretical source which can help rid overly theological descriptions of their
religion-specific significance.[7] So, in the light of what has been said about plausibility
theory a definition of salvation as a theoretical construct may be suggested as the
basis for subsequent analyses of widely differing religious movements. The benefit
to be gained from an essentially non-theological definition of salvation lies not only
in the fact that if the religious sense of one tradition were adopted then the argument
would tend towards a dogmatic perspective, but also in that if a fundamentally
different notion is adopted at the outset then very many theological and religious
phenomena may be illuminated by the critical view brought to bear upon them
'from the outside'. What this implies is that the dominant outlook of this study is
more that of the student of the history and phenomenology of religion than of the
theologian as such. As Werbloswky has argued, it is important to make clear whether
a study of religious phenomena is carried out from the position of religious commitment or, as far as the specific study is concerned, from that of academic detachment.[8]
In order to prevent confusion of aims and criticism this thesis explicitly utilizes
the latter stance.

Accordingly we may say in general terms that 'salvation is a state of cognitive

---

6   Berger, P. L., 1969: 63.
7   Davies, D. J., 1978: 91.
8   Werblowsky, R. J. Zwi, 1976.

and effective well-being within the currently available system of world interpretation'. More formally we might say that 'salvation is that state of sufficiency of durable plausibility existing for an individual or group, under given ideological and social structural conditions, such that no alternative is sought'. One important implication of the phrase 'given ... conditions', as far as the whole argument of this book is concerned, is that it permits an understanding of a religion as one system amongst other systems, in other words, that it admits the importance of arguments from general systems theory which are discussed at length in the Conclusion. What must also be emphasized is that such given conditions always involve the negative aspects of reality which Bowker, as already indicated, identifies as those compounds of limitation through which religions establish themselves as route finding activities. Such compounds of limitation along with Berger's notion of anomic intrusions may, simply, and from the phenomenological standpoint be identified as areas of implausibility. This single category can serve to express in terms of a simple paradigm of meaning notions of 'evil' held and used by scholars in a variety of disciplines; this means that the term evil, like salvation, can be used in a way which stresses no specific theological meaning drawn from any one religious tradition, but a phenomenologically descriptive sense of what contradicts plausibility in any given context. While most perceptions of implausibility are related to and contained within major religious traditions, so that salvation systems might be said to contextualize evil, there will be occasions when the sense of implausibility leads to a fundamentally different kind of response and explanation. There are, then, periods in the history of religions when plausibility is no longer durable enough to withstand the forces of negative questions. Such 'questions' can be of a strictly philosophical or scientific kind, as was the case of Darwinian evolution in the nineteenth century or Durkheimian sociology in the twentieth, or they may result from life experiences and periods of social or autobiographical change as will be shown in the cases of Mormonism and Sikhism. It is precisely because religions are, themselves, systems of meaning construction set within ever changing social contexts that religious doctrines and rites must not be viewed as static phenomena, but as dynamic interpretations of and responses to the external environment. It is just such a perspective which is served well in terms of theoretical justification by a general systems theory approach operating upon a basic paradigm of meaning. A fundamental presupposition of this approach is that analyses of religious phenomena ought not to engage in simplistic reductionist argument with a strict cause and effect mechanism seen as underlying religious 'responses to social pressures' and the like; but ought to be considered as creative systems in relation with, responding to but also causing other systems to respond to it. Religious systems are then seen to be self-regulating in respect of certain goals, and these will vary from group to group, while also influencing institutions apart from itself. To be self-regulating, however, is not to be confused with being autonomous, inasmuch as once a general systems theory approach is adopted then it only makes sense to talk of religious systems as part of a wider complex of systems. It is only because one system coexists with others that it may be said to possess any basis for its own continued existence. Sociological deprivation theories of religion, for example, tend to elevate one principle of explanation above all the available data which are then interpreted solely in terms of that principle. Once a religious movement is subordinated to other social processes as far as explanation is concerned it becomes easy to overlook the influence of that movement on other institutions. As will be shown below, the methodological predilection of historians of religion to evaluate religious phenomena in terms appropriate to them can be seen to be in accord with the general systems theory approach, and also resembles the method adopted by phenomenologists which has already been discussed.

These general comments lead to the question of what factors do enter into the perception of evil and of salvation? Berger and Bowker provide a useful starting point in answering this question and serve to show how academic and philosophical presuppositions cannot be ignored when evaluating scholarly contributions to religious studies. Bowker, for example, in his desire to emphasize the external origin of cues of meaning fails to appreciate fully the fact that the need for meaning, which underlies the process in which man utilizes external cues in constructing meaning systems, lies in man and that it is the very mental process of man which results in plausible frameworks. This is one aspect of the differences existing between the two scholars, for Berger follows Durkheimian orthodoxy in under-standing man's category construction and religious conceptualizations as originating in social experience, while Bowker is prepared to admit the notion of God's existence into his argument. This, perhaps, is what causes Bowker to focus on the positive and constructive cues from the universe which support plausibility, whereas Berger tends to describe human life as possessing an ever-ready tendency to slip into chaos. It is instructive to see that Bowker stresses implausibility not in the structures of general life activities but within religious traditions by recognizing that 'crises of plausibility ... occur far more frequently ... within theistic traditions themselves than being imposed from outside'.[9] Here Bowker is not being sufficiently analytical and instead of considering the wider contexts of social institutions he chooses to focus on the kind of intellectual questioning which, while it does arise in some movements, need not affect the majority of members. He is advancing the notion of plausibility-implausibility in terms of the christian theological perspective of the relation between faith and doubt. That doubt is related to faith is true for many types of Protestant theology, especially those involving an existentialist perspective, but to extend the idea to make it of universal application is hazardous. 'This doubt about the plausibility of projected ways', which Bowker says, 'is possible at any time, even in so called ages of faith', is a different concept from the phenomeno-logically defined notion of evil used in this book.[10] In constructing a phenomeno-logically descriptive system of religions it would be true to say, with Bowker, that the kind of perceived implausibility found in a group will be directly related to the process adopted to overcome it, but it would be untrue to say that the evil itself, or the compounds of limitation themselves, are necessarily part of the transcending process.

Christianity itself can provide an illustration of this contention inasmuch as the Jehovah's Witness, Christian Science and Mormon movements do not admit the

9 Bowker, J., 1973: 84.
10 Ibid, p. 72.

element of doubt in their notions of faith. Some qualification could be made to this assertion since, for example, certain groups of intellectuals in the Mormon church are prepared to acknowledge the role of doubt and uncertainty in their faith and their attitude to certain doctrines, but this type of questioning is seldom found among the mass membership. While this kind of intellectualism can be maintained among small groups of Mormons who continue to act as believers, as far as the ordinary church behaviour is concerned, it is far from that normative stance which sees faith and doubt as antitheses. The very fact of conversion in these groups emphasizes the difference, for converts are usually those who have been in a state of doubt, both of an intellectual and what might be called an emotional doubt or lack of certainty in life commitments, prior to their conversion. Their new found life of certainty possesses a conviction in terms of ideas and behaviour which is characterized by the sectarian affirmation which does not merely assert an 'I believe', but a definitive 'I know'. The universe of meaning which is constituted by sectarian institutions is one of complete and completed significance. Its very existence is owed to the fact that available systems of world interpretation are found by some to be insufficient in terms of explanation and as sources of motivation for life commitment.

So it is that the notion of doubt as belonging to the structures of faith has tended to emerge in traditions which stress intellectualism and undervalue emotional factors, as in Anglicanism and some types of Reformed Protestantism. But this is certainly not a universally found feature of religiosity so that while the theoretical possibility of a co-existing faith and doubt structure must be entertained, the general location of doubt as a manifestation of implausibility ought to be in the world outside the religious plausibility system.

In one sense there is but little point in making this criticism too strongly since the important factor is the recognition of negative factors in religious concerns and this Bowker has done. The real reason for criticism, lies in the fact that no one religious idea should be used as the basis for neutral categories of study, as already argued for the phenomenological use of the terms salvation and evil.

Having already commented upon what both these critical terms can mean in a phenomenological sense it might now be useful to offer one hypothesis, expressed in terms of plausibility theory, concerning the notion of durability of plausibility, and which will be applicable to later discussion of actual religious phenomena. To do this recourse must be taken to the work of structural anthropology and in particular to that of Claude Lévi-Strauss who, as already mentioned in passing, argued a kind of general communication theory with respect to social institutions.[11] He suggested that 'in any society communication operates on three different levels: communication of women, of goods and services, and of messages'.[12] The messages are, obviously, not of the same kind so that women, services of a behavioural kind and words are all of different orders of reality, and can be said to vary in their level of symbolic expression. What is exchanged and those performing the exchange are the same in the case of kinship acts of communication: men exchange women

---

[11] P. 20.
[12] Lévi-Strauss, C., 1963: 296.

but both are human beings. In the case of language, by contrast, the words used are of a high level of symbolic association bearing little obvious resemblance at the material level to the things they represent. Moreover the actual time taken to perform a communication event varies from a rapid exchange in words to entire generations in kinship procedures. If this idea is used in conjunction with Berger and Luckmann's analysis of socialization, which stresses both the linguistic and non-verbal aspects of human being, then the suggestion may be made that what might be called the speed of communication and the durability of plausibility are inversely related, such that the faster the communication event the less plausible will be the durability conferred. The higher the speed the more abstract the message conveyed and the less likely it is that the message will result in effecting the receiver's emotional response. This hypothesis has obvious significance for a paradigm of meaning which is applied to religious phenomena, for it provides a broad theoretical perspective for describing ritual, symbolism and myth. It is somewhat difficult to use the word 'describing' here, however, since the process of discussing phenomena by means of this notion of durability involves a certain degree of explanation as well as description. For the present it is assumed that this communication model does possess explanatory power as well as facilitating phenomenological description.

One particularly important aspect of the idea of speed of communication lies in the fact that it may be seen to emphasize the fact that the notion of meaning applies as much to affective dimensions as to cognitive process of human life. The above hypothesis can then be interpreted as asserting that the higher the speed of communication and the less emotional the affective component of the exchange then the more dependent upon 'reason', or the more strictly intellectual functions, does the communication become. More than this, it may be said that whenever the intellectual element comes to predominate to an inordinate extent then the plausibility conferring power of the communication context is reduced. This is not to say that philosophical arguments do not possess, or cannot come to possess a powerful influence over individual lives, but it does argue that the power of ideas is likely to be maintained only if there is a group or community committed to those ideas. This idea will be developed more in the Conclusion when the relation of abstract notions to concrete social institutions will be explored in the light of recent anthropological studies.

In the various religious phenomena analysed in the following chapters the plausibility model will be drawn upon to show in what way, for example, sacrifice is generally a rite of what might be called 'steady state religions' served by priests, whereas religions associated with periods of social or personal change often manifest phenomena of possession or ecstasy served by mediums and prophets. In both types of condition the phenomenon of evil is differently conceived as are the ways of dealing with it and in analytical terms the notion of speed of communication associated with that of durability of plausibility may be seen to represent one facet of a general paradigm of meaning.[13]

---

[13] Davies, D. J., 1978: 97.

The Perception of Evil

In emphasizing the centrality of the perception of evil for religious studies one is identifying an area in which theological, philosophical and phenomenological interests converge. In one sense this fact illustrates what has already been argued with respect to the paradigm of meaning, for the very fact that negative features of existence are established as problems in these various disciplines attests to the power of the desire for meaning which is thwarted by these very phenomena. As already argued above the mutual relation of meaning and non-meaning ought not to be ignored and, what is more, both aspects require to be taken together as constituting the paradigm of meaning at the pragmatic level of religious phenomena. To argue either the priority of meaning over non-meaning as Berger tends to, or of negative factors over primary ones as the present author has done elsewhere is somewhat misguided.[14] Bowker adopts a more theoretically satisfactory view in which negative phenomena, his compounds of limitation, coexist with and in relation to the positive aspect of religion as a route finding activity. It is precisely because of this close interaction that ideas of evil and of salvation change so specifically in terms of each other. Both the cases of Mormon and of Sikh religion, which will be considered in depth below, provide apt illustration of this fact.

For the present a more abstract point must be made, namely, that differences in ideas of evil and salvation may often be seen as expressing the degree of externalization or internalization of implausibility and plausibility present in a person or group. Both the way of conceiving evil and the methods adopted for its resolution vary according to the degree of personification and abstraction engaged in with respect to negative features. It is not possible to construct any simple continuum with a clearly personified and externalized source of evil at one end and a highly subjective and internalized source at the other, and then to apply such a scheme to, say, western and eastern forms of religion. While this is the case it remains true that eastern forms of religiosity often do stress the subjective consciousness aspect while western forms of Christianity assert the external ontological status of evil. But since there are so many qualifications which would have to be made for such generalizations they must be left simply at the level of helpful labels categorizing trends rather than rules.

One western philosophical study which clearly demonstrates the complexity of these issues is provided by Paul Ricoeur whose *philosophie de la volonté* shows how far the internalization of the notion of evil can be taken in a western work. His second volume of *Finitude et Culpabilité* entitled *La Symbolique du mal* is particularly useful for the present argument for it shows the variety of man's awareness of evil as well as the particular contribution of this existentialist philosopher who, as John Rogerson suggests, also shows similarities to the phenomenologists.[15]

Ricoeur argues that the three notions of defilement, of sin and of guilt (*souillure, péché, culpabilité*), have emerged, the one from the other, in a kind of historical development which demonstrates an increased internalization of a negative self-

---

[14] Ibid., p. 92.
[15] Rogerson, J. W., 1974: 128.

evaluation. The religious sense, which of all kinds of awareness is the one most particularly involved in this act of self-judgement, operates in many spheres of life and especially in confession to bring man to an acknowledgement of his true plight: 'cet aveu est une parole que l'homme prononce sur lui-même'.[16] In his volume, L'homme faillible, Ricoeur expresses this enigma of human existence by saying that in the world of myth man's world is represented to him as already fragmented, while man himself is often characterized as being in a state of internal division of the self. 'Ce caractère global – le concept de faillibilité – consiste dans une certaine non-coincidence de l'homme avec lui-même.[17] As far as Ricoeur the religious believer is concerned, this dividedness must also be viewed as part of man's self evaluation as sinner before God. As will be shown through a later consideration of Australian aboriginal religion it is quite possible for a people to possess a negative self-evaluation without having to express it in terms of sin or of a status presuming the existence of a god or the like. Ricoeur's analysis, inevitably, reflects a particular western theological and philosophical outlook which has limitations. Even so the description of life which he provides offers a form which will be matched by data from non-Christian cultures, despite the fact that its content will vary from others according to the dictates of cultural restraints.[18] The question of myth occupies much of Ricoeur's argument for he sees myths as among the most fundamental modes of expression capable of dealing with the enigmatic nature of human experience. J. W. Rogerson has aptly characterized myths as functioning as symbols in Ricoeur's work, which means that while they refer to certain ideas they cannot be fully interpreted in terms of those ideas in a purely intellectual way. They cannot be interpreted in terms of things other than themselves.[19] A further complexity might be added here, drawing from Lévi-Strauss's study of myth, in arguing that myths can be translated without serious loss of meaning.[20] The use of the terms 'interpret' and 'translate' indicates the centrality of myths to the broad question of meaning while also pinpointing the necessity of correctly identifying the precise status of myths as units of communication. Both Ricoeur and Lévi-Strauss, and the same could be said of Eliade in the history of religions and of Stanner, as will be shown later, in anthropology, regard myths as conveying a kind of knowledge which cannot be gained in any other way. So while a myth may be translated into another language and elicit an appropriate response, it cannot be interpreted by non mythical intellectual means and still function as myth.

   This view shows the significance of the paradigm of meaning in religious studies both in terms of the scholarly level of analysis and that of the acting practitioner. In discovering the meaning of myths as they are found among religious believers, where they function as legitimating phenomena, the scholar sees how 'meaning'

---

16 Ricoeur, P., 1960, Vol. 11, p. 11.
17 Ricoeur, P., 1960, Vol. 1, p. 21.
18 Cf. Ibid. Vol. 11, p. 155. 'Plus fondamentalement encore le mythe veut atteindre l'énigme de l'existence humaine à savoir la disordance entre la réalité fondamentale – état d'innocence, statut de créature, être essential – et la modalité actuelle de l'homme, en tant que souillé, pécheur, coupable'.
19 Rogerson, J. W., 1974: 135.
20 Lévi-Strauss, C., 1963: 206 ff.

possesses more than a simple logical or reasonable significance. For Ricoeur as for Lévi-Strauss that which is explained is none other than the human condition, with the former emphasizing the moral imperfection of man and the latter the basic perceived dichotomy between nature and culture. This emphasis apart both identify myth as the area of communication in which man attempts to solve the most basic problems of his perceived reality, and the resolution need not, and usually does not, take the form of any fully rational explanation of things. A similar point to this is made by the historian J. B. Russell in his analysis of 'the perceptions of evil', where the major concern is with the idea of 'understanding' the work of the devil. Russell is less concerned with the idea of evil than with the experience of evil which underlies the various abstractions made from it. The notion of understanding relates to the way this experience is 'assimilated and integrated' into a person's life such that he knows how to deal with evil, while the process by which that understanding is reached need not to be a fully rational one. Russel's study is a useful contribution to a descriptive phenomenology of evil with the personal focus of evil as its major gain: evil is, he says, 'sensed as hurt deliberately inflicted, it is perceived as personified and is never abstract'.[21] What is more, and here his argument lies close to the burden of this book, 'the perception of a flawed world is as widespread as any that can be ascribed to mankind'.[22]

In discussing components of meaning, or kinds of understanding, the argument approximates to the classical debate in anthropology over the nature of human mentality. From the nineteenth century issue of whether there was a pre-logical mentality operating in primitive tribes which was different from the logical bent of the Victorian intellectual, to the twentieth century interest in rationality anthropological opinions have varied as the present writer has shown elsewhere.[23] One question which may appropriately be drawn out of this rather intractible debate is whether the emphasis ought to be placed less upon the notion of kinds of than on styles of thought, frames of mind, or in more phenomenological terms on tensions of consciousness, that is, on mental sets adopted for and appropriate to specific tasks. To do so is to make it easier to talk of the fact that, for example, primitive peoples are as markedly pragmatic in some aspects of their life as some western urban people are devotionally mystical. So mythopoeic thought could be regarded as a universal mode of mental operation in the same way as pragmatic thought or any other outlook determined by the object of perception and the goal of perception. The problem with the primitive mentality debate lay in the fact that religious endeavours of tribal peoples were compared with the scientific activities of western man, once a correction is made for this inappropriate comparison many of the difficulties are resolved.

Other problems remain, however, and are beyond the scope of this book, not least among these are the psychological issues associated with mental processes. For example, while it may be possible to agree with Lévi-Strauss that 'the same logical processes operate in myth as in science', one could not go on to presume

---

[21] Russell, J. B., 1977: 11.
[22] Ibid., p. 21.
[23] Davies, D. J., 1975.

that logical processes and tensions of consciousness can be equated.[24] Modern studies of meditation would, alone, provide sufficient evidence to suggest that different mental activities are associated with different modes of neural activity and result in altered levels of subjective consciousness.[25] This is not to say that if myth is a *sui generis* category then it always effects a particular experience in its hearers or users, but it does admit the possibility of this occasionally taking place, and certainly advocates the necessity of exploring the function of the phenomenon which may be peculiar to itself. Lévi-Strauss affords a suggestive insight into the specific nature of myth in saying that 'the intellectual impulse' which produces myth may well be exhausted before any true logical resolution of perceived contradiction is attained.[26] In terms of plausibility theory this would be interpreted as the participant achieving a level of sufficient plausibility requiring no further explanation, a level of meaning constituted as much by ritual participation, affective reaction and 'mythical' thought as by rational argument. The rationale of the solution may well take one form in the opinion of the practitioner who, for example, might regard the myth as being historically true and affording a concrete explanation of things, while for the analyst, who is also employing, albeit at a different level of abstraction, a paradigm of meaning, the final level of understanding in the subject is seen as a culmination of factors including non-cognitive ones. It is precisely in acknowledgement of the complexity of religious phenomena contributing to a sense of meaning that the phenomenology and history of religions as disciplines have been acutely aware of the hazards of reductionism in explaining any particular religious event, and it is for this reason that emphasis has here been placed upon the possibility that myth is a category irreducible to any other. Later a similar argument will be advanced for aspects of ritual and other facets of religious life which contribute towards meaning for the practitioner.

   In logical if not in chronological terms, then, the mastery of evil begins with a categorizing of it by any particular religious tradition. Its paradoxical presence is then approached by means of ritual acts and mythical expression in an attempt to remove or at least attenuate it. As far as most religions are concerned at the level of popular devotion and spirituality philosophical problems of evil are entirely secondary to the problem of coping with the very experiences giving rise to abstracted theories of their origin. In practical terms this means that perception and categorization of evil are processes which are closely associated with those of salvation which counter the power of evil. This obvious point has been made by many scholars not least by Sigmund Freud who identified the 'threefold task' of the gods as exorcizing the terrors of nature, reconciling men to the cruelty of fate especially in the form of death, and of compensating them for the sufferings and privations imposed by civilization.

   The wide variety of ways in which religions identify evil and set about its resolution makes a theoretical perspective like that of plausibility theory the more necessary as a way of reducing phenomenological chaos to some order. The definition of salvation given above and the discussion of evil as a kind of flaw in the plausibility

---

24 Lévi-Strauss, C., 1963: 230,; 229 respectively.
25 Benson, H., 1977: T. R. Blakeslee, 1980.
26 Freud, S., 1973: 14.

structures embracing perceived reality will be seen to be advantageous in the specific cases of African tribal religion to which we now turn as well as in the Sikh and Mormon religions discussed in following chapters. Before going on to consider further developments in the general paradigm of meaning, and in particular the notion of identity as one vital aspect of meaning, it will be instructive to consider in concrete terms the applicability of the mode of meaning and plausibility theory in some specific cases of African tribal religions.

CHAPTER THREE

EVIL AND WITCHCRAFT

Reference has already been made in the first chapter to the theoretical significance of E. E. Evans-Pritchard's anthropological work as marking and effecting a change from functionalism to what might be called a weak form of structuralism. This is not the strong form of Lévi-Strauss's work, which itself marks the foremost French contribution to a paradigm of meaning in the study of man, and which presupposes a theory of mind and mental operations, but is more pragmatic in seeking so to analyse social phenomena as to allow their inner structure to be fully manifest to the anthropologist. The 'anthropologist seeks to do more than understand the thought and values of a primitive people and translate them into his own culture. He seeks also to discover the structural order of the society, the patterns which, once established, enable him to see it as a whole, as a set of interrelated abstractions'.[1]

In his most influential early work on witchcraft among the Azande of the southern Sudan Evans-Pritchard demonstrated how this structural order could be identified and communicated to a reader unfamiliar with the native context. The wide significance and influence exerted by this study can be assessed from the fact that the 1968 meeting of the Association of Social Anthropologists was devoted to the theme of witchcraft and the ensuing volume dedicated to Evans-Pritchard. In its editorial Mary Douglas emphasizes the importance of Evans-Pritchard's work, and the significant comment is made that *Witchcraft and Oracles among the Azande* was, in effect, a study in the sociology of knowledge. Because anthropologists had tended to read it as some kind of functionalist analysis Mary Douglas felt it necessary to 'establish that the study of Azande witchcraft was indeed offered as a contribution to the sociology of perception'.[2] Similarly in *The Nuer* and *Nuer Religion* his concern with issues of social values, experience and mind is obvious and in this his intellectual affinity to Durkheim is marked as he seeks the abstract system of thought underlying native culture. Yet he does not present any abstract set of models expressing the rationale of indigenous thought: 'interpretations are contained in the facts themselves, for I have described the facts in such a way that the interpretations emerge as part of the description'.[3] The 'purposive description' presented by Evans-Pritchard is, perhaps, one of the most sophisticated social scientific examples of the paradigm of meaning to be found in ethnographic literature, for in his description of Zande life Evans-Pritchard sets forth the 'how', or the indigenous rationale, of life-phenomena but he does so in a way which itself presupposes, at an academic level, that the culture as a whole possesses a meaning which can be understood by his readers who do not begin with Zande presuppositions.

So it is that Evans-Pritchard discusses the subject of witchcraft as one aspect of the problem of explanation as such, asking why any metaphysical system should

---

[1] Evans-Pritchard, E. E., 1962: 22.

[2] Douglas, M., 1970: xiv.

[3] Evans-Pritchard, E. E., 1937: 5.

be accepted. In an interesting way his basic question is the opposite form of Berger's interest in the nature of social reality: the latter views problematic areas of life as the major tensions on plausibility systems while Evans-Pritchard is more occupied with the constraints supporting belief in a system of explanation.[4]

Mary Douglas identifies three elements of the Azande study as having been significant for later work and which demonstrate the significance of witchcraft as a plausibility maintaining process. In terms of this book these elements also demonstrate the way evil, defined as implausibility, can be viewed and dealt with apart from reference to transcendent sources of evil. In the first place witchcraft accusations 'allowed grudges to be brought out into the open and ... provided a formula for action in misfortune. Secondly such accusations were clearly associated with areas of life and persons involved in conflict and rivalries, while, thirdly, the witch beliefs were directly related to the moral code inasmuch as witches were characterised as possessing anti-social features of behaviour as also of physical appearance. While this kind of analysis is open to criticism focusing on functionalism of too static a kind it nevertheless shows how witchcraft operates as a kind of homeostatic device for social friction. In addition it provides an explanatory framework for evil experienced in social intercourse 'based on the idea of a communication system'.[5] Even when other anthropologists such as Marwick, Middleton and Turner developed witchcraft studies in directions other than a functionalist-like way they, nevertheless, utilized Evans-Pritchard's insight that witchcraft was, 'essentially a means of clarifying and affirmal social definitions'.[6] Whether witchcraft processes led to the maintenance of social relations or their disruption they served the purpose of fostering a system of plausibility.

As far as the Azande study is concerned witchcraft demonstrates clearly that plausibility is a notion relating to both intellectual and emotional factors, and Evans-Pritchard takes pains to show that the emotional and experiental dimension may even predominate inasmuch as witchcraft is a method of actually coping with a problem in terms of action rather than one of elaborate intellectualizing upon a problem. 'In truth Azande experience feelings about witchcraft rather than ideas, for their intellectual concepts of it are weak and they know better what to do when attacked by it than how to explain it. Their response is action and not analysis. The Zande actualizes these beliefs rather than intellectualizes them, their tenets are expressed in socially controlled behaviour rather than in doctrines'.[7] The fact that an entirely coherent and systematic logic of witchcraft is not held by the Azande, not merely an uncompleted system in western terms of system or rationality, but one which they know and feel to be 'peculiar' and which they do not 'profess to understand entirely', in no sense appears to reduce the plausibility conferred by the beliefs'.[8] For the rites performed by the Azande appear to them to achieve the desired end, whatever is wrong is righted and since the very implausibility exists at the level of experience it is at that same level where the resolution occurs.

---

[4] Ibid., p. 4.
[5] Douglas, M., 1970: xvii.
[6] Douglas, M., Idem., p. xxv.
[7] Evans-Pritchard, E. E., 1937: 82-3.
[8] Ibid., p. 99.

The Azande case clearly makes the point that not only will postulated solutions vary according to the nature of evil in particular groups, but that pragmatic causes are as significant as intellectual ones in some instances. Evans-Pritchard is remarkably clear on the way in which Azande attain satisfactory levels of meaning in life, telling of how, in his own participant observation, he adopted their mode of coping with problems and decision making. In attempting to 'think black', or as he corrects himself, to 'feel black', he found it an effort to check his 'lapse into unreason' when using magic oracles in daily life. Yet he urges acceptance of the fact that Azande methods possessed an intellectual consistency when viewed in context, and when it is appreciated that their coherency is to be evaluated as a product of particular cultural contexts. The beliefs in witchcraft, oracles and magic relate to one another as 'loose associations of notions' which operate 'in bits, not as a whole', with the 'plasticity of beliefs' resulting from or being the function of situations and not 'indivisible ideational structures'.[9] It is likely to be true that this kind of situation obtains for practical religion in all societies even though formal theologies advanced by religious specialists tend to ignore the fact. As a type case the Azande material would suggest that the notion of sufficiency of plausibility might well be applied to ritual as to more theoretical means of dealing with life's misfortunes in situations where there are no fully systematized and comprehensive schemes of knowledge.

Witchcraft and oracles are, then, institutions which, according to the basic argument of this book, pertain to salvation, inasmuch as they serve to interpret phenomena of evil to the Azande and go on to help validate the nature of reality by means of ritual processes which serve to overcome the perceived implausibility of the Zande world. What is more, these institutions are in no direct sense associated with the Zande concept of God, which itself is no single and uniform notion.[10] Witchcraft is a physical characteristic of certain persons and is inherited by unilineal descent; the substance causing it can even be located within the dead body of a witch at an autopsy.[11] This witchcraft or *mangu* causes illness and disease of all kinds with only two exceptions which beset infants and which are usually fatal. These infant diseases are vaguely thought to be permitted by the supreme being but do not result from witchcraft. As Evans-Pritchard suggests these babies are scarcely social beings and so are hardly susceptible to witchcraft when it is interpreted anthropologically as the result of social friction arising between established social persons; further than this, as far as the Azande are concerned the child has only recently arrived and his soul may well soon return whence it has but come. For adult persons a different rationale is employed which ascribes all misfortune to witchcraft, and while it possesses a supernatural mode of operation its source is not the supreme being but in man himself.

This is a significant point for the present study for it indicates that even when a phenomenon is not attributed to a deity there may still be a folk explanation which a western observer might regard as supernatural, the fact that *mangu* is of human origin yet operates supernaturally shows that much care must be taken in applying the generalized ideas of plausibility to concrete cases.

9 Ibid., p. 540.
10 Evans-Pritchard, E. E., 1962: 162 ff.
11 Evans-Pritchard, E. E., 1937: 22.

At the folk level of a paradigm of meaning the Azande might be said to engage in the maintenance of a pragmatic plausibility, one which seeks to rectify life's misfortunes in a practical way as the case of death will demonstrate. All Zande deaths must be avenged by kinsmen for all death is believed to be the outcome of witchcraft. The way in which vengeance is enacted does not, however, cause further social strife but leads to a sense of satisfaction on the part of the bereaved kinsmen. This is so even though the apparent logic of vengeance ritual, which involves the death of the offending witch and the questioning of oracles to see whether any recently dead person was that witch, leads to yet another round of magic on the part of the newly deceased's kinsmen. A death brings to an end the questioning of the first group and satisfies them, for at the pragmatic level the issue of death and of man's response to it has met with action deemed appropriate and justifying. Evans-Pritchard emphasizes the intellectual consistency of Azande at the pragmatic level of thought as well as stressing their lack of coordination and systematic logicality in magic as a whole.[12]

The case of the Azande affords an interesting example of western academic approaches to the question of thought inasmuch as studies of their religion have produced integrated systems where none, as far as Evans-Pritchard's extensive ethnography is concerned, seems to exist in the minds of the people. References to prayers used by Zande to *Mbori* or the supreme being have been organized into theological systems by western commentators whereas 'in real life they are never so presented but are dissociated phrases evoked in situations of grief, anxiety and fear'. In such contexts they possess an 'emotional rather than conceptual significance' indeed Évans-Pritchard in criticizing over-schematizations in interpretations of Zande thought expresses the opinion that the 'Azande do not have any clear doctrinal opinions, for they actualize their beliefs, expressing them in rite and prayer rather than intellectualizing them in dogma and myth'.[13] The important feature lies in the 'logico-emotional dependencies between religious categories'.[14] The form of this dependency is what constitutes the system of plausibility, and the relative balance of logical and emotional factors the sufficiency of plausibility, for Azande. Their interest in cosmology, or rather their lack of it, is complemented by the great interest paid to social relations and the factors underlying them. Plausibility is generated against the social background rather than against a cosmic or even divine-satanic scenario.

By contrast with the Azande the Nuer, another Sudanese tribal people, direct their thinking about evil by means of the idea of spirit or *kwoth*. Spirit, unlike *Mangu*, does not originate in man but belongs to another order of reality, and it is with respect to that other order that Nuer direct their religious activity. This particular emphasis permits mention of a theoretically important idea which Evans-Pritchard raises in the concluding section of his 'Nuer Religion', and which bears directly on our argument. In reflecting on the lack of theoretical development in the study of primitive, and one might add advanced, religion he suggests that what is necessary is a comparative study of what he calls primitive philosophies,

---

12 Evans-Pritchard, E. E., 1962: 172.
13 Evans-Pritchard, E. E., 1937: 196.
14 Ibid, p. 197.

of the *weltanschauungen* which include elements that might not normally be regarded as religious. As a basis for such comparison he proposed that the 'dominant motif' of each culture be identified, but since there are so many potential motifs Evans-Pritchard went on to make the significant suggestion that 'the test of what is the dominant motif is usually, perhaps always, to identify that to which a people attribute dangers and sickness and other misfortunes and what steps they take to avoid or eliminate them'.[15] While this criterion might be thought a particularly appropriate choice of topic for Evans-Pritchard to make given the predilections of Azande and Nuer thought, it may well have an application of much broader scope as Evans-Pritchard hoped and as we also hope to establish for groups outside Africa.

One of the areas of weakness in religious studies requires some comment in the light of this expressed hope, and it is one which Evans-Pritchard himself saw clearly, namely the way in which primitive religions tend to be treated as different in kind from the so called world religions. In criticising the late nineteenth and twentieth century intellectualist, emotionalist and projectionist scholars of religion Evans-Pritchard expresses regret that they did not pay attention to contemporary forms of the world religions. Had they investigated the actual functioning of these religions rather than studying only the texts, creeds and formal systems then their relation to primitive religions would have been more obviously apparent and similar, and the primitive religions would not have been treated 'as something so unlike the religions of civilization that they appeared to require a special kind of interpretation and a special vocabulary'.[16] The evolutionary presupposition which directed much of this divorce between kinds of religion has already been considered, and it remains to say that in subsequent discussions no essential difference is postulated in the practical expression of religions. The paradigm of meaning implies that religions are engaged in the basic task of plausibility generation in the context of perceived evil and that this process can be identified despite culturally different expressions of evil and salvation. To reinforce this perspective a rather hard test case will be considered from the field of African ethnography, one which might almost serve to disprove the plausibility generalization.

The Mbuti pygmies of the Ituri Forest in the Congo do not possess any witchcraft beliefs or techniques, neither do they entertain any cosmological explanation for misfortune and evil.[17] This unusual combination contradicts S. F. Nadel's compensatory theory of witchcraft which argues that witchcraft will be employed as an explanation of evil if there is no cosmological or 'scientific' account of it readily available. Mary Douglas's comment on the Mbuti ethnography, that 'people can do without explanations of misfortune. They can live in tolerance and amity and without metaphysical curiosity', is quite critical for the paradigm of meaning offered here in terms of plausibility theory. Yet this is the very exception which proves the rule, for Douglas goes on to say that the apparent precondition for this state of affairs is that the Mbuti 'should be free to move away from each other

---

15 Evans-Pritchard, E. E., 1956: 315.
16 Evans-Pritchard, E. E., Ibid., p. 314.
17 Turnbull, C. M., 1965.

whenever strains appear. The price of such a benign cosmology is a low level of organization'.[18]

In different terms the Mbuti could be described as exhibiting a developed form of pragmatic plausibility which shows the necessity of making explicit reference to affective factors entering into the construction of a world of satisfactory meaning. This pragmatism operates as much at the level of supernatural beliefs as at that of social organization, for as C. M. Turnbull has adequately demonstrated in his extensive ethnography of the pygmies they have no elaborate conception of any world of gods, and even regard abstractions about a future life as without adequate foundation in human experience. Some of the systematized accounts of Mbuti theology which have been constructed Turnbull regards as more the result of western desires 'to present a picture of a system applicable to all Mbuti' than as an accurate assessment of the actual state of affairs.[19] In his criticism of Father Schebasta's over systematizations Turnbull resembles Evans-Pritchard's regrets with respect to similar exercises performed on the Nuer and Azande.

The Mbuti supernatural pragmatism, if it might be so called, is manifested in the fact that the forest itself, which is an immediate phenomenon, rather than some abstraction of it, lies at the centre of all their thought and action. Just as the Azande enact their attitude to misfortune through the rituals of witchcraft and oracles so the Mbuti act out their attitude to life and reality in their forest nomadism. Some comment on the perception of evil is required for the Mbuti since their case appears to be so exceptional.

Perhaps Turnbull's study of the Mbuti provides one of the best examples of a functionalist approach to witchcraft for it demonstrates how the pygmies who normally live in the forest itself have no witchcraft ritual, as already mentioned. But it goes on to show that the tribal villagers, with whom the Mbuti engage in economic exchange, do practise both witchcraft and sorcery, which serve to dispel the social frictions and conflicts engendered by village life. Witchcraft here 'being a concept employed usefully to bring to light hidden sources of dispute and to publically shame troublemakers'.[20] In the social life of the village, as symbolized and expressed in witchcraft, the Mbuti encounter that which is 'totally outside their forest-world experience, conscious malevolence'.[20] This is not to say that the life of pygmy hordes is always calm and illustrative of that lack of noise which they regard as the best way to live in, and without disturbing, the great forest itself. Friction does take place but the social response to it lies in the intentional division of the group with the offending parties withdrawing to different parts of the forest. This response to what must be regarded as a perception of evil as social conflict, is an example of the Mbuti pragmatic outlook, and is possible because, as Mary Douglas rightly says, they possess a low level of social organization. This response is not open to the villagers in the same way, for they live under the restraints of having to build houses in jungle clearings which cannot be abandoned just because trouble arises among neighbours.

The normal absence of crisis among the Mbuti results from their expertise as

---

[18] Douglas, M., 1970: xxxiii.
[19] Ibid., p. 246.
[20] Turnbull, C. M., Ibid., p. 59.

forest livers in an environment which is essentially benevolent, and which makes the basic nature of life appear to be good. They know how to cope with practically all problems they encounter, and illness in particular is something they know how to treat though the basic healthiness of their environment makes this less of a problem than it might be. Turnbull goes so far as to say that there is not a 'solitary instance to show the belief in a malevolent power against which protection must be sought', there is, rather, an intimacy of relationship between the individual Mbuti and the forest which is his father and mother, the source of his life and all his good. The one obvious exception is, inevitably, death itself. Yet unlike the Azande and the jungle villagers the Mbuti do not regard death as caused by the evil intention of one of their number. Witchcraft accusations never follow death, death is accepted as being perfectly natural and in accord with the processes which are forever at work in the forest. There is, nonetheless, the feeling that death is 'the one really imperfect thing in life', and death rites as with those of mourning, serve to restore the normality of life as quickly as possible.[21] The Mbuti would thus appear to present a case in which evil as such, or where perceived implausibility, is not a significant concern as far as the entire scheme of life is concerned. What they do present, however, is the desire to maintain that level of plausibility which forest life makes possible and which is interestingly expressed in the ideas of sound and noise.

Noise, especially loud noise, is said to be disturbing to the forest as such. This is as true of natural noises as to noises made by quarrels, and as far as the Mbuti are concerned one might just as easily express the notion of social friction as social noise as in any other way. It is better, they say, to disperse than to have such noise in the forest. Quiet, by contrast, is good and pleasing to the forest, its social expression through sound is in song. Song is, in terms of their conceptual classification, a form of quiet inasmuch as both quiet and song are 'cool' phenomena whereas noise is 'hot'. As might then be expected song rituals occupy a central place in rites of crisis such as death, and serve to attract the attention of the forest itself to their needs which helps restore the coolness of good order which itself is a feature of normal times. From this it can be seen that Mary Douglas's assertion that people can do without explanations of misfortune is both accurate and misleading; accurate inasmuch as the Mbuti do not have elaborate accounts of why disruptions occur, but misleading since they do possess ideas of what to do when quarrels occur. It is this action framework which characterizes both Mbuti and Azande religiosity, and it might be supposed that similar religious responses obtain much more widely. One way of understanding folk religion in any context is to regard those abstract theorizings which have been the focus of study for scholars of the world religions as less important than usually they are assumed to be, and to consider in more depth the pragmatic responses taken to various life circumstances.[22] The great divide between primitive religions and the 'village' manifestation of the world religions would then assume radically different proportions.

A postscript to this notion of pragmatic plausibility may be provided by drawing

---

21 Ibid., p. 147.
22 Cf. James Obelkevich, 1976.

from another study of Turnbull, one which offers another rather paradoxical test
of the paradigm of meaning. In fact no greater contrast with the Mbuti could be
found than that provided by the Ik tribe of Uganda which, because of particularly
bad climatic conditions, was forced into surviving against the pressures of overwhelming hunger.[23] This later study of Turnbull, which is as much an autobiographical essay on the nature of man as it is an ethnography, illustrates the growing
irrelevance of religious belief and ritual practice under conditions of social disintegration resulting from an increasing individualism itself made necessary to
obtain food for personal survival. Even witchcraft accusations which might have
been expected to increase in number as social conflicts multiplied came to be used
more as a form of abuse than as a social corrective. This would appear to reinforce
the essentially Durkheimian view of religion as a social phenomenon concerned
both with corporate morality and the classification of the world. No morality
remained among the Ik, and social classifications as expressed in religious forms had
virtually been abandoned. It appeared to Turnbull that they had come 'to a recognition of what they accept as man's basic selfishness, of his natural determination
to survive as an individual before all else'.[24] Not only was there no attempt to
improve conditions by ritual means, for actual physical conditions were acknowledged as having passed all bounds of reversal, but the basic categories of good and
evil were themselves made redundant. In this world of social fragmentation all
values were reduced to insignificance beside that of possessing food for oneself.

This example demonstrates the necessity of appropriate constraints in any
society conceived as a communication system and in which processes of plausibility
generation may operate effectively. The extreme environmental conditions made
social existence a practical impossibility and what is witnessed is human life apart
from its normative social context. Precisely because of this the social nature of
plausibility theory is underlined and the general paradigm of meaning established
as a normal human endeavour.

Evil and Sin

With the exception of the Ik ethnography, anthropological and phenomenological
studies of religion possess functioning social groups as their object of analysis, and
in them can be discerned systems of religious communication involving ideas of
evil and methods for its resolution. Because this book urges that the idea of evil
be interpreted non-theologically and in terms of plausibility theory some further
thought must be given to what is implied in this use of terms.

Some distinction must be drawn between the term evil when used in the
sociological sense of implausibility, and sin when employed theologically to refer to
a transgressed divine imperative. The necessity of such a distinction, one which
will facilitate analysis of 'negative' religious phenomena, becomes quite apparent
in the light of an important anthropological contribution to this whole area namely
Christoph Von Fürer-Haimendorf's Henry Myers Lecture delivered at the British
Academy and entitled 'The Sense of Sin in Cross-Cultural Perspective'. His conclusion

---

[23] .Turnbull, C. M., 1973.
[24] Ibid., p. 182.

that 'the concept of sin and with it the sense of sin cannot be common to all branches of humanity' would appear to undermine a central theme of our argument, namely that the perception of evil is the primary process in religions.[25] After a clarification of terminology this will be seen not to be the case.

Once the suggested distinction is drawn between evil and sin it is possible to agree with Fürer-Haimendorf that 'many societies lack a developed sense of sin and the belief in supernatural sanctions for transgressions of the moral code', and to agree with his further assertion to which he wishes to give a near universal status, that men have had to acknowledge that they have to 'struggle in a world beset by evil and imperfection'.[26] This point he elaborates even more in saying 'that the feeling that man was born for a fate better than his present condition is found among populations of all economic levels'.[26] Evil as perceived implausibility in the nature of things is the category which could be used to interpret this universal sense of imperfection, while sin would be a category relating to particular theological interpretations of imperfections including moral transgressions. While this is a far from perfect distinction inasmuch as different theologies require more particular distinctions to be drawn between kinds of 'sin', it does allow an initial phenomenological description to be made which is itself not grounded in any theological definition.

A positive contribution made by Fürer-Haimendorf lies in the final assessment that there is no universal correlation existing between types of social structure and the kind of sin identified by a society; there is no direct or indirect association between social and economic level of development and the form of sin experienced. If the distinction between evil and sin is adopted after the plausibility model it would be easier to make this point and to say that while sin is not a universal feature of human experience evil is, everywhere, a part of man's self-evaluation. Even such a simple redefinition would make one of Fürer-Haimendorf's concluding generalizations more intelligible in the light of his own preceding argument. 'Like other religious beliefs', he suggests, 'the sense of sin is a phenomenon *sui generis* which intertwines with social and economic phenomena but has an existence of its own not determined by conditions in secular spheres'.[27] This could be interpreted as saying that it is the sense of evil as perceived implausibility which is the *sui generis* element rather than the phenomenon of sin as transgressed imperatives which he has already shown to be absent from certain cultures including the Chenchus of the Deccan.

What is particularly significant in Fürer-Haimendorf's position is the ascription of a *sui generis* status to the sense of sin. He does not make it clear as to what exactly this means, yet he appears to offer the idea as a way of describing that which is widely present and yet is not determined by particular features of a social structure. Indeed, he makes it quite clear that anthropologists as anthropologists can make no philosophical or religious assertions about the ultimate nature of reality, and he cites Evans-Pritchard's closing and provocative words in *Nuer Religion* that 'at this point the theologian takes over from the anthro-

---

[25] Fürer-Haimendorf, C. Von, 1974.
[26] Ibid., p. 555.
[27] Idem.

pologist'.[28] While Fürer-Haimendorf's argument remains ultimately undefined its intention is perfectly clear and is that of asserting the universality of the 'fact of human imperfection'.[29] His desire is not to explain 'the ultimate roots of evil and sin' but merely to describe, in a manner which might even be called phenomenological, how various cultures identify the negative features of their existence.[30] His disinterest in engaging in any philosophical debate on the nature of this evil is characteristic of the pragmatic character of British anthropology, yet the very fact that he wants to establish a *sui generis* status for the negative phenomenon which 'has an existence of its own not determined by conditions in secular spheres', shows the impropriety of terminating the discussion at the level of description.

One reason Fürer-Haimendorf does not argue for a universal notion of sin, in his sense of the word, is because some tribes lack appropriate words to describe it. To what degree latent Christian ideas have influenced his search for words corresponding to those expressing guilt and penitence it is hard to say, once, however, any directly Christian model is eschewed as in the perspective of plausibility theory it is much easier to see how the perception of negative features is categorized in world cultures. This would establish the awareness of a lack of perfection as the basis for the *sui generis* category of evil, which might or might not involve a notion of human imperfection in any one social group. In the case of the Mbuti there would be no such indigenous notion of human evil while in most religions of the great traditions there would be such a factor. Some attention must be given to the way in which particular religious traditions develop their idea of implausibility if only to show that to talk of a *sui generis* category is impossible without relating it to concrete instances which both help identify the nature of the general category and assert the distinctive difference of various cultural expressions.

W. J. Boyd has carried out a useful study in this area showing how man's experience of evil is expressed in mythical form. Making considerable use of Rudolph Otto's categories of the holy he begins from an existentialist standpoint to show how Buddhist and Christian frameworks have developed ideas of evil explaining human experience. Christianity is evaluated as maximizing the externality of evil and the *horrendum* aspect of it, while minimizing its *fascinans* element. Buddhism, by contrast emphasizes this element of fascination which he links with the notion of bondage to *samsara*, or the repetitive existence of the unenlightened being. The points of greatest similarity are those which manifest a *numinal* quality attributed to symbolizations of evil, Satan in the case of Christianity and *Mara* in that of Buddhism. Precisely what is meant by numinal quality is hard to say, Boyd describes it as 'an overplus of meaning eluding conceptual analysis', and seems to be expressing the idea of the power and compulsion experienced in and through the symbols of evil as most dramatically portrayed in the phenomenon of possession by *Mara* or Satan.[31] What constitutes this power as evil is its disruptive aspect, the way it opposes what Christians and Buddhists regard as the truest expression of the ultimate. This positive goal or pattern of ideas Boyd identifies as the holy and true

---

[28] Evans-Pritchard, E. E., 1956: 322.
[29] Fürer-Haimendorf, C. Von, Ibid., 556.
[30] Idem.
[31] Boyd, W. J., 1975: 150.

and while their specific meanings are determined by the respective traditions he, nevertheless, regards them as correlates within these traditions.

Analysing Boyd's usage, evil might be said to be a term which identifies the disruption between good and evil, a kind of statement asserting that the holy and true is not easily attained. It does not provide any comment on the specific content of categories of evil, Boyd follows, in this approach, Ricoeur's analysis of evil as a shattering of man's grasp upon the sacred. As far as the present argument is concerned Boyd does not commence his description of evil at a sufficiently early period in the process of religious perception, for it is not necessarily true that 'the meaning of evil is derived from the meaning of the sacred'.[32] While it is impossible to arrive at any knowledge of whether mankind identified evil before identifying good, it is at least feasible to discuss the interrelation between notions of good and evil in any one religious tradition conceived as a communication system. In so doing no priority is given either to the notion of good or evil, both are regarded as necessary for the very rationale of that religious system of salvation to make any sense.

One of the most significant and influential studies to have addressed itself to these central categories of good and evil in an essentially non-theological way was William Robertson Smith's *Religion of the Semites*. In the fourth of those Burnett Lectures Smith began his theoretical analysis of religion in earnest by identifying the central categories without which he felt a study of religion to be impossible. The most important of these he calls 'the distinction between what is holy and what is common.[33] But Smith, and here his caution is at a premium and rather unlike the attitude of many other nineteenth century intellectualists, adds that the precise meaning of the terms holy and common is not easy to establish since it varies from religion to religion and also within any religion over the course of time.

Here Smith seeks to identify a general feature in religious phenomena which can be established in any particular case and yet which need not be of any particular kind, he is postulating the existence of religious structures rather than of any particular content. He exemplifies the principle by asserting that while holiness implies an ethical factor it did not do so in early Semitic religion. The notion of holiness he likens to electricity and to electrical discharge which might be associated with specific places or persons. A fundamental aspect of the category 'holy' lay in the fact of relationship, indeed holiness is the most general notion that governs the relationship between the gods or the divine and human beings.[34]

Inasmuch as holiness has to do with this interaction there may be said to exist rules governing it. These 'rules of holiness' Smith identifies with schemes of taboo, with those 'rules of conduct for the regulation of man's contact with deities'.[35] Not only does he conceive of a positive taboo associated with divinities, but he emphasizes the importance of negative taboos relating to man's encounter with evil spirits and powers, and these taboos he identifies with rules of uncleanness. In practical terms there is a problem in Smith's scheme since the notions of holiness and uncleanness can function in a very similar way in some societies, for what the

---

[32] Boyd, W. J., Ibid., p. 165.
[33] Smith, W. Robertson, 1894: 140.
[34] Ibid., p. 142.
[35] Ibid., p. 152.

rules associated with them are essentially concerned with is man's contact with, or access to, sources of power and influence.

Smith did not appear to recognise the difficulties introduced by his categories of holy and common for while arguing the case for the difference between positive and negative taboos he makes the point both that 'in most savage societies no sharp line seems to be drawn between the two kinds of taboo', and that 'in the Levitical legislation the law of clean and unclean may be brought within the sphere of divine ordinance on the view that uncleanness is hateful to God'.[36]

If it be asked what level or kind of analysis Smith is here engaged in the response would have to acknowledge a certain confusion in his entire scheme. While he is doubtless more concerned with man as a social being than as an individual consciousness he finds difficulty in handling a discussion on the social nature of man, and as will be commented later for Durkheim this lack of conceptual facility led to numerous statements being made about early man and his society which are simply difficult for a twentieth century social scientist to understand. Again, his perspective is decidedly evolutionary, not in the concrete sense of, for example, Frazer who postulated distinct phases through which human society had passed, but in a more general sense of periods and trends through which various ideas had been developed. This emergence of religious conceptions was not in Smith's thinking necessarily a positive and beneficial process. One of the best examples to the contrary being furnished by his belief that ancient religion was in some way more pure because less tainted and influenced by the idea of property in relation to sacrifice and the gods. Here, perhaps, Smith's inherent protestant evaluation of religion is glimpsed in the sense that he disliked the idea of a powerful priesthood whose status was derived from sacrificial ritual.

While Smith is unconcerned about the individual level of religiosity he nevertheless presupposes states of religious awareness in the early and later phases of religion. There is a certain methodological confusion in this for Smith is never able to formulate clearly the nature of the relation between the individual and the group. His constant concern with processes of human thought resembles the general nineteenth century anthropological involvement in the issue of primitive mentality which was not settled satisfactorally. It is for this reason that some of the crucial sections in the *Religion of the Semites* are notoriously difficult to interpret, as, for example, in this representative quotation from the ninth lecture dealing with sacrifice. 'In the beginnings of human thought, the natural and the supernatural, the material and the spiritual were confounded, and this confusion gave rise to the old notion of holiness, which turns on the idea that supernatural influences emanated, like an infection, from certain material things'.[37] A major problem in such sections lies in deciding whether Smith wanted to refer to states of mind or to modes of thought, to kinds of feeling states or to systems of logic. It may be closer to his intention to say that both were included so that the mode of experiencing and the understanding of what had been experienced combined in the lives of early man. What is clear is that Smith had simply not discovered an adequate methodology

---

[36] Ibid., p. 153.
[37] Ibid, p. 395.

and theoretical perspective which could have made his work more subtle and penetrating.

Emile Durkheim, whose work was fundamentally influenced by Smith, was able to achieve greater clarity and precision over the basic classification of humanly perceived reality through his sociological method, though as far as religious studies in the broadest sense are concerned and apart from sociology in the stricter sense, this was at the expense of a complete sociological reductionism. To make religion a mere epiphenomenon of social interaction, albeit a radically important creation of society, would not have satisfied Smith who forcefully argued for an adequate treatment of the supernatural element in Christianity, and who maintained a practical attitude of piety, which witnesses to this dimension, until his death.[38] But this is of secondary importance here, for what is true both of Smith and Durkheim is that the idea of a basic dichotomy, Smith's holy and common, expresses both a perception of phenomena and a means of classifying them. It relates both to the description and identification of experience, and more especially to experience gained within social contexts rather than in isolation. It was precisely this relational perspective which Durkheim developed in his study of *The Elementary Forms of the Religious Life*.[39] There he showed that the source of religiosity lay not in sacred places but in the community itself, not in any awesome power of a sanctuary but in the dynamic of society which itself generated religious power experienced by the participants as something completely different from their mundane existence, indeed for Durkheim this was 'the real characteristic of social facts, their transcendence over individual minds'.[40]

It is quite clear that Durkheim followed Smith in assuming the fundamental significance of a dichotomy in the classification of reality, but Durkheim is much firmer in his grasp of the way in which these categories originate in social life. For him all categories of thought are generated from social experience and in his opening chapter on 'religious sociology and the theory of knowledge' he provides a classical expression of a sociological theory of knowledge. Behind all categories of mind lies the primacy of the dichotomy between the sacred and the profane, terms developed from Smith's holy and common, and which are so profoundly different that in the whole history of human thought 'there exists no other example of two categories of things so radically opposed to one another'.[41] In accounting for the basis of this difference Durkheim grounds it in the nature of social reality as opposed to individual reality, of social goals and private goals. Accordingly magic is classified as profane inasmuch as it works antisocial ends as it achieves some selfish benefit for an individual. In this Durkheim may be seen to clarify one point of confusion in Robertson Smith, namely, that positive and negative taboos are of an essentially different kind. Without any explicit reference to Smith, Durkheim makes the point that even the traditional opposition of good and bad is nothing beside the sacred and profane dichotomy, thereby implying that positive and negative taboos ought not to be classified as members of the same class. Durkheim's obvious and explicit

[38] Black, J. S. and G. W. Chrystal, 1912a, p. 109; 1912b, p. 572.
[39] Durkheim, E., 1912.
[40] Ibid., p. 231.
[41] Ibid., p. 38.

respect for Smith's work is less likely to be the reason for his not arguing directly against his scheme, than the fact that Durkheim continues the argument of *The Elementary Forms* with very few direct references to or confrontations with other scholars.

Since Durkheim regarded his study of religion as one which laid bare the essential features of religion, and since he saw the sacred and profane as the most fundamental features it might seem surprising that he did not go on to discuss, or at least refer to, the idea of salvation. For the sake of the theoretical development of religious studies it is worth commenting upon this omission because it has influenced, albeit after the fashion of an argument from silence, the way scholars have related primitive and advanced religions. Durkheim appears not to have conceived of Aboriginal religion as even possibly containing elements of the idea of salvation, and the sacred-profane dichotomy which might have served as a basis for discussing the phenomenon of evil and the human response to it, is restricted for use in analysing the social nature of religiosity. Whether his avoidance of the idea of salvation results from his sociological rather than theological intention, or from the evolutionist assumption that to discuss the notion with respect to so primitive a level of society was a fruitless task since it was only in later phases of development that such phenomena emerged, it is impossible to say with certainty. It would, nevertheless be true to say that the explanatory framework adopted always determined not only how description and analysis proceeds, but also what is perceived as an appropriate object of study, and not least is this true for the idea of salvation. On the whole it would seem that Durkheim falls into the position held by Fürer-Haimendorf who regarded saviour and salvation motifs as the products of relatively advanced social systems, advanced in terms of economic and cultural technology. This kind of perspective is markedly different from Evans-Pritchard's studies of equally undeveloped societies for he admits the possibility and importance of another dimension to the life of, for example, the Nuer, one which could not be completely explained in terms of any single social scientific theory. This emphasis upon the individual's perception of his relationship to a divinity, noted but not analysed by Evans-Pritchard, marks a significant difference in the way he sees the individual relating to society compared with Durkheim's rather more abstract considerations, this difference is to be understood, in part, in the light of the fact that Durkheim never did study a group in the field.

In terms of the plausibility model of salvation it is possible to interpret Durkheim's study of religion as one which is very much concerned with the reality of salvation as we understand it even though Durkheim did not see the issue in this way at all. The only justification there can be for indulging in an exercise of this sort, given the sound rejection of the ethnographic accuracy of *The Elementary Forms* in modern anthropology, is to show how theoretical perspectives can appear to change the entire significance of the religious phenomena studied.[42] If, then, the category of the sacred originates in the intensity of social experience, salvation can be identified as the state of maximum social involvement, experienced by each participant member of a society. It is, as Durkheim says, the state of transcendence

---

[42] Evans-Pritchard, E. E., 1965: 53 ff.

resulting from ritual activity in which the power of society is encountered but only as perceived in the totems and other sacra.[43] Again in terms of plausibility theory, the profane would represent states of disintegration when the unifying forces of social relationships are no longer present or effective, a condition which indicates Durkheim's evaluation of man whose religiosity is not only a function of his sociality but is actually identified with it. Durkheim describes man as Homo duplex with the two components of individuality and sociability producing the whole, yet as far as he is concerned man is only fully himself when caught up in the central totemic rites which serve to reinforce the individual in his social role, once separated from community interaction the sole person declines from a full measure of humanity. The real significance of what Durkheim is here suggesting can only be appreciated when it is realised that he does make a full equivalence between god and society. Total dependence on god, or god as that which is ultimately significant, is what Durkheim sees society to be in relation to its individual members, so that to be in a state of salvation is to be a fully participant member of society, for outside affective society there is no salvation.

To think of religious ritual only in terms of psychological excitement would, however, be incorrect, an error of understanding which can be rectified by a consideration of Durkheim's analysis of knowledge, and the fundamental premise that true knowledge is to be equated with impersonal reason which itself is a product of historical and collective processes. Durkheim forces the point that all personal and subjective elements must be 'rooted out' of collective representations 'if we are to approach reality more closely'.[44] The means by which the personal factor is eliminated is that of corporate agreement, a form of social consensus which establishes basic ideas while ignoring idiosyncratic elements of thought. Durkheim's reification of the notion 'society' underlies this kind of argument and enables him to believe that what is produced by social action is different from that resulting from individual cogitation. For Durkheim, then, reason itself is a phenomenon, is a social product divested of both personal and collective emotionalism while religious phenomena retain as a basic attribute high levels of affectivity. Religious 'knowledge' and rational knowledge can be seen to occupy different positions in Durkheim's thought such that the categories of thought are, themselves, ever present with individuals whereas religious knowledge or awareness cannot be maintained except on the basis of repeated reinforcement. This means that any notion of salvation as far as Durkheim is concerned would, necessarily, have to involve affective factors as well as a reasonable, that is, a non-emotionally based explanation of what takes place in the ritual process.

This emphasis on mind and affectivity is, interestingly though rather differently, the core of another nineteenth century scholar, Max Müller, whose Hibbert Lectures of 1878 are a model of clear thinking in the history of religions. Mention of Müller serves not only to acknowledge one who has been called 'the father of comparative religion', but also to make the more substantial point that the later nineteenth century and early twentieth century scholars were much given to issues of mind,

---

43 Durkheim, E., Ibid., p. 215.
44 Ibid., p. 444.

perception and the true nature of things.[45] In Müller's case, as in that of Durkheim, there is no interest in the question of salvation or evil in any analytical sense. Müller is fundamentally an evolutionist preoccupied with the problem of how notions of supernatural entities developed from the growth of language. It is, however, to be regretted that he is usually only remembered for his infamous 'disease of language' theory of the origin of divinity which results from the ascription and subsequent reification of personal names and attributes to natural phenomena.

In the first of his lecture a section is devoted to the question of 'religion as a subjective faculty for the apprehension of the infinite' here he takes up a definition of religion presented in 1873 in a lectures to the Royal Institution. The substance of this definition involves the notion of a mental faculty: 'religion is a mental faculty or disposition which, independent of, nay, in spite of sense and reason, enables man to apprehend the Infinite under different names and under varying disguises'.[46] By contrast with Durkheim's social emphasis Müller's argument clearly demonstrates the philosophical and individualistic concern of the intellectualist anthropologists, philosophers and theologians of Müller's period. Yet the dichotomy of emphasis between Durkheim's social processes and Müller's individual dimension should not be allowed to obscure their mutual interest in mind and the structure and origin of religious consciousness. Müller makes perfectly clear with respect to his definition of religion, and to potential criticism of it, that he does not intend saying that the term 'faculty' involves the notion of 'a substantial something', for there is 'but one self and one consciousness' with no 'separate consciousness for religion'.[47] What differentiates religious awareness from any other kind if mental state is the object of consciousness, so the notion of faculty designates a mode of action in relation to an object of general consciousness and for religion this is the most general of all categories, the idea of totality, of all that transcends sense and reason.

While it would be possible to show the intellectual affinity between this view, which focuses upon the relation between consciousness and the object of consciousness, and that of William James in psychology along with subsequent phenomenologists and their notion of intentionality, it is much more appropriate as far as the present argument is concerned to indicate the way in which Müller is attempting to handle questions of meaning through the study of the notion of totality. When he says that 'the history of religion is a history of all human effort to render the Infinite less and less indefinite' he was engaging in the highest level of generalization of a specifically philosophical kind, and in that was but little concerned with practical aspects of religion which might, at the more affective dimension, work towards the elimination of indefinite factors, yet he thereby demonstrated, albeit indirectly and by implication, that religious studies could not ignore the fact that man perceived the world as other than they desired it to be.[48] Later unpopularity of Müller's theory of language and mythology, along with the evolutionistic dimension of his speculative thought, has obscured the basic similarity of intention

---

[45] Sharpe, E. J., 1975: 35.
[46] Müller, M., 1882: 22.
[47] Ibid., p. 21.
[48] Ibid., p. 36.

between Müller and the much more recent work on the paradigm of meaning in religion, especially perhaps that of Hans Mol.

Meaning and Identity

Mol's recent study *Identity and the Sacred*[49] is particularly important as far as the paradigm of meaning is concerned because it positively advances the status of affective phenomena within the entire process of meaning construction. In short this change can be typified in the very terms used, from meaning to identity, where the very notion of identity presupposes an emotional dimension to the human sense of significance. Mol describes this work as a sketch for a general social scientific theory of religion, 'yet one which seeks to avoid the general sociological tendency to relativise the phenomena under consideration by absolutizing the theory adopted'.[50] The desire to avoid reductionist forms of explanation has a dual basis, for Mol is both convinced that vital religiosity is more important a human phenomenon than is theorizing from an absolute position, and that to do so is to fall foul of a central tenet of his own theory. For, as far as he is concerned, absolutized theories, or explanations which claim ultimate validity, are potential religious phenomena themselves.

Mol regards all men, including members of primitive society, as engaged in a 'search for identity', which as part of man's nature as an envolving species implies a contrasting and paradoxical tension through the process of change in which he is involved either as a recipient or instigator.[51] There exists in man a dialectic between 'adaptation and identity, between differentiation and integration', a dialectic which may be evaluated not only in terms of social values and expectations as in Durkheim, but also psychologically at the level of the individual. It is precisely this concern with the individual which leads Mol to emphasize emotional aspects of life associated with the construction of a personal identity, and therein a sense of meaning. He categorizes what might be called this affective dimension of plausibility subsisting in the phenomenon of personal identity as the element of 'commitment', or the 'emotional attachment to a specific focus of identity' which serves the religious individual as the 'pivot or articulation between the transcendent and the mundane'.[52] It is precisely the overemphasis on rationality in scientific method and much philosophy which has lead to the inability of science 'to anchor meaning emotionally'.[53]

Mol follows Talcott Parsons' idea that it is commitment demonstrated in action which makes a religion out of a mere philosophy, but commitment of that kind presupposes the worthwhileness of the endeavour and assumes that a creed or set of values is worthy of implementation on the part of the religious person. This leads the argument to Mol's central thesis that an idea system which provides a definition and explanation of a person's life will tend to be sacralized, and that such sacralized ideologies constitute a religion. In other words and by the way of definition he says

---

[49] Mol, H., 1976.
[50] Ibid., p. x.
[51] Ibid., p. 2.
[52] Ibid., p. II.
[53] Ibid., p. 126.

that sacralization is a 'process by means of which on the level of symbol systems certain patterns acquire ... (a) taken for granted, stable, eternal quality'.[54] So it is that the sacralization process possesses the function of 'objectification', the 'tendency to sum up the variegated elements of mundane existence in a transcendental point of reference', while also engendering a commitment to the focus of identity located in the objectified structures.[55]

Much of this language and material follows the general outline of plausibility theory and Mol acknowledges his debt to Berger through whom most of Mol's phenomenological material, deriving ultimately from Alfred Schutz, has been mediated. Mol's emphasis upon the integrity of the personality in the process of emergent identity leads him to consider the significance of general affective dimensions and to place less emphasis upon language than does Berger for example, this is a useful corrective to Berger's phenomenological sociology. One reason why Mol's discussion of personality is particularly significant for our argument emerges from the idea of integrity, for he believes there to be processes operating against the integrity and identity of the personality of the individual and also of groups. These negative factors are located in, or arise from, both the human being as an individual and the social processes of evolution. The inevitable changes influencing man as he faces new environments, both natural and social, present a perpetual challenge to whatever state of equilibrium obtains, this 'inexorable tendency towards change and differentiation' is, for Mol, to be seen as inevitable because of the very fact of human being in the world.[56] This rather philosophical expression is only a gloss on the basic reality of man as a biological and social creature set within an ever changing and dynamic environment, as part of this environment may also be added the changing understanding of philosophical and theological kinds which call the intellectual *status quo* into question. This is a somewhat better explanation of the immediacy of 'alienation and disorder' than that offered by John Bowker and his notion of religions as route finding activities set amidst compounds of limitation, or at least it provides a more adequate theoretical context for discussing the phenomenon of negative features.[57] In another respect the evolutionary context even aids Bowker's form of argument, for it is primarily concerned with processes of interaction between entities in the present and which may be seen as working towards a homeostatic equilibrium of a dynamic kind. That is to say that Mol's use of evolution is less that speculative developmentalism which has already been criticised in the nineteenth century scholars, than another way of expressing what has already been applauded in the communication theory approach of general systems theory. While Mol does not emphasize the negative aspects of the interaction between man and environment, indeed he stresses that his concern lies on the side of the positive sacralizing processes, their significance remains quite considerable inasmuch as man is seen to be engaged in ascribing differential values to the world in which he is set.

For Mol religion is a term which defines an ideology as ultimate, an ideology

---

[54] Ibid., p. 5.
[55] Ibid., p. II.
[56] Ibid., p. 262.
[57] Ibid., p. 265.

which itself necessarily defines man's status and condition to him including an evaluation of negative features. Moreover 'religion sacralizes any identity', it 'defines man and his place in the universe', functions which are of a positive nature and which symbolize man's 'proclivity for order'; here meaning and order can be seen to be more objective and impersonal notions while identity serves a more subjective and personal end. Hence sacralization of identity presupposes the affective element in any paradigm of meaning, it is a quality perceived in a proposition about the nature of things.[58] To relate Mol to Müller one might say the former is not content merely to show how man comes to understand the Infinite, but how he comes to relate himself, in action, to it. Religious beliefs are placed beyond doubt, as far as practical action on the basis of them is concerned, when they are sacralized, their self-evident and compelling nature determines how men relate to them. Here Mol's notion of validation closely resembles Berger's use of legitimation processes. Mol is not so acutely aware of the problem of evil as was Berger who emphasized factors which challenged legitimizing processes, and also Bowker in his argument that religious systems are those explanatory modes which are expressly directed towards particularly intransigent problems of meaning experienced by man. Mol's particular contribution, despite his underemphasis on negative factors, lies in identifying the quality of the sacred as inhering in statements of identity and of definitions of ultimate reality. Unlike Durkheim Mol did not see that ultimate religious reality, as far as a social scientific perspective is concerned, necessarily involves the profane along with the sacred, the only reason for labouring this point is that Mol's own explanation of objectification processes is hindered by the perpetual accentuation placed upon the sacred. His reference to the notion of *maya* demonstrates the disadvantage under which he has placed himself. Arguing that objectification 'is the tendency to sum up the variegated elements of mundane existence in a transcendental frame of reference where they can appear in a more orderly, consistent and more timeless way', Mol offers several examples of notions which he orders in a ranked manner on what might be described as a basis of the distance of the phenomenon from the mundane world. Thus *mana* is categorized as a 'supernatural power concretized in persons and things', and appears 'only one step removed from the mundane' and hardly distinguishes between the transcendent and the immanent. *Maya*, by contrast, is further removed constituting the 'utmost universalization of mythic being ... unified into a single interpretative system'.[59] In order to make these assertions which, if true would exemplify and substantiate his argument, Mol finds it necessary to engage in some reinterpretation, firstly by taking recourse to the 'original' meaning of *maya* as supernatural power rather than to its more usual sense of cosmic illusion, and secondly by identifying *maya* with the Brahman-atman doctrine which he says represents the notion of cosmic identity. In this double elimination of the notion of *maya* in its sense which might easily be interpreted in terms of plausibility and negativity Mol says that the 'profane is relativized', a relativization which has 'a balancing effect on the mundane'.[60] The consequence of this exercise is that Hinduism comes to be evaluated as possessing 'a weak

---

58 Ibid., pp. 63, 70.
59 Ibid., p. 206.
60 Ibid., p. 207.

potential for active motivation', and as encouraging an 'essentially negative world-view', though exactly why this should be Mol does not say. Similarly in examples from Judaism, Islam and Christianity Mol finds himself having to provide explanations in order to avoid categorizing sacred entities along with profane ones. If once it is admitted that both sacred and profane entities can be sacralized then this problem is removed. But saying that the profane can be sacralized is to employ Mol's terms and means that men act towards the profane in a particular way, it is not to equate the sacred and the profane in terms of their content but of their form as ultimate explanations of mundane phenomena.

Despite these criticisms Mol's study stands as a clear example of how the paradigm of meaning can be seen to underlie modern religious studies, most particularly it shows how high level generalizations about the nature of thought and interpretative categories can be related to the actual commitment of ordinary religious practitioners. It is just this kind of perspective which will be adopted in looking at particular cases of sectarian religion and Indian religion in following chapters. Before that, however, attention must be turned to another aspect of the paradigm of meaning which can best be described as hermeneutics, or the task of interpretation.

CHAPTER FOUR

ANTHROPOLOGICAL HERMENEUTICS

Religious phenomena probably more than any others are subject to a great variety of interpretations at a number of different levels of analysis, this is due not only to the fact that several academic disciplines have interested themselves in this area, but is also due to the fact that religious men seek to understand themselves, and produce theologies and mythologies as well as histories in order to do so. Because this study is not an exercise in systematic theology it does not attempt to comment upon or to contribute any confessional understanding of religion, that task first requires the kind of work which is intended here, namely a critical evaluation of methods used in religious studies and especially with respect to the notion of salvation.

The central concern of this chapter is that of reductionism as a characteristic feature of social scientific explanations of religion. As has already been suggested in the case of the sacred-profane dichotomy all theorizing operates according to certain fundamental principles which once adopted, become difficult if not practically impossible to abandon even if the data encountered prove difficult to interpret by their means. The goal of most anthropological and sociological analyses is fairly clearly defined and, theoretically at least, relatively easily attained. What is more difficult, and this is the issue which must now be taken up at some length, is the question of whether the data themselves should be allowed to influence the way they are interpreted? But what exactly does this question mean in terms of anthropological hermeneutics?

It obviously does not mean that the external observer, be he anthropologist or theologian, must come to accept the religious claims of the movement or society studied; neither, however, does it mean that he ought to set himself the task of disproving whatever claims to truth are made. While most scholars would not explicitly engage in any such destructive task, indeed they generally state that truth claims made by religious groups have nothing to do with them as analysts, it nevertheless remains true that the form of interpretation engaged in by sociologists and anthropologists often presupposes the error of religious assertions, while going on to demonstrate that the significant or 'true' facts of the religion are to be discovered in the way it reflects the social structure or the like. Having said this it is only proper to add that some historians of religion similarly presuppose the ultimate veracity of religion in general when studying any one in particular, and this is, likewise, a dangerous stance especially if they, while ignoring what might be called their own 'religious reductionism', criticize the sociological or psychological reductionism of other scholars.

Mol, as has already been shown, preferred to interpret religion in terms of man's search for identity rather than in terms of social structure; but is it possible to go further than this in religious interpretation? In answering this question it will be possible to clarify further the paradigm of meaning both substantially and also in terms of the similarity of approach shown by anthropologists and historians of religion.

Wilhelm Dupré in his study of ethnophilosophy argued in the same general vein as Mol, evaluating religion as a unitary phenomenon on the basis of man's universal solidarity in the search for meaning. Religion becomes an 'intensive quality of the process of symbolization in general', and may be so regarded as a symbol of symbolization, as such it represents 'the culmination of life in general' in which meaning may be said to be concretized.[1] This argument which resembles so much of what has already been said in respect of the paradigm of meaning, lead Dupré to the obvious point that the study of religion must 'evolve out of an analysis of culture and man', by means of what he designates as an 'unconditioned functionalism', and more significantly to the idea that indigenous terminology should be retained as a reminder to the scholar of 'the hermeneutic situation'.[2] He fully acknowledges the fact of cultural diversity, as this retention of native terms shows, but he also believes in a fundamental human unity manifested in the 'quest for meaning', it is as a result of this paradox of human unity and diversity that Dupré's passing comments on hermeneutics lie in need of further elaboration.[3]

A primary question concerns the very word 'meaning'. This metaproblem, the meaning of meaning, assumes anything but a trite significance once it is realized that cultures might well hold different notions of what ideas and values are worthy of social recognition and validation. How then can the term be so used as to make it viable in cross-cultural contexts? Perhaps the simplest answer to this question consists in establishing a distinction between the form and content of the notion of meaning. By form is intended the presupposition that men and cultures seek an ordered and intelligible world, while content refers to the specific cultural set of values in the light of which order is pursued. So to distinguish between form and content is to raise again the issue outlined much earlier between external and internal observers' models, and to admit that the meaning of a culture established by the analyst may differ from the indigenous understanding, when such a difference occurs it will, usually, be because the observer is engaging in some higher level, and probably reductionist, mode of interpretation. So the question of meaning can be seen to be rather like the problem of the definition of religion, this is because any term which is used cross culturally must possess both general characteristics which admit of comparison, whilst also allowing specific variation.

At the most pragmatic level it might be argued that the form of the notion derives from man's biological and sociological relations through which he orders his environment for the purpose of survival, while the particular features will vary from the kind of meaning content furnished by the forest life for the Mbuti, to the urban complexity of western city dwellers. Both possess meaning and are set on survival even though the precise mechanics of that motivation and its means vary to a marked extent. It is in this connection that accurate phenomenological descriptions of social and religious phenomena become invaluable inasmuch as they do not prejudge the content of indigenous value and meaning systems, and seek

---

[1] Dupré, Wilhelm, 1975: 139; 131; 138.

[2] Ibid., p. 120.

[3] Ibid, p. 119.

only to permit whatever native structure of significance there might be to manifest itself. This also shows the need for the phenomenological act of *epoche* in the task of description, as well as for as full a description as possible, since it may only be at a late stage of observation that otherwise insignificant factors assume a major role in the overall system of meaning.   ✦

If the first stage of study consists in this kind of phenomenological description the second is even more difficult to discuss and to name, for while the term 'analysis' suggests itself it rather begs the question of criteria, while 'understanding' in the sense of *Verstehen* appears at first to be too vague. What Dupré seems to be suggesting as desireable is an analysis which is grounded in the facts themselves, an understanding emerging from the indigenous phenomena. He presumes that the observer will perceive a kind of intellectual *Gestalt* amidst the diverse material such as will enable him to identify several key ideas which can themselves then be utilized in interpreting other, less obvious, aspects of the data.

Dupré introduced the notion of 'constitutive analysis' to embrace this kind of study which is an 'analysis of the particulars that receives its logic from the whole which bears them in their particularity'.[4] In actual fact he is advancing methodologically no further than the level achieved by Evans-Pritchard in the fieldwork already discussed above, except that Evans-Pritchard engaged himself in performing the task rather than identifying and categorizing exactly what he was doing. It is probably significant that the one reference to him in Dupré's work is to his attempt to integrate meaning and ritual, which suggests a rather partial reading of the Evans-Pritchard contribution to the study of religion, especially since the latter's work can be seen as a practical example of both descriptive phenomenology and constitutive analysis without claiming to be either. Evans-Pritchard in both the Nuer and Zande studies uses the data themselves to provide the framework for analysing the indigenous rationale of thought.

This lack of appreciation of Evans-Pritchard's work may be excused Dupré since it is only recently that anthropologists themselves have given it theoretical appraisal. Be that as it may, the point he is eager to make, and which Evans-Pritchard made implicitly, is of the greatest importance, namely that any religious phenomena set within a cultural context must be interpreted in the light of that culture. The system of logic, or pattern of thought, relative to a culture must be discovered and described whether or not it bears a resemblance to any other system of thought. This is one methodological safeguard against postulating primitive or any other kind of mentality to social groups other than that of the observer.

It also safeguards against another methodological fallacy which might be described as the Platonic fallacy of approximation, or in other words the ascribing to mankind essential features or attributes on the basis of observing different levels of manifestation of a phenomenon such as religiosity in a number of different cultures. Observations based on a limited, restricted or selected group of cases could easily present a wrongly balanced evaluation of the nature of man in terms of any one aspect of his constitution be it religious, economic, psychological or that of kinship.

---

[4] Ibid., p. 119.

Homo religiosus

In the context of this chapter it is particularly interesting to observe that the very title Homo religiosus was suggested to replace Homo sapiens in an argument centred on the problem of interpretation. R. R. Marett, who coined this phrase in his 1932-3 Gifford Lectures, was well aware of the critical nature of cultural diversity as far as its analysis and interpretation were concerned, and identified the choice between using european words to describe the thoughts of the un-civilized which might be misunderstood, or those of the natives which might not be understood at all, as 'the dilemma of anthropology'.[5] Marett believed in the unity of man as far as his essential constitution and mental faculties were concerned, preferring the 'old fashioned assumption of the absolute homogeneity of the human mind' to the position he saw represented in Lévy-Bruhl which regarded man as possessing 'as many distinct 'mentalities' as there are distinct social types'.[6] His criticism of Lévy-Bruhl and of the Année Sociologique, which he otherwise tended to favour, resembles the methodological criticism we will raise later in connection with Rodney Needham's study of mentality, inasmuch as Marett reasoned that if 'the mentalities of different men at different levels of culture are in all respects as incommunicable as their passing dreams then Social Anthropology would be utterly inconceivable'.[7]

For Marett anthropology was an eminently conceivable discipline as long as its subject matter was clearly identified and given an intelligible status. It was in attempting to denote the nature of the study that he disagreed with the Durkheimian emphasis upon rather reified notions such as sentiment, for that reification which regarded the products of psychological states as 'things' in themselves Marett saw as part of a process which reduced the significance of the individual as such in the entire system of explanation. It was for this reason that Marett advocated a social psychological approach, one which accommodated the individual to the group and vice versa. As far as the historical development of anthropological theory is concerned, and in terms of the study of religion the implications of this are significant, Marett's paper of 1908 entitled A Sociological View of Comparative Religion, is important inasmuch as he declares that British anthropologists would 'one and all, if challenged, declare (their) method to be, broadly speaking, psychological'.[8]

Marett's fundamental concern was with the problem of reductionism and it was this which led him to criticise both what he called individual psychology with its general philosophical emphasis upon the discrete existence of the single self, and also the 'social morphology' of the Année Sociologique tradition which he saw as reducing the status of the individual by submitting it to that of the social body. There is a kind of pragmatic focus upon the individual in Marett's work which is more reminiscent of the stance of phenomenologists and historians of religion than of many subsequent anthropologists who tended more in the direction of Durkheim and the social nature of human being. It would certainly be true to say that apart from occasional contributions of recent anthropologists such as I. M. Lewis the

---

5 Marett, R. R., 1933: 3.
6 Marett, R. R., 1929: 174.
7 Ibid., p. 175.
8 Ibid., p. 124.

British tradition has not regarded psychological considerations with favour.[9] It will be necessary to return to this issue of psychology later since the very model of meaning can hardly be discussed apart from it. For the present it suffices to say that Marett not only presumed that men were universally similar in thought processes, but that he regarded religious factors as basic to the constitution of human life itself.[10] Religion is what enables man to face the unknown and to deal with it optimistically, especially in periods of crisis.[11] So asserting the pragmatic quality of primitive thought and action, and being fully aware that primitive and advanced men are similar in many mental characteristics, Marett identified the religious factor as a certain attitude to the world which he characterized as being associated with the sacred. Crises and other events may illicit from man a feeling of awe and a sense that he is involved in a realm quite different from that of the workaday world, it is precisely this 'supernormal' dimension, as it might be called, and the attitude of sacredness which attaches to it which constitutes Homo religiosus for Marett.

In his paper on *The Conception of Mana* he takes up this problem of definition with respect to religion and in terms of the sacred by suggesting an alternative minimal definition of religion to that of Tylor, one which involves the necessary complementarity of the notions *mana* and *tabu*. Marett shows himself clearly aware of the delicate decision to adopt alien terms in what he calls comparative religion, yet he feels that the general category of phenomena which can be embraced by the terms *mana* and *tabu* is sufficiently wide and inclusive as to benefit from the description. *Mana* thus designates the 'positive aspect of the supernatural, or sacred',[12] which describes those events or experiences which 'differ perceptibly from the order of ordinary happenings'; *Tabu*, by contrast, serves to identify the negative aspects of such experience.[13] Marett distinguishes between the essential nature of these experiences and the diverse ways in which they are expressed across cultures.

In certain respects the kind of anthropological stance adopted here resembles the outlook of Mircea Eliade in the history of religions, particularly in the way the sacred as a category is thought to be prime as far as the ultimate quality of human perception is concerned. It would also be possible to compare and contrast *mana* and *tabu* in Marett's sense of general categories, with Rudolph Otto's conception of the holy as embracing attracting and repelling elements. The similarity between these ideas and those of Robertson Smith on holy and common, and Durkheim on sacred and profane is quite striking and, perhaps instructive. The obvious fact that Marett was familiar with the work of Robertson Smith and Durkheim is possibly less valuable than the fact that in order to accommodate his argument to the data as he found them it was necessary to adopt a twofold classification.

If Dupré's notion of constitutive analyses be recalled here it might be suggested that if the information gathered in religious studies is to be permitted to influence

---

    9 Lewis, I. M., 1971, 1977.
    10 Marett, R. R., 1933: 3.
    11 Marett, R. R., Anthropology. (Undated).
    12 Marett, R. R., 1909: 99.
    13 Idem.

the way categories are drawn up to handle it, then this dichotomy between essentially distinctive entities might actually correspond to a real *status quo* in the world of religious perception. Were that the case then what might be called the family resemblance between all these terms would represent the attempts made by different scholars to render intelligible a diverse mass of documentation which, nevertheless, appeared to offer the natural division into the two opposing notions which have been perceived by them even when working from significantly different perspectives. To say this is to transgress into more philosophical areas which will be explored at greater length in the final chapter. To raise the issue in a context considering hermeneutics is quite proper, however, especially since these brief comments on Marett's work show that, contrary to recent anthropological expectations and procedures, it is not improper to ask questions about the basic nature of man and of man in relation to his complete environment including that which might be called the supernatural dimension.

But in terms of the paradigm of meaning there is an even more demanding question raised by what we have identified as categories bearing a family resemblance, and it concerns the polarity of positive and negative factors. What would seem to be the case is that both at the level of folk religiosity and at the more abstract level of scholarly analysis there is a consensus as to the twofold nature of human experience. This duality of perception both of plausible and implausible features of reality demonstrates a point made much earlier, that both scholarly and non-reflective considerations of the human condition are one in terms of a general principle of meaning construction even though the mode of expression adopted inevitably varies. The fact of this polarity also reinforces the argument that identification of the sources of implausibility or evil constitutes, in terms of structure at least, the basic element of the initial starting point in the process of redemption. To say that there is a group of categories specifically dealing with the polarity of good and evil is to say that the process of meaning construction shows a certain unity in the area of religion when such categories are also constructed in differing disciplines they mark the trend of the paradigm of meaning as a unifying approach to the study of religion.

Perhaps the best known anthropological contribution which could be drawn upon to reinforce the argument on meaning is that of Claude Lévi-Strauss and his structural analysis of myth. Although it is not intended to embark on any significant discussion of the Lévi-Straussian corpus it is necessary to make several observations which are particularly apposite to the idea of categories embracing fundamental polarities of existence, and to the pervasiveness of the notion of plausibility.

Firstly it should be observed that Lévi-Strauss is concerned to show that all men, irrespective of their so called level of cultural development, exhibit the same kind of mental alacrity and facility in ordering the world in which they find themselves and in the face of the paradoxes of experience they encounter. This implies that all men are engaged in the search for meaning and that it is not significantly different in form even when cultural content varies manifestly. Another interesting issue which emerges indirectly from this is the question of how the mythologist differs from the myth teller? Indeed it became fashionable in reviews and critiques of Lévi-Strauss to suggest, for example, that 'in the final analysis, the intellectually reflective and scientifically deliberate study of the infrastructure and hidden unconscious reality of myth 'is itself a kind of myth'.[14] But to make such comments is not even to score a cheap point, it is, rather, to ignore the fact that both man and anthropologist are human. While Lévi-Strauss is not concerned to argue any explicit phenomenology of the status and function of the anthropologist he is aware that the fundamental human processes are at work in him as his rather autobiographical volume *Tristes Tropiques* amply indicates.[15] So Lévi-Strauss's work could itself be advanced as an example of the way in which the paradigm of meaning operates both in the producer and analyst of culture, albeit at varying levels of insight into the very motives for and processes of meaning construction.

The second major issue raised by Lévi-Strauss's approach is that of the nature of the perceived polarities he believes to be present in many different kinds of culture.[16] It is well known that Lévi-Strauss presupposes that 'mythical thought always progresses from the awareness of oppositions towards their resolution' by means of sets of binary oppositions which serve as mediating notions between the initial distinctions. These primary oppositions are not necessarily those of good and evil in any simple moral sense, they relate rather to the essential ontological awareness of man that he is a creature of nature whilst also being a person of culture. To what extent this distinction could be related to the Durkheimian opposition of sacred or profane, or to the other categories which have been considered, it is difficult to say, what is certain is that Lévi-Strauss finds that he cannot engage in his anthropological analyses apart from this conceptual distinction underlying man's self awareness. Here he shows the power of the evidence itself in compelling the anthropologist to pay due regard to the internal observer's model provided by indigenous informants. This is something he has done in the classic study of Totemism where he emphasizes the point made by E. B. Tylor that 'it is necessary to consider the tendency of mankind to classify out the universe'.[17] The fact remains that Lévi-Strauss pays the closest attention to the ways in which tribal peoples work out their ideas on the realities they experience in life by means of mythological study. The category opposition of nature and culture usually embraces the more obvious distinctions between death and life, earth and heaven and the like.

The final idea in Lévi-Strauss which bears directly upon the present argument concerns the personal level at which meaning is to be sought and which includes an affective dimension. Lévi-Strauss is quite explicit in identifying anthropology as a 'semiological science' which takes 'as a guiding principle that of 'meaning''.[18] He is not only saying that both myths and symbols operate at cognitive as well as at affective levels as far as the native is concerned, though the fact that he has been criticized for overstressing the unconscious mind demonstrates that he has a real interest in both dimensions of being, but he is also suggesting that the anthropologist himself must not ignore the existential dimension of those he studies or of his own life. So it is that he associates anthropology more with 'humanistic

---

14 Scholte, Bob, 1970: 148.
15 Lévi-Strauss, C., 1968.
16 Lévi-Strauss, C., 1963: 224.
17 Lévi-Strauss, 1962: 13.
18 Lévi-Strauss, C., 1963: 364.

studies' than with the social sciences of economics and demography which, he thinks, resemble the natural sciences.[19] This same emphasis can be further exemplified in the work of a lesser known anthropologist, W. E. H. Stanner, whose contribution to the study of religion posesses direct significance to the question of anthropological hermeneutics.

Reductionism and Elementary Forms

The problem of reductionism is central to any consideration of how analysis and interpretation should proceed, and it is also directly related to how the anthropologist views himself. A total reductionism is only possible when the observer and the observed are thought of as belonging to essentially different orders of reality. The style of functionalist anthropology which treats of social institutions as entities independent of the observer is perfectly proper, but certain other social phenomena which include religious entities implicate the observer from the outset. The moment the observer is himself seen as part of the same field as his subjects, or is under the influence of similar restraints, then it becomes impossible for any complete reductionism to take place.

Although anthropologists of religion have been well aware of the problem of ethnocentricity for many years, and while historians and phenomenologists have acknowledged the necessity of understanding alien religious notions in terms appropriate to them, the power of systematizing western intellectual traditions has, nevertheless, tended to impress itself upon analyses of other cultures. Stanner is particularly aware of this for his own subject matter, that of Aboriginal religion, has attracted varying degrees of culture-bound interpretation for over a century. Durkheim's classic work on the nature of primitive religion is an obvious case in point which influenced later traditions in this area, and simply because it is so well known may serve as a constant comparison of the difference in intention between that author's theoretical stance and the one adopted by Stanner.

While in no sense following either an implicit or explicit phenomenological approach Stanner sets out 'to try as far as possible to let Murinbata religion exhibit itself'.[20] He interprets his material in terms of its own inner logic, in terms of the messages conveyed through myths and rituals, for as he says, 'if the main functions of myth are not cognitive I wonder if we can understand them at all'.[21] This is not to say that mythic functions are only cognitive, he argues against that position, but that they are intelligible to other men beyond the group in which the myths are found.

Stanner reversed Durkheim's theoretical approach by avoiding making religious facts of primary concern and social ones of secondary significance.[22] In other words he did not engage in an *a priori* reductionism with religious phenomena being interpreted in terms of social structures and processes. This was the case because he came to the conviction during his fieldwork that Aboriginal religion

---

[19] Idem.
[20] Stanner, W. E. H., 1959: 107. Cf. Obituary Royal Anth. Inst. News Feb. 1982.
[21] Ibid., p. 50.
[22] Ibid., p. 28.

could not be understood unless it was first assumed that it possessed particular and distinctive features which might be said to impress themselves upon the researcher. Stanner describes the groups studied as possessing 'overwhelming convictions about ultimate values', so much so that Aboriginal man might be called Homo convictus.[23] If it be said that Durkheim evaluated Aboriginal religion in terms of emotional release, then Stanner might be regarded as shifting the emphasis more to the philosophical dimension. While it is true to say that Durkheim did deal with the question of the problem of knowledge and the construction of logical categories in association with social organization and structure, it is equally true to say that he remained largely unaware of the meaning of the religion to its Aboriginal practitioners, and it was this which Stanner set at the forefront of his concern. This meaning is the meaning which exists for the practitioners and not primarily for the analyst, it represents the inner logic of the religion.

Implicitly speaking Stanner is disagreeing with any procedure which allows privileged access for the analyst to the real meaning of a phenomenon whilst the participant members of a group only possess some other level of meaning of lesser significance. His study of the Murinbata group of Australian aborigines is instructive both for the actual ethnographic data and for the way he shows how academic analysis entertains certain presuppositions with respect to religious ideas and their configurations. For the purposes of this chapter it will be convenient to focus on one of the many rituals discussed by Stanner, that which concerns initiation from boyhood into manhood and is called the *punj* ritual. Through this rite of passage the young males are brought into direct contact with the basic symbols of Murinbata society, and it is precisely the question of how the individual comes to understand himself and his society through these rites which Stanner takes up with some ardour. His intention is to emphasize the profound significance of initiation rites in this tribe as far as the psychological and intellectual dimension of the youths' life is concerned. By contrast with most aboriginal studies, as Stanner himself admits, he is concerned with 'metaphysical problems' because he sees the data as themselves expressing concern over metaphysical issues. By the term metaphysical he seeks to denote an awareness of non-empirical realities which is related to man's life-pattern in the midst of the empirical world, and which helps man make sense of that world.

This all-embracing reality might be described as possessing two aspects, one which could be denoted as the dimensional and the other as the qualitative components of life. The dimension of reality is the notion of time, which does not possess a linear signification as in the Judeao-Christian tradition or even a more cyclical meaning as in the broad Hindu-Buddhist context, rather it is to be evaluated in terms of the second aspect referred to above, and which is best described as a quality perceived in the present, a quality which results from a direct participation in the social life of the group. This is not as abstract a comment as might first appear since every culture defines the present in terms of something, the western world in the twentieth century and after the nineteenth century emphasis upon history defines the present in terms of an historical past and in the hopes of an 'historic future'. What Stanner is suggesting is a rather different mode of evaluation

---

[23] Ibid., p. 27.

in which the present is best understood as a quality of life rather than as a moment in a passage of time. The Murinbata myths, for example, refer to no golden age, and there is no notion of perfection as such either in 'nostalgia for a past or yearning after a perfected futurity'.[24] That to which the myths do refer is to be found in the present and is expressed by ritual, it is the awareness of the meaning of man's self-reflective life set amidst the realities of social life. So it is that the physical hole or hollow in which a central part of the *punj* ritual takes place is referred to both as a nest and as a wallow, that is, as a place of comfort and refuge expressed in the image of a nest, but also as a site of discomfort and pain symbolized in the wallow. The sacred space of the punj ritual thus 'denotes what seem like positive and negative statements of the same truth about life', for standing at the centre of society this focal point of ritual announces the dual truth of reality that of 'refuge and rotteness'.[25] Stanner refers to this paradoxical message of the rites as the 'covenant of duality' into which the emerging generation is initiated through symbols of life and of suffering.[26] In this process each initiate is 'taken out of his empirical and social self as though to meet something of his essential self', while the connection which is established between this essential self and the equally essential nature of the life he has to live in society and the natural world, is portrayed as one which is inherently implausible. Concrete existence is shown to be of a mixed order and the initiate is brought to a position from which he may obtain an 'intuition of an integral moral flaw in human association'.[27] The reality which exists beyond any individual being and yet in which all participate is one of 'perennial good-with-suffering, of order-with-tragedy', and it is precisely because of the mixed and uncertain nature of the world that the young men are taught, again through the initiation rites, to depend upon the positive feature despite the presence of its negative complement.[28]

It might be argued that through the *punj* ritual certain 'elementary forms' are manifested and experienced in the sense that the initiates are confronted with events which demonstrate the nature of reality as understood by the Murinbata. These are internal observers' models and not those of the anthropologist, yet they furnish the very evidence which underlies his analysis of what is happening in and through the ritual. The significant point about Stanner's argument is that he is attempting to extend or develop the level of philosophical awareness of the anthropologist himself, in the hope that certain of the indigenous elementary forms will be viewed as essential categories which cannot be fully understood by means of being changed to another kind of meaning through a reductionist perspective. What this means, in part, is that the scope of anthropology is broadened to embrace those philosophical issues which have normally been beyond what has been regarded as the proper concerns of the discipline. Such a philosophical anthropology is inevitable once a discussion of meaning is proposed even though it might be regarded by some as too speculative and too far removed from the more pragmatic debates

---

24 Ibid., pp. 45, 58.
25 Ibid., p. 44.
26 Ibid., p. 56.
27 Ibid., p. 44.
28 Ibid., p. 70.

about social structures. As far as most British studies of anthropology are concerned it would probably be true to say that they have, as it were, been satisfied with a middle range of ideological comment. It will be necessary to refer to this point in a later consideration of spirit possession, it suffices to say here that any anthropology which is to contribute to a broader study of religion through discourse with the history or phenomenology of religion will, inevitably, have to engage in some reference to the nature of man in terms other than those of social determinism. This is what Stanner attempts to do in suggesting that in myths man finds a way of expressing a set of meanings which cannot be directly interpreted in terms of any other system of explanation. The full meaning of myth cannot, therefore, be explained by means of propositional statements or by iconographic or other means. If this is true it means that the kind of final analysis sought by scholars is likely to elude their grasp, at least in terms of the existential significance of myths to those using them. It also means that myths must be accorded a certain autonomy as discrete categories of religious phenomena, and to admit this is to comply to a greater degree than usual with the goals and intentions of historians of religions and phenomenologists in viewing religious phenomena as independent variables and not as sociologically or psychologically dependent variables.

As far as hermeneutics in the anthropology of religion is then concerned it would be necessary to consider not only the culturally different values of social groups but also that ultimate point of significance which the anthropologist can only identify as being present for a people, without claiming to grasp from the inside. This is, inevitably, a hazardous area of debate inasmuch as the question of knowledge is seen as involving the factor of commitment. To understand the structural relation of ideas within a culture is the ordinary task of field anthropologists, and the analysis which relates that structure to other aspects of the social world is the one usually presented in studies of cultures. The fact that these patterns of meaning also carry the weight of personal commitment involves what might be called a personal equation which the anthropologist, by the very fact that he is an observer, albeit a participant observer, cannot make. Of the many implications which follow from this is one which would necessitate a reconsideration of the issue of primitive mentality and myth. This is so because the question of the logic of mythical structure cannot be divorced from that of the degree and manner of commitment which exists between individuals and their social mythologies. In other words, it may be less of a question of kind of thought involved than of the nature of commitment to the beliefs and values expressed in the myth, or of the power the myth brings to bear on people who are themselves adherents to the truth it expresses. When that truth diverges from the normative perspectives of the analyst it is quite possible that the latter will regard the whole mythic context as absurd, archaic or perhaps even prelogical.

One of Stanner's most important suggestion is that the system of Murinbata symbols communicates messages concerning the nature of personal reality to each individual in a way which cannot be explained in terms of strict logic. The very fact that no independent stance could be adopted to describe analytically what the symbols did is indicative of what they actually do for the committed individuals concerned. Once a paradigm of meaning is adopted by the student of religion it becomes possible to refer to the fact that such personal meanings are communicated, and even to detail aspects of their contents, while still admitting that the level of individual significance must elude full observation. It was just this kind of anthropological awareness which Evans-Pritchard expressed in the last chapter of his *Nuer Religion*, in referring to the 'intuitive apprehension' of the phenomenon of Spirit by individual Nuer, and in the assertion that 'Nuer religion is ultimately an interior state'.[29] To say this is not to deny the power of anthropological explanation with respect to the ritual data which is in the field of social life, but it is to say that anthropological hermeneutics can, justifiably, be related to the mode of discourse adopted by historians and phenomenologists of religion with respect to notions such as that of myth and also of ritual, in the final analysis of which 'reductionism ... is irrelevant as a hermeneutical tool', as Eliade puts it.[30] The positive acceptance of the paradigm of meaning by these disciplines also involves a further fact, that the emotional dimension of belief is fundamentally important and that it is part of the personal equation mentioned above. The necessary consequence of such a factor is precisely that a degree of irreducible personal significance be identified as part of religious processes. If both myth and some rituals serve the function of correlating diverse aspects of life in the process of meaning construction then it will be true to say that such phenomena which serve unifying purposes will hardly be able to be analysed critically in terms of any one aspect of reality with no loss accruing to their central nature. Stanner does so regard symbols, for example, as uniting together 'several distinct structures of existence, including the cosmological, social and ecological' aspects of life.[31] What can be said in analysing religious phenomena is that they facilitate meaning, but this generalization cannot completely be explained at all levels as far as the individual is concerned. It is the form of meaning which is capable of assertion rather than its manifold content. So the *punj* ritual may be described as a rite which maximizes plausibility in the context of hostile features present in both natural and social environments, while the precise manner in which this meaning is experienced by individuals must be asserted as beyond academic knowledge.

To support the idea that religious phenomena such as symbols and myths may not be completely transparent to critical analysis is not, necessarily, to comply with historians of religion who assert the complete distinctiveness and *sui generis* character of, for example, the idea of the sacred in Eliade's work, of the sense of the holy for Otto or of prayer for Heiler.[32] While such scholars find it easy to chide the reductionist tendencies shown by some sociologists of religion they fail to appreciate that a similar kind of exercise can be discerned in their own work, and that it would not be improper to speak of a religious reductionism. Once an attempt is made to treat any set of phenomena as independent variables it becomes even more incumbent upon the analyst to take care in devising schemes of causation.

The particular strength of, for example, Durkheim's theory of religion lay in the complete reductionism which he openly espoused in the belief that his sociological

---

[29] Evans-Pritchard, E. E., 1956: 321-2. Cf. Andre Singer 1981: 176.

[30] Eliade, M., 1973: xvii.

[31] Stanner, W. E. H., 1959: 167.

[32] Eliade, Mircea, 1957. Otto, Rudolph, 1924. Heiler, Friederich, 1932.

understanding of the nature of man was actually correct, and was the inevitable perspective for anyone hoping to gain insight into the real nature of the human condition. The fact that Durkheim also believed that social phenomena could be treated as discrete entities facilitated his work whereas, for example, Dupré asserts quite categorically that 'an objective description of religious phenomena is a factual impossibility'.[33] The nature of this impossibility is derived from a form of existential awareness of the hazards involved in attempting to discuss the inner meaning of ideas for another person. The difference in emphasis between these two authors can usefully be drawn from their respective definitions of religion.

Whereas Durkheim's definition is eminently sociological and focuses upon the more institutional aspects of life involving systems of ideas so that;

> 'A religion is a unified system of beliefs and practices relative to sacred things, that is to say, things set apart and forbidden – beliefs and practices which unite into one single moral community called a Church, all those who adhere to them',

Dupré's perspective shows a clear understanding of the context in which the scholar is himself set, and manifests an existential dimension quite alien to Durkheim.

> Religion is 'an achievement through which man becomes capable of bearing the burden of existence. Birth and death, suffering and joy, failure and success, threat and trust, all these instances of human life are mediated with one another in the ultimate symbols of myth, cult and life itself. Religion in this sense renders meaning to man under the conditions of the life community. It enables him to accept the necessities of life as a human being. Religion is to be understood as the symbolic structure in which the humaneness of man receives lasting expression. As such it shares in the truth of man as a human being'.[34]

There is no difficulty in showing how Dupré's outlook manifests the general notion of meaning, what needs simple outlining is the fact of the personal philosophical dimension of his argument. The question is not just that of social systems of an integrated kind which confer meaning upon man, a view which could be read into Durkheim's perspective, it is, rather, one which presupposes that the issue of meaning has a direct personal significance. The existential dimension of Dupré's thought is also clear in a statement which shows how his concerns approximate to those taken up by us with respect to the idea of evil; he says that 'in addition to (the) experience of evil as the negation of meaning in the objectivity of consciousness, there is also its affirmation in the subjectivity of conscience'.[35] This definition of religion could easily be applied to Stanner's view of Murinbata religion; what it means for hermeneutics, however, is that care also needs to be taken lest an overly philosophical bias leads to what might be called an existentialist reductionism.

From what has been said about this variety of possible reductionisms it will be obvious that the very idea of 'elementary forms' is far from being a simple one.

---

33 Dupré, Wilhelm, 1975: 2.
34 Durkheim, E., 1976: 47.
35 Dupré, W., 1975: 334.

The nature of elementary forms, or of those essential features which may be said to be the fundamental units of religion, will change from system to system of explanation depending upon the dominant theory adopted in them. It cannot be presupposed from some archemedic point that any particular religion will demonstrate a specific feature of belief or practice. Once it is accepted that cultures may themselves possess interpretations of reality which differ the one from the other, and once it be admitted that the autonomy of a culture is a proper notion to entertain in religious studies, then the question of interpreting the sense of any religion in terms of the cultural perspectives of the analyst becomes quite critical. This is especially true with respect to the question of understanding and commitment. The act of making available to members of one culture data pertaining to another, particularly over religious matters, is an act of translation which emphasizes the conceptual and verbal dimensions of religiosity. It is, *ipso facto*, impossible to communicate the sense of native commitment to value systems apart from the experience of actual commitment. This fact which is an implicit assumption of anthropological work needs to be made explicit in any inter-disciplinary religious study inasmuch as the study of religions in the west has often proceeded along the lines of historical and textual analysis. The reason why the hermeneutical problem has tended to be implicit in anthropology lies, perhaps, in the experience of field-work and in the intuitive, non-verbal, sediments of knowledge accumulated by the scholar in his personal contacts. When one anthropologist then reads an ethnographic study of another he reads it in the light of this experiental dimension and, almost unconsciously, makes the necessary provision of the affective dimension to complement the social-structural account presented in the study itself.

In one sense it was just this process of understanding which, perhaps, allowed anthropologists to be content with the kind of explanations which were provided by their ethnologies. It is when anthropological studies become the basis of discussions engaged in by historians or phenomenologists of religion that a more explicit account of method is required, and this is the reason for devoting much of the present chapter to the issue of anthropological hermeneutics.

Having alluded to religious reductionism, as well as existential reductionism and the more often cited sociological variety of reinterpretation, it remains to say that the accusation of engaging in reductionism can become a tedious and ill-advised repetition since any kind of explanatory system can be subjected to its perjorative tones. The problem of an inter-disciplinary approach to the study of religions is one of accommodating different traditions of interpretation to each other, a task which also involves a process of bringing scholars to see their own convention as potential stumbling blocks to others. One function of the paradigm of meaning is to permit each tradition to contribute its theoretical perspective upon one or another level of meaning present in and for a social group. It may well be that the level and kind of analysis which satisfies anthropologists may not so content historians of religion, while theologians set within a confessional framework will probably require yet further levels of explanation. While the notion of a paradigm of meaning is advocated here as a fundamental outlook shared by most disciplines concerned with religion, it is not offered as an attempt to turn each specific disciplinary contribution into an attenuated version of itself with the intention of resembling others. It is merely suggested in order to show that the notion of meaning admits of many variations, whilst also arguing the fundamental theme of plausibility and implausibility as the form in which the issue of evil and salvation can best be handled theoretically.

CHAPTER FIVE

BROADER HERMENEUTICAL ISSUES

If indigenous groups studied by fieldwork techniques of participant observation characterize the anthropological perspective, and if that kind of critical discipline can permit the data to influence the form of final analysis, then the history of religions which studies the great religions of the world, largely in their classical and systematic expressions, and by philological and historical means, ought to have less difficulty in so doing.

The main question raised in this chapter concerns the presuppositional restraints to be found in the history and phenomenology of religions which might be identified as facilitating or hindering the approach to religious phenomena adopted by the more social scientific disciplines. In particular the question of the applicability of a general paradigm of meaning needs to be raised as far as central models and methods of selected historians and phenomenologists are concerned.

No extensive attempt is made to differentiate between the history and phenomenology of religions inasmuch as practitioners who tend to emphasize either the historical critical method or that which focuses upon the essential relation of specific phenomena often utilize aspects of the other approach when occasion demands it. In general terms it might be said that the phenomenology of religion is to the history of religions as the nineteenth century anthropology with its emphasis on stages of development is to twentieth century anthropology which is more concerned with relations existing between social phenomena.

Because of the difficulty attendant upon generalizing over academic disciplines which cover a wide area it will be useful to consider the approach of several specific scholars in the history and phenomenology of religion in order to establish their basic method and to see how they relate to the themes of salvation and evil as understood in terms of the general theory of plausibility. This is all the more necessary because of the avowed anthropological commitment of history of religions in spite of which distinctive differences have obtained between them. The declaration signed by, among others, Mircea Eliade and J. M. Kitagawa in 1958 to the effect that history of religions 'is an anthropological discipline studying the religious phenomenon as a creation, feature and aspect of human culture', is, itself, indicative of the awareness of differences between the respective academic perspectives.[1] Hultkrantz commented on this declaration that despite the fact of 'no definite barrier' existing 'between anthropology and the history of religions' there still remained 'an important difference of orientation'.[2] As has already been mentioned this difference originated largely in the change of attitude to evolutionary perspectives over the turn of the nineteenth into the twentieth century. While this may have been largely so it was not exclusively so. In what now needs to be said about

---

[1] Schimmel, A. M., 1960: 236.
[2] Hultkrantz, Ake, 1970: 338.

Eliade's perspective it will become   clear that the personal view and ideological perspective of scholars also contributed significantly to the way in which they have conceived and organized their studies of religion.

Mircea Eliade was born in Bucharest in 1907 and having studied in India with Dasgupta returned to the west and worked in England, France and America. Through this international contact and as a result of his prolific publications in both academic and popular areas he came to exert a wide influence as an authority in the history of religions. It is not intended to produce anything like a comprehensive evaluation of Eliade's *corpus* here and the biographical points just mentioned serve only to emphasize Eliade's extensive and pervasive influence in religious studies. It is important, however, to focus upon the central notion used by Eliade and which recurs as a constant theme in his many writings which themselves have come to be accepted as classical works in the history of religions.

Eliade sees the purpose of his writings as influencing western man's fundamental outlook and attitude to the world itself. History of religions aids man's understanding of his true nature, it is no mere neutral discussion of natural phenomena and cannot be a 'detached' discipline in any sense of that word because its very existence effects a change in personal attitude. So radical may this change in the scholar be that Eliade has described the history of religion as a 'saving discipline'.[3] It is a 'total hermeneutics' applied to 'every kind of encounter of man with the sacred from prehistory to today'.[4] This particular quotation precisely identifies Eliade's central notion of and overriding concern with the sacred, and of this category as one with which man is inextricably associated. This means that Eliade's approach to the phenomenon of religion can be described as relational inasmuch as it is neither the object in itself nor the essential nature of the subject which alone determines the character of a religious phenomenon but the way in which they are related in a complete life experience.[5] Eliade is not concerned with discussing this process in any strictly philosophical sense and does not make any serious use of the phenomenological notion of intentionality, yet in practical terms he is much concerned with just this area of perception. Through the hermeneutics of the discipline a growth in personal understanding takes place and the 'degree to which you understand is the degree to which you change', inasmuch as an individual is modified through his understanding and this is 'the equivalent of a step forward in the process of self-liberation'.[6] As far as Eliade is concerned western man lies in need of such a transformation because the Judaeo-Christian tradition led to the denial of the sacred quality of earthly phenomena. In saying this he is largely in agreement with the argument of Max Weber concerning the progressive demystification of the world consequent upon an increase in rational thought and action fostered by puritan forms of theology, and also the even broader hypothesis of Harvey Cox which located the origin of secularization in the old testament view of God.[7]

---

3 Eliade, M., 1978: 296.
4 Eliade, M., 1965: 5.
5 Bettis, J. D., 1969: 199.
6 .Eliade, M., 1978: 310.
7 Cox, H., 1968.

The history of religions may thus, according to Eliade, be seen to possess 'an awakening effect' which enables man to perceive an aspect of reality which has largely been lost to him.[8] This function of the discipline consists in awakening the sense of the sacred which western life has done so much to attenuate, and which for Eliade constitutes the prime nature of religious man and therefore of essential humanity. This notion of the sacred resembles Rudolph Otto's concept of the *sensus numinis* and, in fact, Eliade makes many references to *The Idea of the Holy*, though he criticizes Otto's lack of methodological rigour particularly in his avoidance of the question of myth and mythopoeic modes of thought. For Eliade the sacred is 'an element of the structure of consciousness and not a moment in the history of consciousness' which means that man's essential nature possesses or includes the faculty of perceiving a discrete category of phenomena different from those arising from everyday encounters in the world.[9] The dichotomy inherent in this view of sacred and profane lies at the centre of his understanding of human nature and is directly related to another cognate idea in Eliade's system, that of hierophany. A hierophany is any phenomenon by means of which the sacred is manifest and the history of religions is itself 'constituted by a number of important hierophanies from the most elementary manifestation of the sacred in a rock or tree to the supreme hierophany, the incarnation of God in Jesus Christ'.[10] From these brief references it can be seen that the notion of the sacred is possessed of the two dimensions already alluded to in commenting on the relational nature of definitions in Eliade's work. The first aspect is a function of the phenomenon experienced and the second lies in the act of experiencing the sacred, so both the subject perceiving and the object disclosing constitute the realm of the sacred. It is important to appreciate this complementary constitution of the sacred if Eliade's discussion of modern western man is to be understood, for despite the fact that sacredness is viewed as so significant a component of human life he asserts that urban european man has virtually lost his sense of the sacred. The pragmatic world of empirical causalities has robbed man of this dimension so that he lives in the absence of the sacred, in a state of what might be called profanity. Herein lies the justification of history of religions for it provides such people with ethnographic and historical materials which serve as the requisite hierophanic focus which itself may trigger off the sacred response in man.

It might be argued that Eliade has so over-valued the notion of the sacred that he defines human nature in terms contrary to much of the evidence suggestive of man's basic secularity, or that he is not prepared to conceive of the possibility of a change in human outlook and consciousness in the course of history, but it is not the intention of the present discussion to press these points any further for it has sufficed to show both how Eliade uses the notion of the sacred and how he understands the function of the history of religions as an academic and human discipline.

One illuminating point which emerges from his discussion of the sacred, and which further emphasizes his commitment to the idea of the sacred, as well as clarifying the status he ascribes to that concept, is his lack of reference to Durkheim's

---

[8] Eliade, M., 1978: 233.

[9] Ibid., p. 313.

[10] Eliade, M., 1968: 124.

use of the categories of sacred and profane. He virtually ignores Durkheim's usage despite the fact that it was the French sociologist who populaized the idea. Eliade is, of course, perfectly familiar with Durkheim's work in the *Année Sociologique* as with *Les Formes élémentaires* but it would seem that Durkheim's final reductionist analysis is what makes him so disagreeable to Eliade. Indeed it would also seem to be precisely this distaste which led Eliade to make the rather academically eccentric assertion that *Les Formes élémentaires* does not properly speaking represent a contribution to the sociology of religion'.[11] While the strictly anthropological criticism of this work are well known and are quite devastating in terms of the purely erroneous argument on totemism and clan structure, even the most scathing critics praise its general insights and theoretical contribution to sociological thought.

So it is that Eliade decries Durkheim's endeavours for precisely the reason he praises those of Otto, for the former discourages commitment to the sacred inasmuch as he explains its origin in the social interaction of ritual whereas the latter locates it in the divine. In fact such a simplistic evaluation hardly does justice to Durkheim for whom the idea of God is no less significant in practical terms when that very idea is seen as a social product than it would be were it derived from a self-existing deity, but such a feat of intellectualizing does not appeal to Eliade. It might have been more to Eliade's credit had he been prepared to consider Durkheim's totemic ritual as hierophanic material but his dedication to establishing the history of religions as a means of religious awakening hardly permitted the use of reductionist sociology which that exercise would have entailed. What would have accorded more with his particular desires would have been a closer study of Robertson Smith's original use of the notions 'sacred' and 'common', for he entertained no reductionist notions in his 'Religion of the Semites', the book on which Durkheim's study of religion was based. In fact Robertson Smith is mentioned very briefly and only in passing, for Eliade's final judgment is that this kind of sociological hypothesis, which is also espoused by R. R. Marett, Andrew Lang, J. F. MacLennan and Lucien Lévy-Bruhl, has had 'no lasting influence on historico-religious studies'.[12]

The framework within which Eliade thus works emphasizes the central opposition between the sacred and the profane which must itself be seen as a way of conceptualizing the state of human being. Because the sacred and profane, whether in the forms of space or time it does not matter, correspond to the 'two modes of being in the world' it is difficult to discuss the notion of salvation in Eliade's work despite the fact that it might be said to be the central concern of the entire corpus. Primarily salvation refers to the quality of being which he identifies as the sacred and which admits of many dimensions. For the primitive this involves the belief that the cosmos was made by the gods and is still a place of transcendent significance and power which man experiences through his own initiatory rituals and the more regular cultic activity of his society. The modern, urban Christian, by contrast, has lost the sense of cosmic dimensions and for his salvation he depends upon a

---

11 Eliade, M., 1969: 15.
12 Eliade, M., 1957: 231.

more private and personal relationship with God.[13] Throughout Eliade's studies the problem of meaning might best be categorized as a problem of being, this is the very reason why his notion of salvation is hard to define with any precision, for being admits of many degrees and levels of attainment. Eliade can be seen to arrive at a position not dissimilar from that of the paradigm of meaning once it is appreciated that the notion of meaning is allied with that of transcendent significance. It is the level of awareness of the sacred which constitutes the full category of meaning for him, and this involves the experiential dimension to a large extent.

In his methodology Eliade follows that orientation in the history of religions which concentrates upon the 'essence of religion' rather than upon its 'historical context' desire to 'discover and communicate its history'.[14] Sometimes he uses the which is critical for hermeneutics in the history of religions. He sees historians of religions as being divided 'between two divergent but complementary orientations', those who focus upon the typical 'structures of religious phenomena ... seek to understand the essence of religion' while those who prefer to analyse the 'historical context' desire to 'discover and communicate its history'.[14] Sometimes he uses the notion of essence in a confusing way, however, as in the rhetorical question: 'Does the fact that we cannot grasp the essence of religion also mean that we cannot grasp the essence of religious phenomena?'[15] Here the distinction between the two types of essence is similar to that which in terms of anthropological analysis could be expressed as the difference between the origin and contemporary structure of a phenomenon. While it may be quite impossible to discover the origin of religious consciousness it is possible, for Eliade's whole work shows this, to ascertain the way religious phenomena function in religious groups. This functioning can be studied not only in contemporary contexts but also in religions of the past, for there is a theoretical distinction to be drawn between historical conjecture of the evolutionary style of nineteenth century anthropology, and the approach of the history of religions which traces the development of religious doctrines, practices or, for example, iconography. Criticism of Eliade will always be influenced by the fear that in such historical analysis, as in any discussion of contemporary phenomena, his concern with the notion of the sacred as an essential component of full human being will lead to an undue bias on the importance of commitment in the life of the historian of religion.

This desire to establish the history of religions as something more than a neutral academic discipline is also shared by Wilfred Cantwell Smith whose influence in the field, while not so widespread as that of Eliade, has been quite prominent. For Smith the history of religions should not only study the religious life of mankind but should also contribute to the religious and moral life of man, for 'every time a person anywhere makes a religious decision, at stake is the final destiny and meaning of the human race. If we do not see this and cannot make our public see it, then whatever else we may be, we are not historians of religion'.[16] To think in these terms, let alone to express them in such strong language, is to make perfectly clear

---

13 Ibid., p. 179.
14 Ibid., p. 232.
15 Eliade, M., 1964: 168.
16 Smith, W. Cantwell, 1968. Cited in E. J. Sharpe, 1975: 284.

the approach being adopted to religious phenomena. The goal of the discipline as
he sees it is twofold; to turn our nascent world society into a world community,
and to help individuals find meaning in their lives. These goals, which exemplify
his sense of commitment to the task of the discipline, are reflected in a major
contribution Smith makes to the history of religions through his suggestion that the
very word 'religion' be eliminated from general usage and be replaced by the
notions of 'cumulative tradition' and 'faith'.[17]

Smith resembles Eliade in seeking to avoid any type of reductionist explanation
of religious phenomena and it is this motive which led him to examine the change
in meaning of the word religion through history and to show that it is a most
inappropriate description of what actually counts as significant in the religious
lives of men. The word religion has tended to be used of the actual doctrinal system
of religious traditions rather than of the personal life of faith of particular devotees,
for this reason it is wiser to separate these two aspects of religiosity; the tradition as
an historical development with sets of teachings, rites and forms, and the personal
life of faith at which level the religious tradition becomes meaningful for the
individual member of the tradition. It is also at this level that it is possible to talk
of truth inasmuch as religious systems ought not to be discussed as abstract sets of
propositions whose validity requires verification by philosophical analysis. Religious
beliefs or assertions become true in individual lives in concrete life contexts, while
this argument does not impress some philosophers of religion such as John Hick,
who wishes to emphasize the question raised by contradictory assertions made in
different religions, Smith feels that it does more justice to the complex realities
of religious phenomena at the level of everyday life.

Smith presumes some idea of meaningfulness for the religious believer throughout
his discussion without attempting to analyse it in any detail, what is clear is that he
regards the formal system of doctrines in any religion as gaining in significance
for the historian of religion only when it becomes vitally related to the actual life
of individual believers. Meaningfulness therefore has something to do with the
intuitive apprehension and application of traditional teachings to personal and
contemporary events, and salvation is the state in which these traditional formulae
of spirituality are actualized. Smith is outlining a general kind of argument which,
he thinks can cope with any religion. The precise content of the traditional formulation of doctrines is not important, and their comparison ought not to be regarded
as the central concern of the history of religions. What is more significant is the way
in which traditional forms are related to present realization; it is precisely because
religious studies have 'analysed the externals but missed the core of the matter',
that a redefinition of method is required.[18]

To complete this comment on historians of religion who see their task as one
which elaborates upon the function of religion as a necessary part of life it will
be useful to refer to Joachim Wach who viewed *religionswissenschaft* as a discipline
which opposed secular tendencies in the modern world, and which could serve to
reinvigorate personal religious values. The following quotation demonstrates how

---

[17] Smith, W. Cantwell, 1963: 17.
[18] Ibid., p. 7.

different the approach of the historians of religion is from that of social anthropologists.

> 'To view the multiplicity of religious life and expression, to discover similarities and relationships need not as some fear have a sobering and paralysing effect on one's own religiosity. On the contrary it could become a support and aid in the battle against the godless and estranged powers, it ought to lead to the examination and preservation of one's own religious faith.'[19]

Religious phenomena should thus, argues Wach, be interpreted in terms of their own logic and rationale, and in saying this he is completely in accord with Smith's view that methodology must be appropriate to the object of study.[20] Reductionisms of sociological or psychological kinds are inadmissible as is historicism. When studied in terms of specifically religious schemes the subject matter of the history of religions will broaden and deepen the *sensus numinis* rather than detract from it.

To admit that the subject matter of a study be allowed to dictate the terms of analysis is to introduce a potential hazard into methodology, yet as long as it is possible to state clearly which elements and ideas are so accepted as guidelines it remains a possible way of proceeding. The great difficulty, however, lies in this very point concerning specificity of indigenous categories, this becomes clearer when the criticism of W. G. Oxtoby is recalled to the effect that, for example, the phenomenology of religion has tended to 'endorse religion in general as compared with secularity'.[21] In one sense the historian or phenomenologist is doing nothing different from the anthropologist of Stanner's pursuasion who seeks the essential and intrinsic pattern of ideas present in an indigenous culture, but the difference lies in the fact that the western historian of religion already possesses his own native concept of religion as a general category and it is this which can, so easily, be brought to bear upon and to endorse religion in general. Yet Oxtoby's criticism would not hold for all scholars as the case of J. M. Kitagawa would exemplify. His brief for the history of religions focuses upon the dimension of religious experience and its diverse manifestations in history studied in a historical critical way and as distinct from a 'theological history of religions' which makes some presupposition about religiosity.[22] Kitagawa acknowledges the great difficulty of studying religions while seeking to avoid the influence of one's own tradition and suggests that one way of coping with the problem methodologically is to maintain an explicit tension between one's own religious background, and its theological dimension upon other religions, and the more neutral academic study of religion as such. Here Kitagawa can be seen to approximate more closely to Eliade, Smith, and Wach since their statements about the commitment aspect of the discipline could be said to apply to the ultimate and final level of analysis. In the initial stages of work they, too, desire the neutral observation and documentation of religious phenomena, and it is only at a later stage of analysis that they wish to engage in a form of religious apologetics. But it is this later form which is absent from, for example, anthropological analysis.

---

19 Wach, J., 1968: 128.
20 Smith, W. Cantwell, Ibid., p. 6.
21 Oxtoby, W. G., 1973: 32.
22 Eliade, M. and J. M. Kitagawa, 1959: 28.

It would be incorrect to infer from what has been said concerning the apologetic nature of history of religions that this very emphasis upon the vital nature of religion for mankind constituted anything like a unifying factor in the discipline although this would be an attractive proposition. Eliade argued that the history of religions was a 'total hermeneutics' with respect to man's encounter with the sacred, and reference has been made to this above, but he went on to say that historians of religion did not construct a unified perspective upon this basis. On the contrary he sees the history of the field as a growth in a defeatist attitude which emerged 'precisely in an epoch in which knowledge concerning man increased considerably' through contributions from psychoanalysis and phenomenology, and at a time when knowledge of the eastern world was developing rapidly. In an earlier chapter the argument was advanced that the decline of the evolutionary model contributed significantly to this change of outlook in religious studies so that what did transpire in that broad discipline is quite intelligible in retrospect, and while Eliade might well say that the change was 'tragic' it was not really 'paradoxical'.[23] The reason for the non-paradoxical nature of the change lies in the fact that as a greater wealth of material became available each of the growing disciplines developed appropriate methods of dealing with the new situation, methods which did not always follow the rather traditional western path of history and philosophy. When Eliade argues that the history of religions ought not to conform to models drawn from the natural sciences, or in other words to seek to follow any one of these newer traditions of explanation, he is expressing another kind of paradox which can be understood in the light of what has been said concerning the commitment factor of some scholars of religion.

Eliade's paradox rests upon a personal factor which is none other than the tension between intuitive understanding and critical understanding. On the one hand is found the private history of a thinker including his cultural background, a factor of obvious importance to Eliade's own self-understanding as is clearly shown in his autobiography, while on the other lies the academic tradition to which he is heir and which causes the central problem of deciding upon presuppositions for study. The paradox is confounded because of the difficulty which exists in describing with any accuracy what this tradition is as far as Eliade is concerned. At best it might be called the liberal humanism of historical analysis, but that broad tendency in western academic life is far from acceptable to him. What this means is that his own work has tended away from the abstract neutrality of pure historical study to a position which is rather distinctively his own. That form of history of religions which does endorse religion in general is one which Eliade has done much to foster and develop, because of the somewhat idiosyncratic perspective adopted in it, however, it was inevitable that he should find himself at variance with just those other academic disciplines whose views he could not completely accept. This assertion is not quite as tautologous as might first appear for Eliade does talk in terms of wishing that a more unified study of religion will come about while apparently failing to see that it is precisely because the alternative methods of study were unacceptable to him that he set about constructing his own position.

---

[23] Eliade, M., 1965: 5.

It is impossible to resolve this difficulty inasmuch as it may well represent a permanent problem in religious studies as long as some scholars feel the necessity of asserting the significance of personal religious dimensions for the appropriate evaluation of religious phenomena. Before considering this issue in the case of the best known author in phenomenology of religion, Gerardus van der Leeuw, it might be instructive to see how the same issue has been represented in anthropology, which might be thought of as an area least influenced by personal considerations. By introducing this comment on anthropological hermeneutics here rather than in the former chapter on this very issue it will become even clearer that the breadth of subjects dealing with religious phenomena is beset with similar difficulties.

One of the best known anthropological comments on this problem is that of Evans-Pritchard in the conclusion of his survey criticism on theories of primitive religion where he asks what kind of understanding has been gained from the classical theories of religion which is of any use in helping to explain the nature of personal religious experience. He is clear in asserting that as far as a discussion of religion in the social life of a group is concerned it makes no difference whether the anthropologist is a believer or not, but once the scholar wishes to go beyond this level of analysis then personal religious preferences do become significant. Evans-Pritchard's quotation from Wilhelm Schmidt to the effect that 'if religion is essentially of the inner life, it follows that it can be truly grasped only from within'; is an expression of his own view of the significance of religiosity for the interior life of individuals, a similar point is raised in the closing paragraphs of his study on Nuer religion where the essentially personal aspect of religious experience is emphasized.[24] But these tantalizing comments are nowhere explored and developed, they merely stand as a testimony by a great anthropologist to the fact that even thorough analyses of social structures do not exhaust the complete meaning of religion.

A more extended discussion of the personal values of anthropologists is to be found in Raymond Firth's essays on religion and anthropology.[25] His position differs from that of Evans-Pritchard inasmuch as he is not a religious believer himself but is much concerned with the issue of motivation in religious analyses. He gives as an example the case of witchcraft which anthropologists normally interpret in terms of social tensions, and says that if they actually believed in the existence of malevolent power distinct from the influence of man on man then the interpretation would have to be radically different. The question is precisely that of the status of the final referent. Firth is particularly useful an example to discuss in this context of hermeneutics since he spends much time in considering the question of meaning, and regards the issue of orders of meaning as central to the quest of religious studies. In asserting that 'religion is man's ultimate answer to the problem of meaning' Firth shows how much he is taken up with the notion of social realities as conferring a sense of order upon individual lives.[26] Unlike many British anthropologists Firth wants to analyse the relationship between the level of meaning which operates for and within the individual and that which functions at the level of society at large. While it is not possible to develop Firth's argument here

---

[24] Evans-Pritchard, E. E., 1965: 121.
[25] Firth, R., 1964.
[26] Firth, R., Ibid., p. 232.

it is necessary to say that his concern with the personal level of meaning is directly related to sociological issues inasmuch as individual persons can greatly influence religious movements, but it is also important to add that although he offers no particular scheme for interpreting systems of meaning construction in society he does make it quite clear that meaning systems are as much emotional as intellectual directed processes.[27] In terms of a general paradigm of meaning no more appropriate anthropological an author could be sought than Firth even though the problems he raises are far from being solved and serve to indicate the rather similar group of hermeneutical difficulties also shared by the history and phenomenology of religions.

It is to the more specifically phenomenological issues that attention must now be turned in concluding this chapter on hermeneutics, and in particular to the influential study of Gerardus van der Leeuw entitled *Religion in Essence and Manifestation* and first published in 1933 as *Phänomenologie der Religion*.

Van der Leeuw's contribution to the phenomenology of religion is both a classical example of how descriptive phenomenology with its schemes of classification can be applied to religious entities, and also of the problem of presuppositions. The issue of presuppositions becomes even more problematical in the phenomenology of religion than in the history of religion, since the phenomenologist reckons to maintain himself in a state of suspension of doubt over the nature of the reality and validity of phenomena under consideration in the hope that the essential nature of these objects, rites or beliefs will become apparent through the act of description. Van der Leeuw asserts at the outset that 'no imperiously dominating theory' lay behind his study, yet in the hundredth chapter, the section dealing with 'the religion of love' which is his typological description and categorization of Christianity, he says that both that chapter and all that have gone before it had been written from the Christian viewpoint.[28] How it is that he can achieve the 'attitude of complete intellectual suspense' whilst also including his personal religious standpoint in his study it is difficult to see. The main reason for this problem arising in the first instance can be discerned in van der Leeuw's conception of the phenomenology of religion as a total activity engaged in by the scholar and involving his intellectual and general life commitment. He thus takes personal biases for granted but advocates honesty in making them public so that they can be included in the final evaluation of phenomenological studies.

The basis of van der Leeuw's objection to the notion of the supposed neutrality of scholarly study lies in the fact of man's historical facticity. It is impossible, he argues, not to be ideologically inclined in some direction or other; to attempt an unprejudiced stance is only to adopt some 'interpretation of religion borrowed from some liberal western european Christianity, the deism of the Enlightenment or the so called monism of the natural sciences', but without acknowledging the fact.[29]

So it is that this particular scholar resembles Eliade and Wach in advocating a commitment to a religious perspective of a personal kind as a basis for wider religious studies, at least he is explicit about it, and, as far as much of *Religion in*

---

[27] Ibid., p. 234.
[28] Leeuw, G. van der, 1967: 10.
[29] Ibid., p. 644.

Essence and Manifestation is concerned, this emphasis does not seem to be of very great importance.It is only when the more descriptive categories have been established and he progresses to the more abstract consideration of the idea of salvation that van der Leeuw's belief in Christianity as 'the central form of historical religions', and the gospel as 'the fulfilment of religion in general' becomes particularly apparent.[30] Before discussing exactly how he handles the notion of salvation it might be useful to emphasize the theoretical tension present in this approach which possesses both a religious commitment and a commitment to the phenomenological stance of epoche. E. J. Sharpe has also observed the paradoxical character of van der Leeuw's work pointing out that for him 'phenomenological scholarship was not to be sharply differentiated from metaphysics or from theology'.[31] Sharpe is correct in seeing this unresolved tension as a distinctive feature in the work of religiously committed scholars who cross the boundaries of their own religion in an attempt to gain understanding of other faiths, especially when the exercise takes up the notion of 'religion as such'.[32]

The factors influencing van der Leeuw's perspective are, in certain respects, the same ones present in any study of religion as a general paradigm of meaning makes clear. What is significant is that he gives a specific content to the notion of meaning, one which is religiously informed. This is an important point for the theoretical argument of our thesis which seeks to advocate the notion of meaning construction in the context of negative features without introducing any preconceived content of what counts as meaningful. In other words, it is possible to be committed to the idea that all religious systems are essentially concerned with the process of meaning construction without having any fixed idea as to the precise meaning present in any one religious tradition. When an author goes further than this and allows his own particular content of the notion of meaning to direct the way he analyses other groups then difficulties are likely to follow. The significance of a general paradigm of meaning is that it can help avoid the doctrinal ethos or ideological set of one tradition affecting the way others are studied. It is, for example, the Christian theological predisposition to positive resolutions of life problems which has led van der Leeuw and others into an over-evaluation of the positive and creative aspects of religious phenomena and processes. This has, indirectly, been contrasted with the anthropological view of Stanner which is more truly phenomenological than van der Leeuw's work inasmuch as it identifies the essential conflict of opposing realities in the life-world of the Murinbata.

In conclusion some attention must be paid to van der Leeuw's study of the idea of salvation, not only because it exemplifies the points already made, but because it approaches the question of meaning from a somewhat different perspective, one which utilizes the concept of 'power', and thereby offers the possibility of a fuller and more comprehensive picture of salvation than has been constructed so far. At least this point could be made by saying that the affective dimension of meaning can well be explored by means of the category of 'power'.

Van der Leeuw begins with the theoretically important point that equivalent

[30] Ibid., p. 646.
[31] Sharpe, E. J., 1975: 234.
[32] Ibid., p. 231.

terms are not always easy to find in the comparative study of religious concepts. Even when translating between German, French and English with respect to the notion of salvation there are problems since, for example, the German *Heil* while it may be rendered as salvation can mean deliverance, and its derivatives, *Heiland* or saviour, *heilig* or holy, *Heiligtum* or sanctuary, and *Heilsgeschichte* or salvation history all serve to broaden the notion and thereby to prevent it from being restricted to what he regards as the 'accepted but definitely limited English significance'.[33] He thinks it useful that such a breadth of meaning is present in the term for he does not want to restrict the notion of salvation to explicitly Christian doctrinal terms. This is an admirable intention but is relatively short lived because he goes on to give a narrower definition of the phenomenon of salvation in terms of the idea of power, and of an awareness of a positive force in the self or in the external world; a force possessing a positive moral aspect as is clear in his assertion that 'salvation is ... power experienced as Good'.[34] Van der Leeuw goes on to describe the emergence of this power and its identification in natural phenomena such as water, certain animals and the season of spring prior to its portrayal in saviour figures.

He develops the theme of evil and demons as a result of the fact that power may be experienced not only as good, but as 'terrifying, devastating and incalculable'.[35] He emphasizes the notion of the incomprehensibility of perceived evil and in so doing demonstrates the fact that affective dimensions of religious traditions cannot be ignored in theoretical works.

> 'Belief in demons does not mean that chance rules the Universe, but rather that I have experienced the horror of some power which concerns itself neither with my reason nor my morals; it is not fear of any concrete terribleness, but vague terror of the gruesome and the incomprehensible, which projects itself objectively in belief in demons.'[36]

Evil in this scheme is the emotional response to intellectual uncertainty, it is not simply ignorance but the context of unknowing which results in the potency of the negative sense of power. In terms of plausibility theory the notion of power can be said to include both the cognitive and affective dimensions with the latter serving as the context for the former. What is quite clear is that in van der Leeuw's scheme the notions of meaning and power are closely aligned, so that his basic presupposition about religiosity is that 'man does not simply accept the life that is given to him', but that 'in life he seeks power'.[37] Power has to do with understanding the nature of reality in order to have it firmly under control for 'Homo religiosus betakes himself to the road to omnipotence, to complete understanding, to ultimate meaning. He would fain comprehend life in order to dominate it'. Power is not simply the desire for status and prestige, in the sense in which E. R. Leach in his earlier work postulated that 'a conscious or unconscious wish to gain power is a very general motive in human affairs', where power means the seeking

---

33 Leeuw, G. van der, Ibid., p. 101.
34 Ibid., p. 102.
35 Ibid., p. 134.
36 Idem.
37 Ibid., p. 679.

of 'recognition, of access to office as social persons, the gaining of esteem', but is the general category of man's response to a world which challenges his own superiority.[38] It is in the process of attaining to full power and mastery that man experiences salvation even though during his actual life-time he does achieve that full sense of power which he so much seeks. Van der Leeuw uses the notion of *Ahnung* to describe this firm sense of conviction of the nature of things which still lacks the full grasp of them.[39] Man is thus engaged in a process of becoming, of endeavouring to possess a full sense of meaning but without actually attaining to it. So it is that the religious life is not essentially different from the rest of cultural life which is also a pattern of constructed meanings and power but it is the natural conclusion of other aspects of cultural life. 'The religious significance of things ... is that on which no wider nor deeper meaning whatever can follow', says van der Leeuw, an assertion which resembles the position adopted by Hans Mol and which will be discussed in due course. The distinctive feature of van der Leeuw's argument lies in his view that man comes ultimately 'to stand at the very frontier and perceives the ultimate superiority he will never attain', which as far as meaning is concerned implies that 'the last word is never spoken', and that full power is never achieved.[40] It is, however, just at this point when van der Leeuw has brought man to the limit of his self-perceived boundary of power and meaning that he talks about salvation. Salvation is that desired though unattained state which directs human endeavour and which exerts a present influence upon those who are still seeking it. The religious quest is thus set within the context of the unknown goal so that in Rudolph Otto's terms it might be said that the 'wholly other' is the determining feature of the searching spirit of man. It is as the ultimate is sought after that the 'numinous' is experienced. There is yet another aspect of the context of salvation which merits attention, for it shows the similarity between van der Leeuw's thought and that of John Bowker which has already been considered in association with the problem of evil, and which exemplifies one of our central arguments concerning the centrality of the problem of evil in religious studies.

There is, says van der Leeuw, a fundamental limitation or restriction experienced by man as he pursues his path to power, it is that experience of the boundary which separates man from full awareness and from the sense of possessing the entire meaning of his life and destiny. Knowledge of this limitation also involves as a consequence the 'devaluation of all that has preceded it', as well as the experience of 'the malicious inadequacy of all that happens and the irrationality at the very basis of life'.[31] The precise meaning of limitation in van der Leeuw is not the same as the notion of compounds of limitation in Bowker, however, for the latter such limitations are the very facts of life which religion serves to overcome while for van der Leeuw they are intrinsic to religious processes as such. The idea of the demonic, for example, which is but one manifestation of the 'inadequate' in religion has been conceptually related to, and has come to be contained within the very concept of divinity. 'In the very concept of God the demonic continues

---

[38] Leach, E. R., 1954: 10.
[39] Leeuw, G. van der, Ibid., p. 660.
[40] Ibid., p. 680.
[41] Ibid., p. 681.

to proclaim its presence, whether as absolute incalculability (predestination) or as inestimable mercy'.[42] But these assertions are to be understood more as the passing comments they are in van der Leeuw's study rather than absolutely central notions which he has carefully worked out. In context the emphasis upon negative features occupies a relatively insignificant place and they have been emphasized here because of the theoretical importance which the present argument gives to negative features as the frame within which the general paradigm of meaning can be the more clearly understood. What is evident from this consideration of van der Leeuw's work is that the notion of power along with this reference to limitation permits an easy application of the paradigm of meaning to the entire scheme which serves to demonstrate that hermeneutical exercises in phenomenology are not very far removed from those in both the history and anthropology of religions.

To say this ought not, however, to presume that a general paradigm of meaning can be accepted in an a prioristic manner, or that there is an unquestionable uniformity developing amongst scholars engaged in the study of religion. This is not so as a consideration of the important study by Rodney Needham on the notion of belief will make clear. This particular book entitled *Belief, Language, and Experience*, has been chosen as the focus of study suitable for the conclusion of this chapter not only because it offers a contradiction of the paradigm of meaning but because it raises the most fundamental questions concerning religious phenomena which bear direct relevance to the theorists already discussed.[43]

The criticisms directed against the lack of philosophical sophistication in anthropological studies in chapter four would be completely inappropriate as far as Needham's study is concerned. As a work it is both profoundly anthropological inasmuch as it treats of those categories which pertain to religious institutions while it is, at the same time, profoundly philosophical in the Wittgensteinian tradition of linguistic usage. The fact that Needham devotes the opening paragraphs to an explanation of the inter-disciplinary nature of his discussion, saying that he wanted to 'attract the attention of theologians, linguists and psychologists' as well as anthropologists and philosophers, shows the breadth of intention and intimates the possible scope of its influence.[44] Despite the fact that but little response has, as yet, been forthcoming from these quarters Needham's analysis of the relationship between statements expressing belief in religious entities and inner feeling-states which might be thought to correspond to them stands as an unavoidable demonstration of the crucial issues which must be encountered by any scholar interested in theoretical problems of religious study, and most especially in hermeneutical tasks.

In sympathy with the general approach outlined earlier for the paradigm of meaning Needham explains the desire of the anthropologist as philosopher 'to discern a constant order in the world, and ... to make an orderly determination of the true nature of man'.[45] This hope has not, however, come to fruition for 'from the confident and universal programme of Comte' to his own tentative and

---

42 Ibid., p. 140.
43 Needham, Rodney, 1972.
44 Ibid., p. xiv.
45 Ibid., p. 243.

particular study there has been nothing but 'a series of setbacks and disillusionments' which has removed any 'ground of absolute knowledge'.[46] His own contribution has a sense of finality about it, at least methodologically, inasmuch as the finding of order depends upon language, and his study has demonstrated only the 'phantas-magoric variegation of the collective forms of significance, in grammar and classifi-catory concepts' which 'reflects the essential relativity that marks all ideas about the meaning and determination of human experience'.[47] All this has led to an increase of scepticism and a sense that no ultimate knowledge of the meaning of human being can be attained. It is no longer a question of the necessity for deeper or more extensive research, for the very idea that success is possible must be abandoned. This notion is repeated several times because Needham sees an essential problem in language itself which is also manifested in other areas of human thought. The fact that there are words which signify certain things conduces to the conclusion that meaning is possible given a suitable precision in the use of words. Since his study is seen as an attempt to 'determine (man's) relationship to reality', it might be thought that what is required is a careful consideration of the human condition, but Needham reckons to have demonstrated that language can serve a purpose other than that of clarifying a problem.[48] This being the case it follows that language, by its very nature, cannot be relied upon to furnish accurate descriptions of the human condition, but since language is the only possible medium of analysis it follows that there is no final and true word which can be spoken on the nature of human being. No 'order of orders' is then possible as far as classification is concerned with the result that 'only shifting relativities remain'.[49] To say this is to make an assertion which, inevitably, proves unpalatable to scholars and which lays bare the implications of the paradigm of meaning, in other words, the general human desire for meaning can be seen as consonant with the general function of language as implying that a full meaning can, potentially, be found for any entity or phenomenon while in actual fact it can be demonstrated that this is not the case.

Needham's emphasis upon the notion of belief followed less from a desire to make a study of religion than from the wish to show that notions which might be deemed to be largely psychological in reference could not be given any full and specific verbal expression. In providing a thorough and comparative study of this one term he thinks that a sound case has been made for the unreliability of this general psychological category of notions as far as their inclusion in philosophical argument is concerned. Needham realizes that this finding is unsettling to intellectual pursuits which depend upon the reliability of verbal constructs, and he resorts to a figurative passage replete with topographical metaphors to convey the sense of 'conceptual instability and loss of location' which follows the necessary acknowledge-ment of 'the precariousness of our delineations of the human condition'.[50]

It is particularly instructive to note this use of the word 'precariousness' inasmuch as it occurs in a similarly emphasized position in the work of Peter Berger to which

[46] Idem.
[47] Ibid., p. 244.
[48] Ibid., p. 236.
[49] Ibid., p. 243.
[50] Ibid., pp. 235, 236.

reference has already been made. The exaltation of the phenomenon of language in the work of both these scholars is largely to blame for this conclusion on the nature of the human condition. This is an important point inasmuch as the extreme emphasis on language and the analysis of language is a significant methodological stance to be borne in mind when evaluating the hermeneutical processes adopted by them. One fact which becomes clear through this is that the logical and cognitive dimension of human beings is the one favoured for study as the prime area of significance in the life of man. The tendency to omit the affective realm has already been stressed in advocating the broader dimension of the general paradigm of meaning, and especially in providing the opportunity through studies such as that of Stanner to entertain this other dimension in a positive way. One illuminating consequence of these comments by Needham and Berger, in the light of the position adopted by the historians and phenomenologists of religion, is the way in which the more sociologically oriented thinkers diverge from those who might be said to be more interested in the transcendental aspect of human life. Someone like Rudolph Otto is supremely confident that attributes of God can be 'grasped by the intellect ... analysed by thought (and) admit of definition', in similar vein he is sure that 'mere feeling' apart from precise verbal expression is useless in religion.[51] The fact that he goes on to analyse the importance of the personal and affective dimensions of religious awareness does not detract from his commitment to the importance of clear verbal definition. In fact the ensuing descriptions of the *sensus numinis* witness to his sense of security in employing language to render profound experiences intelligible to all.

It is precisely this sense of security which merits comment, however, for it depends less upon any theory of language which Otto possessed than upon his own general religious certainty of the ultimate existence of the realities with which his study is concerned. In this sense Joachim Wach is just in evaluating Otto as one whose implicit religious convictions are not 'matched by an articulate statement of the methodological aspect' of his analysis of religious phenomena.[52] Needham, by contrast, is all too clear as to his methodology and pushes its consequences into those very areas where they are sensed as unwelcome, which is to reassert the point that theoreticians are not exempt from the inclinations of their fellow men in their desire for security and certainty in the world. Mary Douglas has aptly observed that the notion of relativity is the 'philosopher's bogy' which seems 'to sum up all the threats to our cognitive security'.[53] To follow a strictly sociological understanding, such as that of Durkheim, then necessarily involves abandoning any 'comfort of stable anchorage for his cognitive efforts', something which Needham demonstrably achieves and thereby proving that hermeneutics must be consistent, and that once the nature of human life and religiosity is the subject of study the personal perspective of the scholar, whether that of relativism or 'transcendentalism' cannot be ignored.[54]

One consequence of Needham's study which is of profound significance for the

---

51 Otto, Rudolph, 1924: 1.
52 Wach, Joachim, In J. M. Kitagawa, 1968: 71.
53 Douglas, Mary, 1975: xvii.
54 Idem.

study of religion is the issue of how private states are to be related to public states as far as the perception and expression of human life is concerned. Towards the close of his book Needham makes use of Alastair MacIntyre's notion of 'opacity' in describing the individual personality. Religious studies must, inevitably, face the issue of how the individual relates to the group as far as religious phenomena are concerned even though, from the studies of Robertson Smith in the nineteenth century through the growing sociological approach of Durkheim to the modern studies of Bryan Wilson, the individual has received little specific attention.[55] Just as the power of the sociological perspective tended to reify the notion of society with an inevitable reduction in concern with private persons, so the history of religions tradition, from Max Müller to Eliade, tended to reify a broad notion of the sacred dimension which also offered no real analysis of the role of religiosity in the personal life. This latter comment might seem to contradict the actual evidence in the case of Rudolph Otto, for example, but the point is that where the focus seems to be upon the individual he is presented as an ideal typical case of one in touch with the sacred. If Needham's analysis is correct, then the relationship between the private apprehension of religious phenomena and the public expression of the same cannot be ignored as a factor in the meaning of religiosity itself. There may actually be no univocal correspondence between private and public religious phenomena as Needham's study demonstrated from a technical standpoint and as ordinary self-reflection might suggest to any observer of private religiosity, but to say this does not mean that attention should not be paid to the personal level of meaning. While it is possible to agree with Needham that individuals are 'subjected to opacity' in their mutual relations, it is unnecessary to follow him in stressing the factor of 'misunderstanding' which he sees as essential to the obscurity which attends human communication.[56]

It could be argued phenomenologically that this opacity is necessary because each person is a unique centre of creativity and not simply a *tabula rasa* programmed by socialization, and that largely by means of language. Language might better be understood as serving to unite discrete persons in as common a group as is possible given the individualistic basis of human being on the one hand, and the necessity of social interaction for co-operative life on the other. If it becomes apparent that there is a resistance to language when it is used to investigate private psychological states, then it is as possible to adopt a positive interpretation of this fact in terms of the uniqueness and intransigent creativity of the self, as it is to embrace a sense of hopelessness in understanding anything about man. Theoretically speaking the point will have been made that the opacity of the individual is but one of the restraints acting upon language as a tool of analysis. Because language can more easily be used to further the ends of a rational discourse than of emotional awareness, though poetry is but one literary genre which encourages care in such a gross assertion, it is important to give some place to symbolic and ritual acts when evaluating an overall study of religious phenomena. Care is required in this area of communication acts and their proper evaluation because implicit assumptions

---

55 Needham, Rodney, Ibid., p. 245.
56 Ibid., p. 246.

can rapidly pass unnoticed. Despite the qualifications made here for Needham's argument it must be said that his presuppositions are clear and open to just such critical evaluation. In the history of religions this is not always the case, and when a presupposition is openly acknowledged it can beg as many issues as it resolves.

Ernst Benz, for example, in a paper which shows fine insight into the problem of translating from one language to another falls foul of the tendency to assume a general religiosity on the part of mankind. He says that he experienced the problem of trying to lecture through a translator in Japan as one of being assailed by an enemy. In the lesser task of translating from German to English he 'found that the very structure of language itself seems to impede understanding'.[57] This sentiment is rather like Needham's position though Benz draws no parallels and makes no theoretical analysis of the problem he encountered. It is to his final comment that some attention must be turned for he there comforts himself with 'the thought that we carry within ourselves the most essential condition for the understanding of other religions'. This intuitive faculty turns out to be nothing less than 'a tradition of earlier forms of religious experience and of earlier stages of religious consciousness'. By some means or other which he does not mention this primal knowledge is located in 'the structure of human personality', and serves as the means by which one religious man of one culture can understand or grasp the religiosity of another person from a completely different cultural background.[58] As far as hermeneutics is concerned this sort of assertion is useless and leads to the anthropological refusal to treat history of religions seriously.

A much more satisfactory argument over the relation of the individual to the group has been forwarded by Wilfred Cantwell Smith and has already been alluded to earlier in this chapter. In returning to his hypothesis that a distinction should be made between the cumulative tradition of a religious movement and the personal faith of individual devotees, emphasis is placed upon Smith's view that it is the individual who is confronted by and who is 'the locus of an interaction between the transcendent, which is presumably the same for everyman, and the cumulative tradition which is different for everyman'.[59] Why the transcendent should be the same for all men is difficult to judge apart from the fact that Smith could be said to operate from an implicit Christian tradition which postulates an essential uniform character of God. Be that as it may the prominence he gives to the faith of the individual which is 'unfathomable, too profound, personal and divine for public exposition' provides a valuable basis for considering the problem of meaning and significance in religious persons.[60] Smith is certain that there are differing aspects of religiosity, some being essentially private whilst others are open to the observer for inspection, but he is content merely to assert the fact of the private dimension without having to lay it bear or to regret that it is inviolable. His view can be seen to be similar to that of the phenomenologists of knowledge, at least in the way he describes the process of growth in understanding, and his notion of cumulative tradition could, itself, be interpreted in terms of, and as being similar to that of the

---

[57] Benz, Ernst, 1954. In Mircea Eliade and J. M. Kitagawa 1959: 117.
[58] Ibid., p. 130.
[59] Ibid., p. 186.
[60] Ibid., p. 170.

'stock of knowledge' in plausibility theory. The fact of individual creativity which justifies human opacity is well exemplified in his assertion that 'each person is presented with a cumulative tradition. From it and out of the capacities of his own inner life and circumstances of his outer life, he comes to a faith of his own'.[61]

These deliberations serve to show that the problem of interpretation in religious studies is inextricably associated with the level and kind of analysis which is deemed proper within each academic tradition. Perhaps the most fundamental difference in orientation which has been encountered thus far has been brought to clear focus in this case of the individual in his relation to the religious group. As far as our present argument is concerned this issue is fundamental inasmuch as the question of salvation must always be clearly expressed in terms of the sphere of its operation. Is the notion of salvation to be understood as a personal and private experience, or is it restricted more to the ideals of a social group and with the co-operative action initiated to bring about the desired state of affairs?

Needham's study was introduced as a test case of the notion of plausibility on the grounds that if no sense of meaning and reality could be posited for the individual, then the notion of plausibility and of salvation defined in terms of plausibility would be severely impaired. The argument brought against Needham has suggested that there is no serious challenge offered to the general paradigm of meaning by his analysis of psychological states and their relation to public concepts. As long as a difference is maintained between the significance of private and public states of meaning, or kinds of meaning, there is but little difficulty. The problem emerges only when an analytic device is used in realms where it is essentially inappropriate, and it has been argued that the notion of human individuality and creativity provides a sound basis of defence against any expectation that a univocal relationship between public and private concepts ought to exist. As far as the history and phenomenology of religions are concerned, and the same point needs to be made for anthropology, the prime object of study is that sphere of inter-personal relationships within which language does serve positive functions. It will be perfectly legitimate to develop categories to accommodate states of private sensations even though it will be impossible to elucidate upon their precise nature. This has well established precedents in the history of religions in the case of Buddhism, for example, where there have been many discussions of the notion of enlightenment even though it is acknowledged that any full comprehension of that phenomenon can only be obtained by one who has attained to the state itself.

One aspect of Needham's argument merits a final comment for it adds a further dimension to the general paradigm of meaning, albeit unintentionally. In referring to his final evaluation of the nature of the individual in the light of his analysis of language and explicitness of concept formation, Needham says that the solitary person is 'divided within himself by his very self-consciousness, yet with no guarantee of his own integrity'.[62] Such an assertion is not unlike the evaluation of the Murinbata notion of man already discussed by Stanner, and it raises the notion that a final concept of meaning can, potentially, include within it an aspect of doubt.

---

[61] Ibid., p. 187.
[62] Ibid., p. 245.

The attitude which is adopted towards such a category of final evaluation can, in a sense, change it, or can lead to a new ultimate explanation, but the point is that Needham's assessment of the role of language in self-understanding tends to be nihilistic. Whereas the Murinbata might be content in the knowledge that reality offers conflicting statements which admit of no final resolution, Needham reacts in a kind of philosophical desperation. This re-emphasizes the need to understand meaning as possessing both cognitive and affective factors. Although Needham is careful in his linguistic analysis of affective states yet the dominance and priority is ultimately given to the dimension of propositions and reason. In this book the argument is forwarded that from a phenomenological perspective it is perfectly proper to assert the necessity of meaning in human life and religiosity in the full realization that the affective dimension of ritual, myth and symbol can produce a sufficient level of durable plausibility despite the fact that no perfectly consistent logical explanation of problems is forthcoming.

If it is agreed that the notion of salvation has to do with the final understanding of things, that it relates to Needham's notion of the 'order of orders' which he has not succeeded in establishing beyond doubt, then it can easily be seen that the term has to do with non-philosophical arguments as with statements about the nature of things. It will be necessary to return to this area of human action in the light of insufficient logical justification in the concluding chapter, for the moment something must be said on the logical status of the term 'belief' which may serve as a validation of some of the studies engaged in by historians and phenomenologists of religion.

Since religious studies in the broader sense are concerned both with the historical development of religious traditions and the particular manifestations of religiosity in religious virtuosi, some critical attention needs to be paid to the concepts which relate the realms of public and social systems of meaning on the one hand, and private and individual ones on the other. This does not mean that a simple construction of paired terms is required as in Cantwell Smith's cumulative tradition and personal faith, but that those phenomena which serve the task of relating these dimensions be themselves clarified. Needham's study is a classic expression of how to go about analysing a concept which 'straddles the border between private states and public appraisal'.[63] It is precisely such straddling terms which require careful identification because they can be expected to manifest peculiar properties such that they may not admit of rigorous explication when viewed solely in the context of either private or public life-worlds. The word belief may well be reduced to a complete lack of specificity under the pressure of a linguistic analysis, yet it possesses a remarkable power in its normal usage. This not only means that philosophers of language are making demands of the particular word which it is not called upon to bear in ordinary use, but also that the very significance of the term lies in its power to unite the person and the group within a communication event. The very word 'belief' can thus be seen as charged with emotive significance which enables it to fulfil its task. Needham sees his argument as having uncovered the confusions introduced into man's thought by words themselves, talking of words he says that 'we cannot think without them, but they make it hard for us to think

---

[63] Ibid., p. 235.

with them'.[64] The confusion which some words seem to introduce into discourse may, in fact, be a necessary blurring of concepts without which a particular activity would be impossible. Most especially might this be the case as far as religious phenomena are concerned.

Along with the word belief are several others which bear a family resemblance to one another including the sacred, transcendence, myth and symbol. The word religion may itself share in the paradoxical quality of these words, a quality bequeathed by merit of the fact that they have to do both with the most personal and private aspects of life on the one hand, and with the nature of the gods or of society on the other. (To place the notions of god and society together is not to engage in the Durkheimian reduction of the one to the other, but simply to draw a distinction between the internal life of men and the external realities they perceive as present to their consciousness). The word salvation also belongs to this category for in specific religious traditions it unites personal sentiments and those doctrinal schemes present within religious traditions and which are offered to devotees as ways of facilitating the attainment of the desired goal. In this immediate context the word salvation is used according to its particular religious meaning within the appropriate theological scheme whether it be Christian, Hindu or Islamic. In its general meaning in terms of plausibility theory it might also be said to possess a peculiar status for there, too, it serves the same function of relating private to public schemes. This category of 'straddling' or 'bridging' words shares in the characteristics of that group of terms called performative utterances, at least to a certain degree.

Some care is necessary in making this point because Needham also refers to performative utterances, but he does so in order to demonstrate that the assertion 'I believe' is similar to other usages like, 'I promise', both statements being free from any necessary special emotion or psychological state. In other words Needham asserts the public nature of these assertions and in that he is quite correct. The reason for our taking recourse to this notion of performative utterance is not that one mentioned by J. L. Austin in his original paper on the subject when he bemoaned the fact that 'people are apt to invoke a new use of language ... to help them out of this, that, or the other well-known philosophical tangle', rather it is employed in an attempt to describe a category of phenomena by means of analogy.[65] It is not that the words 'belief, religion, salvation, sacred, myth' and 'symbol' are themselves performative utterances, but that the general category to which they be said to belong itself resembles the general category of performative utterances. Austin's basic intention in coining the name for this group of words was to identify the fact that people actually did something by using them rather than simply saying something, an action is performed by means of the words which describe the nature of the act itself, as in the cases of 'I apologize', or 'I name this ship ...'. What is more, this category of words is not concerned with issues of truth and falsity of assertions, even though there may be what Austin calls 'infelicities' associated with the usage of performatives. The similarity between performative and straddling categories lies not only in the fact that their truth or falsity is not the prime concern

---

[64] Ibid., p. 228.
[65] Austin, J. L., 1961: 221.

of the scholar, although he needs to be aware of the appropriateness of context in which they are used along with potential infelicities, but in the observation that, as Austin pointed out in respect of performatives, there are utterances whose proper status is to be discovered more in what he calls their 'force' than in their strict meaning.[66]

It is precisely because Needham avoids this distinction that he fails to do justice to the full effect of belief terminology. Needham pursues the very philosophical interest in 'the old doctrine about meanings', as Austin labels this general position, rather than seeing the more significant 'new doctrine about all the possible forces of utterances'.[67] If this notion of force may be legitimately applied to the religious phenomena of myth, ritual, the notion of the sacred and salvation and others, then they can be loosely described as performative phenomena. The significance of such a category to the general paradigm of meaning is obvious, for it marks the kind of inquiry which is appropriate to the phenomena themselves. In continually emphasizing the affective and cognitive dimensions of the notion of meaning what has been advocated, albeit implicitly, is this notion of 'force' which is found as a characteristic aspect of many religious phenomena, and without which little understanding can be gained of the actual function they effect both in religious traditions and the personal dimension of faith. One important implication of this suggestion is that it is unnecessary to adopt any particular religious stance in order to emphasize the distinctive features of religious phenomena in human life. The identification of a category such as this one of 'straddling terms' can assist in coping with notions which appear to demand a peculiar response on the part of the devotee, while enabling the observer to maintain a more neutral stance. The mere construction of a category does not, of course, reduce the significance of questions concerning ultimate truths or the existence of God, but it does enable the phenomenologist to attempt an adequate explanation of phenomena without feeling that he has to subscribe to their doctrines. In other words, some categories facilitate description by removing the necessity of reductionism.

In the light of these hermeneutical considerations it is now both possible and desirable to recall the earlier argument on plausibility theory and the notion of salvation, and to attempt a discussion on the issue of salvation with respect to a variety of religious movements. Aspects of primitive religions are first discussed in order to make the theoretical point that they are not different in kind from the so called world-religions, and then the argument turns to one eastern and one western religion in an attempt to show that the perspective grounded in a general paradigm of meaning does, in fact, possess a significant hermeneutical power.

---

[66] Ibid., p. 238.
[67] Idem.

PART TWO

CHAPTER SIX

SALVATION IN PRELITERATE SOCIETIES

The central concern of this chapter arises because of the fact that studies of religion, whether in the tradition of anthropology, phenomenology, or history of religion, have scarcely regarded the notion of salvation in primitive societies as worthy of any significant attention.

For nineteenth century scholars this fact may be relatively easily understood inasmuch as the predominating influence of evolutionary thought led to primitive religions being viewed as representing a relatively undeveloped form of religiosity. Later forms of religion, especially the world-religions as they were called, were thought to represent the outcome of many ages and phases in the development of the human mind, and central to these developments was the phenomenon of salvation which might be sought, but only in vain, in the relatively undeveloped primitive religions. Robertson Smith expressed something of this position in his Burnett Lectures of 1888 by asserting that in its earlier stages 'religion did not exist for the saving of souls but for the preservation and welfare of society'.[1] In Max Müller's influential Gifford Lectures of the same year there is no treatment of the idea of salvation at all, even in sections devoted to the definition of religion.[2] A similar picture emerges from E. B. Tylor's treatment of religion which focuses on the nineteenth century specialities of soul, spirit possession, worship and sacrifice.[3] F. B. Jevons provides further evidence of the peculiar interest in the phenomena of taboo, magic, fetishism, ancestor worship, and mythology, in his well known studies in the history of religion and comparative religion.[4]

Of the early twentieth century scholars Andrew Lang in his *Making of Religion*, and Rafael Karsten in his *Origins of Religion*, demonstrate a similar lack of interest in salvation which is also shared by R. R. Marett.[5] E. O. James, whose work extended into the nineteen sixties and whose interests betray a resemblance to the somewhat antiquarian concerns of the intellectualist scholars of the Victorian period, did address himself to the subject of salvation but did so less in order to explore its theoretical significance than as an approach to Indian religions.[6]

More recently W. G. Oxtoby has expressed surprise at this general lack of theoretical interest in the notion of salvation during what he calls the first phase in the development of the history of religion up to 1915.[7] He suggests that the term salvation was too theological for currency at a time when theology was not a popular pursuit among academics, but as has already been indicated earlier this is a less likely explanation than that which sees the emphasis upon evolutionism

---

[1] Smith., W. R., 1894: 29.
[2] Müller, M., 1889.
[3] Tylor, E. B., 1958.
[4] Jevons, F. B., 1896, 1908.
[5] Lang, A., 1900. Karsten, R., 1935. Marett, R. R., 1929, 1933.
[6] James, E. O., 1933, 1938, 1962.
[7] Oxtoby, W. G., 1973: 32.

as tending to reduce expectations of finding such an advanced form as salvation within primitive religious structures. During the decade of 1960 there was a growth of interest in the notion of salvation among historians and phenomenologists but, as Oxtoby points out for the two key volumes expressing this concern, it was more pragmatic than theoretical.[8] The same criticism could be levelled against other standard works in the history of religion and even the editor of one such collection, which represented the papers given at one world congress of the International Association for the History of Religion, could admit that no theoretical scheme had been advanced or typology advocated.[9]

While it is most appropriate that assent should be given to Oxtoby's observation that it was in the period following the first world war that a growth took place in *Religionswissenschaft* and in the phenomenon of salvation as an object of academic concern, the further point should be added that this interest was almost entirely philological or philosophical with respect to the great religious traditions of the world. Where comparisons have been made they have usually followed the plan of discussing functional equivalences in the meaning of salvation ideas, there has been but little concern with more theoretical issues, a fact which may be explained by the tendency for anthropological and sociological studies, which normally engage in more abstract theorizing, to follow different lines of interest from the history and phenomenology of religion which themselves favour discussion of the more formal systems of religious thought.

The very fact that the methods employed by these rather distinctive academic traditions varied markedly reinforced the notion that primitive religiosity and that of the world religions were of significantly different types. The nature of this difference is not easy to establish with any precision, though it certainly does not rest on the older notions of primitive and developed forms of mentality. Eliade within the history of religions and Lévi-Strauss within anthropology have both established powerful arguments to the effect that, as the former expresses it,

> 'the metaphysical concepts of the archaic world were not always formulated in theoretical language: but the symbol, the myth, the rite, express on different planes and through the means proper to them, a complex system of coherent affirmations about the ultimate reality of things, a system that can be regarded as constituting a metaphysics'.[10]

If there is no essential difference in the ability to conceptualize, there is a difference over the current content of thought, in terms of Eliade's general thesis this could be expressed as the essential sacred ethos of the life-world and therefore world of thought of primitives, and the desacralized world of western, urban man.

The fact that a more abstract consideration of salvation is now possible results from the necessary association of anthropological and history of religions perspectives as a result of more recent studies of world religions at the local level. In order to see how questions are forced upon the observer it will be useful to begin with Kenelm Burridge's study of millenarian movements which is exceptional in

---

8 Abel et al., 1962. Brandon, S. G. F., 1963.
9 Werblowsky, R. J. Zwi, and C. J. Bleeker, 1970.
10 Eliade, M., 1959: 3.

developing an abstract notion of salvation for a preliterate religion, and which, because it is not concerned with a world-religious tradition, can show the elements of analysis which can be applied to those more complex cases where historical traditions are directly involved.

In order to avoid an overly ethnocentric frame of reference Burridge adopted a definition of religious activities based on the idea of power relations in society. Accepting as basic postulates that men seek power and prestige, much as Edmund Leach had suggested in his study of highland Burma, and that they do so through systems of obligation in social interaction, he defined religion as a,

> 'redemptive process indicated by the activities, moral rules, and assumptions about power which, pertinent to the moral order and taken on faith, not only enable a people to perceive the truth of things, but guarantee that they are indeed perceiving the truth of things'.[11]

The notion of redemptive process here serves as a broad category applicable to movements from many parts of the world, it is firmly located in the Durkheimian tradition of sociology and avoids the older definitions of religion which stressed the nature of belief and the objects of belief. It also implies a shift of emphasis from more static functionalist models to a dynamic conception of religious institutions, the particular significance of this as far as the present argument is concerned lies in Burridge's assertion that underlying millenarian movements is a feeling of 'dissatisfaction with the current system'.[12] This phenomenon of perceived implausibility would correspond to the notion of evil which has already been discussed and the succeeding movement could be regarded as the soteriological response after the fashion to be considered at the end of this chapter.

The dissatisfaction once formulated and preached, usually by a prophetic figure in the case of millenarianism, provides the basis for the description of the forces and powers at work on men, and which the ordinary member may grasp as a way of explaining his own plight. A new redemptive process emerges as men act in accord with the new system of power and prestige, but the new order only becomes viable when the former state of things is no longer able to carry the undivided approval of society, a situation which may well arise during periods of cultural contact between groups as the processes of both westernization and sanskritization demonstrate as will be shown in an analysis of Indian religion in a later chapter. Burridge argues that in periods of internal development of society people may feel their current pattern of beliefs concerning their social reality is no longer able to explain, or to cope with the changing situation. In order to maintain integrity and status as individuals they feel the need for a change in the beliefs that will enable them to act in accord with the altered power relations of the new order. He regards the redemptive process as involving three major areas of life and thought, the actual experience of social reality, the working assumptions about that reality, and lastly 'the assumptions we call faith'.[13] It is when the level of actual experience is found to be in conflict with the working assumptions, or even

---

[11] Burridge, K., 1969: 6.
[12] Ibid., p. 14.
[13] Ibid., p. 5.

more significantly with the basic beliefs, that a new system is sought. Burridge's emphasis upon that period of a group's history 'when faith belies experience' corresponds to the emphasis upon the identification of areas of implausibility which, we have argued, constitute the initial factor in religious processes.[14] In terms of the definition of salvation understood according to the perspective of plausibility theory another of Burridge's usages becomes quite clear, for he says that under certain circumstances there occurs 'an unsatisfactory redemptive process', in other words there no longer exists a 'sufficiency of durable plausibility' for members of the community.[15]

Burridge's distinctive contribution to the notion of salvation lies in the idea that it has to do with social obligations. Human life is social life and as such inevitably involves many reciprocal obligations. The redemptive process is one in which men seek to discharge all their obligations, this is the essence of religious activity. Salvation is thus to be understood in terms of unobligedness, and this is regarded as being a future state which can only be experienced during life to a very limited extent, he thus identifies the saved state with the notions of heaven and *nirvana*. In terms of the history of religions this view could be extended quite markedly to embrace present experiences of salvation in a more realistic way than is possible when the prime focus is upon millenarian movements which themselves, necessarily, restrict the terms of theoretical considerations. It is precisely because he deals with such movements that he is concerned with social change and instability in power and prestige systems, as far as societies of a more stable base are concerned the whole issue of obligedness assumes different proportions. In them it would be more appropriate to talk of salvation as consisting in satisfactory expectations of mutual respect based upon an established and maintained set of values, but that is a separate question. As far as Burridge's analysis is concerned it would seem that his notion of power is cognate to the concept of meaning which has already been extensively argued. The similarities between the two notions is quite instructive as far as the general paradigm of meaning is concerned inasmuch as power is used to describe a wide variety of human activities and thereby demonstrates that religious phenomena should not be sought in isolated spheres of human life, but in the broad areas of social life. Further, Burridge sees the search for power as associated with the process of developing personal integrity as a social actor. In so doing he makes the realm of psychological questions an open one for anthropological analysis even though he does not himself pursue it to any great length. He assumes that in the quest for power and integrity human beings act in a basically rational way, this agrees with the notion of meaning as a general goal in life, but gives a useful redirection to it in the sense that to talk of power is to refer to emotional desires and ambitions. To stress this is to substantiate that aspects of this thesis which asserts the affective dimension of the paradigm of meaning. Burridge sees this assumption of a state of rationality among those studied to be in accord with the similar assumption underlying sociological analysis to the effect that social life is potentially intelligible.[16]

---

14 Ibid., p. 14.
15 Ibid., p. 171.
16 Ibid., p. 7.

In slightly less theoretical terms the interesting feature of millenarian movements is that the desire for meaning emerging within a changing social structure is implemented by means of a reconstructed social order. In developed societies, by contrast, change in plausibility tends to occur relatively slowly and to a limited extent, and if a segment of the population requires a more radical change, as the result of deeming their present conditions unsatisfactory, then it may establish a new group or community as the basis for the new way of life. Burridge's work is most useful in emphasizing the relationship between beliefs and the actual social networks within which they are enacted. Such restraints and lack of restraints upon change may well explain in large measure the reason why some religious groups have adopted the response of migration in association with the growth of changing doctrinal perspectives *vis-à-vis* wider society. The nineteenth century emigration of Mormon converts from Europe to Utah, which will be considered later in another context, had the explicit and manifest function of preparing souls for the second coming of Christ, but one of its crucial latent functions lay in the possibility of constructing anew a society of saints freed from the obligation of interacting with gentile neighbours. In this case Burridge's dictum that salvation is unobligedness can be seen as a quite appropriate description of the process of Mormon adventism. Something of a qualification of Burridge's thesis is necessary from a phenomenological standpoint, however, and the Mormon case is but one example which underlines the necessity, for many religious groups stress the significance of service and commitment to other persons. It is not the case that 'redemption itself can only be realized at or after that appropriate death which brings to an end an appropriate mode of discharging one's obligations'.[17] Burridge is not suggesting some subtle reading of these words which might imply a death to self and a new life of dedication to others, he is stressing the entire processual nature of redemption which continues during earthly life.

Phenomenologically speaking it would be wiser to employ a more subtle understanding so that the notion of commitment to the service of others could be seen as an integral part of the state of salvation itself. What this would involve is a twofold notion of power, one relative to the ordinary social world and the other directed towards the religious ideal of inversion of status. The New Testament concept of the first being last and the last first would furnish an example of this concept of power understood as humility.[18] It is then in the fellowship of the saints that the devotee experiences his new found sense of power and personal integrity, it is a perspective which to him is the complete opposite to his previous life. The desire for communitarian groups in the early phases of some sects expresses the rationale of attempting to unite in one entire and self-contained realm the practical aspect of living with the ideal of the doctrine. Utopias are willed because of the feeling that there should be no dichotomy between theory and practice. The ritual of millenarian movements is often the ritual of change, both of the perception of the need for change, and of the accommodation of belief systems to apparent changes. The trance, vision, and as far as the prophet is concerned, the ability to understand

---

[17] Ibid., p. 6.
[18] Matthew 19. xxx.

what others find confusing, these are the important things. The ritual of stable societies tends to be more redressive and seeks to relate the ideal and the actual states of religious life within the context of existing social patterns, a function often fulfilled by sacrifice. At the level of religious functionaries a difference can be established between the prophet who calls men into a radically new form of life, and the priest who seeks to remove the dichotomy between spiritual ideal and the failure of life engendered by social interaction. A classic example of the association of prophets with change in social order under pressure from external sources is provided in Evans-Pritchard's study of the Nuer. There the priests are identified as the major religious functionaries and the prophets as a relative innovation emerging late in the nineteenth century in response to the disruption caused to Nuer life by Arab slave traders, Madhists and by Anglo-Egyptian rule.[19] It is during such periods of culture contact that the system of indigenous meaning and power is called into question, and what is clear from this is that religion is inextricably associated not only with the fundamental social structure, but also with human integrity at the level of the personality. It is precisely because of this fact that the notion of affectivity cannot be omitted from any model of meaning used heuristically for religious traditions.

The case of millenarian movements compared with religions of more stable societies demonstrates the sense of conflict present in the human perception of social relationships. Rather than supporting Burridge in his argument that redemption means freedom from obligation, a more widely applicable notion may be established if it is accepted that what men seek is a particular quality of relationship, rather than no relationship at all. The reference to Christianity and the notion of joyful service could be developed to show that it is the way service is understood that makes the difference between the sense of obligation conceived as an undesired necessity, and that service which is perfect freedom. As will be shown later the Mormon Church is a fine example of obligation as a central feature of salvation.

What Burridge's example is clearly showing is that in the particular social world which engenders millenarianism there is a strong feeling of conflict and negative evaluations of reality which extends to social relations as to everything else. In other religious contexts a movement may maintain, and our basic argument suggests that it will maintain, a strong negative evaluation of some aspect of reality. Just what factors are singled out for judgement is a question which has been taken up in the sociology of sects which will be discussed at the end of this chapter. For the moment the millenarian instance can be firmly established as a most instructive typical case of the identification of evil in religious movements by referring to Peter Worsley's conclusion on Melanesian cargo cults which affirms that the precondition for their emergence lies in 'a situation of dissatisfaction with existing social relations and of yearnings for a happier life'.[20] Such a generalization can, as might be expected, find application in religious movements other than preliterate ones, and so it is that Norman Cohn has demonstrated that the millennium became

---

19 Evans-Pritchard, E. E., 1956: 309.
20 Worsley, P., 1970: 251.

the hope for many European groups of socially deprived persons existing in a marginal relation to a more stable society.[21]

This form of deprivation theory has been most clearly expressed by Vittorio Lanternari in his analysis of messianic movements which argues that it is when primitive societies feel oppressed by the conservative pattern of social life that millenarian responses occur. The sense of oppression meets with a desire for new conditions and if a suitable prophetic figure emerges, who is able to initiate a break with the past, then a messianic movement is likely to occur. 'Salvation (is) the purpose of all religions', says Lanternari, and freedom from oppression is what constitutes a saved state.[22] While many movements seek escape from tensions arising within their natal societies as with the Tupi cults of precolonial Brazil, the Tafari movement of Jamaica as well as the Mormons and Sikhs to be considered later, others result from culture contact and pressure from outside sources as with the Moaris and North American Indians as well as the Polynesian cargo cult groups. Lanternari identifies this response of 'religious escapism' with 'the quest for a way out of the earthly confines' experienced by many for whom it may be said that it 'is inherent in the nature of religious experience that temporary evasion from the world can be achieved while awaiting the final hour of redemption'.[23]

In terms of the general paradigm of meaning, and also to do justice to the wealth of religious data, comment must be made on the fact that Lanternari fails to see that the implied critique of reality which is found in messianic movements possesses counterparts in non-messianic religions. He tends to presuppose that established, world religions which serve members of stable societies and which validate the lives they lead, do not serve this function of judgement and negative evaluation of the world. While it is true that world religions are not usually religions of the oppressed they can be so, but what is more important is that they do contain within their cosmology or theology an analysis of evil. Lanternari is correct in wanting to argue that 'it is not possible to separate the world of the so-called primitive peoples from the world commonly described as historical', and if he had extended his theoretical perspectives in accordance with this view it would not be necessary to issue the caveat on this question of evil.[24]

Despite the fact that both Burridge and Lanternari entertain the notion of salvation for the very specific forms of religiosity they focus upon in preliterate groups, they imply that some significant difference obtains between those groups and others which belong to the traditions of the world religions. This is somewhat less true for Burridge but even so the way in which these studies are presented has not exerted any significant influence upon the history of religions, or upon the general corpus of theorizing in religious studies. As has already been implied this is unfortunate inasmuch as Burridge's use of the notion of power and obligation, which may be interpreted as one application of the general paradigm of meaning, possesses wide theoretical significance both for sociological studies and for those of a more theological or phenomenological interest in the attributes of human

---

[21] Cohn, N., 1970.
[22] Lanternari, V., 1963: 321.
[23] Ibid., p. 314.
[24] Ibid., p. vi.

beings. The way in which he adopts a non-theological perspective enables the whole study to inform theologians about a range of materials and human actions which they can, if they so wish, employ as part of their own theological discussion. This desirable approach differs significantly from that of another scholar who has commented upon the notion of salvation in primitive religion but whose approach, despite the fact that it is supposed to be phenomenological, appears to be rather influenced by Christian theology.

His systematic approach leads him to discuss the significance of the standard phenomena of religion for each major tradition and also for primitive religions, this means that it is likely that he had no particular interest in notions of primitive salvation, or in the theoretical issues involved in discussing them, but simply that the structure of his study inevitably led him to comment upon the ideas of cosmic regeneration and cyclic fertility which is the way he handles salvation ideas among such peoples. His definition of salvation exhibits a theological bias:

> 'The fundamental structure of salvation seems to be a liberation from the senseless and never-ending play of human passions and desires and from servitude of sin, and a hope for reconciliation and integration with the divine, and an attempt to realize the divine. All the attempts in religions to remove the evil and to become united with the divine once and for all constitute the ways of salvation and the final attainment of this goal is salvation itself.'[25]

There is no significant contribution made by Dhavamony in this work, and it is cited to show that even when the subject of primitive salvation was raised in this phenomenological context its discussion remained at the level of non-theoretical interest, which shows just how great is the need for a theoretical model of the paradigm of meaning variety in the study of religion.

By way of contrast to the work of these anthropologists and phenomenologists the studies of Max Weber in the sociology of religion are even more theoretical and provide an important example of material which manifests close affinities with the general paradigm of meaning, and which may also help to relate the more social perspective of Burridge with the more individualistic outlook of Dhavamoney, if these two men may be taken as representative of those rather different, though potentially complementary approaches.

The theoretical basis of Weber's approach is grounded in the analysis of the variety of responses to the world adopted by religious groups in so fas as they affect practical activity in the world.[26] This concern with ideology and action lead Weber to construct a set of types of responses espoused by world religions as a means of attaining salvation. He postulated three central areas within which soteriological action could be identified as a response to particular needs.

The first involved the disprivileged, or those who in terms of deprivation theories turn to religious activities and other-wordly goals to compensate for their lack of material satisfaction in the mundane world. It is this category which covers the case of millenarian movements since the experience of culture contact with those possessing an abundance of desired goods results in a sense of personal privation and in actions

---

25 Dhavamony, M., 1973: 315.
26 Weber, M., 1963: 149.

which seek to overcome it. The second area relates to the middle classes who do not experience any sense of lack as far as possessions are concerned, but who seek a legitimation of their well-being. For such groups the desired psychological reassurance that all is as it should be makes blessedness of mere contentedness. It is to the third category, however, that some thought must be given for it comes closest to expressing the central theme of the general paradigm of meaning.

Whereas the disprivileged and the middle classes seek salvation in response to their life-experience in the world of action, so that Weber can identify types of salvation as 'products of the practical way of life', there is yet another type of person possessing a distinctive style of thought which he calls the 'intellectualist' group.[27] This category denotes those who are engaged in the life of the mind and whose 'metaphysical needs' drive them to reflection upon ethical and religious questions. The basis of this intellectual application is not one of social deprivation, nor does it emerge from a psychological need for legitimation of the life context, it is, rather, grounded in man's 'inner compulsion' both to 'understand the world as a meaningful cosmos', and to adopt an appropriate attitude towards it. This particular need identified by Weber might be said to subsist both at the level of thought and of intentional action. Weber's sociology of religion can be seen as an elaboration of this theme of world understanding and of the action which it initiates, yet he seems but little concerned to analyse the basis of the drive or to relate it to other theories of knowledge. The very fact of meaning and the processes whereby it is constructed are accepted on an *a priori* basis. Talcott Parsons has also observed this aspect of Weber's work and has characterized it as constituting a certain 'ad hocness', though one which finds adequate compensation in the weight of erudition without which Weber's discussions would appear far less satisfactory at the level of methodology. In the light of more recent studies in the sociology of knowledge it is possible to contextualize the notion of drive for salvation within a framework which can reduce the *ad hoc* nature of Weber's study, and this is precisely what we advocate in the notion of plausibility theory. The general paradigm of meaning would suggest that the response to sensed deprivation and the desire for legitimation are not, essentially, different from the intellectualist pursuit of meaning, once it is admitted that cognitive and affective dimensions are necessary for any full notion of meaningfulness.

One other aspect of Weber's approach to the study of religion must be mentioned alongside this notion of drive for salvation, for it is directly related to our emphasis on the perception of evil, namely what he called the 'problem of the world's imperfection'. At least three kinds of imperfection may be identified and they correspond to the three categories of salvation. For the disprivileged imperfection represents the state of desiring but being unable to obtain certain goods or services; for the middle classes it is the fact that they desire validation for what they already possess, while for the intellectualist group imperfection is manifested in the lack of unity and total explanation of the world which they so desire. From this it can easily be argued that the notion of imperfection, as a description of a mode of perception of the world, relates both to intellectual dimensions and to affective

---

[27] Ibid., p. 117.

concerns. Weber distinguished between these poles in terms of 'inner need', experienced by the intellectual who is also one of the privileged classes, and 'external distress' thought to be more indicative of non-privileged classes.[28] Adherence to such a strict dichotomy ought not to be made, in the light of earlier discussions on the notion of meaning, since both groups are ultimately involved in both cognitive and affective dimensions. This point must be emphasized because Weber writes as one who accentuates the realm of thought almost through the style of argument which he chooses to adopt. A similar caveat could be introduced for Talcott Parsons who is well aware of the necessity of discussing affectivity both in ordinary social life and in religious contexts, yet treats of what he clearly calls the 'problem of meaning' in religious acts in a way which subsumes emotional factors to intellectual ones. He speaks of religious *ideas* as answers to the problem of meaning possessing 'cathectic and evaluative' levels of explanation.[29] It is just this kind of emphasis upon the ultimate rational basis which makes such sociological analysis unacceptable to historians and some phenomenologists of religion who regard it as a form of reductionism, even though in its own terms of reference it is not attempting to be so.[30]

So it is that the difference in kind which Weber tries to establish between privileged and disprivileged social groups in their perception of evil and drive for salvation is more a difference of the degree to which rational procedures are resorted to in the process of constructing a satisfactory explanation of the mundane contradictoriness of life. While Weber is correct in arguing that it is 'the intellectual who transforms the concept of the world into the problem of meaning', he is not justified in his implication that there is no problem of meaning for the non-intellectual. Existential questions of the broadest kind obtain for all men even though they may be couched in symbolic, ritual or mythic forms, as was shown in an earlier chapter for the Murinbata as a type case, rather than as explicit philosophical arguments. Indeed, philosophical speculation may serve only to state problems in clearer forms rather than to actually solve them. Religious traditions, by contrast, attempt not only to formulate the nature of evil, whether as a philosophical argument or as a mythical account, but also to provide solutions acceptable at the emotional level of action in the world.

Despite the fact that Weber himself was not concerned with psychological factors in the strict sense he was preoccupied with the way systems of thought related to the actions of individuals, and this is a true of religious actions as of any other type of behaviour. The instructive aspect of his work lies in the fact that he does not enter into that kind of individualism, which informs the argument of Dhavamony outlined earlier, nor does he reify a single concept such as that of obligation in the case of Burridge. His notion of meaning, if qualified in terms already suggested marks a fundamental contribution to a general paradigm of meaning from the area of sociology.

Although Weber did not concern himself with the problem of salvation in primitive religion one aspect of his work did lead to a significant development

---

28 Ibid., p. 124.
29 Parsons, T., 1970: 367.
30 Ibid., p. 6.

influencing that subject through the writings of B. R. Wilson. From his earlier publications in the sociology of religion Wilson employed the notion of orientation to the world as a basic theoretical concept for analysing differences between religious institutions in the process of constructing typological classifications of sects.[31] It was in his later volume entitled *Magic and the Millennium* that the idea came to receive a fuller treatment, however, and was there developed so as to apply to non-Christian religious groups.[32] A particular feature of this study lies in the fact that Wilson explicitly associates the idea of orientation to the world with the notion of salvation. He assumes, again on an *a priori* basis that 'men seek salvation in a world in which they feel the need for supernatural help'.[33] This 'demand for salvation' is a human response to the world perceived as evil, indeed the fundamental meaning of the word 'world' cannot be divorced from the notion of evil which is universally present, and which men everywhere seek to overcome.[34]

One major criticism, or qualification of Wilson's study must be made here despite the fact that his intensions are so similar to the central argument of this book, it may be introduced through the sub-title of the study which refers to 'religious movements of protest among tribal and third-world peoples'. Wilson is here treating such movements as rejections of and protests against established cultural goals, much as sects used to be viewed as protest movements against the established church. This is a perfectly legitimate view to adopt as long as it is realized that those very established systems do themselves advocate a means of identifying and coping with evil. If the assertion that 'men apprehend evil in many different ways, and thus look for relief from it in different forms of supernatural action, and the various responses to the world embrace different conceptions of the source of evil and the ways in which it will be overcome', is taken to apply to all religious traditions then no objection can be raised.[35] Wilson, however, is not saying this, on the contrary he draws a firm distinction between the established cultural norms and those of protest groups. A critical passage makes clear his intention on this point.

> 'There appear to be eight basic supernaturalist responses to the dilemma which men face in asking how they might be saved. The dominant position is that of acceptance of the world, the facilities it offers, and the goals and values that a given culture enjoins upon men. This orthodox response (whether secular or religious) concerns us only as a base-line. Concern with transcendence over evil and the search for salvation and consequent rejection of prevailing cultural values, goals, and norms, and whatever facilities are culturally provided for man's salvation, defines religious deviance.'[36]

Wilson obviously makes some allowance for the existence of processes of salvation within the established religion of a society since he is counting one of the supernaturalist responses to evil as the dominant one of cultural orthodoxy. Yet he says that concern with evil, with its transcendence and with a rejection of normal

---

31 Wilson, B. R., 1959.
32 Wilson, B. R., 1973.
33 Ibid., p. 19.
34 Ibid., p. 492.
35 Ibid., p. 21.
36 Idem.

cultural values is what characterizes religious deviancy, this seems to imply a qualitative difference of perception of evil by those within the established culture and others who are set upon a course of social protest. To what extent it is possible to press this criticism it is difficult to say because Wilson admits that he is not directly concerned with the established pattern of culture but only with the protests against it. Even so Wilson appears to treat salvation as a scarce commodity which is differently evaluated by 'deviants' and by the orthodox, this is a question which could be discussed at some length for each particular case of protest but the point to be made here is that such protest groups are not engaged in any significantly different endeavour, at least as far as a general paradigm of meaning is concerned. In terms of the definition of salvation offered earlier such deviants merely find the institutionalized formularies insufficient as means of conferring durable plausibility. Wilson's interest may, however, lie in saying something different and which involves a qualitative judgement upon the nature of the religious system against which protest is intended. It is as though, 'the very dilute thaumaturgy of Christian orthodoxy', which 'has long been culturally accommodated', is viewed as having forfeited its right to act as a religious process for men. This would apply not only to thaumaturgy but to all religious forms of action, for Wilson sometimes writes as though the fact of secularization must be accepted with all its consequences, including the fact that some established religions cannot be treated with the seriousness they appear to demand.[37] It was in this spirit that he wrote of denominations and churches as having cooled into a state of temperateness and tepidity from one of a passionate state of love.[38] Having made this tentative criticism over the possible influence of a secularization concept upon Wilson's study, it remains to acknowledge the significance of his work, especially that of *Magic and the Millennium*, for its concern with the notion of salvation among tribal and third world peoples.

The sociologically grounded approach of Wilson frees classification from theological overtones and portrays the human response to changing circumstances. Wilson's studies along with those of Burridge have shown the necessity of this non-confessional position, but they have also shown that a general paradigm of meaning inevitably involves a discussion of negative factors of perception. This is quite important for it shows that what might be called phenomenologically descriptive accounts of the nature of religious groups concur with the theological assertions of religious traditions in emphasizing the significance of the perception of evil, or of implausibility as a central motivation in human thought and action, and to this it will be necessary to return in the conclusion.

The major theoretical problem remaining with Wilson's argument is one which must be mentioned in the light of this generalization, and before the discussion proceeds to a case which Wilson's scheme would find hard to interpret and accommodate within itself. It is the difficulty of relating the perception of evil in established religions to the apparently more acute awareness of evil in protest movements. The seven kinds of response to evil, which Wilson identifies as ideal typical of protest movements, can easily be read as a typology of evil, but this

---

[37] Ibid., p. 503.
[38] Wilson, B. R., 1970b: 242. 1982.

typology would not suffice to handle the evidence of primitive societies. The reason for this is, theoretically speaking, quite simple and rests almost upon the tautologous nature of definitions. Wilson is concerned with movements of revolution and protest whereas most primitive religions documented in ethnographies are not in a state of radical change or transformation. This is not to say that they exist in some timeless realm of changelessness, but that whatever transformations are at work are natural to that particular culture.

In terms of the three broad classes which embrace his seven responses the 'objectivist' group of revolutionist, introversionist, reformist, and utopian perspectives would seldom apply to primitive societies for this particular reason. The 'subjectivist' group of conversionist outlook and the 'relationist' class of manipulationist and thaumaturgist views might, however, be open to an interpretation which could admit of tribal cases.[39] The Murinbata, for example, might be said to encourage a change of outlook in the minds of the initiates which befitted adult members of their society. So too some of the features of witchcraft and magic which have already been considered for the Azande could be regarded as possessing manipulationist and thaumaturgical elements. The theoretically important point arising from this is that protest movements, whether they be tribal or part of urban, western societies, exhibit similar responses to evil which is conceived in a particularly emphasized manner. This is useful information because it provides another reason for advocating the position that primitive and advanced societies ought not to be distinguished in terms of fundamental differences in their religious structures. The real issue concerns the way in which evil is perceived within either kind of tradition during periods of ordinary social life on the one hand, and periods of social change on the other. This is why some caution was expressed over Wilson's emphasis upon evil in protest movements which suggested that it was a different species from evil as found in the orthodox and relatively stable social context. The determining feature which governs the significance of evil in any movement is the degree to which the existing system of plausibility is able to contain the perception of negative factors on the part of its members.

Because societies are seldom completely closed systems there may well occur moments when external factors bring about a situation which cannot be met by the normal means; it may even be the case that the evil which is regarded as operative upon people is of an essentially new kind. Millenarian responses of the cargo cult variety can be such novel reactions to formerly unheard of circumstances, but even when this is the case the underlying processes which work towards a new resolution, are the same as the ones for ever operative in the case of stable societies. So the plausibility theory of salvation can be seen to be applicable in both types of case.

A somewhat different social context can now be considered in the light of these deliberations, which will make even clearer the necessity for theoretical precision over the notion of salvation. This example is all the more usefull because it demonstrates the problematic nature of another hermeneutical issue in religious studies which arises from the same debate over the relation between primitive and advanced religions. The case is that of Burmese village religion as studied by Melford

---

39 Wilson, B. R., 1973: 27.

Spiro and the hermeneutical problem is that of relating a so-called world religion to specific, local examples of the same.[40] The basic presupposition required for this case to achieve any validity is that such an instance of village religion can be equated with the religions of preliterate societies which are themselves completely unrelated to any of the major religious traditions of Islam, Christianity, Hinduism or Buddhism. In anthropology at least this is now an acceptable assumption as E. R. Leach makes quite clear in his editorial introduction to the significantly titled *Dialectic in Practical Religion*.[41] There he argues that grave misunderstandings had developed in the study of comparative religion because the distinction between the philosophical expression of a religion and the religiosity of ordinary believers had not been sufficiently recognized. Accordingly the pure and true form of a religion, say Buddhism, was to be found in the classic texts and the philosophical exegeses of them, while the religious life of village Buddhists was said to be deeply influenced by animistic survivals or Hindu superstitions. The title 'practical religion' was used in order to emphasize the mundane and pragmatic dimension of religiosity, and it would be true to say that since the late nineteen sixties, when Leach's volume was published, there has been a growing realization among historians and phenomenologists of religion that this area is of fundamental importance.

The significance of this distinction between what might be called the world and village levels of a religion for the notion of salvation will be immediately apparent, and Spiro's study will serve to bring it into sharp focus. Spiro's ethnographic evidence makes the question of the two levels of a single religion and their relation even more complex because he finds that the village Buddhists also embrace to a certain extent another form of religion under certain conditions of their everyday life. This was a religion involving the idea of spirits called *nats*, hence the name *Nat* religion.

Arguing against the notion that Buddhism is merely a thin veneer overlying indigenous animistic religion, Spiro seeks to demonstrate that both Buddhism and Nat religion are important for the Burmese villagers, and that ultimately Buddhism is given primacy of place as far as religious power is concerned. He prefers to describe Burmese religion as permitting 'dual religious adherence' rather than manifesting some form of syncretism, and this duality is related to the two central concerns of his study, namely the idea of salvation and the fact of suffering. In analysing the relations existing between these, both in theoretical and theological, as well as practical and sociological terms, he portrays an interaction between what he calls Burmese Buddhism and Burmese supernaturalism. Buddhism is primarily concerned with salvation while Nat religion is taken up with problem of man's preoccupation with things causing him pain and difficulty in his everyday life. This supernaturalist religion expresses man's immediate existential concern which results in the desire for a present solution to his problems. Spiro distinguishes between these proximate goals and the more distant ones of Buddhism, the former are contrary to Buddhist teaching which relegates the desire for pleasurable states

---

[40] Spiro, M., 1967.
[41] Leach, E. R., 1968.

to an unworthly outlook which is antipathetic to the true religious path and to its ultimate goal.

Spiro begins his analysis of Burmese religion by saying that religions function to help devotees in their experience of suffering both by 'offering an explanation for suffering, and by providing techniques by which suffering may be avoided or its burden diminished'.[42] It might be thought appropriate for him to apply this statement to Nat religion in a direct and straight-forward way, such that its explanation of illness and the methods of cure through offerings and exorcism, might be regarded as a central religious tenet. He does not do this, however, but chooses to emphasize the idea that 'for the Burmese religion means the Path to salvation, and the nats are totally and completely irrelevant for even finding, let alone walking along the Path'.[43] Salvation is thus taken as a notion pertaining essentially to Buddhism, indeed it is 'on the crucial dimension of salvation (that) the distinction between these systems is absolute'.[44] 'As a religion of radical salvation ... the Buddhist attitude to the world is unambiguous, the world is to be renounced'.[45] Thus the realm of worldly existence, *lokika*, is for Buddhism the world of illusion, and represents the sphere of *samsara* and recurrent rebirth, which results from a persistent desire for things and personal well-being. But this is also the very world of supernaturalism, it is the realm of the *nat* cultus, of witches, possession, and exorcism. Contrasting with this is Buddhism's concern with *lokuttura*, the reality grounded in escape from illusion, and with the extinction of desire in the attainment of nirvana. It is the world of *lokika* which is both the barrier to Buddhist salvation and also the dominant concern of the lay Burmese. At best their Buddhist religiosity seeks the attainment of a better rebirth in their next worldly existence. 'Contrary to Buddhist teaching in which these pleasurable states are but temporary way stations on the Path to its ultimate goal, most Burmese take these stations as their ultimate goal'.[46]

In interpreting the relationship between these forms of religion Spiro tends to accept as the central and determining feature of what constitutes true religion in this context the Buddhist notion of salvation. For an anthropologist this is an unwarranted assumption and demonstrates the continued influence of nineteenth century presuppositions about religious orthodoxy. It might be justified if the ethnographic data showed that interpretation was impossible without making such a claim, but on the evidence of Spiro's own material this can be seen not to be the case. He actually says that, 'Buddhism in both its Theravadist and Mahayanist forms is never the exclusive religion of its lay devotees', and that such an assertion can be accepted almost as a truism in Buddhist cultures.[47] If this is so, and if, for example, rites concerning spirit possession and exorcism are of positive significance in the life of a people, then it is unwise to enforce a conceptual orthodoxy upon them when other explanations are readily available and which do not presuppose any religious norms.

---

[42] Spiro, M., 1967: 2.
[43] Ibid., p. 267.
[44] Ibid., p. 266.
[45] Ibid., p. 263.
[46] Ibid., p. 269.
[47] Ibid., p. 2.

If the plausibility model of salvation is employed in this context it makes better sense of Spiro's own material and in particular of his assertion that 'man seeks for meaning even more than he seeks for order'.[48] In terms of the Burmese Buddhist laity this means that illness, which is thought to be caused by spirits and which can be cured by exorcism, is what causes an immediate loss of meaning in the world as far as a state of general plausibility is concerned. It may well be part of the overall Buddhist scheme of illusion but the villager prefers to accept an immediate kind of meaning than some philosophical scheme of doctrinal order. There may be a contradiction between the nat religion and that of Buddhism propounded by the monks, but the villager opts for the immediate relief rather than a future state of bliss. What this means is that the salvation they require or demand is not always in agreement with what in orthodox terms they actually need. It is more realistic to discuss the notion of salvation in one way for the Buddhist laity and in another way for the monks. The Buddhist goal of ascetic detachment and the attainment of merit sufficient to achieve *nibbana* is the prerogative of the *sangha*, and in this context it is perfectly appropriate to employ the orthodox religious notion of salvation. Then the plausibility view of salvation can be applied to the doctrine as such with evil being grounded in *tanha*, or the desire for things which emerges from the perceived self, and salvation being understood as the cessation of this desire which causes pain and transmigration. So too the *sangha* can be understood as that context within which the necessary state of plausibility may be achieved. The total frame of reference necessary to understand what Buddhism means for the monks must include the role of the laity who actually support them. Spiro's approach can be read as evaluating the laity as somewhat parasitic upon the monks in terms of wanting to achieve merit from them so that their own future lives will be happier. Even if this is true, and the ethnographic evidence would suggest that it is, it ought not to lead to a view of the laity as being failed Buddhists who could not manage the life of renunciation. Rather it should be seen as demonstrating a far more complex situation in which the monks could only set about their duties directed towards *nibbana* because the laity possessed such an attitude to merit that it resulted in their supportive role. The fact that the laity could be regarded as inconsistent Buddhists is quite irrelevant to anthropological analysis. If the facts of the case are that the belief in *nats* 'permits the Burmese to obviate the painful consequences of a consistent belief in karma', the question must be asked as to whether the notion of salvation can play any part in evaluating the role of religion in their lives. In terms of the plausibility model the answer is an unequivocal yes, for within the limits of the social and ideological conditions in which the Burmese find themselves they employ notions and rites of the *nat* religion to complement aspects of Buddhism in such a way that they possess a sufficient state of durable plausibility such that no alternative is sought. The model of Buddhist renunciation is ever present in the *sangha*, but the continuous presence of pragmatic trouble is also experienced as a present reality, and to that area of life, perceived as evil, Buddhism has no immediate practical solution.

This case throws into sharp relief the problem of what might be called two

---

[48] Ibid., p. 8.

dimensions of religion and what was referred to earlier as the world and village levels of religiosity. The reason why the distinction is especially prominent in Spiro's case is because the *nat* supernaturalism appears to belong to a different species of religiosity when compared with the Buddhism of the *sangha*. Yet both dimensions coexist for the Burmese layman in his life-world. If only the Buddhist dimension is thought to be, potentially at least, capable of effecting salvation, then the *nat* supernaturalism is categorized by default along with other primitive religions, which offer no explicit soteriological hope, as a phenomenon of an essentially different kind. Yet what seems to be the case is that within a single community different groups identify evil in such divergent ways as to react to it in a non-uniform manner. To presuppose that the religiously orthodox way is the right one is to import evaluative criteria which should be alien both to the anthropologist and to the historian of religion. What Spiro's case shows clearly is the tendency to classify the so called world-religions differently from religiosities which do not belong to such a clear historical tradition.

This methodological error has also been prevalent in similar cases but has been identified in rather different terms, namely those of 'the grand literary tradition' on the one hand and 'village religion' on the other.[49] S. J. Tambiah's study on a similar theme to that of Spiro, namely *Buddhism and the Spirit Cults*, but this time in North-east Thailand, provides an admirable basis for considering this problem. After outlining the background to the theoretical problem Tambiah offers his own analysis of the interrelation between kinds of religiosity in a way which is much more in accord with anthropological tradition and which also contributes to methodology in religious studies.

Tambiah identifies the major contributors to the discussion as Robert Redfield and his Chicago school's approach which refers to the great-tradition and little-tradition opposition in Indian society on the one hand, and to Dumont and Pocock who utilize the notion of Sanskritic Hinduism and Popular Hinduism on the other. Both perspectives presuppose that some kind of two-level distinction is necessary, they differ in the way the wish to relate these elements to one another. The fact that these authors are concerned with Hinduism while Tambiah was working on Buddhism presents no problem as far as the theoretical issues at stake are concerned. Indeed it accentuates the fact that when practical studies of religion involve the major religious traditions of the world similar problems have to be dealt with.

While Tambiah locates the various terminologies of this debate very firmly in relatively recent studies, largely from the nineteen fifties, it is likely to be the case that the inherited perspective of nineteenth century scholars has exerted a significant influence on the very notion of what counts as a religion. If this is so then the problem is less one of having to distinguish between a discrete literary form of a religion and an actual popular or village manifestation of it, than it is one of realizing that it has become customary to think in terms of the two levels as a result of the two kinds of religious study which now influence the approach of scholars of religion. In Srinivas' work, which Tambiah cites, there is ample evidence of the more classical style of Indology informing his conceptual categories. At least this is

---

49 Tambiah, S. J., 1970: 367.

a factor which must be entertained as a theoretical possibility, for Tambiah cannot be completely accurate in saying that the notion of two levels 'is a fabrication of anthropologists which they have bequeathed to the modern Indian consciousness', if only because scholars like Max Müller stimulated Indian scholars to think of their own religious history in terms of systems and texts.[50] Furthermore, the existence of indigenous notions of religiosity cannot be ignored, and both Hindu and Buddhist religions contain dynamic traditions which are aware of their mutual distinctions. The problem of levels of truth and religiosity cannot for these reasons alone be regarded as the product of anthropological study and theorizing. Indeed, this is something which Tambiah ought to have seen more clearly for in arguing against the two-level model he says that it is 'frequently inapplicable to the anthropologist's field data and experience'.[51]

Tambiah's wish is to treat the notion of two-levels in terms of the relation between historical religion and contemporary religion'.[52] Contemporary religion, which is the dimension of practical and lived religiosity, would include the historical factor in the sense of texts, ritual traditions of the priesthoods as well as temples. The basic requirement is to develop a way of handling the fact of continuity between the past and present. When the society concerned is of an homogenous type this approach will be relatively easy to adopt, but when there appear to be several sorts of religion present it becomes more difficult. Tambiah's analysis of the mutual interrelation of Buddhist and Hindu functionaries in Thailand provides a model example of how to set about studying such a complex issue. The case is made more difficult still when one element in the contemporary religious life bears no direct relationship to the more distinctive historical tradition, as is the case with Buddhism and the spirit cults. Yet as far as the phenomenologist and historian of religion is concerned it would be methodologically improper not to treat all the elements present in a society with equal validity and seriousness. As far as the notion of salvation is concerned this means a much more complex form of analysis, for no single theological stance can be adopted, after the fashion of Spiro, if the evidence suggests a variety of views on the question of evil along with what might be regarded as a few varied responses to it. It is precisely in this kind of situation that the plausibility theory perspective becomes significant, so that it would not be inappropriate to regard the exorcism aspect of the *nat* cultus as one aspect of the soteriological process directed towards the elimination of an immediately perceived ill, despite the fact that it might contravene orthodox Buddhist teachings. Such recourse to spirit agencies not only provides an explanation of troubles but also makes available the means for resolving them. This being so it could be said that while the *nats* may be irrelevant for walking the nirvanic path they are more than relevant for making sense of the life-world of the Buddhist laity. In phenomenological terms the fact that the life of the monks is markedly different from that of the peasantry would suggest that different explanations and means of coping with problems might be forthcoming.

Spiro agrees with this indirectly for he views the supernaturalistic aspect of

---

50 Ibid., p. 371.
51 Ibid., p. 372.
52 Ibid., p. 374.

Burmese religiosity as one way by which that dimension of the Burmese personality which he calls the Dionysiac comes to be expressed in a form that permits Buddhism to remain uncontaminated by the non-renouncing excess of cultists. It is precisely in reaction against the ascetic ideal that the *nat* cult with its ceremonies involving emotional release and licence finds acceptance by the laity, and, as Spiro says, 'permits the Burmese to obviate the painful consequences of a consistent belief in karma'.[53] The actual life-world of the laity does not easily fall to a simple analysis and Spiro himself provides evidence which belies his rather rigid view which espouses Buddhist norms. This becomes particularly clear in that part of his work where he draws upon culture and personality perspectives to aid his interpretation. The psychological model he adopts views the individual as one seeking resolution of inner conflicts and tensions resulting from frustrated desires. Unresolved frustration results in states of unconsciousness in which the personality is overwhelmed and 'hallucinatory and dissociational behaviour' is viewed as 'defence mechanisms by which (this) inner conflict is expressed or resolved'.[54] What this psychological model implies is that both emotional and intellectual factors are involved in the relationship between the personality and society, a dual factor which has already been stressed as a fundamental presupposition of a plausibility theory approach to religion. The postulated conflict can, itself, be seen as a form of implausibility involving the emotional desire of the person and the cognitive evaluation of those social norms which prevent its realization. Rituals of exorcism and theories of witchcraft are thus indicative of the attempt to remove the emotional dissonance resulting from the clash of behavioural norms originating in Burmese folk tradition on the one hand, and Buddhist morality on the other, and, in having this plausibility generation as their goal, merit consideration as soteriological phenomena.

From this discussion it will be clear that if the notion of salvation possesses any social effect within the context of the world religions, then religious effects which may be observed in societies not associated with them could also, potentially at least, be discussed in terms of salvation if those effects manifested similar functions. Since the function of religious institutions as meaning construction devices is postulated as of fundamental importance and since, in this case of Burmese religion as in that of Thailand, the establishment of meaningful life-worlds in the face of perceived evil is what is taking place, it would seem eminently appropriate to expand the notion of salvation to embrace religions outside the great traditions of the world. Because this notion of salvation is not dependent upon any one theological meaning, its sociological context, and the new meaning in terms of plausibility which is being ascribed to it, must be explored in some detail for particular examples of religious phenomena.

In attempting this task it will be necessary to portray what might be called the relational nature of the notions of evil and salvation, or of implausibility and plausibility, in each particular context under consideration. This point is often ignored yet it lies quite central to the notion of meaning in religious systems, especially when the approach is of a phenomenological kind. The basic distinction

---

[53] Spiro, M., 1967: 256.
[54] Ibid., p. 169.

which needs to be drawn is between the nature of phenomena as they are in and of themselves, and the nature of phenomena in relation to each other. If, for the sake of argument, it be accepted that Western thought in general, and Christian theology in particular, emphasizes the nature of things in and of themselves, while for example Indian thought focuses upon the nature of the relation existing between entities, then there would be available a distinction between essentialist and relational definitions which could provide the basis for a categorization of evil. What is thus being sought is a phenomenological description of ideas including notions of evil and salvation, which shows how they are related one to another. Such a pattern of ideas, or configuration of doctrines may well differ in content, that remains to be seen, but it is hypothesized that they will manifest similarity in form in terms of the appropriateness of relation between perceived implausibility and postulated mode of its resolution.

CHAPTER SEVEN

EVIL AND SALVATION IN SIKH RELIGION

Throughout the preceding discussion the emphasis has returned on numerous occasions to this notion of evil and to the fact that the common experience of men is that the world is other than they would have it to be. For Turnbull it was 'the one really imperfect thing in life' as far as the Mbuti were concerned, Fürer-Haimendorf referred to it as the 'fact of human imperfection', while for van der Leeuw it was the 'malicious inadequacy of all, the irrationality at the basis of life'.[1] Stanner in his aboriginal study talks of the 'intuition of the integral moral flaw in human associations while Worsley identified man's state as a 'situation of dissatisfaction with existing social relations and a yearning for a happier life'.[2] Max Weber simply refers to the 'problem of the world's imperfection'.

The purpose of citing this list is to introduce the suggestion that, phenomenologically speaking, there are certain phenomena which may be called structures of implausibility. Any discussion of the notion of salvation must relate these structures to their complementary structures of salvation. The necessity of carefully relating the one to the other arises from the fact that a single phenomenon, as is also the case with any single symbol, only comes to reveal its significance and full meaning when understood in the context of other, complementary, phenomena. To discuss the notion of salvation, in its sociological sense of plausibility, without also referring to the negative aspects in relation to which alone it makes sense, is to commit a methodological error grounded in a lack of awareness of the context dependent nature of phenomena. While this is quite obviously true it has often been the case that a variation of the assertion has often been ignored, namely that to discuss the notion of evil, as exemplified by studies in witchcraft, spirit possession and some forms of magic, without also referring to its positive aspect, of the goal towards which the negative aspect relates, is to fail in understanding the symbolic whole of which negatives features are but a part.

Why it is that such experiences of negative phenomena occur in the first instant is a question beyond the scope of the present argument, for answers could be sought from a variety of sources, from the philosophical realms of idealism through psychological debates on integrated fields of perception, as advocated by Gestalt theorists, to a pragmatism grounded in an evolutionary theory according to which man might be said to seek a cognitive niche and an orderly mental environment just as he seeks, in his animality, a well comprehended territory of a physical kind. The present concern is less with the essential nature of human imperfection, for ultimately that question must be answered from a committed religious or philosophical standpoint, than with the pattern of notions of evil and of good in specific societies. What is more, it is precisely because such patterns or configurations of symbolic

---

[1] Cf. cap. 2.
[2] Cf. cap. 4.

expressions of positive and negative features vary significantly from group to group that some kind of higher order analysis is required to help discover their basic rationale. Hence the employment of plausibility theory as a means of describing structures of implausibility and their associated modes of resolution which may be deemed to be processes of salvation.

Irrespective of why notions of negative factors emerge in the first instant it is true to say that they possess great power in the lives of men. The earlier reference to the relational nature of man becomes significant at this point in the sense that attention must not simply be given to the way in which ideas of good are related to those of evil, but to the actual life contexts in which men are related to or perceive themselves to be involved with negative phenomena. To say that man is related to evil is only to describe the nature of his relation to a class of phenomena in much the same way as man has been described in the numerous titles ascribed to him by the social sciences, for example, man is *Homo economicus, faber, convictus*, without mentioning the more usual epithets of *sapiens* and *religiosus*.

This wide variation in the use of 'Homo nouns' indicates the breadth of man's relational nature as much as it identifies any one essential attribute of his being. While this particular process of categorization proceeds by means of isolating distinctive kinds of human activity, the present argument seeks to perform a similar function as far as man's religious actions are concerned. This involves a more sociological kind of phenomenology, more in the tradition of Alfred Schutz than of Edmund Husserl, and means that the categorization of a phenomenon, in this case evil, involves a consideration of human action as much as of human perception.[3] It is precisely for this reason that anthropological perspectives are regarded as of fundamental importance in determining the significance of religious phenomena. The precise significance of this dynamic perspective will be explored at greater length in the Conclusion, but one consequence must be stated here, and that is the supposition that a complex interrelation exists between sources of evil and the perceivers of evil.

To refer again to Peter Berger and John Bowker it might be said that the meaning 'poured into' men or the 'cues' provided for them by the external world, are not always of a positive kind, and that the sense of evil which is so widespread is actually the result of sources of implausibility which confront human perception. These sources may change and need not be regarded as uniform in any sense, and it is certainly not supposed that they provide any justification for arguing for the existence of a devil or any other theologically grounded concept of evil. If the systematic theologian wishes to use such data for his own arguments, in the way Bowker urges the notion of cues of meaning to imply the existence of God, that is quite appropriate, but it would be out of place in a more phenomenological study.[4]

These theoretical arguments should not remain at an abstract level of significance, but must be applied to actual religious phenomena so that their real value might become apparent. The first case chosen for study is that of Sikh religion which will afford an example of eastern religiosity, and the second case will be drawn from the

---

[3] Roche, M., 1973: 33.
[4] Bowker, J., 1981.

Mormon religion which presents a peculiar type of western religion. The hermeneutical considerations of chapters four and five underlie this present analysis, and in addition a firm historical perspective is adopted so that the emergence of different configurations of ideas of good and evil can be clearly traced.

Contemporary Sikhs possess an image of their own history which serves a kind of mythological function within the Sikh community. Sometimes this folk history is also used as more concrete historical data by Sikh scholars and others which leads to the inevitable question of validity and historical reliability.[5] To say this is not merely to comment on contemporary issues in Sikh studies but brings to clear focus another more significant point, namely, that there are elements of the past which Sikhs regard as necessary for existence in the present. The problem posed for Sikh scholars lies in the fact that certain of these elements which are, at present, of deep significance to Sikh religiosity are idealized and projected into the past as a form of history even though it is practically impossible to establish them as historically valid. It is often the case that the idealized notion of the past is very different from that constructed by historical scholarship. There is nothing surprising in this fact for similar divergencies of view may be found in most religious movements, and it is mentioned here only because the past is a most significant dimension in Sikh thought and enters into the notion of evil as will be shown below.[6] It would not be completely inappropriate to say that Sikh religion is historical in a way which resembles the historical character of Christianity, though care is vital in making this generalization since Sikhism is not bound by any doctrine of historical incarnation, nor could it be said to possess any form of salvation history. Nevertheless, unlike its parent Hinduism it is committed to its own past in a particularly concrete way.

The nature of this commitment is twofold, consisting in a devotional attachment to the historical gurus from Nanak (1469-1539), to Gobind Singh (1666-1708), on the one hand, and in a 'patriotic' zeal which binds the individual Sikh to his community, on the other. The problem of historical criticism of Sikhism, as already mentioned, lies in the way the form of community which emerged during the lives of the last two gurus in particular, and which has contributed to the ethos of contemporary Sikhism, is projected into the earliest period and is regarded as normative even for guru Nanak. While this process could be identified in many religions, and in Christianity would take the form of folk religiosity assuming that contemporary Protestant practice was normative even in New Testament times, or that Martin Luther's spirituality was just like that of a contemporary church leader down to the habit of teetotalism, a distinctive feature in Sikhism is that it provides a legitimation of this exercise in as much as it teaches the essential unity of all ten historical gurus, speaking of the first, second, and third Nanak etc., as well as referring to these men by their actual and individual names of Nanak, Angad, and Amar Das and so on. This notion supposes that the essential truth incorporated in the identity of the first guru was transmitted to the others, and was ultimately deposited in the continuing Sikh community of the *khalsa* brotherhood of 'pure' and dedicated disciples, as well as in the volume of sacred scriptures containing

---

[5] Cole, O. and P. S. Sambhi, 1979.

[6] Ling, Trevor, 1973: 93. Ling suggests that such projections are made with respect to the 'conversion' of Guatama.

the devotional poetry of the gurus. So according to Sikh ideology the very nature of the guru, which constitutes the central element in Sikh thought, is now to be identified with the essential reality of the continuing community. The present thus cannot be understood apart from the past, indeed, it gains it very meaning from the historical origin. But the present also contributes to the earliest guru period of the late fifteenth and early sixteenth century ideas which historical criticism cannot validate as truly pertaining to that era. This problem can be simply exemplified in terms of two models used by the Sikhs to describe their religion, or to be more specific when representing the true characteristics of Sikh individuals.

These models portray the Sikh as a 'saint', and as a 'soldier', but in the combined expression of saint-soldier. Such internal-observer's models, as this kind of indigenous self-understanding can be called, provide an instructive insight into the self-evaluation of Sikhs in terms of the ideas of evil and salvation, while also offering a way of seeing how Sikhs interpret their own past.

The period of the first five gurus is, characteristically, that in which the idea of a devoted band of pious disciples constitutes the picture of the Sikh religion.[7] It would not be truly accurate, however, to see this period from 1500, when Nanak's public ministry was beginning to be effective in creating a popular response, until the first decade of the seventeenth century when, after the death of the friendly emperor Akbar, his successor Jehangir set about attacking the Sikh population which had itself grown in size and sense of identity since Nanak's day, as being a completely 'spiritual' age in which devotees hung on the sublime words of their living gurus. Change inevitably took place and each of the early gurus contributed to the emergence of that Sikh population which was later found to be preadapted for a militaristic response to the new conditions of hostility from both Muslim and Hindu sources. Nanak's teaching that 'there is no Hindu, there is no Muslim', was without a doubt a significant factor in providing an aspect of Sikh identity which was, later, to constitute a fundamental element in Punjabi identity. Kushwant Singh's admirable study of Sikh history is correct in evaluating this ideal of non-conformity as being essential to the rise of 'Punjabi consciousness and Punjabi nationalism', but it required the political changes which followed long after Nanak to make this latent feature manifest its powerful implications.[8] In no real sense can it be argued that the political ideal was dominant, and perhaps not present in any significant sense, during Nanak's lifetime.

The same can be said for guru Angad's proclivity for physical fitness and organized games among his followers, for while all this was far removed from military training when such exercises became necessary some sixty years later under the leadership of guru Har Govind it was not completely alien to the Sikh outlook on life. Indeed it could be argued that one of the features of early Sikhism lay in the provision of a pool of potential orientations which served as a ready source for later use, and

---

[7] The dates of the ten historical gurus of Sikhism are: Nanak, 1469-1539; Angad, 1504-1552; Amar Das, 1479-1574; Ram Das, 1534-1581; Arjan, 1563-1606; Har Govind, 1595-1644; Har Rai, 1630-1661; Har Krishan, 1656-1664; Tegh Bahadur, 1621-1675; Gobind Singh, 1666-1708.

[8] Singh, Kushwant, 1977. Vol. I, p. 48.

which enabled subsequent Sikh generations to feel a sense of continuity with former brothers in the faith.[9]

Inevitably, this first period of Sikh history saw the emergence of many of its basic doctrines, and may be said to have emphasized the more obviously religious factors which would justify the accent being placed on the saint model as a description of the activity of this era. The third guru, Amar Das, established the institution of the free communal kitchen and dining facilities called the *langar*, which sought to establish equality of status among Sikhs as a contrast to the commensality prohibitions of the Hindu caste system. Guru Arjan, as fifth Nanak, provides one of the most clearly identifiable models of the saint figure after Nanak himself, and also serves to provide an historical marker, for after him conditions changed in a way which led to an increase in political activity. Arjan built the renowned golden temple at Amritsar which was to become the centre of Sikh religious life, and there in 1604 was installed the compiled writings of his predecessors. This work called the *Granth Sahib* not only expressed the devotionalism of the gurus' teachings, including those of Arjan, but also symbolized the relation between Sikh, Muslim and Hindu spiritual amity. Nanak's religion had started as one example of the North Indian *nirguna sampradaya* or Sant tradition which stressed the attributeless nature of God and the necessity of meditating upon His reality through song and poetic recitation, caste and idolatry had been abandoned for the free fellowship of likeminded seekers. With the establishment of the *Hari Mandir*, more commonly called the Golden Temple, at Amritsar, the religion attained to a significant level of institutionalization, and this temple with its sacred book enshrined at its centre constituted another example of preadaptation within the pool of potential orientations which was to prove invaluable as a means of organizing the Sikh community when it finally abandoned the idea of living gurus. Meanwhile the saintly religiosity was concretely expressed by the devotion shown to the words of the gurus and to the ideal of life contained within them.

The change of emphasis which brought the soldier motif to the fore was a consequence of the change of political events in India. Just as the goodwill of Akbar had facilitated developments within the Sikh communities of the Punjab, so the malevolence of Jehangir, his successor in the high office of Emperor, precipitated the emergence of the militaristic ethos among the Sikhs.[10] Guru Arjan serves as a kind of transition stage between these emphases of saint and soldier, which themselves involve rather different notions of good and evil as will be shown later, and this not only in an historical sense, but also in a structural way in as much as his imprisonment and death while in Muslim custody first initiated the idea of martyrdom in Sikh religion and culture. This category of religious action prepared the way for that of outright heroism and military gallantry which assumed its fullest expression in the last guru, Gobind Singh.

From the moment of Arjan's death his son Har Gobind became the leader of the Sikhs both in the spiritual and political realms. Perhaps the clearest example of the transition in the ethos of Sikhism represented through his leadership may be

---

[9] Davies, D. J., 1972: 28 for notion of pool of potential orientations.
[10] Binyon, L., 1932: 110.

observed in the fact that whereas Arjan built the Golden Temple as a focal point of Sikh religiosity and installed the scriptures in it, Har Gobind built another structure at the Temple, namely the *Akal Takht*. Despite its meaning of throne of the eternal one, this edifice served a most temporal purpose as political and military headquarters of the guru, within it as a throne-room the guru became increasingly more like an emperor or district ruler with military intentions and resources. The large number of Jat caste farmers who had entered the Sikh fellowship under Arjan's ministry were not slow to see the advantage of serving the gurus in a military capacity, and from this time on the question of a Punjabi population comes to the fore. As Kushwant Singh says of Har Gobind, 'the change of emphasis from a peaceful propagation of the faith to the forthright declaration of the right to defend that faith by force of arms proved to be extremely popular'.[11] The force of Mughal power, however, forced him into retreat and after his death in 1644 guru Har Rai continued living in the mountains of eastern Punjab. His son and successor in office, Har Krishan, had not escaped the attention of the Emperor Auranzeb quite so easily and died while under a not very strict house arrest in Delhi.

Tegh Bahadur had been named as the next in line of guruship but, rather like Har Rai, was more of the saint then the soldier, and it was only after Auranzeb began a programme of destroying temples and removing Sikh organizations in the Punjab that he was recalled to the Punjab from Bengal where he lived with his family, and began to provide a focus and rallying point for the oppressed Sikhs and Punjabis. As a result of this he was summoned to Delhi, sentenced to death and executed. This act of martyrdom, as it was understood by the Sikhs, led to his son, Gobind Singh who was then only nine years of age, becoming guru leader and as it turned out the absolute idealization of Sikh warriorhood.

Gobind Singh led the Sikhs along with many other low caste groups against the Islamic powers with a first victory taking place in 1686 at Bhangani. The history of the next twenty years is incredibly complex but the significant outcome was that Gobind Singh ended the line of living gurus and transferred the guru authority both to the scriptures, which he edited to include the works of later gurus, and also to the community of the *khalsa* which has already been mentioned. In the dual concept of *Guru Granth*, and *Guru Panth*, is expressed the two-fold nature of Sikh culture, with the Granth expressing the saintly aspect and the panth the soldierly nature of the community commitment, it is only through a historical analysis that this dual expression of the notion of guru can be appreciated. While it might be argued that the Panth represents the older notion of *sangat*, or that assembly of the saints in which the divine praises were sung, it is more likely to be true that it mirrors the later Sikh experience of that unified community possessed of a distinct identity which had emerged around the scriptures and ideals of the earlier gurus but which had come to a definite form only as a result of the pressure exerted by military hostility. The major new element which entered Sikh thought as a result of the seventeenth century hostilities was that of the identifiable community. The experience of the subsequent centuries, and particularly the bloody partition of the Punjab in the nineteen forties has served only to reinforce this identity and to make

---

[12] Singh, Kushwant, Ibid., p. 66.

the religious aspect of Sikh culture something different from what it was during the earliest period of Sikh history.

Before attempting to show the precise influence of this historical development of Sikh society upon the notion of evil it will be as well to present an analysis of this notion from two other perspectives. Firstly in a way generally espoused by Historians of religion, offering a formal description of evil as presented in the Sikh scriptures, and secondly, a view of evil from the more strictly anthropological perspective which demonstrates how the notion of evil is understood in a life-context. The first of these comments is from a timeless perspective of texts, and the second from the rather timeless perspective of ethnography. Both dimensions find a place in the historical analysis which has already been initiated and with which a final comment will conclude this chapter.

Allusion has already been made to the spirituality to which guru Nanak was heir; this *Sant* tradition of North India, which rejected Brahmanic authority in both scripture and ritual much as Guatama Buddha had done some two thousand years before, provided the all pervasive ethos out of which the devotional piety of Sikh religion was to emerge. The *Sants*, and in this they also resemble Gautama, rejected Sanskrit and used the colloquial languages for teaching their interested followers who were largely of rural, low caste, status rather than the more urban elite group which constituted early Buddhism.[12] The *Sants*, and Kabir is often cited as an example of this outlook, insisted upon the freedom of the individual to grasp, through methods of devotion and meditation, the sense of a god who was *nirguna*, without attributes, but who could be experienced directly through an intuitive love relationship grounded in meditative devotionalism. One of the great facts of love, as the reflective knowledge resulting from this union might be called, was that god was but seldom truly found by men. The *nirguna sampradaya*, or Sant tradition, and after it the Sikh tradition, came to possess what might be called a negative evaluation of ordinary life, or at least of ordinary states of consciousness. Most men were regarded as existing in an undesirable fashion, not only the masses who paid but little attention to god but also the priests and supposed religious virtuosi of Hinduism and Islam.[13] Nanak's religion thus involved a radical critique of established religion and advocated a path to salvation which depended more upon the subjective state of a man than upon his social status, in this too he resembles the Buddha's teaching. The one who truly knows *Brahm* is the Brahman, mere caste membership is not to be relied upon.[14] Indeed, the Vedas themselves contribute but illusion to the one not truly given to the inner praise of the Lord.[15]

In general terms the Sikh view of evil follows the broad Indian notion of *maya*, and regards man as existing within a form of consciousness which represented things as they appear to be and not things as they really are. The best way of portraying this phenomenon is by describing the way in which the self is related

---

12 Ling, Trevor, 1973: 59 ff.

13 The following references follow Ernest Trumpp's translation of 1877. The final brackets indicate page numbers for ease of references. Adi Granth. Siri Rag; mahala III. 1. Ghar. III. XXXVI. (3). (p. 42).

14 Adi Granth. Siri Rag; mahala. Ghar. VI. XXII. (8). (p. 94).

15 Adi Granth. Gauri; mahala IV. XXII. (1). (p. 333).

to other entities, in other words, a relational mode of explanation is best suited to a phenomenon which is, itself, concerned with qualities of relations between things. The self in Sikh thought is called the *man*, this is the active centre of individuality which includes both the dimension of thinking, feeling and motivation, it cannot be divided into distinct cognitive and affective aspects.[16] What is more it cannot be defined in and of itself, but must always be seen in terms of that to which it is related. Accordingly mankind may be divided into two categories depending upon the object to which consciousness or the *man* is directed. The majority may be described as *manmukh*, those whose attention is directed towards themselves in attitudes of self-will, self-love, and pride. In this condition an individual may be said to be under the influence of *haumai*, a concept closely related to that of *maya* in Sikh religion.[17] It describes that condition which exists when the *man* is directed to objects and goals other than the ultimate and transcendent god or guru. It is the normal and usual condition of life in which most men live most of the time. As a state of life it is to be contrasted with that condition which comes into existence when the individual undergoes a change of attitude, in which the *man* becomes focused upon the true guru, and is said to bẹ *gurmukh*. This transformation involves a reorientation to the world itself.

For Sikhism the world is not mayic in the sense that it is total illusion. It certainly exists as a reality to be dealt with but the view of it held by the *manmukh* person is inaccurate and false, and only by a transformation into a *gurmukh* status does a true perspective upon reality emerge. The deceived *manmukh* individual becomes *gurmukh* by means of disciplined meditation and the dwelling upon the name of the true guru, in practical terms this means the recitation of the words of the scriptures, while in the early period of Sikh history before the compilation of the *Adi Granth* it meant singing the compilations of the gurus themselves. Such recitation is both private and public, and the public form is particularly important since the sense of corporate fellowship in pursuit of the divine union has been a central component of Sikh spirituality from the earliest times. But the disciplined activity of the devotee will not ensure freedom from *haumai* unless the true guru, or god himself, admits the seeker into the realm and court of his presence by an act of benevolent incorporation. This notion of the grace of the guru, or *gurprashad*, is central to Sikh notions of salvation, and reinforces the point already made concerning the relational nature of self-identity in the process of spiritual advance.

In classical Sikh thought those things are evil which prevent meditation on the true name and which hinder that divine union which in Sikhism, as in all bhakti religiosity, is the ultimate goal of man. In one sense it is inappropriate to refer to such hindrances, or indeed to any problem area, as constituting a 'problem of evil' in Sikh religion, because that phrase possesses such a specific meaning within Christian theology, particularly so since there is nothing which could be called a problem of theodicy in the strict sense as far as Sikhs are concerned.

Responsibility for evil is firmly identified with men even though the very world of illusion in which they live is regarded as being part of the divine play and intention.

---

[16] Adi Granth. Majh; mahala III. XXIII. XXIV. (7). (p. 172).
[17] Adi Granth. Siri Rag; mahala I. XIV. (1). (p. 29).

It is for the individual to discover within himself the yearning after the Lord, and to set about finding that blessed union which the Lord will, himself, be pleased to consummate. It is quite improper to import as a hermeneutical device the Christian issue of whether salvation results from the labours of the disciple, or whether it is the free and unconditioned act of the guru, it is much more appropriate to see the issue in terms of a feedback or mutual interaction between the parties. So it is that Sikh thought does not recognize the category of natural evil, and in order to account for natural catastrophe, illness, death and misfortune, recourse is taken to the notion of *karma*, or that cosmic process of merit accumulation or loss by which men receive in any one existence and life that which accrues to them from the experience of former lives. But Sikh religious thought does not simply hold to this rather impersonal model of causation, for it employs the idea of the divine will or *hukam*, which introduces the element of freedom on the part of the true guru or god in his relations with men. In this respect Sikh thought follows Islamic rather than Hindu traditions, and probably marks the Sufi influence upon Guru Nanak and his successors.

The apparent evil which befalls man is, thus, to be understood both in terms of the desert of the individual and of the will of god for him. In analytical terms it could be said that the personification of causation, whether in terms of good or evil, might be expected within essentially devotional traditions. Unlike the more logical schemes of Vedanta where personalized conceptions of deity are undervalued, the bhakti traditions operate on a model of relationships rather than one of conceptualizations, this being so it is perfectly natural for the Sikh tradition to speak of a divine knowledge involved in human destiny.

Whatever form evil takes, be it natural disaster, illness, or moral evil the ultimate Sikh recourse is to consciousness, and to the application of that consciousness to the words of the true guru. This characteristic response leads to a corresponding lack of interest in theories of material reality so that, for example, no theory of creation has been generated to any significant extent. Similarly it is not possible to talk of doctrines of creation and salvation in Sikh religion as in Christian theology. What Sikh thought does is to offer a practical solution to the implausibility of the life-world; through meditation and the focusing of life on god the psychological and spiritual fruit of union with the divine, *sahaj*, is attained. To a person so settled in an awareness of the guru, who is *gurmukh*, all circumstances can be borne with equipoise. What is required is such a transformation of the self that its view of adverse circumstances is altered in such a way that the ultimate demands of god take the preeminence. Again the main factor is the quality of relationship obtaining in the partners involved in the act of perception. Perhaps the simplest way to understand the nature of both good and evil as it affects men is to specify the quality inhering in each partner as they are related now in a context regarded as evil, and now in one which is essentially soteriological. This clumsy form of expression may be better understood through an example which might be drawn from Christian theology. Faith on the part of the Christian may be said to correspond to grace on the part of god, they are attributes similar in kind and serving a particular end. Similarly there are qualities of relationship in Sikh thought both as far as evil and as far as the saved state are concerned.

It is necessary to preface a further comment on *maya* in this way because of the apparently paradoxical element in that notion which locates *maya* within the province of activity of god himself. As W. H. McLeod says, 'maya is, of course, the work of God, for it consists in the creation and is inseparable from it', but when he goes on to add that, 'even evil is from God and is to be regarded as an aspect of man's opportunity', he slips into the essentialist form of definition which is ill-suited to an understanding of what Sikh thought is striving to express.[18] The doctrine of *maya* and its cognate *haumai* might be said to be a definition after the event, in the sense that the essentially negative evaluation of the world which it advances follows from the changed perspective of the one who has achieved the enlightened union with god. This means that *haumai* in the individual life and *maya* in the world itself constitute a matching pair of evil categories which contrast with the positive categories of man as released from *haumai* and god perceived as entirely good and gracious. This last pair of categories is normally referred to only as the fact that the individual is *gurmukh*, in other words it emphasizes the union existing between the two partners. If the first pair are also seen in this relational way then the question of how can god initiate *maya* never arises. Indeed so to phrase the point is to express the ethnocentricity of a Christian theology rather than truly to reflect the manner in which the Sikh scriptures portray the problem. That there are verses which assert that, 'the infatuation of *maya* is made by the Lord', cannot be denied but the whole context in which they are used shows that the question is not understood in terms of aetiology, and there is no developed issue of theodicy as a result.[19] That the world is deluded, infatuated, and encircled by *maya* is but one way of expressing the fact that individual men are themselves captive to *haumai* which is a kind of thirst, filth and passion of the self.[20] The Sikh concern is always with the necessity of exchanging one set of these conditions for the other, rather than on seeking to explain the nature and origin of evil, or indeed of good.

Such an account of evil and salvation constitutes a rather classic expression of the way the history of religions tends to approach religious phenomena, many more texts and authorities could be cited to demonstrate the formal system of thought underlying Sikh notions of religious values, but these few will suffice. While this kind of study is perfectly acceptable in itself it only goes part of the way as far as a full understanding of evil in Sikh religion is concerned, and this is because the phrase 'Sikh religion' embraces more than the texts and formal explanations provided of them by Sikh scholars. So, in accordance with the methodological arguments advanced earlier, it is wise to give some account of the phenomenon of evil at a more pragmatic level, if any balanced description of the reality of Sikh religion is to be forthcoming.

In 1974 P. S. Jammu published one of the first anthropological studies of what might be called village Sikhism, in the 'Journal of Religious Studies' of the University of Patiala in the Punjab. Both the content of that study, and the identity of the publishers are important facts in the history of Sikh religion, in as much as they

---

[18] McLeod, W. H., 1968: 187.
[19] Adi Granth. Siri Rag; mahala III. V. XXII. (1). (p. 93).
[20] Adi Granth. Siri Rag; mahala III. V. XXXVIII. (1). (p. 43); VII. XL. (3). (p. 44).

herald an acknowledgement that Sikh religion did not exist only as some ideal kind of religiosity. The influence exerted by respected Sikhs on the act of publishing such material may be viewed as a significant step in the direction of a more critical self-evaluation of the religion as it is, as opposed to, or at least as differing from the religion as it is often said to be. The interesting fact about Jammu's *Religion in a Malwa Village*, at least as far as the present argument is concerned, is that while it is not explicitly directed to the issue of evil as such, it possesses numerous references to phenomena of evil.[21] In fact the article could have been written with that as its focal point, or so its content would suggest. What this fact illustrates is that a study which set out to document a village religiosity could not avoid the concern of the people studied with practical perceptions of evil.

The kinds of rituals referred to might be broadly classified into three major groups with each reflecting a distinctive life-concern with what might be said to involve the perception of evil, defined in terms of implausibility. The first concerns death and the welfare of the deceased soul. After the death of elderly persons a week long reading of the 'Granth Sahib' takes place, and after that of a childless or single person whose remains are buried under a tree, offerings are made to the dead by women. These rites of *saptahik path*, the recital of scripture, and *mahri lippna*, or the offerings, serve both to aid the progress of the dead and also to protect the living from any evil influence exerted by the departed. The second group of rites relate to human well-being, this time in the form of avoiding illness. Here the rite of offerings made to *biberian* or the female deities, serves to protect women from *chhaya* or possession by spirits, while that paid to *gugga* the snake deity serves to guard against snake-bites. The third and last group of rites concerns animal welfare and aspects of husbandry, factors which obviously relate to human success. The *basarias* rite, for example, is performed by women in offerings made to female deities for the health of cattle and for good milk yields.

Other rites which are not so much concerned with the above categories but which are directed more specifically at human relations with spirits and spirit power also occur. Jammu briefly mentions the *tara lahuna* and *sive jaguna* rites but, unfortunately, he does not provide sufficiently detailed ethnographic data to make any full description and analysis possible. It must suffice to mention that the latter rite makes use of mantra chanting, a form of activity used in many other Sikh ritual contexts and serving to show the dominant symbolic role of verbal ritual in Punjabi society. In part this is due to the high evaluation placed upon the sacred scriptures and the reading of them in Sikh religion, and this, in turn, reflects the earlier respect paid to Vedic rites and scriptures. The precise extent to which Islamic emphasis upon the Quran has affected such rural Sikhism it is hard to assess, yet it can hardly be an insignificant contribution.

Another issue which anthropological study has brought to light in the Punjab, but which bears no obvious relation to classical and scriptural Sikhism, is that of ritual purity in social relations between the sexes. Without developing much of Paul Hershman's good ethnographic analysis mention should be made of the two basic ideas he identifies as underlying Punjabi moral and social values. Firstly that

---

[21] Jammu, P. S., 1974.

man is essentially pure while woman is impure, where the notion of impurity arises largely from the physiological processes of intercourse, menstruation, birth and lactation, and secondly that fertility is a dominant concern of Punjabis since it is only through birth that a woman becomes a mother and achieves full status as a member of society.[22]

What both these ethnographic studies clearly demonstrate is the distance which might be said to exist between the formal, doctrinal ideas of Sikh religion, as expressed in the systematic expositions of Sikhism, and that form of the religion which is actually practised by members. This reinforces the point that any satisfactory analysis of a religion ought to consider both the classic and folk aspects of religiosity, since either taken alone presents only a partial picture of the reality as it is. That there should be a complex relationship between the formal and pragmatic dimensions of religions is not surprising, but that either one of these aspects should be omitted from comprehensive studies can only be regretted in terms of hermeneutics whether in the phenomenology or history of religion.

The abiding fact is that religions are historical phenomena, and where that history is known then it must be incorporated into any study so that the formal definition of the theological system, which has usually emerged under specific historical conditions, can be related to contemporary religious structures. It is precisely because many preliterate societies did not possess any documentary or archaeological history that their religions were studied in a fundamentally different way from that which held for the established and historic faiths.

What the historical study of Sikh religion shows is that its emergence among a relatively small group of devotees of devotional pursuasion in fifteenth century Punjab led, after some two hundred years, to a militaristic and relatively distinct cultural group which may be identified as the Punjabi Sikh community. The implications of this transformation are many and various, but one of the important issues emerging from it concerns the change in the doctrine of evil which accompanied the social transformations.

The essentially new element which entered Sikh thought as a result of the seventeenth century hostilities was that of the identifiable community. To say that it was essentially novel is to comment more on the qualitative nature of the group's self-identity than upon the existence of a group as such, for from the earliest days the gurus had possessed bands of devoted followers. But the very experience of aggression served to forge a sense of identity which had not obtained before, and which in later years was to grow even stronger through events like the bloody partition of the Punjab in the nineteen forties. Because of these changed social conditions the older *sant* notions of evil expressed as *haumai* must be complemented by reference to the important fact that evil, again viewed as structures of implausibility, came to assume different meanings as the Sikh community grew and as political pressures were applied to it. This might be expressed in terms of the evil of oppression and the resulting response of a desired freedom from such restraints.

Accordingly, consideration must be given to the role of membership in the khalsa, to the potential evil in the sense of political aggression which this involved,

---

[22] Hershman, P., 1977.

and to the responsibilities attendant upon such membership, if any sense is to be made of the relation of evil to salvation in later Sikh history. A useful way of doing this is through a consideration of the question of ethics in the life of the Sikh community.

The emergence of the expanded Sikh community in eighteenth century Punjab led to an unprecedented interest in the question of social order, welfare, and ethics. One of the best examples of this is furnished by the Prem Sumarag document written by a near contemporary of Gobind Singh and attributed to him. This outlines a theory of society and social order applicable to, and needful for a Sikh state, and as J. S. Grewal has pointed out its prologue seeks to encourage the khalsa in the defence of Sikh religion and resistance to external hostilities.[23] The major concerns of this treatise include the moral duties of Sikhs, their attitudes to those of other groups, to women and to caste, all of which are concerns indicating the dominant interests of a group gaining autonomy of political and social power, while also experiencing a far reaching search for self-identity. Nevertheless it was not until Ranjit Singh assumed power as Maharaja of the Punjab in 1801 that such ideals could find practical expression within an established and extensive Sikh community, for he supervised the development of a national state from disparate groups of Sikhs. This newly ordered community, in which the Maharaja maintained close relations with the ordinary people through the style of life he adopted, was regarded as built upon an authority vested not in Ranjit Singh's intrinsic power of conquest, but in the fact that he had been chosen by the panth khalsaji, or the venerable Sikh congregation itself, acting on divine principles of decision making. All of this is somewhat far removed from the simple sangat, or small group of disciples surrounding guru Nanak and singing the divine praises which conferred enlightenment. This emergent society provided the basis of all future Punjabi political though as well as the moral code of the individual Sikh to which it will be necessary to return later when discussing the notion of Sikh identity and the processes of its development by means of Sikh mission endeavours.

In the light of this brief historical analysis it is possible to see that the Sikh internal observer model of soldier and saint can also be usefully employed by the non-Sikh student of the religion. Not only can this model serve, in its divided form of saint and soldier motifs, as an ideal typical expression of particular historical periods, with the saint element portraying the first five gurus and their disciples' style of life, and the soldier element the last five, with Nanak and Gobind Singh providing pivotal models of each type, but they may also be seen to express aspects of contemporary Sikhism. What is more significant as far as the present discussion is concerned is that they may be evaluated in terms of the notions of salvation implicit in each of them, ideas which are, themselves, not very closely related. In terms of the history of religion this is a point of some importance for it indicates how an idea of salvation can be subject to change under the influence of altered social conditions, conditions which ought not to be thought of as purely external influences, which in the case of Sikhism would involve Mughal hostility or the earlier influence of Sufism, but also including internal factors which are the product

---

23 Grewal, J. S., 1965.

of the change in structure of the institution itself. Thus the large number of Jat peasant farmers entering the guru's band during the late sixteenth and especially during the late seventeenth century resulted in a positive emphasis upon a more militant attitude and, ultimately, contributes to the emergence of an ethnic Sikh community. Once a movement attains such a status involving a fixed geographical homeland which can easily became the basis of a definite subculture, then its interest in political activity is assured.

In one most significant sense this is what occurred in the Punjab, and it heralded a quite new departure in Sikh history in as much as it necessitated political involvement in social relations with other sub-cultural groups, as well as in its own future planning. This meant that 'religion' which, for the early saint gurus and Sikhs, was an endeavour carried out while one lived ones life in the workaday world now became inextricably associated with that world. In other words, the saint model of religiosity presupposes a life-world within which the individual sets his mind on gaining an intuitive knowledge of God, while the soldier model unites that religious quest with ordinary life, including its political aspects. In the first case religion and society, or the world, are rather distinct entities, while in the latter they merge together.

As far as the notion of salvation is concerned, the most significant difference between these types is to be found in the fact that whereas the earlier tradition had presupposed a personal commitment to the living guru, who taught as much by his presence as by his actual words, it now involved the individual as a member of an established social institution which itself possessed goals other than the specifically pietistic and supernatural. While it would not be completely true to say that religious status in the former system was achieved while in the latter it was ascribed, it would nevertheless be suggestive of the way in which the notion of salvation was developing in the emergent ethnic group of Sikh Punjabis.

Much caution is required in making this point because it could be argued that both the saint and the soldier models exist in contemporary Sikhism, and that they provide the parameters for religious and social action. It could also be said that they function as ideal types even for those who do not act upon them, so it is that contemporary ideas of salvation are related to earlier ones, but with the addition of significant new dimensions born out of the social history of Sikh society. The dual nature of the contemporary Sikh ideal is clearly expressed in Punjabi *gurudwaras* or temples especially the larger ones serving as major religious centres, where the presence of armed attendants at the entrance symbolizes the soldier motif, whereas the *granthis* who read the sacred book represent the saint ideal. The ritual of initiation also presents a dramatic lesson to the young with the five members of the khalsa who serve as initiators representing the historical five first members of the khalsa, and incarnating the soldierly ideal. But at the same time the centrality of the sacred book draws attention to the devotional and saintly life of the Sikh. It would thus appear that Sikhs have a choice, which is always readily available to them, and which is able to provide legitimation for different kinds of life activity. Political engagements, for example, are readily validated by means of the soldier theme and in the politics of the Punjab this is no small concern. Similarly in Britain and other peripheral areas, as will be argued below, problems of community identity, especially when they relate to any opposition from the dominant non-Sikh culture, are readily couched in terms of military aggression. But at the same time these political endeavours cannot be divorced from a religious meaning, for they are often interpreted as the means of maintaining Sikh cultural values, and thereby the truth of the sacred guru teaching. In terms of popular Sikhism, for example, Gobind Singh stands as the perfect guru and as the model for imitation in every Sikh's life. Nowhere is this better seen than in the literature produced for Sikh children in Britain where one of the best known little books published by the British Sikh Missionary Society is entitled *The Saint-Soldier* in which there is an explicit identification made between the two named principles. 'Like Guru Nanak, Guru Gobind Singh attached the utmost importance to purity of life; but on a level with it he placed brave deeds and devotion to the Sikh cause. There was no higher duty for a Sikh than to die fighting in defence of his faith'.[24] Large pictures of this man are to be found in many Sikh homes, and the values enshrined in them inform many Sikhs in their sense of social behaviour.

It might be said that the pool of potential orientations of a religion, to which reference has already been made, is largely constituted by the person of Gobind Singh as far as Sikh religiosity is concerned. This source provides a ready supply of differently emphasized doctrines which can be selectively utilized as occasion demands. Political activism, community concern, devotion to parents, love of the khalsa, sincerity, as well as learning and knowledge, are all to be seen in his life. Again no better illustration of this could be found than that furnished by the same children's book in which some one hundred and twenty six adjectives are provided as apt descriptions of this ideal Sikh man, who was also the guru.

This discussion shows that the structures of implausibility which predominated in early Sikh traditions were those of a wrong consciousness, and that the process of salvation lay in so hearing the words of the guru and meditating upon them as to be granted release from the power of maya. The company of disciples which constituted the institutional plausibility structure was merely a means of fostering the company of the guru and striving to attain the blessed state of union or *sahaj* with god himself. The growth of the khalsa as a military power and then as an ethnic community brought about significant changes in this scheme so that evil came to represent not only the darkness of the mind, but also the very existence of enemies who challenged the Sikh community. The various verses composed by Gobind Singh attest to this and address god as the sword who smites the enemy.[25] The notion of salvation thus experienced a shift in meaning and came to embrace a social dimension of group membership. In order to develop the implications of this assertion as far as plausibility theory is concerned it will be useful to consider the growth of the Sikh community in Britain, at least in general terms, and in particular to show how the notions of both evil and salvation depend for their meaning upon the precise context of their usage. In particular it will be shown that these notions bear particular connotations as far as ethnic religions are concerned.

In order to show the theoretical importance of such issues another case of ethnic

---

24 Sidhu, G. S., et al., 1974: 56.
25 Radhakrishnan, S., 1960: 270.

religiosity will be drawn upon for comparative purposes, that of the Mormon religion, and both traditions will be evaluated by means of the notion of mission. In other words it is suggested that the phenomenological category of mission can be used to advantage in comparing the notion of salvation in two, apparently different, religious traditions.

CHAPTER EIGHT

IDENTITY IN SIKH AND MORMON SOTERIOLOGY

Enough has already been said to show that the notion of salvation varies according to the way in which evil is conceived in specific social contexts. If it is accepted that the idea of salvation can be expressed in terms of plausibility theory, then it is possible to go on and argue that a close relation exists between the notion of meaning and that of identity. This chapter seeks to establish just such a point in the cases of Sikh and Mormon religions, and argues that processes of mission exhibit specific concern with identity as they are engaged in the task of forwarding a particular idea of salvation.

Because the problem of defining the terms identity and mission is not easy, and because these two religions might initially appear very different in character it will be useful to begin by discussing them separately and then attempting to see whether there are similar processes at work in both of them.[1] Once again a historical perspective is adopted to provide the basic context for understanding the development of the religions in question, and a particular anthropological notion, that of rank concession, is invoked in an attempt to discuss the idea of mission in terms which are not usually applied to it, in the hope that aspects of the phenomenon of mission which have hitherto eluded observation will be revealed.

Despite the apparent distinctiveness of these religious traditions in terms of their Eastern and Western origins the phenomenological similarity between Sikhism and Mormonism is considerable. Each possesses an identifiable charismatic leader, guru Nanak and the prophet Joseph Smith; distinctive geographical centres in Punjab and Utah serving as foci of subcultures, at the heart of which exist important temples, at Amritsar and Salt Lake City; sets of scripture believed to have come directly from god and lacking any error due to scribal transmission, the *Guru Granth Sahib* and the *Book of Mormon*. Both were founded movements emerging in periods of religious interest and zeal, and have manifested considerable changes in practice and belief during the five hundred life period in the case of Sikhism, and the less than two hundred year duration of Mormonism. Along with these similarities are to be found others associated with the process of mission which can now be discussed for each tradition, and which will enable the significance of the general paradigm of meaning to be seen for this dimension of religious action.

Mormon Mission

Conceived during the religious revivalism of New York State in the eighteen twenties, and officially born in eighteen thirty, this religious movement reflected the book based millenial ideals of several protestant parents as well as the notion of priestly status, authority, and church structure of Roman Catholic origin, for that Church too was engaged in active revivalist work on the American

---

[1] Mol, Hans, 1976: 55.

Frontier.[2] Not least significant in contributing to this family resemblance was American Freemasonry whose initiatory ritual provided the basis for Mormon temple ritual at a later date. For Joseph Smith and his successors these foundations of belief constitued the rationale for mission, the basic proclamation involved the necessity of emigration to a place appointed by the Lord for his imminent return to America. Temples were built wherever the Mormon community happened to reside, and as they were driven out by local popular opposition they built new ones until they finally arrived in the relative security of the Salt Lake Valley. These temples served as foci of the adventist hope, and can be interpreted in terms of the idea of sacred space which was intimately associated with sacred time. During the last decade of the nineteenth century the Mormon mission, which had been established in Europe from about eighteen forty, was producing far fewer converts, and of these fewer still actually emigrated to the American Zion. The great stream of Scandinavian and British converts which had largely populated Utah had now become a mere trickle. As the present author has shown elsewhere the doctrine that the second coming of Christ was imminent had virtually ceased, and so had many of the economic and social ills which had influenced many a doubting convert to emigrate for his safety's sake.[3] Some few Saints maintained a languishing Mormon community in Europe but it was scattered and disorganized. The first great mission period was over, but it had produced an entire Mormon sub-culture in Utah.

This picture remained largely unchanged until after the second world war when a new mission programme, instituted as early as nineteen thirty, was implemented by the sending out of pairs of young missionaries to serve two year periods of evangelism in many parts of the world. During the first quarter of the new century some central aspects of the millenial doctrine had changed so that the divine kingdom was no longer expected to descend from the heavens, but would emerge as the church extended its institutionalized structure across the world. As a result of this the message preached by the missionaries was very different in effect from that of their nineteenth century counterparts. Converts were encouraged to remain in their homeland, there to establish holy Zion. The subsequent building of temples in Europe, New Zealand and elsewhere symbolized the shift in significance of the notion of Zion, for they represented the sacred space of Utah's Zion now located across the world and amidst the world's evil. In them the faithful received rituals which were of soteriological power having been performed by the Melchisedek priests.

Not only did this new mission venture result in revivifying the languishing Mormon communities and in creating new ones, but it also contributed most significantly to a revitalization of Utah Mormonism, in as much as the mission period served a kind of reflexive purpose in converting the missionaries themselves, in an affective way, to the very doctrines they preached to the so called Gentiles. Many of these young missionaries came from rural Utahn townships and could be called nominal Mormons who, through the process of mission and its attendant experience of opposition from those canvassed, as well as the equally

---

2 Dolan, J. P., 1978.
3 Davies, D. J., 1973

psychologically reinforcing experience of seeing people come to faith, became convinced and converted Mormons. These, in turn, provided many of the personnel for the central church bureaucracy and were totally convinced of the necessity of the mission period for the youth of the church.

The mission period thus served a major function in the process of creating a self-identity among the missionaries themselves, and this was inextricably associated with the phenomenon of salvation. It was often through mission work that the young people entered into a sense of the truth of their religion in an affective as well as an intellectual way. More than this the mission period has served to establish the identity of the church as a whole as a missionary minded body. In 1978, for example, some 2,000 missionaries were operating in Britain with a Mormon population of 104,000 while across the world there were 26,000 missionaries in the total church population of 4,000,000.

The phenomenon of mission in the Mormon religion can usefully be approached by considering the individual missionary as a phenomenological category. He or she, viewed as an ideal type, may be regarded in Victor Turner's usage as a polysemic symbol, one which expresses a series of meanings at different levels of abstraction and in different contexts.[4] At the family level the missionary represents the ideal son or daughter who puts the concerns of the gospel before any personal considerations in completing the two year period away from home. On returning home marriage tends to follow quite quickly and the young person assumes the status of husband and father, a status highly desired by his own parents. The mission period is thought to prepare people for marriage in the sense that it aids personality development through the experience of bearing church responsibilities. This experience also serves as preparation for office in the home church, so the missionary bears a powerful meaning as a potential leader in the higher echelons of the bureaucracy. Not only at the ecclesiastical level, but also at the historical level the missionary expresses a basic aspect of the nature of the church, for he manifests an activity, that of proselytizing, which has been a major endeavour of Mormons from the beginning. This traditional aspect has the further twist of significance in that it represents a kind of reverse emigration, for whereas their ancestors may have come from Britain to Utah the missionaries now return to their native parts to propagate their message. In one sense, then, this activity is a kind of pilgrimage for the young person.

In and through these levels of meaning the missionary demonstrates the nature of Mormon spirituality, and may be viewed as an expression of what the idea of Homo religiosus can mean for Mormons. This is especially true in mission areas where the missionary is more socially visible and plays a larger part in the running of services than he would in established areas. A later discussion will take up the precise meaning of soteriological doctrines in Mormonism and for the moment it will suffice to say that the missionary as a completely dedicated Melchizedek elder, who takes the message to the people and thereby getting them to begin the complex ritual process which culminates in a heavenly salvation, presents a clear example of Mormon spirituality, and of Mormon truth. In terms of body symbolism it could

---

4 Turner, Victor, 1967.

be said that the well groomed missionary exemplifies the submission to both the doctrine and authority of the church which guarantees salvation to those who, similarly, will adopt an identity which involves faithful acceptance of the church and its 'ordinances'. The identity of being a Mormon is much more specific than that of merely being a Christian. That aspect of sectarianism deemed to be exclusivist is fully operative in this case, for the revelation deposited in the church is quite unique and thought to be necessary for final salvation. To be saved in the eternal world involves being identified as a Mormon in the material world of temple ritual and ordinary social life. Some of these points will be considered again when Mormonism is analysed as a possible exception to the plausibility theory definition of salvation, but enough has been said here to show that the sense of meaning which constitutes Mormon status cannot be divorced from the mission process which involves a distinct sense of identity in terms of belonging to an exclusive group possessing access to a unique body of truth. It can thus be argued that the message and the messenger bear a particularly close relation to each other, so self-identity and truth are notions which need to be considered as inextricably associated concepts within the entire scheme of salvation.

The nature of mission, understood as the planned diffusion or application of a religious message to a target population, is thus determined to a large extent by the precise nature of the message and of the sense of self-identity obtaining among those propagating it. The phenomenologist needs to pay particular attention to the content of the message and to this means of propagation, as well as to changes in both areas. It has already been shown how the early Mormon message of an imminent advent of Christ led to a strong proselytizing mission resulting in an entire American sub-culture, and how that message changed to one of a slowly emergent kingdom apart from emigration.

It is now possible to go on to analyse processes of mission by means of a general communication theory, viewing them as sets of messages exchanged between groups and persons whose statuses need to be defined. Indeed the way the various partners in mission exchanges are identified is an important concern for it directs the kind of communication event deemed appropriate by them. In the Mormon case it quickly established itself on an in-group, out-group basis of Saint and Gentile, with aggression and hostility accompanying the actual conversion of persons, and the migrations of the Mormon community. The case of the Sikh religion resembles that of Mormonism in several respects and it will be as well to document these before engaging in an analysis of both.

Sikh Mission

As in the case of the Mormons, the Sikhs have also engaged in a variety of relations with their geographical neighbours during the course of their history to date, some of these relations can be interpreted in terms of the notion of mission, and more particularly in terms of mission as an aspect of the development of a self-identity.

The social context of medieval Punjab was very different from that of frontier America. The *nirguna sampradaya* or Sant tradition, which W. H. McLeod has done much to establish as the basic soil from which Sikh religion emerged, was certainly not millennialist, the focus was upon the individual grasp of the one god in an intuitive love-grace union.[5] If the activity of guru Nanak is to be categorized as a form of mission then it ought to be identified more as the mission of mystic necessity to express his profoundly located experience of god, than as a vital proclamation to be rapidly conveyed to men for their response and immediate salvation. The very notions of *karma* and *samsara* rather than that Christian idea of the one life after which comes judgement, introduces a significant difference to the process and study of the logic of mission.

As has already been suggested, Nanak's mission led to the formation of a group of seekers whose fellowship constituted the context for religious experience of the divine. Whether his religion would have become the birthright of an entire sub-culture solely on the ethos and teaching of Nanak is at least questionable, what is historically certain is that after the fifth guru, Arjun and the rapid growth in numbers due to the incursion of large numbers of Jats, its religious aspect could no longer be separated from political issues between Moghul power and Punjabi interests. By the time of the last guru and the establishment of the khalsa warrior community at the close of the seventeenth century, the message of the gurus was as much a group demarcator of Punjabi sub-culture, as it was a ship which, by god's grace, the terrible ocean of existence might be traversed. This brief historical recapitulation is necessary if the twentieth century activity of Sikhs is to be at all comprehensible. The two aspects of Sikh mission which will now be outlined show the extent to which the growth of the religion in the modern world has both led to a continuation of past traditions and identities and also to some basic discontinuities. A major intention of this particular part of the analysis is to show how some very basic sociological factors are inextricably associated with the notion of salvation, understood in terms of identity and plausibility, and that the notion of salvation should not be restricted to the more philosophical perspectives of a religion.

Of first consideration is what might be called mission to the Punjabi 'dispersion', and to the community integrating process which it serves. The trickle of emigrant Punjabis leaving India during the British Empire period increased somewhat after the second world war as single men, or married men without their spouses, made their way to America, Britain, Canada, and parts of East Africa. Seeking the patronage of the host community for jobs, many of them abandoned the turban, long hair, and beards, and adopted the style of dress appropriate to the culture concerned. Very few *gurudwaras* or Sikh temples existed, but since weekly attendance at a temple was hardly an established custom in the Punjab, the British pattern of non-attendance was hardly significant in evaluating patterns of changed religiosity. Despite the difficulty attending any attempt to categorize periods of history, the later nineteen sixties may be identified as one which marked a change in Sikh religion outside the Punjab, and especially in Britain. To a large extent this was due to the immigration of Sikh women and children who came to join their husbands who had arrived earlier. The immigration statistics for Indians, the majority of whom were Sikhs, demonstrate this change with the increased numbers of the mid-

---

[5] McLeod, W. H., 1968: 151 ff.

sixties representing incoming families of resident immigrants.[6] This period resulted in the establishment of Sikh homes which replaced the earlier and utilitarian 'dormitory' use of houses for workers. This demographic change resulted in an increase of Sikh social visibility, and resulted in a renewed sense of group identity. Indeed it was this factor which was so important in the apparently minor debate as to whether Sikhs should be forced to wear crash-helmets for driving in place of the customary turban which many men were now increasingly wearing.

At the same time growing numbers of *gurudwaras* provided centres of worship, instruction and political activity. They served as important community centres for the largely Punjabi speaking and tradition-bearing womenfolk, who also found in them the therapy of a home-land institution amidst the potentially confusing new reality of urban Britain. The Sikh Missionary Society in Britain, founded in 1969, may serve as a clear expression of this new zeal for Sikh values and culture, and which resulted in language classes for the children as well as a growth of literature aimed at conveying the richness of the cultural heritage. This institution and others like the Sikh Research Centre of Canada, which was also founded in 1969, came to function as agencies of social solidarity and applied themselves to the question of how the Sikh teaching could be applied in western, urban, contexts. The Sikh Students' Federation of Britain, for example, which was established in 1977 has taken up the issues of caste status, the elimination of marriage of convenience for immigration purposes as well as party divisions among Sikhs.

In all these issues the community is clearly the focus of concern, and it is just this self-directed factor which offers the clearest distinction between Mormon and Sikh notions of mission, understood as 'the planned diffusion of religion'.[7] Theoretically it might be said that the focus and the object of the message are different in one important respect, namely, that while for Mormons the missionary is the focus and the gentile community of unbelievers is the object of the teaching, for the Sikhs the khalsa is both the focus and object of the guru teaching. In other words a relatively small number of dedicated Sikhs have sought to maintain their religion and culture amongst the larger number of resident immigrants. In addition to this direct service to the Sikh community in an attempt to maintain it as a community with distinctive features of language and religion, there is what might be called an indirect service which members can provide through their relations with non-Sikhs, and that is by attempting to establish the status or identity of the khalsa in the eyes of the host population. In this aspect of mission there is no attempt to make converts to the religion, indeed, most Sikhs almost deny any intention of so doing. What is more the very notion of a convert is difficult to handle in Sikh religious terms since Sikh life presuppose to a very large extent membership in Punjabi culture. A positive discontinuity in cultural attachment is involved in conversion as is aptly demonstrated by some American converts who have adopted Punjabi dress and language. This reference to white American Sikhs

---

[6] Number of Indian Immigrants coming to Britain. From Banton, M., 1972: 70. 1958, 6,200; 1959, 2,900; 1960, 5,900; 1961, 23,800; 1962, 21,100; 1963, 1,800; 1964, 15,500; 1965, 18,800; 1966, 18,400; 1967, 22,600; 1968, 28,300; 1969, 12,300; 1970, 8,400; 1971, 6,600.

[7] Heise, David, 1967.

leads naturally to the second major aspect of Sikh mission, namely mission to non-Indians.

While only a few Britons have converted to Sikh religion America has seen a more substantial interest shown in the guru teaching as might be expected in the wake of interest in eastern thought associated with the counter-cultural attitudes of the nineteen sixties. The establishment of Sikh Dharma, a religious movement grounded in the guru teaching and meditation practice, indicates this interest while also demonstrating some interesting features of American religiosity as such.[8] For example one aspect of the rationale underlying the creation of Sikh Dharma in America was the belief that Punjabi Sikhism was entering a decadent phase under the impact of western materialism, and that just as Buddhism had emerged and virtually vanished in India to be continued elsewhere, so too the pattern would be followed by Sikh religion. The American championing of the Sikh tradition demonstrates the denominationalizing tendencies of American religion, as well as the tendency to canvass members from unbelievers which conflicts with the more usual Punjabi reflectiveness in the religious life. But this is only one aspect of a much broader and more significant issue, that of the relation between the idea of mission and that of ethnic religiosity, factors which are closely related to the problem of salvation espoused in this book.

No historian of religion would ever think of discussing the notion of mission with respect to a primitive society and its indigenous religion, yet in many ways that kind of relatively closed society with its group related and restricted religiosity resembles groups which are normally viewed as ethnic communities but which are neither preliterate nor remote. While some of these ethnic groups are also not generally regarded as mission minded, as in the cases of Judaism and to a large extent Hinduism, there can be cases of ethnic mission. Both Mormonism and Sikhism offer interesting examples of what might be called mission processes, though some care is required in the way in which the term mission is used in each case.

When religion is one aspect of a total culture, religious status and social status tend to be coterminus, it is for this reason that Judaism is as non-conversionist as Punjabi Sikhism, rural Utahn Mormonism, or parochial Anglicanism. Conversionist movements presume that the world in which most men live is other than it should be, there is, in other words, a fundamental judgement served upon the generally accepted life-world, and this perspective is essentially different from that of ethnic religions which validate the way things are. Notwithstanding this difference, there remains an underlying similarity in the concern for meaning and the creation of a sense of identity in both types of religiosity. This fact makes it easier to understand the community validating aspect of the Sikh Missionary Society, as it does the conversionist outlook of American Sikh Dharma which is, essentially, an American conversionist perspective applied to an Indian religion. In this latter case, as also in the Hare Krishna movement, the question of identity lies with the converts who seek a personal sense of identity apart from the one immediately given them by their natal society. While mission could be said to serve the purpose

---

8 The movement *Sikh Dharma in America* publishes a magazine entitled *Beads of Truth*.

of changing an individual's identity in conversion movements, in ethnic groups it serves to reinforce the traditional identity. This is not to say that only conversionist religious movements bring about radical changes in individual lives. The earlier discussion of Aboriginal religion stressed the change which took place through the process of initiation, similarly the change in Mormon missionaries themselves could be paralleled to the sense of growing commitment to the traditional ideals of Sikh religion and culture which some Sikhs report both in Britain and the Punjab. Whether or not the same term, namely mission, should be employed in discussing both ethnic and other religions will remain a moot point; but the significant fact, which the present argument wishes to bring to the surface by so adopting it for both, is that there are similar processes operating in the direction of creating a sense of identity which is itself intimately associated with the state of salvation as already defined.

By taking recourse to the anthropological concept of rank concession it will now be possible to extend this discussion of identity and mission, and by so doing to disclose yet another aspect of salvation as a phenomenon relevant to ethnic communities. This concept of Martin Orans relates as much to psychological as to sociological aspects of life and in this resembles the width of application found in plausibility theory. In the present context the sociological dimension is stressed but only because the object of concern is the way in which one social group evaluates another.[9]

Both mission as the action of a religious group and conversion as the reaction of the proselytized population involve the process of rank concession. In his ethnographic study of the East Indian Santal tribe, Orans analyses the complex reactions of the Santal to urbanization and to rapid industrialization. In particular he showed how they began by conceding rank to the superior and dominant Hindu ethic and religion which resulted in the Santal emulation of Hindu abstinence from beef eating and excessive alcoholic indulgence, this emulation involved a radical rejection of the traditional Santal emphasis upon 'pleasure'. The Santal initially adopted what Orans calls an economic rank path, through which some individuals made considerable personal advantage at the expense of community solidarity. The political changes which were associated with movements towards Independence in India made it possible for Santal to engage in concerted action for political status as a distinct group in the new government. This involved a switch from the economic to political rank paths, a change which increased internal solidarity and facilitated the reconstruction of a tribal identity, a process which included the creation of an alphabet, codification of religious ideas and of former tribal customs.

In what sense can such rank concession and its attendant responses be identified as part of any distinctively religious phenomenon? Primarily, it might be suggested, in the way one group evaluates and responds to truth claimed by another. As far as a conversionist religious group is concerned it tends to presume possession of a truth which confers upon it the right and duty to propagate a particular teaching and style of life. In doing this a lower status is ascribed to the target population, at least as far as religious ideas are concerned, though this devaluation may also extend

---

9 Orans, Martin, 1965.

to the economic and political aspects of life of the group concerned. The success of a proselytizing mission depends not only on this labelling of the 'pagan' by the missionary, but also and perhaps more significantly, on the way in which the target population evaluates him. It is precisely in this context that the concept of rank concession becomes significant, for mission becomes feasible only when rank is conceded to the missionary; when, that is, the message and often a style of life are seen as desirable goals. According to Orans concession of rank leads to the adoption of a particular rank path which enables the desired goal to be attained, such paths vary in a complex process involving several possible combinations of responses. The fact that rank has been conceded does not mean that only the path preached by the missionary will be followed, though Orans' basic postulate is that rank concession produces a tendency to emulation. Here the Santal ethnography is informative for it shows that the later, political, rank path adopted by them led the Santal back to their own culture and to the construction of a 'great tradition' of their own. This involved a strong assertion of their tribal identity against that of the neigbouring Hindus.

Indeed the question of identity is always important and must be approached with care. For while in this chapter we are taking a fairly high level of generalization in talking about Sikh community, identity and tradition, it must be appreciated that in specific cases the data is more complex than initially appears. Recent studies in Sikh culture outside the Punjab as well as within it have shown wide variation in practice from those ideals of Sikh life and theology which are often propounded in works on Sikhism.[10] The relation between ideal and actual forms of religion is one that can be obscured by the practitioners of religion and by those seeking an ideal-typical description.

In Nottingham for example research has shown the significance of caste groups in the community organisation of Sikhs, and thereby in their self-identity. It is not the case that Sikhs define themselves solely in terms of the host population, but part of their identity construction derives from the one sub-group's view of other sub-groups. In Nottingham there were three basic groups roughly corresponding to sub-castes; the Bhatra, Jat and Tarkhan (or Ramgarhia).[11] These attended separate temples and constituted relatively distinct groups, with the Bhatra Sikhs being the most discrete. Although the Bhatras settled in Britain before the others, they have maintained their distinctive forms of dress and behaviour longer and in a more conservative way. Having first arrived in the 1920s and 1930s and living as pedlars they soon become more involved in semi-skilled work. It is in the view of their womenfolk that the Bhatras are most clearly distinguished from the other two groups. Very few go to work outside their home despite the fact that the community's longer residence means that their women often speak more english than the others. No Bhatra women were in fact employed outside their own family. From puberty the girls are carefully controlled lest the loss of virginity impair marriage possibilities and the family honour. Bhatra women wear more brightly clothes than other Sikh women and are more likely to be veiled in public gatherings. Whereas Jat and

---

10 Juergensmeyer, M. and N. G. Barrier, 1979.
11 Nesbitt, E. M., 1980.

Ramgarhia women often wear western style dress at home the Bhatras retain traditional garments.

While the Bhatras migrated to Britain from India the Ramgarhia and Jat groups often include those with an East African background. Despite the fact that Ramgarhia and Jat are socially compatible groups in terms of history there is practically no relation through marriage, they are endogamous. They will meet at each other's gurdwaras whereas the Bhatra Sikhs keep to their own temple.

The distinctive rites which Bhatra Sikhs possess in connection with festivals and rites of passage serve to remind the other groups that differences do exist between them, and this itself is one factor entering into the entire process of identity construction. The Bhatras were said by the others to eat meat in their gurdwaras which in fact they do not do. This internal evaluation of one Sikh group by another carries an implicit assumption of value and must feedback to a self-evaluation in terms of adaptation to the host society. Not least is this true in the fact that the Bhatra community is geographically located in a relatively restricted area while the Jat and Ramgarhia Sikhs are much more widely distributed throughout the local population. One important function of close community relations is that the power of gossip and of social sanction on deviance from the traditional norm can all the more easily come into play.

So within the overall Sikh group in Nottingham it can be argued that the Jat and especially the Ramgarhia Sikhs are deeply involved in processes of emulation of the host society in an economic and rank path to a certain extent whereas the Bhatra group is in no real search for equal status. Indeed the Bhatras are not engaged in any rank path exchanges with the other Sikh groups let alone with the wider society. The precise reasons for this significant difference have yet to be analysed and for this more data is required, especially historical data which might aid the antecedents to identity values.

In what we go on to say about rank concession and subsequent rank paths adopted we restrict comment to the Jat and Ramgarhia groups. Enough has been said to indicate the necessity of specific and detailed information for any full discussion of social movements. But even so the inner relations of these three groups does produce a larger picture of the broader community which itself can be seen as involved in processes of identity formation.

Some of the implications of this case can now be drawn for both the Sikh and Mormon religions. As far as the Sikhs are concerned the situation within the Punjab varies from that obtaining in Sikh communities elsewhere. From the period of Partition in 1947 Sikhs in the Punjab followed a political rank path with the goal not of emulating British, Islamic, or Hindu patterns of life, but of establishing a Sikh State. The historical fact that Sikhs already possessed the historical example and precedent of Maharaja Ranjit Singh in the early nineteenth century as one who ruled the Punbaj as a Sikh, made it difficult to concede rank in any submissive sense. The political rank path which they did adopt was more a reaction to the fact of lost power than any acknowledgement of basic powerlessness. Following the success of Indian Independence many Punjabi Sikhs became set on economic improvement and assumed an economic rank path, this was to be associated with that emigration of workers which has already been discussed, and which resulted in much money being invested in the Punjab economy by those resident abroad. The fact that there has been no significant decline of Sikh solidarity in Punjab as a result of economic pursuits is probably the result of the proximity to Pakistan and to the aggression engendered over the period of Partition which resulted in a strong sense of Sikh community solidarity.

In Britain the process of rank concession with respect to mission is clearer. In the period of Sikh residence and work leading up to the nineteen sixties an economic rank path was assumed. The Sikh men conceded rank to the host community whose patronage was sought for work, in this process the life-style of the dominant society was emulated in the sense that turbans were abandoned and the long hair was cut. From the mid sixties and following the advent of relatives and the consequent replacing of more dormitory like accommodation by Sikh homes and households, the nature of the rank path adopted changed significantly.

Though money was still a major goal the issue of Sikh community identity in the maintenance of Punjabi language and social values led to the assumption of a political rank path. This was apparent in the erstwhile trivial episode of whether Sikhs should wear turbans or not while riding motorcycles. The question was conceived in terms of whether rank was to be conceded or not, and by contrast to the early Sikhs in Britain who shaved their beards, the general opinion was that their present status should be respected and recognized. As a result of this internal solidarity increased and the whole process of mission came to represent a reinforcement of Punjabi identity. That there was a strong emphasis on calling the khalsa to live up to its high ideals cannot be doubted during this period, and visiting holy men and politicians from the Punjabi aided this vocation.

Just as for the Santal the rise of a new tradition, following political success, led to a revival in their religious beliefs and practices as a focal point of the new situation which was, thereby, seen as a continuation of the earlier way of life, so too for the Sikhs whose major concern with mission was directed towards their own community and to the growth of a sense of solidarity and identity. The new situation was one which could be described as conferring a satisfactory level of plausibility upon khalsa members and thereby to constitute a state of salvation. The whole issue of self-identity associated with this development in Sikh communities resembles that found in the growth of the Mormon religion.

From its inception in 1830 Mormonism has been preoccupied with the question of its status and real significance as a social movement. The preaching of Joseph Smith led to a rapidly growing community of believers, and while Smith's initial concern was with the simple preaching of a religious message he was soon taken up with the problems attending the organization of an expanding social group. This group was opposed by non-Mormons on many occasions, for the growth in Mormon power was thought to endanger the freedom of non-members. Throughout the nineteenth century Mormons adopted a political rank path with respect to the American government. Joseph Smith had been mayor of Springfield, Illinois, while Brigham Young had been territorial governor and church leader simultaneously. The decade of eighteen eighty witnessed direct political confrontation between church and nation and was overtly focused on the question of polygamy. It resulted in the formal abandonment of that institution in 1889. Throughout this period there was a growth of internal solidarity amongst Mormons whilst they also greatly improved their economic status. In this case, then, it would appear that both economic and political rank paths entered into the Mormon response to their immediately given social world. The full significance of the corporate identity of Mormons for their doctrinal system has yet to be demonstrated, and in the next section of this chapter some attention will have to be paid to this important question of how the very notion of salvation generated within Mormonism is related to their view of their own social structure. For the moment the major difference between Mormon and Sikh religious structures in terms of rank paths requires comment, most particularly to make the point that Mormonism did not develop dispersed groups of an ethnic type. Dispersed Mormonism, if the world-wide congregations may be so identified, was largely convert Mormonism, and what differentiated these members from their neighbours was their peculiar form of religious adherence. For them religion was the focal point of activity and life, it was primary and did not possess the secondary function, so central to Sikh groups, of establishing and reinforcing community identity. In the light of this difference it would seem useful to make a formal distinction between rank paths involving religious features as a secondary concern and those in which religious factors are of primary importance.

The central meaning of mission which has emerged from this comparison of Mormon and Sikh traditions is that of the self-conscious awareness on the part of religious groups in applying their understanding of truth to their immediate social context. In the more general terms of the history of religions this might be expressed as the desire to communicate the idea of the holy; the precise nature of that notion being couched in millenarian terms in the case of Mormonism, and of intuitive union of the individual with god in that of the Sikhs. Mission, understood as the self-conscious action resulting from a notion of having gained possession of a significant truth, is thus inextricably associated with the process by which a sense of self-identity is gained. The fact that in the Christian traditions this process is often aligned with that of proclaiming the message to non-believers would not prevent a similar process being identified as operating in non-Christian cultures. In as much as the message possessed relates to the state of salvation it has been shown that such a state needs to be maintained within a group as well as being extended to others. When the notion of salvation is interpreted in terms of plausibility theory the maintenance of community or ethnic identity by reference to religious ideas can readily be viewed as a mission by parts of the group to the whole group with salvation being the desired state of integration. Just as the notion of rank concession involves an act of judgement between the parties concerned, and in proselytizing mission this means that the proclaiming group deems others to be lacking in certain fundamental respects, so in ethnic communities it is possible for one interest group to deem the community as a whole as being in need of transformation. It is in this sense that the Sikh mission can be understood as a mission process.

As a final comment on the process of identity and soteriology some consideration will now be given to the Mormon doctrine of salvation, and in particular to the basic negative features which appear in it. This concern arises from the point just made about the judgement which is served upon reality by religious groups, for while the argument of this book has emphasized the negative factors pin-pointed by religions, the case of Mormonism would, initially, seem to contradict the importance of such a stress. As it stands Mormon theology presents a clear case of an optimistic world-view coupled with a world-affirming way of life. So if religion is to be defined by means of negative features and in terms of a plausibility theory some qualification would seem to be necessary in setting these positive factors in some kind of intelligible context. At the same time a detailed study of this aspect of Mormonism will demonstrate how one Christian doctrine of salvation can be almost completely different in meaning from others within the same general tradition. This variation alone will reinforce the assertion that a non-theological definition of the notion of salvation is necessary in religious studies.

Theologically speaking Mormonism rejected the established doctrines of both Catholic and Protestant traditions concerning original sin, predestination and grace. The idea of the Fall was retained but rather than stress the shame and catastrophic aspect of the doctrine Joseph Smith developed it, not as might have been expected more in the direction of the *felix culpa* theme which argued that without the Fall, man would never have known the blessedness of salvation in Christ, but in terms of offering man the opportunity for sense experience and fuller potential for enjoyment. Had Adam not sinned by indulging in sexuality itself then no children would have ensued, and pleasure would have been impossible. The Fall itself thus served a positive end, and the humanity which resulted from it enables pre-existent souls to prove their allegiance to god while they also gain experience by inhabiting material bodies on earth. This too, benefits them in their own future state. Every living man comes into an earthly existence because he has already demonstrated his worthiness in the pre-existent world of souls. Man thus begins life in the flesh with a history of success already behind him, what is more, he is under no influence or contagion of sin resulting from a historic fall of man from grace. While the orthodox Mormon does believe in a historic event through which evil entered the world this does not mean that all the descendants of Adam are implicated in the evil there perpetrated. On the contrary, Adam alone is responsible for his personal act of disobedience, and that no evil consequence befalls other men is assured by the doctrine of general salvation, for to all men, irrespective of whether they seek it, there comes the benefit of Christ the Redeemer's work. As a consequence of that work all men are free to live as they will.

Mormon theology inevitably finds itself in something of a dilemma at this point in its soteriology since it wants to lay claim both to human endeavour and to the work of Christ. While this paradox is never truly resolved it is the case that in exegesis of the Bible and the Book of Mormon the emphasis comes to be laid upon individual activism which is thought to be a worthwhile commitment of the individual because of the preparatory work of Christ. It is as though Joseph Smith saw a clear distinction between the doctrines of justification by faith and salvation through works, and desired to transform the former into a version of the latter; accordingly each man was made responsible for acquiring for himself salvation from his personal sins by means of trust in Christ's work and the ritual processes of the church. Salvation results from 'obedience to the laws and ordinances of the gospel', as the third of the Articles of Faith expresses it, and by ordinances is meant faith and the rituals performed in the temples without which salvation is impossible.

Even a brief consideration of some aspects of this ritual will clearly show how significantly different the Mormon religion is from practically all other traditions of Christianity when it comes to soteriological issues. This is largely due to a distinction drawn in Mormon theology between the term salvation and another which introduces a radically different element, that of 'exaltation'. In this complex notion is to be found a resolution of the paradoxical treatment of faith and works already referred to as one of Joseph Smith's central interests, but more significantly than this, in describing the ideas constituting the doctrine of exaltation, it is possible to show how the entire system of Mormonism is, itself, a salvation process grounded in and arising from negative factors.

As is the case with any cultural system Mormonism is more than a mere sum total of its constituent parts, parts which were drawn very largely from contemporary sources of religious activity. Protestantism is represented by the intense emphasis laid upon the written word which is thought to be devoid of any error because of the contemporary nature of divine revelation to Smith. By producing the Book of Mormon and later the Inspired Version of the bible, Smith circumvented that biblical criticism which fixed upon errors of translation and text and caused so many difficulties in Christian churches from the later nineteenth century. Moreover, his rewriting and rephrasing of certain paradoxical sections of scripture made the written word even more self-authenticating to the Mormon community which accepted that these changes were of divine origin. Good examples of this are found in the Prologue to St. John's gospel and in the sections of the Epistle to the Hebrews concerned with Melchizedek and the notion of high-priesthood.[12] Another fundamentally Protestant notion which he developed with much success was that of the priesthood of all believers. In Smith's formulation the essentially private and personal dimension of this doctrine, which asserted the immediacy of relationship conceived to exist between god and man, was transformed into a charter for operating within the church bureaucracy. Each person was given the right to inquire of god with respect to his role within the church organization. By means of this idea Smith retained his position as the foremost prophet, but permitted others an intimacy with god in so far as their formally appointed office in the church required it. This example of Weber's notion of the routinization of charisma shows how Smith both protected his own status while allowing all church members a sense of immediacy of contact with god.[13]

Along with these Protestant motifs Mormonism came to contain some distinctively Roman Catholic features, their inclusion tended to reduce the plausibility of Catholic criticism of the new movement, and further validated it in the eyes of converts from Catholic and Anglican traditions who were taught to view these elements as aspects of their old religion which had been freed from error through the miraculous intervention of god through the ministry of Joseph Smith. Foremost among such factors was that of the doctrine of priesthood, which came

---

12 Inspired Version, 1965. John. 1. i-iv, Hebrews. 5. vi-vii.
13 Weber, Max, 1968.

to be the focal institution of Mormon religion and which contained within itself both metaphysical and pragmatic meanings. It combined features of the Catholic doctrine of authority vested in men through the indelibility of ordination by properly empowered persons, with the immediacy of access to god already referred to as a basic protestant belief. The ritual of ordination was believed to have been restored to earth by the biblical figures of John the Baptist, Peter, James, and John, and Christ Himself, and functioned on an *ex opere operato* basis. The context of its use came to be restricted to the temples and to the action of the Melchizedek priests, in fact the power of priesthood was thought to underlie the entire life of the church in this world and the next. The line of succession in the priesthood is carefully maintained and validates the process of salvation in which the church members are involved whilst it also calls into the question the existence of all priesthoods and ministries existing in other religious bodies. It is just this kind of act of censure which Smith passed upon the religions of his day which indicates the significance of negative features in the growth of the Mormon religion.

As far as Joseph Smith and those who first accepted his message were concerned evil could be defined as much in terms of the conflicting truth claims of the frontier religions as in the more accepted phenomena of moral and natural evil. Joseph Smith's own perception of implausibility began when he could not decide which religion was preaching the truth. His desire for salvation, whatever else it contained, included a yearning for an assured way of knowing the truth of god and of having a determined way of following it. Salvation and certainty were two closely aligned notions for Smith, and in that fact the orthodox Christianity of his environment manifests itself, for there was no place for doubt in the life of faith. Doubt constituted the unsaved condition and was represented by the competing truth claims of religions known to him, in personal terms this meant that Smith was not prepared to concede rank to any religious group, in fact he did just the opposite and deemed them all to be imperfect. The fact that many of the elements he incorporated into his own formulation came from these very religions may be counted as an example of emulation, but one which involves a radical reinterpretation of the doctrines and rites so borrowed.

In the case of Mormonism there is, then, a twofold perspective which can be adopted with respect to the problem of evil. The one concerns the movement as a sociological phenomenon, while the other emphasizes the actual doctrines held by the church. As far as the former is concerned it can be seen that the problem of evil is no simple matter when any single religious movement is concerned. For in this case it is the very existence of ways of salvation, for that is how the religious movements of Smith's day regarded themselves, that proved to be the stumblingblock to Smith. This particular example is, and this point merits emphasis, not the only one of its kind. The analysis of the emergence of Buddhism offered by Trevor Ling, for example, shows how the Buddha formulated his prescription for the enlightened life not only in the light of the traditionally repeated encounters he is supposed to have had with sickness and death, but also in the conflicting presence of competing truth claims vested in the contemporary religious environment.[14] A

---

[14] Ling, Trevor, 1973: 64 ff.

similar picture may be found in the early phases of Sikh religion, when Nanak often referred to representatives of Hindu and Muslim religions being deceived by their own religious lives and as deceiving others. The teaching of Jesus is also not without parallel as his denunciation of the Pharisees would suggest.[15] This means that while Mormonism might appear, at first sight, to be an exception to the rule suggested in this study that religions as salvation processes have their major point of focus upon the phenomenon of evil, it transpires on further analysis that the entire enterprise was initiated by a fundamental perception of implausibility in the confused competition amongst frontier religions.

The second perspective upon the problem of evil follows from this historical issue and concerns the actual doctrines of evil contained within the movement, and it may be seen that here, too, the historical origin is not without significance. There can be no doubt that as far as Mormonism is concerned the doctrine of priesthood is central to the understanding of any major doctrine and religious rite. This is true even in the way Mormons interpret history, including their own history. Briefly, this may be described as the history of priesthood, for shortly after the time of Christ, priesthood which had been possessed by Adam and other major old testament figures, was removed from the earth, and was not restored until the time of Joseph Smith.

The specific identity of the Mormon church arises from the belief that it alone possesses the priesthood, and that it is only through the power of this priesthood that final salvation may be attained. So strong is the sense of identity that the notion of salvation is, itself, not thought of apart from community membership. Whilst the notion of individuality is emphasized as the basis for self-development, achievement and progress it nevertheless occupies a secondary position in the overall scheme of salvation, and this is why genealogical work, family gatherings and the like are important to Mormons. Salvation is understood as a corporate activity, and the ritual performed by the Melichizedek priests in the temples is of fundamental importance to the creation of an integrated and saved community. Personal endeavour is important for it may influence the salvation of another soul insofar as the vicarious rites performed for the dead, and these include ordinations and marriages as well as baptism, enable the departed to enter the various states of salvation obtaining in the eternal world.

Priesthood itself is better understood as an ontological attribute of persons than as a description of institutional office, it is, in fact, a divine attribute. Priesthood is, 'the eternal power and authority of Deity by which all things exist, by which they are created, governed and controlled'.[16] Mormonism knows of no essential difference between god and men, indeed all men are gods in embryo and only await a sufficient amount of experience before they attain to divine functions, because of this it is not thought inappropriate that human action should result in the salvation of souls. The power of priesthood is thus the central phenomenon regarded by Mormons as directing the process of salvation, it operates through specific

---

15 Matthew, Caps, 15, 16.
16 McConkie, B., 1961.

rituals and seeks to bring about the attainment of specific states on the part of those undergoing the rites.

For Mormon theology evil is less the presence and influence of malevolence than it is the absence of good. Sloth, idleness, and similar inattention to duty are the problems which Mormon teaching addresses and seeks to overcome. As already mentioned, Joseph Smith rejected an emphasis on salvation which seemed to consist in an act of faith of a personal and private kind. For him, every man's merits must be fully àppreciated and a suitable reward accorded. As a result of this view the idea of the after-life which emerged, and in accord with western religiosity it was pictured as a supernatural reality beyond that of this present life, was of a tripartitely divided heaven, along with a hell of a limited constituency. It is in the way in which this division is established that the full import of Smith's thought becomes apparent. In terms of a specifically sociological analysis it would be possible to say that this was an example of a millenarian sect which appears to hold a universalist doctrine of salvation but which made possible an exclusivist attitude to outsiders by positing that complete salvation came only to those located within one of the three heavenly planes.

The highest so called heaven is named the celestial kingdom, the second the terrestial kingdom, and the third the telestial kingdom. The precise meaning and significance of these 'degrees of glory' results from the dual wish to reward all according to their deeds, but also to differentiate between Mormon and Gentile, for only married Melchisedek priests may attain to the celestial kingdom. There is a Mormon aphorism to the effect that, 'salvation without exaltation is damnation', and this gains its significance from the fact that the celestial kingdom is also called the state of exaltation. Man, as one whose nature is of progressive development on an eternal perspective will find that if he does not achieve the highest state then he will experience a sense of being thwarted in his development. Only those in this highest state will experience the presence of God the Father, while the second sphere enjoys that of the Son, and the third that of the Spirit, a fact of basic importance in understanding the Mormon doctrine of god which is completely distinct from the creedal confessions of ancient Christianity. What this scheme does clearly indicate is the qualitative difference which is thought to exist in the future world, and how that is related to contemporary achievement, and in particular to the rituals performed by the Melchisedek priests, for as has been stated it is only those married by the appropriate temple ritual who so attain the highest realms of eternal glory.

Just as ritual action works against sloth in the Mormon scheme of salvation, so the acquisition of knowledge works against a state of ignorance. 'It is impossible for a man to be saved in ignorance', so he must apply himself to study and learning on a permanent basis.[17] Salvation is, essentially a process and not a state, this means that the notion of grace is also interpreted as an ongoing change taking place in the developing personality. In the state of exaltation the individual Mormon finds himself in intimate association with his family, for the temple rites of marriage 'seal' husband and wife together not only till death parts them, but for ever. Similarly

---

[17] Doctrine and Convenants, 131: 6.

children are sealed to their parents, and in the context of the heavenly extended family develop their capacities for all eternity. The event of death is not seen as a radical transformation by which earthly realities are transformed into heavenly ones, rather the Mormon concept of matter as constituting all things means that all realities participate in essentially the same nature. All that is evil lies within the slothful and rebellious nature of man, and this it is the task of the church to change by bringing all men under the rituals, or 'ordinances of the gospel'. So it is that the Melchisedek priesthood, which emerged from Smith's confusion with the religious bodies of his day, came to be central in the process of salvation which has been defined in terms different from those present in any other recent Christian tradition. The entire meaning of reality is subsumed within the meaning of priesthood, just as priesthood constitutes the basis for the Mormon community and sense of identity.

What this brief discussion has made clear is that the notion of evil, understood in terms of plausibility theory, is a factor which relates not only to the internal value system of a religion, but also to the context out of which the religion emerged. It has also demonstrated the fact that the notion of salvation cannot be divorced from that of identity, itself a notion which is closely aligned with community membership. All this makes clear the point that the idea of evil cannot be discussed simply as a philosophical problem, or as a question of theodicy, but necessitates a discussion of the nature of the community within which persons are set and as members of which they produce their thoughts about good and evil. To have argued that the perception of evil and the adoption of particular salvific responses cannot be dissociated from the process of self-identity and community membership is to have made preparation for the final chapter of this study which analyses the general paradigm of meaning in greater depth, and especially in the way the individual person is related to socially accepted values about the nature of evil and to processes of salvation which follow from that.

CONCLUSIONS AND CONSEQUENCES

Our task has gone some way to show how the swing from the 1880s to the 1980s has been from man as an evolving entity to man as a meaning making creature. It now lies to us to show how, as a moral being, he has found it necessary to engage in processes of salvation as well as of rationalization and symbolization.

What we say is necessarily tentative for while in the field of anthropology for example, Malcolm Crick has demonstrated the change of perspective from functionalism to the semantic position the precise weight of interpretation offered by that outlook remains questionable.[1] Yet we cannot but agree with Basso and Selby who, in commenting on the American context, say that while they cannot identify any unified official paradigm of meaning they feel that to 'wait until a qualitative mathematics is devised for the full and proper axiomatization of a general theory of meaning', would mean that a great deal of necessary work would be left undone.[2]

One is, however, encouraged to engage in the following concluding arguments for the reason already adduced in the preceding chapters, and in particular by the lead set in John Bowker's Wilde Lectures which demonstrate the power of a communication theory approach to the study of religions.[3] Reality is presumed to exist as an organization and not as a chaos, while man is taken to be an active personality system in dynamic interaction with other systems of his environment be they biological, psychological or social. He is no robot acting strictly and mechanically upon messages received from either society or his genes. This line could be extensively pursued psychologically or theologically, in terms of personality and self-hood or of man's freedom in relation to his knowledge of God.[4] In fact this perspectivist approach, as it was called by Ludwig Von Bertalanffy the originator of general systems theory, has innumerable applications. Whether in biological, human, or theological disciplines a way is provided of looking at the mutual relations between man and the objects of his interactions apart from a simple cause and effect mechanism. As this more dynamic approach to phenomena replaces the more static and mechanistic view of cause and effect much less room remains available for simple reductionist explanations.

Gregory Bateson's anthropological studies afford a clear example of this shift in paradigms, for in 1958 he added an epilogue to his original 1936 work on the Iatmul culture of New Guinea. Bateson speaks of the post-war reorientation in theory, and in particular of the contribution made by cybernetics in interpreting human behaviour.[5] His summary of the change not only reinforces what we have said about meaning but also underlies the fact of evolutionary demise. 'The ideas themselves', he says, 'are extremely simple. All that is required is that we ask not

---

[1] Crick, Malcolm, 1976: 3. Also Edmund Leach, 1976.
[2] Basso, K. H. and H. A. Selby, 1976: 9.
[3] Bowker, John, 1973, 1978.
[4] Cf. Abner Cohen in Ioan Lewis, 1977: 117.
[5] Cf. 1973 Part IV for cybernetics and epistemology.

about the characteristics of lineal chains of cause and effect but about the characteristics of systems in which the chains of cause and effect are circular or more
complex than circular.[6] Different properties inhere in such systems so that one
must speak of, for example, self-corrective feedback systems and not of purpose
and adaptation working towards some teleological end. This is a crucial point for
our explanation of meaning as a human attribute.

If we are intending to apply this general paradigm to the field of religious
studies it must embrace the notion of man as a symbolic animal. In particular it
must be asked what is being maintained or corrected through the systems at the
centre of which is man himself? Perhaps an analogy will facilitate the answer we
wish to give to this centrally pertinent question. It is easy to see that the homeostatic
or feedback systems of mammalian bodies serve, among other things, to maintain
a constant blood and body temperature as the creature enters into innumerable
relations with various environments. And as it is possible to talk of other physical
systems as maintaining energy levels, so we may say that meaning or power comprises
that state maintained by the ritual, symbolic, social and psychological systems
centred on the religious individual.

The general paradigm of meaning may be interpreted alongside general systems
theory to show that man and meaning are inextricably linked concepts. From the
history of religions perspective Werblowsky has said that 'the notion of man as a
builder of systems of meanings is a commonplace of philosophical as well as of
social and cultural anthropology', so too Zijderveld assumes that one of the essential
insights gained from philosophical anthropology is the fact that man bestows
meaning upon his environment.[7] But we need to go further than this if we are to
shed any light on the phenomena of evil and salvation. In fact we must emphasize
the qualitative aspect inherent in the negative valuation man places upon the
chaotic and frustrating facts of life. For the process of defining evil and of seeking
salvation involves more than a simple desire for order, it involves a moral dimension.
Man is not only semantic man but is also moral man. It is this element that is overlooked in much recent work in philosophical anthropology, even Clifford Geertz
whose work on the problem of meaning is exemplary refers in passing to moral
issues as theologically substantive ones.[8] That is to say, morality is left as an
essentially theological and varied datum rather than seen as intrinsic to the human
semantic endeavour. The notion of morality ought perhaps to be retrieved from
any specific theological usage so as to serve on a larger front, in much the same
way as we have redefined salvation. J. H. Morgan in his specific study of meaning
in anthropology and theology fails to see the necessity of this development being
overly concerned to demonstrate the semantic nature of man. But Morgan's book
does make one very clear contribution to our argument, albeit indirectly, in organising
a body of material all witnessing to the paradigm of meaning. The significance
of our present stress on the moral factor is in trying to make room for it in the

---

6 Bateson, Gregory, 1958. In a recent work, 1979, he discusses thought as an extension
of biological and natural systems.

7 Werblowsky, R. J. Z., 1976: 108. Zijderveld, A. C., 1970: 36. Cf. Roland Robertson,
1978: 84.

8 Geertz, Clifford, 1966; 24. 1971: 91 ff.

body of material which will inevitably become established and institutionalized as properly definitive of the bounds of meaning.[9]

So man is moral as he is semantic. He both identifies objects or states as evil and then sets himself against them, he possesses a commitment to what is ordered and deemed good and assumes an intellectual and emotional antipathy to whatever radically disrupts his life. But in no sense is this a modern thought for it lies at the very centre of Durkheim's view of the dichotomy between the sacred and the profane. His definition of religion refers to a moral community, and the positive valuation of aspects of life is essential for his conception of the role of religion in social solidarity. This is not the place for a full analysis but it would be an instructive exercise to reconsider Durkheim's sociological theory of knowledge in the light of more recent studies in meaning. One of the outcomes would be a deeper grasp of emotion or sentiment in the otherwise socially framed modes of cultural thought.

The interdisciplinary consequences of the moral and semantic issue are quite numerous. For example we might ask to what extent the religious quest for order in doctrines of creation and redemption are extensions of and qualitative transformation in the animal quest for a defined territory. Theologians would already find established traditions of interpretation as far as order is concerned, for according to Augustine order along with mode and form constituted the meaning of the good.[10] So too with John Calvin for whom the restoration of order by means of the church marks a restoring of the *imago Dei* in mankind.[11] The religious sense can in no way be divorced from that moral sense which is an inevitable component of social life. What the religious motivation does is to raise the level of significance of meaning to a point at which order may be viewed as invested with a divine quality, whether in the cosmos as a creation or within the soul as a redeemed and perhaps even recreated entity.

This is to view religious activity as an extension of ordinary human endeavour and it raises again the question of form and content as far as any comparative study of religions is concerned. For while all religions may be said to engage in similar activities the content of doctrinal or traditional schemes varies to a marked extent. Similarly while commitment to goals is a common feature of life it would be worthwhile analysing the distinctive features of commitment to religious foci of meaning and the identity ensuing therefrom. This would provide a sound basis for a theological discussion of religious anthropology. In this more directly religious direction we can cite as an example the great nineteenth century theologian and pastor P. T. Forsyth whose view that man possessed a 'deep human passion to be redeemed' could easily be explored through the paradigm of meaning, but who went further in a theological way to consider the 'holy passion of God to redeem'.[12] This theological opinion lies beyond the scholar of religion but is not alien to the mode of discourse we have been advocating as a general method. Involved in the question is the fact that man as Homo religiosus must be viewed additionally as both semantic and moral.

---

[9] Morgan, J. H. (Ed), 1979: 87 ff.
[10] Augustine, De natura boni. Cf. Thomas Aquinua, Summa. 1a. 103-109.
[11] Milner, B. C., 1970: 193.
[12] Forsyth, P. T., 1907: 81.

Man's semantic inclination can, of course, be divined in the world of mythology as Lévi-Strauss has done much to demonstrate. But the moral factor is itself often clearly manifested through the use of mythology in religions. So too in the case of symbolism, where emotional elements are affixed to both positive and negative evaluations of life. Theology as a formal discipline would be entirely emasculated if the groups possessing it were devoid of mythology and symbolism. Not only because any theology must entertain myths and symbols as basic data, but also because these very modes of religious life facilitate the implementation of abstract ideas, and mobilize the affective dimension of human response. It is this capacity to release emotional and personal responses to ideas which contributes to the difficulty in giving a specific definition of symbolism, as to the word 'meaning' itself.

Malcolm Crick has referred both to Chomsky who said that meaning was a 'catch-all term for those aspects of language which linguists knew very little about', and Max Black and his 'extraordinary shiftiness of the word meaning.[13] Similarly Dan Sperber thinks it 'impossible to circumscribe the notion of meaning in such a way that it may still apply to the relationship between symbols and their interpretation'.[14] Despite the fact that Sperber uses the word meaning in a more technical sense he highlights one feature of meaning construction involved in symbolic processes. As far as he is concerned 'meaning' should only be used to refer to 'intuitively perceived relations between signs – that is to say in particular those of paraphrase and analyticity'.[15] He disagrees with Lévi-Strauss' procedure of treating myths, along with social institutions like kinship, as semiological systems in any strict sense. Myths are not signs, the symbols of which myths are composed are not 'paired with their interpretations in a code structure; their interpretations are not meanings'.[16] Myths function more for individuals than for groups, they are open to idiosyncratic understanding. Even so we can argue that the understanding of myths and symbols is essentially part of a meaning construction process in terms of the general paradigm we have pursued in this book.[17] Symbolism is the product of a cognitive process which incorporates within itself a tacit knowledge of how to interpret myths and other discrete phenomena in much the same way that analytic statements in ordinary use are accepted as being self-evidently true. Here we are in fact following Sperber who believes that 'without explicit instruction all humans learn to treat symbolically information that defies direct conceptual treatment'.[18]

This defiance is significant and draws attention to the reason why symbolism, and mythology, and the idea of meaning, are all difficult to define and appear to possess a confused area of function. Primarily it is because these concepts refer to processes which relate the individual with his own sediments of private knowledge to the social group with its public consensus of ideas. Symbols and myths facilitate the communication of ideas which are concerned with emotional and commitment

---

13 Crick, Malcolm, 1976: 11.
14 Sperber, Dan, 1975: 13.
15 Ibid, p. 10.
16 Ibid, p. 85.
17 Cf. Ross Fitzgerald 1978 for a literary application of semantics.
18 Ibid., p. 148.

inducing factors. At the personal level they deal with notions which cannot be fully explicated by the individual to himself, let alone to another. For myths and symbols are much rooted in the implicit aspects of autobiography within the wider historical ground of a society. The question of definition can be answered by giving a clear understanding of what processes are at work without being able to offer full description of their inner working. What symbols and myths do is clear, how they effect it is necessarily vague because of the model of man adopted in this book and to which we turn in a moment.

So Sperber argued that the inherent drive for meaning directed into symbolic processes of thought those data which defied a directly logical solution. This would place the 'reasons of the heart' and other human modes of thought on a continuum of interpretation with the strictly rational types, in an overall scheme which admitted the need of both explicit and implicit; verbal, non-verbal, and pictorial and discursive schemes of handling ideas.

Not only so but the embarrassment over the fact that 'the term meaning has various meanings' can be dispelled by the paradigm of meaning inasmuch as man can be accorded a class of his own as a meaning constructing animal.[19] We have sought to describe the form of man's activity in creating and maintaining an integrated life rather than to specify doctrinal content, for as Bateson argued, anthropologists 'deal with meta relationships between messages' and not simply with ethnographic descriptions.[20] This theoretical and descriptive distinction is precisely what we have sought to embrace in the two parts of this book. Bateson was helped in his analysis of the Iatmul culture through the simple assertion that a class cannot be a member of itself. Taking this notion from Russell's theory of types he was enabled to relate the ethnographic material to his theoretical concerns, and this is also something which applies to our more phenomenological analysis of the notion of meaning. That which appears through the creative ordering and reordering of a self-conscious agent is of a logically different type than is found in any one preliminary set of data. In other words, the product of human meaning construction represents more than the sum total of each constituent part. It is at that high point of the meaning generation process that salvation is perceived as the outcome of many other kinds of life activity. Systems of cognitive and affective ideas involving symbolic, philosophical, and moral factors combine in that higher order system which manifests the attribute of salvation. Reductionism thus becomes quite inappropriate as a means of discussing this state of identity and integrity through which the life-world is held in a particular form of intentionality. By analogy, meaning in the human class would correspond to the temperature level maintained by a vascular system, and salvation itself would be the attribute of that achieved level of organization. Salvation could not be defined in terms of any one of the sub-systems contributing to its higher order existence. So even if it was argued that salvation is that state arising from a sense of identity conferred by some person or event it would not reduce the significance of that identity at all. The genetic fallacy must ever be borne in mind when looking at possible mechanics of

---

[19] Barnhardt, J. E., 1977: 159.
[20] Bateson, Gregory, 1958: 293.

religious life. Hans Mol's argument that man tends to confer a sense of awe and a status of sacredness upon whatever gives to him a strong sense of identity is an interesting and powerful thesis, but need not be read in a reductivist way.[21]

Several studies of salvation carried out through a comparative method at the beginning of the century go some way in identifying a variety of phenomena which were perceived as vehicles of salvation. But whatever the form of *der Heilbringer* it is the creative utilization of folk heroes or nature myths by semantic and moral man that leads to a sense of salvation.[22] The precise material comprising the information of each religious salvation process is the subject matter of the history and phenomenology of religion and many good examples of such studies have been carried out. But it is the theoretical and more interdisciplinary aspect of the semantic and moral processes of life that we have sought to develop in this book.[23]

Such a philosophical anthropology which is able to handle the human perception of a higher order state of meaning might be particularly useful to scholars of religion in enabling them to continue their own discussion beyond the point usually reached in customary argument. Once factors from a wide range of subjects are introduced into a narrow field the possibility of fruitful results at least presents itself for testing.

For example, it is interesting to ask whether studies on the consequences of literacy have anything to contribute to the emergence of abstract and idealized concepts of salvation. Jack Goody has shown that 'literacy and classroom education brings a shift towards greater abstractness, towards the decontextualization of knowledge'.[24] This implies that as legitimating events and procedures have been subject to increasing systematic abstraction, so the notion of salvation – interpreted as a state of ultimate identity and security – has become less associated with ordinary life-world structures. As religions become applicable to non-tribal or non-ethnic groups so the conception of salvation becomes less immediately relative and specific. It is perhaps not insignificant to observe that it was the cosmopolitan Mediterranean world that saw the birth of a Christian idea of universal salvation effected by a divine man whose significance transcended his Jewish origin. The rise of texts and of exegetical, dogmatic, and apologetic traditions all make possible a positive decontextualization of salvific events. Indeed the much later institutionalizing of the eucharist in the Mass effected a universal recontextualizing of the sacrifice of Christ, but this was possible only because the theological ideas underpinning the rite had been arrived at through abstract philosophizing.

Much of what we have said so far could be summarized in Mircea Eliade's position adopted in his magnum opus *A History of Religious Ideas* where he asserts that 'every rite, every myth, every belief or divine figure reflects the experience of the sacred and hence implies the notion of *being*, of *meaning*, and of *truth*'.[25] Eliade stresses the positive side of life here, while we have emphasized in addition the negative elements in relation to which the sense of salvation arises. Indeed our

---

21 Mol, Hans, 1976
22 Breysig, K., 1905; Ehrenreich, P., 1906; Van Deursen, A., 1931.
23 Werblowsky, R. J. Z. and C. J. Bleeker, 1970.
24 Goody, Jack, 1977: 13.
25 Eliade, Mircea, 1979: 2. Original emphases.

argument might be seen as an extended gloss on William James' conclusion to the study of religious experience that man's religiosity is grounded in a basic uneasiness about life and in a consequent search for a resolution to the wrongness.[26]

It now remains to take up the question of the focus of action in processes of meaning construction and in the emergence of a sense of salvation. The two obvious ways of approaching the issue are essentially deficient. On the one hand we could invoke the notion of society as the basic context within which meaning is generated, this was the way followed by Durkheim and Berger. On the other hand we could identify the private self as the source of all significant thought and reflection, the way adopted by Déscartes and the whole rationalist tradition which culminated in Kant's Copernican revolution. The reason why we chose another view is the same reason why the dichotomy between society and self is inadequate.

If we adopt the word social-person for the unit central to our concluding comments we will be able to bridge this gap between self and society, and also make it clear that the unit or concept represents a higher order phenomenon than is usually conceived when reference is made to the individual as a lone entity. The social-person requires an identification as of a different order from that of any single system comprising its total reality. Both Déscartes and Durkheim serve as typical exponents of that reductionism which isolates a sub-system of the human creature and magnifies it to a prime position. The reductionist fallacy can only be seen in its full error in the light of a general systems theory and the paradigm of meaning and salvation. Déscartes for example employed language as a neutral tool rather than as a socially existing and given phenomenon. A more truly phenomenological approach assumes that language is essentially social and therefore presupposes the existence of other interacting selves. Déscartes felt able to use language as the means of his private meditations by which he could seriously doubt that existence of others. Similarly Durkheim reified the notion of society, rather than that of self, though at least he recognised the difficulty involved in this as his concept of man as Homo duplex shows. Durkheim's problem lay in integrating the individual and social aspects of Homo duplex, a task in which he ultimately failed. Stephen Lukes thinks this difficulty arose from Durkheim's conviction that there was 'an underlying ontological distinction between levels of reality', with individuals and society occupying discrete locations. Lukes cites Ginsberg's comment on Durkheim to the effect that the notion of society 'had an intoxicating effect on his mind'.[27] For Durkheim there does exist a firm dichotomy between the bodily aspect of persons, which he calls 'the organism', and their social or collective aspect.[28] It is as though the latter had been superimposed upon the former dimension during the process of evolution.

It was unfortunate that William Robertson Smith, who so influenced Durkheim, himself introduced a distinction between the self and group in his famous dictum that for primeval man 'religion did not exist for the saving of souls but for the preservation and welfare of society'.[29] This accords well with Philip Rieff's shrewd

[26] James, William, 1902: 508.
[27] Lukes, Stephen, 1975: 417.
[28] Durkheim, Emile, 1976: 16.
[29] Smith, W. R., 1894: 29.

aligning of Freud with D. H. Lawrence as sharers in that sociological position dominant from the second quarter of the nineteenth century according to which 'the self is society individualized'. Rieff has cogently and powerfully shown how the 'historic Western binge of inwardness, the socialized individual self' lies at the heart of modern neuroses, for the inner man is set at odds with his outer social self and conduct.[30] In our concept of the social-person the focus of integrity is not restricted to either the private or public domains but to their transcending synthesis and transformation. The term social-person emphasizes man's bodily aspect with all its organic systems, and the social dimensions with their contributory systems. Thus both affective and cognitive, as well as intuitive and socially understood ideas and sensations can be coped with through this view. In one sense it is the secularization of discourse that has made the choice of name necessary, for one of the benefits of the word soul lay in that very degree of autonomy and transcendence devoid of nihilistic introversion which we seek to establish in the concept of the social-person.

So while partial descriptions of the social-person as enshrined in the Homo nouns such as H. economicus, H. socialis, H. religiosus etc., may serve useful heuristic functions in restricted cases, they have 'nothing to do with the essence of man' as Ralph Dahrendorf says, but only with models of social action.[31] In similar vein Dorothy Emmett has questioned the opposite tendency to overemphasize the romantic notion of the bare subjective 'I'.[32] More within the context of theology Reinhold Niebuhr sees no place for individuality in either pure mind or pure nature.[33] Indeed this brings us back to a powerful undercurrent in Wilhelm Dilthey's view of man. For him *individuum est ineffabile* and cannot ultimately be approached in any way other than that of a hermeneutics of the human spirit which transcends and invalidates all partial explanations.

In the realm of literature this point has been well made by George Steiner who thinks the 'least inadequate' definition of man is *zoon phonanta*. By this Steiner directs attention to the semantic realm which he thinks will afford an overcoming of any simple psychological distinction between a mind-body empiricism.[34] On the theological front much attention has, of course, been given to language, but perhaps Austin Farrer might be singled out in his emphasizing the role of language in man's spiritual self-evaluation, in the emergence of reason and even in the possibility of the birth of ideas of God.[35]

It is precisely because the social-person is the irreducible unit of phenomenological analysis, being the point of convergence of many systems, that it is appropriate to describe this category as integrated and intransigent. Integrated inasmuch as it is the social-person who assimilates environmental systems to his internal system, and intransigent because no amount of reductionist explanation can fully give account of the total entity. One of the earliest sociologists of religion to urge this position was Joachim Wach who draws on Kierkegaard's notion of the individual (*der*

---

30 Rieff, Philip, 1973: 174.
31 Dahrendorf, Ralph, 1973: 88.
32 Emmett, Dorothy, 1966: 178.
33 Niebuhr, Reinhold, 1943: 15 ff.
34 Steiner, George, 1971: 73, 76.
35 Farrer, Austin, 1966: 106 ff.

Einzelne) as the basic sociological and religious category.[36] Because of the potential for individual creativity, a creativity which can issue into a public movement, Wach was careful to assert the peculiar dialectic of religious experience.[37] Once the entire complexity of the social-person is admitted it becomes improper to talk of man as, for example, possessing a body. That very verb implies a dualistic and potentially reductionist tendency to divide between body and mind. So too references to people holding beliefs rather than expressing or manifesting them can give a biased impression of abstract realities purveyed by materialistic agents. Man's complexity also admits of a certain opacity of the individual both towards himself and towards others. He cannot fully explicate himself nor can he fully comprehend others.[38] In Alfred Schutz' phenomenology this means that other selves along with the realms of nature and culture transcend the individual. Here symbolic processes come into their own as a means of interaction and communication between discrete agents, whilst also allowing individual interpretation of some aspects of the shared units of communication. What this implies is not that symbolism is undefinable but that its defined processes reach to opaque areas of life.

Several major criticisms could be made of this emphasis upon the notion of social-person. First it could be said to be nothing other than an ethnocentric model of the individual. D. M. Schneider, although in a different context, has spoken of the 'Western conception of the person as a bounded, unique, more or less integrated motivational and cognitive universe, a dynamic centre of awareness, emotion, judgement and action organized into a distinctive whole and set contrastively both against other such wholes and against its social and natural background'.[39] He thinks this ideal type, however incorrigible it may seem to us, to be a rather peculiar idea within the context of the world's cultures. Our desire in this book has not been to perpetuate a cultural model but to arrive at a model which can cope with a variety of data. The fact that the social-person approximates to a cultural ideal is gratuitous to the fact that it is an expression demanded by the paradigm of meaning.

Occasions may well arise when the scholar's model of man resembles that of his own culture. While the sociologist of knowledge will always be interested in such correlations the negative preoccupation of relativizing the relativizers should not be allowed to disqualify any potentially useful model. The social anthropologist is not, of course, immune from his hated error of ethnocentrism but his own concern with problems of classification and cultural translation of ideas does alert him to potential dangers.[40]

A final point of criticism is more orthodoxly sociological in its focus on culture as that concept to which the individual needs to be related. Marshall Sahlins affords a clear example of this stance which replaces our notion of social-person with the primacy of culture. 'Meaning', he says, 'is the specific property of the anthropological object' which is nothing less than culture itself.[41] Sahlins is aware of the idealist tendency of thought which almost inevitably attends any abstract discussion

---

[36] Wach, Joachim, 1944: 33.
[37] Ibid, p. 110.
[38] Jourard, S. M., 1971 discusses self-disclosure and transparency.
[39] Schneider, D. M. in K. H. Basso and H. A. Kelley, 1976: 225.
[40] Ellen, R. F. and David Reason, 1979.
[41] Sahlins, Marshall, 1976: x.

and he wants to avoid it. His well intentioned desire is also ours and motivates the stress on the concept of the social-person rather than that of culture or the sacred, for it must be admitted that Eliade reifies the notion of the sacred at least as much as Durkheim did that of society. It is the social-person who remains the integrated and intransigent locus of meaning and of salvation, whether as a creator and innovator of salvation for himself and others, or as a follower who engages in established means of salvation.

Having adopted this model of man and religious man it becomes possible to reconsider many problems which have caused an impasse in religious studies. The question of world and village levels of religiosity can, for example, be re-examined in terms of the individual who integrates varied strands of the great and little tradition. And who does so under the restraints of the drive for moral meanings set against negative obstacles. Or again Cantwell Smith's important suggestion that religious men mediate between accumulated tradition and their personal faith.[43] Similarly our model goes some way to show why the phenomenology of the religious individual has been so significant in the work of men like Rudolph Otto and Friedrich Heiler, and why some anthropologists such as Stanner and Evans-Pritchard have felt that even when a full sociological account has been rendered there remains an unaccounted for aspect of life. While it may be appropriate to turn the study over to the professional theologian at that point for him to paint his particular picture on the dark canvass unearthed by the phenomenologist and anthropologist, it would be quite inappropriate to end the study in a confused methodological cul-de-sac. We have sought to identify the basic features of salvation states as constituting a level of meaning which is perceived as salvation. That is, the form of a salvation state irrespective of any particular theological content. Whether that content is shamanic possession for the purpose of community healing, or one of 'being grasped by an ultimate concern ... which contains the answer to the question of the meaning of our life' is irrelevant.[43] Indeed Tillich's notion of ultimate concern and ultimate meaning is a theological model closely aligned to the paradigm of meaning in sociology. Both express the power of existentialist thought over wide ranges of academic endeavours.

Throughout this book we have sought to enliven the 'silence lying between anthropology and the history of religions', and to describe religious phenomena in a way that will enable theologians to reconsider their own doctrines of man and knowledge.[44] While much has been left unsaid and the praise of many, including Mary Douglas whose discussion of the symbolic body has much to contribute to the paradigm of meaning in theology, has remained unsung, we have sought to draw attention to the nature of salvation as an extension of the human drive for meaning, and have indicated that moral factors cannot be ignored in man's perception of a world with which he is not totally content.

---

42 Smith, W. C., 1963.
43 Tillich, Paul, 1963: 4. Cf. Wells, D. F., 1978.
44 Douglas, Mary, 1978: 81. Cf. Douglas, 1970 for symbolic bodies.

BIBLIOGRAPHY

Abel, et. al. Religions de salut. Annals du Centre d'Etude des Religions, 2, 1962.

Allen, Douglas. Structure and Creativity in Religion. Mouton, The Hague, 1978.

Aquinas, Thomas. Summa Theologiae. Blackfriars, Oxford, 1970.

Austin, J. L. Philosophical Papers. Clarendon Press, Oxford, 1961.

Banton, Michael. Anthropological Approaches to the Study of Religion. Tavistock, London, 1966.

--------. Racial Minorities in Britain. Fontana, London, 1972.

Barnhardt, J. E. The Study of Religion and its Meaning. Mouton, The Hague, 1977.

Basso, K. H. and H. A. Selby (Eds). Meaning in Anthropology. Univ. of New Mexico Press, 1976.

Bateson, Gregory. Naven. California Univ. Press, 1936. Second Edition, 1958.

--------. Steps to an Ecology of Mind. Paladin, 1973.

--------. Mind and Culture. Wildwood, London, 1979.

Beattie, John. In M. C. F. Bourdillon and Meyer Fortes, 1980.

Bellah, R. N. Beyond Belief. Harper and Row, New York, 1970.

Benson, Herbert. The Relaxation Response. Collins, London, 1977.

Benz, Ernst. 'On Understanding Non-Christian Religions' in Mircea Eliade, 1959.

Berger, P. L. The Social Reality of Religion. Penguin, London, 1969.

--------. Rumour of Angels. Pelican, London, 1971.

Berger, P. L. and Thomas Luckmann. The Social Construction of Reality. Penguin, London, 1967.

Bertalanffy, L. v. General Systems Theory. Allen Lane, London, 1971.

Bettis, J. D. Phenomenology of Religion. S. C. M. Press, London, 1969.

Binyon, L. Akbar. Peter Davies, London, 1932.

Black, J. S. and G. W. Chrystal. William Robertson Smith. A. and C. Black Edinburgh 1912 (a).

--------. William Robertson Smith, Lectures. A. and C. Black, Edinburgh 1912 (b).

Blakeslee, T. R. The Right Brain. Macmillan, London, 1980.

Bourdillon, M. C. F. Meyer Fortes. Sacrifice. Academic Press for the Royal Anthropological Institute, London, 1980.

Bowker, John. The Sense of God. Oxford University Press, 1973.

--------. The Religious Imagination and the Sense of God. Oxford Univ. Press, 1978.

--------. Believing In The Church, S. P. C. K. 1981.

Boyd, W. J. Satan and Mara. E. J. Brill, Leiden, 1975.

Brandon, S. G. F. Man and His Destiny in the World Religions. Manchester University Press, 1963.

------. The Saviour God, Comparative Studies in the Concept of Salvation presented to E. O. James, Manchester Univ. Press, 1963.

Breysig, K. Die Entstehung des Gottesgedankens und der Heilbringer. Berlin, Bondi, 1905.

Burridge, Kenelm. New Heaven New Earth. Blackwell, Oxford, 1969.

Cohen, A. In Ioan Lewis (Ed), 1977.

Cohn, N. The Pursuit of the Millennium. Paladin, 1970. First published by Secker and Warburg, 1957.

Cole, O. and P. S. Sambhi. The Sikhs. Routledge and Kegan Paul, London, 1979.

Cox, Harvey. The Secular City. Pelican, 1968. The Feast of Fools. Harper and Row, 1969. The Seduction of the Spirit. Wildwood House, 1974.

Crick, Malcolm. Explorations in Language and Meaning. Malaby Press, 1976.

Dahrendorf, Ralph. Homo socialis. Routledge and Kegan Paul, London, 1973.

Davies, D. J. The Mormons of Merthyr Tydfil. Oxford B. Litt Thesis, 1972.

--------. 'Aspects of Latter Day Saint Eschatology' in Michael Hill, 1973.

--------. 'Frank Byron Jevons and Primitive Mentality'. In DYN, The Journal of the Durham Univ. Anthropological Society, 1975.

--------. 'Sacrifice in Leviticus'. Zeitschrift für die Alttestamentliche Wissenschaft, 89. Band 1977.

--------. 'The Notion of Salvation in the Comparative Study of Religions'. RELIGION Vol. 8. 1978.

--------. The notion of Meaning and Salvation in Religious Studies. Nottingham Ph. D. Thesis, 1979.

Davies, D. J. 'Theologies in Code'. Research Bulletin Univ. of Birmingham Institute for the Study of Worship and Architecture. Edited by J. G. Davies, 1981.
——. 'Sacrifice in Theology and Anthropology'. Scottish Journal of Theology, Spring 1982.
Davis, Charles. Christ and the World's Religions. Hodder and Stoughton, 1970.
Deursen, A. van. Der Heilbringer. Batavia, 1931.
Dhavamony, M. Phenomenology of Religion. Gregorian University Press, Rome, 1973.
Dilthey, Wilhelm. Einleitung in die Geisteswissenschaften, 1883.
——. Ideen über eine beschreibende und zergliedernde Psychologie, 1894.
——. Das Erlebnis und die Dichtung, 1905.
——. Die Typen der Weltanschauungen, 1911.
Doctrine and Convenants. Independence Missouri: Herald Publishing House, 1970.
Dolan, J. P. Catholic Revivalism and the American Experience. Notre Dame University Press, 1978.
Douglas, Mary. Purity and Danger. Routledge and Kegan Paul, London, 1966.
——. Natural Symbols. Pelican, London, 1970.
——. (Ed). Witchcraft Conflicts and Accusations. Tavistock, London, 1970.
——. Implicit Meanings, Routledge and Kegan Paul, London, 1975.
Dupre, Wilhelm. Religion in Primitive Culture: A Study in Ethnophilosophy. Mouton, The Hague, 1975.
Durkheim, Emile. The Elementary Forms of the Religious Life. Allen Lane, 1976. (1st Ed. 1912).
Durkheim, Emile and M. Mauss. Primitive Classification. Cohen and West, London, 1963.
Ebeling, Gerhardt. Introduction to a Theology of Language. Collins, London, 1973.
Ehrenreich, P. Gotter und Heilbringer. Zeitschrift für Ethnologie. 38. 1906.
Eliade, Mircea. Sacred and Profane. Harper and Row, New York, 1957.
——. Cosmos and History. Harper and Row, New York, 1959.
——. 'Crisis and Renewal in the History of Religions'; in HISTORY OF RELIGIONS Vol. 4, No. 1, 1964.
——. 'The Quest for the Origin of Religion'; in HISTORY OF RELIGIONS Vol. 5, No. 1, 1965.
——. Myths, Dreams and Mysteries. Fontana, New York, 1968.
——. The Quest. Chicago University Press, 1969.
——. Australian Religions. Cornel University Press, 1973.
——. No Souvenirs. Routledge and Kegan Paul, London, 1978.
——. A History of Religious Ideas. Collins, London, 1979.
—— and J. M. Kitagawa. The History of Religions. Chicago University Press, 1959.
Ellen, R. F. and David Reason. Classifications in their Social Context. Academic Press, London, 1979.
Elliott-Binns, L. E. Religion in the Victorian Era. Lutterworth, London, 1946, 1964.
Emmett, Dorothy. Rules, Roles, and Relations. MacMillan, London, 1966.
Evans-Pritchard, E. E. Witchcraft, Oracles and Magic among the Azande. Clarendon Press, Oxford, 1937.
——. The Nuer. Clarendon Press, Oxford, 1940. Nuer Religion. Clarendon Press, Oxford, 1956. Essays in Social Anthropology. Faber, London, 1962. Theories of Primitive Religion. Clarendon Press, Oxford, 1965.
Farrer, Austin, Love Almighty and Ills Unlimited, London, 1966.
Feuerbach, Ludwig. The Essence of Christianity. Harper and Row, London, 1957.
Firth, Raymond. Essays on Social Organization and Values. Athlone, London, 1964.
Fitzgerald, Ross. Ed. What it Means to be Human. Pergamon Press, 1978.
Forsyth, P. T. Positive Preaching and the Modern Mind. Independent Press, 1907.
Foster, M. L. and S. H. Brandes. Symbol as Sense. Academic Press, 1980.
Fraxer, J. G. The Golden Bough. MacMillan, London, 1963.
Freud, Sigmund. Totem and Taboo, Routledge and Kegan Paul, London, 1960.
——. The Future of an Illusion. Hogarth Press, 1973 (Ed).
Fürer-Haimendorf, C. von. 'The sense of sin in cross-cultural perspective'. In MAN, Vol. 9, No. 4. 1974.
Geertz, Clifford. 'Religion as a Cultural System'. In Michael Banton, 1966.
——. Islam Observed. University of Chicago Press, 1971.
Glock, C. Y. and R. Stark. Religion and Society in Tension. Rand McNally, New York, 1965.
Goody, Jack. The Domestication of the Savage Mind. Cambridge Univ. Press, 1977.
Grabner-Haider, Anton. Semiotik und Theologie. Kosel-Verlag München, 1973.
Grewal, J. S. 'The Prem. Samurag: A Theory of Sikh Social Order'. In PROCEEDINGS OF THE PUNJAB HISTORY CONFERENCE, 1965.

Hayes, E. N., and Tanya Hayes. Claude Lévi-Strauss. The Anthropologist as Hero. Cambridge Massachusetts University Press, 1970.
Hebblethwaite, Brian. Evil, Suffering and Religion. Sheldon, London, 1976.
Heiler, Friederich. Das Gebet. München, 1920. (Eng. tr. Prayer. 1932).
Heise, David. 'Sociology of Mission'. JOURNAL OF THE SCIENTIFIC STUDY OF RELIGION. Spring, 1967.
Hershman, Paul. 'Virgin and Mother'. In Ioan Lewis, 1977.
Hill, Michael. (Ed.). The Sociological Yearbook of Religion. S. C. M. London, 1973.
Hultkranz, Ake. 'Anthropological Approaches to Religion'. In HISTORY OF RELIGIONS, Vol. 9, No. 4. 1970.
Huxley, Aldous. The Perennial Philosophy. Chatto and Windus, London, 1947.
INSPIRED VERSION OF THE BIBLE. Herald Publishing House, Independence Missouri, 1965 (1884).
James, E. O. Christian Myth and Ritual. John Murray, London, 1933 (a).
‐‐‐‐‐‐‐‐‐. Origins of Sacrifice. John Murray, London, 1933 (b).
‐‐‐‐‐‐‐‐‐. Comparative Religion. Methuen, London, 1938.
‐‐‐‐‐‐‐‐‐. The Social Function of Religion. Hodder, London, 1940.
‐‐‐‐‐‐‐‐‐. Sacrifice and Sacrament. Thames and Hudson. London, 1962.
James, William. The Varieties of Religious Experience. Longmans, London, 1902.
Jammu, P. S. 'Religion in a Malwa Village'. JOURNAL REL. STUDS. Patiala, 1974.
Jevons, F. B. Introduction to the History of Religions. Methuen, London, 1896.
‐‐‐‐‐‐‐‐‐. Introduction to the Study of Comparative Religion. MacMillan, 1908.
Jourard, S. M. Self-Disclosure. Wiley, New York, 1971.
Juergensmeyer, M. and N.G. Barrier. Sikh Studies. Graduate Theological Union, Berkeley, 1979.
Karsten, R. The Origins of Religion. Kegan Paul and Trench, London, 1935.
Kitagawa, J. M. Understanding and Believing. Essays by Joachim Wach. Harper, New York, 1968.
‐‐‐‐‐‐‐‐‐. 'The History of Religion in America'. In Eliade and Kitagawa, 1969.
Kuhn, T. S. The Structure of Scientific Revolutions. Chicago University Press, Second Edition, 1976.
Lang, Andrew. The Making of Religion. Longmans, London, 1900.
Lanternari, V. The Religions of the Oppressed. Alfred Knopf, New York, 1963.
Leach, Edmund. Political Systems in Highland Burma. Bell and Sons, London, 1954.
‐‐‐‐‐‐‐‐‐. Dialectic in Practical Religion. Cambridge Univ. Press, 1968.
‐‐‐‐‐‐‐‐‐. Culture and Communication. Cambridge Univ. Press, 1976.
Leeuw, G. van der. Religion in Essence and Manifestation. Peter Smith, Glucester Mass., 1967. First Published in 1933 as Phanomenologie der Religion.
Lévi-Strauss, C. Les structures elementaires de la parente. Paris, 1949.
‐‐‐‐‐‐‐‐‐. Tristes Tropiques. Paris, 1955; New York, 1968.
‐‐‐‐‐‐‐‐‐. Totemism. London Merlin Press, 1962.
‐‐‐‐‐‐‐‐‐. Structural Anthropology. Allen Lane, London, 1963. The Raw and the Cooked. Jonathan Cape, London, 1964.
‐‐‐‐‐‐‐‐‐. Structural Anthropology, Volume Two. Allen Lane, London, 1977.
Lévy-Bruhl, L. La mentalité primitive, Paris, 1923.
Lewis, Ioan. Ecstatic Religion. Pelican, London, 1971.
‐‐‐‐‐‐‐‐‐. (Ed). Symbols and Sentiments. Academic Press, London, 1977.
Ling, Trevor. The Buddha. Temple Smith, London, 1973.
Lukes, Steven. Emile Durkheim. Peregrine, London, 1975.
Mannheim, K. Essays on the Sociology of Knowledge. Routledge, London, 1952.
Marett, R. R. The Threshold of Religion. Methuen, London, 1909. (4th Ed. 1929).
‐‐‐‐‐‐‐‐‐. Sacraments of Simple Folk. Clarendon Press, Oxford, 1933.
‐‐‐‐‐‐‐‐‐. Anthropology. Williams and Norgate, London. Undated.
Martin, David. The Religious and the Secular. Routledge. Kegan Paul, London, 1969.
‐‐‐‐‐‐‐‐‐. A General Theory of Secularization, Blackwells Oxford, 1978.
‐‐‐‐‐‐‐‐‐, J. O. Mills and W. S. F. Pickering. Sociology and Theology. Harvester Press, 1980.
McConkie, B. IMPROVEMENT ERA March 1961. Church of Jesus Christ Latter Day Saints.
McKinney, R. W. A. (Ed). Creation, Christ, and Culture. T. & T. Clark, Edinburgh, 1976.
McLeod, W. H. Guru Nanak and the Sikh Religion. Oxford Univ. Press, Delhi, 1968.
‐‐‐‐‐‐‐‐‐. Evolution of the Sikh Community. Oxford Univ. Press, Delhi, 1975.
‐‐‐‐‐‐‐‐‐. Early Sikh Tradition. Clarendon Press Oxford, 1980.
Milner, B. C. Calvin's Doctrine of the Church. Brill, Leiden, 1970.

Mol, Hans. Identity and the Sacred. Blackwell, Oxford, 1976.
----------. (Ed). Religion and Identity. Sage Publications, London, 1978.
Morgan, J. H. Understanding Religion and Culture. Univ. of America Press, 1979.
Müller, Max. Origin and Growth of Religion. Longman's London, 1882.
----------. Natural Religion. Longman's London, 1889.
Munz, Peter. Relationship and Solitude. Wesleyan Univ. Press, 1964.
Natanson, M. (Ed). Alfred Schutz. Nijhoff, The Hague, 1973.
Needham, Rodney. Belief, Language and Experience. Blackwell, Oxford, 1972.
Nesbitt, E. M. Aspects of Sikh Tradition in Nottingham. Unpublished M. Phil. Thesis of
    Nottingham University, 1980.
Niebuhr, Reinhold. The Nature and Destiny of Man. Nesbit, London, 1943.
Nock, A. D. Conversion. Clarendon Press, Oxford, 1933.
Obelkevich, James. Religion and Rural Society: South Lindsey 1825-1875. Clarendon Press
    Oxford, 1976.
Orans, Martin. The Santal. Wayne University Press Detroit, 1965.
Otto, Rudolph. The Idea of the Holy. Oxford University Press, 1924.
Oxtoby, W. G. 'Reflections on the idea of Salvation'. In E. J. Sharpe and J. R. Hinnells, 1973.
Parsons, T. Introduction to Max Weber's The Sociology of Religion, Methuen, London, 1922.
Popper, K. The Open Society and its Enemies. Routledge and Kegan Paul, 1966.
Radhakrishnan, S. Sacred Writings of the Sikhs. Allen and Unwin, London, 1960.
Rickman, H. P. W. Dilthey Selected Writings. Cambridge Univ. Press, 1976.
----------. Wilhelm Dilthey: Pioneer of Human Studies. Cambridge Univ. Press, 1979.
Ricoeur, Paul. L'Homme faillible. Vols. 1 and 2. Aubier, Paris, 1960.
Rieff, Philip. The Triumph of the Therapeutic. Penguin, 1973.
Robertson, R. The Sociological Interpretation of Religion. Blackwells, 1978.
Roche, M. Phenomenology, Language and the Social Sciences. Routledge and Kegan Paul, 1973.
Rogerson, J. W. Myth in Old Testament Studies. De Gruyter, Berlin, 1974.
----------. Anthropology and the Old Testament, Blackwell Oxford, 1979.
Russell, J. B. The Devil. Cornell University Press, 1977.
Sahlins, M. Culture and Practical Reason. Chicago Univ. Press, 1976.
Saliba, J. A. Homo Religiosus in Mircea Eliade. Brill, Leiden, 1976.
Schimmel, A. M. 'Summary of the Discussion'. NUMEN 7, 1960.
Schmidt, W. The Origin and Growth of Religion. Methuen, London, 1935 (2nd Ed.).
Schneider, D. M. In K. H. Basso and H. A. Kelley, 1976.
Scholte, B. 'Levi-Strauss's Unfinished Symphony'. In E. N. Hayes, 1970.
Schutz, A. Collected Papers. In Maurice Natanson, 1973.
Sharpe, E. J. Comparative Religion. Duckworth, London, 1975.
--------- & J. R. Hinnells. Man and His Salvation. Manchester University Press, 1973.
Sherrington, C. Man on His Nature. Cambridge Univ. Press, 1946.
Sidhu, G. S. et al. The Saint-Soldier. Sikh Missionary Society, Gravesend, 1974.
Singer, Andre. Evans-Pritchard. Faber, 1981.
Singh, Kushwant. A History of the Sikhs. Oxford University Press, Delhi, 1977.
Smith, W. C. The Meaning and End of Religion. MacMillan New York, 1963.
Smith, W. R. Religion of the Semites. A. and C. Black Edinburgh, 1894.
Sperber, Dan. Rethinking Symbolism. Cambridge University Press, 1975.
----------. In M. L. Foster and S. H. Brandes, 1980.
Spiro, M. Burmese Supernaturalism. Prentice Hall, Englewood Cliffs, 1967.
Stanner, W. E. H. 'On Aboriginal Religion'. OCEANIA, Vol. 30.
Steiner, Franz. Taboo. Penguin, London, 67. (First Edition, 1959).
Steiner, George. Extraterritorial. Faber and Faber, London, 1972.
Tambiah, S. J. 'The Magical Power of Words'. MAN Vol. 3 No. 2. 1968.
----------. Buddishm and the Spirit Cults. Cambridge Univ. Press, 1970.
Tillich, Paul. Systematic Theology. Nisbet, London, 1953.
----------. Christianity and the Encounter of World Religions. Columbia Univ. Press, 1963.
Troeltsch, E. The Social Teachings of the Christian Churches. MacMillan, New York, 1931.
Trumpp, E. The Adi Granth. Manoharlal, Delhi, 1970.
Turnbull, Colin. Wayward Servants. Eyre and Spottiswoode, London, 1965.
----------. The Mountain People, Pan Books, London, 1972.
Turner, V. The Forest of Symbols. Cornel University Press, 1967.
----------. The Ritual Process. Routledge and Kegan Paul, London, 1969.
Tylor, E. B. Primitive Culture. Harper, New York, 1958.

Uberoi, J. P. S. Sikhism. Patiala University Press, 1969.
Wach, J. Sociology of Religion. Chicago Univ. Press, 1944.
————. The Comparative Study of Religions. Columbia Univ. Press, 1958.
————. Ed. J. M. Kitagawa. Understanding and Believing. New York, 1968.
Wansbrough, J. The Sectarian Milieu. Oxford University Press, 1978.
Weber, M. The Sociology of Religion. Methuen, London, 1963. (1st. Ed. 1922).
————. The Protestant Ethic. Allen and Unwin, London, 1976.
Wells, D. F. The Search for Salvation. I.V.P. London, 1978.
Werblowsky, R. J. Z. Beyond Tradition and Modernity. Athlone Press, London, 1976.
———— & C. J. Bleeker. Types of Redemption. Brill, Leiden, 1970.
Werner, Karel. Yoga and Indian Philosophy. Motilal Banarsidas, Delhi, 1977.
Whitehead, A. N. Religion in the Making. Ca Brodge Univ. Press, 1930.
Wilson, B. R. Religion in Secular Society. Pelican, London, 1966.
————. Rationality. Blackwells, Oxford, 1970 (a).
————. Religious Sects. World University Library, 1970 (b).
————. Magic and the Millenium. Heinemann, London, 1973.
————. Contemporary Transformations of Religion. Oxford, 1976.
————. Religion in Sociological Perspective. Oxford Univ. Press, 1982.
Worsley, P. The Trumpet Shall Sound. Paladin, London, 1970.
Zijderveld, A. C. The Abstract Society. Allen Lane, London, 1970.

INDEX

DATE DUE

JAN 07 1997		
APR 06 2000		
		Printed in USA

TECHNOLOGY, TRUST, AND RELIGION

Cover design: Maedium, Utrecht
Lay out: V-3 Services, Baarn

ISBN   978 90 8728 059 8
e-ISBN 978 90 4850 792 4
NUR   706

Technology, Trust, and Religion

Roles of Religions in Controversies on Ecology and
the Modification of Life

Edited by
Willem B. Drees

LEIDEN UNIVERSITY PRESS

Table of Contents

Preface and Acknowledgements

Technology is a major dimension of human existence, and a major force for change, for better or for worse. Ecological concerns have become prominent in the last decades. They thus become issues of human concern and of human values – issues that merit religious reflection, and thus also trigger reflections on the role of religions in modern, secular and pluralist societies, where the appeal to traditions has been challenged.

In the context of the programme *The Future of the Religious Past* by NWO, the Netherlands Organisation for Scientific Research, a project was funded on religion, ecology and technology. The project is titled *Misplaced Vocabularies: Scientific and Religious Notions in Public Discourses on Ecology and Genetics.* The principal researcher of the project is Willem B. Drees, professor of philosophy of religion and ethics at Leiden University. As a postdoctoral fellow in this project, Tony Watling surveyed the multireligious literature on ecology. The project also encompasses a PhD project by Olga Crapels on religion in public discourses on genetics.

Drees, Watling, Crapels, and Taede Smedes, another postdoctoral fellow working on religion and science, formerly at Leiden University, organized a conference on religion, technology and public concern, which was held at Leiden University, the Netherlands, in October 2006. Several essays from this symposium were selected for this volume. In the editorial process, Drees received extensive assistance from Renée Reitsma, a masters student in the philosophy of religion, and John Flanagan, a Ph. D. candidate in Old Testament Studies, both at the Faculty of Religious Studies of Leiden University, now the Leiden Institute for Religious Studies. The conference, their careful editorial help, and the publication of this volume has been made possible by the grant from NWO, the Netherlands

Organization for Scientific Research. Drees is also grateful to the Center of Theological Inquiry, Princeton, USA, where he was the J. Houston Witherspoon Fellow for Theology and the Natural Sciences in 2008-2009, while completing the editorial work on this book.

Technology, Trust, and Religion

Willem B. Drees

We live in a technological culture. Our identities and our responsibilities, our hopes, dreams, and nightmares are all shaped by rapidly evolving technology and its impact on our environment. What is it to be human if we are dependent upon technological artifacts and systems? What concepts of 'the natural' and 'the sacred' are invoked by the accusation of 'playing God'? Will technology transform our religious and humanistic traditions? And will our traditions shape our technological culture? What is the role of religion in relation to public concerns about technology? Is religion a brake upon technological possibilities, a valuable guide that might helps us in the choices we face, or, is religion itself in flux, slowly adapting to new powers?

Are we destroying our natural habitat with biotechnology, or with civil engineering and human greed? Does the ecological crisis call for more refined technology, or should we change our behaviour and values instead? What role might there be for religious traditions in responding to the ecological crisis? And should we be concerned about our abilities to modify living beings: crops, animals, and even ourselves? How might we reflect upon the challenges that have arisen?

Last but not least, how should we make decisions about our common future, in light of ecological challenges and new technologies? And who should make these decisions: scientists and engineers, since they possess expert knowledge? Or are they too narrow minded, concentrating on their inventions as if they were children playing with new toys? What do we use our technology for? This does not seem to be a question reserved for experts only. How can the general public be involved? Can it work with the experts? Do these two groups trust each other? Is the public ignorant, in the perspective of the scientists? Or are the engineers too narrowly focused, in the eyes of the general public? Matters of trust, expertise and involvement need to be addressed again and again.

These are the issues we will address in this volume: our technological condition (part one), religious resources for the ecological crisis (part two), biotechnology (part three) and matters of trust between scientists and the general public (part four). In this introductory chapter I'll offer some preliminary reflections on these issues, especially on our technological condition, while arguing for a positive appreciation of our technological abilities 'to play God'.

Religion in an Age of Technology

The standard view of technology's place in relation to 'religion and science' can be illustrated well with the titles of two books by Ian Barbour: *Religion in an Age of Science* and *Ethics in an Age of Technology.* This may seem an obvious pair of titles, but it is nonetheless a particular and consequential way of dividing the field; I owe this observation to Ron Cole-Tuner in a private conversation when these books had just appeared. Why not *Religion in an Age of Technology*? And does the absence of *Ethics in an Age of Science*, to take the fourth combination of the pairs {science, technology} and {religion, ethics}, imply that there is no moral issue in relation to scientific knowledge, but that one exists in relation to technological applications?

The underlying issue is in part the understanding of 'science'. There is substantial interest in the religious implications of cosmology and fundamental physics – our attempts to understand the nature and origins of physical reality. Furthermore, there are many books on religion and evolutionary biology, on our understanding of the natural history of our world. In focusing on cosmology and natural history, we deal with aspects of reality that we may seek to understand but (being history) cannot change. But science is not only about understanding reality. Science is also about *transforming* reality. That may not be obvious when cosmology is our prime example, but it is clear when one thinks of chemistry – with its roots in alchemistic practices, seeking to purify reality by transforming elements. Disciplines such as the material sciences are clear examples of this active, reality-transforming side of science, rather than of science as the quest to understand reality.

The case for including engineering among the sciences has become far more serious over time, with a fundamental transition somewhere in the eighteenth and nineteenth centuries during the rise of chemistry and the control of electromagnetism. Modern technology is interwoven with science; the computer would not be possible without the understanding provided by quantum physics, and genetic engineering depends on understanding the double helix of DNA – and vice versa: progress in understanding depends upon progress in construction.

The underlying issue is in part also the understanding of 'religion'. If the interest in religion, in the context of 'religion and science', is defined by an apologetic interest in arguing for the plausibility of the existence of God as 'the best explanation' of reality and its order, then the prime interest in science for the understanding of reality it aspires to offer. But religious traditions not only fulfil such an 'explanatory' function, they also often have an evocative function and a transformative interest – they call people to work for a better world or to work for this world in a better way, by seeking to liberate beings from bondage. Such liberationist theologies certainly should have an interest in the way we humans transform reality, for better or for worse. Cosmologically oriented theologies and worldviews also need to accommodate the fact that our world turns out to be as flexible and as malleable as technology reveals it to be.

Dimensions of Technology

When speaking about technology, most people at first refer to *devices* such as the telephone, the car, and the refrigerator. We live in the midst of such technological artifacts, machines, as materially present entities. But technology is more. These devices cannot function without *infrastructure.* Think of telephone lines, electricity, and gas stations, and behind those, more infrastructure: refineries, ships and pipelines, oil wells – and there the sequence ends, as the oil deep down in the ground is not itself a product of human technological activity. That is where we touch upon natural resources, at the beginning of the line. And in using oil as fuel we also have to get rid of excess heat and waste products, and thus need not only a well but also sinks to get rid of what we do not use, which generates ecological problems for the atmosphere and the soil.

Technology is also a *social system*, for the kind of actions it requires and for the services it provides. And technology depends on *skills* (and thus on educational systems) as much as on hardware. Highly technical medical disciplines such as surgery are certainly also about technical skills of the humans involved. And skills are also involved for ordinary people; driving a car is a technical skill.

So far, I have referred to two 'layers' of technology: the material manifestations of technology in devices and infrastructure, and the social, human dimension of organization and skills. There is a third layer when we consider the psychological level. We can also consider particular *attitudes* to be 'technological'. It refers to a way of life in which a problem – whether it's a leaking roof, an illness, or a miscommunication – is not the end of a story, to be accepted as a fact of life, but rather perceived as a problem to be addressed. An active attitude, sitting down to analyse a problem in order to solve it by practical means, is part of our lives. To us this is such a self-evident part of our lives that we may find it hard to understand cultures in which a tragic or fatalistic attitude is more common. The 'technological attitude' brings us to a major aspect of some of the contributions in this volume: do we wait for God to rescue us, or should we do it ourselves? How do we see human action in relation to the wider understanding of reality?

Last but not least, technology is more than devices and infrastructure, organization, skills, and attitudes. We live in a *technological culture*. Technology pervades and shapes our lives. Antibiotics, sewage systems, anti-conception pills, refrigerators, and central heating systems are more than new means. Antibiotics and sewage systems changed our sense of vulnerability (limiting enormously the number of parents who had to bury their own infants). The pill changed relations between men and women and between parents and their children. Thanks to the refrigerator and the microwave we can eat whenever it suits us, individually, and each according to his or her taste, and thus the common meal as a major characteristic of the day has lost significance. Central heating has made the common room with the fireplace less important; we can each spend our time in our own rooms in the way we like. Technology makes life easier and more attractive; with stereos and iPods, music is available without effort. Such developments were considered by the philosopher Albert Borgmann in his *Technology and the Character of Contemporary Life* (1984). His concern is that while consumption has become easier, some more demanding but meaningful and rich experiences are lost.

History of Technology as Cultural History

That technology and culture are intertwined can be made clear by considering the history of technology as cultural history, and not just as a history of inventions (e.g. Diamond 1998; McNeil 1990). In a sense, technology has made us human, just as tool making and the ability to make, maintain, and use fire are tied up with the emergence of our own species, including its social structures. In a more recent past, the transition from copper to iron some 1500 years bce changed social structures. Copper was relatively rare and thereby created an elite, whereas iron was more widely available and thus more democratic; iron, however, required a more demanding manufacturing process, which strengthened the emerging division of labor. Interaction between cultures revolved around trade, and thus with technologies of transport, production, and use. Agricultural technologies such as the domestication of animals, the improvement of wheat and other crops, and much later of farming tools such as the plow increasingly allowed for greater production with fewer workers, thus creating the opportunity for the emergence of cities.

In more recent European history, accurate timekeeping and the invention of the printing press may have been major factors in the transition from the medieval to the modern period. The Protestant Reformation made good use of the printing press, and in subsequent centuries, new labor relations arose due to the introduction of machines. Working with machinery owned by the master, installed at premises belonging to the master, was the beginning of the factory system. A good example can be seen in the shift in location of the production of textiles from the home to factories. When textile producers shifted from using water power, with locations spread out along the river, to coal, factories were concentrated close to the coalfields. In the absence of affordable passenger transport, workers had to live nearby, in houses they had to rent from their masters. Thus, we see the rise of the major industrial cities, with social arrangements such as regular working hours and standardization.

The steam machine and the 'railway mania' were followed by the freedom of internal combustion. What the car has done to social relations is enormous: for all commuters, the spheres of home and work were separated, and at the same time, the possibility for children to play safely outside was diminished. Controlling electrons in the late nineteenth century (telephone and electrical light) with subsequent developments in the twentieth century (radio and TV, computers and the Internet) added to the enormous cultural transformations of our time. As just one indication of how quickly the developments are going: the very first 'www'-type of communication took place between two computers at CERN in Geneva on Christmas Day of 1990 (Berners-Lee 2000, 30).

The way we speak about technological possibilities influences our perception of what is happening. Talking about the Internet as creating 'cyberspace' suggests a new domain, floating free and remote from traditional human activities, as if we are starting all over with a new reality (see also the contribution by Karen Pärna, this volume). This language was severely criticized by Michael Dertouzos in an essay in 1981 (incorporated in Dertouzos 1997,11):

> The press and most soothsayers tell us we must prepare ourselves to enter Cyberspace – a gleaming otherworld with new rules and majestic gadgets, full of virtual reality, intelligent agents, multimedia, and much more. Baloney! The Industrial Revolution didn't take us into 'Motorspace'. It brought motors into our lives as refrigerators that preserved our food and cars that transported us – creations that served human needs. Yes, there will be new gadgets, which will be fun to use. But the point is that the Information Marketplace will bring useful information technologies into our lives, not propel us into some science fiction universe.

Technology also influences our self-understanding: who has never felt a 'huge pressure'? Do you occasionally need 'to let off steam'? These are images from the steam age. We may consider ourselves as made in God's image, but we speak of ourselves as if we were made in the image of machines. This is not exclusive to the steam age. The early radio receivers also left their traces in our language – we need to 'tune in' – and computers and the Internet are modifying our vocabulary and self-understandings right now. How do we appreciate new technologies: as opportunities, or as problems?

Technology: Liberator or Threat?

When technology is seen as a liberator, we may speak of technological *optimism.* We expect positive contributions to human lives from technology, contributions that will liberate us from various burdens and increase standards of living around the world. We expect a longer and healthier life, with more choices for the individual and more spare time as machines take over various tedious tasks, with better communication (e.g.

telephone and Internet) and more direct forms of democracy. There may be problems, for instance with the environment, but these problems can be resolved by technology. One should not idealize the past; we may want to camp outdoors occasionally, but we would not like to be cut off from modern medicine when needed.

Technology may also be seen as a *threat* to authentic human lives. Technology promotes uniformity and efficiency, undermines social networks, and increases the possibilities for tracing and manipulating individual behaviour. Earlier philosophies of technology, for example those of Lewis Mumford and Jacques Ellul, tended to be of such a more pessimistic kind. More recently, the Unabomber (Chase 2000) and Bill Joy from Sun Microsystems can be mentioned as adherents of such a view. The structure of their messages is often double, just as with messages on predestination or genetic determinism: we are unable to resist, but still we ought to resist. Technology is perceived as a force in its own right, with human behaviour, individually and collectively, following in its trail. This pessimism concerns not only what technological devices may do, but also how they make us look at problems, at fellow humans and at our selves. Technology has overtaken the way we think about ends and values.

Whereas optimism may be aligned with the tradition of utopian thought, we also have a dystopian tradition; there is, alongside the social utopia of Thomas More's *Utopia* (1516), the social dystopia of George Orwell's *Animal Farm* (1948) and, alongside the technological utopia of Francis Bacon's *Nova Atlantis* (1627), the technological dystopia of Aldous Huxley's *Brave New World* (1932). It has been argued, in my opinion convincingly, that the *technological* utopian dream has been far less disastrous in its consequences than the *social* utopian one (Achterhuis 1998); technology always has unexpected consequences, it may be used for other purposes, and it leaves one free to think and explore, unlike the desire to improve behaviour and attitudes, which deteriorates into one-sided control of humans.

A third view of technology, discussed with the other two (in Barbour 1993, chapter one), is more modest and less loaded with a positive or negative valuation. Technology may be seen *instrumentally* or *contextually*, emphasizing the human responsibility for design, deployment, and consequences. This view may be held naively or it may be more reflective, for example when design and use are subject of public discourse. Each context may have many dimensions, including incentives and inhibitions, desires, biases, and prejudices. In this volume we are not presenting technology as a liberator in itself, nor as a threat that happens to humans, but as a social domain where humans need to take responsibility.

Technological and Human Competences and the God-of-the-Gaps

A surgeon stands by my bed. She explains what they intend to do tomorrow. When she has left for the next room, the man in the bed beside me begins to talk. 'You know, my son was in medical school with her. When she had to do her exams, the professor said that she should have failed, but that he would let her pass just to be rid of her.' I am down.

A pastor stands besides my bed. She reads Psalm 139, words of trust and consolation. 'If I take the wings of the morning and dwell in the uttermost parts of the sea, even there thy hand shall lead me, and thy right hand shall hold me.' I see my life in the light of eternity. My mood goes up again. When she has left for the next room, my neighbor begins again. 'You know, my daughter was in seminary with her. When this chaplain had to do her exams, the professor said that she should have failed, but that he would let her pass just to be rid of her.' This does not bother me at all.

We demand professional competence from a surgeon, a pilot, and an engineer who designs a bridge, and rightly so. (The example of the surgeon was made up; it does not do justice to the professional responsibility of those who train doctors.) With the pastor, and in everyday human contact, the issue is not so much particular knowledge and skills. I depend on the surgeon; when she has not slept well, I am at risk. I no longer depend on the pastor; our conversation opened resources in myself (if adequate; sometimes, pastors and friends can also close such resources, and do more harm than good; read the book of Job in the Bible). The surgeon is, to speak religiously, a mediator who stands between me and my salvation.

In daily life we do *not* put our trust in prayer and pious words. When something needs to be done, we want an engineer, a doctor, a pilot: a professional who is competent in the practice at hand. Only when the doctor is unable to offer a hopeful perspective, some may be tempted to spend money on aura reading, powdered shark cartilage (in the Dutch pseudo-medical circuit a 'cure' for cancer), prayer healing, or whatever. When life becomes difficult we look for something to hold on to, but we prefer to begin with strategies that play by regular professional standards.

In conversations on religion and science, there is the critical expression 'god-of-the-gaps'. This refers to the tendency to focus on the holes in our knowledge, on limitations of our current understanding, and to assume that such gaps are where God is at work. Far more satisfactory, in my opinion, would be to see reality as we understand it as God at work. Emphasizing gaps is a risky strategy, like building upon ice; whenever we become blessed with greater understanding, the role of any god-of-the-gaps will be diminished.

Not only in our dealings with science is there a god-of-the-gaps. In our dealings with technology we are also tempted to fall back upon a god-of-the-gaps. Occasionally with some gratitude, but often without paying much attention, we use the fruits of science and technology – antibiotics, electrical light, water drainage, computers, the anti-conception pill, and so on. When the doctor fails, when there is no cure yet, we fall back upon God or upon other elements from the rich treasury of (pseudo-) religious offerings. The expression 'god-of-the-gaps' may have its home in conversations on the theoretical side of science, where too many believers are anxiously looking for that which science is yet unable to explain. However, a similar danger arises in the context of the practical side of science – to look for God when our human skills still fall short of what we wish we could achieve. Introducing God when technology fails results in an instrumental type of religiosity; God is supposed to help us when we need help, but to keep out of our way as long as we do well.

Rather than the tendency to assume that the religious dimension comes into play when the engineers and doctors are finished, it seems preferable to appreciate the efforts of the professionals – and not only appreciate them commercially, but also religiously. When the computer in the plane or on the intensive care unit of the hospital fails, I hope that the staff of the service department will not pray 'that thou wouldst slay the wicked, o God' (Psalm 139: 19). We look to the engineers for our salvation. This is not to be seen as an anti-religious move, as we may appreciate their knowledge and skills as gifts of God, as possibilities to serve one's neighbor 'with all your heart, and with all your soul, and with all your strength, and with all your mind' (Luke 10: 27).

Playing God

Sometimes the concern is voiced that we go too far in our technological activities; we are 'playing God'. This metaphor has been used recently in debates on genetic modification and on cloning. Less than a century ago similar labels were used against those who put up lightning rods. Frederick Ferré tells the story of his father who, in 1922 as a young boy in a farming community of Swedish immigrants in the US, heard the preacher fulminate against the 'shiny spikes of faithlessness'. 'Thunderbolts were God's to hurl, not man's to deflect. The fires of hell, deep under the earth on which the congregation now sat and quaked, were even then being stoked for those who insisted on rising in rebellion against God's will by installing newfangled lightning rods. Amen.' Even if one would have no doubts about hellfire, there seems to be something deeply problematical about such a sermon. 'Could God's will truly be foiled by a steel rod and a grounding wire? Was it really wrong to protect family and livestock from the storms that swept in from the prairies with such seemingly undiscriminating force? ... Should he believe that the God Jesus called "our Father in heaven" really would punish farmers for taking whatever meager technological precautions might be available?' (Ferré 1993, 27).

Why would even non-believers find 'playing God' a useful metaphor in criticizing new technologies? The American philosopher Ronald Dworkin suggested in *Prospect Magazine* in May 1999 that this is because those new technologies do not merely raise ethical issues, but create insecurity by undermining a distinction that is vital to ethics. Underlying our moral experience is a distinction between what has been given and what our responsibility is. What is given is the stable background of our actions. We cannot change those issues. Traditionally this has been referred to as fate, nature, or creation: domains of the gods or of God. When new technologies expand the range of our abilities, and thus shift the boundary between what is given and what is open to our actions, we become insecure and concerned. It is especially in such circumstances that the phrase 'playing God' arises. There is a reference to 'God' when something that was experienced as given, not up to our choices, becomes part of the domain of human considerations. We accuse others of playing God when they have moved what was beyond our powers to our side of the boundary. The fear of 'playing God' is not the fear of doing what is wrong (which is an issue within the domain on our side of the boundary), but rather the fear of losing grip on reality through the dissolution of the boundary. Dworkin argues that this fear is not necessary; humans have always played with fire, and we ought to do so. The alternative is, still according to Dworkin, an irresponsible cowardice for the unknown, a weak surrender to fate.

New technologies imply a different range of human powers, and thus a changing experience of fate, nature, creation or God. For instance, *if* God is associated with that which has been given – often identified as 'creation' – our technological activity will be perceived as pushing God back into the margin. Antibiotics and anti-conception have contributed more to secularization in Western cultures than Darwin; practices are more important than ideas. This God who is pushed to the margin is a god-of-the-gaps, as considered above.

Going beyond the Given: Technology and Religion

If we do not accept this god-of-the-gaps, then how should we proceed? Theism with its root pair of metaphors of power (on the side of the transcendent God) and dependence (on our side) is challenged to rethink itself in the light of the powers we have acquired. If we draw upon the Christian heritage, we find a variety of attitudes.

Stewardship may be interpreted as a call to conserve this world, which then is appreciated as the best of all possible worlds, just as in arguments of traditional natural theology (see Brooke and Cantor 1998). However, in the biblical traditions, God is also associated with a vision of a kingdom of peace and justice, a city of light and glory, where death will be no more. Images of redemption and liberation are integral to the Christian understanding of God. In this light, humans are not merely stewards who are to keep and preserve what has been given. Humans are also addressed as people who should abandon their old ways and take up the risk of living in a new way, as witnessed by the narratives on the Exodus and on Pentecost. Humans are called to renew themselves and the world.

Since the very beginning of the Christian tradition (as the first major heresy, that of Marcion, testifies) there has been a tension between the focus on God as creator – and thus on the world as a God-given created order – and on God as the gracious, loving father of Jesus Christ, who longs for the renewal of the world. Distrust of technology springs from emphasis on what has been given; in contrast, technology could be part of the Christian calling. Additionally, to shift to a naturalistic vocabulary, morally sensible 'naturalists' might share this responsibility by not emphasizing the given as normative, but thinking through the possibility of improving the natural.

Preview

Our lives will change, for better or for worse. And so will our ideas and practices. We are not merely bystanders, but may contribute to this development. Biotechnology and ecological problems are contexts within which these developments are clearly visible in our time. This interplay of technology and tradition, of ecology and religion, of self-understanding and moral vision is what the essays in this volume are about.

The essays in part one of this book address our technological human condition. **Bronislaw Szerzynski** sets the tone by speaking of the religious roots of our technological condition. Technology is not some development by itself; its rise to prominence relates deeply to our values, our notions of nature, of the secular and of transcendence, as he argues, in the light of human history. **Taede Smedes** goes even farther back, to the early evolution of humans, but in the same article speaks of us as cyborgs, that is, organisms which have technology (cybernetics) built into their existence. **Karen Pärna** speaks of technophilia, the love of technology, in the case of 'the Internet age' – again, not just a practical technology, but a new context for religious dreams and meanings.

The second part deals with religious resources that people appeal to in relation to ecological concerns. **Tony Watling** gives an overview of the multiple ways humans have appealed to religious traditions of East and West and to scientific insights such as the 'Gaia theory' to re-imagine the human situation and role relative to nature. **James Miller**'s analysis of the role of Daoism in China's quest for a sustainable future provides an in-depth example of such an appropriation of an ancient religious vocabulary in relation to modernization and in relation to ecological challenges. **Francis Kadaplackal** addresses the issues in a Christian context. His main focus is on the idea of human nature, drawing on the classical *imago Dei* concept and a more recent 'created co-creator' designation to speak of human embeddedness, freedom, and responsibility. **Forrest Clingerman** considers a variety of approaches, and speaks of a 'theology of nature' as well as of 'religious naturalism'. The main focus is, however, not on these positions but on the preliminary question of how one comes to such positions, and what may be expected of religious or secular schemes. Thus, he speaks of the way we build religious models, in this case models of nature, that have sufficient depth of meaning to serve us well descriptively as well as prescriptively – conceptualizing our place as well as our responsibilities.

The third part deals with biotechnology as a context in which similar questions regarding our values and visions arise. **Frank Kupper** reports on public debates on animal biotechnology, and thus addresses the fundamental issue of how discussions on sensitive issues can be organized such that the various voices are heard. Their methodology, 'the value lab', seems able to explore value diversity. **Michiel van Well** considers another Dutch debate, on genetically modified (GM) food. Following Martijntje Smits, Van Well interprets concerns about GM food with categories drawn from religious studies, such as concerns about purity (Mary Douglas) and the danger of monsters. Humans, and especially the possibility to extend the human lifespan, are the topic of **Peter Derkx**'s contribution. How do those possibilities extend with views on meaning and fulfillment, and what moral issues of distributive justice arise in terms of access to life-extending technologies? **Annika den Dikken** considers not extension but enhancement technologies in relation to ideas on care, suffering, and limitations. An ethos of care will remain of utmost moral importance, even if we accept more enhancement technologies.

In the fourth part, the focus continues on the public debate around these issues. What role might religious arguments have in a pluralistic democracy? **Patrick Loobuyck** draws on modern political philosophy, where calls for the exclusion of religious arguments as too particular have been countered by arguments for weaker or stronger forms of inclusion of such expressions of values and concerns. The contribution by **Olga Crapels** focuses on experts and lay people in public debates. Is there a knowledge deficit on the side of lay people involved in public debate on new technologies? Or are the experts insufficiently attentive to the values articulated in religious or other ways? **Franck Meijboom** takes up a similar issue of trust in relation to the acceptance of new technologies, for instance food technologies. **Nancie Erhard** considers the dynamics of multi-faith alliances, through which lay people are politically engaged in a secular democratic society and explores how these could contribute to the larger issue of human engagement with new technologies and the ecological challenges of our time.

Acknowledgements

This chapter draws extensively on (Drees 2002a; 2002b). It arose in the context of the project 'Misplaced Vocabularies: Scientific and Religious Notions in Public Discourses on Ecology and Genetics', which was sponsored by the Netherlands Organisation for Scientific Research, NWO, in the context of its programme 'The Future of the Religious Past'.

References

Achterhuis, H.J. 1998. *De erfenis van de utopie.* Baarn: Ambo.

Barbour, I.G. 1993. *Ethics in an Age of Technology.* New York: HarperCollins.

— 1990. *Religion in an Age of Science.* New York: Harper & Row.

Berners-Lee, T. 2000. *Weaving the Web: The Original Design and Ultimate Destiny of the World Wide Web.* New York: HarperCollins.

Borgmann, A. 1984. *Technology and the Character of Contemporary Life.* Chicago: University of Chicago Press.

Brooke, J.H. and G. Cantor. 1998. *Reconstructing Nature: The Engagement of Science and Religion.* Edinburgh: T & T Clark.

Chase, A. 2000. Harvard and the Making of the Unabomber. *Atlantic Monthly* 285 (6, June), 41-65.

Dertouzos, M. 1997. *What Will Be: How the New World of Information Will Change Our Lives.* New York: HarperCollins.

Diamond, J. 1998. *Guns, Germs and Steel.* London: Random House.

Drees, W.B. 2002a. 'Playing God? Yes!' Religion in the Light of Technology. *Zygon: Journal of Religion and Science* 37 (3, September 2002), 643-654.

— 2002b. Religion in an Age of Technology. *Zygon: Journal of Religion and Science* 37 (3, September 2002), 597-604.

Ferré, F. 1993. *Hellfire and Lightning Rods: Liberating Science, Technology and Religion.* Maryknoll, NY: Orbis Books.

Frye, Northrop. 1982. *The Great Code: The Bible and Literature.* San Diego: Harcourt Brace Jovanovich.

Joy, Bill. 2000. 'Why the Future Doesn't Need Us', *Wired* (April).

McNeil, Ian, ed. 1990. *An Encyclopedia of the History of Technology.* London: Routledge.

Smits, M.W. 2002. *Monsterbezwering: De culturele domesticatie van nieuwe technologie.* Amsterdam: Boom.

Part One

OUR TECHNOLOGICAL HUMAN CONDITION

1   The Religious Roots of Our Technological Condition[1]

Bronislaw Szerszynski

Religion, Environment, and Technology

The relationships between religion, technology, and the environment are
at least as important now as they were when Lynn White published his
seminal essay 'The Historical Roots of Our Ecologic Crisis' in *Science*
about forty years ago – an essay to which my own title is, of course, an
homage (White 1967).

For a start, *religion*, far from fading away as theorists of secularization
would have us believe, seems to be becoming more significant than ever,
even more so than when Peter Berger published the collection *The Desecularization of the World* in 1999 (Berger 1999). For example, the events of
the last years have seen various forms of Islam become hugely significant
forces in world affairs; in the US, too, the influence of religion on politics
was felt throughout the Bush administration; there is growing awareness
of the numerical significance of the global south in Christendom, especially due to conflicts within the Anglican Church over gay priests – an
estimated two-thirds of the world's Christians live in Asia, Africa, and
South America; and there is a growing awareness of how even apparently
secularized Western societies contain an extraordinary range of alternative spiritualities (Heelas et al. 2004).

Similarly, the *environment* too is now moving back up the political
agenda: global climate change is becoming more recognized as a reality
rather than a hypothesis; the spectre of 'peak oil' is prompting a revival
of interest in issues about resource depletion; economic growth in China
and India is raising the question of how the spread of Western-style levels
of consumption can be supported by an increasingly overstrained planet.

Against this background, there is, understandably, increasing policy interest in finding new ways of changing people's behaviour to reduce ecological footprints, in areas such as energy and water use.

It is perhaps worth dwelling on this last point a little. The seasoned environmental campaigner Tom Burke has recently suggested that environmental politics is moving into a new and more challenging era.[2] For its first few decades, Burke argued, environmental politics was primarily concerned with issues such as air and water pollution, hazardous wastes, toxic chemicals, and radioactive substances, issues in respect of which there was a clear case for action, there were obvious courses of action to take, there were more winners than losers when action was taken, and there were easily identifiable victims and villains. However, with what he calls the 'hard politics' of the environment that we are now having to tackle, in relation to issues such as climate change, deforestation, ocean degradation, water scarcity, food insecurity, and biodiversity loss, the case for action is not always clearly perceived and the policy tools are far less obvious. If action is taken, there are more immediate losers than winners: it is far more difficult to find win-win solutions, and the victims and villains are often the same people in different roles, such as citizen and consumer.

This hard politics of the environment will require institutions to find radically new modes of intervention, ones that involve not pulling a few big regulatory levers, but influencing the micro-texture of human behaviour, shaping billions of unreflexive micro-decisions distributed across the social fabric. In such a context, it would not be surprising to see a renewed interest in using religion to help meet conservation goals. In September 1986 the World Wildlife Fund organized a two-day retreat for leaders of world religions in Assisi, Italy, to mark its twenty-fifth anniversary, a meeting that led to the Assisi Declarations on ecology from the major world religions, and to the creation of the Network on Conservation and Religion. It is said that Prince Philip, the president of the WWF, initially came up with this idea largely because of the numerical and hierarchical power of the world religions to shape human behaviour. Such moves might seem less likely twenty years later, in an increasingly globalized world, one in which modern society, as Zygmunt Bauman puts it, is turning from solid to liquid – from a society organized through communities, institutions, and certainties to one of individualization, mobility, and uncertainty (Bauman 2000). But, ironically, in the broader context of globalization and neo-liberalism, many states, stripped of conventional regulatory levers with which to control their territories, are indeed starting to turn to 'faith groups' for the delivery of policy objectives. So it should not surprise us to see bodies like the UK Sustainable Development Commission exploring the role that faith leaders and faith communities might play in advancing sustainable development objectives (SDC 2005). We could see religion increasingly turned to as a possible way of achieving the massive behavioural change needed if we are to avert mounting ecological problems.

Technology is of course of huge significance in policy debates – particularly in those parts of the world that, like the European Union, are currently under the thrall of a particular political-economic imaginary, that of the knowledge-based economy, which sees future economic prosperity as depending on a continuous technological innovation underpinned by high investment in research and development, in order to prevent any temporary high-technology advantage evaporating as developing world economies 'catch up'. And under the influence of this imaginary, when the public fails to welcome new technologies enthusiastically, this is typically seen as a kind of failure of nerve which threatens economic performance. One thing that has been particularly striking in the policy discourse since the EU agreed on its Lisbon Agenda in 2000, which committed it to the goal of making Europe 'the most competitive knowledge-based economy in the world by 2010',[3] is the way that the European public is repeatedly cited as one of the reasons for not meeting the targets towards that goal, with European resistance to the introduction of genetically modified organisms (GMOs) into European agriculture and food an oft-cited example. For example, the 2006 Aho Group Report, *Creating an Innovative Europe*,[4] lists as one of the key actions necessary for meeting the challenges of globalization 'fostering a culture which celebrates innovation'. It argues that:

> Europe must break out of structures and expectations established in the post-WW2 era which leave it today living a moderately comfortable life on slowly declining capital. This society, averse to risk and reluctant to change, is in itself alarming but it is also unsustainable in the face of rising competition from other parts of the world (Aho et al. 2006, 1).

Whether explicitly or implicitly, religion is often invoked as part of this anti-innovatory culture. Religious opposition to medical biotechnology such as stem cell technology has, of course, been particularly prominent amongst Catholics and Evangelicals in the US. By contrast, much less of the opposition to agricultural biotechnology has been explicitly religiously motivated,[5] though it is interesting that Lord Robert May, formerly chief scientific advisor to the UK Government and president of the Royal Society of London, recently described European opposition to GMOs as 'theological' in nature – meaning presumably that it was not grounded in empirical proof of harm, but in less tangible, even metaphysical concerns over what DNA technology might signify. And, given the *schadenfreude* with which the UK biotechnology sector has viewed the slowing down of stem cell research in the US, we can surely expect other cases in which religious beliefs are seen as an exogenous brake on the seemingly 'natural' process of technological innovation.

So it is not only the case that the three terms on which I will be focusing in this chapter – 'religion', 'environment', and 'technology' – are each of significant interest in public discourse; we can also see that links are starting to be made between religion and environmental policy, and between religion and technology policy. But note that, whereas in terms of environmental policy, religion is often seen as part of the *solution*, when it comes to economic strategy, religion is more often seen as part of the *problem*. I want to argue that common to *both* sides of this contrast is an unhelpful assumption about the relationship between religion, science and technology. I can perhaps best indicate what I mean by looking more closely at these framings of religion as tool and as impediment, in turn.

On the one hand, with the enrollment of faith groups in the promotion of environmentally benign lifestyles and practices, there is a danger of religion being instrumentalized. In 1992 Robin Grove-White and I published an article warning against the use of values and beliefs simply as non-rational determinants of behaviour that can be manipulated through public policy instruments in order to gain policy objectives (Grove-White and Szerszynski 1992). According to this instrumental view of religion, and of values more broadly, the task is to identify which religious or secular world views are ecologically 'destructive' and which are 'benign', and to find ways of discouraging the first and encouraging the latter. In our paper we suggested that this is an ultimately technocratic project – as if science can tell us how we should live, what our goals should be, and then values are only manipulated to achieve those goals. Much literature in the religion and environment area is still vulnerable to that critique, often because it takes for granted the account of nature offered by science, thus making the sacred subordinate to the secular. It yokes religion into the service of the technical administration of the earth's life processes as understood by science, instead of seeing religion and values as involving the inquiry into what is valuable in the first place.

On the other hand, in the case of technological innovation, there is an equal but opposite danger of religion being positioned not as a useful instrument but as an annoying hindrance. In the imaginary of the knowledge-based economy, an extraordinary emphasis is placed on one particular aspect of what Gilbert Simondon (1958) called the 'mode of existence' of technological objects – their capacity to mutate, combine, and diverge into new forms. In short, within this discourse, technology is all but synonymous with *new* technology, and technological change is seen as an absolute good. Furthermore, technological innovation is understood as a process which is driven by knowledge processes purely internal to the world of science and engineering; the world of culture, religion, and public meanings is only relevant as a realm of potential reception for the technological products produced by the world of technology and commerce. The public, with their meanings and values, are thus relegated to a passive role, that of simply welcoming, and adapting to, these new arrivals in the family of created beings.

These two worries are at once diametrically opposed and intrinsically connected. First, how can we overcome the enchantment which scientific and technical accounts of nature hold over environmental politics, both secular and sacred? How can we create and defend an intellectual space for religious ideas to have more than a purely instrumental role in environmental politics? Must religion be relegated to simply offering new reasons *why* we should behave differently to nature, rather than offering anything new concerning *how* we should behave? Second, how can we counter an understanding of technology as an inevitable, autonomous process, which positions culture and meaning as on the outside of that process? And, specifically, can the promissory nature of modern technological development *itself* be subjected to a religious analysis? In the rest of this chapter I will argue that the first step in thinking through *either* of these challenges is problematizing the idea of the ontological primacy of the secular.

The Critique of the Secular

In 2005 I published a book on this topic, *Nature, Technology and the Sacred* (Szerszynski 2005), and one of the main contributions I hoped it would make to the literature on the relations between religion, environment, and technology is as an exploration of the religious roots of the apparently secular cultural meanings that underpin and sanction the modern domination of nature. In this, the book was influenced by the argument made by the postmodern theologian John Milbank in his *Theology and Social Theory* (1990). Milbank sought to turn the tables on secular accounts of human beings and of society, suggesting that, rather than understanding religion as a distinctive cultural phenomenon within a fundamentally secular world, it is the *secular* we should problematize, understanding it as a historically contingent cultural development within a fundamentally religious cosmos – and, most importantly, that the modern secular can never shake off its origin in, and dependency on, specific religious ideas.

Milbank suggested that this has profound implications for the way we think about modern society. In particular, religious discourse, rather than being one which is open to being explained by reference to secular realities such as psychology, interests, or ideology, becomes a kind of master discourse – once again theology is the queen of the sciences. In my book I take Milbank's basic idea (without necessarily taking on board his specific normative commitments) and extend it into the areas of our relationship with nature, especially as mediated through science, technology, and environmental politics – and argue that it has equally profound implications here.

Let me explain the Milbankian move in a little more detail. Modern thought is dominated by a particular picture of the relationship between the sacred and the secular. Firstly, the secular is understood as a self-dependent reality, one might say a self-evident reality – a world full of empirical beings, both animate and inanimate. The particular sacralizations offered by the religions of the world are then seen as cultural meanings which supervene on this shared, secular reality that is described by the empirical sciences. Here, the secular is the 'unmarked' term, the side of the secular/sacred contrast which is in no need of explanation. Secondly, seeing the world this way, understanding the natural world in terms of cause and effect, through physics, biology, and chemistry, and understanding human beings through sociology, psychology, and economics as mortal, rational animals driven by a combination of animal instinct and rational calculation, is seen as a universal form of thought that was always waiting within human history as a potentiality – indeed the destiny – of humankind.

Instead, we need to see the modern secular world as a peculiar and distinctive product of the religious and cultural history of the West, and as inextricably shaped by its religious roots. Originally, the concept of the profane presupposed the sacred; conceptually, they operated as a pair, with the contrast between them only relative, and one that could be switched around as a person moves through different life stages and circumstances, so that he [sic] 'one day sees the sacred where before he has seen the profane, or vice versa' (Van Gennep 1960, 13). In its original sense in the Classical world, the profane or worldly was thus *itself* understood religiously – indeed, the Latin term *pro-fanum* originally referred to the space in front (*pro*) of the temple (*fanum*) (Gadamer 1975, 150).

Yet modern secular thought and action understands itself as secular or profane in an *absolute*, not a relative sense – not as a pragmatic relaxing of sacral norms, or as heresy, idolatry, or apostasy within a shared sacral horizon, but as purely *non*religious, to be understood in its own, immanent terms, with no need of any sacral reference point to make it intelligible. One way I have described this move is to say that with the onset of modernity the world was turned inside out; once, the secular was simply a space within a sacral horizon, within a world understood in sacral terms; now, our cosmic horizon is secular, and sacrality, belief in religion, is understood as a phenomenon within that secular horizon. Indeed, I have suggested that this turning inside-out of the world is the reason we find it so hard to define religion. The secular, we can define. Religion, we can't; we can't find any core characteristics that are shared by everything we think of as religion, but not by anything we think of as secular. Any definition of religion either casts the net too widely, or too narrowly. And this, I suggest, is because the concept of religion is a *political* term. Before the elevation of the secular to constituting the horizon of our world, there was no such thing as religion in the modern sense; the category emerged as the result of an extraordinary piece of cultural labor, a gathering together of a huge range of phenomena, ideas, and practices, an immense othering performed by emerging secular modernity, as the vast and incommensurate panoply of beings, ontologies, and practices that once existed *outside* that space were herded into the space that has come to be called 'religion' (Szerszynski 2006, 813-16).

The Secular and Nature

So, what are the implications of applying this sort of approach, one that rejects the ontological priority of the secular, to the domination of nature? In my book I explored this through a critical reinterpretation of the idea of the 'disenchantment of nature' – the idea that in the modern era nature has been disenchanted, stripped of sacral meaning, rendered calculable and manipulable. This idea, most famously formulated by the sociologist

Max Weber as *die Entzauberung der Welt* (Weber 1989, 14, 30) has a long history, indeed is as old as modernity itself. This, I suggested, is the 'creation myth' of modern society, told in order to justify modernity's sense of its own exceptionality, its discontinuity with earlier, 'traditional' cultures, its wiping the slate clean so as to start afresh (see Toulmin 1992). But a more-or-less standard version of this narrative also runs through the literature on religion and the environment. So, both those who see modern rationality and technology as liberating forces, and those who see them as a source of profound alienation, generally accept that nature has become disenchanted – that the way nature is understood underwent a decisive break with Western religion.

My suggestion in the book is that the story of the disenchantment of nature is only a half-truth. It is *true* that the dominant way that nature is understood was transformed in the seventeenth century. It is *true* that nature is no longer understood as being filled with gods, demons, or spirits who might assist, hinder, or terrify us. Nature is no longer shot through with occult connections between one object and another. Neither is it any longer seen as one of the two books of God,[6] filled with signs and lessons for human beings from its creator (though with the rise of molecular biology with its idea of genetic codes and commands, that metaphor has seen a bit of a renaissance).

Instead (and here I am grossly simplifying the modern view of nature), today nature is mathematical – something to be counted, measured, and mapped. Nature is immanent – it operates according to its own internal processes, rather than being shaped or guided by a supernatural hand. It is mechanical – behaving according to cause and effect, not seeking teleological goals. It is a resource – to be owned or held in common, to be used or preserved. It is to be understood through careful observation and scientific theory, not through mythology or divination. This is a nature whose being is mastered by science, whose value is measured by economics, and whose potentiality is determined by technology.

So I grant that, and some. But this is not because nature has been *stripped* of meaning, somehow rendered bare, rendered how it has always been, no longer hidden from view by the consolations of religion. On the contrary, the natural world has been *filled* with particular cultural meanings – and it is at least as important to interrogate *those* cultural meanings as those which we think might hold technology in check.

Of course, something like this idea was already present in Lynn White's essay (1967), as he suggested that the domination of nature arose in Western Europe because of the particular theological ideas of Western Christianity. But what was dominant in White's paper and the subsequent literature was the idea that Christianity simply permitted something which was being held back by religious ideas – that Christianity banished the spirits from nature, and thus removed taboos against its exploitation. Implicit or explicit in this literature has been the idea that the reason *why* in the past humans enjoyed less exploitative relations with nature (although it is not always agreed how far back we have to go) was because they had religious beliefs about nature that acted as a constraint on their technological domination of nature: for example, the belief that nature is alive, that nature is God's body, or that it is full of spirits. The implication here is that once these beliefs are removed, and you move thereby to a secular understanding of nature, then the latent technological attitude is somehow introduced. To use a metaphor with which I open my book, it is as if in the modern world religion simply recedes, like the sea of faith in Mathew Arnold's poem of the same name, leaving a denuded, unprotected nature.

Instead, in the book I develop the argument that, in modernity, nature is not disenchanted but is held under a different enchantment; not stripped of meanings, but has been *filled, constituted*, through particular meanings. I draw on religious studies, history, anthropology, philosophy of technology, and empirical sociology to suggest that contemporary society is characterized by not so much a disappearance as a *reorganization* of the sacred, and that contemporary ideas and practices concerning nature and technology – whether associated with the technological exploitation of nature, or with resistance to that exploitation – remain closely bound up with religious ways of thinking and acting.

Western Religion, Nature, and Technology

So, part of my argument is that the modern scientific view of nature takes shape within the womb of Western religion. To summarize the argument I developed in *Nature, Technology and the Sacred*, Western thought has passed along a highly distinctive historical trajectory through its two millennia of transcendental monotheism, one without which our modern ideas of nature and technology would not take the form that they do. In contrast to the unified cosmos of primal religions, this trajectory saw the establishment of a vertical, transcendent axis in thought and cosmology, one that divided that cosmos into an empirical world and a transcendent, other-worldly reality. As this axis emerged, the supernatural powers of ancient divinities were progressively gathered together into the idea of the monotheistic God, and expelled from the empirical world into a supernatural reality. This axis, along with its correlate in the philosophical reason of classical Greece, established a new dimension in human experience which had a profound impact on ways of thinking about the world. Without such an axis it would not have become possible, as happened later, to regard nature as *nature* – as a unified secular realm, the laws of which can be discovered through empirical inquiry, and which can be manipulated technologically.

But central to this story is also the *radicalization* of this axis in the Protestant Reformation and the scientific revolution. The Reformation stripped away the institutional and supernatural hierarchies that both constituted and spanned the gulf between the transcendent divine and the world, making that gulf at once infinite and infinitesimal, absolute and vanishingly small. With the divine's even more absolute removal from this world, it became apprehended under the figure of the *sublime* – as infinite, unconditioned, and unknowable. But at the same time as the Reformation radicalized the gulf between the empirical and transcendent worlds, the transcendent was also brought close to each individual, and to nature. Then, with the emergence of modern thought, the transcendent axis was pulled into the very empirical world that was constituted by its ejection, and both the human subject and the natural world came to take on attributes that had previously been assigned to the divine (Szerszynski 2005, ch. 2).

So, rather than the emergence of modern science in the seventeenth century being a decisive event in the *separation* between religious thought and natural philosophy, it was the moment of a spectacular *fusion*. The scientific revolution did not simply jettison God; rather, its proponents drew their sublime and distant God even closer, into the empirical world, and in doing so changed the meaning of theological language. In order to carry out their project of reconfiguring the human understanding of nature to make it capable of mathematical certainty, figures such as Descartes, Newton, More, and Leibniz took language about God's attributes, being, and action in the world, stripped them of what medieval theologians such as Aquinas had seen as their analogical character, gave them clear, univocal meanings, and progressively absorbed them into their emerging account of the empirical world (Szerszynski 2005, 48). Thus the modern scientific idea of nature was born through a particular transformation of theological discourse, although these theological roots become progressively obscured as decades and centuries passed.

The emergence of this new understanding of nature was closely linked with that of modern technology (Heidegger 2003). For classical thinkers, *techne* – craft, or art – provided an inferior kind of knowledge than that promised by contemplation, because of its concern with particulars rather than universals, and with changing rather than unchanging things. Individual crafts were regarded as intrinsically uncertain and unpredictable in their outcomes, partly because of an almost animistic classical conception of matter as having its own desires, its own *telos*. The process of manufacturing an object, of combining form with matter, involved not just imposing a form on matter but cooperating with matter, almost conversationally, so was not reducible to formal principles and had to be learned through experience (Mitcham 1994, 118-23). Crafts were thus tentative, quotidian activities located in the context of non-technical understandings of human flourishing which incorporated ideas of beauty, justice, and contemplation.

But after the Reformation we see the rise of 'technology' in the modern sense as a project of reducing the arts to universal methodological principles – of finding the *logos* of *techne* itself, of overcoming the recalcitrance of matter and making it subservient to *logos*, thus bringing human activity into the realm of 'clear, voluntary and reasoned concepts' (Ellul 1964, 20). The idea of a transcendent God provided an Archimedean vantage point outside the empirical world at which the experimental scientist sought to stand to gain objective knowledge of the world, knowledge untainted by the perspectivism suffered by empirical creatures dwelling within the world (Arendt 1958, 257-68). In this new ordering of nature and technology, *Homo faber*, the human as fabricator, is no longer one who co-operates with matter as another creature with its own desires and goals; instead, he acts on it from outside, yet as one who knows it more intimately than it does itself, as if he were its creator.

So the quintessentially modern idea of 'technology' emerged as a fusion of craft practices with ideas from transcendental monotheism, effecting a radical transformation in ideas of knowledge. But this emergence also radically changed the meaning of the practical arts. From Francis Bacon's *Advancement of Learning* ([1605] 1960) onwards, technology became conceived as a project to liberate humankind from finitude and necessity, allowing it to share in the unconditionedness of a deity understood in increasingly sublime terms (Noble 1999; Song 2003). Modern technology was thus framed from the outset as a soteriological project. Initially, the technological relation with nature came to be seen not just as a way of easing the human condition, but as a way of radically transforming it, of returning to the prelapsarian condition of ease and harmony between humans and nature – ultimately, as a fusion of art and reason, of *techne* and *logos*, which promised to bring the certainty of reason to humanity's technical dealings with matter. But with the later loss of a supernatural reference, the ends and purposes of this technological project come to be understood in purely technical ways, as requiring the adaptation of the human to technological imperatives. Technology became measured against neither quotidian nor supernal human needs and interests, but against its own, technical criteria. Technology became the measure of man – became autonomous, became sublime.

Conclusion

I started this chapter by talking about the importance of religion, environment, and technology in contemporary public discourse. All three, for different reasons, are of importance in policy discussions; but also, I suggested, connections are increasingly being made between them. In the case of the environment, I suggested that there are signs that religious beliefs and what are called 'faith groups' are being enrolled in the difficult task of effecting radical behavioural change in order to meet environmental targets. Regarding technology, I commented on the way that technology policy tends to construct public beliefs and values such as those labelled 'religious' as an impediment to the acceptance of new technologies, and thus to economic productivity and competitiveness in the knowledge economy. I suggested that *both* constructions of religion – as tool or as impediment in relation to secular goals – were equally unhelpful, and rested on problematic assumptions about the relationship between the secular and the sacred. I then sketched an argument that problematized the idea of the ontological primacy of the secular, arguing in particular that modern, secular ideas of nature and technology are profoundly shaped by the religious history of the West.

What are the implications of this move for debates around religion, environment, and technology? Firstly, it implies a rather different picture of the role of 'religious' voices in critical debates about environmental and technological priorities than the dominant picture; rather than referring to scientific and technical definitions of environmental problems and technological effects, and purely remaining at the level of 'values', critique should involve exposing and engaging with the theological roots at the very heart of modern science and technology. The anthropologist and philosopher of science Bruno Latour has recently called for a 'secularization' of Science (with a capital 'S') – the abandonment of science's mythical claim to have privileged access to objective truth (Latour 2004, 30-1). He suggests that the sciences (with a small 's'), the particular, fallible ways we have of generating knowledge about the world, need saving from this myth, not least so that we can dispel the dangerous illusion that scientific knowledge-making can, and should, ever be insulated from politics and debate. Latour calls this 'secularization' to indicate that this would be a removal of science's transcendental epistemic privilege, bringing it down to the level of the world, and leveling the terms of engagement between science and politics. Yet, ironically, this very secularization of science could also facilitate a more productive engagement between science and *religion*, by bringing to the level of conscious reflection and debate shared and conflicting theological assumptions about time, finitude, matter, and human epistemic powers.

Secondly, the distinctive temporal structure of contemporary technology, its promissory and autonomous character – at once promising humanity progressive liberation from the limits of finitude, and requiring humanity to be subject to its dynamic – cannot solely be analysed in terms of the institutional organization of contemporary science and technology, but also requires us to see how the meanings of nature and technology have been conditioned by religious ideas. The promise of science and technology to enable humans to transcend the limits of creaturely existence has emerged out of a cultural history profoundly shaped by transcendental monotheism and associated ideas of salvation. This was by no means a necessary development; the emergence of what I have been calling the technological condition depended on a contingent transformation in Western religious and intellectual ideas associated with the Protestant Reformation and the scientific revolution, which relied on a highly voluntarist image of God imposing his will on passive matter without remainder. Such ideas closely link together issues of epistemology, ontology, technics, and social power, as is very evident in the hopes pinned on contemporary biotechnology. Witness the similar rhetoric deployed by succeeding generations of social actors as traditional plant and animal breeding has been overtaken by scientific Mendelian breeding, then by genetic modification, and most recently by the promise of the biological engineering being pioneered at MIT.[7] In each case, the 'promise' of the new technological paradigm has been the introduction of unprecedented levels of certainty and control in the production of traits and functions. As Lily Kay comments in relation to the rise of molecular biology as an industrial paradigm in the twentieth century, '[t]here is seductive empowerment in a scientific ideology in which the complexities of the highest

levels can be fully controlled by mastering the simplicity of the lowest'
(Kay 1999, 17, 18). An exposure of the substantive theological assumptions
that underlie such dreams of control, and equally underlie the elevation of
the technical as the highest form of knowledge, can play an important role
in 'humanizing' technological development, so that we can begin to see
alternative technological futures, grounded in very different social imagi-
naries and theologies.

Notes

1   Many thanks to Brian Wynne and Larry Reynolds for conversations which
    have greatly helped me formulate parts of my argument.
2   http://www.tomburke.co.uk/docs/GA250205TXT[1].doc. The concept of the
    'easy' and 'hard' politics of the environment was developed in an earlier ar-
    ticle (Burke 1997).
3   http://ec.europa.eu/growthandjobs/index_en.htm
4   http://ec.europa.eu/invest-in-research/action/2006_ahogroup_en.htm
5   But see the essays in (Bruce and Bruce 1998) and (Deane-Drummond and
    Szerszynski 2003).
6   Acccording to many of the Church Fathers, nature, like the Bible, was a book
    through which God reveals his glory and his commands to us – see Tanzella-
    Nitti (2005).
7   See http://www.guardian.co.uk/science/2005/mar/10/science.research.

References

Aho, Esko, Josef Cornu, Luke Georghiou, and Antoni Subirá. 2006. *Creat-
    ing an Innovative Europe: Report of the Independent Expert Group on
    R&D and Innovation Appointed Following the Hampton Court Sum-
    mit.* Luxembourg: Office for Official Publications of the European
    Communities.
Arendt, Hannah. 1958. *The Human Condition.* Chicago: University of Chi-
    cago Press.
Bacon, Francis. [1605] 1960. *The Advancement of Learning, and New At-
    lantis.* London: Oxford University Press.
Bauman, Zygmunt. 2000. *Liquid Modernity.* Cambridge: Polity Press.
Berger, Peter L. 1999. *The Desecularization of the World: Resurgent Religion
    and World Politics.* Washington, D.C.: Ethics and Public Policy Center.

Bruce, Donald and Ann Bruce, eds. 1998. *Engineering Genesis: The Ethics of Genetic Engineering in Non-Human Species.* London: Earthscan.

Burke, Tom. 1997. The Buck Stops Everywhere. *New Statesman*, 20 June, 14-16.

Deane-Drummond, Celia and Bronislaw Szerszynski, eds. 2003. *Re-Ordering Nature: Theology, Society and the New Genetics.* Edinburgh: T&T Clark.

Ellul, Jacques. 1964. *The Technological Society*, tr. John Wilkinson, New York: Vintage.

Gadamer, Hans-Georg. 1975. *Truth and Method.* New York: Seabury Press.

Grove-White, Robin and Bronislaw Szerszynski. 1992. Getting Behind Environmental Ethics. *Environmental Values* 1 (4), 285-96.

Heelas, Paul, Linda Woodhead, Benjamin Seel, Bronislaw Szerszynski, and Karin Tusting. 2004. *The Spiritual Revolution: Why Religion Is Giving Way to Spirituality.* Oxford: Blackwell.

Heidegger, Martin. 2003. The Question Concerning Technology. In *Philosophy of Technology: The Technological Condition: An Anthology*, eds. Robert C. Scharff and Val Dusek. Oxford: Blackwell, 252-64.

Kay, Lily E. 1999. In the Beginning Was the Word? In *The Science Studies Reader*, ed. Mario Biagioli. London: Routledge.

Latour, Bruno. 2004. *Politics of Nature: How to Bring the Sciences into Democracy*, tr. Catherine Porter, Cambridge, MA: Harvard University Press.

Milbank, John. 1990. *Theology and Social Theory: Beyond Secular Reason.* Oxford: Blackwell.

Mitcham, Carl. 1994. *Thinking through Technology: The Path between Engineering and Philosophy.* Chicago: University of Chicago Press.

Noble, David F. 1999. *The Religion of Technology: The Divinity of Man and the Spirit of Invention.* Harmondsworth: Penguin.

Simondon, Gilbert. 1958. *Du Mode D'existence Des Objets Techniques.* Paris: Aubier.

Song, Robert. 2003. The Human Genome Project as Soteriological Project. In *Brave New World? Theology, Ethics and the Human Genome Project*, ed. Celia Deane-Drummond. Edinburgh: T&T Clark, 164-84.

Sustainable Development Commission 2005. *Sustainable Development and UK Faith Groups: Two Sides of the Same Coin?* London: WWF UK and the Sustainable Development Commission.

Szerszynski, Bronislaw. 2005. *Nature, Technology and the Sacred.* Oxford: Blackwell.

— 2006. A Reply to Anne Kull, Eduardo Cruz, and Michael Delashmutt. *Zygon: Journal of Religion and Science* 41 (4), 811-23.

Tanzella-Nitti, G. 2005. The Two Books Prior to the Scientific Revolution. *Perspectives on Science & Christian Faith* 57 (3), 235-48.

Toulmin, Stephen. 1992. *Cosmopolis: The Hidden Agenda of Modernity*. Chicago: University of Chicago Press.

Van Gennep, Arnold. 1960. *The Rites of Passage*. Chicago: University of Chicago Press.

Weber, Max. 1989. Science as a Vocation. In *Max Weber's 'Science as a Vocation'*, eds. Peter Lassman and Irving Velody. London: Unwin Hyman, 1-31.

White, Lynn, Jr. 1967. The Historical Roots of Our Ecologic Crisis. *Science* 155, 1203-07.

2   Technology and What It Means to Be Human

Taede A. Smedes

Introduction: Technology and Nature

Sitting in my study, looking around me, all I see are human-made items – artifacts such as books (lots of them), book shelves, a computer and a PDA, a desktop lamp, pens and pencils, and so on. When I look out my window, I see houses, but also gardens with plants and trees. Plants and trees are generally regarded as natural phenomena, yet the way they are planted as parts of the town in which I live is purely artificial. As far as I can see, except for the blue sky and the sunshine, there is nothing in my direct vicinity that is not, in some sense, the product of human design and engineering. I am an inhabitant of what I term the *technosphere* – a place that itself is an artifact, designed and technologically manufactured by humans. Even more, there is hardly a place on earth that is not in some way touched by human influence.

For many people, the influence of humanity in and upon nature is something that should be kept to a minimum as much as possible. Human influence on nature, especially involving technology, is somehow considered to be 'unnatural'. The way many people speak about the relationship between humans and nature is as if humans are not part of nature; as if humans are somehow above or against nature, so that human actions that affect nature are 'interventions'. Nature – traditionally a very slippery and vague concept – can in this context be described as that which develops by itself without the interference of humans. This concept of nature also seems to be tacitly present in many discussions concerning conservation of natural habitats: humans have to take a step back and should not interfere. Nature should be able to take care of itself.

This is a strange and even paradoxical situation. On the one hand (and I will say more about this later), Darwin's evolutionary theory in a sense destroyed the dualism between humanity and nature. The ascent of humans was just as much a natural process as the evolution of fishes, insects, birds, and so on. As Michael Ruse (1986, 104) describes,

> If you take Darwin seriously – accepting evolution through natural selection and not merely some Spencerian bastard version of evolution – then the special status of *Homo sapiens* is gone forever. Any powers we have are no more than those brought through the crucible of the evolutionary struggle and consequent reproductive success. It is true that, as a species, we are unique, with our own special combination of powers and abilities. But then, so also is *Drosophila melanogaster* (a species of fruit fly).

Darwinian evolutionary theory (most recently in the form of sociobiology) has shown human culture to be just another dimension, or even product, of biological evolution. Yet in many discussions concerning the relationship between technology and nature, human influence is still considered to be somehow unnatural, or not part of natural processes.

This deep ambiguity is especially prominent in discussions concerning the human use of technology. It often seems as if the technosphere (as the realm of human technology) is not a part of the biosphere, but is a separate realm or layer. This view, of course, has deep roots, going back at least to the Puritan tradition that followed Francis Bacon, who in his *Novum Organum* (1620) foresaw technology as a means of regaining a lost paradise. Bacon's ultimate goal with technology 'was to redeem man from original sin and reinstate him in his prelapsarian power over all created things' (Paolo Rossi, quoted in Noble 1997, 50). The philosopher René Descartes wrote in his *Discourse on Method* (1637) that, through science and technology, 'we might be able ... to use [the actions of fire, water, air, the stars, the heavens, and all the other bodies that surround us] for all the purposes for which they are appropriate, and thus render ourselves, as it were, masters and possessors of nature' (Descartes 2000, 4). John Milton, in his *Paradise Lost* (1667) argued that humans with their mechanical arts and science would have dominion over nature. The view that science and technology are meant to give humans dominion over nature has since then become a deep-seated view of the relationship between humans/technology and nature.

One example: the historian Thomas Hughes writes that early American settlers believed they were called to create the Promised Land for themselves, which meant taming the wilderness they found when they arrived in America. The view that humans stood against a wilderness they needed to tame and control became entrenched in the American mind. Americans in the nineteenth century 'conceived of the transformations wrought by technology as a manifestation of mind over matter. ... Full of self-satisfaction, they believed that the human mind was ordering chaotic nature, a wilderness, into a world of enlightened culture' (Hughes 2004, 29f.). In effect, 'Americans would become the lords of creation. Human design was supplementing the Creator's plan for the universe' (29). America's nature was to become a paradise that was to be regained.

As the French philosopher Rémi Brague writes, such a view of technology as the human potential to tame wild nature is now generally accepted. Modern technology has become defined by domination.

> Technological activity was considered up until the modern era as a perfection of nature. It was a matter of delivering nature of that which it could not produce by itself. One then appealed on behalf of effective nature to a superior jurisdiction, which might be seen as the not completely accomplished intent of nature, or the plan of the Creator. Henceforth it was a question of imposing external order upon nature. If technology could set out to ameliorate nature, it was because nature left a lot to be desired. Modern technology thus accepted a fundamental premise of Gnosticism. (Brague 2003, 209)

Such views of technology in human hands to regain dominion and control over nature presuppose and, to some extent, even promote a dualist view of humanity and nature.

A Conceptual Exercise in Philosophical Anthropology

The dualist view of nature and human culture (including technology) thus seems to be engraved in the Western mind, although Darwinian evolution seems to question this dualism. In the following section, I want to suggest a perspective on technology according to Darwinian lines, a view of technology as a part of human culture and, as such, a part of and continuous with nature. Instead of seeing technology as merely an epiphenomenon of human culture, I argue that technology is a central and irreducible aspect of our human existence, even to such an extent that the philosopher Andy Clark has argued that humans are 'natural-born cyborgs'. Developing and using technology is something that apparently comes quite naturally to humans. I will argue that these scientific developments should stimulate us to reconsider the questions what it means to be human, and how humans and their technology relate to nature. As a consequence, this chapter is a conceptual exercise in philosophical anthropology.

As for the use of the term 'technology', I will use this term broadly to designate 'the intelligent use and development of material elements which are designed, made, used, and modified for some purpose'.

The Evolutionary Roots of Human Technology

An appropriate and interesting question to start with is this: Where does our capacity for developing technology stem from? Archeologists, paleontologists, and paleoanthropologists all seem to agree that the use of tools, and thus of technology as defined above, is a defining characteristic of human nature. Humans have never been without technology. The famous periodization of human history into *Paleolithic* ('ancient stone' age, the period of chipped stone artifacts), *Mesolithic* ('middle stone' age), *Neolithic* ('new stone' age, the period of polished stone artifacts), *Bronze Age* (when copper and bronze artifacts appear), and *Iron Age*, was inspired by human tool production and tool use. That division has become part of our culture, even though it has been modified several times including the addition of several subdivisions.

This periodization mirrors the belief that all species of *homo* that have ever existed have been able to use, manufacture, and/or modify tools. This is, of course, a conjecture, since we can only make inferences about tool use in early hominids because of the discovery of stone tools (Schick and Toth 1993). It is possible and even likely that some human species used tools made of wood, bone, grass, fur, and so on, instead of, or in addition to, stone tools. However, unless these were fossilized, there are little to no remains of such tools because they were not preserved.

By looking at these stone tools, an expert can tell how they were made and where they came from in both place and time. On the basis of such information, some have argued that one can even discern developments in the way stone tools were fabricated. For instance, in 1968, the archeologist Grahame Clark argued that one can discern five technological modes in the production of stone tools (Clark 1977, 21-38 and *passim*; Clark's book was originally published in 1968; see also Foley and Mirazón Lahr 2003, 113ff.). These five modes 'express more complex ways of making stone tools, leading toward greater control and a more effective use of raw material to produce particular end products' (Foley and Mirazón Lahr 2003, 113). In other words, Clark's classification mirrors a progression in the fabrication and refinement of stone tools, from simply striking a flake off a core without much concern about shape (mode 1, Oldowan industry, 2.5-1.4 million years ago) to the complex fabrication and refinement of multi-functional blades of various sizes and lengths, involving microlithic technologies (mode 5, transitional phase between the Ice Age and the Holocene period). Different hominid species are associated with each different mode: for example, *Homo habilis* and *Homo ergaster* are associated with mode 1 technologies; *Homo erectus, sapiens, heidelbergensis,* and *neanderthalensis* are associated with mode 2 tools. *Homo sapiens* probably had the flexibility to use tools from all five modes.

The pervasiveness of tool use among humans raises an interesting question: is the capacity to use tools restricted to humans? In his famous book, Kenneth Oakley wrote that 'man may be distinguished as the tool-making primate' and that 'employment of tools appears to be his chief biological characteristic' (Oakley 1972, 1). Oakley points to tool use among chimpanzees, but argues that this 'is a far cry from the systematic making of stone tools, the earliest known examples of which evidently required much premeditation, a high order of skill and an established tradition implying some means of communication' (2f.). Nowadays, there is much evidence that shows that tool use among animals is ubiquitous. There are examples of otters using stones to crack crab shells, birds that use stones to crack snail shells, and chimpanzees that use twigs to catch termites, ants, or to extract honey from honeycomb. In all these cases, artifacts are being used to manipulate nature. Humans, thus, are not the only species that use technology.

If that is agreed upon, then the question is: how special are *we* in *our* use of technology? Does our tool use differ qualitatively from those of other species, and if so, in what way? Or are we simply expanding the possibilities that are also present in 'lower' creatures? Otters and birds are using stones to acquire food, but they may have mastered the use of stones as tools through trial-and-error learning. If so, does this imply that they comprehend the underlying principles of the problem? Are they 'aware' of the cause-and-effect relations inherent in their tool use?

There are still many questions here that are unanswered and many venues for further research. Yet it seems that the Tanzanian chimpanzees that are so fond of termite fishing and ant dipping at least have some clue about what they are doing. Ian Tattersall (2000, 52f.) writes,

Twigs of different kinds are selected for different purposes, and recent observations reveal that stouter branches are used as levers or to dig out honey from bees' nests. Significantly, twigs are not necessarily discarded when they become bent or frayed; as long as they can, chimpanzees will usually break off the end of such a tool to 'refresh' it and will continue using it as long as such modification is possible. Chimpanzees have also been observed to break off branches for use in hooking in fruit from otherwise inaccessible tree limbs, for attacking potential predators, and for expelling the occupants of holes in trees. Branches [instead of twigs] are also brandished to enhance the effectiveness of aggressive displays, and rocks and sticks are thrown in attempts to intimidate competitors or predators.

Clearly then, as Tattersall acknowledges, those chimpanzees have some insight into the principles of using twigs and, perhaps, using the power of analogous reasoning, the use of branches. Yet, as Tattersall writes,

This does not mean that chimpanzees are toolmakers (or even tool users) in the sense that modern humans are – clearly, they are not – but it shows that chimpanzees are capable of *forming a mental picture* of what attributes some simple tools, at least, need to have to accomplish a particular aim. (53; italics added, T.S.)

Shaping tools to improve their function shows insight into its workings and knowledge of the underlying principles. This, however, seems to involve cognitive functions of a quite advanced type. These cognitive feats may have emerged from trial-and-error learning, but they go much further. If stone-using otters or birds ever come to a territory in which there are no stones for them to use, they are facing a real problem. Because there are no stones they can use, these animals might even starve to death. They lack the cognitive capacities for improvisation and flexibility, for adapting their actions accordingly, because they lack the cognitive capacities for insight into the principles underlying the use of stones.

Non-human primates such as chimpanzees do seem to grasp the underlying principles. However, one of Tattersall's central claims is that the cognitive abilities of humans even go beyond those of chimpanzees and other non-human primates. There seems to be a 'cognitive gap' between humans and chimpanzees. Ian Tattersall, Richard Leakey, and Stephen Mithen, for instance, argue that human tool use is somehow connected to the complexity of the brain (Tattersall 2000; Leakey 1995; Mithen 1996).

There thus seems to be a consensus among scientists that the human species, which already had made a cognitive leap compared to other species such as the chimpanzee, somewhere and somehow during its evolution made another cognitive leap. It crossed a critical threshold, which led to the 'big bang of culture'. And this 'big bang' led eventually to art, religion, science, and advanced technology (cf. Klein and Edgar 2002).

If true, what does this say about technology? Perhaps there really is a cognitive gap between humans and other creatures. Nevertheless, if we agree that it was nature that caused the 'big bang of culture', can we plausibly defend the modern idea that culture and technology stand opposed to nature any longer? Especially since we can see the use of basic stone tool technology by non-human species such as otters, birds, and chimpanzees. I agree with Frans de Waal (2001, 271) when he writes: 'Thinking of nature and culture as distinct and separate domains is tricky: there's plenty of nature in culture, just as there is plenty of culture in nature.'

Technology and What It Means to Be Human

So, on the one hand, technology seems to be an entirely natural process. In the course of evolution, different species have managed to use tools in quite advanced ways. However, scientists seem to agree that, in the case of humans, something peculiar is going on. There seems to be a cognitive gap between tool use among non-human primates and other animal species, and the advanced and flexible ways that humans are able to use tools.

In the last couple of hundred years, technology has advanced up to a point where we seem to have lost contact with our natural environment entirely. In our times, our habitat has become the technosphere which seems remote from nature, from which we emerged. Guided by economic rationality we have become estranged from nature, and downgraded nature to nothing more than a set of resources that we can use for our own well-being. There is a constant threat that we will see nature as the realm of the wild that has to be tamed, of that which does not belong to culture or has not (yet) been cultivated, of that over which humankind has dominion. Such an attitude that mirrors an existential remoteness of culture from nature can lead to patterns of behaviour that result in the destruction of other living beings, the biosphere, and even the destruction of our habitat and of our own species through technology.

Getting rid of technology is not an option, for we can no longer survive without it. We have grown dependent upon the existence of technology, as much as our technology depends on our cognitive abilities. Our relation to technology – whether we like it or not – has become one of symbiosis between humans and machines. What we need, then, is a perspective that is able to reconnect us, our culture, and our technology to the natural environment in which we are embedded. Such a perspective should also be able to guide our attitudes towards that natural environment when using technology. One such perspective that I find attractive and would like to explore further (although I do not have the space here to do so) is that of humans as natural-born cyborgs.

Just think about it – think about cochlear implants or 'simple' hearing devices. Think about the pair of glasses that you're wearing (or contact lenses), a pacemaker, an artificial heart or hip, or the medical application of steel pins in a human body. Human lives depend on these technological artifacts. And as theologian Gregory Peterson (2003, 217) writes, using medication 'merges us in the most intimate way with our technology, as our bodies absorb chemicals that may never have existed in nature'. 'Enhancement technology' – technology that supplements and sometimes replaces biology – is especially prominent in the medical sciences. In many medical applications there is truly a merging between humans and technology.

The symbiosis between a human being and machine is described by the term *cyborg*, the abbreviation of 'cybernetic organism', which was coined in 1960 in a paper on space travel by Manfred Clynes and Nathan Kline (Clynes and Kline 1995, 29-33). Clynes and Kline wrote that because people were not biologically adapted to survive the harsh conditions of outer space, science should alter human biology so that people would be able to survive in space. Such an alteration would result in what Clynes and Kline call a cyborg, an organism that 'deliberately incorporates exogenous components extending the self-regulatory control function of the organism in order to adapt it to new environments' (31). Clynes and Kline describe a cyborg as an entity that incorporates external elements in its physical constitution as a survival strategy to adapt to changing influences from the surroundings.

Cyborgs are no longer merely considered creatures in science fiction films or books; nor are cyborgs the ideals of 'transhumanists.'[1] Indeed, being a cyborg nowadays may be an appropriate metaphor for describing our technological human condition, as cognitive scientist and philosopher Andy Clark argues (Clark 1997; 2001a; 2001b; 2003). Clark draws heavily on the recent neuroscientific approach of 'embodied' or 'situated' cognition – an approach that strongly emphasizes the role of *embodiment* and in cognitive processes. Clark (2003, 10) argues that 'What makes us distinctively human is our capacity to continually restructure and rebuild our own mental circuitry, courtesy of an empowering web of culture, education, technology, and artifacts.' For Clark, the term cyborg is not limited to the inhabitants of science fiction stories and films such as *The Matrix*; instead it signifies the fundamental human ability 'to enter into deep and complex relationships with nonbiological constructs, props, and aids' (5). Humans possess a peculiar though natural flexibility in being able to use all kinds of external objects to solve certain problems (in the broadest sense of the word). Therefore Clark speaks about humans as *natural-born* cyborgs: the use of technology comes as natural as walking, talking, eating, and having sex.

Consider, as an example, a blind person using a stick to find her way around in the world. How are the person and the stick related? On a physical level, there may be a demarcation between body and the tool (stick). However, in *using* the tool that demarcation disappears: the tool at hand becomes an extension and hence part of the body. As a matter of fact, this example of a blind person and a stick is used by philosophers such as Michael Polanyi (1962, 55f., 58f.) and Maurice Merleau-Ponty (1962, 143) to argue the same point: that our 'body scheme' – to use Merleau-Ponty's phrase – is not spatially fixed, but dynamic. What I see as belonging to 'me' (i.e. inherent to my body scheme) and not belonging to 'me' (i.e. external to my body scheme) is highly context dependent. The boundaries between our bodies and the world can become – and often simply are – fluid. The car that is parked on my driveway is external to my body scheme. Yet, when I drive my car, my car becomes part of my body scheme, and what happens to my car feels like it is affecting me directly.

In a sense then, and following Andy Clark, I believe we can agree with theologian Gregory Peterson (2003, 217) that we have always been cyborgs: 'Human beings are tool users, and modern human beings are tool users par excellence. So familiar has our technology become that it is often invisible to us. But any individual who wears glasses or contacts is in a sense a cyborg.'

Cyborg technology can be seen as a *replacement* of biology, for example in the case of cochlear implants. Someone who has such an implant is (after a long and sometimes arduous process of getting used to it) no longer consciously aware that the implant is present – unless it malfunctions. On the other hand, cyborg technology is also an *extension* of biology. Telescopes and microscopes extend our visual senses because when we look through them, we see things that under normal circumstances are hidden from sight. Our flexibility in adapting to such technology is amazing. Centuries ago, scientists literally could not believe their eyes as they gazed through Galileo's telescope. They thought that Jupiter's moons were artifacts produced by the telescope, and that they were witnessing an optical illusion. Nowadays you can go to any mall and buy a cheap telescope that will reveal the craters of the moon in vivid detail. Glasses and contacts also extend biology. With the help of cars we extend our motor capacities and jet planes give us the wings we never had. A tennis racket extends a sports star's arm, and so on.

The notion of technological extensions of the body is not exactly new among philosophers of technology. In 1877 the German philosopher Ernst Kapp (1808-1896) wrote that many technological developments were rooted in 'organ projection' (Kapp 1877). A hammer looks like a fist, a saw like a row of teeth, and the telescope is a technological copy of the eye. Much of technology was, according to Kapp, an enlargement and externalization of human organs, such that technology supersedes human capacities. The link between technology and human embodiment was also perceived by the philosophical anthropologist Arnold Gehlen (1904-1976). In 1957 Gehlen wrote a classic essay on the relationship between humans and technology, in which he introduced three terms: *Organentlastung*, *Organverstärkung*, and *Organersatz*. (Gehlen 1957). Gehlen speaks of *Organentlastung* ('organ relief') in the case of a car or a boulder car, which makes the physical pulling or lifting of objects unnecessary. *Organverstärkung* ('organ reinforcement') is the case when technological artifacts enhance and reinforce human capacities, as is the case with a hammer or a microscope. In the case of *Organersatz* ('organ replacement') there is the adding of functions that are otherwise not present to humans: we are able to fly with airplanes, which 'replace' our absent wings.

But Clark wants to go further. He believes humans as natural-born cyborgs are not only capable of creating extensions of their physical bodies, they also *extend their minds*. Pens and pencils are extensions of our hands. The paper on which we write things down, however, becomes an extension of our cognitive apparatus. By writing things down, we no longer need to remember them. Papers with notes, but also paper calendars, electronic PDAs that synchronize with Outlook, reference books and encyclopedias (whether made of paper or in electronic form) – Clark believes these are all external elements that are being used by us as extra-neural memory banks. And what about computers and the Internet? Cyberspace is starting to become a collective memory bank.[2] E-mail and chat rooms extend our communicative abilities (as did the telegraph, telephone, and fax machine before) – and the end of these developments is not yet in sight; one example of this is 'telepresence' (the projection of one's physical appearance in, for instance, a global business meeting) is one of the future possibilities that may make business trips unnecessary.

We have to remember, however, that Andy Clark speaks about humans as *natural-born* cyborgs. It is easy to forget that this fascinating technology has a biological basis, and that it all began with the stone tools that early human species started to use as technology some 2 million years ago:

> It was at this time that some of the early hominids equipped themselves with tools and moved into new evolutionary niches that proved to be enormously successful. This was the start of a new adaptation, seemingly insignificant at first, that continued and evolved over the next few million years and finally led to what and where we are today (Schick and Toth 1993, 18f.).

Clark's concept of the natural-born cyborg is a powerful and imaginative metaphor to emphasize this natural character of human technology and the continuity between humans and the rest of nature without denying or ignoring the peculiarity of human tool use in comparison with animal tool use. There is a fundamental but natural ability in humans to build up a very intimate and flexible relationship with non-biological external tools and technologies. Using technology apparently is what comes naturally.

Conclusion

I am still sitting in my study. And when I look around I still see human-made items – artifacts such as books (lots of them), book shelves, a computer, a desktop lamp, pens and pencils, a PDA, and so on. However, their nature has now changed. I look upon them as being somehow a part of me. The books, my PDA – they all are somehow intimately connected to my biology, including the cognitive processes going on in my mind. When I look out my window, I see houses, but also some gardens with plants and trees. Plants and trees are generally regarded to be natural phenomena, yet the way they are planted, as parts of the town that I live in, is purely artificial. However, the arrangement of the town may be artificial, but the way humans have made their own environment strikes me now as quite natural: this is what humans have done from the emergence of the human species onwards.

Does the use of technology equal the exercise of dominion? Certainly, technology has become dominion, but only at the moment people started to forget that they had emerged from nature. Religion (especially the Christian religion) has done a lot of harm to nature by placing humans halfway between the beasts of the earth and the angels of heaven – that is something I as a theologian have to admit. Moreover, because we have severed the bonds between technology and nature, we have let technology gain control over us, and allowed nature to become a demonic force. We need to find a way to reconnect ourselves to nature, to change our perspective and not perceive nature as a resource for economic benefit, but as a partner with which we need to cooperate in order to survive in the long run.

I am an inhabitant of a technosphere, of a place that is itself an artifact, designed and technologically manufactured by humans. Yet this technosphere is not opposed to nature, but is a part of it, as the theologian Philip Hefner (1993, 154) writes: 'The hybridized navel orange, the automobile, the asphalt parking lot, the computer – these are nature. We call them *techno-nature*, recognizing that techno-nature is, in a real sense, the only nature that now exists on our planet.' The technosphere has *emerged* from nature, it is an emergent property. Through our technology we have gained a certain freedom from biological and evolutionary constraints. However, that freedom is not something that exceeds nature, but is, to use Hefner's phrase (1998, 179), 'nature's way of stretching itself toward newness'.

Perhaps the metaphor of the natural-born cyborg is a way of overcoming the dualism between nature and culture, or between nature and technology, although it may inevitably be a metaphor that for some sounds too technological. The dualism between nature and culture represents an alienation that needs to be overcome: it is not only an alienation from the nature that bore us, but, moreover, an alienation from our own nature. The metaphor of the natural-born cyborg can reframe the continuity of humans and their technology and nature in modern terms, and hopefully thereby give people a new sense of being at home in the universe.

Notes

1   'Transhumanism', according to Wikipedia, 'is an international intellectual and cultural movement supporting the use of new sciences and technologies to enhance human mental and physical abilities and aptitudes, and ameliorate what it regards as undesirable and unnecessary aspects of the human

condition, such as stupidity, suffering, disease, aging and involuntary death.'
See: http://en.wikipedia.org/wiki/Transhumanism.

2   Moreover, the virtual reality of cyberspace is an extension of physical spatiality. This again is an aspect that forces us to rethink certain aspects of Western metaphysics. See: Wertheim 1999; Heim 1993; Heim 1998.

References

Brague, R. 2003. *The Wisdom of the World: The Human Experience of the Universe in Western Thought.* Chicago: University of Chicago Press.

Clark, A. 1997. *Being There: Putting Brain, Body, and World Together Again.* Cambridge, MA: MIT Press.

— 2001a. *Mindware: An Introduction to the Philosophy of Cognitive Science.* New York: Oxford University Press.

— 2001b. Reasons, Robots, and the Extended Mind. *Mind and Language* 16, 121-145.

— 2003. *Natural-Born Cyborgs: Minds, Technologies, and the Future of Human Intelligence.* New York: Oxford University Press.

Clark, G. 1977. *World Prehistory in New Perspective.* Cambridge: Cambridge University Press.

Clynes, M.E. and N.S. Kline. 1995. Cyborgs and Space. In *The Cyborg Handbook*, ed. C.H. Gray. New York: Routledge, 29-33.

De Waal, F. 2001. *The Ape and the Sushi Master: Cultural Reflection by a Primatologist.* London: Allan Lane The Penguin Press.

Descartes, R. 2000. *Philosophical Essays and Correspondence*, ed. R. Ariew. Indianapolis: Hackett Publishing.

Foley, R. and M. Mirazón Lahr. 2003. On Stony Ground: Lithic Technology, Human Evolution, and the Emergence of Culture. *Evolutionary Anthropology* 12, 109-122.

Gehlen, A. 1957. *Die Seele im technischen Zeitalter: Sozialpsychologische Probleme in der industriellen Gesellschaft.* Hamburg: Rowohlt Taschenbuch Verlag.

Hefner, P. 1993. *The Human Factor: Evolution, Culture, and Religion.* Minneapolis: Fortress Press.

— 1998. Biocultural Evolution and the Created Co-Creator. In *Science & Theology: The New Consonance*, ed. T. Peters. Boulder: Westview Press, 174-188.

Heim, M. 1993. *The Metaphysics of Virtual Reality.* Oxford: Oxford University Press.

— 1998. *Virtual Realism.* Oxford: Oxford University Press.

Hughes, T.P. 2004. *Human-Built World: How to Think about Technology and Culture.* Chicago: University of Chicago Press.

Kapp, E. 1877. *Grundlinien einer Philosophie der Technik.* Braunschweig: George Westermann.

Klein, R.G. and B. Edgar. 2002. *The Dawn of Human Culture.* New York: John Wiley.

Leakey, R. 1995. *The Origin of Mankind: Unearthing our Family Tree.* London: Phoenix.

Merleau-Ponty, M. 1962. *Phenomenology of Perception.* London: Routledge.

Mithen, S. 1996. *The Prehistory of the Mind: The Cognitive Origins of Art, Religion, and Science.* London: Thames and Hudson.

Noble, D.F. 1997. *The Religion of Technology: The Divinity of Man and the Spirit of Invention.* New York: Alfred A. Knopf.

Oakley, K.P. 1972. *Man the Toolmaker.* London: The British Museum for Natural History.

Peterson, G.R. 2003. *Minding God: Theology and the Cognitive Sciences.* Minneapolis: Fortress.

Polanyi, M. 1962. *Personal Knowledge: Towards a Post-Critical Philosophy.* Chicago: University of Chicago.

Ruse, M. 1986. *Taking Darwin Seriously: A Naturalistic Approach to Philosophy.* Oxford: Basil Blackwell.

Schick, K.D. and N. Toth. 1993. *Making Silent Stones Speak: Human Evolution and the Dawn of Technology.* New York: Simon & Schuster.

Tattersall, I. 2000. *Becoming Human: Evolution and Human Uniqueness.* Oxford: Oxford University Press.

Wertheim, M. 1999. *The Pearly Gates of Cyberspace: A History of Space from Dante to the Internet.* New York: W.W. Norton.

3   Technophilia: Internet as a Vessel of Contemporary Religiosity

Karen Pärna

Introduction

The front cover of an October 1999 issue of the American magazine *Business Week* features a rendering of the *Creation of Adam* by Michelangelo, a scene from the ceiling of the Sistine Chapel in Rome. On a dark blue background we see God's finger reaching for Adam's hand. This is a mod-

ern version of a familiar detail from the *Donnadio* and it has an unmistakable high-tech aesthetic to it. Both hands are drawn in a style that reminds one of the wire frame models used in three-dimensional computer graphics, and because of the bright yellow lines that delineate them the hands appear electrified. A spark of light emerges from the point of contact and from the space between the two hands the text 'the Internet age' comes to the fore.

Figure 1. Artist: J. Calviello. *Business Week* 4 October 1999. Front cover image. *Business Week* 3649.

It is not hard to decode the message; the religious undertones of the image are immediately recognizable. Associations with godly inspiration, new life, enlightenment and the zenith of creation come to mind. In this elevating scene a parallel is drawn between the potential and genius of the Internet and the biblical miracle of creation. A divine invention has been born, bringing about a new era – 'the Internet age'. However, *Business Week* is not a messenger for any specific religious organization or set of beliefs; it is concerned with the corporate world, finance and world affairs. Bearing this in mind, the allusion to a biblical tale in the otherwise strictly secular setting of a business publication is striking, for it suggests a connection between religion and the domain of technology and commerce.

This seemingly contradictory relationship generates a number of questions that I shall tackle in this paper. Namely, what might be the significance of religiously charged terminology in public representations of technologies such as the Internet? Which kinds of sentiments are being articulated and what, if anything, does the use of religious imagery and analogies in discourses about new technology say about religiosity in contemporary Western society?

In what follows I will argue that, while the Internet is an exemplary product of the modern, rational-scientific mindset, in the (mostly enthusiastic) tales about it, it serves as a vessel of religious sentiments. As has been the case with several other technological inventions throughout history (Corn 1986; Czitrom 1982), the Internet was credited with extraordinary powers to change and improve many aspects of life and it was granted a special, even sacred, status. A look at reports about the Internet in articles from international general interest and news publications, ranging from *Time Magazine*, *The New York Times* and *The London Times* to *Forbes* and *Business Week*, in the biographies of leading inventors and Internet visionaries, and in books on the history and future of this new technology reveals that it was perceived as an object that transcended what was hitherto thought to be within the grasp of humanity. Placed on such an elevated pedestal, the Internet became an object of reverence to which truths and beliefs about the future of the society could be attached. At the heyday of the hyperbolic interest in, or 'hype' around, the Internet, this technology was granted a significance that, to all intents and purposes, can be called a religious one. Let us look at this expression of religiosity and consider how the Internet acquired the special status that it had.

The Internet Age

The 'Internet age' edition of *Business Week* was but one specimen in a veritable avalanche of publications devoted to the Internet that marked the public interest for this new technology throughout the latter part of the 1990s. A lively utopian discourse emerged in the journalistic media and other popular publications in North America as well as in Europe, Australia, and parts of Asia. Although there were exceptions, much writing about new information and communications technology (ICT) in general and the Internet in particular overflowed with visions of wealth, enlightenment, and boundless freedom. Age-old dreams of comfort and the betterment of human existence, transcendence beyond the limitations imposed on people by time and matter, and hopes of greater harmony and growth of knowledge were attached to this technology.

The aforementioned *Business Week* cover typifies the sort of language and imagery that was employed regularly in articles about ICT and the Internet. Accounts of the powers and anticipated effects of the Internet on society were often padded with (quasi-) religious notions and epithets. Some visions, such as the ideas expressed by the American ex-Vice President Al Gore in his 'information superhighway' speeches, where he promoted the Internet with phrases such as 'the network of networks ... ultimately linking all human knowledge' (Gore 1998), may call forth vague associations with some form of supra-human entity. Throughout Al Gore's terms in government, the Internet and the knowledge economy were important points on his political agenda. In several speeches he used the term 'information superhighway', and promoted the Internet as a powerful force that would make the world a better place. For instance, in a speech given at the conference of the International Telecommunication Union in 1998, Gore praises the Internet, or 'the Global Information Infrastructure' as the means of realizing some age-old dreams:

> For all the stunning capabilities of the Global Information Infrastructure, we must remember that at its heart it is a way to deepen and extend our oldest, and most cherished global values: rising standards of living and literacy, an ever-widening circle of democracy, freedom, and individual empowerment. And above all, we must remember that – especially in this global economy and Information Age – we are all connected, from Minnesota to Mongolia, from Madrid to Mali (Gore 1998).

Other enthusiasts have made use of more explicit religious terminology: the Internet has been described as a 'demiurgic force' (Gilder 1997), the conditions expected to be created by this technology as 'heaven', 'paradise', 'nirvana', and so forth. (Kaplan 1999; Quittner 1999; Baker & Beaton 1997; *Economist* 1995), and those active in the branch have been profiled as 'messiahs', 'evangelists', and 'prophets' of a new worldview (*Economist* 1999; 2000; Pennar 1997; Malone 2000). For instance, in the articles 'Nerd theology' (1999) and 'God Is the Machine' (2002), the former editor of the technology magazine *Wired*, Kevin Kelly, speaks of computer technology as a deity. In the same vein, in their book *The Long Boom* (1999) the American economists Schwartz, Leyden, and Hyatt refer to the Internet as the 'Great Enabler', an all-powerful agent of change and the prime cause of an era of unprecedented wealth (Schwartz et al. 1999, 19). Similar language is used in commending prominent computer scientists, web programmers and e-business innovators, who are variously portrayed as 'mini-gods' (Kelly 1999a) and virtuosi (Berger 1996). The business publication *Forbes* even describes Tim Berners-Lee, one of the main inventors of the World Wide Web as 'St. Tim of the Web' (Reiss & Levine 1999). References were also made to strong faith in the Internet, the spreading of its 'gospel' and evangelical missionary fervour (Alexander 1999; Clarke 1999; *Guardian* 1998). Finally, it was not unusual for journalists and various experts to speak of 'Internet religion', 'web religion', or 'digital religion' (Cortese 1995; Mack 1999; Reinhardt 1999). For example, in his biography *A Very Public Offering* (2001) the youthful Internet entrepreneur Stephan Paternot describes the early days of e-commerce as follows: 'It was a potential new religion. This was a religion being invented' (Paternot 2001, 57).

In short, rhetoric about the Internet was filled with religious analogies and some felt able to describe feelings inspired by it as religious. But was this not a case of mere florid metaphor? Looking at the examples just mentioned, can one really speak of religion? In line with Paternot's suggestion that the craze for Internet-related businesses was giving birth to a new religion, I would posit that the public interest for the Internet was indeed a religious affair. However, unlike Paternot, I would not claim that *a new religion* was being invented. No religious organization or dogma in the conventional sense was born. Rather, the discourse concerning the Internet was a manifestation of a more implicit form of religion. By that I mean that, without any exclusive links to religious institutions, the technology concerned was nonetheless charged with characteristically religious notions: transcendence, salvation, and a strong belief in the power of one's object of admiration to transform one's existence. Above all, the trust in the great potential of this technology fulfilled a basically religious function: it presented a frame of reference for making sense of the world.

The Relocation of the Religious

The idea that religion need not manifest itself exclusively in an especially designated domain (i.e. within the boundaries of organized congregations) has been acknowledged by a number of sociologists. Thomas Luckmann and Robert Bellah, among others, have argued that instead of the claimed complete secularization of the contemporary Western society, a shift in religiosity is taking place. Religion is being relocated from its traditional institutions to the everyday, secular world.

Both authors employ a functional definition of religion and hold that it is a system of meanings that is anchored to certain notions or objects that serve as transcendent guarantees of the truths and values of a particular worldview. The defining task of religion, then, is to present frames of reference for making sense of the world and to provide answers to basic existential questions. It can be fulfilled by a variety of seemingly non-religious phenomena. Accordingly, Luckmann uses the term 'invisible religion' to denote the kind of 'hidden' religious sentiment that a variety of contemporary ideals, such as 'familism' (the veneration of the family unit), the cult of the individual, the social mobility ethos, and the democratic ideal entail (Luckmann 1967, 106, 113). Bellah's concept of 'civil religion' in public life reveals a similar understanding that certain secular phenomena display religious facets. According to Bellah, secularized versions of traditional (Christian) religious thought can be found in a variety of American social phenomena: Memorial Day, presidential inaugurations, rituals at veterans' cemeteries, the ideal of the 'American way of life', and so on. He indicates that although references are made to religious convention (martyrdom, charisma, evangelism and the Promised Land), civil religion is divorced from this context and ultimate meaning is found in objects that belong to the secular world (Bellah 1970, 175-179).

Technophilia and the Internet

Collective 'technophilia' is another example of such relocation of the religious in the modern world. In the book *The Internet. A Philosophical Inquiry* (1999) the British philosopher Gordon Graham refers to the cultural theorist Neil Postman's use of the term 'technophile' when speaking of individuals 'who gaze on technology as a lover does on his beloved, seeing it without blemish and entertaining no apprehension for the future' (Postman quoted in Graham 1999, 9). Graham describes technophilia as the activity or attitude of technophiles: blind love of technology that implies complete trust in its omnipotence (Graham 1999, 9).

According to the French philosopher Jacques Ellul, such love of technology is an ideology. As he sees it, technology and applied science have such a prominent position in today's society that they have become its guiding myths. In *The Technological Bluff* (1990) he argues that modern-day belief in technology is based on the conviction that it is essential to society and can provide solutions to all of humankind's dreams. Anticipating the hopes that were to be pinned to the Internet some five years after the publication of the book Ellul asserts:

> Not only is technology good, not only is it indispensable, but also... it alone can achieve all that human beings have been seeking throughout centuries: liberty, democracy, justice, happiness (by a high standard of living), reduction of work, etc. (Ellul 1990, 30).

In other words, Ellul holds that, in the modern world, technology has been granted a significance previously associated with mythical, heavenly forces. First, it is thought to have powers that go beyond human capacities and it holds the promise of delivering what we long for. From this perspective, technology can be seen as an agent of salvation – it offers hope of a world better than the one we know. Second, being the point of reference to which our culture measures its truths and ideals, technology moulds and steers society's beliefs and values in a specific direction.

To use Neil Postman's formulation, in the contemporary world one can observe the 'deification of technology' (Postman 1992, 71). By this he means that technology has a growing influence on how life and the world are given meaning in Western societies. What he describes as a 'technological culture' 'seeks its authorization in technology, finds its satisfactions in technology, and takes its orders from technology' (Postman 1992, 72). In short, a technophiliac society refers to technology as a somehow transcendent, omnipotent power that forms the framework for definitions of what is important, desirable, and meaningful.

In this process of constructing meaning, a number of facets come to the fore that mark technophiliac discourses as religious. Namely, the construction of objects with a superhuman status, shared convictions and (utopian) beliefs, trust in the power of certain objects or individuals to bring about radically new and better ways of existence, and collective excitement about the objects or ideas in question.

The intense public fascination with the Internet was a prime case of technophilia and an exemplary manifestation of the religious dimensions just mentioned. Since its popularization and speedy commercialization from the mid-1990s onwards, this new technology has been praised as a radically new business opportunity, as the ultimate platform for democracy, as a cornucopia of self-generating riches, and as an agent that will make work and communication easier and more pleasant. Media reports and various popular-scientific and futuristic publications, with titles such as *Being Digital* (Negroponte 1995), *Meganet: How the Global Communications Network Will Connect Everyone on Earth* (Dizard 1997), *The Death of Distance: How the Communications Revolution Is Changing Our Lives* (Cairncross 1997) and *Telecosm: How Infinite Bandwidth Will Revolutionize Our World* (Gilder 2000), reveal the popular sentiment that with the introduction of the Internet something extraordinary and marvellous had started to take place. As early as in 1995, in an article entitled 'Technomania', a bewildered but enthusiastic journalist at *Newsweek* refers to the Internet as the mysterious and powerful entity that is bound to have far-reaching effects on our lives: 'as we grappled with the unanswered questions [with regard to the Internet], we're in for the ride of a lifetime' (Levy 1995). The author regards the introduction of digital information technology, such as the Internet as a momentous historical event. As he sees it, a 'Bit Bang' – the Big Bang of information technology – has taken place that 'will change every aspect of our lives' (Levy 1995).

In the years to follow, the Internet continued to be portrayed in these terms: as a fascinating and awe-inspiring force of exceptional capacities. The belief that it was the prime agent behind the birth of a new kind of society formed one of the central themes of the public discourse about the Internet. Albeit for a brief period, this technology was presented as *the* object that defined the nature of modern society. To speak with Neil Postman's words, the Internet became deified: it was seen as a superhuman force, an object capable of making sweeping changes in the world as we know it and thus worthy of worship.

Transcendence by Paradigm Shift

The Canadian scholar historian of technology, David Noble, describes technologies that are granted such extraordinary capacities to change the world as 'technologies of transcendence' (Noble 1999). To Noble, these are technological inventions upon which great hope is pinned and, typically, they are hailed as the means of overcoming the uncertainties and shortcomings of the human condition. In *The Religion of Technology* (1999) he argues that throughout history such 'technologies of transcendence' have been approached as the means to 'the recovery of man's lost divinity' (Noble 1999, 6). He shows that since the beginning of the second millennium crafts and skills, scientific knowledge and technology have been regarded as a step closer to divine powers and knowledge: ever-greater control over nature, space, the fate of humanity, and even mortality. Noble's examples from the more recent history are atomic weapons, space travel, artificial intelligence, and genetic engineering. In all these cases he recognizes the desire to transcend: to triumph over the forces of nature, to reach the heavens and rise above the limitations of the earth, to create life and overcome death. In short, when revered as a vehicle of transcendence, technology is seen as a means of reaching further than what was thought to be within the grasp of humans. Visions are sketched of how the world will be transformed under the influence of a new invention and often, utopian scenarios of a new world are born.

In the book *The Digital Economy. Promise and Peril in the Age of Networked Intelligence* (1997) by the Canadian writer Don Tapscott, one encounters a typical formulation of the feelings associated with the imminent rise of a new kind of reality where the Internet would play a key role:

> We are at the dawn of an Age of Networked Intelligence – an age that is giving birth to a new economy, a new politics and a new society. Businesses will be transformed, governments will be renewed, and individuals will be able to reinvent themselves – all with the help of information technology. (Tapscott 1997, 2)

Tapscott attributes remarkable powers to what is described as 'Networked Intelligence': it will transform society and redefine the very identity of individuals. In this new world ICT is to be the key to meanings, beliefs, and ways of acting. Of crucial importance to his argument is the emphasis on the radical break with the current, familiar worldview that the Internet era implies. As Tapscott sees it, new technology will be the cause of an all-encompassing revolution (Tapscott 1997, 4). This understanding of technology reveals a belief in its capacity as a vehicle of transcendence. In Tapscott's vision of the future, technology will take humanity beyond the hitherto known and give birth to new systems of meaning. However, in the secular tale of transcendence that Tapscott's book tells, we encounter an alternative, more scientific term for the process of exceeding the world as we know it: a 'shift', change or innovation in 'paradigm' (Tapscott 1997, 29; 54; 95).

Originally derived from Thomas Kuhn's *The Structure of Scientific Revolutions* (1962), the idea of paradigm change was a favoured metaphor in attempts made in the public discourse to emphasize the far-reaching influence of the Internet on various aspects of society (Burman 2003; Grow 2001; Tapscott & Caston 1992;). For instance, the 'high-tech high priest' (Goodman 2001) and 'techno-evangelist' (*Economist* 2000b; Helmore 1999) George Gilder, who saw cause for a 'paradigm party' to celebrate the rise of new technologies, spoke of a new, 'Gilder paradigm' in defining wealth and scarcity in the Internet era (Gilder 1996; 1998). Similarly, the *Financial Times* writes of a 'paradigm-shift in our cognisance of reality' (Pearson 1995), in trade (Authers 1998) and in institutional hierarchies (Taylor 1999). If Kuhn's term refers to fundamental changes in the set of accepted truths and practices that form a scientific discipline, then the paradigm of the Internet era also was associated with a revolution in truths and values.

Fashionable catch phrases and neologisms of the era, such as information superhighway, cyberspace, online world, electronic frontier, New or Knowledge Economy, network society, and so on all referred to this shift in paradigm. These terms suggested pioneering discoveries, innovation, and whole new conceptualizations of space, time, distance, social interaction, and of doing business. They carried the connotation that with the implementation of networked information technology society would be lifted above its *status quo* to a novel kind of existence. For example, in the best-selling book, *New Rules for the New Economy* (1999), Kevin Kelly describes the so-called New Economy as a new reality and he mentions three ways in which it differs from anything preceding it. First, it is disembodied and weightless, meaning that its main resource and object of trade are non-material products – 'information, relationships, copyright, entertainment, securities and derivatives' (Kelly 1999b, 3). Second, he considers information technology and 'ubiquitous electronic networks' (Kelly 1999b, 2) to be *the* sources of hitherto unknown wealth. Kelly notes that 'the network economy will unleash opportunities on a scale never seen before on Earth', and adds that this is not a far-fetched utopian statement

(Kelly 1999b, 156). Third, he describes the New Economy as global. With much excitement and some pretence of prophecy he makes it clear that the current point in history is an important one for the whole world: 'we are now at a moment when a cloak of glass fibres and a halo of satellites are closing themselves around the globe to bring forth a seamless economic culture' (Kelly 1999b, 156).

A number of distinctive themes become clear from the optimistic visions that informed this notion of a paradigm shift. If we recall Jacques Ellul's allusion to the promise of technology to fulfil a range of dreams, then the Internet was indeed regarded as the long-awaited answer to age-old aspirations: wealth and the betterment of standards of life, freedom and equality, the redefinition of space, and finally, harmony among humans and better mutual understanding. I shall discuss two of these themes – the belief that the Internet would radically transform our notions of space and distance, and the trust in its capacity as a liberating force.

Control over Matter and Space

In *Cyberspace and the American Dream: A Magna Carta for the Knowledge Age* (1994) a number of outspoken Internet visionaries affiliated with the Progress and Freedom Foundation (Esther Dyson, George Gilder, Alvin Toffler, and George Keyworth) expressed their belief that the Internet would play an active part in the 'overthrow of matter' and the ascendance 'of the power of the mind' (Dyson et al. 1994). In this collective statement an idea is presented that formed an important ingredient of the optimism about the Internet: in the information age greater emphasis would be on knowledge and digital data. 'Intangibles' – 'intellectual capital, skills, research and development (R&D), brands, relationships and reputation' (Zadek 2001, 28) – would eventually reduce the relevance of physical things.

Accordingly, Don Tapscott imagines that 'in the new economy, more and more of the economy's added value will be created by brain rather than brawn' (Tapscott 1997, 7). In a similar vein, in his *New Rules for the New Economy* Kelly posits that the influence of the Internet and other networked ICT will diminish the role of physical things in the world:

> The principles governing the world of the soft – the world of intangibles, of media, of software, and of services – will soon command the world of the hard – the world of reality, of atoms, of objects, of steel and oil, and

the hard work done by the sweat of brows. Iron and lumber will obey the laws of software, automobiles will follow the rules of networks, smoke-stacks will comply with the decrees of knowledge (Kelly 1999b, 2).

Such visions of a new kind of spatial experience were not propagated by science fiction and popular science writers alone. Reputable authorities from the academic world, such as Nicholas Negroponte and William Mitchell – both professors at MIT – claimed that bits and software were shaping the physical environments in which we live, and that they were increasingly transforming matter into data. As Negroponte says in *Being Digital* (1995): 'Digital living will include less and less dependence on being in a specific space at a specific time, and the transmission of place itself will start to become possible' (Negroponte 1995, 165). He imagines that in the near future, as the possibilities of cyberspace and the Internet are developed further, physical distances will become irrelevant for face-to-face experience: one will be connected with far-away places as if they were just outside one's window and even be able to smell the Swiss Alps and their '(digital) manure' when on the other side of the planet (Negroponte 1995, 7, 165).

As the Canadian author Vincent Mosco observes in the book *The Digital Sublime* (2004), Negroponte's writings on the digital world represent an unshakeable belief in the rise of a new way of life (Mosco 2004, 73). Indeed, no questions are asked about the move to a more immaterial kind of existence: 'the change from atoms to bits is irrevocable and unstoppable' (Negroponte 1995, 4). Digital technology and the Internet, then, run a course that appears independent of human intervention. They are astounding objects of trust and admiration that are elevated to a position higher than banal, daily existence, and have their own 'sacred and sublime mission', as Mosco puts it (Mosco 2004, 75).

Related to the idea that the material world was being marginalized was the notion that, as the Internet was 'fundamentally and profoundly *anti-spatial*' (Mitchell 1995, 8), it would have the effect of diminishing or even eliminating distances. This idea was elaborated in many publications, such as Frances Cairncross' *The Death of Distance: How the Communications Revolution Is Changing our Lives* (1997), *The Road Ahead* (1995) by Bill Gates, and various best-selling books by the 'digital guru' George Gilder. The recurrent theme in these books was that the Internet would not only make contact between great distances possible but facilitate instant exchange of materials digitally. Thus, Cairncross foresees that 'the death of distance loosens the grip of geography', causing borders and barriers to break down (Cairncross 1997, 5), Gilder describes networked information technology as the agent behind the 'overthrow of matter' (Gilder 1990, 15-58), and Gates hails new ICT and the 'global information market' (Gates 1995, 6) as the means of making distance and geography less relevant or eliminating them altogether (Gates 1995, 6, 152, 181). Again, one can detect hopes of transcendence: the Internet is expected to give us power over matter and be the agent of a new kind of existence.

Internet, a Liberating Force

The idea that the Internet would grant humanity access to new powers was a recurrent theme in accounts about this new technology. In addition to the anticipated control over space and matter, hopes of greater personal power and autonomy were projected onto this technology. The Internet was expected to bring about a general de-centralization of power, eliminate all manner of intermediaries, lift limitations set on people by gender, race, social class or physical disability, and further democracy (Barlow 1996; Cairncross 1997; Dizard 1997; Dyson 1998; Mitchell 1995; Negroponte 1995; Rheingold 2002). *Newsweek* summarizes the ethic of the Internet as follows: 'voraciously free expression, a drive for individual empowerment, a loathing for authority and a strong libertarian strain' (Levy & Hafner 1995). At long last, what the American author Andrew Shapiro describes as 'control revolution' was to take place and make it possible for private persons to participate directly and more actively in decision making processes (Shapiro 1999).

The Internet and related new technologies would facilitate unknown freedom, create space for individual development and break down established social hierarchies. For instance, *Newsweek* imagined that they had potential to topple dictatorships:

> Obviously, the decentralizing nature of the computer poses a threat to dictators... But the same dynamic confounds managers everywhere, as computers and networks amplify the powers of individuals and twist the corporate organizational charts (Levy & Hafner 1995).

As Hand and Sandywell put it in their criticism of what they call 'e-topia' (utopian thought relating specifically to electronic communications media), under the influence of the Internet, future civic life was imagined as 'a continuous "town meeting" where active citizens devote most of their time and energy to debating the public good to create a genuinely communitarian culture of self-reflexive civic subjects' (Hand and Sandywell 2002, 201).

The above-mentioned publication 'Cyberspace and the American Dream' is an exemplary illustration of such an e-topia. In this collective statement, ICT and the Internet are linked to aspirations that constitute American mythology. As the title of the document suggests, the Internet is presented as the next step in the realization of the American Dream and an appeal is made to the frontier mentality. The authors of the statement envision the Internet as the new American frontier, a fresh realm that has no established constraints and where everything is still possible. This is a place of complete pre-modern freedom: '[The Internet] spells the death of the central institutional paradigm of modern life, the bureaucratic organization' (Dyson et al. 1994). Together with the promises of new riches and domains to discover and conquer, the Internet was to offer liberty and self-determination. It came to be associated with one of the highest values current in the United States: the freedom achieved by the first settlers.

Internet, a Vessel of Religiosity

According to the authors of 'Cyberspace and the American Dream' and others, such as John Perry Barlow, the author of 'A Declaration of the Independence of Cyberspace' (1996), long-term dreams of liberty would be fulfilled and barriers would inevitably disappear. Others have claimed that the Internet would make us less dependent on the limitations of space and distances. Others still have declared the Internet to be the carrier of a lasting 'age of prosperity' (Schwartz et al 1999, title) and predicted a future of 'ultraprosperity' for everyone (Kelly 1999c). As Kevin Kelly puts it, 'the good news is, you'll be a millionaire soon. The bad news is, so will everybody else' (Kelly 1999c).

But, typically for the rhetoric of Internet enthusiasm, the precise reasons for these developments remain unclear. As Mosco points out, the discourse about the influence of digital technology, including the Internet, on society was filled with charismatic sentiments (Mosco 2004, 74). The Internet had gained special authority and its enigmatic powers were not questioned. With examples of writings by Barlow, Dyson and her co-authors, and others, such as MIT professor Negroponte, Mosco shows that the enthusiastic rhetoric about the Internet throve on stories of 'mythic transcendence' (Mosco 2004, 75). That is, the optimistic tales about the Internet celebrated digital communications technology as a force that rises above the banal and is capable of performing wonders. As Mosco says, the idea propagated among a number of Internet pundits was that this technology represented a historically unique phenomenon that could not be compared to anything preceding it and therefore had an exalted value of its own (Mosco 2004, 82). Technology was deified: it had a logic of its own; it could not and needed not be explained.

Looking at the high expectations for the Internet, one cannot help but recognize an old vision of a long-awaited liberator that will eliminate oppressive systems and install a reign of freedom and independence. Without any clear links to religious tradition, this strong belief in better times nonetheless contains an essentially religious message: an all-powerful and awe-inspiring phenomenon will transform how we understand and experience the world. It will bring salvation, help us transcend to a new kind of existence and, above all, it will confirm with great clarity the defining values of our society: liberty and equality.

Judging by the amount of media coverage and the infiltration of the theme of the Internet beyond specialist literature into general popular culture, the belief in the power of the Internet to bring about great changes to life as we know it was a source of shared, public exhilaration. During the heyday of Internet enthusiasm a number of dedicated lifestyle magazines were born (*Fast Company, Mondo 2000, Wired*, and *Red Herring*) and the Internet was subject to intense attention from established general interest magazines as well. For instance, between 1993 and 2002, *Time* magazine featured the Internet and its many visionaries and heroes on its cover on at least twenty occasions. The election of Jeff Bezos, the founder of the web-based bookstore Amazon.com, as the magazine's Person of the Year in 1999 is a telling sign of the special status granted to the Internet in the public discourse. With Bezos' title, the Internet and enterprises related to it are honoured as phenomena of historical import for the world. Similarly, when *Newsweek* calls 1995 'The Year of the Internet' (Levy & Hafner 1995) or when *Wired* magazine claims that 'We're facing 25 years of prosperity, freedom, and a better environment for the whole world' (Schwartz et al. 1997), the emphasis is on the collective experience of something of great social and emotional significance.

According to Emile Durkheim, high-spirited communal expression of emotion or shared 'effervescence' is a key to the rise of religious feelings (Durkheim 2001, 164). It is at these instances that sacred objects are created, shared beliefs arise, and ties between individuals in a community are forged and strengthened. In the case of technophile enthusiasm for the

Internet, this sort of effervescence arose in the public discourse carried out via the journalistic media and publications by various visionaries. Albeit a completely different setting than the corroborees of the Australian Aborigines to which Durkheim refers in his discussion of effervescence in *The Elementary Forms of Religion* (1912/2001), the same processes were at work. Namely, in the discourse about the Internet, a transcendent object of reverence was constructed and a set of values and aspirations were articulated that served as the defining points in the formation of a specific worldview, that of the Internet Age.

Conclusion

As several authors have shown, in some form or another, religiosity continues to play a role even in secular areas where modernization and rationalization seemingly reign supreme (Alexander 2003; Aupers 2004; Szerszynski 2005; Wertheim 2000). In various disguises forms of religion exist that are uncoupled from official religious institutions and whose religiosity has therefore been obscured or ignored. While one may accept the claim that in some parts of the world, organized religion has lost the importance it once had, religion as such shows no signs of disappearing. In the modern, Western world religious sentiments are often integrated and implied in seemingly non-religious social phenomena.

The collective love for the Internet as it took shape in discourses in the media and other publications throughout the second half of the 1990s was one such vessel of religiosity. Religiosity manifested itself in the tales of paradigm change that envisioned the rise, or transcendence of humanity to a different kind of existence; there were religious facets to the representations of the Internet as a force capable of diminishing distances and controlling matter. Equally, the role of an agent of freedom and equality that was granted to the Internet has a religious significance, as it links technology to hopes of salvation. Furthermore, the techno-utopian dreams related to the Internet gave rise to collective emotions, provided shared objects of admiration and (re)articulated values that constitute the modern Western worldview (freedom, equality, progress).

As to the allusions to biblical tales, such the *Business Week* cover mentioned in the introduction to this paper, phrases such as 'the John the Baptist of the Digital Age' (Malone 2000), the characterization of a manager at Cisco Systems as an 'evangelist of the Internet gospel' (*Economist* 1999) or the description of the Internet as 'God's gift to marketing' (Millar

1996), these are primarily rhetorical tools. Although there are recognizable echoes of religious tradition, the use of such vocabulary does not necessarily mean that an explicitly religious agenda is pursued that binds the described object to specific dogmas. Rather, it is often a token of a more implicit form of religion, which is embedded in secular phenomena and institutions. In discourses concerned with technological inventions such as the Internet, terminology and analogies that refer to religious traditions are expressions of strong faith in the extraordinary power and the special, even sacred status of technology. They are employed in order to express technophile sentiments and values with familiar and suitably emotive vocabulary.

References

Alexander, A. 14 October 1999. Bill Gates points the way to his brave new world. *Daily Mail*, 79.

Alexander, J.C. 2003. The Sacred and the Profane Information Machine. In J.C. Alexander, ed., *The Meanings of Social Life. A Cultural Sociology*. Oxford, etc.: Oxford University Press, 179-192.

Aupers, S. 2004. *In de ban van moderniteit: de sacralisering van het zelf en computertechnologie*. Amsterdam: Aksant.

Authers, J. 24 June 1998. From DIY to branded broking on the net. *Financial Times*, 28.

Baker, R. and J. Beaton. 1997. Surfer's paradise. *Inc. 19*(16), 57-64.

Barlow, J.P. 1996. A Declaration of the Independence of Cyberspace, retrieved 17 August 2008, from: http://www.eff.org/Misc/Publications/ John_Perry_Barlow/ barlow_0296.declaration.txt

Bellah, R.N. 1970. *Beyond Belief: Essays on Religion in a Post-Traditional World*. New York: Harper & Row.

Berger, B. 2000. The Wunderkind. *NetGuide, 3*(3), 152-153.

Burman, E. 2003. *Shift!: The Unfolding Internet – Hype, Hope and History*. Chichester: John Wiley & Sons.

Cairncross, F. 1997. *The Death of Distance: How the Communications Revolution Is Changing our Lives*. Boston: Harvard Business School Press.

Calviello, J. and *Business Week* 4 October 1999. Front cover image. *Business Week 3649*. Cover.

Clarke, H. 1998. The Hillary Clarke interview: I'd like to teach the world to surf. *The Independent*: 29 (22.11).

Corn, J.J. ed. 1986. *Imagining Tomorrow: History, Technology, and the American Future.* Cambridge, MA: MIT Press.

Cortese, A. 1995. The software revolution. The Internet changes everything. *Business Week* (3453): 78.

Czitrom, D.J. 1982. *Media and the American Mind. From Morse to McLuhan.* Chapel Hill: University of North Carolina Press.

Dertouzos, M.L. 1997. *What Will Be: How the New World of Information Will Change Our Lives.* New York: HarperEdge.

Dizard, W.P. 1997. *Meganet: How the Global Communications Network Will Connect Everyone on Earth.* Boulder: Westview Press.

Durkheim, E. 2001. *The Elementary Forms of Religious Life.* Oxford: Oxford University Press.

Dyson, E., G. Gilder, G. Keyworth, and A. Toffler. 1994. Cyberspace and the American Dream: A Magna Carta for the Knowledge Age, retrieved: 17 August 2008, from: http://www.pff.org/issues-pubs/futureinsights/fi1.2magnacarta.html

Economist 1995. A new electronic Messiah. *Economist, 336* (7926), 62.

— 1995. Paradise by the modem lights. *Economist, 336* (7921), 14-15.

— 1999. Cisco's reluctant evangelist. *Economist, 351* (8118), 65.

— 2000. The accidental messiah. *Economist, 354* (8163), 73.

— 2000. Praise the baud. *Economist, 356* (8187), 103-104

Ellul, J. 1990. *The Technological Bluff.* Grand Rapids: William B. Eerdmans Publishing.

Gates, B. 1995. *The Road Ahead.* London: Viking Press.

Gilder, G. 1990. *Microcosm: The Quantum Revolution in Economics and Technology.* New York: Free Press.

— 1996. The Gilder Paradigm, *Wired,* 4 (12), 17 August 2008, from: http://wired-vig.wired.com/wired/archive/4.12/gilder.html

— 1997. Inventing the Internet again. *Forbes, 159* (11), 106-120.

— 1998. Paradigm Party. *Forbes, 162* (4), 94-100.

— 2000. *Telecosm: How Infinite Bandwidth Will Revolutionize Our World.* New York: Free Press.

Goodman, W. 04 March 2001. Miracle Workers. *The New York Times,* 3.

Gore, A. 1997. Remarks by Vice President Al Gore at the Internet/Online Summit. Renaissance Hotel, Washington DC. Tuesday, 2 December 1997, retrieved 17 August 2008, from: http://www.usdoj.gov/criminal/cybercrime/gore-sp.htm

— 1998. Remarks prepared for Vice President Al Gore at the 15th International ITU Conference, Monday, 12 October 1998, retrieved 17 August 2008, from: http://clinton3.nara.gov/WH/EOP/OVP/speeches/itu.html

Graham, G. 1999. *The Internet. A philosophical inquiry*. London: Routledge.

Grow, B. 2001. A Net Apostle Keeps the Faith. *Business Week Online*.

Guardian 10 September 1998. Europe's wired isle. *Guardian*, 2.

Hand, M. and B. Sandywell. 2002. E-topia as Cosmopolis or Citadel On the Democratizing and De-democratizing Logics of the Internet, or, Toward a Critique of the New Technological Fetishism *Theory, Culture & Society 19* (1-2), 197-225.

Helmore, E. 10 January 1999. Internet on line for new revolution. *The Observer*, 8.

Kaplan, D. A. 1999. Silicon Heaven. *Newsweek, 133* (24), 48-52.

Kelly, K. 1999a. Nerd theology. *Technology in Society 21*, 387-392.

— 1999b. *New Rules for the New Economy: 10 Radical Strategies for a Connected World*. London: Penguin Books.

— 1999c. Prophets of Boom. George Gilder. Wealth Is the Right Thing to Do, *Wired*, 7 (09), retrieved 17 August 2008, from: http://wired-vig.wired.com/wired/archive/7.09/prophets.html

— 2002. God Is the Machine, *Wired*, 10 (12), retrieved 17 August 2008, from: http://wired-vig.wired.com/wired/archive/10.12/holytech.html

Kuhn, T. 1962. *The Structure of Scientific Revolutions*. Chicago: University of Chicago Press.

Levy, S. 1995. Technomania. *Newsweek, 125* (9), 24-30.

Levy, S. and K. Hafner. 1995. This Changes...Everything. *Newsweek, 126/127* (26/1), 22-30.

Luckmann, T. 1967. *The Invisible Religion. The Problem of Religion in Modern Society*. New York: Macmillan.

Mack, T. 1999. Paul Allen Bandwidth Believer. *Forbes, 164* (12), 186-192.

Malone, M.S. 2000. The Gildered Age. *Forbes, 165* (4), 124-130.

Millar, I. 04 July 1996. Never mind the quality, feel the bandwidth. *Guardian* , 11.

Mitchell, W.J. 1995. *City of Bits: Space, Place, and the Infobahn*. Cambridge, MA: MIT Press.

Mosco, V. 2004. *The Digital Sublime. Myth, Power, and Cyberspace*. Cambridge, MA: MIT Press.

Negroponte, N. 1995. *Being Digital*. London: Hodder & Stoughton.

Noble, D. 1999. *The Religion of Technology. The Divinity of Man and the Spirit of Invention*. London: Penguin.

Paternot, S. 2001. *A Very Public Offering. A Rebel's Story of Business Excess, Success, and Reckoning*. New York: John Wiley.

Pearson, K.A. 29 July 1995. Journey to the heart of cyberspace. *Financial Times*, 10.

Pennar, K. 1997. Info-age evangelist. Esther Dyson. *Business Week* (3549), 92.

Postman, N. 1992. *Technopoly: The Surrender of Culture to Technology.* New York: Knopf.

Quittner, J. 1999. An Eye on the Future. *Time, 154* (26), 56-66.

Reinhardt, A. 1999. MR. INTERNET: Cisco Systems CEO John Chambers has a vision of a New World Order. *Business Week, 3646,* 128.

Reiss, S. and J. Levine. 1999. St. Tim of the Web. *Forbes, 164* (2), 314-317.

Rheingold, H. 2002. *The Virtual Community: Homesteading on the Electronic Frontier.* Cambridge, MA: MIT Press.

Schwartz, P. and P. Leyden. 1997. The Long Boom: A History of the Future, 1980-2020. *Wired, 5* (07), retrieved: 17 August 2008, from: http://www.wired.com/wired/archive/5.07/longboom.html

Schwartz, P., P. Leyden, and J. Hyatt. 1999. *The Long Boom. A vision of the coming age of prosperity.* Cambridge, MA: Perseus Publishing.

Shapiro, A.L. 1999. *Control Revolution: How the Internet is Putting Individuals in Charge and Changing the World We Know.* New York: The Century Foundation.

Szerszynski, B. 2005. *Nature, Technology and the Sacred.* Oxford: Blackwell.

Tapscott, D. 1995. *The Digital Economy. Promise and Peril in the Age of Networked Intelligence.* New York: McGraw-Hill.

Tapscott, D. and Caston, A. 1992. *Paradigm Shift. The New Promise of Information Technology.* New York :McGraw-Hill.

Taylor, R. 16 December 1999. Back to a more prosperous future. *Financial Times* , 16.

Wertheim, M. 2000. *The Pearly Gates of Cyberspace.* London: Virago.

Zadek, S. 2001. *The Civil Corporation: the New Economy of Corporate Citizenship.* London: Earthscan.

Part Two

RELIGIOUS RESOURCES FOR THE ECOLOGICAL CRISIS

4   Re-Imagining the Human-Environment Relationship via Religious Traditions and New Scientific Cosmologies

Tony Watling

Introduction

This article explores how a number of religious traditions and science-based cosmologies (as represented in a 'field of religion and ecology') understand nature, particularly in response to the environmental crisis, using metaphors, myths, and symbols, to 're-imagine' it, attempting to create new environmentally-friendly meanings and actions.[1] The environmental crisis in this sense is seen as being not only economic or technological but also moral and spiritual, based on a modern, Western, Enlightenment worldview (and associated secular/scientific myths) that sought to liberate humanity from dependence on nature, via reason and progress, but has, however, developed into an anthropocentric desire to master and transcend nature, replacing previous animistic, experiential, holistic, ways of perceiving the environment, with a mechanical, objective, reductionist view, with humanity separated from a commodified nature (separating mind/body, matter/spirit). This has led to a disenchantment and ecological illiteracy (the earth being denied spirit or subjectivity, being measured by economic or technological standards).[2] Such perceptions about humanity and nature, then, have been seen to become dominant, defining reality, leading to destructive ecological responses. However, such a way of looking at the world is also seen as socially constructed; nature is a diverse and malleable concept, always a social practice. It is argued therefore, that what is needed is a critique of the construction of reality, dialogue about and counter views of (a politicization of) nature; new worldviews with new ecological myths, embracing organic, subjective, or spiritual, views, reconnecting humanity with nature, enabling ecologically orientated lifestyles, respecting and caring for the environment (Cronon 1996; Callicott 1997; Gardner 2002; Maxwell 2003; McGrath 2003; Metzner 1994; Oelschlaeger 1994; Soule 1995; Tucker 2002; Tucker and Grim 2001; Weiming 1994).[3]

It is argued that a new imaginative language is needed to re-root humanity in the earth. Metaphors are seen as being fundamental to this process. They express fundamental concepts through which humans understand and organize experience, having the power (rational, emotional) to create (personal, social) reality. They may thus be crucial for re-creating the conception of the world and the human place within it. Cosmogonies, or creation stories, for example, locate the present in sacred time, providing a common cognitive legitimacy and meaningfulness, linking moral orientations to cosmic origins. They create feelings of belonging, divulging humanity's connection to a wider scheme, highlighting its role and destiny. Rethinking or re-appropriating accounts of creation may thus stimulate a rethinking of ecological behaviour. Such ideas link to myth in that they provide a meaningful and powerful imaginative or symbolic narrative that orients humanity, providing the basis for knowledge and wisdom, and evoking ways of interpreting and acting within the world. Such images are cosmological, relating to the origin, order, and meaning, of the cosmos and the human condition. They relate 'truths' and principles that define possibilities and limitations, being the basis of creative activities of cultures. Humanity in this sense has been described as a 'mythopoeic' species, unable to exist without narratives or stories through which to understand, engage, and order, the world. Hence, to effectively address the environmental crisis it is argued that humanity must attend to its stories; creating a (metaphoric) re-imagination of the world and the role of humanity within it (Bolle 2005a; 2005b; Callicott 1997; Lakoff and Johnson 1980; Long 2005; Oelschlaeger 1994; Tucker 2002).

Traditionally, religion has provided such narratives, but in the modern world religion is seen to be in decline and lacking relevance; religious traditions are losing control of social life to secular bodies, their beliefs no longer providing existential meaning (e.g. secularization). However, religion may not be so static or unitary a phenomenon as previously thought (neither may secularization; such ideas may be a consequence of an objective, rational Western bias, creating an 'official' 'religious' category and ignoring unofficial views). It may rather be a complex, dynamic process of individual and social, official and unofficial, actions in particular contexts. Religion may thus be capable of interacting with new developments, creating new meanings, and re-ordering personal and social beliefs and identities (albeit in more diverse and fluid forms) (Beyer 1994; Casanova 1994; Woodhead and Heelas 2000). This may be especially so as recent social changes (economic, scientific, technological), and their often deleterious effects on the environment, cause instability and moral dilemmas while isolating individuals from the moral resources needed to address them. In particular, it has been argued that religion can be useful (even essential) in addressing the environmental crisis. Religious traditions (with histories of ethical reflection and frameworks of myths and symbols) are seen to go beyond egoism and materialism, stressing the sacredness and order of nature, defining humanity's place in it, highlighting its obligations to it, providing meaningful guidance. They are thus thought to have the (metaphoric) means, the critical and prophetic potential, and the influential moral authority to re-imagine the environment (and humanity), to contest dominant views of it, and to provide new values and social direction through creating, recovering, and expressing, ecologically oriented metaphors, myths, and symbols (Beyer 1994; Gardner 2002; McGrath 2003; Oelschlaeger 1994; Tucker and Grim 2005).[4]

To provide such ecological re-imagination, however, religions traditions may need to be re-interpreted in a more eco-centric way. Judeo-Christianity, for example, has been seen as being too anthropocentric, and possibly anti-environmentalist, stressing humanity as dominant and nature as passive. Many religions have been seen as world-denying, concentrating on human salvation alone, or as being part of political regimes that are ecologically destructive.[5] Such an ecological awareness of religions – what is seen as religion entering an 'ecological phase' – has been growing over a period of time, and has been termed the 'greening of religion' (Nash 1989; Tucker 2003). In particular, there is a growing 'field' of 'religion and ecology', a range of academic and religious literature and actions exploring and promoting eco-religious ideas, deepening spiritual awareness of nature, and encouraging ecological activism (Tucker 2003; Tucker and Grim 2001; 2005; Watling 2008a).[6] Such initiatives aim to engage the transformative possibilities of religion, reclaiming and reconstructing traditions so as to promote flourishing human-earth relations. They aim to reconceptualize religious attitudes to nature and to create a cross-cultural reservoir and mutually enriching dialogue of imagination, commitment, and wisdom, providing interdependent ecological ethics based around the common ground of the sacred reality of the world, while still being sensitive to the cultural and historical context (assessing and using religions in a self-reflective, not self-promoting, way; respecting claims to truth, but exploring different avenues to truth) (Callicott 1997;

Oelschlaeger 1994; Tucker 2003; Tucker and Grim 2001; 2005). In this way, new 'religious' views may emerge alongside traditional ones. In particular, in this light, science is seen as a possible source of new views, offering meaningful resources for understanding the world and humanity's role in it, as well as combating environmental problems by suggesting new ways of acting, particularly since it is considered as having plausibility as well as global reach, and as being able to co-exist with and encompass other views. Such science is not envisaged as materialistic, objective, or reductionist, however, but rather interdisciplinary, holistic, and organic, possibly spiritual and teleological, what has been called 'deep' science, an imaginative epistemology of rational empiricism and spiritual awareness (a 'scientific paganism'). This is seen as science entering its 'wisdom phase' and encountering mystery and meaning (possibly synthesizing with religion), going beyond purely rational explanations and objective facts, and using metaphor, myth, and symbol, to inspire new (subjective) visions of the environment and the human place in it, creating intimacy and inspiring reverence (Barlow 1997; Brockelman 1999; Callicott 1997; Griffin 1988; Maxwell 2003; Metzner 1994; Taylor 2001).[7]

It is argued, then, that cross-cultural comparisons of (and dialogue between) religious and scientific concepts of nature, human nature, and human/nature interaction, are needed to enable engagement with ecological issues. New 'earth literate' religious or science-based cosmologies, highlighting the (holistic, organic, spiritual) cause, nature, and purpose of life, reconnecting and re-integrating humanity and nature (mind/body, matter/spirit) are seen as possible foundations for ecological ethics and actions in relation to the environment and the human place in it, able to inspire new visions and provide new guiding myths. In this article, therefore, I qualitatively and ethnographically explore such ideas by analyzing and comparing new ecological views being stressed among two Eastern and two Western religious traditions, Buddhism and Chinese religions and Judaism and Christianity,[8] as well as two science-inspired cosmologies, Deep Ecology and Gaia[9] (stressed in the field of religion and ecology).[10] I analyse and compare the ecological metaphors, myths, and symbols stressed, exploring what they say about nature and the human place in it and examine what this may mean for future (ecological, scientific, religious) identities and actions. I will examine how religious and scientific individuals and traditions may be re-assessing their views, recovering forgotten ecological themes or stimulating new ones, while exploring and highlighting how religion and science are creatively and dynamically being re-addressed in the modern context.

Eastern Religious Traditions and Ecology

Buddhism

'The Six Great Elements are interfused and are in a state of eternal harmony. The Four Mandalas are inseparably related to one another. When the grace of the Three Mysteries is retained (our inborn mysteries will) quickly be manifested. Infinitely interrelated like the meshes of Indra's net are those we call existences' (Ingram 1997, 75).

These lines of an esoteric Shingon Buddhist poem are, for Ingram (1997), seen as highlighting a Buddhist, organic, holistic view of nature. Here the six elements, earth, water, fire, wind, space, and consciousness, highlight the timeless, non-dual, harmony of the universe, all life arising simultaneously with mutual causality via their interaction, with the aim of existence the awareness and experience of this. To achieve this awareness, four mandalas (paintings of Buddha in colours representing the interpenetrating elements) encourage meditation towards harmony with nature, integrating the three mysteries, body, speech, and mind. This is correlated with 'Indra's net' of many-sided jewels, each reflecting the other, highlighting their (and the world's) interdependence. If one jewel becomes cloudy (e.g. environmental pollution, species decline) or clear (e.g. environmental clean-up, species protection) this is reflected in the others (unbalancing or balancing the whole, emphasizing humanity's wider connections and responsibilities) (Barnhill 1997; Callicott 1997; Kaza 2002; Loori 1997; Sponberg 1997; Swearer 2001).

Such ideas highlight 'Green Buddhism', a movement using Buddhism as a source for eco-friendly advice. In this scheme, Buddhism is seen as an 'ecological religion' with concern for nature integral to its beliefs and practices. Buddha's Four Noble Truths – the universal reality of suffering, the cause of suffering through desire, freedom from desire as freedom from suffering, and freedom as lying in moral discipline and spiritual depth – are especially highlighted for their ecological importance. In this sense, the basis of any Buddhist 'eco-ethics' is the recognition that suffering is caused by *trishna*, a selfish attachment to existence ('I self'; alienation from the world), and that to overcome this requires moral and spiritual learning in order to realize the 'true' nature of reality, which is the ontological interrelation of the world ('we self', uniting with the world), and hereby experience 'enlightenment'. These ideas are linked to Buddhist teachings of *dharma*, meaning a path to truth and things in nature, highlighting interdependence, that all inner and outer phenomena are inseparable: all beings are *dharmas* or have '*dharma* nature', a universal essence, and the potential to attain enlightenment through acting compassionately, cultivating interdependence, and creating *sangha*, or community. In line with this the doctrine of *karma*, or cause and effect, and the concept of *samsara*, or rebirth, where all thoughts, words, or deeds, shape experiences, affecting the whole, are also seen to link life in the (moral) continuum of the enlightenment process (and stress human responsibility to wider nature) (Barnhill 1997; Callicott 1997; Gross 2002; Kaza 2002; Loori 1997; Sponberg 1997; Swearer 2001).

Enlightenment, then, is the path not only to truth and a fuller realization of existence, but also to environmental, personal, social, and spiritual health. To achieve it involves, for Swearer (2001), a 'particular-general principle' process, following the Buddha's example: understanding personal karmic history, then the karmic history of humanity, and finally the principle underlying the cause of suffering. This is seen, by Sponberg (1997), as a 'hierarchy of compassion' where, unlike Western individualistic views, 'progress' is an evolution of consciousness toward the awareness and cultivation of interdependence: more evolved beings accept inter-dependence and thus have greater compassion, wisdom, and responsibility, towards life. This is a progress that moves away from selfishness and consumerism, a 'virtue ethic' involving the 'threefold learning' of morality, meditation, and insight, leading to a 'mindful awareness' and 'middle path' moderate lifestyle, overcoming dualism (self-denial/self-indulgence), providing stability and balance. To achieve it involves using nature as a teacher of balance and interrelation, or abiding by traditional 'precepts' such as not creating evil, practicing good, or being truthful (the 'eight-fold path' of right understanding, intention, speech, action, livelihood, effort, mindfulness, and concentration). In this scheme simplicity and discipline of lifestyle is a moral virtue, something highlighted by Buddhist temples and monasteries, which are seen as ideal eco-friendly *sanghas* or communities (and whose example can be enlarged globally in a 'Great Earth *Sangha*') (Gross 2002; Kaza 2002; Loori 1997; Maguire 2000; Palmer and Finlay 2003; Sponberg 1997; Swearer 2001).

Chinese Traditions (Confucianism and Daoism)[11]

In ecological terms, Chinese religions are stressed as sharing a worldview that is organic, vitalistic, and holistic, seeing the universe as a creative, harmonious process (what is termed *sheng-sheng*, or 'production and reproduction'). In this scheme the universe is complete and self-generating, combining heaven and earth, spirit and matter, with all things interdependent via ongoing relationships, and the aim of life is to realize harmony with natural rhythms of the cosmos – what is seen as 'the Way' (*Dao*), the 'primeval wisdom of reality'. This dynamic of harmonic relationships is seen to occur through the cosmos being filled with *qi*, a vital energy that links the material and spiritual, composed of and expressed via two complementary elements, *yin* and *yang*, in balanced interaction (represented in opposites, e.g. positive/negative, male/female). Relational change, therefore, is the principal characteristic of nature and (correct) human existence is the process of flowing with rather than resisting this change (in this sense there may be good and bad ways of channeling *qi* with Chinese gardens, medicine, painting, or *feng shui*, argued as producing relational balance between landscape or objects, allowing *qi* to flow) (Kinsley 1994; Maguire 2000; Tucker 1994; Weiming 2002; Weller and Bol 1998). Confucianism and Daoism are seen to interpret and experience this worldview in different ways: the former stressing the secondary causality of humans and a harmonious human society via social and political commitment, the latter stressing the primary causality of the *Dao* and a withdrawal from social and political affairs and spontaneous closeness to nature. Confucians thus encourage a rethinking of individual/society/ nature connections, stressing moral education and responsibility and a moral ruler representing humane government and ethical practice, while Daoists encourage re-examination of human/earth relations and the unfolding of natural processes and see the non-involved hermit as an ideal (Tucker 1994; see Callicott 1997; Kinsley 1994).

Confucian views are seen to involve 'cosmic humanism', focusing on human society and virtues. Humanity forms 'one body' with the cosmos (virtue of *qi*) but has a special role: it has the highest expression of *qi* and most sentience, and is, therefore, charged with enhancing the balance of nature. This is seen as an 'anthropocosmic' view – a unity and mutual responsiveness of Heaven-Earth-Humanity. Humans are situated within the organic processes of nature and exist in concentric circles of relationships – family, community, nature (a kinship based on *qi*) – with a mutual reciprocity of obligations and larger sense of common good. The Mandate of Heaven, or moral law, thus enjoins humans to take part in cosmic transformation. This requires a 'relational resonance' in tune with a 'cosmic resonance' – a mutual (moral) response to myriad things. In this scheme, human thoughts, feelings, and actions, respond to movements of *qi* in the world. Furthermore, there is a proper or appropriate response to this in accordance with *li*, or patterns of the cosmos. 'Authentic' Confucian humanity, then, involves continuous self-transcendence, overcoming egoism through practicing *jen*, or 'humaneness', something that is exemplified by the 'sage', who is attuned to the environment (with the *Dao*), instantiating the perfection of natural order in thought and action (Adler 1998; Callicott 1997; Cheng 1998; Maguire 2000; Weiming 2002; Weller and Bol 1998).

Whereas Confucianism is seen to stress cultivation of self and nature, Daoism is seen to stress nature for its own sake, seeing simplicity, spontaneity, intuitive knowledge, and non-interference as appropriate ways of interacting with the world. This is described as *wu-wei*, a 'non (assertive) action' that is indirect and respectful, involving 'feminine' behaviour (yielding rather than asserting, soft rather than hard), eliminating competition or desire. In this sense 'appropriate' actions are those that produce the best results from minimum effort, avoiding over-doing. The aim is to penetrate beyond the physical to the primordial essence of *Dao* and mirror its operation (something termed 'self-so'). The aim is to be like water – soft and yielding, yet able to wear away rock – a potentiality of generative action. This follows the *Dao*, which is empty and full of potentiality, allowing things to develop in their own ways. 'Daoist ecology' then, in this sense, is not an intellectual principle; 'knowing' involves comprehending existence though relationships attending to the rhythms of the cosmos, not 'improving' them. Daoism trusts the world and natural processes to operate as they are supposed to – in harmony. Non-action is compassionate whereas action can cause unintended problems by upsetting the harmony (therefore, if things run counter to the harmony of nature they must be abandoned even if they are in human self-interest). The practical result of this is asceticism, training the will to follow nature's ways (Ames 2001; Callicott 1997; Kinsley 1994; Kirkland 2001; Tucker 1994).

Western Religious Traditions and Ecology

Judaism

Jewish ideas on ecology are seen as integral to relationships between God, humanity, and the world. In this scheme, the world belongs to God, who created it (and renews this creation daily), and created everything 'according to its kind', assigning unique value to species and arguing for their conservation; all species thus have meaning and purpose and need to be respected and cared for due to their God-given place and role. God thus has regard for all of creation, its individual species and its overall pattern.

Bio-diversity in this sense relates to the rightness of God's pattern for creation which meets His intent independent of human concerns or notions of cause and effect. The world in this sense is an allusion to God, full of His glory, and an object of divine concern (inspiring amazement and humility, tempering human egoism) (Goodman 2002; Hutterman 2002; Rose 1992; Solomon 1992; Tirosh-Samuelson 2001; Waskow 2002).

In line with this, the concept of *bal tashchit*, or 'do not destroy', is stressed. This is seen to emphasize that creation is to be conserved and not wasted. This is also seen as highlighting a Jewish 'tradition' of moderation, limiting lavishness and conspicuous consumption – creation is God's gift, humanity is to help preserve and improve it, being of the earth but also (virtue of *imago Dei*) its crowning achievement, this conferring privilege and also responsibility; humanity is a caretaker or steward leasing the land in covenantal trust (not the owner of it) (Goodman 2002; Jacobs 2002; Solomon 1992; Tirosh-Samuelson 2001). Maguire (2000) highlights the theme of exile in this, seeing humanity being alienated (via egoism) from its true role and its destiny of a harmonic Eden, which is a vision of the future, a 'promised land' not yet reached. Judaism's historical escape from destruction, in this sense, thus mirrors humanity, which exists in a lost desert at present. Along these lines, Jacobs (2002) emphasizes *teshuva*, repentance or 'beginning again', and argues for an 'ecological *teshuva*', restoring harmonious ecological balance (also related to *tikkun olam* or 'repair of the world'). Such a new, repentant humanity creates justice (*sedaqah*, argued as being the heart of Judaism), for people and nature, via the cultivation of both. In a similar vein, Palmer and Finlay (2003, 115) argue that all creation deserves mercy (Psalm 89: 3 'the world is built on tender mercy'). Humanity, therefore, is restricted in its use of nature, forbidden to show cruelty, or take excess, but rather has to prevent suffering (Goodman 2002; Solomon 1992).

Along similar lines *kashrut* or the kosher code – food obligations and restrictions as a connection between Jews, the land, and God – is stressed and extended in an 'eco-kosher' code. Humanity's consumption of coal, oil, and wood, in this sense, may be seen as a form of idolatry, and needs to be consumed in a more sacred (less polluting, wasteful) way. In line with this blessings, festivals, prayers, or rituals (*Rosh Hashanah, Sukkot, Tu B'shevat*) that purify the body via consumption of food and express gratitude for creation, are seen as creating a sacred connection to the earth (and bearing witness to God's power in it; similarly biblical injunctions to avoid cutting fruit bearing trees are symbolic cynosure of human responsibility to nature). In line with these ideas *Shabbat*, the sabbath or rest day (month/year), a retreat from labour or consumption and mnemonic of humanity's ties to nature (argued as the last thing God created but first in intention), is seen as restoring nature's balance (Goodman 2002; Green 1996; Jacobs 2002; Pick 1992; Rose 1992; Tirosh-Samuelson 2001; Waskow 1996; 2002). Such ideas highlight that religio-moral purity is necessary for residence in God's land; the flourishing of nature and humanity are causally linked; following God's ordinances, especially the Torah, ensures prosperity, doing otherwise causes suffering. In this light Fishbane (2002) envisages an 'Oral Torah', where the world is an expression of God's breath, a syntax of His wisdom embodied in existence, and argues for (emotional, physical, spiritual) alignment to its natural rhythms via prayer or ritual. Such ideas link to the Jewish mystical tradition that respects and reveres nature through seeing God revealed in it, highlighting communion with nature as being communion with God. Kabbalism, for example, sees an underlying divine reality behind the corporeal world, connecting the many (creation: H-W-Y-H) to the one (God: Y-H-W-H, the 'primordial Torah') with humanity's task being the realization of this. Such ideas are also linked to the Hasidic ideas of Martin Buber, especially the 'I-Thou' relationship, where the aim of existence is to relate to nature via the 'whole being', nature being a 'waiting Thou' (connected to God, the 'eternal Thou') not an 'It' (Gellman 2002; Green 2002; Hutterman 2002; Tirosh-Samuelson 2001; Waskow 2002).

Christianity

Within Christian attitudes to nature, several themes are stressed: God created a good (harmonious) world; God created humans in His image (*imago Dei*) from the world to have a relationship with Him (and creation); humanity sinned against this by seeking self-awareness, becoming alienated from God (and creation); God provides the means to overcome this in a 'new creation' in Jesus (God dwelling and suffering in creation) and the subsequent passing on of the Holy Spirit to the Christian community. To these themes can be added Jesus' commandments to 'love God' and 'love your neighbour', and the Old Testament statement that the 'fear of God' is the beginning of wisdom. These themes provide the groundwork for what has been described as an 'ecological reformation' to an earth-centered Christianity that values and cares for nature. Central to such ideas is the 'integrity of creation', the idea that the world is created and sustained by God (His 'breath', *ruah*), being a gift and covenant, to reveal His creativity. God, in this sense, loves nature and its creatures and cares for their well-being (giving them intrinsic value). To love and care for them is thus to love and care for God, to abuse them is to abuse God. Nature in this sense worships God in its being and to worship God in a human sense means caring for it. Nature in this respect is also a means to know God (His 'Book of Works'), not only by the learning of it but also by 'experiencing' its 'being' (subjectively interacting with it) (Callicott 1997; Deane-Drummond 2004; Kinsley 1994; McFague 2000; McGrath 2003; Page 1992; Reid 200; Wallace 2000).

Humanity's role in creation is a somewhat privileged virtue of *imago Dei*. However, this is interpreted not as giving it dominion over nature but as giving it responsibility for it: humans are seen as 'stewards', in fellowship (being neighbours) to other creatures, embedded in nature yet given the task of tending it, being channels for God's grace. This is God's intention for them, a benign authority exercising power with praise and humility (hence biblical sayings emphasizing this, such as 'salt of the earth' or Jesus as 'vine', and the 'sabbath' principle, letting the earth rest and recover, as well as rituals using earth elements, such as bread, oil, water, wine). However, the effects of sin are seen to have affected this, with humanity not caring for creation as God intended; humanity is seen as fallen and self-centered, alienated from creation, and harming it. To recover a right (harmonious) relationship to creation (God), in this sense, means overcoming sin. To this end God became incarnated in Jesus and embodied in nature, highlighting its special-ness and pointing to its redemption (ideas of the 'cosmic Christ' also see Jesus redeeming not only humanity but all of (cosmic) creation). Nature in this respect is also seen as part of God's body or a sacrament of God, such ideas arguing for a sacramental approach to it, accepting it as evoking/mediating the sacred and interacting with it in a relational (Trinitarian) 'I-Thou' relationship (Callicott 1997; Deane-Drummond 2004; Kinsley 1994; McFague 1996; McGrath 2003; Page 1992; Reid 2001; Ruether 2000).

Along similar lines the Holy Spirit, present at creation as a life-giving force and still dwelling in the world, courtesy of Jesus, is seen as providing a useful approach to nature, giving intrinsic value to life and providing the 'power of becoming', the possibility of redemption and capability of attaining the perfection of (a new) creation. In this sense it guides humanity in discerning the appropriate (harmonious) way of interacting with nature (fulfilling humanity's role of bringing creation to fulfillment). In a similar way the concept of 'Wisdom', also seen as inherent in creation and dwelling in the world, is seen as providing an eco-friendly Christianity. A 'wise' interaction with nature, in this sense, is seen to be based on a 'practical wisdom' or 'virtue ethic' of justice, prudence, and temperance; a natural law in dialogue with human inclinations (Deane-Drummond 2004). Wisdom is also seen as female, and eco-feminist ideas have also been seen as a way of being critical of the modern worldview and creating care for nature. In this sense, there is a need to overcome patriarchal dominance (God as transcendent, male) and its dualism (mind/body, matter/spirit separation), which destroys nature, through seeing God/nature as mother, something that is seen to highlight God's immanence and promote ideals of care and harmony. Such ideas also link social justice to environmental justice; nature becomes the 'new poor' with ecological and social degradation occurring in 'sacrifice zones' while 'eco-living' requires social inclusion and 'fair consumption' (Edwards 2001; McFague 2000; McGrath 2003; Ruether 1992; 2000; Wallace 2000).

New Scientific Cosmologies and Ecology

Deep Ecology

Deep Ecology has been described as a philosophical, political, scientific, and social movement as well as a nature religion, rethinking human identification with nature (traced to intuitive experiences of nature (of ecological diversity/symbiosis) by field ecologists). Inspired by the science of ecology that holistically studies ecosystems it sees nature as intrinsically valuable, rather than for use as in 'shallow ecology', with humans embedded in it. Its worldview, 'Ecosophy T', is seen as an ecological wisdom (combining 'eco' or earth and 'Sophia' or wisdom), based around a 'wide identification' thesis and an ultimate norm of 'Self-realization', being a 'relational total field image' stressing 'bio-spherical egalitarianism'. Its essence is to ask questions about humanity, society, and nature, going beyond factual science to the level of self and earth wisdom, leading to an awakening of wholes greater than the sum of their parts, seeing through what it sees as the illusory and erroneous modern worldview (Devall and Sessions 1985; Kinsley 1994; Macy 2002; Naess 1991, 1995; Sessions 1994; Taylor 1996). This is seen as a 'transpersonal ecology', moving from personal identification, the experience of commonality through personal involvement, to ontological identification, the experience of commonality through a sense of or openness to being; a wide, field-like, sense of Self with no ontological divide in existence, no bifurcation between human/non-humans. This is argued as leading to 'Self-realization': nature (and all the individuals, human/ non-human, of which it is comprised) realizing itself (becoming fulfilled). This is seen as a psychological/social/ecological maturity, stressing that humanity underestimates itself by equating self with ego; with sufficient maturity it cannot avoid identifying with nature as it is in, of, and for it, in its very being. Self in this sense equates to organic wholeness, an 'ecological self', where humanity is grounded in the metaphysical fact of interconnectedness, this leading to an ecological lifestyle of harmony or equilibrium. Thus it is natural for humanity to care for nature, for its true humanness is part of it; acting more environmentally friendly in this sense creates greater happiness and satisfaction (Devall and Sessions 1985; Fox 1990; Kinsley 1994; Naess 1991, 1995; Sessions 1994).

Such a deep-ecological self is seen as possibly tapping into an innate eco-friendly humanness, what has been termed 'Biophilia'; a tendency to focus on and care for life and lifelike processes (opposite is 'biophobia', aversion to nature). This is a human dependence on nature, an emotional need for a deep and intimate association, something that is seen as part of humanity's evolutionary heritage, evolving in a bio-centric, not machine-regulated, world (and shaped by cultural patterns through which 'primal (indigenous, tribal) cultures' integrated into the world). Such a love of life and right relation to nature is seen as the key to (continued) human existence, a sign of mental/physical health; humanity's sanity depends on it (environmental degradation is thus a deprived existence). An ethical responsibility for nature, then, in this sense, is an aesthetic, biological, cognitive, emotional, and spiritual, imperative (Kellert 1993; Wilson 1984). Such a view of humanity and nature has been seen as 'eco-psychology', exploring the foundations of human nature, expanding the human self, and healing its alienation from nature. This sees the needs of the planet and the person as a continuum (human nature being embedded in the world, as it is often thought to be so by primal peoples). Here, psychosis is an environment-deficiency disease with modern humanity 'ontogenetically crippled', immature, and neurotic, separated from true (sane, mature) feelings of connection. Thus the aim is to awaken healthy (earth-connected) human nature; a transactional, relational, ecologically grounded form of animism (Macy 1996; Roszak 1993).

Ritual is highlighted as a practical part of this, reconnecting humanity to nature through re-experiencing the earth. Examples of these types of ritual are: shamanic or traditional healing rituals as practiced in primal peoples, discoursing with the spirits of nature; or in a modern sense, the Council of All Beings, a communal 're-earthing' ritual, creating an experience of intimate connection to nature, giving voice to the earth's suffering, and creating a commitment to defend it, awakening a 'shamanic personality' (Roszak 1993; Seed, et al. 1988; Macy 2002). Deep Ecology thus also embraces spiritual aspects of reality, having Buddhist, Christian, Confucian, Daoist, Hindu, and Jewish influences, especially with regard to self-realization and the oneness of/reverence for life. For example: the right to live and blossom for all and the desire to achieve liberation from egoism and cultivate/realize an interconnected self, based on a harmonious underlying principle, where order is emergent, and diverse parts enrich each other via non-violence instead of destruction. In this sense it has an ethical and religious attitude of valuing nature for its own sake and seeing it as divine or spiritual. It thus may be the newest and oldest religion and an emerging corpus of myth, symbol, and rite, awakening human nature to its connections with, and responsibility for, the environment (Barnhill and Gottlieb 2001; Gottlieb 1996).

Gaia

The Gaia hypothesis considers the activities of living organisms using the earth's atmosphere and changing its composition. The earth – named 'Gaia' after the Greek earth goddess – in this sense is a complex 'cybernetic' or feedback system seeking an optimal physical and chemical environment for life. It is a self-regulating (autopoietic), interdependent, entity, an organic whole greater than the sum of its parts, possibly a living thing (a super-organism). It is served by its constituents, adjusting and regulating itself in the same way that the organs of a body serve a person (what is seen as 'geo-physiology' or 'wisdom of the body'; and it may thus have vital organs, e.g. rain forests, keeping the whole stable and needing to be protected). The earth can be considered the unit of colligative evolution, with self-regulation emergent, and it may thus be organized or behave purposely, being animate, with spirit or consciousness (the culmination of a living process, analogous to an embryo). In this sense, understanding and enabling the processes of regulation, rather than unbalancing them, may be planetary medicine, something that may be humanity's natural role; acting within the system rather than outside it (Callicott 1997; Joseph 1991; Lovelock 1979; 2000; Midgley 2001).

This idea of the world as alive has been held throughout history: Goddess religion especially celebrated the ongoing rhythm of life, death, and regeneration, seeing the earth as the source of being, a living force, concerned with creative, peaceful interaction. A Gaian 'rebirth of the goddess' thus stresses humanity as part of nature, able to call forth its power, such intuition of the aliveness and interconnectedness of the earth seen as able to lead to a responsibility to all that lives, inspiring a less materialistic society. Re-embodying the goddess in the human self in this way is seen as a sacred psychology recovering intimacy with and tapping into a natural earth creativity; an awakening, re-birthing, re-indigination, recovering a lost sense of place, and 'primal perception' leading to a 'primal mind' in healthy interdependency (humanity's natural experience, exemplified again by primal/tribal peoples) (Callicott 1997; Christ 1997; Gadon 1989; Joseph 1991; Lovelock 1979). Such female-centered views are seen as partnership based, being about connection and wholeness, nourishment and therapeutic action, enabling and enhancing, not dominating and destroying life. They are related to eco-feminism, analyzing ecology from a female point of view, locating environmental degradation in (rational, dualist) male thinking, seeking to reintegrate humanity with nature and create life-sustaining mutuality and relationality through (intuitive) care, compassion, and empathy; a cultural, psychological and spiritual earth healing; healing relationships between men/women, humanity/earth. A healed society in this sense is one of non-dominating relations, a biospheric community of biophilic mutuality (humanity's destiny is of and for the earth and it needs to listen to the voice of Gaia and respect other life-forms as inherent parts of the energy that it is a part, acting with responsibility) (Adams 1993; Eisler 1990; Ruether 1992; Spretnak 1989).

Such an ethic of care links to autopoietic or ecosystem ethics, an ethical holism where individual interest lies within the whole. Life in this sense is a process of autopoiesis, or self-production, constantly renewing parts (organisms) to form a whole (the earth); humanity therefore co-evolves and is dependent on other life/earth in a 'Gaian body wisdom'. The world is thus a pattern of reciprocal relations, or 'gift events', impelling responsibility and commitment. Related to religion, this sees God (autopoietic and participant in the evolutionary process) as the original giver in an ontological or relational theology of the sacred whole. Such a Gaian perception shifts the locus of creativity from humanity towards the world, the two being living presences in reciprocal interaction. Human creativity thus is an elaboration of a deeper (holistic) creativity and it may be psychologically (and evolutionary) rewarding to interact with the earth in a particular (balanced, co-operative) way (or unrewarding to do otherwise) that has been termed 'Gaiasophy' (linking Gaia to another female concept, Sophia or wisdom). This idea of communicating with an animate earth is seen as shamanic wisdom; an innate ability to tap into a 'supersensory' awareness or energy field of the earth (dissolving the boundaries of ordinary perception, divining the spirit of the earth), rediscovering the reciprocal energetic relationship with a dynamic earth – a 'shamanic renaissance' or 'geomantic revival' that Deveraux et al. (1992) call 'Earthmind' (Abram 1990; Callicott 1997; Joseph 1991; Lovelock 2000; Midgley 2001; Primavsi 2000; Sahtouris 1989; Zoeteman 1991).

Conclusions

The present environmental crisis is seen to be a result of a dominant modern worldview delineating assumptions about reality that are anthropocentric, materialist, economic and technology-based, separating humanity from and devaluing nature. Addressing this crisis is seen as requiring a challenge to this worldview, a politicization of nature and an ecological re-imagination; creating new empowering conceptual schemes reconnecting humanity (psychologically, socially, spiritually), to a re-envisioned nature and simulating new ecological ethics and environmentally friendly thought and action. Religious traditions (reinterpreted, beyond anthropocentrism, embracing the whole of creation) and new scientific visions (more holistic, interdisciplinary, spiritual) are thought to be able to provide such challenges and new conceptual schemes, acting as channels for humanity to reconnect to nature and articulate ecological concern, being avenues for the re-imagination of nature and the human role in it (both religion and science are seen as pertaining to the construction of reality, with emotional and rational, personal and social, influence, frameworks of metaphor, myth, and symbol, moral authority, and plausibility). Such a 'greening' of religion and science is occurring within a field of religion and ecology that seeks to inspire religious traditions and science-based cosmologies to explore and express ecological metaphors, myths, and symbols, and provide a mutually enriching dialogue between them.

In this article I have analysed such ecological re-imagining among two Eastern and two Western religious traditions and two science-inspired cosmologies (as represented in the field of religion and ecology), exploring the ways they (metaphorically) express ecological awareness. Eastern religions, like Buddhism and Chinese traditions, see nature as a balanced, interconnected, process, an egalitarian, reciprocal, web of life. Humans have (natural) abilities to enhance this ecological balance, through tapping into a natural underlying life energy via an expanded sense of self, freed from selfish desires, through awareness of a particular/ general, person/cosmos, linked and acting in a careful, sensitive way, creating community. Western religions, like Judaism and Christianity, by contrast, envisage God as creating and sustaining a harmonious nature (that alludes to God), giving it intrinsic value. Humanity has a special but flawed place; charged with tending nature but failing due to sin, only recovering by embracing the spirit of God/nature and behaving in a caring, humane manner. Lastly, the cosmologies of Deep Ecology and Gaia stress identification with an earth that is a living, self-regulating, symbiotic organism. Humanness, in this sense, is realized in interconnectedness, via an innate attachment to existence, that is psychological, social, and ecological, and related to health, maturity, and sanity; a primal perception of biophilic mutuality, achieved via myth and ritual, compared to (Goddess) religion and female ideas of caring relationality.

Such religious and scientific re-imagining challenges dominant modern conceptions of humanity, nature, and human-nature interaction, both personal (ideas of self-identity) and public (consequences of ecological problems). Although expressed in diverse ways, such re-imagining has a common purpose and commitment (re-enchanting nature, curtailing human action by tying human morality (and prosperity) to (prosperity of) the environment, seeing progress in an ecologically holistic way). Common (possibly convergent, syncretic) ideas and themes can thus be witnessed (science-inspired views in particular incorporate religious or spiritual ideas, while both converge on the overall ecological ideal of a harmonious, sustainable humanity and environment): the environment is seen as having intrinsic worth, virtue of (continuing) creation, independent of human values, being envisioned as an interdependent whole; it is a reciprocal web of life infused with a flow of energy or spirit embodying the divine; humanity, virtue of self-consciousness, has a limited but special role, being part of the web of life yet also enabling creation to achieve its harmonious state, something egoistic action upsets; humanity, therefore, needs to experience the flow of energy/ spirit and interdependent being, widening its boundaries, embracing relationality and selflessness (a life of self-sacrifice, its natural evolutionary state).[12] Such re-imagining may fulfill a priestly and prophetic role, conceiving of environmental balance and justice, envisioning and stimulating an ongoing (metaphoric) dialogue about/between humanity and nature (and religion, science, and secular society). New religious and scientific ecological visions may thus act as arenas of ecological dialogue; powerful, influential, efficacious symbolisms through which to re-imagine the world, being both cosmological and moral, situating humanity in nature as well as defining its role in it, providing new organizing principles and epistemologies, fusing scientific insight and religious imagination.[13] They may thus (be used to) inform, inspire, empower, and unite new views and actions, stimulating new cultural outlooks or paradigms, and heightening awareness of ecological necessities and responsibilities, hereby (ideally) revitalizing religion, science, and society.

Notes

1   The terms 'environment' and 'nature' tend to be used interchangeably to denote the non-human world (although the latter seems to show a somewhat more all-encompassing and subjective use; other terms also used in this way are 'cosmos', 'creation', 'earth', or 'world'). Following the field of religion and ecology I also use the terms 'ecology', 'ecological', and 'ecologically' as these are seen as including humanity in the definition, implying a holistic interdependent, process of human, animal, and world (and possibly the sacred), sentient and non-sentient (rather than objectifying or externalising an 'environment' or 'nature' outside and unrelated to humanity, which is seen as part of the problem) (see Tucker and Grim 2001).

2   Szerszynski (2005) argues that the modern worldview, instead of being a disenchantment, may be an enchantment, a product of the sacral history of the West, building upon Judeo-Christianity's separation of a transcendent God from immanent nature and Protestantism's concentration on individual human action leading to secular rationality. Nevertheless, the modern worldview did in some respects challenge and disenchant the previous (dominant, Christian) worldview (which itself may have disenchanted an earlier animistic worldview) and replace it with a new one that became hegemonic. The problem, then, may be the dominance of one view over others (which may still coexist with it); thus challenging the dominant view may, in Szerszynski's terms (this volume), 'open up a space' for new visions in a diverse 'post-modern' worldview, allowing diverse constructions of reality in mutual dialogue and action.

3   Changing worldviews and 'protecting' the environment or nature, in this sense, may not be as simple as it seems. There is the danger that such changes may also treat the world as an object, similar to (but opposing) the modern worldview (e.g. 'romanticism' opposing 'rationalism'). It is argued, therefore, that what may be needed is a reconnection of humanity to nature while recognizing diversity. Thus the aim may not be to wholly overcome the modern worldview (to be hegemonic) but to channel its successes (e.g. better health, greater freedoms) in new, creative (diverse, eco-friendly) directions, which is

seen as the liberating impulses of the enlightenment grounded in earth processes (see Cronon 1996; McGrath 2003; Soule 1995; Tucker 2003).

4   By coalescing around global ethical issues such as the environmental crisis, religions may thus regain (provide) moral, cultural, political, and social (and transcendent) capital. They may engage the opportunities (or problems) created by modernity (i.e. its ethical, environmental, or social, consequences) and create innovative responses, going beyond the ideas articulated in modern discourse (including the official definition of environmentalism), providing alternative (ecological) ideas with a larger qualitative frame of reference, becoming resources for recreating private beliefs (e.g. existentially re-connecting individuals to the environment), as well as publicly addressing (e.g. ecological) issues. Such eco-religious action may thus have eschatological implications for all humanity, inspiring new attitudes and actions with respect to nature, defining and maintaining the common good, giving meaning to the environment and promising the power to overcome environmental problems (Beyer 1994; Casanova 1994; Oelschlaeger 1994; Woodhead and Heelas 2000).

5   Lynn White (1967) famously goes so far as to argue that Judeo-Christianity may have been a root cause of the ecological crisis through *imago Dei* and the command in Genesis for humans to have 'dominion' over the earth, with the latter serving man. Other authors have pointed out that Judeo-Christianity's overcoming of pagan animism (and its interdependence of humanity and nature) and anthropocentric, dualistic, hierarchical, and patriarchal, ideas may also have had such an effect as well as leading to an avoidance of environmental issues and lateness in engaging with them. It may also be that *interpretations* of biblical texts, linked with Greek sources and later secular scientific ideas, may have contributed to such views. However, such ideas have been seen to be somewhat biased and oversimplified. They may ignore the Bible's and Judeo-Christianity's views of God sustaining nature, the need to overcome sinful humanity, and other commands to *care* for life, seeing *imago Dei* as involving responsibility for creation, mirroring God's care, with humanity's role being to serve God (and creation). Interpreted differently, therefore, Judeo-Christianity may be said to have theocentric rather than merely anthropocentric views (see Callicott 1997; Deane-Drummond 2004; Kinsley 1994; Nash 1989; Oelschlaeger 1994).

6   There is a large and growing body of literature and actions in this area. For a wide-ranging overview see (Taylor and Kaplan 2005); www.religionandnature.com, as well as the *Forum on Religion and Ecology* (www.yale.edu/religionandecology).

7   Such a 'new science' that converges, discourses, and/or embraces, with religion or spiritual ideas is seen to result from developments within biology, cos-

mology, genetics, neuroscience, and physics, as well as the history/ philosophy of science, that lead to a questioning of the modern, rationalist, mechanical worldview and awareness of and involvement with ethical and religious issues (especially questions of transcendence, value, and meaning). This has led to what has been described as the 'field of science and religion' a diverse interdisciplinary dialogue, with science and religion in creative mutual consonance, co-operation, interaction, or harmonization (see Van Huyssteen 2003).

8   Religions are diverse and thus there may be no definitive Buddhist, Confucian, Daoist, Jewish, or Christian perspective on the environment. Rather there may be a (cultural, geographical, historical, social, theological) diversity of (possibly competing/contradictory) perspectives. Interpretations of religious traditions within the field of religion and ecology then are new ecological-based or inspired interpretations of Buddhism, Confucianism, Daoism, Judaism, and Christianity, made by individuals or groups concerned with environmental issues, using them as constructive sources of environmental ideas. They are new religious forms, not the whole story and have not been without challenge. The idea of unified 'religious traditions' or 'world religions', themselves, following Talal Asad (1993) and Tomoko Masuzawa (2005), may be questioned (especially when assessing Eastern forms which are quite diverse), these being seen as Western-based concepts and constructions appropriating and unifying contextual and diverse social forms. Nevertheless, it can be said that there are (diverse, dynamic) historical processes that are self-identified as Buddhist, Confucian, Daoist, Jewish, or Christian, and which transmit narratives and written records of interactions between human communities and local ecosystems which are distinct from one another and from secular approaches and which can be explored. Furthermore, as religions are diverse and dynamic, not monolithic and static, new interpretations and forms have always occurred (although not always recognized or legitimated) and thus those expressed in the field of religion and ecology may be accepted and become influential.

9   Deep Ecology is traced to philosopher Arne Naess (plus Bill Devall and George Sessions). Other influences include eco-centric (Eastern) religions, Christian thinkers (e.g. St Francis of Assisi); 'primal' (tribal) peoples; the philosophers Heidegger and Spinoza; the romantic movement and literary tradition of naturalism; the eco-centrism and social criticism of Aldous Huxley, Henry David Thoreau, John Muir, D.H. Lawrence, and Robinson Jeffers; and the 'ecological perspective' of ecologists and conservationists, such as Aldo Leopold, Rachel Carson and Dave Brower. Leopold especially is seen as influential, his 'Land Ethic' stressing the web-like interrelated complexity of the earth and urging humanity to 'think like a mountain'. The Gaia hypothesis is traced to scientist James Lovelock (plus microbiologist Lyn Margulis).

Historical antecedents to it are seen in the philosophies of Hegel, Spinoza, and Whitehead, Herbert Spencer and Aldo Leopold, all of whom spoke of nature in terms of an organism, Russian scientist Vernadsky, who viewed the biogeochemistry of the earth as a unity, and scientist James Hutton who saw the earth as a 'super-organism'. Gaia ideas are also seen to be 'resonant' with 'primal' peoples, animism, Buddhism, paganism, shamanism, and totemism, as well elements of Theosophy.

10 This is an inevitably selective group, dependent on space and chosen for contrast and comparison. Other religious traditions, such as Baha'i, Hinduism, indigenous traditions, Islam, Jainism, Shinto, Sikhism, or Zoroastrianism, could be explored in this way, of course, (and are) as could a scientific concept such as the 'Epic of Evolution' (see Callicott 1997; Gottlieb 1996; Kinsley 1994; Watling 2008b).

11 Chinese terminology involves two systems, the 'Pinyin' (e.g. *Dao*, Daoism, *qi*) and 'Wade-Giles' (e.g. *Tao*, Taoism, *ch'i*), used by different Daoist and Confucian scholars. For clarity I use the former.

12 Bassett et al. (2000, 78) see 'Points of Religious Agreement in Environmental Ethics': the natural world has value in itself and does not exist solely to serve human needs; there is a significant continuity of being between human and non-human living beings (which can be experienced), even though humans have a distinctive role; non-human living beings are morally significant, in the eyes of God and/or in the cosmic order; the dependence of human life on the natural world can and should be acknowledged in ritual; moral norms (justice, compassion, reciprocity), apply both to human and non-human beings; the well-being of human and non-human beings are connected; there are legitimate and illegitimate uses of nature; greed and destructiveness are condemned, restraint and protection are commended; human beings should live in harmony with nature (via their traditions). Similarly, Kinsley (1994, 227-232) suggests common recurrent religion and ecology themes: reality being viewed as organic; an emphasis on knowledge of and rapport with the land; a stress on human kinship with nature; mutuality and reciprocity as the appropriate framework for relating to nature; the embeddedness of humanity within nature; existence envisioned as a unity; a stress on an underlying moral or ethical unity; the need for human restraint in dealing with nature; a criticism of the prevailing worldview; a recognition that ecological concerns have religious meanings.

13 Questions, of course, may be raised concerning such religio-scientific ecological ideals and activities. For example, there is the challenge of comparing or reconciling different religious or scientific beliefs, theories, or traditions, or differences within them over the authority to use traditions or create new

visions. Secondly, there is the question of whether it is inevitably an academic, liberal initiative, with overarching ecumenical concerns, based on dualist Western assumptions (of an objective 'nature' needing protection, or of a singular 'religion' or 'science'), this overriding non-Western assumptions, imposing a universal eco-ethic on them (and possibly simplifying religious or scientific concepts and traditions, ignoring diversity or depriving them of deeper meaning or relevance). Counter-arguments to such points are that neither religion nor science is static; they always adapt and change, which means they are open to re-interpretation (as are concepts of nature) and adherents themselves interpret them in different, complex or simple, ways, dependent on context. Furthermore, any ecumenical commonalities or practices with respect to ecology may be seen as legitimate new forms of religion or science. It may be, then, that such ideas and activities may need to be viewed as a process, a variety of beliefs, dialogues, and movements, in mutual communication, posing possible future directions (see Tucker 2003; Tucker and Grim 2001). In this sense, then, I stress these visions as 'arenas' and 'dialogues' to emphasize that they are dynamic, evolving visions, collages constantly being reinterpreted. They may be challenged (particularly the religious-based visions) and (in the science-inspired visions) the people and theories within them may not always explicitly identify or be identified as active 'members' of them. Nevertheless, they may be linked to, referenced, or interpreted and used, encouraging, influencing, and stimulating, new thought and action, within an ever-evolving (co-ordinated, diverse, expanding) discourse.

References

Abram, D. 1990. The Perceptual Implications of Gaia. In *Dharma Gaia: A Harvest of Essays on Buddhism and Ecology*, ed. A.H. Badiner. Berkeley: Parallax Press, 75-92.

Adams, C.J. 1993. Introduction. In *Ecofeminism and the Sacred*, ed. C. Adams. New York: Continuum, 1-9.

Adler, J.A. 1998. Response and Responsibility: Chou Tun-i and Confucian Resources for Environmental Ethics. In *Confucianism and Ecology: The Interrelation of Heaven, Earth and Humans*, eds. M.E. Tucker and J. Berthrong. Cambridge, MA: Harvard University Press, 123-149.

Ames, R.T 2001. The Local and the Focal in Realizing a Daoist World. In *Daoism and Ecology: Ways within a Cosmic Landscape*, eds. N.J. Giradot, J. Miller, and L. Xiaogan. Cambridge, MA: Harvard University Press, 265-382.

Asad, T. 1993. *Genealogies of Religion: Discipline and Reasons for Power in Christianity and Islam.* Baltimore: John Hopkins University Press.

Barlow, C. 1997. *Green Space, Green Time: The Way of Science,* New York: Copernicus.

Barnhill, D.L. 1997. Great Earth *Sangha*: Gary Snyder's View of Nature as Community. In *Buddhism and Ecology: The Interconnection of Dharma and Deeds,* eds. M.E. Tucker and D.R. Williams. Cambridge, MA: Harvard University Press, 187-217.

Barnhill, D.L and R.S. Gottlieb, eds. 2001. *Deep Ecology and World Religions: New Essays on Sacred Ground,* Albany: State University of New York Press.

Bassett, L., J.T. Brinkman, and K.P. Pedersen, eds. 2000. *Earth and Faith: A Book of Reflection for Action,* New York: Interfaith Partnership for the Environment/ United Nations Environment Programme.

Beyer, P. 1994. *Religion and Globalization.* London: Sage Publications.

Bolle, K.W. 2005a. Myth: An Overview. In *Encyclopedia of Religion,* ed. L. Jones. Farmington Hills, MI: Thomson Gale, 6359-6371.

— 2005b. Cosmology: An Overview. In *Encyclopedia of Religion,* ed. L. Jones. Farmington Hills, MI: Thomson Gale, 1991-1998.

Brockelman, P. 1999. *Cosmology and Creation: The Spiritual Significance of Contemporary Cosmology.* New York: Oxford University Press.

Callicott, J.B. 1997. *Earth's Insights: A Multicultural Survey of Ecological Ethics from the Mediterranean Basin to the Australian Outback.* Berkeley: University of California Press.

Casanova, J. 1994. *Public Religions in the Modern World.* Chicago: University of Chicago Press.

Cheng, C. 1998. The Trinity of Cosmology, Ecology and Ethics in the Confucian Personhood. In *Confucianism and Ecology: The Interrelation of Heaven, Earth and Humans,* and M.E. Tucker, J. Berthrong. Cambridge, MA: Harvard University Press, 211-235.

Christ, C.P. 1997. *Rebirth of the Goddess: Finding Meaning in Feminist Spirituality.* New York: Routledge.

Cronon, W. 1996. Introduction: In Search of Nature. In *Uncommon Ground: Rethinking the Human Place in Nature,* ed. W. Cronon. New York: Norton, 23-56.

Deane-Drummond, C.E. 2004. *The Ethics of Nature.* Oxford: Blackwell.

Devall, B. and G. Sessions. 1985. *Deep Ecology: Living as if Nature Mattered.* Salt Lake City: Gibbs M. Smith/Peregrine Smith Books.

Deveraux, P., J. Steele, and D. Kubrin. 1992. *Earthmind: Communicating with the Living World of Gaia.* Rochester, VT: Destiny Books.

Edwards, D. 2001. For Your Immortal Spirit Is in All Things: The Role of the Spirit in Creation. In *Earth Revealing, Earth Healing: Ecology and Christian Theology*, ed. D. Edwards. Collegeville, MN: The Liturgical Press, 45-68.

Eisler, R. 1990. The Gaia Tradition and the Partnership Future: An Ecofeminist Manifesto. In *Reweaving the World: The Emergence of Ecofeminism*, eds. I. Diamond and G.F. Orenstein. San Francisco: Sierra Club Books, 23-34.

Fishbane, M. 2002. Toward a Jewish Theology of Nature. In *Judaism and Ecology: Created World and Revealed Word*, ed. H. Tirosh-Samuelson. Cambridge, MA: Harvard University Press, 17-24.

Fox, W. 1990. *Towards a Transpersonal Ecology: Developing New Foundations for Environmentalism*. Boston: Shambhala.

Gadon, E.W. 1989. *The Once and Future Goddess: A Sweeping Visual Chronicle of the Sacred Female and Her Reemergence in the Cultural Mythology of Our Time*. San Francisco: Harper & Row Publishers.

Gardner, G. 2002. *Invoking the Spirit: Religion and Spirituality in the Quest for a Sustainable World* (Worldwatch Paper 164). Washington, D.C: Worldwatch Institute.

Gellman, J.Y. 2002. Early Hasidism and the Natural World. In *Judaism and Ecology: Created World and Revealed Word*, ed. H. Tirosh-Samuelson. Cambridge, MA: Harvard University Press, 369-388.

Goodman, L.E. 2002. Respect for Nature in the Jewish Tradition. In *Judaism and Ecology: Created World and Revealed Word*, H. Tirosh-Samuelson. Cambridge, MA: Harvard University Press, 227-260.

Gottlieb, R.S., ed. 1996. *This Sacred Earth: Religion, Nature, Environment*. New York: Routledge.

Green, A. 1996. Vegetarianism: A *Kashrut* for Our Age. In *This Sacred Earth: Religion, Nature, Environment*, ed. R. Gottlieb. New York: Routledge, 301-302.

— 2002. A Kabbalah for the Environment Age, In *Judaism and Ecology: Created World and Revealed Word*, ed. H. Tirosh-Samuelson. Cambridge, MA: Harvard University Press, 3-16.

Griffin, D.R. 1988. Introduction: The Re-enchantment of Science. In *The Re-Enchantment of Science: Post-Modern Proposals*, ed. D.R. Griffin. Albany, NY: State University of New York Press, 1-46.

Gross, R.M. 2002. Toward a Buddhist Environmental Ethic. In *Worldviews, Religion, and the Environment: A Global Anthology*, ed. R.C. Foltz. Belmont, CA: Thompson/ Wadsworth, 163-170.

Hutterman, A. 2002. The Most Misunderstood Part of the Bible. In *World-*

views, *Religion, and the Environment: A Global Anthology*, ed. R.C. Foltz. Belmont, CA: Thomson/Wadsworth, 280-289.

Ingram, P.O. 1997. The Jeweled Net of Nature. In *Buddhism and Ecology: The Interconnection of Dharma and Deeds*, eds. M.E. Tucker and D.R. Wiıliams. Cambridge, MA: Harvard University Press, 71-88.

Jacobs, M.X. 2002. Judaism and the Ecological Crisis. In *When Worlds Converge: What Science and Religion Tell Us about the Story of the Universe and Our Place in It*, eds. C.N. Matthews, M.E. Tucker, and P. Hefner. Chicago: Open Court, 261-272.

Joseph, L.E. 1991. *Gaia: The Growth of an Idea*. London: Arkana.

Kaza, S. 2002. Green Buddhism. In *When Worlds Converge: What Science and Religion Tell Us about the Story of the Universe and Our Place in It*, eds. C.N. Matthews, M.E. Tucker, and P. Hefner. Chicago and La Salle: Open Court, 293-309.

Kellert, S. 1993. Introduction. In *The Biophilia Hypothesis*, eds. S.R. Kellert and E.O. Wilson. Washington, D.C.: Island Press/Shearwater Books, 20-27.

Kinsley, D. 1994. *Ecology and Religion: Spirituality in Cross-Cultural Perspective*. Englewood Cliffs, NJ: Prentice Hall.

Kirkland, R. 2001. 'Responsible Non-Action' in a Natural World: Perspectives from the Neiye, Zhuangzi, and Daode jing. In *Daoism and Ecology: Ways within a Cosmic Landscape*, eds. N.J. Giradot, J. Miller, J, and L. Xiaogan. Cambridge, MA: Harvard University Press, 293-304.

Lakoff, G. and M. Johnson. 1980. *Metaphors We Live By*. Chicago: University of Chicago Press.

Long, C.H. 2005. Cosmogony. In *Encyclopedia of Religion*, ed. L. Jones. Farmington Hills, MI: Thomson Gale, 1985-1991.

Loori, J.D. 1997. The Precepts and the Environment. In *Buddhism and Ecology: The Interconnection of Dharma and Deeds*, eds. M.E. Tucker and D.R. Williams. Cambridge, MA: Harvard University Press, 177-184.

Lovelock, J.E. 1979. *Gaia: A New Look at Life on Earth*. Oxford: Oxford University Press.

— 2000. *The Ages of Gaia: A Biography of Our Living Earth*. Oxford: Oxford University Press.

Macy, J. 1996. Faith, Power, Ecology. In *This Sacred Earth: Religion, Nature, Environment*, ed. R. Gottlieb. New York: Routledge, 415-422.

— 2002. The Ecological Self: Post-modern Ground for Action. In *Worldviews, Religion and the Environment: A Global Anthology*, ed. R. Foltz. Belmont, CA: Thompson/Wadsworth, 441-446.

Maguire, D.C. 2000. *Sacred Energies: When the World's Religions Sit Down to Talk About the Future of Human Life and the Plight of the Planet.* Minneapolis: Fortress Press.

Masuzawa, T. 2005. *The Invention of World Religions.* Chicago: University of Chicago Press.

Maxwell, T.P. 2003. Considering Spirituality: Integral Spirituality, Deep Science, and Ecological Awareness. *Zygon: Journal of Religion and Science* 38, 257-276.

McFague, S. 1995. The Scope of the Body: The Cosmic Christ. In *This Sacred Earth: Religion, Nature, Environment,* ed. R. Gottlieb. London: Routledge, 286-296.

— 2000. An Ecological Christology: Does Christianity Have It? In *Christianity and Ecology: Seeking the Well-Being of Earth and Humans,* eds. D. Hessel and R.R. Ruether. Cambridge, MA: Harvard University Press, 29-46.

McGrath, A. 2003. *The Re-enchantment of Nature: The Denial of Religion and the Ecological Crisis.* New York: Doubleday/Galilee.

Metzner, R. 1994. The Emerging Cosmological Worldview. In *Worldviews and Ecology: Religion, Philosophy, and the Environment,* eds. M.E. Tucker and J.A. Grim. Maryknoll, New York: Orbis Books, 163-172.

Midgley, M. 2001. *Gaia: The Next Big Idea.* London: Demos.

Naess, A. 1991. *Ecology, Community, and Lifestyle: Outline of an Ecosophy.* Cambridge: Cambridge University Press.

— 1995. The Shallow and Deep, Long-Range Ecology Movements: A Summary. In *Deep Ecology for the Twenty-first Century: Readings on the Philosophy and Practice of the New Environmentalism,* ed. G. Sessions. Boston: Shambhala, 150-155.

Nash, R. 1989. *The Rights of Nature: A History of Environmental Ethics.* Madison: University of Wisconsin Press.

Oelschlaeger, M. 1994. *Caring for Creation: An Ecumenical Approach to the Environmental Crisis.* New Haven: Yale University Press.

Page, R. 1992. The Bible and the Natural World. In *Christianity and Ecology,* eds. E. Breuilly and M. Palmer. London: Cassell, 20-34.

Palmer, M. and V. Finlay. 2003. *Faith in Conservation: New Approaches to Religions and the Environment.* Washington, D.C: The World Bank.

Pick, P.L. 1992. Tu Bi Shevat: A Happy New Year to All Trees. In *Judaism and Ecology,* ed. A. Rose. London: Cassell, 67-9.

Primavesi, A. 2000 *Sacred Gaia: Holistic Theology and Earth System Science.* London: Routledge.

Reid, D. 2001. Enfleshing the Human: An Earth Revealing, Earth Healing

Christology. In *Earth Revealing, Earth Healing: Ecology and Christian Theology*, ed. D. Edwards. Collegeville, Minnesota: The Liturgical Press, 69-84.

Rose, A. 1992. Introduction to the Jewish Faith, In *Judaism and Ecology*, ed. A. Rose. London: Cassell, 9-18.

Roszak, T. 1993. *The Voice of the Earth: An Exploration of Ecopsychology.* New York: Touchstone.

Ruether, R.R. 1992. *Gaia and God: An Ecofeminist Theology of Earth Healing.* New York: HarperSanFrancisco/HarperCollins.

— 2000. Conclusion: Eco-Justice at the Center of the Church's Mission. In *Christianity and Ecology: Seeking the Well-Being of Earth and Humans*, eds. D. Hessel and R.R. Ruether. Cambridge, MA: Harvard University Press, 603-613.

Sahtouris, E. 1989. *Gaia: The Human Journey from Cosmos to Chaos.* New York: Pocket Books.

Seed, J, J. Macy, P. Fleming, and A. Naess, eds. 1988. *Thinking Like a Mountain: Towards a Council of All Beings.* Gabriola Island, BC: New Society Publishers.

Sessions, G. 1994. Deep Ecology as Worldview. In *Worldviews and Ecology: Religion, Philosophy, and the Environment*, eds. M.E. Tucker and J.A. Grim, Maryknoll, NY: Orbis Books, 207-227.

Solomon, N. 1992. Judaism and the Environment. In *Judaism and Ecology*, ed. A. Rose. London: Cassell, 19-53.

Soule, M.E. 1995. The Social Siege of Nature. In *Reinventing Nature? Responses to Postmodern Deconstruction*, eds. M.E. Soule and G. Lease. Washington, D.C: Island Press, 137-170.

Sponberg, A. 1997. Green Buddhism and the Hierarchy of Compassion. In *Buddhism and Ecology: The Interconnection of Dharma and Deeds*, eds. M.E. Tucker and D.R. Wiliiams. Cambridge, MA: Harvard University Press, 351-376.

Spretnak, C. 1989. Towards and Ecofeminist Spirituality. In *Healing the Wounds: The Promise of Ecofeminism*, ed. J. Plant. London: Green Print, 127-132.

Swearer, D.K. 2001. Principles and Poetry, Places and Stories: The Resources of Buddhist Ecology. *Daedalus* 130 (4), 225-242.

Szerszynski, B. 2005. *Nature, Technology and the Sacred.* Oxford: Blackwell.

Taylor, B. 1996. Earth First!: From Primal Spirituality to Ecological Resistance. In *This Sacred Earth: Religion, Nature, Environment*, ed. R.S. Gottlieb. New York: Routledge, 545-557.

— 2001. Earth and Nature-Based Spirituality (Part II): From Earth First! and Bioregionalism to Scientific Paganism and the New Age. *Religion* 31, 225-245.

Taylor, B. and J. Kaplan, eds. 2005. *The Encyclopedia of Religion and Nature.* London: Thoemmes.

Tirosh-Samuelson, H. 2001. Nature and the Sources of Judaism. *Daedalus* 130 (4), 99-124.

Tucker, M.E. 1994. Ecological Themes in Taoism and Confucianism. In *Worldviews and Ecology: Religion, Philosophy, and the Environment,* eds. M.E. Tucker and J.A. Grim. Maryknoll, NY: Orbis Books, 150-160.

— 2002. Religion and Ecology: The Interaction of Cosmology and Cultivation. In *The Good in Nature and Humanity: Connecting Science, Religion, and Spirituality with the Natural World*, eds. R.S. Kellert and T.J. Farnham. Washington, D.C.: Island Press, 65-90.

— 2003. *Worldly Wonder: Religions Enter Their Ecological Phase.* Chicago: Open Court.

Tucker, M.E. and J.A. Grim. 2001. Introduction: The Emerging Alliance of World Religions and Ecology. *Daedalus* 130 (4), 1-22.

— 2005. Ecology and Religion: An Overview. In *Encyclopedia of Religion*, ed. L. Jones. Farmington Hills, MI: Thomson Gale, 2604-2616.

Van Huyssteen, W., ed. 2003. *The Encyclopaedia of Science and Religion.* New York: MacMillan.

Wallace, M.I. 2000. The Wounded Spirit as the Basis for Hope in an Age of Radical Ecology. In *Christianity and Ecology: Seeking the Well-Being of Earth and Humans,* eds. D. Hessel and R.R. Ruether. Cambridge, MA: Harvard University Press, 51-72.

Waskow, A. 1996. What is Eco-Kosher? In *This Sacred Earth: Religion, Nature, Environment*, ed. R. Gottlieb. New York: Routledge, 297-300.

— 2002. And the Earth Is Filled with the Breath of Life. In *Worldviews, Religion, and the Environment: A Global Anthology*, ed. R.C. Foltz. Belmont, CA: Thomson/Wadsworth, 306-317.

Watling, T. 2008a. The Field of Religion and Ecology: Addressing the Environmental Crisis and Challenging Faiths. In *Religion: Beyond a Concept*, ed. H. de Vries, New York: Fordham University Press, 473-488.

— 2008b. New Cosmologies and Sacred Stories: Re-Imagining the Human-Environment Relationship via Religio-Scientific Metaphor and Myth. In *Creation's Diversity: Voices from Theology and Science*, eds. W.B. Drees, H. Meisinger, and T.A. Smedes. London: Continuum, 89-112.

Weiming, T. 1994. Beyond the Enlightenment Mentality. In *Worldviews and Ecology: Religion, Philosophy, and the Environment*, eds. M.E. Tucker and J.A. Grim. Maryknoll, NY: Orbis Books, 19-29.

— 2002. The Continuity of Being: Chinese Visions of Nature. In *Worldviews, Religion and the Environment: A Global Anthology*, ed. R.C. Foltz. Belmont, CA: Thompson/Wadsworth, 209-217.

Weller, R.P. and P.K. Bol. 1998. From Heaven-and-Earth to Nature: Chinese Conceptions of the Environment and their Influence on Policy Implementation. In *Confucianism and Ecology: The Interrelation of Heaven, Earth and Humans*, eds. M.E. Tucker and J. Berthong. Cambridge, MA: Harvard University Press, 313-341.

White, L. 1967. The Historic Roots of Our Ecological Crisis. *Science* 155: 1203-07.

Wilson, E.O. 1984. *Biophilia: The Human Bond with Other Species.* Cambridge, MA: Harvard University Press.

Woodhead, L. and P. Heelas, eds. 2000. *Religion in Modern Times.* Oxford: Blackwell.

Zoeteman, K. 1991. *Gaiasophy: An Approach to Ecology Based on Ancient Myth, Spiritual Vision, and Scientific Thinking.* Husdon, NY: Lindisfarne Press.

5   Religion, Nature, and Modernization in China

James Miller

One of most important concepts in the Weberian theory of modernity is summed up in the German term *Entzauberung*, usually translated into English as 'disenchantment' or 'rationalization'. A concise summary of this concept can be found in an essay published in 1987 by the British sociologist Ernest Gellner. He writes:

> The modern world is organized in a rational way. This means that clearly specified goals are pursued by a calculated allocation of means; the means include not only tools but also human activity and men themselves. These things are treated instrumentally and not as ends in themselves. Effectiveness and evidence are kings. The procedures are also rational in the sense of being orderly and rule-bound: like cases are treated alike. (Gellner 1987, 153)

According to this view, therefore, modernity presupposes a rational, logical and orderly view of the world, one that is best managed by rational procedures and gives rise to the legalistic, bureaucratic institutions of the modern state. Rationalization, moreover, is not something that 'happens' to society. It also has consequences for the way that moderns view and engage the natural world. Gellner continues:

> It is not only the procedures of organizations which are in this sense 'bureaucratised'; the same also happens to our vision of nature, of the external world. Its comprehensibility and manipulability are purchased by means of subsuming its events under orderly, symmetrical, precisely articulated generalisations and explanatory models. *This* is Disenchant-

ment: the Faustian purchase of cognitive, technological and adminis-
trative power, by the surrender of our previous meaningful, humanly
suffused, humanly responsive, if often also menacing or capricious
world. *That* is abandoned in favour of a more a more predictable, more
amenable, but coldly indifferent and uncosy world. (Gellner 1987, 153)

As Gellner's explanation makes clear, the Weberian concept of *Entzauberung* has at least two aspects to it, evident in the two English terms that
are commonly used to translate it, rationalization and disenchantment.
On the one hand, *Entzauberung* involves a belief in the possibility of the
rational ordering of the world; on the other hand this belief is predicated
on an instrumental view of nature, one in which nature is not valued as
an end in itself, but becomes a means for the attainment of rationally cal-
culated ends. *Entzauberung* is thus more than a process that takes place
within the ordering of society. Rather it also 'happens to our vision of nature' conceived as the world that is 'external' to the self. Thus, according
to this theory, the rationalization and bureaucratization of society that we
are familiar with in the modern period, is also accompanied by the secularization of space and the disenchantment of nature.

Recently, however, this understanding of disenchantment has begun
to be questioned by social theorists. In particular, Bronislaw Szerszynski
(2005) has argued that the reordering of society and nature in modernity
should not be viewed as a final stage in the process of disenchantment and
secularization, but rather as a moment within the ongoing transformation of the sacred throughout history. This transformation is not so much
a gradual process of the sacred's absenting itself from society and from
nature, but rather a continuous reordering of the sacred within the world.
The view of modern society as the highest stage in some gradual evolution
towards rationality and secularism is a view from a particular evolutionary perspective, one that has been informed by centuries of Western theological history, or as Szerszynski terms it, 'the long arc of monotheism'. As
Szerszynski writes:

> The illusion that the sacred has disappeared is arguably a feature of all
> historical transitions from one form of the sacred to the next in a given
> society. Each transition can seem like an eclipse of the sacred in the
> terms in which it was organized in the closing epoch; from a larger his-
> torical perspective, however, it can be seen as the emergence of a new
> sacral ordering. (Szerszysnski 2005, 26)

The secularization of society and the disenchantment of nature summed up in the concept of 'absolute profane' are thus not to be seen as a final stage in history but as 'an event *within* the ongoing history of the sacred in the West' (2005, 27).

This paper aims to consider the disenchantment of nature in modern China from the perspective of this debate within social science theory. First it examines the process of modernization in China as a self-conscious process of disenchantment and rationalization. In this process the state assumed rational control over religious spaces and religious organizations. It was able to do so in part through the development of the concept of 'superstition' in which the religious activities associated most overtly with nature were prohibited. All this seems to indicate the value of the Weberian view of modernization. This chapter follows Szerszynski, however, in arguing that this process should not be understood as the absolute secularization of Chinese society but rather as the creation of a new form of the sacred in Chinese society, this time the creation of a transcendent monotheism focused on the abstract concept of the state and concretely embodied in the Communist Party. In effect, therefore, the process of modernization in China has not been about secularization but rather about the establishment of a new sacred order in which the diversity of Chinese religious values became increasingly subordinated to a new transcendent monotheism.

The Rationalization of Sacred Space

In an article entitled 'Knowledge and Power in the Discourse of Modernity: The Campaigns against Popular Religion in Early Twentieth-Century China' Prasenjit Duara (1991) argued that the newly emerging modern Chinese state in part based its ascendancy on its ability to destroy the local religious associations and local geographies of power so as to reorganize them within a monolithic ideology of the modern nation state. Even before the establishment of the People's Republic of China in 1949, the modernization of the Chinese state was achieved through a reorganization of local power and social networks, chiefly by appropriating land owned by local temples. 'Monks and priests who had depended on religious properties were deprived of their sources of livelihood; local religious societies that fulfilled social as much as spiritual needs were dispossessed and replaced by government offices that seemed mainly interested in extracting revenues and uncovering unregistered property' (Duara 1991, 76). Duara viewed this reordering of local religion as socio-economic activity, with the state assuming control over the economic resources and social structures previously under the control of the religious organizations. But perhaps this was not simply a reordering of the religious economy, but also a reordering of the sacred. Perhaps in crushing the social and economic power of the local temple networks, the modern Chinese state was also establishing itself as the only legitimate source of spiritual authority within the nation. In short, this transformation might not be about secularization, as Weberian theory understands it, but, in Szerszynski's terms, as one of these various moments in human history when an old sacred order gives way to a new one.

In order to understand how this forced disenchantment of China's countryside could legitimately be viewed as a transformation within the sacred in modern China, it is necessary to understand the relationship between the sacred, nature and geography in traditional China. In the history of China, power was not only constituted ideologically and theologically, but geographically too. This was evident most clearly in the sacred cosmography that held China to be the 'middle kingdom'. This term originated in the Warring States period, and was originally understood in the plural. It referred to the various 'central states' that shared the culture of writing in characters. These 'central states' were thus distinguished from outer regions who did not share the same literary and cultural traditions. After unification under the first Qin emperor, these 'central states' became the 'middle kingdom', that is, the single China that is familiar to us today. At the centre of this middle kingdom was the capital, and at the centre of the capital was the imperial palace, and at the centre of the imperial palace was the court from which the emperor governed the distant corners of the empire. This cosmology was replicated everywhere. The magistrate had his offices in a courtyard at the centre of the city. The city was surrounded by walls. Outside the walls was the countryside that provided the food to keep the city functioning and beyond the countryside was the wilderness inhabited by bandits, beasts, and barbarians. This cosmology was replicated also in the heavens, which were viewed as a circular canopy rotating around a central ridge-pole known as the Great Ultimate (*taiji*), an *axis mundi* connecting the pole star down through the earth into the underworld. In some Daoist religious movements, the most significant deities were thus the ones associated with the stars of the Big Dipper (*Ursa Major*) who lit the way to the apex of heaven and around which the lesser constellations revolved. Power, in earth and on heaven, was manifested in the construction of space. It was about the disposition of things, structuring human relations in a certain way within their surroundings so as to promote a cosmic vision of order and harmony (see Lewis 2006).

Central to this worldview was the network of sacred mountains that symbolized the centre and the four corners of the empire. In addition, both Buddhists and Daoists claimed their own sacred mountains and established monasteries and retreat houses there. At certain times and in certain locations these sacred geographies overlapped with each other. Mt. Tai in Shandong province, the Eastern mountain of the imperial cult was also sacred to both Buddhists and Daoists. On this mountain, the Qin emperor who reunited the country following the dissolution of the Warring States period instituted new sacrifices to the supreme cosmic rulers. Only the emperor was permitted to offer these *feng* and *shan* sacrifices. Through this exclusive ritual the emperor asserted his own personal connection to the cosmic powers that governed heaven and earth. He established himself not only as the chief mediator between the gods and the people but as an indispensable element in the theological geography that constituted the Chinese understanding of their place in the universe. The Wu emperor of the Han dynasty reinstated these sacrifices and built a temple at the base of the mountain where the entire cosmic pantheon could assemble to witness the rituals over which the emperor personally presided (see Bokenkamp 1996). The imperial cult thus served to reinforce the authority of the emperor over his people, an authority vested in the ritual construction of sacred space by means of which the nation could orient itself in relation to the heavens above and the peripheral spaces to the north, south, east and west.

This network of sacred spaces, however, should not solely be interpreted in ideological and epistemological terms about what Chinese people *believed* about the nature of the cosmos. Rather we should interpret this construction of sacred space as the way in which power and authority were actually constituted in terms of the geography of the nation. The significance of the *feng* and *shan* sacrifices did not lie solely in the symbolic nature of the liturgy and the ritual, but in the fact that they were performed at the base of a vast and imposing mountain reaching vertiginously up into the sky. Through the ritual the emperor was appropriating power vested in the physical geography of that particular space.

The technological limits of the pre-modern era, however, meant that the official state orthodoxy was not imposed uniformly throughout China. China was thus a land of religious diversity in which local religions constructed their own interpretations of sacred space and competed with each other for the allegiance of the people. Dynasties were established on the back of religious fervour and were destroyed in the same way. As much as the Imperial court sought to impose its vision of unity and harmony on the empire, such an imposition was inevitably imperfect, fracturing at its various intersections with the authority of local cults and popular religions. In order for this vision to become a reality, it was necessary for the modern state to dismantle the networks of theological power and religious authority traditionally associated with the sacred mountains and local cults. This was made possible part by rapid developments in communications technology that, for the first time, enabled the central authorities to impose their vision of the world upon the various regions of China. Although from the perspective of traditional Chinese religious history this could be viewed as the secularization of these natural and local spaces, the campaigns against popular religion could equally be interpreted as the reordering of the sacred into a single, overarching, transcendent monotheism constructed around the abstract notion of the state.

It would come as no surprise, therefore, that religion and the state would come into conflict where the function of religion was not clearly allied with that of the state. In such cases religion had to be controlled by the state because it was, in effect, a theological competitor. Duara traced the modern history of conflict between religion and the state to an official document published in 1928, called the 'Standards for Preserving and Abandoning Gods and Shrines' (Duara 1991, 79). This document marked a milestone in the process of legitimating certain forms of religion and delegitimizing others. Some gods such as Confucius, Guandi, Laozi, and Buddha were permitted to be worshipped. Other gods, such as the city god and the god of wealth were proscribed. The main distinction to be drawn between these two lists of gods is that the former could be identified in terms of their function with the overarching goals of a nation state, whereas the latter list contains gods who chiefly serve the interests of individuals or localities. In short, some gods had a place within the temple of nationalism and other gods were seen as subversive of the overarching agenda of the state. Just as the rise of the nation state in Europe has been seen as a theological consequence of the Protestant Reformation (Loy 2002, 94), so also the invention of the modern Chinese nation state could be seen a type of theological activity that demanded the restraint of religious competitors.

Religion, Nature, and Modernization

The debate about the place of religion in the modern Chinese state was not, however, understood simply within the framework of the overarching theology of the nation state. It was also an ideological conflict predicated on competing visions of nature. This conflict was made possible by the invention of the category of 'superstition' (*mixin*). Duara demonstrates in the same article that although popular cults and local religions had previously been regarded with disdain by elite religious leaders and categorized as 'heterodox' (*xie*) they were now increasingly placed under the new category of superstition (*mixin*). The category of 'superstition' thus functioned as an ideological tool by means of which the state was able to make normative judgments about religious institutions so as to assert power over them. It did so by framing the ideology of local and popular religious movements as 'superstition', that is to say, 'deluded beliefs'. A deviant or unorthodox institution might have the possibility of being aligned, reformed or normalized in some way. An organization founded on superstition, or deluded belief, would face a far harder task of surviving in the modern state. Just as the birth of the nation state in Western Europe and North America was accompanied by the proscription of witchcraft and magic, so also the birth of the modern Chinese state witnessed a violent struggle over the ideologically correct way to view and engage the natural world. In both cases, magic and superstition were seen as the direct enemies of technology and science.

The attempt to define superstition in China began in 1930 with the 'Procedure for the Abolition of Occupations of Divination, Astrology, Physiognomy and Palmistry, Sorcery and Geomancy,' the 'Procedures for Banning and Managing Superstitious Objects and Professions,' and the 'Prohibition of Divinatory Medicines' (Duara 1991, 80). The so-called superstitions of divination, astrology, physiognomy, palmistry, and geomancy were all key elements of popular religion in China, frequently conducted in local temples, and were not generally associated with the foreign religions of Buddhism or Christianity. In effect the proscription of these activities was designed to promote the demise of traditional Chinese popular religion. But there was also a significant ideological component at stake here that revolved around the philosophy of nature. Although astrology and physiognomy are generally dismissed in modern society as 'fortune-telling', in traditional Chinese religion they were part and parcel of the fabric of religious meaning that enabled people to make sense out of their lives, and also part of the local temple economy. What binds all these forms of 'fortune-telling' together, however, is a shared philosophy of nature, one that is diametrically opposed to the ideology of science and rationality on which the modern Chinese state was building its authority. All the proscribed activities described as 'superstitious' held in common the view that physical nature, whether in the form of human bodies, the stars or geography, had the capacity to reveal truths that are of value for human beings. As such they were sources of religious meaning and moral capacity that originated beyond the control and authority of the state, or, indeed, any formal religious institution. The development of science, on the other hand, was accompanied by an instrumental rationality that viewed nature not as the revealer of spiritual truths but as neutral, value-free space capable of being shaped by human will through technology and so forth. In the former case, nature revealed truths to humans through religious processes; in the latter case, humans imposed their values on nature through technological and economic processes. In the modern nation state the imposition of values on nature is directed by the organs of the state through its various science and technology research institutes and the modern university system.

The attack on superstition persisted in modern China through to the Communist period. At the Eleventh Party Congress in 1979, freedom of religion was restored in China only for the five state-sanctioned religions of China. All other forms of traditional religious culture were deemed superstition. The policy on the regulation of religions adopted in 1979 states that:

> By superstition we generally mean activities conducted by shamans, and sorcerers, such as magic medicine, magic water, divination, fortune telling, avoiding disasters, praying for rain, praying for pregnancy, exorcising demons, telling fortunes by physiognomy, locating house or tomb sites by geomancy and so forth. They are all absurd and ridiculous. Anyone possessing rudimentary knowledge will not believe in them. (Document 3 from *Selected Documents of the Third Plenary Session of the Eleventh Party Congress, 1979*; MacInnis 1989, 33-4)

From this excerpt we can see that the principal question about the relationship between religion and the state has been formulated around the capacity of nature to shape and direct people's religious experiences. The so-called superstitious activities mediate the relationship between humans and nature in a way that lies outside of the bureaucratic processes of the state, or the established religions with solid institutional structures that could more easily be brought into line with the goals of the modern Chinese state.

Thus the conflict between religion, science and superstition was not just about epistemology, or the rational procedures for verifying belief. They were also about the capacity of nature to be a source of sacred power and even moral authority outside of the structures of the state and the rational procedures of science. The campaigns against superstition and local religions that were begun in the Republican period and carried through most forcefully in the Communist period were not only contesting ideological and epistemological space within the Chinese psyche; nor were they solely struggles to assert central power over local areas; rather they were also struggles over the value of nature, and the capacity of nature to function in some way as sacred space, as a source of divine revelation, or as a theological reality.

It would be a mistake to underestimate the serious nature of this conflict between science and 'fortune-telling'. The various activities proscribed under the rubric of 'superstition' were by no means fringe activities restricted to a few uneducated people. Rather, they expressed a fundamental aspect of the traditional Chinese worldview, namely the view of nature as a source of sacred power. This view is neatly summed up in a third-century poem by Cao Zhi. The subject is Mt. Tai, the sacred mountain of the east, mentioned above as the location of the *feng* and *shan* sacrifices.

> I roamed the mountain in the dawn
> Secluded in its misty depths
> When suddenly I met two boys
> With faces that were fair and fresh.
> They gave me herbs of the immortals
> The Numinous Supreme had made,
> Medicaments that when absorbed
> Revive the seminal essence and brain,
> So life, like a rock's or metal ore's,
> Passes through eons, but does not age.
> (Trans. Elvin 2004, xxii-xxiii)

Here nature, in the form of Mt. Tai, is the space in which the poet encounters two boys. They are described as having 'fair and fresh' faces, which is the clue that they are not ordinary mortals but immortal beings. This view is confirmed when they give the author 'herbs of the immortals' to 'revive the seminal essence and brain'. Here, nature is not simply the location for an encounter with divine beings, but is also the source of cosmic power which has the capacity of conferring immortality on the one who ingests the herbs. Finally, nature in the form of unchanging rock is a metaphor for the sacred ideal of immortality. In these three cases, nature is not valued in terms of some rational economic calculus but as the medium through which the adept can transcend the mundane world. Nature is sacred inasmuch as it is the Way to attain a transfigured and more perfect reality. When the state proscribed 'divination' and 'magic medicine' it was in effect proscribing this view of nature, which formed the bedrock of traditional religious culture.

Remarkably, however, this view of nature was never extirpated from the Chinese mentality; instead it continued, albeit in a transformed way, into the modern period. Despite the ideological rhetoric of the modern Chinese state, the view that nature is a source of sacred power and moral authority continues into the present day. Take for instance, the following song from the Great Leap Forward in the 1950s:

> Let's attack here!
> Drive away the mountain gods,
> Break down the stone walls
> To bring out those 200 million tons of coal.
> (Zhang Zhimin, *Personalities in the Commune*; quoted in Shapiro 2001, vii)

At first glance it would seem that this song supports the Weberian hypothesis that modernization involves the disenchantment of sacred space. Here modernization, in the form of coal mining, demands the secularization of the mountain space where the mining takes place, described as 'driving away the mountain gods'. From the perspective of traditional Chinese religion this indeed is tantamount to the secularization of sacred space, but from a larger perspective it is more accurate to interpret this as the reordering of the sacred. Driving away the mountain gods does not reveal the mountain to be an inert place devoid of any sacred power. Rather it reveals the mountain to be harbouring a new form of sacred power, that of coal. Coal is not here simple 'stuff', but during the Great Leap Forward was the means by which China would achieve its Great Leap Forward into the future. It was, in effect, the numinous substance that was essential in the concoction of a new elixir of immortality: steel. The view of nature as harbouring secret powers, whether conceived as 200 million tons of coal, or herbs with numinous powers remains constant. The only thing that changed from the time of Cao Zhi to the time of Mao was the understanding of the role of the traditional gods as guardians or mediators of the sacred power of nature. These were dispensed with and replaced by the gods of the human will. As Jasper Becker writes in *China's Hungry Ghosts* (1996, 308; quoted by Shapiro 2001, 68):

> Mao wanted to modernize China but could not grasp the basis of modern thought, the scientific method: that the way in which the natural universe behaves can be proved or disproved by objective tests, independent of ideology or individual will.

Becker's critique of Mao, and also Shapiro's, was that Mao did not in fact secularize nature in the 'correct' way. Rather he simply replaced one form of ideology with another, asserting the supremacy of the human spirit, not the celestial gods, over nature.

Reading Chinese modernization not as 'secularization' but as an enduring theological contest over the location and power of the sacred might also help explain contemporary Chinese leaders' fascination with grand works of environmental engineering. Projects such as the Three Gorges Dam can be understood as modern equivalents of the acts of mythological heroes who brought order out of the watery chaos. Such projects continue to reveal the enduring power of sacred mythology in modern China. Thus the destruction of the natural environment continues not through the rationalization and disenchantment of nature, as conservative religious critics of modernity might suggest, but because of the enduring power of 'secular theologies' to subordinate human interests to irrational ideals (see Gray 2004).

Religion and Nature in Contemporary China: Three Cases

The debate over the place of religion and nature in modernity was not, therefore, decisively settled in the twentieth century and has begun to take on new forms in an era of relative religious freedom in China. The following three brief case studies display something of the complex situation of religion, nature and modernity in contemporary China.

The first case concerns that of religious sites located in areas of outstanding natural beauty, which have been developed and reorganized chiefly as tourist attractions in China, and function under the authority of local tourism offices. Although the reopening of temples might lead one to think that religion is somehow resurgent in China, the fact that religious spaces are often contained firmly within tourist economic development zones makes clear that the sacred is secondary to the economic. The recent flourishing of religious activities in China thus leads, paradoxically, to serious problems faced by wealthy monasteries located in tourist development zones. Referring to Buddhism, Jing Yin (2006, 90) writes:

> Problems associated with the impact of the market economy on Buddhism can be divided into two categories. The first can broadly be termed external problems that arise when government officials, particularly low ranking local ones, infringe upon the rights and interests of the monasteries. The more wealthy monasteries become the more frequently this occurs, and this constitutes a rather serious problem in some areas. The second category of problems are internal disputes that arise when the state returns property to the monasteries following the implementation of the policy of religious freedom in 1979.

The recent freedoms bestowed on religious institutions in China have thus come at a price, that of keeping sacred space contained within the bureaucratic control of the state as a means to achieving rational economic ends. Jing Yin (2006, 91-92) goes on:

> From a Buddhist perspective, one can say that the one-sided economic development in many monasteries has made them lose their distinctively Buddhist characteristics. I have accompanied many overseas Buddhist delegates on visits to monasteries in China. In my experience, visitors often feel that despite the proliferation of monasteries, there is a lack of character here. Monasteries commonly operate vegetarian restaurants, guest houses, souvenir shops, and food and drink booths. Some even go to the extreme of running factories and operating companies. The long-term effect is that the market economy is seriously hurting the religious nature of the monasteries. Once monasteries become large-scale enterprises, it is difficult for them to back out. And when monasteries become principally tourist attractions, the danger is that the energy of the monks becomes devoted chiefly to receiving tourists, leaving no time for the *sangha* or to engage in Buddhist practice.

In other words, even in an era of religious freedom, it seems that religious activities continue to be subordinated to rational, economic functions and are increasingly unable to stand as moral or ethical challenges to the dominant values of the state. Such a view is borne out by the Chinese state regulations on religion issued in 2004, which paint a clear picture of the place of religion within the secular space of the Chinese state. These new regulations do not deal with the thorny theoretical questions such as the definition of religion, or the relationship between religion, superstition and scientific belief. Rather they tend to focus on more bureaucratic questions such as which government agency is the competent authority for dealing with various types of religious issues, and economic questions such as the relationship between religious pilgrimage and secular tourism. Article 18 of the new regulations, for example, governs the management of religious sites and typifies well the new direction in Communist policy towards religion:

> A site for religious activities shall strengthen internal management, and, in accordance with the provisions of the relevant laws, regulations and rules, establish and improve the management systems for personnel, finance, accounting, security, fire control, cultural relics protection, sanitation and epidemic prevention, etc., and accept the guidance, supervision and inspection by the relevant departments of the local people's government. (State Council 2004)

As this regulation indicates, the overall goal now is to promote the smooth management of religious spaces in such a way that they do not disrupt social harmony or pose a threat to the authority of the government. It seems that party officials are no longer concerned with understanding the nature of religion in terms of political theory, but only with managing its social and economic functioning. In contrast to the divisive ideological debates of the May Fourth and early Communist era over secularization, tradition, and modernity, the contemporary framework for understanding the relationship between religion and society emphasizes economics, management and social harmony. The CCP no longer seems intent on attempting to control the religious beliefs of Chinese citizens, but rather on ensuring that religious organizations, whatever they believe, work to support the nation and its economy

The second case study concerns the revival of interest, at least in a theoretical sense, of the value of traditional religions in contributing to the emergence of environmentalism in contemporary China. Most notable in this regard has been the work of Pan Yue, Vice-Minister of the State Environmental Protection Administration (SEPA). In a notable speech in 2003, he called for the creation of an 'environmental culture and national renaissance' that forged traditional views of nature with the demands of the modern Chinese state into a nationalistic vision of Chinese development, and one that would avoid the ecologically destructive excesses of Western modernization. He quoted chapter 16 of the Daoist classic, *The Way and Its Power* (*Daode jing*), 'The myriad creatures all rise together / And I watch their return / The teeming creatures / All return to their separate roots' to argue for a 'circular economy,' his vision of an ecologically sustainable society (Pan 2007, 11). Such a society would be at once at the forefront of ecological economics and sustainable development theory, and at the same time indigenously and authentically Chinese:

> The pursuit of harmonious relations between man and nature is the mainstream of traditional cultures in the past thousands of years. The Confucian school advocated 'the unity of nature and man', which emphasizes that all human behaviours must conform to the law of nature.
>
> ...
>
> The Daoist school proposed the theory of 'Tao following nature', which elevates the concept of 'nature' to a metaphysical height. ... According to Laozi, natural laws shall not be violated, and human principles must conform to the natural laws. (Pan 2007, 6-7)

In Pan's view, therefore, China's religious traditions are sources of moral capacity and intellectual authority which could be reconfigured to fit in with China's new goals of sustainable development. China's economic development, its accompanying environmental and social pressures, and its state-sponsored nationalism are thus ushering in new transformations of the sacred.

Finally, the contemporary Chinese scene reveals a popular interest in understanding the relationships between religion, science and nature. Such an interest has most recently been evident in the 2005 debate about whether environmental protection in China was best served by an attitude of reverence (*jingwei*) towards nature. He Zuoxiu, a prominent scientist, argued that reverence for nature was the product of anti-scientific thinking and was not helpful in fighting diseases or natural disasters (He 2005). Liang Congjie, the founder of the Chinese NGO Friends of Nature, on the other hand, argued that nature cannot be viewed simply as a tool, and that having a sense of reverence for the natural world was itself natural and rational (Liang 2006). Although Liang was careful to define his use of the word 'reverence' in a humanistic way, the very use of the term 'reverence' or 'awe' (*jingwei*) in the first place, clearly struck a negative chord with some members of the scientific establishment. The very debate reveals that issues of the environment are not simply a matter of science and technology in China, but also ethics and values.

These three examples from the contemporary Chinese scene reveal that in China's quest for modernization, religion and nature continue to be sites of ideological conflict. Religious organizations continue to be actively managed by the state's religious affairs administration. This oversight is especially strong where religious sites are located in areas of natural beauty and there is thus a large potential for making money by developing the local tourist economy. On the other hand, there seems to be a willingness among some of the elite to consider the value of traditional ideas in helping to solve China's dire environmental problems. Their views are regarded as controversial because they seem to contradict the official ideology of modernization and scientific development (*kexue fazhan*) and yet figures like Pan Yue hold senior positions within the government. At the same time the question of respect for nature remains highly contested among scientists and environmentalists. All this seems to suggest that despite the rhetoric of science and modernity, there has not been an irreversible process of disenchantment in China. Some traditional values persist, whereas others have been transmuted into nationalism and scientism. The relationship between science, nature, and religion continues to be contested both theoretically and practically.

References

AsiaNews. 2005. Sixty Thousand People Protest Against Chinese Pollution. *AsiaNews.it* 14 April 2005. Internet: http://www.asianews.it/view_p.php?l=en&art=3036

Bokenkamp, Stephen. 1996. Record of the Feng and Shan Sacrifices. In *Religions of China in Practice*, edited by Donald S. Lopez Jr. Princeton: Princeton University Press, 251-60.

Duara, Prasenjit. 1991. Knowledge and Power in the Discourse of Modernity: The Campaigns against Popular Religion in Early Twentieth-Century China. *Journal of Asian Studies* 50 (1), 67-83.

Elvin, Mark. 2004. *The Retreat of the Elephants*. New Haven: Yale University Press.

Gellner, Ernest. 1987. *Culture, Identity and Politics*. Cambridge: Cambridge University Press.

Girardot, N.J., James Miller, and Liu Xiaogan, eds. 2001. *Daoism and Ecology: Ways within a Cosmic Landscape*. Cambridge: Harvard University Press.

Gray, John. 2004. The Future of an Illusion. *Daedalus* 133 (3), 10-17.

He Zuxiu. 2005. *Ren yu ziran yi shui wei ben, wuxu jingwei daziran*. Internet: http://www.kxwsl.com/ReadNews.asp?NewsID=1915

Jing Yin. 2006. The Impact of Economic Reforms on Buddhism in China. In *Chinese Religions in Contemporary Socities*, edited by James Miller. Denver: ABC-CLIO.

Lewis, Mark. 2006. *The Construction of Space in Early China*. Albany, NY: State University of New York Press.

Liang Congjie. 2005. *Bu neng jinjinde ba ziran kanzuo renlei de gongju*. Internet: http://www.kxwsl.com/ReadNews.asp?NewsID=1915.

Loy, David. 2002. *A Buddhist History of the West: Studies in Lack*. Albany, NY: State University of New York Press.

MacInnis, Donald, ed. 1989. *Religion in China Today: Policy and Practice*. Maryknoll, NY: Orbis Books.

Pan, Yue. 2007. *Thoughts on Environmental Issues*. Beijing: Chinese Environmental Culture Protection Association.

Shapiro, Judith. 2001. *Mao's War Against Nature*. Cambridge: Cambridge University Press.

State Council of the People's Republic of China. 2004. *Decree no. 426: Regulations on Religious Affairs*. Adopted at the 57th Executive Meeting of the State Council on 7 July 2004, promulgated 30 November 2004, effective as of 1 March 2005.

Szerszynski, Bronislaw. 2005. *Nature, Technology and the Sacred*. Oxford: Blackwell.

6   In Search of an Adequate Christian Anthropology

Francis Kadaplackal

Introduction

We currently live in challenging times. The role of the human being should be placed under scrutiny due to the rising tide of progress and development, scientific discoveries, technological innovations, and the reality of ecological catastrophe. Our unquenchable thirst for profit and for making our life more comfortable, cosy, and easy, has a direct relation to the degradation of the natural environment (McDonagh 1986, 8-9; Wirzba 2003, 62). The Judeo-Christian tradition has been accused of perpetrating an inhuman, careless, environmentally unfriendly, and even destructive attitude towards nature and the natural environment. In this essay, I intend to enter into a theological investigation regarding the place and task of human beings in creation. First, Christianity's theology of creation seems to propose a strongly anthropocentric worldview, as a result of the extreme personalistic character of the operational theological categories, which can be considered as theologically insufficient, one-sided, and inadequate. Second, we can identify *imago Dei*, which is considered to be the backbone of the prevailing theological anthropology, as theologically insufficient, too broad and too exclusivist, because it does not really provide enough grounds to care for the whole creation. Third, this means that we need to plunge into a reinterpretation of *imago Dei* in order to suggest a compatible theological anthropology, which can help us to value the creation as a whole. Only an adequate theo-anthropology can maintain the equilibrium between the unique role of human beings in creation (in their relationships with God, other human beings, and nature) and the care for nature as God's creation. Based on these hypotheses, I will take a two-fold step to reinterpret the human beings in creation. In the first part, I will expound upon the theological nature of the problem. Here, I will also dwell on the limitations of 'mago Dei because of which I argue that it cannot function properly in theological anthropology. In the second part I will present the 'created co-creator' as a better theo-anthropological category. I shall conclude my theological reflection by comparing both these categories to prove why I opt for the 'created co-creator'.

The Theological Nature of the Problem

Christian theology finds its basis in the fundamental tenets of our faith that were formulated already in the earlier centuries of Christianity, especially in the Creed. The Niceno-Constantinopolitan Creed (381) sets out the basis of our belief in a God who is described as '...Deum, Patrem omnipotentem, factorem caeli et terrae, visibilium omnium et invisibilium' (Denzinger and Schönmetzer 1963, 67). Whenever Christians use the word 'credo', it is pregnant with the full meaning of the belief in a God who is Almighty and who causes the whole world into 'being'. As Houtepen says: 'Het geloof in de scheppende God wil juist fundamenten leggen onder alle religieuze en esthetische ervaring en richting geven aan ons gedrag' ['Faith in the God of Creation aims to give good foundations for all our religious and aesthetic experience and guide our behaviour'] (Houtepen 1990, 59). It is therefore our task to understand rightly and to interpret our traditions properly in order to discover our place in creation.

Many scientists and philosophers have charged the Judeo-Christian creation theology as guilty of perpetrating a dreadful exploitation of nature. So, for example, Lynn White published an article in 1967, 'The Historical Roots of Our Ecological Crisis,' which was a great attack on Christianity's way of treating nature and nonhuman beings. White was of the opinion that the crisis can be traced back to the way Christianity taught its believers about the creation of the world (White 1994, 9-14). 'By destroying pagan animism', says White, 'Christianity made it possible to exploit nature in a mood of indifference to the feelings of natural objects. ... Man's effective monopoly on spirit in this world was confirmed, and the old inhibitions to the exploitation of nature crumbled' (White 1994, 12). Scholars like Douglas John Hall and René Coste do recognize that there is a problem, a grave ecological crisis, which is 'the distorted relationship between human and nonhuman nature' (Hall 1986, 5-13; Coste 1994, 42-47; Moltmann 2001, 172; Oelschlaeger 1994, 19-26; Ratzinger 1995, 33-39).

While recognizing the crisis and a certain culpability, Hall goes on to ask if we have been good and faithful stewards of the earth (Hall 1986, 24; Hall 1990, 188-191; Cobb 1972, 34-36). It is not enough that we look at the technologists and scientists with indignation, but we must evaluate the whole lot of our beliefs and actions and we should 'begin in the spirit of self-examination and *metanoia*'. (Hall 1986, 24; Grenz 1994, 168; McEvoy 2001, 196). In my opinion, we must clarify, reinterpret and redefine the operational theo-anthropology that regulates our relationship with each other, God, nature, and nonhuman beings.

Imago Dei

Imago Dei is a theologically loaded term that expresses the relationship between God and human beings. From the early history of humankind, this has adopted a technical, *theo-anthropological* connotation in the confession of faith within the church (Hall 1986, 61; Langemeyer 2000, 369-371; McGrath 2000, 379-382). Humanity becomes the point of attention based on the *Wirkungsgeschichte* in the book of Genesis, 1: 1-2:4, since the image of God is imprinted on us as human beings. The concepts 'stewardship' and 'dominion' were used and interchanged in an effort to specify the role of the human being. It is the staunch wish of God to raise the place of humans above all creation and to give him control and power over all creation. The Judeo-Christian tradition argues that humans receive the most prominent place in creation and the human assignment in nature is to 'dominate' and 'control' the creation by being a 'master and ruler' just like God is a master for him. This 'dominion thesis' is often seen to be the fundamental cause of the ecological crises in the world. This ethical imperative for upholding 'dominion and stewardship' is strongly coloured by deep anthropocentric convictions, inspired by the Judeo-Christian faith traditions and encourages the exploitation of nature.

As *imago Dei*, humans have a unique and privileged place within creation, with special authority that also brings along due responsibility. This implies that creation as a whole can be a promise as well as a threat, since 'human beings are the most vulnerable aspect of creation, the linchpin of success and failure' (Fern 2002, 167). According to Joseph Ratzinger, the human being is the venue where heaven and earth meet each other. As the image of God, 'in the human being God enters into his creation; the human being is directly related to God. The human being is called by him' (Ratzinger 1995, 45). Being confronted with the enigma of the 'human condition', argues Grenz, we end up in an identity problem. But we must realize that 'our foundational identity rises from the fact that our ultimate origin lies in God' (Grenz 1994, 166).

The theological world reckons *imago Dei* as the 'backbone of theological anthropology', as that which is foundational in determining humanity's relationship with God, each other, and nature. Furthermore, it is considered as the qualifier, determinant, and regulator of how we should discover our place in the world. It is precisely this that I want to bring into question. I am of the opinion that this cannot be accepted as the only theological standard to regulate, to assess, and to make sense of our role in creation, unless it has been subjected to theological reflection, moral analysis, and evaluation. Can it render us with the possibilities to cope with the challenging situations that we face today? Does it provide us with a framework to bring together theology and anthropology (and ecology) for shaping a coherent vision about the role of the human being?

Theological Limitations of Imago Dei

In my opinion, *imago Dei* does not provide us with an adequate anthropology. First, as God's images, our origin lies in a God who creates human life, the whole world and everything in it. This belief forms the very foundation of our existence. But in my opinion, *imago Dei* overemphasizes the dignity of human beings. It is here that I would like to make my first theological argument. Our 'being in the world' is not just a presence, but it should be a theologically qualified presence, that reflects and radiates the dignity that we have received from Him in love. In this way, dignity is not only an ontological category, but also a call and a vocation at the same time. An overemphasis of the concept can endanger the theological ideas behind it, that is, that we have our origin in God. Taking part in the dignity of God should not be a reason for us to exploit nature without restrictions. We need to realize that every creature has its own place in God's circle of love. God found all created things 'good' and therefore we must respect this 'goodness' in nature. In my opinion, in spite of its many positive aspects, *imago Dei* does not seem to succeed in this.

Second, being *imago Dei*, the human being is created not to be alone, but to be in communion and relationship with the Creator, with other humans, and the natural world. It is through these spectrums of relationships that we realize our dignity as persons. Creation is valuable not just because it is useful to us, but also because it is valued by God and is found to be 'good' (Grenz 1994, 186). We must value nature through our relationships, and as Houtepen (1990, 75) says, we need to foster a caring attitude towards the natural world. *Imago Dei* gives importance to the relational dimension, but restricts it mostly to the interpersonal level. Relationship with other human beings and God are important, as *imago Dei* upholds, but stopping there would be against the plan of God for creation. It is therefore necessary that we go beyond interpersonal relationships and extend our care to the rest of creation. Fostering relationships and respect for all life are fundamental theological choices that the human being should make, so that we may improve the quality of our relationship with the Creator and the whole of creation. Any sound theological anthropology must take account of this holistic dimension. In my opinion, *imago Dei* does not recognize this sufficiently.

Third, we can emphasize that the capabilities for moral reasoning, free choice and responsible activity differentiate the human being from the rest of creation. This brings humanity not only to a privileged position, but also to a responsible one. The human capacity to think rationally and critically cannot be seen as a licence to exploit the natural world according to one's whims and fancies (Labuschagne 1990, 10-11). As beings endowed with rationality and freedom of choice, we are to act in a morally responsible manner in dealing with nature. Every human action, therefore, that does not comply with the demand for responsibility has to be brought into question. To image God responsibly, the human being has to extend the sphere of responsibility beyond its kin (mankind), to the non-human world. In my opinion, *imago Dei* closes down the avenues for an inclusivistic approach with regard to nature, by overemphasising the role of the human beings and thus falls into a theological fallacy.

Fourth, theologically speaking we have good foundations to encourage the human being's creativity. True freedom means that our talents and capabilities should be at the service of God and directed towards the enhancement of His creation. By sharing in this creative activity, we share in the fullness of life that God has willed for us. Humans are called to become themselves. 'Human persons are not to be understood merely from the perspective of their past histories or from that isolated moment that we refer to as the present. They are oriented towards their future' (Ratzinger 1995, 49). This opens up the horizons from the distant past, to the present and from there to the future, to that which is not-yet. Very often people understand the role of the human being as a passive one. But I am of the opinion that we have enough theological foundation to promote the human being's active role in creation. In my opinion *imago Dei* does not succeed in maintaining a proper balance between human being's 'creative capacity' on the one hand, and the 'createdness' on the other. With the abilities received from God, the human being is called upon to perfect the earth and to continue God's creative action (*creatio continua*) in the world (Labuschagne 1990, 16).

I do acknowledge that *imago Dei* has played an important role in regulating our relationships with God, with other human beings and with the natural world (Case-Winters 2004, 813-826; Wirzba 2003, 123-124). In spite of the many positive aspects, it fails on several grounds and turns out to be theologically incompetent, ethically inadequate and strongly anthropocentric in regulating our relationships and our treatment of nature. This has to do with its overemphasis on the dignity of the human being, the inclination to be exclusive in attributing value and concern, its partiality in dealing with creation by maintaining an extremely personalistic viewpoint and through its unbridled glorification of interpersonal relationships. In the following part, I would like to suggest 'created co-creator' as a more viable, theologically qualified and morally competent theo-anthropological category.

Towards a More Adequate Anthropology: The 'Created Co-Creator'

As is evident from our previous discussion regarding the limitations of *imago Dei,* it is a necessity that the role of the human being be rethought and redefined from a theological perspective. What should be the role of the human being within the natural world? Should the human being play the role of a servant, of a steward or that of a tyrant? The question as to the 'rightful place of the human being' is a very pressing issue. The interesting part of the whole discussion is that sometimes these questions are asked by humanity itself and at other times, these are addressed to humanity (Hefner 2004, 733). On the one hand, we ask how the situation can be improved, how our relationships can be bettered, how the environmental degradation can be reduced and how we can contribute to the protection of nature. On the other hand, as Hefner says, 'in their mute and yet dramatic way, *our fellow citizens in the commonwealth of the natural world* – plants and animals – ask us the question (Hefner 2004, 733)'. These questions need to be answered, because we cannot afford to wait any longer. In this section, I will attempt to reinterpret and rediscover the rightful place of human beings within creation, based on a theological reflection on the 'created co-creator'.

Historical Development of the Term 'Created Co-Creator'

The beginnings of the proposal for understanding the human being as created co-creator can be traced back to 'Unsere Verantwortlichkeit gegenüber der Schöpfung', an article published by Frits Blanke in 1959. In this article he called for the acceptance and appreciation of 'co-createdness' which he called *'Mitgeschöpflichkeit'* and suggested that we all belong to the one family, no matter if we belong to the human race or not.

> Alles, was da lebt, ist vom selben Schöpfergeiste durchwaltet. Wir sind, ob Mensch oder Nichtmensch, Glieder einer großen Familie. Diese Mitgeschöpflichkeit (als Gegenstück zur Mitmenschlichkeit) verpflichtet. Sie auferlegt uns Verantwortung für die anderen 'Familienglieder' (Blanke 1959, 198).

In 1970, Karl Rahner used the same idea in his discussion about the problem of genetic manipulation in his article 'Zum Problem der genetischen manipulation aus der Sicht des Theologen', although the explicit use of 'created co-creator' was not yet introduced as such (Rahner 1970, 135-166). The term 'created co-creator' as is presently used in scholarly circles was introduced in 1984 by Philip Hefner. This was developed into a full-fledged theory through the publication of his book *The Human Factor. Evolution, Culture, and Religion* in 1993. In this book he develops a theology of the 'created co-creator' and brings it in relation to divine purposes for all creation. The term has attracted wide attention not only from theologians, but also from philosophers, scientists, and people who have been on the lookout for finding a category that could do justice to the unique role of the human being, while taking the whole creation into account. From the time of its introduction, it has exerted a lot of influence in theological anthropology. Just as with anything new, people have reacted very differently to this new term. Many accepted it with great satisfaction. Some rejected it since they looked at it from the point of view of 'playing God' and yet others have found it a vital concept that should be developed further (Willer 2004, 844-847). In my opinion, this concept is significant to make breakthroughs in understanding our role in creation.

Theological Core of the Vision: Interpreting Human Beings

Philip Hefner's efforts to come to an adequate theo-anthropological category can be considered as an original contribution in understanding the place of humans in creation. According to him:

> Human beings are God's created co-creators whose purpose is to be the agency, acting in freedom, to birth the future that is most wholesome for the nature that has birthed us – the nature that is not only our own genetic heritage, but also the entire human community and the evolutionary and ecological reality in which and to which we belong. Exercising this agency is said to be God's will for humans. (Hefner 1993, 27)

It is interesting to note that this concept is very original, useful and compact in several ways. First, it puts forward *'one unified image'* in theological anthropology by which we can summarize the whole lot of our understanding about the human being. Second, it makes room for the *'conditionedness of human existence'* and suggests that the human being can be seen as the crucial element in the evolution of the whole world. Third, we can see *'freedom as the qualifier'* of this conditionedness, through which God enables His creation and achieves His purposes (Hefner 1993, 31-32; Hefner 2005, 186). In my opinion, the theory opens up new horizons and offers us new possibilities to reinterpret the role of human beings within creation. Hefner points out the three important elements of his theory as follows:

1. The Human being is created by God to be a co-creator in the creation that God has brought into being and for which God has purposes.
2. The conditioning matrix that has produced the human being – the evolutionary process – is God's process of bringing into being a creature who represents the creation's zone of a new stage of freedom and who therefore is crucial for the emergence of a free creation.
3. The freedom that marks the created co-creator and its culture is an instrumentality of God for enabling the creation (consisting of the evolutionary past of genetic and cultural inheritance as well as the contemporary ecosystem) to participate in the intentional fulfilment of God's purposes. (Hefner 1993, 32)

Human Beings Are 'Created'

In the term 'created co-creator', both the noun and the adjective are equally important. The *created* in the 'created co-creator' calls for some explanation. The term 'created' refers to our own 'createdness' which affirms that ultimately we are also creatures, and as such, dependent. This dependency is to be referred to God and we are totally dependent on the creative grace of God for our very origin and existence (Hefner 1988, 522). The terms 'the way things really are' and 'what really is' are to be used in reference to God. Since we are 'created', we belong to 'the way things really are' through our conditionedness and freedom. This also acknowledges the fact that as 'created' beings, we are not the designers of our own place and role in the world. As Hefner says, 'to be created is to be derived, to be dependent upon antecedent factors (environmental, biological, cultural) as well as contemporary sources (environmental, cultural)' (Hefner 1993, 35-36). The term gains its theological significance when we make the reference to 'God'. The conditionedness of our existence that we experience has its origin in the divine creative activity. God should be seen here as the foundation and the corner stone of the process from which the human beings have emerged (Hefner 1993, 36-38).

> *Homo sapiens* did not emerge to be conquistador, dominating and pillaging as the opportunity arose. Rather, as creature, the human serves the process of the creator, and all of the possibilities, activities, and achievements of the creature are to be referred to the created order and the purposes with which it has been endowed. (Hefner 1993, 36)

Two qualities that characterise this being 'created' are the aspects of *belonging* and *receptivity*. We must be conscious of the fact that for long, the human being has been thought of and understood in dualistic terms. More than ever, our times insist on the fact that 'we can no longer tolerate understandings of human nature that insist upon separating us from our fellow human beings, from the natural ecosystem in which we live, or from the evolutionary processes in which we have emerged' (Hefner 1997, 198). Our belonging to the world is a specific property of our existence. This also brings us in contact with the other human beings and surpasses the interpersonal realm and extends the sphere of concern and care to the nature and other living beings. I am of the opinion that a coherent vision on the human being should certainly take into account not only the relationship to God and to other human beings but also to the natural world and nonhuman beings.

Human Beings Are 'Co-creators'

By using 'created co-creator' as a new category in theological anthropology, we emphasize not only the 'created' dimension (with reference to God, other human beings and the natural world), but also the 'creative' one. The term 'co-creator' refers to the freedom of the human being, which is a fundamental condition of existence. Through this freedom, human beings are capable of facing situations in which they have to make choices, which have an enormous influence in shaping their life. They are called to make these choices in freedom and furthermore, they also need to give good reason for these choices. The specificity of the human being consists in the fact that it is only humans who are able to make the decisions, and are in charge of shaping their life and are called to justify their choices (Willer 2004, 841-858). To put it in Hefner's own words:

> Humans cannot avoid the freedom to make the choice, and only humans can construct the stories that justify such choices... environmental policies require a myriad of value judgments concerning the comparative values of the earth and of humans and other forms of life. Humans cannot avoid such policy-making and the value judgments inherent to that policy. Further, only humans can construct the stories that provide the justifying arguments for such judgments. (Hefner 1993, 38)

Richard Fern offers similar ideas in *Nature, God and Humanity* where he speaks about the freedom of the created order. The possibility to make choices is a gift that God has given His creation:

> God grants creation its own, creative freedom for the sake of a love, a mutuality, that cannot exist apart from genuine freedom and risk. It is not enough to have created creatures with whom he can talk, creatures capable of grasping creation and analogically, himself in thought, God must give these creatures and, thereby, creation, the nature he has so lovingly made, the capacity to choose their own future, to form and act for reasons, ends, and goals, of their own... Having placed the future of creation in its own reflective awareness, God waits for the free reciprocity of his continuing, sustaining love. (Fern 2002, 160)

The qualities of belonging and receptivity are morally qualified since human beings are self-conscious and are therefore able to plan their life in the world. While carrying out their plans, they are conscious of their sense of belonging to the natural world of which they are part of and they are able to receive feedback and alter the process by making use of the accumulated wisdom. The freedom of the human being is a determined human condition. (Hefner 1993, 97-98) Rational reflection and moral action are essential elements herein. This also emphasizes the possibilities for 'human becoming'. Without freedom, the human beings will not be able to play a creative and constructive role in the world to which they belong. They are designers of their own destiny, but always in reference to God and his purposes for the world. As creatures, human beings are called to be 'co-creators' with God, in fulfilling God's purposes for creation.

Freedom as the defining condition of the human beings highlights the extraordinary characteristics of the human creature and the special place that this creature has within the ecosystem of the planet. But this freedom should not be mistaken for equality with God, the Creator. As we have described above, human beings are creatures and can therefore never be considered equal to God, since they are dependent on the Creator for their creative activity (Hefner 1993, 39). The 'co' in the co-creator has to be emphasized sufficiently if we are to take the term in its right meaning. This suggests that we are participating in the creative action of God, not on our own, not in subordination, but in partnership. It also confirms that the future is open and undetermined. The human being can give it direction whenever needed, or change the course whenever found necessary (Hefner 1989, 524; Peterson 2004, 829). As is explained above, the creative activity of the human being finds its source in God the Creator who gives it to humanity with love. It is an essential characteristic of human beings as 'co-creators' that we can participate actively in the unique plan of God.

To have a proper understanding of the 'created co-creator' we have to place it in the context of creation and its purposes. Without this essential dimension, 'created co-creator' loses its meaning. The purposes of God for creation connect the human beings to the destiny willed by God. 'Both the creation and the human being have purposes for their existence, and the two are intertwined within the larger notion of God's destiny for the entire creation' (Doncel 2004, 794; Hefner 1993, 39; Russell 1994, 148-150). From a theological point of view, nature is to be understood and valued as God's creation. Nature is actually all that we have in our efforts to understand the world. Hefner opines that even those religions that speak of revelation, have to recognize 'that revelation happens within nature, and that it is received, understood, and interpreted through the thoroughly natural structures of a natural animal, *Homo sapiens*' (Hefner 1993, 41).

As human beings we are embedded in this world, out of which we ourselves have evolved. The world (nature) becomes the stage for all our operations. From this perspective, Sittler considers the world as the 'theatre of God's grace'. Viewing nature in this way can help us to value nature and to care for it (McFague 1997, 153-154). The natural web of interrelationships and interdependence, within which we find our place, suggests that the purpose of human existence should be referred to this web of interrelationships. The human construction of purposes has a great influence in the natural world especially if we place it in the circle of relationships. The concept of 'wholesomeness' can help us to find an appropriate manner in which humans can contribute to the purposes in creation. In our understanding of the human being, nature receives great significance.

> ... nature is the arena for human purpose and that concern for nature's wholesome state provides a pragmatic criterion for our thinking... Nature is the medium through which the world, including human beings, receives knowledge, as well as grace. (Hefner 1993, 42)

The idea of *'wholesomeness'* should be scrutinized thoroughly in order to come to a consensus regarding what is good for nature. Our behaviours have different effects and outcomes and therefore, they do not bring the same result for human beings and the whole of nature. This is true especially with regard to the application of technological innovations and possibilities. We have to make choices in this technological civilization within which we live. This particular aspect demands of us that we take decisions that are scientifically and technologically responsible and theologically coherent. If we take the evolution of humans into account, we can understand the meaning of nature as follows: '... the appearance of *homo sapiens* as created co-creator signifies that nature's course is to participate in transcendence and freedom' (Hefner 1997, 197). Human beings are called upon to discern the requirements for adequate living and they must learn to meet the challenges that are posed to them. The environmental collapse that we face today can be seen as a result of our incapacity to cope with the technological era. It is not enough that we make choices and transform them into actions. We need to be morally responsible and give justification for our actions.

Christian theology reiterates the fact that God is the ultimate source of everything. The belief in God as 'Creator' is the most fundamental statement of our Christian faith, and it is the foundation on which our life as Christians revolves around. The emergence of the 'created co-creator' opens up new horizons in theology, in our thinking about God as the Creator, the place of the human being as 'created co-creator' within it and the value of nature as creation. The 'created co-creator' is the plan of God for the world and it is through the human being as created co-creator that God wants to bring His purposes for the world to fulfilment. Keeping this in mind, I would like to reflect on the possibilities that the created co-creator can offer us in dealing with the environment.

First, the created co-creator emphasizes the fact that the human being is first and foremost a creature, together with the natural world. Humankind is not to be seen as an autonomous entity, but has to be seen in relationship with a God who creates in love. In this way, we are dependent on the Ultimate Reality, God. This dimension of *'createdness'* and *'dependence'* qualifies our existence in the world. The correlation between the nature of the world and the nature of the Creator manifests itself fully in the human being. It is this 'createdness' that connects the human being to God and to the natural world (Hefner, 1988: 522; Hefner 1997, 203; Peterson 2004, 828-829).

Second, the 'created co-creator' opens up new avenues for taking care of nature. As we have already stated, creation is grounded fully in God who has freely desired and caused everything into being. The fact that we are 'co-creators' with God is not a licence to act as we like. Furthermore, there is no reason for us to be arrogant as 'co-creators' because we need to acknowledge that this gift comes from God and that it is a state of 'givenness'. It should be seen as *'God's will for human beings to be co-creators'*. Nature, together with the human beings, as creation should be seen as the realm of intentionality, which is to be perceived within the realm of God's intentionality. As Hefner says, 'this theological framework illuminates the fact that human intentionality exists not for its own sake, not only for the sake of the human species, but as the expression of and for the sake of the larger intentionality of God's creation, nature' (Hefner 1997, 203).

Third, the concept *'creatio continua'* acquires its fullest meaning in the human being as 'created co-creator'. Creation has to be understood, not only as that which is present here and now, but it also refers to the manner in which God sustains His creation continually. The world depends continuously on the ongoing grace of God. From the point of view that God continues to care for the natural world, we can accept that the nonhuman creation is valuable and that it is an entity that humans can trust. We are not to view the natural world as antagonistic to our life and progress, but as complementary, supportive, and strengthening to our well-being. The earth has to be seen as a friendly home for humans (Hefner 1989, 523; Lobo 1991, 79-80, Russell 1994, 144). The earth is not an enemy whom we have to fight, but a friend who needs our care and concern. There is also a correlation between God, humans, and the natural world because these three are partakers in the creative activity. We are called to make choices and to direct the course of events as 'created co-creators' (Grenz 1994, 168-172; Hefner 1989, 523). Humans have to keep in mind that our creative activity and the way we are able to develop and bring things into being, is a 'dependent' creation, which is in no way a restriction, but a possibility to contribute our share constructively in the continuation of creation. The use of the latest modes of science and technology are encouraged here, only if they are in consonance with the freedom that God has given and the responsibility this demands of us (Drees 2002, 643-654).

Fourth, through the creation of the 'created co-creator', God lays bare his plan for the further evolution and future of the world. Our example in this undertaking is Jesus Christ, the new Adam, who can also be called the 'prototype of the true *humanum*'. It is in and through Jesus our model that God reveals to us the possibilities and potentialities of humans and what humanity can yet become. The Christ event can be taken as the event to which we are called to adapt ourselves. 'In his life, death, and teachings, Jesus offers us the possibilities for raising human living to a higher plane, one which will reveal new ways of adapting to the reality system of nature and of God' (Hefner 1989, 524; Stone 2004, 761-762). The love principle that Jesus proposed and the Trinitarian relationship can be seen as guidelines to go beyond the boundaries of our interpersonal relationships and to extend our love also to the natural world. Going beyond the boundaries of kinship is a basic Christian attitude that can be of enormous importance in caring for nature and in building up the natural environment (Hefner 1989, 524; Hefner 1997, 203; Hill 1998, 263; Irons 2004, 777-778; Ruether 2005, 112-113). By taking Jesus as our role model, we can bring about changes in our attitudes towards nature and inculcate qualities that can strengthen our relationship with God, other human beings, and nature.

From a theological perspective, we can summarize this new theo-anthropological concept, created co-creator, as follows:

Homo sapiens is God's created co-creator, whose purpose is the 'stretching/enabling' of the systems of nature so that they can participate in God's purposes in the mode of freedom, for which the paradigm is Jesus Christ, both in respect to his life and to his understanding of the world as God's creation. (Hefner 1997, 203-204)

Conclusion

In this essay, I have attempted to reinterpret the role of human beings within the framework of Christian theology. It is beyond doubt that *imago Dei* is too broad and ambiguous as a theo-anthropological category. It lays too much emphasis on the dignity of human beings, to the extent that the nonhuman nature has no possibility to enter into the sphere of concerns. Besides, it takes only humanity into account and the rest of creation is sidelined and easily forgotten. But the 'created co-creator' opens doors and windows and allows the nature and natural systems to enter its sphere of concerns. This is based on the belief and realization that creation has its origin in God and that the human being is also a 'created entity', just like the rest of nature, taking its place in the evolutionary process. Due to its anthropocentric overtones, *imago Dei* encourages an arrogant attitude towards nature, by glorifying the interpersonal dimension beyond limits. It does not really open up possibilities for entering into a relationship with nature. But the 'created co-creator' is situated within the nature and its processes. The 'created co-creator' is truly part of nature and thus enters into relationship with it. The relational dimension is not restricted here to God and other human beings only, but is extended towards the natural world.

One of the drawbacks of *imago Dei* is that the sphere of concerns and thus also the sphere of responsibility are restricted to the human beings. The 'created co-creator' acts in freedom and exercises responsibility not only for oneself or for one's own species. The realm of responsibility is extended here to the whole creation. This holistic view of creation enables the 'created co-creator' to take a holistic view of responsibility as well. The human being is placed within creation with the responsibility to be a 'co-creator' with God, with the ethical imperative to care for the whole creation. As part of God's creation, the human being is within the creation, not above it. The concept 'created co-creator' accepts the fact that humans are special, but this speciality is to be placed within creation and is to be realized by being at the service of creation.

Imago Dei does not give enough room for the human being to realize fully the creative dimension, which is a gift of God. Though Christian theology emphasizes the significance of this creative dimension, there seems to be a hesitation in taking it up as our legitimate role in creation. The 'created co-creator' accepts this gift of creativity from God with gratitude. The human being is in close collaboration with God in order to bring God's purposes for creation to fulfilment, in freedom and responsibility. It is not seen as the chance to become equal to God, but as a possibility to take part in God's creative activity so that the act of creation may go on. *'Creatio continua'* is an existential condition of the world and the role of the 'created co-creator' is to bring this condition to its full realization and fulfilment.

To conclude, I do not intend to suggest that we have to get rid of *imago Dei* as a category altogether, because I am conscious of the fact that it has a number of positive aspects which are significant. In my proposal of the 'created co-creator' as a better category in theological anthropology, I have tried to integrate the positive aspects of *imago Dei* and I have attempted to go beyond its limitations and to expand the realm of possibilities. The theological arguments that I have presented above make the case for the affirmation of the 'created co-creator' as a better, theologically qualified, and constructive theo-anthropological category to reinterpret the role of human beings in creation.

References

Blanke, F. 1959. Unsere Verantwortlichkeit gegenüber der Schöpfung. In *Der Auftrag der Kirche in der modernen Welt. Festgabe zum siebzigsten Geburtstag von Emil Brunner.* Zurich: Zwingli Verlag, 193-198.

Case-Winters, A. 2004. Rethinking the Image of God. *Zygon: Journal of Religion and Science* 39, 813-826.

Cobb, J.B. 1972. *Is It Too Late? A Theology of Ecology.* Beverly Hills: Bruce.

Coste, R. 1994. *Dieu et L'écologie. Environnement, théologie, spiritualité.* Paris: Les Editions De L'atelier.

Denzinger, H. and A. Schönmetzer, eds. 1963. *Enchiridion symbolorum definitionum et declarationum de rebus fidei et morum.* Barcinone: Herder.

Doncel, M.G. 2004. The Kenosis of the Creator and of the Created Co-Creator. *Zygon: Journal of Religion and Science* 39, 791-800.

Drees, W.B. 2002. 'Playing God? Yes!' Religion in the Light of Technology. *Zygon: Journal of Religion and Science* 37, 643-654.

Fern, R.L. 2002. *Nature, God and Humanity: Envisioning an Ethics of Nature.* Cambridge: Cambridge University Press.

Grenz, S.J. 1994. *Theology for the Community of God.* Nashville: Broadman & Holman Publishers.

Hall, D.J. 1986. *Imaging God. Dominion as Stewardship.* Grand Rapids, MI: William B. Eerdmans.

— 1990. *The Steward. A Biblical Symbol Come of Age.* Grand Rapids, MI: William B. Eerdmans.

Hefner, P. 1988. The Evolution of the Created Co-Creator. *Currents in Theology and Mission* 15, 512-525.

— 1989. The Evolution of the Created Co-Creator. In *Cosmos and Creation. Theology and Science in Consonance,* ed. T. Peters. Nashville: Abingdon Press, 211-233.

— 1993. *The Human Factor: Evolution, Culture and Religion.* Minneapolis: Fortress Press.

— 1997. Biocultural Evolution of the Created Co-Creator. *Dialog: A Journal of Theology* 36, 197-205.

— 2004. Editorial. Human Being: Questioning and Being Questioned'. *Zygon: Journal of Religion and Science* 39, 733-735.

— 2005. Can the Created Co-Creator Be Lutheran? A Response to Svend Andersen. *Dialog: A Journal of Theology* 44, 184-188.

Hill, B.R. 1998. *Christian Faith and the Environment. Making Vital Connections.* Maryknoll, NY: Orbis Books.

Houtepen, A. 1990. 'Integrity of Creation': naar een ecologische scheppingstheologie. *Tijdschrift voor Theologie* 30, 51-75.

Irons, W. 2004. An Evolutionary Critique of the Created Co-Creator Concept. *Zygon: Journal of Religion and Science* 39, 773-790.

Labuschagne, C.J. 1990. Het bijbelse scheppingsgeloof in ecologisch perspectief. *Tijdschrijft voor Theologie* 30, 5-17.

Langemeyer, G. 2000. Image of God. In *Handbook of Catholic Theology,* eds. W. Beinert and F.S. Fiorenza. New York: Cross Road Publishing, 369-371.

Lobo, G.V. 1991. *Guide to Christian Living: A New Compendium on Moral Theology.* Westminster: Christian Classics.

McDonagh, S. 1986. *To Care for the Earth: A Call to a New Theology.* London: Geoffrey Chapman.

McEvoy, J. 2001. Situating Humanity: Theological Anthropology in the Context of the Ecological Crisis. In *Earth Revealing-Earth Healing.*

Ecology and Christian Theology, ed. D. Edwards. Collegeville: The Liturgical Press, 195-212.

McFague, S. 1997. *Super, Natural Christians. How We Should Love Nature.* London: SCM Press.

McGrath, A.E. 2000. *Christelijke Theologie. Een Introductie.* Kampen: Kok.

Moltmann, J. 2001. The Destruction and Healing of the Earth: Ecology and Theology. In *God and Globalization. The Spirit of the Modern Authorities*, vol. II, eds. Max L. Stackhouse and D.S. Browning. Harrisberg: Trinity Press International, 166-190.

Oelschlaeger, M. 1994. *Caring for Creation. An Ecumenical Approach to the Environmental Crisis.* London: Yale University Press.

Peterson, G.R. 2004. The Created Co-Creator: What it is and is not. *Zygon: Journal of Religion and Science* 39, 827-840.

Rahner, K. 1970. Zum Problem der genetischen manipulation aus der Sicht des Theologen. In *Menschenzüchtung: das Problem der genetischen Manipulierung des Menschen*, ed. F. Wagner. Munich: Beck, 135-166.

Ratzinger, C.J. 1995. *In the Beginning... A Catholic Understanding of the Story of Creation and the Fall.* Edinburgh: T&T Clark.

Ruether, R.R. 2005. *Integrating Ecofeminism, Globalization, and World Religions.* Oxford: Rowman & Littlefield.

Russell, C.A. 1994. *The Earth, Humanity and God.* London: UCL Press.

Stone, J.A. 2004. Philip Hefner and the Modernist / Postmodernist Divide. *Zygon* 39, 755-772.

White, L. 1994. The Historical Roots of Our Ecological Crisis. In *Environmental Ethics. Readings in Theory and Application*, ed. L.P. Pojman. Boston: Jones and Bartlett, 9-14.

Willer, R.A. 2004. Created Co-Creator in the Perspective of Church and Ethics. *Zygon: Journal of Religion and Science* 39, 841-858.

Wirzba, N. 2003. *The Paradise of God. Renewing Religion in an Ecological Age.* Oxford: Oxford University Press.

7　Seeking the Depth of Nature in a Scientific World

Forrest Clingerman

While differences of opinion abound on how religion ought to confront environmental issues, one potential point of agreement is that contemporary scientific knowledge and religious knowledge are all too often detached from each another – to the detriment of the environment. The divide between scientific and religious thinking (starting with the rise of mechanical philosophy and in some respects culminating in various nineteenth-century tracts on the 'warfare' between science and religion) can be correlated with a 'secularization' of nature by science. Technological advances created new ways of changing and destroying the environment, especially after scientific thinking was freed from religious strictures and conceptualizations. However, the 'environmental crisis' that has resulted from modern technological living has forced us to rethink our almost exclusive reliance on such 'calculative thinking', even as such large problems (to name a few, climate change, loss of biodiversity, resource depletion, wide-scale drought) are discussed prominently in the media. A completely secular foundation for our scientific worldview has been found wanting, yet we cannot simply return to pre-reflective religious views on science and nature (cf. the essay by Szerszynski in this volume). As heirs to both the Enlightenment and postmodernity, contemporary Christian theology must re-evaluate how it interprets the meaning of nature in light of the impossibility of returning to a pre-modern garden paradise. In other words, we must reintroduce spirituality and religion in our understanding of nature, without denying the power and usefulness of scientific knowledge.

But how might Christian theology work toward a re-evaluation of its understanding of nature? To be sure, most 'eco-theologians' recognize that both the sciences and theology together are necessary for interpreting nature. What is often lacking is the elaboration of an adequate method through which 'eco-theology' can bring these disciplines together. In this regard eco-theology can learn from recent discussions on modelling that have occurred in religion and science dialogues. The contemporary debates over the environment show the need for a reinvigorated religious and spiritual interpretation of nature, just as they show the continued need for scientific and other forms of knowledge. In many cases, however, scholars subordinate theology to science, or vice versa. Allowing for parity across disciplines can occur only through a reflective and systematic methodology. If we are to overcome the scientific and religious dogmatic 'calculative thinking' of the past, this method cannot grant primacy to either scientific or theological dialogue. Instead, the method of an ecological theology must place disciplines into true dialogue, finding a mediation between scientific explanation and theological understanding. The present essay thus enters the methodological debate by arguing for a more hermeneutical eco-theological method – a method that emphasizes theological modelling and the use of 'emplacement' as an organizing principle.

As a contribution to this methodological debate, this essay first will present a characterization of the context of types of environmental theology and explain how the method of modelling can be advantageous for environmental theology. Next, I will explain a specific process of theological modelling that will be beneficial for environmental theology, drawing on the work of Klemm, Klink, and Scharlemann. Finally, I will argue for the use of 'emplacement' as a way of identifying the domain of a theological model of nature. Theology, in dialogue with other disciplines, can advance our understanding of nature only when it becomes more conscious of the process of constructing theological models. Theological models, using methods akin to those found in the construction of scientific models, offer a nuanced comprehension of nature and open the possibility of a testable and clearly defined theological knowledge of the natural world. Using the process of modelling, theology can determine the depth dimension of the abstract and lived elements that conjoin the human relationship with nature.

Theological Modelling and the Theology of Nature

Many theological projects have emerged in an effort to address the ecological crisis and the religious dimensions of nature more generally. Assessing these attempts, we find that several theological projects unwittingly create barriers between theology and science through their conception of the communication between the two areas of study – perhaps partially a result of the complex history of the 'disenchantment with nature'. At the risk of oversimplification we can divide these projects of environmentally-focused theology into two broad categories. In both cases, what often occurs is that one discipline dictates the parameters of discussion for the other discipline. In effect, science or theology presents a monologue without allowing for dialogue.

The first type of environmental theological project might be described as what Ian Barbour calls, in the context of the field of religion and science, a 'theology of nature' (Barbour 1990, 26). A theology of nature, says Barbour, starts from Christian theology and tradition in an effort to understand our contemporary experience. Thus, some theologians address environmental problems by revivifying confessional and biblical language as a means to alter Christian attitudes (e.g. H. Paul Santmire). Others seek to identify a spiritual or mystical dimension within the tradition, seeing nature as a sacramental subject (e.g. Larry Rasmussen) or lifting figures like St Francis up as exemplars (e.g. Lynn White, Jr.). Thus, one theological approach to nature is found in the attempt to mine the tradition in order to justify Christianity as a worldview that is adequately explanatory and continually relevant for ecological concerns. But this conceptual reliance on tradition can obscure the way in which we live in a secularized world, and thus how we can see nature independently of its supposed mystical or traditional dimensions. Further, this method often fails to examine or to understand concrete instances of nature and the environment, and instead relies on vague generalizations or idyllic portrayals of the natural world.

The second broad type of project moves in the opposite direction, beginning with scientific understanding (broadly speaking) as the framework by which to redefine Christian theology. While Barbour identifies this with forms of natural theology, we might better identify this with recent programmes of 'religious naturalism'. Religious naturalists such as Ursula Goodenough focus on scientific understanding to rebuild doctrines consonant with a scientific paradigm. In order to develop religious doctrines derived from science, a minimalistic definition of religion is often required. Science is argued to be the most valid and persuasive description of the world and thus scientific understanding provides the basis for any adequate religious worldview. But religious naturalism might also present problems. Often religious naturalism uses a minimal definition of its object of description, which does violence to religion. Under such a definition, the complex interaction between thought, ritual, belief, morality, community and individual is frequently rendered largely invisible. Equally as troublesome, it can move from a clear understanding of the norms and canons of scientific knowledge to an unclear and imprecise definition of what constitutes religious knowledge.

Both of these categories move between religion and science in a single direction, implying that our knowledge of nature arises from either religion or the scientific disciplines first and foremost. Not only does this inaccurately show the complexity of our understanding of the natural world, this can produce an estrangement between the work of theology and that of other disciplines. To avert this estrangement, therefore, environmental theology must focus on a method that draws on the strengths of both of these categories, while offering a way that avoids the flaws that might arise in each. Foremost, ecotheology must find a method that systematically fosters mutuality and parity among disciplines while simultaneously seeking knowledge of nature within the context of theology. Put otherwise, environmental theology must seek a method that instantiates a true dialogue on nature.

I would like to argue, thus, that a more hermeneutical and dialectical framework is the preferred alternative to the two categorizations of environmental theology noted above; what is needed is a method that offers critical reflection on the dialogue between theological understanding and scientific forms of knowing. This, I further argue, is found in the process of constructing theological models.

Why are theological models relevant in light of the current concerns? Theological models demand a rigor that allows for a common ground between theology and the sciences, thereby promoting an equal footing between disciplines while also maintaining their uniqueness. The creation of models in both science and theology has several important qualities. Building models requires knowledge of the given domain, providing a 'fit' with the data. It also requires imagination and creativity – something that Sallie McFague's work on modelling has pointed out. Echoing McFague's emphasis on metaphor and imagination in modelling, David Klemm and William Klink point out: 'Models participate in the metaphorical capacity of provoking the mind to think something new by seeing a resemblance previously unnoticed and unthought' (Klemm and Klink 2003, 503). Further, models are constructed and are developed in light of both cultural and historical conditions, are innovative, and open to change pending new data. Models are unable to portray the entirety of the data, and thus can be placed alongside competing models. Even when successful, models are continually questioned and tested in an effort to determine new facts and blind spots. Ultimately, a model that is successful and more encompassing becomes a paradigm, or an 'overarching conceptual framework' for the domain.

These qualities of theological modelling are exemplified in the proposals of Robert Scharlemann, David Klemm, and William Klink. Klemm and Klink elaborate and systematize the idea of models initially brought forth in Scharlemann's essay, 'Constructing Theological Models'. Scharlemann begins by noting that theories (defined simply as 'well-established models') and models get data from the two places: their 'basic structure of domains' and the conjunctives that arise from these structures. Scharlemann sets the rationale for utilizing models in any discipline: a model is not an observational description or placeholder, and it doesn't seek to be a replica of how a thing really is. Instead, a model is a construction that attempts to show how we can cognitively deal with an object. Thus, models are constructed, non-natural, and they are testable. 'In sum, what we mean by a model is a construct that provides us with a methodological way of dealing with an object being investigated' (Scharlemann 1989, 130). The difference between theological and other models is found in the *domain* to which the model belongs. Theology can build models independently of other areas of study, but it is dependent on other domains for *content* – theology has no material domain of its own.

Klemm and Klink argue that such models offer an opportunity to move beyond certain impasses present in the contemporary theological scene. For them, this is the challenge: 'Theology is often perceived as a marginalized discipline in contemporary intellectual life' (Klemm and Klink 2003, 495). According to the authors, modelling is a way for theology to address its previous silence regarding the perils confronted by contemporary society. As Klemm and Klink state it: 'the silence of the theologian has consequences. Thinkers who do try to understand and to interpret what is happening in our world today do not look to theology to assist them in the task of making sense of our cultural and social lives' (496).

Consequently, contemporary theology is forced into the horns of the secular and the confessional, causing a 'marginalization of theology' in the academy. What is needed to overcome this is a way of showing how theological discourse constitutes *knowledge* in the contemporary world. By moving beyond social constructivism and naïve realism, science maintains a critical stance that has allowed the scientific disciplines to dominate intellectual discourse in contemporary culture. For Klemm and Klink, theology must move in similar fashion to reclaim its place in the *cognitive* sphere of cultural discourse. 'We claim that theology can and should assume an important place in the current scholarly debates. However, the price of admission is the capacity both to make testable knowledge claims and to justify the possibility of so doing' (498). This emphasis on *testability* is a key dimension of modelling, but it is not often adequately addressed. For Klemm and Klink, testing is an activity that places theology squarely as a scholarly discipline: 'The point we are making is that at each stage of evolution and development of a model, it must be testable; that is, it must be capable of making predictions that can (perhaps only in principle) show the model to be wrong' (504).

Testing is at the heart of legitimating theology in the context of contemporary intellectual discourse, therefore, and it is by way of models that theology offers testable claims. Models – both scientific and theological – are constructed to manipulate and test data; thus, it is not the case that theological models have not been used in the past, but that they have not been constructed in such a way that we can independently verify and test them. The main purpose of a model is to 'investigate the structure of a domain... More generally, models enable one to 'see' why something behaves the way it does' (503). It is the 'why' question that makes models unique, for their purpose centers on showing why certain things are correlated. In other words, models provide a sense of meaning to a given correlation. Further, a model is built in an attempt to show the structure of a domain; 'a structure is what gives unity to the essential elements that constitute a determinate domain' (502). Models are not dogma or inalienable propositions, but rather 'models are created as tentative exploratory means for understanding new phenomena' (507).

The broader situation in which theology as a discipline finds itself is analogous to the two broad categories of theological approaches to nature and ecology; the division between theologies of nature and forms of religious naturalism echoes the bifurcation between confessional and secular theologies noted by Klemm and Klink. Therefore, if the method that Klemm and Klink offer assists in overcoming these problems, then it should also suggest an alternative position at the divergence between confessional and secular theologies on the topic of nature. What makes theological modelling a unique and viable alternative for studying the natural world? It offers a way for theology to present knowledge claims that take seriously environmental science and other disciplines, in such a way that offers legitimacy, uniqueness, and independence to both science and theology. In other words, modelling resolves the methodological situation by presenting a way of systematically placing theology and the sciences in dialogue in a truly mutual way.

The Procedure of Modelling for Environmental Theology

If modelling is an appropriate and advantageous method for an environmental theology, what is the process through which one models nature? To begin, we must remember that the domain of theology is unique, because theology does not have a domain of its own. It seeks to find the religious and spiritual dimension of all other domains, without having a domain that is demarcated as exclusively theological. Therefore, the purpose of a theological model of nature is to find the religious dimension of nature, which entails accepting and valuing the variety of ways we understand nature's other dimensions. Theology must account for the work of other disciplines, but it is not beholden to them; there is an openness to dialogue within theology.

The process of constructing a theological model has several steps. Scharlemann presents a basic view of modelling originating from the claim of the lack of domain in theology. For Scharlemann, theological models are built through two tasks. First, one identifies the basic structure of a domain, and second, one adds a 'theological conjunctive' (the phrase, 'God is...') to the structure. In theology, *models form an identity in difference, allowing us a dimension of transcendence in the midst of disparate facets of the structure* – in other words, a different unity, 'one established by the transcendence or depth in the domain' (Scharlemann 1989, 132). Such a model can potentially start from any domain, although some domains might be more useful than others. Scharlemann is careful to point out that theological models can use material from any domain without having to give a metaphysical reading of it. '"Theology", then, refers either to the whole set of conjunctives, in whatever domain, or to a theologics that, like mathematics, is an a priori symbol system needing some incorporation into models before it can provide knowledge of actual reality' (Scharlemann 1989, 139).

Klemm and Klink take Scharlemann's basic outline and elaborate on it, showing five steps for the construction of a theological model. The first step is that a domain must be chosen; since theology has no material domain of its own, this means that any domain of study can be used as the basis for a theological model. Next, we must describe the *structure* of the chosen domain. At this point, there is no substantial difference between theological and scientific models. Furthermore, there is not a sense that theology is a different or complementary science. Instead, the researcher seeks to identify and describe the structure of a domain in ways that accurately reflect the framework of the domain itself.

Third, we must identify and outline the *depth* of this structure. By 'depth' of the structure, Klemm and Klink are making a contrast with the 'surface' of the structure, which simply posits the different elements without presenting their overall meaning or identity. 'The 'depth,' therefore, means the standpoint from which the investigator can see the unity in difference of the structural elements. This standpoint enables one to see how the elements in the structure are necessarily related yet irreducible to each other. *The depth of the structure is a presentation of the fundamental principle according to which the basic elements of the structure are seen as both unified and preserved in their difference.* In this sense the concept of depth is always implied in the concept of structure: any structure has depth insofar as the structure is a unified, coherent structure. The depth of the structure is thus immanently present in the structure itself as its ground, basis, and principle' (Klemm and Klink 2003, 515).

The usage of the metaphor of 'depth' is greatly indebted to Paul Tillich's theology of culture. In turn, Tillich's discussion of 'depth' is based on a correlational understanding of theology, which offers a more nuanced and dialectical understanding of interdisciplinary scholarship. Klemm and Klink thus move past many objections found in other proposals. Foremost, if their understanding of the relationship between structure and depth is accurate, then it allows theological models to move beyond being mere metaphors for a specific confessional community. A theological model of nature offers a structure that is testable, in order to then study the depth of this structure. In the case of theological treatments of nature, a model is valid only if it coincides with the results of models of nature from other disciplines. The importance of the depth of the structure is that it provides a unique element to theological discourse, but it simultaneously shows us how theology can participate within a unified epistemology wherein it can be questioned by other disciplines.

The fourth step correlates the depth of a structure with its religious dimension. That is to say, Klemm and Klink make explicit that the theological connection of God and world is paralleled in the model's connection of depth and structure. A model is theological when a theological conjunctive, such as 'God is…' (Scharlemann) or 'God appears as…' (Klemm and Klink), is added, for this correlates the depth of meaning with God. 'God is not literally equated with the depth of the structure, nor is the depth of the structure predicated of God. Rather, the formulation asserts that in God's being God, God appears as what is literally not God but the depth of the structure. The depth of the structure is where we find the manifestation of God's being as God' (Klemm and Klink 2003, 516). This correlation presumes reflexive thinking about God, in other words; it is thinking that 'bends back reflexively on itself: thinking thinks its own act of thinking' in reflexive thought in such a way that the here-and-now act of thinking is conscious of itself (516).

The final step is that the model is critically viewed and tested. There are several tests for models. Models in any domain must be tested for fruitfulness, coherence, and fit. A model must adequately present that which it models in order to be useful – it 'must account for all of the details at the surface of the phenomenon under analysis' (517). There are also discipline-specific tests. For theology, we must test the model to ensure that the depth acts as both the 'principle on the basis of which one can see the opposing structural elements as both unified and different,' while simultaneously pointing toward a transcendence within the structure (517). That is to say, the depth must be tested to show its being as an 'is/is not' of the structure. For this test, Klemm and Klink outline the use of Anselm's 'that than which none greater can be thought'. The second type of test for a theological model should show that the depth is able to '...manifest the being of God when presented as part of a complex symbol' (518) of the theological conjunctive. This test attempts to show that the depth is an adequate symbol for 'God's being as what God is not' (Scharlemann 1989). This relates to a final test, which is to show that the symbol created out of the theological conjunctive of the model enables our thinking of God – that is, that the model is useful as a model.

The method of modelling described above presents a fruitful way for theology to investigate nature because it allows for a theological conception of nature that accounts for scientific ideas, without simply co-opting scientific results or collapsing into scientific domains of study. We can build a model of nature that reflects theologically on the scientific, religious, and other discourses concerning nature, precisely by seeing the fruitfulness of science as science, aesthetics as aesthetics, economics as economics, and the like. The theological model attempts to discover and test the depth of a given domain, but thereby does not negate the value or independence of a multifaceted study of the domain itself. Thus, ecological science (and other dimensions of the study of nature) contributes to a theology of the environment when theology models the sense in which the structure of nature – seen in the dialogue between varieties of fields – has a 'depth' that theology identifies and studies.

Emplacement and the Modelling of Nature

Developing a fully adequate model of nature is impossible in the limited space available here. What *is* possible is to explain how theological modelling can identify a fruitful domain in order to overcome some of the problems that overwise plague environmental theologies. The choice of domains is difficult when investigating nature, principally because humans are strangely both detached observers and entrenched participants in the natural world. Thus, a theological model of nature must focus on a domain that explicitly accounts for humans as subjects and nature (including humans) as objects. Thus, the concern is to strike a proper balance: a naïve objectivity (assuming nature is an object apart from humanity) would lead to a narrowly confessional or secularized perspective, while a naïve subjectivity (focusing on the human alone) would not allow for appropriate testing.

To identify a domain for the theological study of nature, then, we must resolve a principal problem of the human-nature relationship: humans are simultaneously within and apart from nature, acting through and upon natural processes. We are 'biohistorical' (Kaufman 2001 and elsewhere) or 'biocultural' (Hefner 1993) creatures of nature and culture, an embodiment of the dialectical relationship between the two. In other words, nature can be modeled only insofar as it is understood in light of the complex relationship between subject and object, overcoming both naïve objectivity and subjectivity in favour of a more nuanced viewpoint. Thus a purely objective model is effectively impossible, for no other reason than that we are participating in the thing we study. That is, our very experience of nature includes an interpretation of experience. Humans do not behold nature in simple, passive immediacy, but through a complex mediation that defines our experience of the world. But nature is more than our interpretations – it is, at least in some respects, 'out there'.

Examining this need for mediation between human and nature, I argue that we must focus on the similarity between our relationship with texts and our relationship with nature. There are parallels between the way humans encounter a text and the way that they encounter the natural world. Harkening back to the medieval metaphor of the 'Book of Nature', the parallels between text and nature offer an entry into the modelling of natural places. Just as the interaction between reader and text rests upon the sense of a shared world, so also the 'reading' of nature opens up a shared space that can be studied. Further, just as we read particular texts but not the concept of 'text', so also can we not investigate 'nature' in the abstract. We 'read' nature in terms of particular places, and in light of our embodied relationship within a given space and time (or 'place'). Our model must account for the experience of the dimensions of place, its textuality, its emplacement. The recognition of a sort of 'textuality' of nature opens the way for the construction of a model, by highlighting how nature presents itself in an exchange of conceptualization, experience, and interpretation. This is done *reflexively*, meaning that the model concentrates on 'thinking about thinking' or 'thinking about what it means to think'. Such reflexivity in thinking means that theology does not seek a model of nature (a form of thinking), but a model of how we think and experience nature (a form of thinking about thinking). Such a reflexive model recognizes the hermeneutical situation in which we relate to nature, rather than attempting to develop an objective model of nature.

What we are delineating amounts to a hermeneutical approach to the natural world. But how are we to model the 'Book of Nature' as a more focused domain of study? It is here that the concept of 'emplacement' becomes essential as a characterization of our reflexive place in the world. 'Emplacement', closely tied to a hermeneutical account of nature, describes how nature arises from the mediation between human and the natural places they live within. As defined here, emplacement identifies the *form* of the interaction between human and nature. More specifically, 'emplacement' is a hermeneutical mediation between (1) a general conceptual framework of place, (2) a concrete instantiation of a particular place, and (3) our (i.e. the experiencing subjects) place in place. We can further clarify these three elements of emplacement. Emplacement includes (1) our objective and abstract conceptualization of nature. Generalized concepts, categories, and theories are a necessary element of our study, even though they are ideal constructs. Our observational frameworks must be systematically analysed and included as constitutive elements of our understanding of place. Emplacement also includes (2) individual, subjective experience of specific natural places. The manifestation of nature is not an abstract concept, but lived and embodied – including the participation of humans as natural beings within the context of a locale. We must also reflect on specific instantiations of nature, such as a particular tree, ecosystem, or place. Emplacement finally (3) includes the structured conversation that occurs between the previous two points. Emplacement reflexively thinks through the existential manifestation of how the human observer relates conceptual thinking with experiential engagement, generalized explanation and specific encounters with nature.

'Emplacement,' as it might be used in modelling nature, echoes a concept that comes from Paul Ricoeur's description of narrativity: 'emplotment' (Ricoeur 1984 and elsewhere). 'Emplotment' identifies the ways in which narrative resolves the tensions between discordant and concordant elements, especially those found in temporal elements of the story. In the present circumstance, it is important to note that we cannot assume that emplacement is merely a temporal or verbal description; rather, it adds a spatial dimension that is absent in Ricoeur's concept of 'emplotment' and other accounts of narrative. That is, it includes human presence and absence within the physical manifestation of *a place* as *place*. This manifestation is seen in the ways that the inscription of place extends into spatial features and elements.

Nature is almost the paradigmatic theological text when structured via emplacement: the intention of the text (versus an 'author'), its ending, and our understanding of its truth and meaning can obtain only within the mediation between subject and object. Yet, unlike other texts, we inhabit the text of nature not only figuratively, but quite literally – we are emplaced in it, such that the meaning that is negotiated is both from within and without, and questioning the simple necessity of past and openness of future. Ultimately, emplacement offers a textual structure that overcomes the tendencies of 'technical thinking,' and without denying the paradox of nature overcomes it. In sum, the domain of our model is not nature as such, nor is it a particular natural place or manifestation. Rather, given our desire to model nature for theology, *the appropriate domain for a theological model is the text of nature as it is manifested in a place and in light of our experience of 'emplacement' within (a) place.* Emplacement, then, provides a beginning point for modelling the textuality of nature. However, the price of this interpretation is that nature does not present itself in a purely objective or immediate way.

The benefits for using 'emplacement' as a domain of study, I argue, are readily apparent, insofar as 'emplacement' presents a discernable structure that can be modeled and tested. Emplacement offers a core concept for structuring nature. Not only do we see the formal structure of emplacement as a systematic way of describing the structure of our encounters with nature, we also see how (for reasons explained below) our emplacement entails aesthetic, ecological, utilitarian and communal forms of interaction. Emplacement moves beyond its own structure toward a meaningful depth of nature – and thus, the cornerstone for gaining theological knowledge from the natural world.

If we conceptualize nature in terms of 'emplacement,' a discernable rational structure emerges through conversation with Tillich's understanding of reason. For Tillich, reason combines the static and the dynamic, the subjective and the objective. 'In every rational act three elements inhere: the static element of reason, the dynamic element of reason, and the existential distortion of both of them' (Tillich 1951, 78). The interplay between subject and object divides reason into four sub-types, which are based on how the mind corresponds with reality: cognitive, aesthetic, organizational, and organic. We can furthermore argue that reason confronts the 'Book of Nature' – at least, when reason moves beyond mere technicality – through a similar division. When taking up the concept of place and the manifesting experience of a place, each of these four aspects or types of reason reflect aspects of the mind (or the subject) and reality (or the object). This means that reason itself defines the way that we integrate the concept of place, the manifestations of a place, and the mediation of these two with our experience of them as subject. Therefore, we can identify four types of emplacement, as manifestations of more general types of reason.

If reason structures the human-world relationship as cognitive and aesthetic, organizational and organic, then our view of nature – as place and emplaced – is structured as place of science and place of aesthetics, as place of community and place of resource. These four aspects of emplacement each constitute a dimension of how humans understand the meaning of the text of nature, when nature is encountered as place (through space and time) and as a place (as defined by the event of dwelling and migration). The first two are, as stated, based on the theoretical, grasping, or reactive side of reason. First, nature can be seen as a place of ecology. Ecologically, place is defined through concepts taken from biology, chemistry, geography, and other sciences. The place can be described through, for instance, its ecological function in a watershed, or its habitat value. Second, apart from our scientific encounter with place, we can 'appreciate' nature as, for example, landscape, scenery, or as a 'vista'. When nature is a place of aesthetics, the place is constituted in ways akin to – but not identical to – aesthetic encounters with cultural works such as art. The second pair of categories of emplacement stem from the practical, shaping, or molding side of reason. The third dimension is best seen when we describe nature through concepts of resource or 'raw material' – in ways that resonate with Heidegger's remarks of the world as 'standing reserve' (Heidegger 1977; cf. Heidegger 1966). Finally, there are views of nature where nature is seen as communal. In this, nature is shaped according to its use as participant in or setting for communal constitution or self-understanding.

If we seek to model nature in these terms, we are seeking to model how we approach 'nature' in a variety of perspectives: through environmental science, for example, or in terms of technology, no less than as 'creation' or other religious terms. While each of us has different experiences, we nonetheless can attempt to model the general ways that we interact with that experience – and how a depth of meaning emerges.

Conclusion: Value and Meaning in the Depth of Nature

I have argued for a methodology and a domain of study as the first steps toward a successful environmentally focused theology. The strengths of this approach are several. Most importantly, a model focused on emplacement can include a diversity of voices – scientific, aesthetic, political, communal, and pragmatic, among others – while at the same time presenting theology as a vital participant in any conversation about our understanding (and implicitly, our treatment) of nature. Unlike other approaches, however, modelling the domain of emplacement is a more hermeneutical enterprise, meaning that these disciplines are in dialogue with each other, contributing from their own spheres of expertise without one discipline holding a place of priority. By arguing for such a model of nature, we also supply expectations for theological discourse in the form of testability, which presents the possibility of furthering our understanding. Furthermore, a model of emplacement takes seriously the complexity of the human participation in the environment – especially given the realities of religious commitment and our scientific, technological worldview. In sum, what I have argued is that theological reflection on nature is best served through the modelling of our emplacement in place, as the way to provide a systematic and testable approach to nature.

What is left undone is a presentation of a specific model of nature for theological use. The presentation of such a model was not the purpose of this essay, but it is the logical next step. What would such a model look like? Foremost, it would take seriously the particular places of our experience, by describing a particular place or ecosystem. Through this, any theological model of nature identifies the ecological, aesthetic, utilitarian, and communal aspects of that place. It would also place these descriptions into conversation with our theological and scientific concepts, as well as our mediation of experience through interpretation. That is to say, insofar as it is a model, it would describe the structure in such a way as to be both interpretive and testable – we must interpret the given locale based on the concepts of the categories we use, but these descriptions are open for verification. Importantly, this structure would seek to ascertain the depth of emplacement and place this depth in relation with a 'theological conjunctive'. We might posit that, on a more general level, the depth of emplacement is the unity of (a) the envelopment of the transcendent subject in the complexity and order of place/space, and the (b) participation and mutual transcendence of place and emplaced from each other in time.

For every place, the possibility of finding and delineating a depth is potentially present. This means that the general statement above would be tailored to the experienced realities of the particular place itself. This 'is/is not' understanding of the depth of emplacement might be seen to hold for emplacement *simpliciter*. Particular places exemplify this depth in different ways. The theological element that is presented by this basic structure is found in the statement that God appears in the unity of transcendence and immanence that coexist in the way that humans participate and discover order (in light of the perspectives of science, humanistic concerns, etc.) in the places of nature around them. Constructing a model along the lines described above provides the opportunity to expand and test this basic description, as well as to explore how values emerge from competing perspectives on nature.

In sum, this type of model offers a new way of opening the metaphorical 'Book of Nature' – taking seriously the theological tradition – while also affirming the importance of scientific knowledge of nature as primary for our contemporary understanding. By taking science, aesthetics, technology, and other disciplines into account, the role of a theology of nature becomes to seek the unity in difference of these dimensions. By using modelling as a method for seeking this unity in difference, theology can offer its voice to the important intellectual debate on the environment.

References

Barbour, I. 1990. *Religion in an Age of Science*. San Francisco: Harper & Row.

Clingerman, F. 2005. *Emplaced in the World: Theological Modelling and the Concept of Nature*. Ph.D. diss., University of Iowa.

Goodenough, U. 1998. *The Sacred Depths of Nature*. Oxford: Oxford University Press.

Hefner, P. 1993. *The Human Factor: Evolution, Culture, and Religion*. Minneapolis: Fortress.

Heidegger, M. 1966. *Discourse on Thinking*. New York: Harper & Row.

— 1977. *The Question Concerning Technology and Other Essays*. New York: Harper & Row.

Kaufmann, G. 2001. On Thinking of God as Serendipitous Creativity. *Journal of the American Academy of Religion* 69, 409-25.

Klemm, D. and W. Klink 2003. Constructing and Testing Theological Models. *Zygon: Journal of Religion and Science* 38, 495-528.

Klink, W. 1992. Nature, Technology, and Theology. *Zygon: Journal of Religion and Science* 27, 203-10.

— 1994. Ecology and Eschatology: Science and Theological Modeling. *Zygon: Journal of Religion and Science* 29, 529-45.

McFague, S. 1987. *Models of God: Theology for an Ecological, Nuclear Age*. Philadelphia: Fortress Press.

Rasmussen, L. 1996. *Earth Community, Earth Ethics*. Maryknoll, NY: Orbis.

Ricoeur, P. 1984. *Time and Narrative*, 3 vols. Chicago: University of Chicago Press.

Santmire, H.P. 1985. *The Travail of Nature: The Ambiguous Ecological Promise of Christian Theology*. Minneapolis: Fortress Press.

Scharlemann, R. 1989. *Inscriptions and Reflections: Essays in Philosophical Theology*. Charlottesville, VA: University of Virginia Press.

Tillich, P. 1951. *Systematic Theology*, vol. I. Chicago: University of Chicago Press.

White, L., Jr. 1967. The Historical Roots of Our Ecologic Crisis. *Science* 10 March: 1203-07.

Part Three

MORALITY AND THE MODIFICATION OF LIFE

8 The Value Lab: Deliberating Animal Values in the Animal Biotechology Debate

Frank Kupper

The development of animal biotechnology is shaped in the interaction between knowledge, technology, and the choices of the actors involved (Nowotny et al. 2001; Jasanoff 2005). The complexity of the biotechnological system makes its development an open-ended, inherently uncertain process. At the same time, it bumps into the limits of values and lifestyles. Democratic societies like the Netherlands have a diversity of views on what is 'right'. Regarding the execution of biotechnological procedures on animals, a plurality of perspectives has been present since its introduction in the Netherlands in the early 1980s. Different stories are told that each express a different vision on the animal, technology, and the relation between humans and animals. Furthermore, what is valued within these perspectives is expressed using different concepts and vocabularies. In other words, various ways of framing are present in the Dutch public debate. They each construct a different interpretation of the value of animals and thereby even of the animal itself. They constitute a typical way of thinking and talking about animals, referring to a distinctive framework of moral values considered to be important with respect to animals and the human-animal relationship. By this act of thinking and talking citizens are making the human-animal relationship meaningful to themselves and others.

This chapter introduces the interactive workshop methodology we have developed to articulate (possible) value conflicts in the Dutch public debate about animal biotechnology. We have dubbed this method the *value lab*. We focused on the deliberation of values regarding animals, although values about humans and about technology also play a role in this debate. Ultimately, this methodology is a first step to transform the public discussion of animal biotechnology into a moral dialogue in which moral values are deliberated. The value lab reconstructs the various value frameworks that are in possible conflict with one another. These frameworks should not be regarded as mental entities, thematic wholes inside the heads of people. Their use is instrumental, in order to facilitate moral deliberation. The reconstructed value frameworks are means for further inquiry by providing structuring insight into the morally problematic dimensions of the pluralistic social context in which animal biotechnology develops.

An extensive methodological discussion of the value lab has been published elsewhere (Kupper 2007). Here we will discuss the major reasons for choosing a discursive method to explore value diversity as well as the most important elements of the method. The chapter ends with a short description of the moral value frameworks we reconstructed and some implications of these frameworks for animal biotechnology ethics.

The Dutch Public Debate: Talk about Intrinsic Value

The Dutch government has made a considerable effort to incorporate the concern for animals in their legislation on animal biotechnology. Since 1997, the Dutch government has recognized the 'intrinsic value' of animals as the central tenet of their regulatory policy. Another objective is to promote public deliberation of the biotechnological use of animals. Despite these efforts, values are not the central theme of discussion. Although they do of course operate in the background, they are not deliberated explicitly. This observation correlates with Van Well's analysis of the adjacent Dutch public debate on GM food. Also here, the organizing committee 'Biotechnology and food' reported that broader moral concerns were not discussed (van Well, this volume). Van Well analyses that even the committee itself excluded moral values from the discussion by conceptualizing ethics as a separate – and thereby empty – category of deliberations.

The debate on animal biotechnology has been largely framed as a legal discussion rather than a process of moral deliberation. One of the main reasons is the opacity of meaning of the concept 'intrinsic value'. Introduced by philosophers and legal experts to reinforce the moral position of the animal, the concept acquired various meanings in the public arena. Different social actors refer to different animal values when they use the concept of 'intrinsic value' to express their concerns about animals (De Cock Buning 1999). In the Dutch parliamentary debate on the ethical regulation of animal biotechnology it was noted that 'intrinsic value is not an issue: what we are concerned with here is its interpretation, which is different for everyone' (see Brom 1999). The floating meanings of the 'intrinsic value' concept hamper moral deliberation because they fail to provide a conceptual framework to structure public debate. Therefore, the only possible structure of the Dutch public debate is legal hegemony. It is the one available framework for social actors to meet for discussion (Paula 2001). Because violation of their ethical values can only be disputed within this juridical context, these actors find themselves repeatedly trapped in a 'ritual dance' against licensing procedures. The legal framework does not provide the appropriate grips to engage in an in-depth moral discussion about values. It does not contain the proper concepts and language to do so. As a result, the (possible) underlying value conflict is not articulated nor deliberated.

'Intrinsic value' served as the conceptual opposite of the instrumental value animals have for their human users (Musschenga 1994; Dol 1999). The concept seemed to address perfectly the moral concerns that go beyond the animal's health and welfare. Its monistic conceptual structure however, appears to limits the consideration of the relevant variety of relationships between humanity and non-human nature. If we want to engage in a meaningful social dialogue on animal biotechnology, applied animal ethics should take a different turn. In order to take the apparent value pluralism into account, we argue for a shift to 'contextualism', encouraging an open and experimental approach to moral inquiry, inspired by the philosophical pragmatism of John Dewey (see the final section of this chapter). A first step in this process of moral inquiry would be the identification and articulation of the (possible) value conflicts between various social actors. As Loobuyck indicates in this volume, the negotiation of positions and the exchange of perspectives can only take place when the identity of the other has become clear.

Social Interaction and In-Depth Understanding

Involving the public in policy-making about animal biotechnology implies listening to what citizens have to say. We were interested in the diversity of value frameworks. Therefore, we chose to look at the widest range of interested publics and to discuss the broader moral concerns. The participants in this study were explicitly addressed as citizens, members of the Dutch democratic society in which animal biotechnology is developing.

One of the assumptions of this research project was the idea that unprofessionalized citizens did indeed have an important contribution to make in the moral deliberation of animal biotechnology, since the discussion is about values that we all exhibit.

In cross-national studies of European consumer attitudes towards genetically modified food, it was observed that an individual's opinions and beliefs about animal biotechnology are deeply embedded in more general attitude domains like the attitude towards nature and the attitude towards technology (Bredahl 1999; Bredahl 2001). Also, values, beliefs, and ideals are among other factors dependent on their context of expression (Potter 1996). From a discourse analytical perspective, the meaning of value concepts is seen as emerging in the process of social interaction (Potter & Wetherell 1987; Burningham 1995). When people talk about their perceptions of animals they will do so in highly complex ways (Waterton & Wynne 1999) have argued that values, beliefs and ideals, that is, the frameworks we set out to explore, are generally expressed in relation to a relevant social context and also as a process of negotation of trust. They are actively negotiated and constructed during the course of interaction with others. Therefore, according to these authors, research into the meaning structure of values, beliefs and ideals needs a more reflexive research framework than is offered by surveys or individual interviews. Adopting this perspective, we felt that the value frameworks underlying public perceptions of animal biotechnology in the Netherlands can at best be investigated by a close examination of the social interaction process through which the meaning of values is constructed.

So we set out to create a setting that enabled social interaction as well as in-depth understanding. In recent years, the focus group interview has been recognized as a powerful site of social interaction through which meaning and understanding are co-constructed (Madriz 2000). Focus groups are distinguished from ordinary group interviews by the explicit recognition of group interaction as a crucial part of the research process. The group is 'focused' in that it involves some kind of collective activity (Barbour & Kitzinger 1999). They are also 'focused' in the sense that a selective set of individuals discusses a specific topic from their own experience (Morgan 1997). Usually, they are set up as once-only meetings that take up to three hours. The recommended number of participants varies between five to twelve participants (Greenbaum 1998). Data derived from focus group discussions relies to a large extent on the interactions between participants themselves (Barbour & Kitzinger 1999). As Kitzinger puts it, the 'group work ensures that priority is given to the respondents' hierarchy of importance, *their* language and concepts, *their* frameworks for understanding the world' (Kitzinger 1994).

The objective of this research project was to articulate the (possible) underlying value conflicts in the public debate on animal biotechnology. This entails listening to what citizens themselves have to say. So, in line with the experiences with focus groups we organized small group discussions in order to reconstruct moral frameworks. This way the participants of the value lab acted as co-researchers, reconstructing their own frames of reference while reflecting and deliberating on animals with others. These frameworks involve the concepts, beliefs and ideals about animals that people personally value. Our qualitative research design aimed at understanding the various meanings participants themselves assign to their own life-worlds and experiences. Following a grounded theory approach we aimed at the inductive development of theoretical concepts from the ways our participants themselves order their thoughts and experiences (Glaser & Strauss 1967).

Designing the Value Lab Method

The objective of the value lab method was the exploration of the width and depth of different ways in which citizens in the Netherlands frame the value of animals. In order to facilitate a fruitful discussion of moral values we had to take several steps. First, we had to establish conditions that created a conversational context in which participants would feel at ease and deeper values could be discussed freely. Then, the selection and grouping of participants had to preserve the fruitful conversational context and warrant inclusion of the diversity of viewpoints. In the actual workshop design we strived for a balance between free-floating discussion and structured exploration. The final step in the value lab methodology was the systematic analysis of the discussion products. All together, the value lab is an interactive methodology merging social interaction and in-depth exploration.

Creating a Conversational Context

In this research process we aimed at encompassing diversity as well as *in-depth* exploration of ideas about animals. In order to enable this process, it was of great importance that a fruitful conversational context was created. According to the literature on public participation mechanisms, such a conversational context is characterized by an atmosphere of mutual respect and openness, and by equal opportunity for every participant (Abelson et al. 2003; Rowe & Frewer 2000; Webler & Tuler 2000; Caron-Flinterman 2006). Mutual respect and openness require a safe and relaxed environment in which participants would feel at ease and open to freely express their thoughts and beliefs. If personal values were to be shared, the conversation environment has to be trustworthy and non-threatening (Greenbaum 2000). Equal opportunity entails a fair deliberative process in the sense that it provides every participant the opportunity to put forward her position and to reflect on the position of others.

These conditions were met by the implementation of two guiding principles. First, we strived for homogeneity *within* the groups and heterogeneity *between* the groups. In this study, homogeneity meant that the participants joining in a particular focus group meeting more or less shared the same worldview. Our results show that working with homogeneous groups indeed showed a positive effect on the group process, creating group adhesion and a strong sense of solidarity. Generally, participants indicated they felt free to express their thoughts. Furthermore, they mentioned that it felt good to discuss these matters among like-minded people. The mixed groups we also organized showed less of the sense of solidarity and spent more time on convincing instead of clarifying one another. Because of the waste of time and energy, mixed groups had a tendency to become superficial, compared to the homogeneous groups.

The second principle entailed working with structured exercises during the focus group sessions. There is always a balance between structure and freedom. Although a free floating discussion certainly helps in the creative construction of ideas, sometimes a directive structure is needed to allow in-depth examination of what has come forward or to prevent dominant participants to claim superiority over other participants. One of the participants of the value lab discussions put it like this: '*I appreciated the idea that the exercises granted everybody's opinion equal attention.*' Another one: '*There was a fair division of attention.*'

Our experience with the value lab discussions demonstrates that the use of structured exercises contributed to an equal distribution of attention during the discussion.

Selecting and Grouping the Participants

Representativeness is regarded as one of the most important criteria for evaluating the effectiveness of participatory mechanisms (Rowe & Frewer 2000; Abelson et al. 2003). In our study, we were explicitly interested in cognitive representation, inclusion of the qualitative diversity of views on animals and the human-animal relationship.

Range of viewpoints	Group	Thematic grouping parameters
	hg1	industrial farming
	hg2	animal research in the laboratory
	hg3	pet breeding & retail/ fishing sports/ zoo workers
	hg4	farming/ countryside/ hunting/ foresting/ veterinary medicine
	hg5	Catholic and Protestant Christianity
	hg6	Islam
	hg7	organic farming/ nature conservation/ nature protection/ nature recreation/ vegetarianism/ humanism
	hg8	pet owners/ assistance animals/ animal shelter/ animal protection
	hg9	Buddhist/ Hindu/ Baha'i religions
	hg10	biodynamic farming/ veganism, deep ecology, anthroposophy, nature religion
	mg1-5	random cross-sections of society

Table 1   Selection and grouping of discussion group participants for a range of viewpoints. hg: homogeneous group; mg: mixed group.

As was mentioned, we aimed for homogeneity within the groups and heterogeneity between the groups to facilitate open and in-depth exploration of ideas. To achieve these aims, we have made use of various criteria to establish groups of congenial minds. We grouped on profession, membership of social organizations and anticipated worldview.

Using a cognitive representation sampling strategy probably entails missing out on some socio-demographic categories. In line with Fishkin (1995), this is only a problem when these groups would provide new or not yet described ideas about animals. Fishkin has argued that if not every person, at least every view must be represented.

We expanded our research population to groups of a specific religion or philosophy of life, because their voices are often considered unheard in the public debate about technology issues, a phenomenon also denoted by the contributions to this volume by Van Well (with respect to the GM food debate) and Loobuyck (with respect to political decision making). A remarkable result of the value lab discussions however, is that the Christian and Islamic discussion groups appeared not to be homogeneous with respect to their ideas about animals, despite the fact that they shared their religion. Apparently, religion was not the strongest determinant of animal values in these groups. On the level of process, these groups did show the same pattern as the other homogeneous groups. There were no observations that this heterogeneity disturbed group interaction.

Qualitative research literature recommends to conduct a series of discussion groups, while simultaneously monitoring the development of a range of issues to see whether new issues come up or the development of themes and categories becomes 'saturated' (Krueger 1994; Sim 1998). We started out with the two groups we expected to construct the two outer extremes of value patterns (see table 1: hg1 and hg10). The homogeneous groups we conducted subsequently showed no transgressions of these extremes. Also the mixed group discussions, which were cross-sections of society, did not show additional value patterns. The range of value categories observed in the homogeneous groups has been produced in the mixed group discussions as well. These results indicate that the selection strategy utilized in this study encompassed the width of ways in which Dutch citizens frame the value of animals.

The Discussion Workshop

The value lab design was standardized for all groups, and was semi-structured. Each group discussion was guided by a facilitator. The facilitator was accompanied by a monitor, who observed the group dynamics and, roughly, form and content of the discussion. Also, the monitor assisted the facilitator in carrying out the assignments. The overall structure of the programme was designed to enable in-depth exploration of animal values in a relaxed and trustworthy environment where participants can easily share their thoughts and beliefs.

The collective activity of the focus group consisted of a step-by-step circling in on the variety and richness of ideas. The focus group programme therefore moved from intuitions to conceptualized values through the repetitive use of structuring exercises.

A session started out with sharing and collecting the participants' direct intuitions and associations about animals. The next step was to articulate the stories behind the associations. The facilitator therefore repeatedly asked 'why questions' in order to move from intuitions towards value concepts and the articulation of contextual stories. The next step was to systematize the value concepts by clustering them in value categories and ranking them in order of importance. Then, the group focused on a specific category and the process of association, articulation and systematization recommenced. Working this programme, the participants constructed an interrelated network of concepts, beliefs and ideals they particularly valued about animals. The facilitator and monitor continually visualized the outcomes of discussions and exercises on flip-over sheets to make sure the group was able to continue working on the material that had come up in their interaction. Furthermore, the workshop design made sure that value frameworks were constructed by the groups themselves, using their own language and concepts.

Mixed Group Sessions

As was mentioned above, three of the mixed groups worked the same programme as the homogeneous groups did. For the other two mixed groups a different setup was chosen. In the standard programme, discussed above, the participants started at the level of intuitive association and slowly moved towards making moral intuitions explicit in a group-specific conceptualization of the intrinsic value of animals. The two remaining mixed groups started directly with an introduction of the intrinsic value concept and its role in the public debate. Subsequently, these groups completed the same exercises but now from the perspective of the intrinsic value concept. We wanted to find out what meaning the participants would attribute to this concept and whether they would use it at all if they were to give their ideas and opinions about animals.

The Reconstruction of Value Frameworks

The value lab discussions yielded a collection of group stories encompassing the variety and richness of ideas about animals in the Netherlands. The next step in the research process was to reconstruct the value frameworks in which the group stories were grounded. First of all, during the group discussions, the participants themselves worked on the articulation and structuring of their own beliefs and ideas. Second, the group stories were analysed by the researchers using a grounded theory approach (Glaser & Strauss 1967). A basic qualitative coding system was developed in an iterative process in a continuous exchange between raw data and the analytical and theoretical ideas researchers developed during the study (Strauss & Corbin 1998; Baarda 2005).

There are three different levels of interpretation in the coding system: value descriptions, value concepts, and value categories. *Value descriptions* are phrased in the participants' own language and correspond to the explanation that was given by the participants to convey why *they* felt a particular animal value was important. It was crucial to preserve this language because our investigation specifically aimed at understanding the language and concepts citizens themselves use to express their thoughts.

Value concepts refer to the values underlying the expressions of the participants when they talked about what they appreciated in the animal. *Value categories* comprise specific sets of value concepts, linking them through a common feature they share. The systematic coding procedures produced relationships between various value concepts and categories. Through this process of categorization and linkage a complex network of interconnected value concepts was reconstructed. This activity of coding, categorizing and linkage clarified which value concepts were used in the participant stories. During the sessions participants already ranked the priority of value concepts. Furthermore, the frequency by which a particular concept was expressed was taken as a measure for the relative weight of value concepts. Comparing concept maps and concept frequencies showed to what extend groups exhibited a mutual coherence. Of course, each of the focus groups went through a unique process of interaction, producing singular differences in how value concepts are framed and how often they are expressed. However, in line with Kitzinger (1994), using the same structured exercises for every group made it possible to compare their stories. Iterative cycles of interpretation by independent interpreters warranted the shared interpretative validity of research process and products (Maxwell 1992) and established the reconstruction of four distinctive value frameworks.

Four Ways to Frame the Value of Animals

Each of the frameworks constitutes a typical way of valuating, thinking and talking about animals. It comprises a descriptive sense (a vision of what an animal is) and a normative sense (a vision of why animals are important and how people should treat animals). The frameworks assemble a set of value categories concerning specific elements of the image of the animal itself or the human-animal relationship. The value categories contain a specific subset of animal values. These values are broadly defined as those features of the animal or the human-animal relationship that the participants of the value lab cared about, that mattered to them. The four frameworks are named after their central value concept: Use, Relation, Balance, and Source.

We consider the value frameworks produced in the value lab to be deliberated constructions of the value of animals and the human-animal relationship. In line with a discourse analytical perspective (Frouws 1998; Layder 1997) we regard those constructions as social representations. Whenever actors like farmers, scientists or other kind of citizens make sense of the issue of animal use, articulate their ideas, they selectively use a reservoir of social representations (i.e. value concepts and categories.) Whether a particular representation is used depends on the ideas and interests of the actor as well as on the changing context of discussion. Probably, for everyone a specific pattern is predominant or functions as a default mode. Other social contexts may however invoke a use of language and concepts that belongs to one of the other patterns.

Four Perspectives

The four frameworks put their emphasis on different levels of their respective worldviews. We have distinguished the level of the individual animal, the species, the ecosystem and the greater whole. Table 2 on page 170 shows the resulting perspectives for these four frameworks. The emphasized level colours the entire perspective on the animal and its relationships to humans and the surrounding world.

frame perspective	Use	Relation	Balance	Source
	I	I-you	i-WE	i-THOU

level		Use	Relation	Balance	Source
	animal	relation experience	relation experience functionality individuality		individuality being
	species	bio-capa-cities use		functionality	
	ecosystem			life naturalness	
	whole			system	naturalness system

Table 2 Four different perspectives on the animal. For each frame, the important value concepts are depicted at the level they address. The arrows indicate that for each of the frames the entire meaning of the animal is perceived from a certain level.

The Use framework draws on an I-perspective. The interests of humans shape the meaning that is attributed to the animal itself. Furthermore, the individual animal is approached as a manifestation of its species. Not the individual but the general is what is perceived and appreciated.

On the contrary, the Relation framework first and foremost values the individual qualities of the animal. The perception of an animal as an individual being colours the entire Relation view. Furthermore, the I-YOU perspective focuses on the relationship between humans and animals.

The Balance framework exhibits an I-WE perspective, focusing on the role of individual animals and species in the ecosystem they inhabit. A balance is sought between human and animal needs.

Also the Source framework holds a system perspective, the I-THOU perspective. However, also the individuality of the animal is recognized. The valuation of the system here acquires a spiritual dimension. The individuality of every animal is perceived as a manifestation of the supremacy of the whole of which both humans and animals are a part.

Different Interpretations of Intrinsic Value

The concept of intrinsic value acquires a different position and meaning in each of the four frameworks described above. Of course, aspects of the different interpretations also overlap. Even when two frameworks refer to the same aspect however, differences remain in how this aspect is precisely understood. Furthermore, the different perspectives on the animal and its relationships to humans and the world colour the understanding of each aspect of a particular intrinsic value interpretation.

In the Use framework interpretation the intrinsic value of animals particularly as the recognition of the animal as a sentient being. The concepts of health and welfare are therefore valued as the most important (and relevant) interests of the animal itself. The capacity for species-specific behaviour is valued in so far as it contributes to the animal's welfare. The Relation framework shares the recognition of the animal's health and welfare as an important element of the animal's intrinsic value. Additionally, the animal's individual quality is seen as a part of the animal's intrinsic value. The animal is appreciated as an independent companion in the human-animal relationship. This idea contributes to the quality of this relationship. Due to the human-centeredness of the perspectives of both the Use and Relation frameworks, some elements of the animal's intrinsic value are simultaneously appreciated for their instrumental value. The Use framework for example perceives the animal's species-specific character and behaviour as something that belongs to the animal but also gives humans the opportunity to use animals in order to fulfil human needs. The Relation framework also appreciates this character and behaviour in an aesthetic sense, referring to the joy it grants the human spectator.

The Balance framework interpretation of intrinsic value primarily emphasizes the animal's independent role and position as a co-inhabitant of the greater whole of 'system earth'. Further constituents of the animal's intrinsic value are the appreciation of the animal as a subject of life, with its own subsequent needs and interests, and the animal's naturalness, grounded in the concepts of species-specific character and behaviour but particularly in the recognition of the animal as a part of a natural environment. A similar 'system' perspective can be observed in the language and concepts of the Source framework. However, there is a more spiritual dimension to it. The greater whole of which man and animal are part is conceived as incomprehensible to us human beings. The interconnectedness of animals with all other things is perceived as one of the most important elements of the animal's intrinsic value. The other element is the animal's individuality. Together, interconnectedness and individuality are viewed as a manifestation of the animal's purpose.

Implications for Animal Biotechnology Ethics

Each of the four reconstructed ways of framing conveys its own narrative of the value of animals and their relationships to human beings and the surrounding world. These narratives are grounded in different frameworks of animal values. The diversity of values between the four frameworks provides a strong validation of moral pluralism in the reflection on animals in the Netherlands. The value diversity observed in this study includes both instrumental values, like the animal's functionality, and non-instrumental values, like the animal's being a subject of life. It is important to note that not only between frameworks but also within each one a mixture of instrumental and non-instrumental values is expressed. Like Smith (2003) noted with respect to environmental politics, both individuals and groups simultaneously appreciate values of nonhuman nature that are difficult to reconcile and pull them in contradictory directions. The ethical monism of intrinsic value theory is proposed to expel this uncertainty and settle the conflicts. In the meantime, it needlessly limits the broad range of interactions between humans and animals and thereby misrepresents the diversity of moral experiences and values. The dichotomy of intrinsic vs. instrumental value construes participants in the moral debate as adversaries on either side of a dilemma. This results in a mere simplification of the morally problematic context. Minteer and Manning (1999) have argued that any form of rigid monistic ethics runs the risk of jeopardizing the democratic tolerance of public ethical pluralism. Above, we already mentioned that the current practice of animal biotechnology ethical regulation in the Netherlands indeed does not provide the framework to incorporate the diversity of values into ethical decision making.

With the undeniable complex and uncertain character of animal biotechnology in mind, we believe a more pragmatic and pluralistic approach to animal biotechnology ethics would be better equipped to engage in moral deliberation of the wide range of moral concerns about the biotechnological use of animals. Here we join up with the fairly recent pragmatic turn in environmental ethics (Light & Katz 1996; Minteer & Manning 1999; Keulartz et al. 2003). These writers are inspired by the school of philosophical pragmatism, originating from the work of Charles Sanders

Peirce, William James, and John Dewey in the late nineteenth and early twentieth century. Mainly the work of John Dewey, offers some fruitful options to deal with the flaws of ethical monism and intrinsic value theory. In Dewey's view the world is a continuous and contingent process of change. His philosophical pragmatism therefore is anti-foundational. In an ever-changing world, the response to a morally problematic situation cannot be justified by some external and absolute criterion. Creative-intelligent inquiry into the context of the morally problematic situation is what is needed. Thus, Dewey aims at an open, flexible and experimental approach to moral problems. Like Minteer (2001) noted, Dewey's philosophical project demonstrates a strong faith in the ability of human experience to produce from within itself the justification of values and beliefs. Moral deliberation in this view ultimately rests on the potential of individuals to collectively engage in the creative-intelligent activity of moral inquiry. We believe incorporating value pluralism through the activity of public debate and criticism is central to the justification of any animal biotechnology policy in a democratic society like the Netherlands.

Application of the value lab method produced in-depth understandings of the various ways in which Dutch citizens frame the value of animals and the intrinsic value in particular. Our results show that in each of the value frameworks the concept of intrinsic value acquires a different place and function. The Dutch Ministry of Agriculture, responsible for animal biotechnology policy in the Netherlands, operationalized the concept of intrinsic value as the health, well-being, and integrity of the animal. Integrity is further operationalized in three aspects: the wholeness and intactness, the capacity for species-specific behaviour and self-sustainment. All of the framings produced in this study are different from the legislative framing of intrinsic value used by the government. The concept of integrity does not play a role in the Use and Relation frameworks. It is not perceived to be a meaningful concept in the evaluation of animal biotechnology practices. At the same time, the Relation framework expresses valuation of the individuality and uniqueness of animals, concepts not reflected in the operational definition. The idea that animals are taking part in a greater whole, important concepts in the Balance and Source framework, is also not reflected in the definition used by the government. In further public deliberations about animal biotechnology, this legal definition will therefore remain subject to critique. Adopting a different definition however will not be likely to change this.

It is strongly advisable to actively incorporate this insight in devising and facilitating the public debate on animal biotechnology. There will never be one absolute truth about the intrinsic value of animals. Given the pluralistic reality of the Dutch public debate, it would be better to create a platform for democratic communities to deliberate the implications of various interpretations then to strive for justification from a detached, external perspective.

As Walzer (1987) once put it: 'It is better to tell stories, even though there is no definitive and best story'. According to Beekman and Brom (2007) modern societies are not used to the discussion of these kind of ethical issues. They argue that ethics as a platform for value debates is therefore necessary in pluralist democracies. In line with the ideas of deliberative democracy (see for example Dryzek 2000), it would be a platform for citizens from all directions and orientations to meet for discussion. Like Crapels is saying in this volume, quoting Nowotny et al. (2001), a real dialogue about biotechnology is a way for society to speak back to science in the production of contextualized, robust knowledge. Benhabib (1996) writes that all citizens must feel free to bring up any moral argument to such a discussion. In his contribution to this volume, Loobuyck too states that pluralism is 'the very essence of the right to exist of our democracy'. But, he also rightfully acknowledges that it requires a deliberative attitude. Like Dewey advocated, it requires the critical appraisal of the values and beliefs of oneself and others. This would be the role of biotechnology ethics. Ethics as a platform for value debates should facilitate such appraisal and criticism. It is the task of animal biotechnology ethics to change a dogmatic clash of belief systems into a critical process of moral inquiry and open democratic deliberation. To fulfil this role, it needs the development of ethical tools, instruments to structure a collective process of moral inquiry. The value lab method we have discussed here can be understood as such an ethical tool. The frameworks produced in the value labs are heuristic tools for understanding the relationship between different values and positions in the public debate. They are instruments that provide a structuring insight into the morally problematic dimensions of the pluralistic social context in which animal biotechnology develops. Development and trial of the value lab was the first phase of a larger project, commissioned by the Dutch Ministry of Agriculture. The second phase of the project focused on the articulation of (possible) value conflicts by organizing dialogue sessions in which participants using different frames had to make decisions on biotechnology cases (in preparation). The project aims to contribute to integrative and context-sensitive policy-making on animal biotechnology. Ultimately, we hope to contribute to the development of a pragmatic and pluralistic approach to animal biotechnology ethics.

References

Abelson, J., P.G. Forest, J. Eyles, P. Smith, E. Martin, and F.P. Gauvin. 2003. Deliberations about deliberative methods: issues in the design and evaluation of public participation processes. *Social Science & Medicine* 57 (2), 239-251.

Baarda, D.B., M.P.M. de Goede, and J. Teunissen. 2005. *Basisboek kwalitatief onderzoek: Praktische handleiding voor het opzetten en uitvoeren van kwalitatief onderzoek.* Groningen: Stenfert Kroese.

Barbour, R.S. and J. Kitzinger. 1999. *Developing Focus Group Research: Politics, Theory and Practice.* London: Sage.

Beekman, V. and F.W.A. Brom. 2007. Ethical tools to support systmatic public deliberations about the ethical aspects of agricultural biotechnologies. *Journal of Agricultural & Environmental Ethics* 20, 3-12.

Benhabib, S. 1996. *Democracy and Difference : Contesting the Boundaries of the Political.* Princeton, NJ: Princeton University Press.

Bredahl, L. 1999. Consumers' cognitions with regard to genetically modified foods. Results of a qualitative study in four countries. *Appetite* 33 (3), 343-360.

— 2001. Determinants of Consumer Attitudes and Purchase Intentions with Regard to Genetically Modified Foods – Results of a Cross-national Survey. *Journal of Consumer Policy* 24, 23-61.

Brom, F.W.A. 1999. The use of 'intrinsic value of animals' in the Netherlands. In *Recognizing the Intrinsic Value of Animals. Beyond Animal Welfare*, eds. M. Dol et al. Assen: Van Gorcum, 15-28.

Burningham, K. 1995. Attitudes, Accounts and Impact Assessment. *Sociological Review*, 43 (1), 100-122.

Caron-Flinterman, J.F. 2006. Stakeholder participation in health research agenda setting: the case of asthma and COPD research in the Netherlands. *Science and Public Policy* 33 (4), 291-304.

De Cock Buning, T. 1999. The real role of 'intrinsic value' in ethical review committees. In *Recognizing the Intrinsic Value of Animals. Beyond Animal Welfare*, eds. M. Dol et al. Assen: Van Gorcum, 133-139.

Dol, M., M. Fentener van Vlissingen, S. Kasanmoentalib, T. Visser, and H. Zwart, eds. 1999. *Recognizing the Intrinsic Value of Animals. Beyond Animal Welfare.* Assen: Van Gorcum.

Dryzek, J.S. 2000. *Deliberative Democracy and Beyond: Liberals, Critics, Contestations.* Oxford: Oxford University Press

Fishkin, J.S. 1995. *The Voice of the People: Public Opinion and Democracy.* New Haven; London: Yale University Press.

Frouws, J. 1998. The contested redefinition of the countryside. An analysis of rural discourses in the Netherlands. *Sociologia Ruralis* 38 (1), 54-68

Glaser, B.G. and A.L. Strauss. 1967. *The Discovery of Grounded Theory: Strategies for Qualitative Research*. Chicago: Aldine Pub.

Greenbaum, T.L. 1998. *The Handbook for Focus Group Research*, 2nd ed. Thousand Oaks: Sage.

— 2000. *Moderating Focus Groups: A Practical Guide for Group Facilitation*. Thousand Oaks: Sage.

Jasanoff, S. 2005. *Designs on Nature: Science and Democracy in Europe and the United States*. Princeton, NJ: Princeton University Press.

Keulartz, J., M. Korthals, M. Schermer, and T. Swierstra. 2003. *Pragmatist Ethics for a Technological Culture*. Dordrecht: Kluwer Academic Publishers.

Kitzinger, J. 1994. The Methodology of Focus Groups – The Importance of Interaction between Research Participants. *Sociology of Health & Illness* 16 (1), 103-121.

Krueger, R.A. 1994. *Focus Groups: A Practical Guide for Applied Research*, 2nd ed. Thousand Oaks: Sage.

Kupper, F., L. Krijgsman, H. Bout, and Tj. de Cock Buning. 2007. The value lab: exploring moral frameworks in the deliberation of values in the animal biotechnology debate. *Science and Public Policy* 34 (9), 657-670

Layder, D. 1997. *Modern Social Theory: Key Debates and New Directions*. London: UCL Press.

Light, A. and E. Katz. 1996. *Environmental Pragmatism*. London: Routledge.

Madriz, E. 2000. Focus groups in feminist research. In *Handbook of Qualitative Research*, eds. N.K. Denzin and Y.S. Lincoln. Thousand Oaks: Sage, 835-850.

Maxwell, J.A. 1992. Understanding and Validity in Qualitative Research. *Harvard Educational Review* 62 (3), 279-300.

Minteer, B. A. 2001. Intrinsic value for pragmatists? *Environmental Ethics*, 23 (1), 57-75.

Minteer, B.A. and R.E. Manning. 1999. Pragmatism in environmental ethics: Democracy, pluralism, and the management of nature. *Environmental Ethics* 21 (2), 191-207.

Morgan, D.L. 1997. *Focus Groups as Qualitative Research*, 2nd ed. Thousand Oaks: Sage.

Musschenga, A.W. 1994. Antropocentrisme en de intrinsieke waarde van de niet-menselijke natuur. *Filosofie en Praktijk* 15, 113-129.

Nowotny, H., P. Scott, and M. Gibbons. 2001. *Re-thinking Science: Knowledge and the Public in an Age of Uncertainty*. Cambridge: Polity Press.

Paula, L.E. 2001. *Biotechnologie bij dieren ethisch getoetst? Een onderzoek naar het functioneren van het Besluit Biotechnologie bij Dieren*. Den Haag: Rathenau Instituut.

Potter, J. 1996. *Representing Reality: Discourse, Rhetoric and Social Construction*. London: Sage.

Potter, J. and M. Wetherell. 1987. *Discourse and Social Psychology: Beyond Attitudes and Behaviour*. London: Sage.

Rowe, G. and L.J. Frewer. 2000. Public participation methods: A framework for evaluation. *Science Technology & Human Values* 25 (1), 3-29.

Sim, J. 1998. Collecting and analysing qualitative data: issues raised by the focus group. *Journal of Advanced Nursing* 28 (2), 345-352.

Smith, G. 2003. *Deliberative Democracy and the Environment*. London: Routledge.

Strauss, A.L. and J.M. Corbin. 1998. *Basics of Qualitative Research: Techniques and Procedures for Developing Grounded Theory*, 2nd ed. Thousand Oaks: Sage.

Walzer, M. 1987. *Interpretation and Social Criticism*. Cambridge, MA: Harvard University Press.

Waterton, C. and B. Wynne. 1999. Can Focus Groups Access Community Views? In *Developing Focus Group Research: Politics, Theory and Practice*, eds. R. Barbour and J.E. Kitzinger. Thousand Oaks: Sage.

Webler, T. and S. Tuler. 2000. Fairness and competence in citizen participation: theoretical reflections from a case study. *Administration and Society* 32 (5), 566-595.

9 'Not by Bread Alone' – Religion in the Dutch Public Debate on GM Food

Michiel van Well

Introduction

Religion plays a role in every debate on innovative food technologies. These debates cannot be understood well without paying attention to the religious aspects of these debates. I will demonstrate this with the help of the work of the anthropologist Mary Douglas and by analysing the Dutch public debate on GM food as organized by the Terlouw Committee in 2001.

Food and Religion

Food is a central theme in almost every religion, and food and religion have been closely intertwined for ages. There are many religious stories and references in which food plays an essential role. Food has been a religiously loaded theme in different ages and places. In the Bible, more specifically in the Torah, the first reference to food is made immediately after the stories of creation, in Genesis 2: 16-17; in the words of the King James version: 'And the LORD God commanded the man, saying, Of every tree of the garden thou mayest freely eat: But of the tree of the knowledge of good and evil, thou shalt not eat of it: for in the day that thou eatest thereof thou shalt surely die.' In the Qur'an (2:35) a similar story is told and also in Hinduism there are numerous stories in which food plays a central role. But not only in words, also in religious practices, rituals, and experiences food plays an essential role, in fasting, feasting, and offering. Connected to those stories and practices many religions have dietary rules and purity laws describing which food is pure and which is impure and therefore not to be eaten (or to be sacrificed).

That practically every religion relates to food does not necessarily imply that religion plays a role in all debates on food. However, a closer look at especially the religious dietary rules and purity laws gives at least theoretical reasons to conclude that religion plays a role in every debate on innovative food technologies.

Dietary rules and purity laws are a good entrance to see the intricate connections between food technology and religion. For modern people, dietary rules and purity laws at first sight seem to have an obscure or arbitrary nature. Many theologians and scholars of religion have tried to come up with a clear interpretation of the purity laws of the Israelites. Many interpreters based their interpretations on motives of hygiene, blood, death, and creation order (Boersema 2001). The anthropologist Mary Douglas gives another interpretation of the purity laws that is different from those her predecessors. She divides those former interpretations into two categories. The first she coins 'medical materialism'. In this approach it is implied that if we only knew all the circumstances, we would find a rational basis of primitive ritual amply justified. Douglas denies this line of reasoning a she states:

> Even if some of Moses' dietary rules were hygienically beneficial, it is a
> pity to treat him as an enlightened public health administrator, rather
> than as a spiritual leader. (Douglas 2002, 37).

As to the second and opposite view in which primitive ritual has nothing whatever in common with our ideas of cleanness, this is by Douglas deployed as equally harmful to the understanding of ritual:

> One cannot state that our modern practises are solidly based on hy-
> giene, and theirs are symbolic: we kill germs, they ward off spirits
> (Douglas 2002, 40).

Yet, for Douglas the resemblance between some of their symbolic rites and our hygiene is sometimes uncannily close. For Douglas, purity and danger are closely related to classification schemes that order the world and are grounded in religion. As I will show in this article, this gives a new entry to modern debates on high tech food as GM food. Therefore an analysis will be made of the Dutch public debate on GM food caled 'Eten en genen', which was organized by the temporary governmental committee 'Biotechnologie en voeding' chaired by Jan Terlouw in 2001.

Introducing Monsters

The debate 'Eten en genen' was not an isolated event; it was part of broader developments in the field of biotechnology and the public debates that were connected to them. In the 1970s, recombinant DNA technology was developed. With this technology it became possible to change an organism at a genetic level and by this it became possible to steer its phenotypical appearance and functions. It also became possible to implant human genes in micro-organisms which therewith produced human insulin. The technology was further developed and in 1983 the first plant with recombinant DNA was constructed. At that time the technique of DNA recombination was known, both in science and in society, as genetic manipulation.

This development opened up a broad range of possibilities for new food products and food production methods. Since then, biotechnology has been booming. New research fields appeared, new companies opened up and new industries have developed. In 1995 the first soy and tomatoes with recombinant DNA were presented for sale. The tomatoes and soy were made herbicide resistant which was expected to give production profits. In 1996 the first ships loaded with recombinant soy tried to enter the Netherlands via the Rotterdam harbour. Greenpeace campaigned strongly against harbouring the ships and especially against unloading the recombinant soy.

In the media a huge debate developed on the topic of genetically manipulated food. The debates were fierce and had some name calling in them. Proponents of the recombinant DNA technology started to use the term *genetic modification* instead of the till then common term genetic manipulation. This made the opponents call for and defend the name *genetic manipulation*, which from that moment on had a more negative connotation. In this essay I will use the inconclusive abbreviation GM. The names and their connotations did not end the debates. They just started a new phase in the debate. The Dutch debate on biotechnological food has shown to be an ongoing story ever since – a story in which names like 'Frankenstein food' came up and got much attention, but too little reflection.

In the media the name 'Frankenstein food' was frequently used and debated. In one way or another it gave expression to severe feelings about GM food which were hard to express in another way. With the name 'Frankenstein food', GM food acquires the connotation of being an abomination, a monster. In this chapter I will argue that it is not a bad name for GM food, without implying that GM food should or should not be eradicated. There are other ways to treat a man-made monster.

Douglas on Dirt

To find out why it might be appropriate to call GM food a monster, let us delve into the work of Mary Douglas on purity. Douglas explains that a precise reading of Leviticus shows a strict classification scheme behind the purity rules and dietary laws. This classification scheme was used by the old Israelites to order the diversity of creation. Distinctions were made between land animals, water animals and air animals with their separate characteristics and their own way of moving. The Israelites saw it as their duty to live to this order. Animals that could not be categorized because they had characteristics of different categories were considered an abomination. The pig for instance, was considered impure because it was the only animal that did not ruminate but does move on four legs without cloven hoofs, and therefore did not fall into any category of the creation order. Impurity is a breach of ruling classifications (Douglas 2002).

The object of Douglas' comparative religion is order. The way people order their world by classification is a central theme in the work of Mary Douglas. Interestingly enough, she does approach this theme via disorder and chaos. What is considered as impure or dirty gives, according to Douglas, insight into ideas about what is clean, pure, and ordered (Reis 1996). Or as she states it herself:

> Reflection on dirt involves reflection on the relation of order to disorder, being to non-being, form to formlessness, and life to death. Wherever ideas of dirt are highly structured, their analysis discloses a play upon such profound themes. This is why an understanding of rules of purity is a sound entry to comparative religion (Douglas 2002, 7).

In daily life dirt or impurity are mostly seen as properties of goods. Douglas however relates them to actions in a specific context. Shoes are not intrinsically dirty; it is dirty to put shoes on the dining table. Impurity and dirt is that what is situated in the wrong place of the classification scheme. Or as Douglas summarizes it, dirt and impurity are 'matter out of place'. The boundaries of the order in which humans, animals, and goods all have their place, are exceeded. This place does not necessarily mean an actual location; it mostly refers to a cultural or material order (Douglas 2002).

Following Durkheim it can be stated that religions give classification and order an objective or God-given status. Essential therefore is the concept of the holy which has an untouchable and autonomous character and conceals human aspects of the classifications. Religion unites the different classifications used by a group (Durkheim 1995). Durkheim applies this view only to non-modern societies. Durkheim was primarily interested in the question how modernity was different from primitive or pre-modern societies. Douglas applies Durkheim's approach also on modern societies and her central question is therefore no longer about the difference but about the similarities between societies. Douglas denies the conventional idea that traditional ideas about impurity are the result of ignorance, superstition and religious imagination, while modern ideas about hygiene would be the result of scientific knowledge and true insight into nature. For Douglas both traditional and modern forms of impurity are the result of the same cultural mechanism. The central notion of this mechanism is that impurity is 'matter out of place'. It is the result of an unsuccessful classification. Impure are objects that do not fit in the cognitive classification scheme. And since the activity of classification is a human universal, which implies unclassifiables, those cannot be eradicated. Dirt, impurity and as we will see 'monsters' are part of every culture and of everyday life.

The Dutch philosopher Martijntje Smits uses Douglas' ideas on religion, classification, and purity to understand responses on new technologies (Smits 2002). Like dirt, impure animals, or food, new technology can be unclassifiable 'matter out of place'. Technologies are innovative, not only in a technological sense but also on a cultural level. With reproductive technologies for example, new ways to become pregnant are introduced, but with it also embryos 'out of place'. Embryos are now held outside the womb inside a test tube. Technological innovation can challenge existing ideas about ourselves, our environment and our relations. Smits considers these new and unclassifiable technologies and their products as monsters. Monsters are ambiguous, they combine elements that are or at least were not combinable (like *bio-technology* or *in vitro fertilization*) and therefore bring both *tremendum et fascinans* – fear and fascination. Monsters may not be classifiable, that does not mean they are considered to have a bad nature. Monsters can be appointed both as sacred and as a taboo. Monsters not only represent the destructive force in the existing order, they can also be taken as a creative shapelessness with the force of creation (Smits 2002). For the Lele (a Congolese tribe), the holy pangolin (scaly anteater) is a contradiction of all categories used. It has scales like a fish, climbs trees, looks like a lizard and is a mammal. It is apparently highly impure, but practically most sacred. The pangolin is prepared and eaten by initiates and considered as a source of fertility. Monsters are ambiguous, but that does not necessarily mean they cannot be attractive.

Monsters!

In what ways is GM food a monster? In the debate, a recurring theme was if GM was fundamentally different from classical ways to improve the species, or if GM could be considered to be just a next step in a longer tradition of improvement. With existing classifications there is no straightforward answer to that question. GM food cannot easily be categorized in an existing classification, it is matter out of place or, due to its innovative character, matter without a place. It transcends boundaries that were taken for granted until then.

In GM qualities of different species are exchanged. In response to that, people bring up worries about contamination. For instance in biological agriculture there are 'especially many worries about "contamination" by blowing over of pollen from plants that are genetically modified' (Terlouw 2002). Others apply great value to the preservation of original species and are worried about irreversible changes. GM food does make an appeal on ideas of naturalness and does not fit into the existing 'natural' categories used by people in the debate (Terlouw 2002).

Besides the 'unnatural' character, GM food also brings up a lot of questions about the risks, dangers and uncertainties of this type of food. In June 2001 the Terlouw Committee asked the public by advertisements in newspapers which aspects should be part of the public debate. Most brought up the matter of safety for humans and the environment (Terlouw 2002).

Purity and danger, risk and safety are directly brought up when GM food is debated. I would state that these themes illustrate that GM food has a monstrous character. We cannot classify GM food in existing categories. To a lot of people GM food is an ambiguous product, which brings in both unprecedented options and changes but also unknown risk and dangers. GM food can be fascinating but also fearsome.

One can reasonably state that GM food is a monster, at least in the way Smits uses the term. Frankenstein food is therefore not a bad name for GM food. Especially when we consider that the problem of Mary Shelley's Frankenstein was not that he created a monster, but that he did not care enough for it (Bijker 1995). With that, the question that comes to the fore is: how does one relate to this monster?

Organizing Open Debate

In 1999 a resolution was passed in which A.M.A. Van Ardenne-van der Hoeven and other members of the Dutch Parliament asked to organize a public debate on GM food. The second cabinet of Prime Minister Kok incorporated the request in the *Integrale Nota Biotechnologie* (Ministry of VROM 2000). Minister of Agriculture, Nature, and Food Safety, Laurens Jan Brinkhorst of the political party D'66, carried out the resolution on behalf of the cabinet.

The motive for the debate was formulated by the minister of Agriculture, Nature and Food Safety in a letter to the parliament (all translations from Dutch are by the present author):

> The cabinet sees modern biotechnology as a key technology, which should be used in a responsible and careful way. The introduction of genetically modified corn and soy a few years ago ... has given rise to discussion in society. It is expected that new uses of modern biotechnology in the future will lead to recognizable advantages for consumers, such as health advantages. The process of opinion making about the formerly mentioned uses has till now not taken place in a structured manner...Much of these discussions are hardly accessible to the broader public. (Brinkhorst 2001)

The outspoken position on biotechnology as a key technology taken by the cabinet does structure the agenda for the debate. The goals of the debate as formulated by minister Brinkhorst are informative on this matter. The cabinet sees the goal of the debate as twofold:

> Primary goal for the public debate (is) ... to make clear the conditions under which biotechnology for food is acceptable by the public. This does not mean the cabinet aims to stimulate the acceptance of the use of modern biotechnology in food in society via the debate. To accentuate this, the organization of the debate is distanced from the government. This stimulates independent information dissemination and facilitates the public debate in an objective manner. The public debate about biotechnology and food aims primarily to spread information under a public as broad as possible. (Brinkhorst 2001)

The cabinet denies aiming at acceptance of biotechnology with the organizational argument of placing the committee at a distance from the government. However, the leading question for the debate clearly anticipates the acceptance of modern biotechnology by the public. Only when acceptance is presumed, does the question regarding under which conditions biotechnology is acceptable for the public make any sense. This does not mean that a free exchange of ideas and opinions is not a value for the cabinet as it states a bit further in the memo:

> The first goal of the public debate is to disseminate information under a public as broad as possible. The second goal of the debate is to give the public and other involved parties the opportunity, by structured discussion, to exchange and formulate opinions and standpoints about the question under which conditions the use of modern biotechnology in food is acceptable to them. (Brinkhorst 2001)

Although the debate should be open to public and other parties involved, the agenda is directly limited to the conditions under which the use of modern biotechnology in food is acceptable to them. The goals of the debate seem to be halted between two options: an open debate and or a campaign for this key technology.

Minister Brinkhorst installed the Committee for Biotechnology and Food under the chair of former minister of Economic Affairs, Jan Terlouw. Both Brinkhorst and Terlouw are members of D'66, which characterizes itself as a progressive-liberal party. It is a pragmatic party which has little affinity with traditional political ideologies or religion. It purports to build on rationality and aims at governmental reform. Together with the liberal party (VVD) and the socialist party (PvdA) they formed a so-called 'purple' cabinet, the first cabinet since 1918 in the Netherlands which reigned without the Christian democrat party (CDA) or its predecessors. In 2001, this purple coalition began its second term. It was, as they characterized themselves, pragmatic rather than ideological.

In this political constellation the Committee is installed and after installation, the Committee closely stuck to the formulated assignment. They used both qualitative and quantitative methods to get insight into public opinions and arguments, organized several debates and offered help to other organizations who would do the same. From their report it is clear the Committee put a lot of work in informing people about the debate and was successful in that. But it became also clear that the Committee had difficulties to get and keep organizations involved in the debate.

Managing Monsters: Monster Adaption by the Committee

Given the presumption that biotechnology is a key technology, which is here to stay, the question for the Committee to answer becomes how to deal with this innovative technology and public opinions on it. The advice of the Committee to the government after the debate can be characterised as a procedural programme for monster management. The Committee formulates it as follows:

> Genetic modification is an impressive new technology, but the application needs the support of the public... The government and political parties have to learn to deal with that. Recovery of trust in the government is most important, because the government sets the boundaries for science and industry. The committee has taken this into account in her recommendations. The recommendations will be summarized here:
> – A national or European Food Authority should be installed which can operate completely independent.
> – The government should develop better methods to start a dialogue with the broader public in an early stage.
> – Freedom of choice should be optimally guaranteed by making good accessible, detailed product information obligatory (Terlouw 2002, 4).

Based on her work on order and religion, Douglas concludes that the way cultures react to monsters is related to the character of the group. Smits translates this to a 'theory of monsters' in which four ideal typical styles of monster management are introduced. As we will see, the style of the Committee can easily be characterised as a ritualistic style.

The four styles that Smits describes are:

a) Dogmatic style – monster exorcism: Cultural classification is in the dogmatic style strict and permanent. Knowledge and morals are inflexible. Monsters are in the most positive case ignored; more often will they be handled as aberrations and therefore exorcised.

b) Ritualistic style – monster adaptation: The cultural classification is less rigid and more subtle; the dichotomy is less straightforward. Instead there are rituals and a complex structure of rules. When these are closely followed it is normally possible to fit in the monster. The monster is considered nothing – fundamentally – new.

c) Pragmatic style – monster assimilation: In this style both monsters and classifications can be adapted. Cultural boundaries are considered as human conventions, and become more instrumental than fundamental. Monsters are assimilated and in the process of assimilation both the monster and the cultural classification are modified.

d) Romantic style – monster embracement: Fascination instead of fear is the leading idea in this style. Contradictions are considered to be of a higher order which cannot be reached with mundane rationality. Cultural classification will be kept intact since there is no urge to solve the contradictions. Monsters are not refused but accepted (Smits 2002).

The advice of the Committee is a good illustration of the ritualistic style of the Committee. This style is well suited for an utilitarian approach of ethics. Although the Committee's use of the concept of ethics is not very straightforward or explicit, it shows an utilitarian idea of ethics. The Dutch philosopher Swierstra once characterized utilitarian ethics as 'regulatory ethics'. Regulatory ethics is easily incorporated in policy making and procedural regulation, since its goal is to answer the practical question how to live together without doing (unnecessary) harm to each other. Regulatory ethics is much less interested and involved in virtues or questions about the good life (Swierstra, Bruggen, et al. 2000).

Although ethics is not considered to be the most relevant aspect of the debate by the Committee, it is still very present in the report of the Committee. But they use ethics in a peculiar way. Reading the report one gets the impression that 'ethics' is an autonomous category of arguments and deliberations in the debate, which have no connection whatsoever with other themes like freedom of choice, health, risks, use of nature and environment or fair relations between the Netherlands and developing countries. This boxing of ethics is most clearly illustrated by the statistics done on reply forms filled in by grammar school students. The results of the statistics were presented in a matrix. In this matrix the advantages and disadvantages of biotechnology in food were given for several categories. 'Ethics was one of the boxed categories and put besides categories as "agricultural production, environment, third world, safety, consumers"' (Terlouw 2002, 45). The Committee makes ethics a special category to such an extent that it disappears as a relevant part of the debate:

> As far as there are objections to biotechnology for food, it appears that only for a few people they arise from ethical or principal sources. Utilitarian deliberations are for the Dutch public in general more important. (Terlouw 2002, 19)

In the eye of the Committee utilitarian deliberations seem not connected with ethics. Already before the actual debate objections are made to this way of conceptualizing ethics.

> Mr Meijboom from the Centrum voor Bio-ethiek en Gezondheidsrecht at Utrecht University stated in the first debate of this series that the government in the Integrale Nota Biotechnology (INB) wrongly makes no relation between ethics and questions about safety, transparency of government and freedom of choice of the consumer. Ethics is presented as an isolated domain; the domain in which complicated identity-defining questions are at stake. In reality discussions about the acceptability of risks and the autonomy of the consumers (expressed in his freedom of choice) are not isolated from morality, states Meijboom; to the contrary. (Terlouw 2002, 74)

Since Meijboom makes his remark early in the first debate of a series (Wageningen, March 2001) he cannot and does not draw conclusions about the debate itself. But by referring to the Integrale Nota Biotechnologie, he criticizes the concept of ethics as used in governmental policy making on biotechnology in general. His remarks can be taken as an advice to the Committee to act differently.

In the report of the Committee the remark of Meijboom is presented as an individual statement, with little use for the debate. The Committee does not give any reflection on its own use of ethical concepts and insights. Meijbooms remark is placed in annex G, meaning that it was heard by the Committee but did not have much impact on its work.

By its focus on utilitarian arguments, the conclusions by the Committee that other than utilitarian arguments have little relevance in the debate, seems to be much guided by presuppositions, and less a result of the debate itself.

The strict but implicit boundaries between utilitarian arguments and fundamental arguments or arguments of principle conceal the interaction between those (analytic) categories. Utilitarian arguments are closely related to more fundamental ideas. The argument of safety of biotechnological food may be utilitarian in nature but it implies also more fundamental ideas about the value of life and relevance of human health or the environment.

The Committee presents the mentioned utilitarian arguments of the participants in the debate as a decision of the participants to have a debate on a utilitarian level. However, for many participants in the debate those

utilitarian arguments are directly related to principles and more fundamental ideas:

> For most participants, when the goal is considered sufficiently useful
> the end justifies the means of genetic modification, irrespective of the
> fundamental judgement one has on improvement (Terlouw 2002, 7).

> The application of gene-technology on animals for food production ap-
> pears to raise much more opposition for many people compared to ap-
> plications with plants. Only when very urgent matters are at stake, like
> medical use for a genuine problem (and not only fighting symptoms),
> the public is willing to deviate from this principle (Terlouw 2002, 7).

Besides that, several participants in the debate used both more fundamental and utilitarian arguments in the debate. Several NGOs who resigned
from the debate organized by the Committee, brought up both missing
utilitarian arguments on safety and risk but also criticized the absence of
fundamental questions as stated before.

Monster Exorcism by NGOs

> Of this aselect group, 37 per cent held that these crops should not be
> grown at all (Terlouw 2002, 13).

This thirty-seven per cent of the public has a dogmatic style towards GM
food. They do not want any relation with this monster. There is no place
for GM food at all in society. The monster should be exorcised. Greenpeace has a similar dogmatic style in its advocacy of a strict interpretation
of the precautionary principle. This states as long as risks are not clear,
one is not allowed to use the technology on a larger scale (Smits 2002).
The monster can only be hold captive in a well-guarded laboratory and
should not be around in society.

With Greenpeace, fifteen NGOs from the fields of environmental issues, third world aid and animal welfare[1] were critical about the assignment of the Committee from the start but they were prepared to give
the debate a chance. Their critique was both on form and content of the
debate. They formulated their main point of critique most clear in a press
announcement:

The public debate (as organized by the Committee) deals with the conditions under which genetic manipulation is acceptable; it does not address the question whether genetic manipulation is desirable (Greenpeace, Alternatieve Konsumentenbond, et al. 2001).

In the assignment of the Committee and the agenda for the debate the conditions under which GM food is the central topic, leaving insufficient space for more fundamental discussion and for the more dogmatic stance of monster exorcism. Besides critique on the agenda of the debate, the information used by the Committee in the debate is criticized. The video the committee showed was considered more like a promotion movie than a source of objective information.

These objections are discussed with the Committee and adaptations were made by the Committee. Having seen the new information material and having visited the opening event of the debate, and in accordance with their dogmatic style, these NGOs decided to no longer participate in the debate organized by the Committee since they still could not agree with the information provided on GM food, the methodological set up of the debates and the agenda used for the debates.

Monster Assimilation by *Kerk en Wereld*

Without being dogmatic, one can still ask fundamental questions. *Kerk en Wereld*, a church and society organization of the main Dutch Protestant churches, stated, for instance:

> Kerk en Wereld pleas for giving attention to presuppositions from philosophy of life and to the questions hidden behind ethical aspects. That does not mean particularly questions as about 'playing God' or 'to go against the order of creation', since these are not live questions for church members. More relevant are questions like: how do we relate to our own vulnerability and to the 'imperfections' of nature, do we keep fighting against these of do we accept limits? Are we still able to handle the (inevitable) tragic aspects of life? What are our moral values and judgements based on? What do we give our deepest trust: our own capabilities, science, nature, God? These questions lead to the fundamental question whether we want to continue with genetically modified food. This question too asks for attention in the debate (Terlouw 2002, 99).

These questions are not aimed at exorcising the monster, nor at stating that there is nothing new under the sun and accepting the monster after some ritual debate and regulatory ethics. This is a plea for a debate on how one wants to live and how we want to live together with monsters. These are questions of 'ethics of life', as Swierstra calls them. They are hard to answer, and often even harder to agree on, but fundamental if one wants to position oneself to the monsters we create and meet. With these fundamental questions, the answers are open. Nothing is God given or a natural fact, an open debate becomes possible. Both the monster and the cultural conventions are open for debate and can be, if decided upon, be modified according to new insights and or experiences. With these fundamental questions the pragmatic style comes to the fore.

No Religion?

It is not coincidental that Kerk en Wereld introduces ethics of life questions. These questions are religious questions, questions about the fundaments of life and living together in this world. This makes the public debate 'Eten en genen' interesting for those interested in the relations between technology, religion and food. This may not be clear at first instance since in the 131-page-long final report and conclusions of the Committee the word 'religion' does not appear once and there are only three references to 'philosophies of life' of which two just deny its relevance:

> There were hardly any purely ethical or 'philosophy of life' discussions. But during the debates ethical deliberations were made. A big majority of the participants is reasoning from a utilitarian perspective (Terlouw 2002, 45).

> A minority of the participants reasons from principles like holding out the boundaries of species. An even smaller minority reasons from principles based on philosophies of life (Terlouw 2002, 45).

The Committee has a hard time appreciating the religious layers in the debate. The utilitarian agenda, where the conditions under which biotechnology for food is acceptable are central, leaves little space for questions about views on life, let alone religion. To see the religious layers and connections becomes even harder if one searches for purely ethical or philosophical views on life in the discussion. Pure religion is not to be found, nor is pure science, politics, ethics, or economics. These are analytical and not empirical categories. One misses the religious agenda when one uses a utilitarian agenda and boxes religion as an autonomous category. However, that does not imply there are no religious layers.

The focus of the Committee on utilitarian aspects results in several leftovers in the debate. The category of 'ethics' as referred to by the Committee is one such leftover. These cannot be denied, but in the utilitarian eye of the Committee they cannot be valued nor used in its analysis of the debate. The same counts expression in which GM food is related to the idea of playing for God, feelings of disgust and discomfort, unnatural behaviour or characterizing names as 'Frankenstein food'.

These leftovers are to be better understood when we take Douglas' ideas on purity and danger once more into account. The leftovers all refer to feelings or ideas of transgressing natural or God given boundaries. Things become out of place and monstrous. There is an order in the leftovers of the Committee. As Douglas has shown, all ideas on purity and danger are connected to the order we create with our cosmologies. Monsters have no intrinsic monstrous character. Monsters are the result of our ideas about life and what we think is natural, God given or an abomination. It is religion with which we decide what is monstrous, dangerous or pure. One can be dogmatic and live strictly to the precautionary principle, or adopt a ritualistic style relying on self-appointed rationality and regulatory ethics. It is no less religious than asking fundamental questions about how to live with monsters and being open to discuss all options. Every style produces and uses its own order and leftovers.

Conclusions

Since this monster called GM food was constructed and now does exist in our world, it is not fruitful to deny its existence nor to deny its monstrous character. We have to learn to deal with the monster. The question that should be discussed is how do we relate to this monster and (where) do we want to place it in our society and culture? The answer can be that we choose to destroy or exorcise the monster, but we can't deny its existence.

We have to relate to the monster and place it in the world. To decide on our style of managing the monster, functional insights and utilitarian arguments are not enough. One could even say that, in case of a monster, information on functions, risks, and dangers are not available in detail. The monster is too new, unknown, and ambiguous for that. From its nature it does not fit in our classifications and orders of thinking. We cannot simply reproduce our ideas and insight into order and classification on the monster. Monsters challenge our institutions, intuitions and knowledge. The challenge is to decide on our approach of the monster, without the backup of scientific knowledge, strict procedures or fit institutional structures.

Managing monsters is about dealing with purity and danger and these are directly related to order and classification. For Douglas, classification is a human universal and part of religion. This view makes our approach of monsters a religious endeavour. Managing monsters is about making connections and relations between us, the monster and others. It is about reserving a place for monsters but also for ourselves and others. One could say that in Mary Shelley's story of 'The monster of Frankenstein' this has been the problem. The monster was created but not domesticated and given a place. If Frankenstein had educated and domesticated his monster well, it may have become a more pleasant and cooperative monster to the world and thereby could have contributed to a better world.

The idea that monster management is a religious activity, means that one has a new perspective on the role of religion in the debate. For the Committee, religion was not part of the debate. With Douglas, I would state the contrary. Religion is fundamental to the debate, although in the set-up of the Committee this fundament is disguised. 'Kerk en Wereld' tried to put the religious aspects on the agenda of the debate. The Committee did not incorporate these points. Religion became marginalized and went 'underground' in the debate. Regularly uttered terms and phrases as 'unnatural', 'disgusting', or 'playing God' gave expression to that. Besides that, one could claim that religion's questions on purity and our relation and role in the world were translated into more utilitarian terms on risks, health and need and necessity for GM food.

Connected to the problem of 'religion' going underground in the debate, is the problem of the religion of the Committee. The Committee makes the ritualistic style and utilitarian ethics starting points and reference points for the debate. This leaves little room for other opinions, approaches, questions and styles. The study of the religious aspects of the debate can be a valuable source to develop a debate that is more informative and in which all participants and subjects are done justice. Anthropological approaches (like Douglas' and Smits') can help us to rediscover the relations between monsters/technology and religion and besides that give insight in the dynamics of debates. This can help us to track down our (presupposed) ideas, values and practises about specific monsters. It might also inspire us to new ways and lead us to useful traditions in this world full of unclassified monsters.

Note

1   Alternatieve Konsumentenbond, Both Ends, Platform Biologica, Dierenbescherming, Greenpeace, Hivos, ICCO, Inzet, Kerken in actie, Milieudefensie, Natuur en Milieu, Nederlands Platform Gentechnologie, Novib, Proefdiervrij, XminY.

References

Bijker, W.E. 1995. *Democratisering van de technologische cultuur*. Maastricht: Rijksuniversiteit Limburg.

Boersema, J.J. 2001. *The Torah and the Stoics on Humankind and Nature: A Contribution to the Debate on Sustainability and Quality*. Leiden: Brill.

Brinkhorst, L.-J. 2001. *Het publieke debat biotechnologie en voedsel*. The Hague: Ministry of Agriculture

Douglas, M. 2002. *Purity and Danger: An Analysis of the Concepts of Pollution and Taboo*. London: Routledge.

Durkheim, E. 1995. *The Elementary Forms of Religious Life*. Oxford: Oxford University Press.

Greenpeace, Alternatieve Konsumentenbond, et al. 2001. *Maatschappelijke organisaties zeggen vertrouwen in commissie Terlouw op*. Press release. Amsterdam: Greenpeace.

Ministry of VROM (Housing, planning and environment). 2000. *Integrale nota biotechnologie: veiligheid waarborgen bij kansen biotechnologie*. The Hague.

Reis, R. 1996. Inleiding. *Focaal: tijdschrift voor antropologie* 28, 7-16.

Smits, M.W. 2002. *Monsterbezwering: De culturele domesticatie van nieuwe technologie*. Amsterdam: Boom.

Swierstra, T. and K. van der Bruggen, et al. 2000. *Kloneren in de polder: het maatschappelijk debat over kloneren in Nederland februari 1997 – oktober 1999*. The Hague: Rathenau Institute.

Terlouw, J.C. 2002. *Eten & genen: een publiek debat over biotechnologie & voedsel: verslag van de tijdelijke commissie biotechnologie en voedsel*. The Hague: Temporary committee on biotechnology and food.

10 Substantial Life Extension and Meanings of Life

Peter Derkx

Introduction

Substantial extension of the human lifespan has become a subject of lively debate. One reason for this is the completion of the Human Genome Project in 2001 and the experimental avenues for biogerontological research the project enables. Another is recent theoretical progress in biogerontology (Austad 1997; Hayflick 1994; Holliday 1995; Kirkwood 1999; Ricklefs & Finch 1995). The character of modern culture is at least as important a factor in explaining why life extension intervention is currently debated. Three existential factors that play a role here are fear of death (fear of no longer existing), fear of the suffering involved in the process of dying, and the sometimes obsessive desire to preserve good health in order to pursue personal life projects and goals (Turner 2004). The historical background of this motivational pattern is 'the decline since the Renaissance of faith in supernatural salvation from death; concern with the worth of individual identity and experience shifted from an otherworldly realm to the "here and now", with intensification of earthly expectations' (G.J. Gruman quoted in Post 2004a, 82, see also Baumeister 1991, 77-115).

There is a lot of interest in substantial life extension, but would it really be a good thing? Experience with other revolutionary technologies shows us that once they exist, they can no longer be stopped. Too much has been invested in them: once research has produced an effective technology catering to all-too-human desires, there is seldom a way back. So we had better investigate the worldview aspects of considerable human lifespan extension now, before this extension has become genuinely practicable, or, before large sums of money have been spent on it.

In this article I will first consider what 'substantial life extension' and a 'meaningful life' means. After that I will deal with some arguments and considerations concerning the relationship between the two.

Substantial Extension of Human Lifespan: What Are We Talking About?

Before embarking on a discussion about the meaning of 'substantial extension of human lifespan', it has to be clear what we mean by it. We can distinguish between four possible outcomes of a biotechnological enhancement of the human lifespan. Drawing on work by Harry Moody (1995) and Eric Juengst and others (Juengst et al. 2003) we can name these extended morbidity, compressed morbidity, decelerated senescence, and arrested senescence.

Extended morbidity means that the average human life becomes longer because the period of (co)morbidity at the end is lengthened. Through good hygiene, nutrition, education, housing, medical care, welfare arrangements, and social services, old people with one or more chronic diseases stay alive longer. This means that average life expectancy increases, but this need not be an increase in human flourishing or a cause for joy. Extended or prolonged morbidity does not imply an increase in maximum human life expectancy. A typical time structure for a human life with extended morbidity could be: growing up from 0 to 20, adult health span 20 to 55, period of growing morbidity up to 95 as the average age at death and with an unchanged maximum of around 120. Some scientists (Baltes 2003) fear extended morbidity as the most likely scenario, with Alzheimer's disease as one of the main threats. Since nobody wishes it to become reality, we shall not discuss the desirability of this type of life extension here.

Compressed morbidity is a scenario in which the onset of serious age-associated maladies, the infirmities at the end of life, is delayed as long as possible and thus these are compressed into a shorter period. The maximum human lifespan of around 120 is accepted as fixed. The focus of compressed morbidity is that the average human health-span is extended to a much longer period from 20 up to 'the ideal average lifespan, approximately 85 years' (Fries 1980, 130), followed by a relatively short period of decline before death, a period of one or two years at the most. The feasibility of compression of morbidity for the life stage between 55 and 85 was first argued for by James Fries in 1980 and it has been embraced by many, for example the biogerontologist Robert Arking (Arking 2004).

Not long ago three officials of the World Health Organization wrote that Fries's tenets and vision 'now lie at the heart of today's approach to NCDs [non-communicable diseases], ageing and health with its focus on the life course, health promotion, and "active ageing" [use it or lose it]' (Kalache, Aboderin & Hoskins 2002). Because its original assumption is that the maximum human lifespan is biologically predetermined at around 120 and that death at an average age of 85 is 'natural' and even 'ideal', compression of morbidity is not a form of substantial life extension. It has to be noted, however, that several gerontologists think that compression of morbidity is actually impossible. They think it is highly unlikely that we will be able to increase the health-span without simultaneously increasing the lifespan and the period of morbidity at the end (Neugarten 1996). Compression of morbidity would then be practically the same as delayed or decelerated senescence.

In *decelerated senescence* the processes of biological ageing are slowed down, resulting in a higher average life expectancy and probably a higher maximum life expectancy. Decelerated senescence means that the period of good health in a human life is extended (as in the scenario of compressed morbidity), but the period of morbidity remains the same or is lengthened as well (as in extended morbidity). The average pattern of a human life in this case could be: growing up 0-20, adult health-span 20-90, and period of decline after that with death at an age of about 110. Maximum life expectancy at birth might be 140 years. Richard Miller is a respected biogerontologist who thinks that such a decelerated senescence is the most likely development. 'Nature can slow down aging, and so, it turns out, can we. There are so far two approaches that work for sure: diminished total caloric intake and changes in genes that regulate the rate of early-life growth' (Miller 2004, 233). A recent and clear manifestation of the idea of decelerated senescence can be found in an article by Jay Olshansky and others, including Miller. They can be regarded as representatives of a growing chorus of scientists calling themselves 'moderate', 'modest', and 'realistic'. They firmly believe that a current investment of 3 billion US dollars annually will make it possible to decelerate ageing and to delay the onset of ageing-related diseases and disorders among the baby boom cohorts by seven years.

> People who reach the age of 50 in the future would have the health profile and disease risk of today's 43-year old; those aged 60 would resemble current 53-year-olds, and so on. Equally important, once achieved, this seven-year delay would yield equal health and longevity benefits for

all subsequent generations, much the same way children born in most nations today benefit from the discovery and development of immunizations (Olshansky et al. 2006, 32).

Arrested senescence refers to relatively complete control of the biological processes of senescence. In this scenario, ageing in the sense of senescence or physical and mental deterioration does not occur anymore, or the human organism is cared for very well (maintenance) and the senescence that occurs is periodically repaired by a rejuvenation cure. For decades, or centuries, the chance (probability) of dying does not increase with age anymore, but stays rather constant. People still die, but they no longer die from the slow accumulation of damage and chronic deterioration. Instead they die from accidents, murder, or war. In this scenario people can become very old. Average life expectancies of 150, 500 or even 5000 years are thought to be possible. Talking about engineering arrested senescence may sound as if we have entered the field of quackery, pseudo-science, or science fiction. However, one of the strongest defenders of the scientific credibility of Strategies for Engineering Negligible Senescence (SENS), Aubrey de Grey (De Grey 2003; 2005; De Grey et al. 2002), forcefully argues that humanity needs to set aside massive sums of money for a War on Aging. He has also, together with relevant specialists, outlined and embarked on detailing a set of biotechnological measures we could use to beat the 'seven deadly things' that accumulate with age as side effects of metabolism. According to De Grey these seven problems together constitute the core of aging. The seven categories of damage to be solved are: 1. cell death without matching replacement (especially important in the heart and the brain); 2. unwanted cells, e.g. visceral fat and senescent cells (important in arthritis and diabetes); 3. nuclear (epi)mutations causing cancer; 4. mitochondrial mutations; 5. extracellular protein/protein cross-links (e.g. leading to high blood pressure); 6. extracellular aggregates (e.g. resulting in amyloid involved in Alzheimer's disease); and 7. intracellular aggregates (e.g. resulting in hardening of the arteries). De Grey proposes to remove and repair the damage that has accumulated every ten years or so. He does not believe in prevention of damage. His type of arrested senescence is rejuvenation. He expects that in the period between 2025 and 2040 we will be able to fix the seven problems of senescence (to a large extent through genetic interventions and stem cell therapies) and that around 2050 'robust human rejuvenation' will be generally accessible. He realizes that the first fixes will not be perfect, but they will give us time to develop better repair methods. Highly respected biogerontologists have attacked De Grey's ideas forcefully (Estep et al. 2006; Warner et al. 2005). It is important to note, however, that the difference of opinion is mainly political, ethical, and related to funding and estimates about the speed of future developments, not about the possibility of substantial life extension in itself. A last remark to conclude this preliminary section: the [US] President's Council on Bioethics has taken 'the possibility of extended youth and substantially prolonged lives' very seriously. In its 2003 report *Beyond Therapy* (President's Council on Bioethics 2003, 159-204) the Council warns against substantial life extension as a threat to the meaning of human lives.

Meanings of Life: A Theory

Before going into arguments on life extension and meanings of life we also have to explicate the concept of meanings of life. A useful point of departure is social psychologist Roy Baumeister's book *Meanings of Life* (Baumeister 1991) in which he develops a theory which gives us some grip on the elusive concept of a meaningful life. According to Baumeister, meaning is about connection. People have a need to put things, actions, and projects in a broader context and this need can be subdivided into a number of needs for meaning. An important one is the need for *purpose*. The vital thing here is to interpret one's current activities in relation to future or possible goals or fulfillments. A second need for meaning is the need for *moral worth*. People want their life to be of positive value and their choices to be right and good and morally justifiable. A third need is for *efficacy*, competence or control. People do not only want to have purpose in a life of moral value, they also want a certain capability or power to achieve these goals and realize these values. They want to feel free and competent and able to make a difference. They do not want life to happen to them, they want to direct it at least to some extent, and often people prefer the illusion of control over a more realistic sense of powerlessness. The last need for meaning mentioned by Baumeister is the need for self-respect, self-esteem, or *self-worth*. Humans not only want a life of positive moral value, they also want to have worth themselves. They want to find some basis for positive self-worth, they want to have some claim on respect, both self-respect and the respect of others. Usually this need takes the form of finding an aspect in which one is better than others, a reason to be respected by others. But this reason need not always be moral. Although self-worth is often related to a combination of moral worth and efficacy, it is not the same as this combination. Someone who has left his or her partner, may feel greater self-worth because of this tough decision (it feels better than being rejected and abandoned by the other), but he or she may feel guilty at the same time, in doubt about the moral value of the act.

Baumeister's theory has been improved by others. Jan Hein Mooren (1998) has argued that a meaningful human life is a life that is sufficiently understood as part of a world with a certain structure and causality. People have a need for *comprehension*. They want to be able to understand and explain the world they live in, what happens to them and why they act as they do. They want to be able to create a coherent life narrative, to tell an intelligible story about their life. They want their new experiences to fit their past and to conform to what they know about their environment, their world. Through 'interpretive control' the need for comprehension can be linked to the need for efficacy. Adri Smaling (unpublished) adds a last need for meaning; the need for *(comm)unity*, which to some extent can be seen as the flip side of the need for efficacy. People not only have a need for controlling things, but also a need for release, for abandonment, they want to let go. They do not want everything to depend on themselves, but they also want to be part of something bigger, to feel connected and as one with others or the other. Altruism is related to the need for moral worth and the need for (comm)unity.

Baumeister has argued that it is very implausible to think of *the* meaning of life as one single overarching good thing everything in life connects with, completely and eternally. This is what he calls the myth of higher meaning. Life is bound to have several meanings and to have trivial, meaningless, and unruly fragments as well. Moreover, it often happens that meanings of life conflict with each other (Berlin 1991). Life is inescapably characterized by absurdity, conflict, and change. However, human beings keep searching for meaning, which is often woven together into *a connecting narrative, a story to live by* (Dresden 1990; McAdams 1997). Living your story turns out to be important, even though your life story is not your whole life and even though your story has more than one important plot. Meaning is one of life's principal tools for stability, continuity, and identity.

This theory of a meaningful life is partly based on findings of empirical psychology, but it is obvious that a fully fledged theory needs historical, sociological and ethical input. Baumeister's conviction that in modern Western society the self has become the major base of values (not needing further justification itself) shows this clearly. Baumeister thinks that seeking, knowing, or finding yourself (personal identity), creating your-self (self-actualization), and self-worth have become more important than religion, morality and tradition. He also indicates (1991, 127) that in mod-ern society it is more difficult to satisfy the needs for moral worth and purpose than those for efficacy and self-worth. In this context, Charles Taylor's *Sources of the Self* (1992), Anthony Giddens's *Modernity and Self-Identity* (Giddens 1991), and Joep Dohmen's *Het leven als kunstwerk* (*Life As a Work of Art*) (2008) raise important philosophical issues about au-tonomy, authenticity, life politics, the art of living, hypergoods, and tran-scendence. Moreover, a meaningful life is not equally within everybody's reach, and some social circumstances are more favourable for achieving it than others. '[I]n many societies that we call advanced, such as the United States, whole segments of the population grow up with so much chaos and so little order that "planning" is a foreign word' (Hagestad 1996, 208). Given all these issues, it is clear that the theory of meanings of life is still in its infancy, and that much more empirical, theoretical, and philosophi-cal research needs to be done.

An important issue is how a meaningful life relates to the quality of life, to happiness, life satisfaction, or *subjective well-being* (Diener 1984; George 2000; 2006; Pavot & Diener 2004; Ryff 1989; Ryff & Singer 1998; Veenhoven 1996), and to the more objective concept of *human dignity* as proposed in human rights theories or human capabilities theories (Buiten-weg 2007; Nussbaum 2001; 2006; Nussbaum & Sen 1993; Pogge 2002). In this context, Baumeister's analysis of the parenthood paradox, described in the following paragraph, is relevant (1991, 160-166).

A large amount of evidence supports the conclusion that having chil-dren produces worries and reduces happiness, but in spite of this many people want children. The difference between a happy or satisfactory and a meaningful life may largely explain the parenthood paradox. However, much here depends on the meaning given to the concepts 'happy' and 'meaningful'. Baumeister's parenthood paradox seems to presuppose a he-donic interpretation of happiness, life satisfaction, and subjective well-being, as argued for by Ed Diener (1984) and Ruut Veenhoven (1996). Life satisfaction, positive affect, and absence of negative affect are central here. If, following Carol Ryff (1989), subjective well-being is interpreted eudai-monically, emphasizing purpose in life and thus 'clearly imposing a defini-tion of life quality on individuals who may or may not evaluate their own lives on those criteria' (George 2000, 7), the difference between 'well-be-ing' and 'meaningfulness' becomes smaller. Ryff's eudaimonic subjective well-being originally had six dimensions: self-acceptance, purpose in life, personal growth, positive relations with others, environmental mastery, and autonomy. After some more empirical work she reduced the relevant dimensions to four, of which the first two are primary: purpose in life and quality connections to others, and the other two are secondary: positive self-regard and mastery (Ryff & Singer 1998).

To my knowledge little theoretical and empirical research has been done to improve Baumeister's theory of 'meanings of life'. The alternative theory of 'eudaimonic subjective well-being' has turned out to be much more fruitful, up to now. Starting from this theory a considerable amount of research has been and will be published (see www.midus.wisc.edu). However, as indicated above, Ryff's concept of subjective well-being shows much overlap with Baumeister's and our theory of a meaningful life. The most important remaining difference appears to be our emphasis on the need for moral worth. And because in my considered opinion morality and ethics posit objective or at least intersubjective norms for relations with others, moral worth makes a meaningful life – in the same way as human dignity – a more than purely subjective concept. To achieve progress in the theory of meanings of life interdisciplinary research, which combines psychology, philosophy (especially ethics), and other academic disciplines such as sociology, history, cultural anthropology, and evolutionary biology, is necessary.

In the remainder of this article I will indicate a few important considerations around the meanings of life that regard effective substantial extension of the human lifespan; a detailed examination of all of these considerations is not my purpose here, nor is it even possible. By substantial extension I mean decelerated senescence and arrested senescence as outlined earlier on in this chapter. Decelerated senescence is much more probable as the scenario for decades to come, but arrested aging certainly is an interesting scenario. It cannot be completely ruled out for the long run and it is interesting because it forces us to think in new ways about what we think most important in our lives and societies. This is important even if arrested aging will never happen.

Life Extension and Sense of Purpose

A very 'natural' argument in favour of substantial life-extension is that in a very long life we will be able to complete important projects we have planned and embarked upon (Hagestad 1996). For example, at conferences I have met quite a few biogerontologists and philosophers who argued that it is unfortunate that when we finally start to understand the topic we study, our cognitive abilities begin to dwindle and our death comes near. However, a sense of purpose does not depend on finishing our projects. When we complete a project or see a long-standing desire fulfilled, this will bring a sense of satisfaction and sometimes efficacy, but to experience a sense of purpose in life it is necessary that we keep striving for something in the future, for something that is unachieved but imagined to be possible. As every scientist and scholar knows, achieving better knowledge of a subject is possible, but it always opens up new questions we had not yet thought of before. Complete knowledge always has the character of a receding target. This means that a much longer life will make it possible to finish larger projects, to plan longer careers, to not only see our children and grandchildren grow up but also our great grandchildren. Essentially, however, the situation will not change as far as sense of purpose is concerned.

Authors criticizing substantial life extension often point to loss of meaning. Thus, Hans Jonas wrote: 'Perhaps a non-negotiable limit to our expected time is necessary for each of us as the incentive to number our days and make them count' (Jonas 1985, 19). The objection to life extension seems to be that, when we have a lot of time to reach our goals, reaching these goals becomes meaningless, because we have known all along that we would reach them, this year or another. Yet much can be said in response to this. What does 'making our days count' exactly mean? Horrobin (2005, 14) points out that it is an odd argument to assert that people enjoy playing football today and experience no ennui in doing so only because they are aware that they cannot do it three centuries hence. Perhaps the most fundamental criticism of Jonas's argument is expressed by Christine Overall (2004). She states that we should not argue against increasing human longevity by reference to the limited parameters set by current life expectancies. According to her, this is the fallacy of begging the question. When the context changes and life expectancies become much longer, our judgment of life's possibilities and meanings will also change. Not only will childhood and age be redefined, but concepts like schooling, education, marriage, partnership, friendship, sexuality, gender, father, mother, parent, grandparent, family, career, retirement, nationality, and citizenship will also take on other meanings. Together these changes will constitute new moral systems, purposes, and contexts for meaning. But I think Overall exaggerates. The way we think about human fulfillment now, of course, is relevant to our well-considered present-day judgments on prolongation of life. I would agree with her, however, if she argued that we ought not to evaluate substantial life extension *only* by reference to the kind of life that we know now. Certainly, a comprehensive evaluation of future possibilities requires not just norms, values, facts and extrapolations, but also imagination.

It is a fact, of course, that lives with less than the average life expectancy can be experienced as meaningful. But even if life extension would not increase the possibility to lead a meaningful life, it might result in new (better?) ways of having a meaningful life, as has happened in the past:

> [T]he increase in life expectancy [since 1900] means that individuals now have a greater chance of growing old. In a sense, the course of people's lives has become more predictable. People expect to reach a respectable age and they live their lives accordingly. The growing certainties in life have been accompanied by a shift in norms and values. In the early twentieth century, people had a more fatalistic approach to life: things simply happened, and changes in life unavoidably befell people (...) This fatalistic approach to life has been replaced by a more proactive attitude, or 'choice biography', the notion that people can shape their own lives (Dykstra 2002, 10; see also Hagestad 1996, 208).

Another round of substantial life extension might cause people to take on an even stronger managerial attitude towards life. However, that human lives can be planned towards chosen purposes in the future will remain a matter of degree. Human vulnerability remains. A society with more (expensive) health care technology for its members creates the conditions for more instead of fewer insurance policies and other risk-averting strategies. New risks (among them corporate and state uncertainties transferred to individual citizens, see Dannefer 2000, 270) and the old risks that remain, might even become more oppressive and threatening because there is more to lose. That is why Aubrey de Grey does not want to lecture in dangerous countries and why he thinks that the prevention of traffic accidents will be given absolute priority in societies with greatly extended life expectancies.

Life Extension and Efficacy

Research shows that having a fair amount of control over life's circumstances and having a relatively high degree of self-esteem are factors in determining a more than average life expectancy (Marmot 2005). So having (a sense of) control is good for longevity. But do control, life extension and a much longer life contribute to a more meaningful life? The desire for control can go so far as to be self-defeating and counterproductive. Furthering longevity might involve such hard and manifold efforts that life becomes meaningless rather than meaningful. A body repair every ten years, as envisaged by De Grey, is not too big a price to pay for a long and healthy life, but when a substantially extended lifespan and health-span demands constant attention every day, the gain in years might be offset by a loss in quality of life. Medicalization could turn out to be a serious problem connected with life extension (Porter 1999; Verweij 1999). A good balance would have to be sought, as otherwise the controlling efforts needed for a longer life might start to make human life meaningless (and lives experienced as meaningless might tend to become shorter again).

Life Extension and Moral Worth: Distributive Justice

An important aspect of a meaningful life is that it can be justified morally, and one of the most important moral problems concerning the engineering of substantial life extension relates to justice. Justice is about the distribution of (the lack of) things we value. At the beginning of this article I distinguished between different kinds of life extension, but I left out one very important factor: the 'social gradient' of longevity. Life expectancies differ according to social status. Michael Marmot's recent summary starts with an illustration from the United States capital:

> If you take the Metro from the southeast of downtown Washington to Montgomery County, Maryland, in the suburbs – a distance of about 14 miles – for each mile traveled life expectancy rises about a year and a half. This is the most life-enhancing journey in the world. There's a twenty-year gap between poor blacks at one end of the journey (male life expectancy fifty-seven), and rich whites at the other (Marmot 2005).

Such inequalities in life expectancy at birth exist all over the world (Mackenbach & Bakker 2003; Marmot 2004). How do we understand these inequalities? Marmot's analysis comes down to this. An important determinant of an individual life's longevity is (1) a favourable genetic endowment and early life history, but, though important, this is only a small part of the story. Other important elements are: (2) living in a country above the absolute poverty level – a GDP of about USD $5,000 – above this, level differences in GDP between countries do not matter very much; (3) high relative social position (as regards status, employment grade, relative wealth and extent of social participation); and (4) high relative freedom, autonomy, or control over life's circumstances – in many Western countries this still means for men especially at work, for women at home. The third and fourth factors are connected with the fact that a more equal distribution of household income in a country seems to be related to a higher average life expectancy. The second factor indicates a similar thing, but then with reference to a threshold kind of equality between countries. In some countries infant and child mortality is still terribly high, while the means to do something about it have been known to humanity for a long time, which shows that we live in a world full of injustice. What counts as injustice depends on the theory of justice that is used. However, whether one refers to human rights (Buitenweg 2007), Rawls's theory of justice as fairness (Rawls 1999a; 1999b), Dworkin's equality of welfare and resources (Dworkin 2000), or Nussbaum's capabilities theory (Nussbaum 2001; 2006), differences in average life expectancy at birth of forty years between countries (Japan and Zimbabwe) and more than twenty years for socio-economic groups within countries – differences which can be removed and prevented by collective social action – are hard to defend as morally acceptable. Now imagine what would happen if in such a world substantial life extension became possible through initially very expensive biotechnology such as longevity pharmaceuticals or gene therapy. The demand, backed by purchasing power, certainly in the beginning, would mainly come from young adults, the better educated, wealthier and higher-income individuals and those with higher initial endowments of health. Socioeconomic and health inequalities would be amplified. A small group of people with an already high life expectancy would have access to lifespan and health-span extension, but many less-privileged people would not. Surely this is ethically undesirable, is it not? 'The need-based claims of the worse off to have reasonably long lives have more moral weight than the preference-based claims of the better off to have longer lives' (Glannon 2001, 167, see also McConnell & Turner 2005, 61 and Mauron 2005).

The existence of social injustice can never be a valid reason for morally objecting to any improvement in the fate of human beings who do not belong to the most underprivileged ones. 'If we were to insist that technological developments of all sorts wait until the world becomes perfectly just, there would be absolutely no scientific progress' (Post 2004b, 537, see also Harris 2003 and Davis 2004). This is true, but I think one should not stop there. Demanding equality and perfect justice within and between countries as a prerequisite to the development of life-extension technology is asking too much. Here, as often, 'perfection' would be the enemy of the good. The remedy for injustice is not denial of benefits to some with no corresponding gain to others, but redistribution (Dworkin 2000, 440). Not being able to do everything, or enough, should be no excuse for doing nothing. Efforts like the UN Millennium Development Goals are very important. It is important before 2015 to try to reduce the proportion of people living on less than a dollar a day by half, to reduce the mortality rate among children under five by two-thirds, to try to reduce the maternal mortality ratio by three-quarters and to halt and begin to reverse the spread of HIV/AIDS and the incidence of malaria and other major diseases (Garrett 2007, 32). These are challenging goals, but they are technically feasible and mainly depend on political will. In the same vein, ambitious but feasible goals could be formulated to do something about the shocking disparities in longevity between and also within countries. Christine Overall proposes a qualified prolongevitism (expanding the 'natural' maximal lifespan) within countries, one that will genuinely be for all, a kind of affirmative action in the field of life extension. She writes that increased research into conditions and diseases that affect groups of people with low life expectancy, like people of colour and poor people, is morally indicated (Overall 2003, 200). However, note that for longer life expectancies of less-privileged people more equality of income is more important than new achievements in high-tech biomedicine. As highlighted by Marmot, only three of the thirty-nine recommendations in the Acheson Report to the British government – *Inequalities in Health: Report of an Independent Inquiry* (1998) – are related to health care. 'The others covered the tax and benefit system; education; employment; housing and environment; mobility, transportation, and pollution; and nutrition' (Marmot 2004, 251). Reducing health inequalities might both be the ethically indicated and the most effective way to substantially extend the (remaining) life expectancies of many people; it will be more effective than biotechnological approaches aimed at decelerating or arresting senescence of human beings as a species. Many healthy human years can be gained by this heavily neglected form of life extension: *more equal longevity*.

One should realize, however, that priorities do not have to be absolute and generally allow for compromise. Serious and strenuous attempts to tackle the national and global social gradient of longevity certainly do not require that biogerontological research into the diseases of the oldest old and into the general underlying processes of senescence is stopped completely. As far as international injustice is concerned, one should not forget that the numbers of the old and oldest old in developing countries will also increase rapidly. Already the remaining life expectancy of a woman who has managed to reach the age of sixty in Brazil (21 more years), India (18 years) and Nigeria (17 years) is not so different from the number of years an average sixty-year-old female inhabitant of the United States can expect to add to her life (24 years). The WHO anticipates that the per centage of people over sixty living in developing countries between now and 2050 will rise from 60 to 85 per cent of the total global number (Kalache, Barreto & Keller 2005, 36, see also Aboderin 2006 and Kirkwood 1999, 8). In China and India the elderly will outnumber the total current population of the US by mid-century (Olshansky et al. 2006, 31). It is possible that understanding the fundamental processes of biological ageing is the most effective way of fighting age-related diseases such as Alzheimer's (Post 2004b). Because of this, because we do not really know how to make the distinction between biological processes of 'normal' ageing and age-associated diseases, and because this distinction continues to change, it would be short-sighted to stop fundamental biogerontological research (Derkx 2006; Izaks & Westendorp 2003; Juengst 2004).

This whole section about justice relates to the sense of moral worth, an important component of a life which is experienced as meaningful. All things considered it should be very difficult for human beings to enjoy a substantially extended and at the same time meaningful life without contributing anything to the fight against ethically unacceptable longevity inequalities in the world.

Life Extension, Subjective Well-Being, and Meanings of Life

I have already made some remarks about the relation between life-extension and sense of purpose, but more has to be said. A longitudinal survey done in the US showed that people over 64 reported significantly lower levels of life purpose than younger adults. In addition, physical and emotional health were perceived as decreasing with age, and people over 74, especially women, rated themselves substantially lower on sense of control than younger age groups. At the same time, however, women over 54 and men over 64 rated their relationships with others more positively than younger adults did, and overall life satisfaction of men and women over 54 was more positive than that of younger people (Ryff 2006). Despite a decline in many areas, overall subjective well-being is as good, if not better, for older people as for their younger counterparts. This has been regarded as strange, but socio-emotional selectivity theory shows that there need not be a contradiction here:

> The theory maintains that two broad categories of goals shift in importance as a function of perceived time: those concerning the acquisition of knowledge and those concerning the regulation of feeling states. When time is perceived as open-ended, as it typically is in youth, people are strongly motivated to pursue information. ... In the face of a long and nebulous future, even information that is not immediately relevant may become so somewhere down the line. In contrast, when time is perceived as constrained, as it typically is in later life, people are motivated to pursue emotional satisfaction. They are more likely to invest in sure things, deepen existing relationships, and savor life (Carstensen 2007, 45).

Not so much a preoccupation with the past but with the present may be a sign that a person's life is felt to be coming to an end (see Hagestad 1996, 207). The decisive factor in socio-emotional selectivity theory is not chronological age but perceived remaining life expectancy. When conditions create a sense of the fragility of life, for example after the September 11 attacks in the US, or during the SARS epidemic in Hong Kong, younger as well as older people prefer to pursue emotionally meaningful experiences and goals in the short term (Fung & Carstensen 2006). So, what does this mean for substantial life extension? It is plausible that with a substantially higher life expectancy people will keep making plans and for a longer time will have a sense of purpose in life, but they will also pay the price of having to wait longer before they reach the state of more positive relations with others and higher overall satisfaction with life. When the expectations of the longevity of life increase, people will be more inclined to keep gathering information that might be useful some time in the future and to postpone gratification of emotional needs. However, it is not immediately clear what is the better situation. Is it more important to have a meaningful life or a happy life? Will later life be more emotionally gratifying if one has had a longer period of (successful?) striving for goals and fulfillments? Will 'old age' be happier if one has had a longer 'youth'? Will it be possible to live longer and at the same time to learn to be 'older and wiser' at a relatively early stage? Part of the answers will depend on the socially expected life course. 'The life course has become a principal cultural connection between individual lives and the larger society through an image not only of the good life, but of the timetable according to which it should be achieved' (J. Keith and others quoted in Hagestad 1996, 209).

A Final Issue: Is Life Extension Unnatural?

Important authors on life extension such as Hans Jonas (1992), Leon Kass (2004), Francis Fukuyama (2002), Daniel Callahan (1995), and Bill McKibben (2003) have exhorted us

> to live more or less according to nature, and warn that our efforts to depart from what we are will result in new evils that are more perilous than old ones. (...) Our focus (...) should be on the acceptance of aging rather than on its scientific modification. The intergenerational thrust of evolution, by which we are inclined toward parental and social investment in the hope, energy, and vitality of youth, provides the basis for a natural law ethic that requires us all to relinquish youthfulness (Post 2004b, 536-537).

It is very easy to dismiss these 'natural law positions' as an untenable deontological stance by pointing out that if substantial life-extension starts to occur in nature it begins to be 'natural', or by emphasizing that humans have always changed nature (including their own natural features) in the course of civilization. More or less the same goes for the religious versions of these arguments, referring to a God who has established the natural law. That humans should respect the will of God or that they should not attempt to play God, runs into similar intellectual difficulties as the exhortation to respect nature, and into additional difficulties as well. Referring to the will of God is not a very strong argument in a pluralistic democratic society that includes atheists and agnostics.

However, it is possible to discover something important behind these arguments from nature or God, even if one rejects the absolute deontological positions and is more inclined towards consequentialist ethics. Human nature is not blank, nor completely and always easily malleable. It is the result of millions of years of natural selection. Human beings are the result of evolution and as such they are very complex organisms with many trade-offs involved, referring back to environments of the past. We cannot design humans from scratch. Stressing that we ought to be wary of bad unintended consequences is not the same as claiming that nothing should be changed. It is possible for a society to opt for a less-than-one-child-per-family policy to counteract undesirable effects of population-growth due to increasing old age survival, but will its individual citizens accept this policy and live up to it? Human nature is very flexible, but it is possible to ask too much of human beings. It seems relevant, for example, to consider the emotional implications of a population scenario with 9 billion people in 2300 with an average life expectancy at birth of about 100 years, few children and a high proportion of very old people (Basu 2004, 93). And we should not only be talking about what is possible for human beings, individually and as a group. We should also consider what is good for them and what makes their lives meaningful. To ask what desires and emotions are humanly 'natural' can be translated into a question about what desires and emotions are good and proper for human beings to have and deserve the opportunity to be acted upon.

More discussion about meanings of life is needed. But in individualistic secular societies people have many different ideas about what constitutes a meaningful life, so it will be difficult to reach consensus or even understanding about the value of life extension. Part of the difficulty is that in modern Western societies it is rather generally accepted that meanings of life are a private matter, not something about which to engage in public debate.

The variety of ideas about meanings of life will be very difficult to handle in a democracy, because the differences can be wide and not a matter of degree. 'Transhumanists' like Ray Kurzweil (Kurzweil & Grossmann 2004), Nick Bostrom (2003; 2005), Gregory Stock (2002), and Aubrey de Grey (De Grey & Rae 2007) feel that we should not accept biological ageing as inevitable. They argue that the fundamental biology of human beings should be changed in order to get rid of death caused by senescence. Other thinkers, not only of the natural-law variety, see this as a dangerous illusion, holding that the propagation and cultivation of ideas like this are very detrimental to the meanings of human lives. This difference in worldview is a crucial aspect of the debate on substantial extension of human life expectancy. Much of what is involved is expressed in these words of Michael Lerner:

> [We] need to do the spiritual work as we grow older to accept the inevitability of death rather than acting as though aging and death could be avoided if only we had a better technology. The enormous emotional, spiritual, and financial cost of trying to hang on to life as long as pos-

sible (and to look as though we were not aging) is fostered by a market-place that tries to sell us endless youth. It is also fostered by our cultural failure to honor our elders, provide them with real opportunities to share their wisdom, and combat the pervasive ageism with its willing-ness to discard people long before their creative juices have dried up, to stigmatize the sexuality of the elderly (...), and to provide little in the way of adequately funded and beautifully conceived long-term care facilities (Lerner 2006, 308-309).

Acknowledgements

Supported by grant 050-32-570 from the NWO (Netherlands Organisation for Scientific Research). I would also like to thank Jan Baars (University for Humanistics, Utrecht), Dale Dannefer and Robert Binstock (Case Western Reserve University, Cleveland), Dick Knook and Diana van Heemst (Leiden University Medical Center) and my colleagues in the research project 'Towards a *lingua democratica* for the public debate on genomics', especially Cor van der Weele and Harry Kunneman, for some helpful remarks in discussions about the topic of this chapter.

References

Aboderin, I. 2006. Ageing in Africa. *Wellcome Focus 2006. Ageing: Can We Stop the Clock?* 1 September 2006. Retrieved 24 January 2007, from http://www.wellcome.ac.uk/doc_WTX033903.html

Arking, R. 2004. Extending Human Longevity: A Biological Probability. In *The Fountain of Youth: Cultural, Scientific, and Ethical Perspectives on a Biomedical Goal,* eds. S.G. Post and R.H. Binstock. Oxford: Oxford University Press, 177-200.

Austad, S.N. 1997. *Why We Age: What Science Is Discovering about the Body's Journey through Life.* New York: John Wiley.

Baltes, P.B. 2003. Extending Longevity: Dignity Gain – or Dignity Drain? *MaxPlanckResearch 2003,* 14-19.

Basu, A.M. 2004. Towards an Understanding of the Emotions in the Population of 2300. In *World Population to 2030,* edited by United Nations – Department of Economic and Social Affairs – Population Division. New York: United Nations, 89-98.

Baumeister, R.F. 1991. *Meanings of Life.* New York: Guilford Press.

Berlin, I. 1991. The Pursuit of the Ideal. In *The Crooked Timber of Humanity: Chapters in the History of Ideas*. London: HarperCollins, Fontana-Press, 1-19.

Bostrom, N. 2003. Human Genetic Enhancements: A Transhumanist Perspective. *Journal of Value Inquiry 37* (4), 493-506.

— 2005. Recent Developments in the Ethics, Science, and Politics of Life-Extension. *Aging Horizons* (Sept/Oct).

Buitenweg, R. 2007. *Human Rights, Human Plights in a Global Village*. Atlanta, Georgia: Clarity Press.

Callahan, D. 1995. *Setting Limits: Medical Goals in an Aging Society* (Expanded ed.). Washington, D.C.: Georgetown University Press.

Carstensen, L.L. 2007. Growing Old or Living Long: Take Your Pick. *Issues in Science and Technology* (Winter), 41-50.

Dannefer, D. 2000. Bringing Risk Back In: The Regulation of the Self in the Postmodern State. In *The Evolution of The Aging Self: The Societal Impact on the Aging Process*, eds. K.W. Schaie and J. Hendricks. New York, NY: Springer, 269-280.

Davis, J.K. 2004. Collective Suttee: Is It Unjust to Develop Life Extension If It Will Not Be Possible to Provide It to Everyone? In A. D. N. J. de Grey Ed., *Strategies for Engineered Negligible Senescence: Why Genuine Control of Aging May Be Foreseeable*. New York, N.Y.: New York Academy of Sciences, 535-541.

De Grey, A.D.N.J. 2003. The Foreseeability of Real Anti-Aging Medicine: Focusing the Debate. *Experimental Gerontology, 38* (9, 1 September), 927-934.

— 2005. Foreseeable and More Distant Rejuvenation Therapies. In *Aging Interventions and Therapies*, ed. S.I.S. Rattan. Singapore: World Scientific Publishing, 379-395.

De Grey, A.D.N.J., B.N. Ames, et al. 2002. Time to Talk SENS: Critiquing the Immutability of Human Aging. In *Increasing Healthy Life Span: Conventional Measures and Slowing the Innate Aging Process*, ed. D. Harman New York, N.Y.: New York Academy of Sciences, 452-462.

De Grey, A.D.N.J. and M. Rae. 2007. *Ending Aging: The Rejuvenation Breakthroughs That Could Reverse Human Aging in Our Lifetime*. New York: St. Martin's Press.

Derkx, P. 2006. Ouder worden: te aanvaarden natuurlijk proces of te bestrijden ziekte? *Tijdschrift voor Humanistiek – Journal for Humanistics, 7* (28, december 2006), 82-90.

Diener, E. 1984. Subjective Well-Being. *Psychological Bulletin, 95* (3), 542-575.

Dohmen, J. 2008. *Het leven als kunstwerk*. Rotterdam: Lemniscaat.

Dresden, S. 1990. De biografie als valstrik. *Maatstaf* (9/10), 46-52.

Dworkin, R. 2000. *Sovereign Virtue: The Theory and Practice of Equality*. Cambridge, MA: Harvard University Press.

Dykstra, P.A. 2002. Ageing in the Netherlands in a Macro and Micro Perspective. In *Ageing in Europe: The Social, Demographic and Financial Consequences of Europe's Ageing Population*, ed. R. de Bok. Breda: PlantijnCasparie, 6-17.

Estep, P.W., III and M. Kaeberlein, et al. 2006, July 11. Life Extension Pseudoscience and the SENS Plan. Retrieved 15 August 2006, from www.technologyreview.com/sens.

Fries, J.F. 1980. Aging, Natural Death, and the Compression of Morbidity. *The New England Journal of Medicine 303* (July 17), 130-135.

Fukuyama, F. 2002. *Our Posthuman Future: Consequences of the Biotechnology Revolution*. New York: Farrar, Straus and Giroux.

Fung, H.H. and L.L. Carstensen. 2006. Goals Change When Life's Fragility Is Primed: Lessons Learned from Older Adults, the September 11 Attacks and SARS. *Social Cognition 24* (3), 248-278.

Garrett, L. 2007. The Challenge of Global Health. *Foreign Affairs 86* (1), 14-38.

George, L.K. 2000. Well-Being and Sense of Self: What We Know and What We Need to Know. In *The Evolution of The Aging Self: The Societal Impact on the Aging Process*, eds. K.W. Schaie and J. Hendricks. New York, NY: Springer, 1-35.

— 2006. Perceived Quality of Life. In *Handbook of Aging and the Social Sciences* (6th ed.), eds. R.H. Binstock, L.K. George, S.J. Cutler, J. Hendricks, and J.H. Schulz. Amsterdam: Elsevier, Academic Press, 321-336.

Giddens, A. 1991. *Modernity and Self-Identity: Self and Society in the Late Modern Age*. Stanford: Stanford University Press.

Glannon, W. 2001. *Genes and Future People: Philosophical Issues in Human Genetics*. Boulder, Colorado: Westview Press.

Hagestad, G.O. 1996. On-time, Off-time, Out of Time? Reflections on Continuity and Discontinuity from an Illness Process. In *Adulthood and Aging: Research on Continuities and Discontinuities. A Tribute to Bernice Neugarten*, ed. V.L. Bengtson. New York: Springer, 204-222.

Harris, J. 2003. Intimations of Immortality: The Ethics and Justice of Life Extending Therapies. In *Current Legal Problems 2002*, ed. M.D.A. Freeman. Oxford: Oxford University Press, 65-95.

Hayflick, L. 1994. *How and Why We Age*. New York: Ballantine Books.

Holliday, R. 1995. *Understanding Ageing*. Cambridge: Cambridge University Press.

Horrobin, S. 2005. The Ethics of Aging Intervention and Life-Extension. In *Aging Interventions and Therapies*, ed. S.I.S. Rattan. Singapore: World Scientific Publishing, 1-27.

Izaks, G.J. and R.G.J. Westendorp. 2003. Ill or Just Old? Towards a Conceptual Framework of the Relation between Ageing and Disease. *BMC Geriatrics, 3* (7).

Jonas, H. 1985. *The Imperative of Responsibility: In Search of an Ethics for the Technological Age*. Chicago: University of Chicago Press.

— 1992. The Burden and Blessing of Mortality. *Hastings Center Report, 22*(1), 34-40.

Juengst, E.T. 2004. Can Aging Be Interpreted as a Healthy, Positive Process? In *Successful Aging through the Life Span: Intergenerational Issues in Health*, eds. M.L. Wykle, P.J. Whitehouse, and D.L. Morris. New York: Springer, 3-18.

Juengst, E.T., R.H. Binstock, M. Mehlman, S.G. Post, and P. Whitehouse. 2003. Biogerontology, 'Anti-aging Medicine', and the Challenge of Human Enhancement. *Hastings Center Report, 33* (4, July-August), 21-30.

Kalache, A., I. Aboderin, and I. Hoskins. 2002. Compression of Morbidity and Active Ageing: Key Priorities for Public Health Policy in the 21st Century. *Bulletin of the World Health Organization, 80* (3, March), 243-244.

Kalache, A., S.M. Barreto, I. Keller. 2005. Global Ageing: The Demographic Revolution in All Cultures and Societies. In *The Cambridge Handbook of Age and Ageing*, eds. M.L. Johnson, V.L. Bengtson, P.G. Coleman, and T.B.L. Kirkwood. Cambridge: Cambridge University Press, 30-46.

Kass, L.R. 2004. L' Chaim and Its Limits: Why Not Immortality? In *The Fountain of Youth: Cultural, Scientific, and Ethical Perspectives on a Biomedical Goal*, eds. S.G. Post and R.H. Binstock. Oxford: Oxford University Press, 304-320.

Kirkwood, T. 1999. *Time of Our Lives: The Science of Human Aging*. Oxford: Oxford University Press.

Kurzweil, R. and T. Grossmann. 2004. *Fantastic Voyage: Live Long Enough to Live Forever*. Emmaus, PA: Rodale.

Lerner, M. 2006. *The Left Hand of God: Taking Back Our Country from the Religious Right*. New York: HarperCollins, HarperSanFrancisco.

Mackenbach, J.P. and M.J. Bakker. 2003. Tackling Socioeconomic Inequalities in Health: Analysis of European Experiences. *The Lancet, 362* (25 October 2003), 1409-1414.

Marmot, M. 2004. *The Status Syndrome: How Social Standing Affects Our Health and Longevity*. New York: Henry Holt, Times Books.

— 2005. Social Determinants of Longevity and Mortality. Retrieved 24 August 2006, from http://www.SageCrossroads.net, 28 June.

Mauron, A. 2005. The Choosy Reaper: From the Myth of Eternal Youth to the Reality of Unequal Death. *EMBO Reports* 6 (Special Issue, July), 67-71.

McAdams, D.P. 1997. *The Stories We Live By: Personal Myths and the Making of the Self*. New York: The Guilford Press.

McConnell, C. and L. Turner. 2005. Medicine, Ageing, and Human Longevity: The Economics and Ethics of Anti-ageing Interventions. *EMBO Reports* 6 (Special Issue, July), 59-62.

McKibben, B. 2003. *Enough: Genetic Engineering and the End of Human Nature*. London: Bloomsbury.

Miller, R.A. 2004. Extending Life: Scientific Prospects and Political Obstacles. In *The Fountain of Youth: Cultural, Scientific, and Ethical Perspectives on a Biomedical Goal*, eds. S.G. Post and R.H. Binstock. Oxford: Oxford University Press, 228-248.

Moody, H.R. 1995. The Meaning of Old Age: Scenarios for the Future. In *A World Growing Old: The Coming Health Care Challenges*, eds. D. Callahan, R.H.J. ter Meulen, and E. Topinková. Washington, D.C.: Georgetown University Press, 9-19.

Mooren, J.H. 1998. Zingeving en cognitieve regulatie: een conceptueel model ten behoeve van onderzoek naar zingeving en levensbeschouwing. In *Schering en inslag: opstellen over religie in de hedendaagse cultuur*, eds. J. Jansen, R. van Uden, and H. van der Ven. Nijmegen: Katholiek Studiecentrum voor Geestelijke Volksgezondheid (KSGV), 193-206.

Neugarten, B.L. 1996. Social Implications of Life Extension [1978]. In *The Meanings of Age: Selected Papers of Bernice L. Neugarten*, ed. D.A. Neugarten. Chicago: The University of Chicago Press, 339-345.

Nussbaum, M.C. 2001. *Women and Human Development: The Capabilities Approach*. Cambridge: Cambridge University Press.

— 2006. *Frontiers of Justice: Disability, Nationality, Species Membership*. Cambridge, MA: Harvard University Press.

Nussbaum, M.C. and A. Sen. 1993. *The Quality of Life*. Oxford: Oxford University Press.

Olshansky, S.J., D. Perry, R.A. Miller, and R.N. Butler. 2006. In Pursuit of the Longevity Dividend: What Should We Be Doing to Prepare for the Unprecedented Aging of Humanity? *The Scientist* 20 (March), 28-36.

Overall, C. 2003. *Aging, Death, and Human Longevity: A Philosophical Inquiry*. Berkeley: University of California Press.

— 2004. Longevity, Identity, and Moral Character: A Feminist Approach. In *The Fountain of Youth: Cultural, Scientific, and Ethical Perspectives on a Biomedical Goal*, eds. S.G. Post and R.H. Binstock. Oxford: Oxford University Press, 286-303.

Pavot, W. and E. Diener. 2004. The Subjective Evaluation of Well-Being in Adulthood: Findings and Implications. *Ageing International*, 29 (2, Spring), 113-135.

Pogge, T.W. 2002. *World Poverty and Human Rights: Cosmopolitan Responsibilities and Reforms*. Cambridge: Polity.

Porter, R. 1999. *The Greatest Benefit to Mankind: A Medical History of Humanity from Antiquity to the Present*. London: Fontana Press.

Post, S.G. 2004a. Decelerated Aging: Should I Drink from a Fountain of Youth? In *The Fountain of Youth: Cultural, Scientific, and Ethical Perspectives on a Biomedical Goal*, S.G. Post and R.H. Binstock. Oxford: Oxford University Press, 72-93.

— 2004b. Establishing an Appropriate Ethical Framework: The Moral Conversation around the Goal of Prolongevity. *Journal of Gerontology: Biological Sciences, 59A* (6, June), 534-539.

President's Council on Bioethics. 2003. *Beyond Therapy: Biotechnology and the Pursuit of Happiness*. New York: HarperCollins.

Rawls, J. 1999a. *The Law of Peoples, with 'The Idea of Public Reason Revisited'*. Cambridge, MA: Harvard University Press.

— 1999b. *A Theory of Justice: Revised Edition*. Cambridge, MA: Belknap Press of Harvard University Press.

Ricklefs, R.E. and C.E. Finch. 1995. *Aging: A Natural History*. New York: HPHLP, Scientific American Library.

Ryff, C.D. 1989. Happiness Is Everything, or Is It? Explorations on the Meaning of Psychological Well-Being. *Journal of Personality and Social Psychology 57* (6), 1069-1081.

— 2006. In *The MIDUS Times*, 1-8. Madison, WI: University of Wisconsin. Retrieved July 5, 2007, from http://www.midus.wisc.edu/newsletter/

Ryff, C.D. and B.H. Singer. 1998. The Contours of Positive Human Health. *Psychological Inquiry 9* (1), 1-28.

Stock, G. 2002. *Redesigning Humans: Our Inevitable Genetic Future*. Boston: Houghton Mifflin.

Taylor, C. 1992. *Sources of the Self: The Making of the Modern Identity*. Cambridge: Cambridge University Press.

Turner, L. 2004. Life Extension Research: Health, Illness, and Death. *Health Care Analysis* 12 (2, June), 117-129.

Veenhoven, R. 1996. Happy Life Expectancy: A Comprehensive Measure of Quality-of-Life in Nations. *Social Indicators Research* 39, 1-58.

Verweij, M. 1999. Medicalization as a Moral Problem for Preventive Medicine. *Bioethics* 13 (2, April), 89-113.

Warner, H., et al. 2005. Science Fact and the SENS Agenda: What Can We Reasonably Expect from Ageing Research. *EMBO Reports* 6 (11, November), 1006-1008.

11　Enhancement Technologies: An Opportunity to Care?

Annika den Dikken

Critics of enhancement technologies emphasize that enhancement technologies essentially differ from medical treatment in the sense that their aim is not to sustain or restore good health. Enhancement technologies produce interventions designed to improve human form or functioning beyond what is necessary to sustain or restore good health (Juengst 1998). Examples of so-called enhancement technologies are cosmetic surgery, genetic manipulations, psycho-pharmaceuticals, and genetic drugs. Discussion about the distinction between medical treatment and enhancement has become a large part of the ethical debate.

The treatment versus enhancement debate takes place in the context of at least two larger backgrounds. First, the quest for a just distribution of scanty resources in the health care system asks for criteria to appoint the care most needed. Ethicists see it as their task to define these criteria. Second, the debate seems to be a touchstone for those who search for the moral boundaries of the growth of biotechnology. In the treatment-enhancement distinction some claim to have found a definable boundary for the acceptable use of human creational powers. Remarkably, the enhancement debate thus seems to be focused mainly on political, philosophical and theological objectives: political objectives, because moral boundaries must be transferable into a policy; philosophical, because moral distinctions can only be made through the rules of logic; and theological, because the conclusions of the debate have to coincide with larger worldviews. The above-mentioned contexts are of great importance, but ethicists and theologians in their search for definitions seem to have forgotten one of the main objectives of the bioethical origin, namely to protect vulnerable people from the social practices that arise in modern medicine (Cahill

2005). Central to the ethical work should be the people who are affected, those who need care, and those who suffer. Their situation should be the core of ethical interest.

A more important question than finding the differences between medical treatment and enhancement therefore seems to be whether so called 'enhancement technologies' can provide a possibility of care. Therefore it is necessary to describe what we understand as care and how we can estimate whether care is needed. When is it morally obliged to give care? I will show that social norms related to the body – such as norms of beauty, health, and performance – can cause human suffering and stimulate people to use enhancement technologies. Therefore these body-related values should be included in the ethical debate. An ethics of care and theological notions of love and redemption could shine another light on this topic, for they show responsibilities related to the social contexts of people who wish to alter their bodies. The task of ethics is not only to better the lives of people who have a disease, it also cares for people who suffer as a whole being.

Suffering, Illness, or Needs?

Why would we use the word 'suffering' in the context of the enhancement debate? It is more common to speak of 'illness', or 'needs' as a cause for moral responsibility. I choose not to use the term '*illness*', because I want to move away from the treatment-enhancement distinction. Illness is a medical term. Thereby it is not the simple opposite of health, when we, for example, use one of the holistic approaches of health as written down in the definition of 'health' used by the World Health Organization (WHO): 'Health is a state of complete physical, mental, and social well-being, and not merely the absence of disease or infirmity' (Preamble to the Constitution 1946). Social well-being is thus also an important factor in the concept of health formulated by the WHO. Because 'health' itself also has a medical connotation, I would rather use the general term 'well-being'.

Some examples will show that it is problematic to use the term 'illness' in cases where we can hardly deny that the well-being of people is at stake. The first example comes from the book *From Chance to Choice* where the authors use it as a case in their argumentation about the treatment/enhancement distinction:

Johnny is a short 11-year-old boy with documented growth hormone (GH) deficiency resulting from a brain tumor. His parents are of average height. His predicted adult height without GH treatment is approximately 160 cm (5 feet 3 inches).

Billy is a short 11-year-old boy with normal GH secretion according to current testing methods. However, his parents are extremely short, and he has a predicted adult height of 160 cm (5 feet 3 inches). (Buchanan 2000, 115)

The authors of *From Chance to Choice* assume that Johnny and Billy will 'suffer disadvantage equally if they are not treated. There is no reason to think the difference in the underlying causes of their shortness will lead people to treat them in ways that make one happier or more advantaged than the other'. (Buchanan 2000, 115) Although Johnny obviously stays short because of an illness, Billy does not. No biomedical malfunctioning is measured to cause his predicted shortness. It would be awkward to call Billy ill, just because he will be shorter than the average male person.

Other examples can be found in the field of reproduction as we can see in the next case:

Mary is a lesbian woman of 28 years old. She and her partner Clare have been together for six years now and they both feel a strong wish to have children. Mary speaks of her biological clock ticking. She also knows how much a grandchild would please her mother, who was not too happy to hear that Mary was a lesbian. Furthermore, Mary and Clare often have to listen to their friends who all had children during the last few years. Those friends often tell them how sad it is that they have to miss this joy. The couple understands that they have only a few years left to try to have children. They hope to find a sperm donor and to become pregnant through reproductive technology methods.

Obviously, there is no illness preventing Mary and Clare from having children together. There is no biomedical malfunction, but they cannot conceive a child together because they are both women. However, although it is not a case of illness, these women experience the same problem as infertile women. Whether caused by medical indication (such as a blocked fallopian tube) or by social indication (such as the lack of a male partner), these women can suffer from the inability to conceive a child of their own.

These examples show that 'illness' is not an appropriate term for all cases in which people's well-being is at stake, even if the suffering involved is equal to cases where we can speak of illness and the alleviation of the suffering could be reached through the same methods.

One could of course consider the use of the term 'illness' for all cases of absence of health or well-being. This would mean an even further medicalization of social life than we already have in our society nowadays. Furthermore it would not clear up the moral debate. Calling Billy, Mary, or Clare 'ill' does not bring us any nearer to the problem they experience, which mainly has a social character, not so much a medical one. It seems more appropriate to acknowledge that their suffering equals the suffering of those who do have a diagnosed illness.

I mentioned above that the term 'needs' as an alternative for 'suffering' is more commonly said to evoke moral responsibility. Needs, however, is a very broad term. Nussbaum, for example, made a distinction between primary needs and secondary needs based on the core capabilities that are necessary to live a human life with dignity (Nussbaum 2006). If closely scrutinized, the distinction between primary needs and suffering will not be great. The use of the word 'suffering', however, has some other implications. First, it brings us to a moment that precedes our speaking about needs. Suffering concerns the core experience of a person who might not yet know what she needs. And second, whereas there are needs that do not necessarily oblige others to satisfy those needs (for example secondary needs), suffering always calls for care, whether by alleviating the cause of suffering or by just supporting the person who suffers.

Suffering and the Problems of Using Suffering as a Moral Compass

To speak of suffering seems to be problematic in the medical field. Eric J. Cassell (2004) claims that 'the relief of suffering is considered one of the primary ends of medicine by patients and the general public, but it is not by the medical profession, judging by medical education and the responses of students and colleagues' (31). Cassell emphasizes that physicians are primarily concerned with the physical, and that medical and social literature mostly explain 'suffering' in connection to pain. But pain and suffering are not synonymous. Physical pain does not have to lead to suffering and suffering does not only consist of pain, although pain can be a large factor in suffering. Cassell describes suffering as follows: 'Suffering occurs when an impending destruction of the person is perceived; it continues until the threat of disintegration has passed or until the integrity of the person can be restored in some other manner' (32). Suffering is experienced by people. A person is not merely mind, but consists of many facets. Cassell sums up: a person has a past with life experiences, a family, a cultural background, roles, relationships with others, a relationship with himself or herself. A person is a political being, people do things, a person is unaware of some things happening to her. A person has regular behaviours, a body, a secret life, a perceived future, and a transcendent dimension. Suffering occurs with the (impending) destruction of one or more of these facets and when the intactness cannot be maintained or restored (36-43). The integrity of a person as a whole is at stake.

This comprehensive concept of suffering can make physicians sceptical about their task to alleviate suffering in general. In part this is with good reason, for how should they offer care when people lose a relative or their job? However, only emphasizing physical conditions has a risk of overlooking important facets that undermine physical or mental health and contribute to personal suffering.

To use this understanding of suffering in the context of ethics raises several problems. How to define when people suffer? How to know what aspects of a personal life cause suffering and how to relieve this suffering? Some people say they suffer when we would not expect them to, whereas others deny that they suffer in situations from which we would expect them to. We should also consider that 'suffering' is a loaded term and that many people will not admit that they suffer. Can we use such a subjective experience as a moral compass? Although suffering is person-related, we can recognize factors in human life that sooner evoke suffering than others. Physicians, psychologists, and pastoral workers are specialized in finding these factors in their field of work. But it is not possible to make general claims about suffering. Only the context of the person involved, and if possible her own opinion about it, can show whether a person suffers, whether facets of her personhood are harmed.

If we think suffering is important in the context of moral responsibility, we have to acknowledge there can be no general rules that define when moral responsibility has to be taken. One of the tasks of ethics should be to explore which factors in life cause personal suffering, and analyzing the role of several actors and social practices that influence these factors.

Body-Related Values

In the context of the enhancement debate at least one group of factors that cause suffering seems to be neglected, namely 'body-related values'. Different values are related to our bodies, depending on culture and period of time. Roughly we can divide body-related values into three categories:

First we can think of values that influence the evaluation of our bodies. According to these values we consider ourselves or other people healthy, attractive, or beautiful. Those values for example mark whether we have desirable bodies and whether we consider ourselves as being a real man or woman.

Second, body-related values can be values that influence the evaluation of ourselves in general. With this I do not want to make a distinction between our bodies and ourselves as if our bodies do not belong to ourselves, but in the first category the body-related values are directly aimed at the body as a specific part of ourselves, while the second category is more general and focused on character or moral evaluation of the person as a whole. Eve Ensler provides an example of this second category by speaking about herself: 'I have bought into the idea that if my stomach were flat, then I would be good, and I would be safe' (Ensler 2004, x). People connect personal values to bodily appearances: when a person is thin she is good. When she is fat, she is bad and lazy. A tanned skin is a sign of health and wealth. A trained body shows a person to be disciplined.

Third, other values we adopt can be body-related. The wish for having children is body- related, because bodies have to come together to realize this wish and a woman's body has to carry the child for nine months. In the case where reproductive technology is used, bodily interventions are performed in order to fulfill the wish for a child. Values of performance can also be body-related, when the body has to be trained and put on a diet to obtain the best performance. Another example of a body-related value in this category is the wish to have control over life. If a society highly values a control over all aspects of life, this will also concern the body, for instance by controlling the aging process.

These three categories overlap and influence each other. It is hardly possible to categorize a value in only one of the categories. The three categories mainly show the different kinds of influence body-related values can have.

If we look at the first case described above, we can see how such culturally determined body-related values can cause suffering. For example, we assume that both Billy and Johnny will not meet concrete physical disadvantages like pain or dysfunction from their being short. But they will both most likely encounter comparable practical and social discomforts. We can find examples of this at the Short Persons Support's website:

> Research has shown that short men have fewer opportunities for romantic relationships, have fewer children, and on average are paid less. Finding adult fashion clothes is difficult. Short women report that they are not taken as seriously as their taller peers (www.shortsupport.org, 29-08-2006).

Some of these situations can cause suffering when social practices push people into situations they cannot integrate with their self-image. Although we assume that both Billy and Johnny suffer equally, because they will both stay short, this assumption is too easily made. Whether they will suffer is dependent on many circumstances. Perhaps one of them lives in an environment that teaches the boy to cope with his shortness, to be self-confident, and maybe he will meet other short people and in that way find comfort.

An Ethics of Care

If we think that it is a moral responsibility to respond to human suffering, as in fact all ethical theories defend, there needs to be an attentiveness to recognize suffering. Such attentiveness is a core concept of an ethics of care. Feminist ethicists, who have developed different kinds of care ethics, make the attentiveness to a person's needs the centre of their ethical theory. Attentiveness to needs is an important aspect of the concept of care. Nel Noddings places emphasis on this attitude of caring:

> Caring involves stepping out of one's own personal frame of reference into the other's. When we care, we consider the other's point of view, his objective needs, and what he expects of us. Our attention, our mental engrossment is on the cared-for, not on ourselves (Noddings 1984, 24).

Although it is common in care ethics to speak of needs, I prefer to use the word 'suffering', for reasons mentioned above. If I do use the word 'needs', I use it related to suffering, as those needs that aim to relieve or prevent suffering. Of course, caring does not only occur in the context of suffering. If a woman cares for her child, her care will in general not be seen as a reaction to suffering. However, her care will prevent her child from suffering, even if this will not explicitly be her conscious motivation to provide care. By caring we relieve or prevent suffering.

What is care? The *Encyclopedia of Ethics* describes care as a distinct moral sentiment – an emotional attitude embedded in a relationship with another person. 'Caring for another individual involves a concern for the other's well-being' (Becker 2001). This description of care, however, seems to be too narrow. Caring does not only consist of the concern for another person. Care ethicists have described 'care' as both an attitude or value and a practice. Caring without action is not real care. One could not say: 'I care for my children' without being prepared to actually provide them care. Such an inconsistency would immediately question the value of care. Daniel Engster describes caring as a practice aimed at helping individuals meet their basic needs, developing and maintaining basic capabilities, and living free from suffering as much as possible (Engster 2005). Examples of caring practices are child raising, educating people, nursing wounds and cultivating social relations. Although care ethicists have put the attention on caring practices, Virginia Held urges that '[M]oral theorizing is needed to understand the practices and to reform them' (Held 2006, 37). Many practices are not seen as caring practices. In this paper we question whether the use of enhancement technologies could be regarded as a caring practice.

Caring can only take place in the context of relationships. People care for other people. The central aim of an ethics of care is to determine the conditions of good caring relationships, with others but also with oneself. However, standards for a concept of care cannot be found in abstract principles or rules guiding us what good care should look like, which is congruent with the context-specific character of suffering. Rather, values of care can shape a framework showing us what caring relationships look like. Care ethicists motivate to establish a mutual caring relationship between the caregiver and the cared-for. 'Caring is a relation in which carer and cared-for share an interest in their mutual well-being' (Held 2006, 34-35). Providing care is therefore informed by the contexts of both the cared-for and the caregiver. Good care is only possible if caregivers are attentive, but also when care receivers are open to receive care and to support their caregivers as far as possible. The task of caregiving is often very difficult and takes a lot of energy from the caregiver (Kittay 1999; Levine 2004). Care receivers can therefore support those who offer care by not demanding too much from them.

Critics of an ethics of care claim that care ethics cannot offer any content because care does not mean anything else than a general term such as 'good'. If we say that we have to care about X, we do not yet know what we should do (Reich 1978). It is not correct to say that 'caring' is an empty concept. Caring attitudes and practices can be verified by affirming that they are attentive for needs, aimed at the other or oneself, part of mutual relationships and informed by the context of persons as a whole (including the body-related values). Caring attitudes and practices relieve or prevent suffering, which is defined as an impending destruction of the (integrity of a) person. Suffering shows when care is needed and when it is our moral responsibility to care.

So we can determine when care is called for and we have set the conditions care needs in order to form good caring relationships, but as for content we still do not know what good care is exactly, because good care is not based on rules and principles but is directly context-related. This can be seen as a problem, as most ethical theories wish to provide clear answers and boundaries. At the same time it can be seen as a big advantage for ethical consideration, because it offers openings to particular contexts, personal experiences, and creative thinking. Although I agree with the last option, I do recognize the problematic aspect of a concept of care that is too open. Without limiting it, through the addition of rules or principles, I hope to offer some guiding tools to recognize good care. This I will do by introducing the theological concepts of love and redemption.

Love

Although 'love' is a central aspect of social behaviour, modern ethicists hardly reflect on the topic of love, for several possible reasons. Love seems to be the opposite of rationale, and could often even be considered as non-rational. Love can be seen as an individual emotion, and love is mostly associated with romantic love. For feminist theologians the latter has been a reason to avoid speaking about love. They stressed that in the name of love power relationships were justified and they preferred to rethink concepts of a relationship, by using other terms. The absence of thorough reflection on love can be considered an inadequacy in the field of ethics, as our understanding of what love is influences our social relationships. What is considered to be love? Who do we love, who may we love, how do we act out of love? How does love for another influence our moral considerations?

The Protestant debate about love (agape) has emphasized the concept of other-regard in contrast with self-regard. This distinction was initiated by Anders Nygren's *Agape and Eros* in which Nygren understands Christian love as moving in two directions: God and the neighbor (Nygren 1953). This is in contrast with natural self-love, which is presented as a morally negative quality (Andolsen 1981). The grounding for Nygren's understanding of love can be found in the traditional understanding of love through the Christological explanation of the crucifixion of Jesus, which understands Jesus' self-sacrifice at the cross as the salvation of humankind. This selfless love of Christ should also be present in the actions of his followers. Feminists have criticized this understanding of agape because it did not do justice to women's experiences. They described women as already being inclined to self-abnegation, having serving roles and not being able to develop themselves. In contrast to the distinction between self-regard and self-sacrifice they offered the concept of mutuality (Andolsen 1981). Focusing on mutuality, friendship, kinship, and relationships, they avoided speaking about love.

In this context, however, I prefer to speak about love. Kinship and friendship refer to particular relationships and although it is possible to transfer the characteristics of kinship relationships to broader contexts of social behaviour, the Christian concept of love is appropriate in this context precisely because it is not limited to particular relationships. Christians are called to love even those who do not return love, because it has no merit to love those who give love in return. The value of love can be found in its general character.

Interestingly, the Christian concept of love seems to correspond with the concept of care in many aspects. Both concepts share the necessity of relationships and mutuality. Just as care requires attentiveness, love is not possible without an open attitude towards the other and the self. Like care, love is not only a value, it is also a practice. Love directly implies action. But if care and love are so much alike, why bother speaking about love? A theological concept of love can offer care ethics some values that are less obviously derived from the concept of care.

Care ethicists emphasize the importance of an attentive attitude for needs. Attentiveness can still be understood as being rather detached, involving no particular emotions of the caregiver. Love on the other hand requires that the loving person is deeply moved. Love is a deep affection. The Protestant ethicist Margaret Farley uses the concept of compassion to refer to this being moved by the other (Farley 2002). But compassion directly refers to already existing suffering, not so much the suffering that needs to be prevented. We do not feel compassion for children we care for, we love them. A person who loves allows herself to be deeply moved. Furthermore, the Christian concept of love is always placed in a larger context. The love between people is a reflection of God's love for people. Our love is a part of the divine love, which binds human love together as a network aimed at redemption.

Love differs from care in one important aspect. Love cannot be a moral responsibility. We cannot be obliged to love, we can only be inspired to love. We might consider calling it a religious or spiritual responsibility. Anyway, love can function as a strong motivation and inspiration to be attentive and provide care.

Redemption

Susan Frank Parsons in the *Cambridge Companion to Feminist Theology* writes about redeeming ethics based on the *Dialogue* with God of St Catherine of Siena (Parsons 2002). Catherine's prayer shows Parsons how knowledge of God's goodness is followed by love and the desire to be turned into this goodness. In this movement from knowledge of God's goodness towards the desire to be turned into this goodness Parsons recognizes the intrinsic connection of ethics with redemption. The theological concept of redemption traditionally has been connected to Jesus' crucifixion. The tremendous love of the Son for his Father and the world made him accept the cross. His crucifixion and resurrection counted as the salvation of humankind. Radford Ruether summarizes it as:

> For traditional Christianity redemption means the reconciliation of the fallen soul with God, won by Christ in the cross, applied to the soul in baptismal regeneration, and developed through the struggle to live virtuously sustained by grace. Salvation is completed after death in eternal contemplative union with God (joined by the spiritual body in the resurrection). (Ruether 1998, 273-274)

This understanding of redemption has been forcefully criticized by feminist theologians, for it did not change the actual oppressed situation of many women. In modern feminism redemption shifts from otherworldly hope to this-worldly hope, according to Radford Ruether:

Redemption is not primarily about being reconciled with a God from whom our human nature has become totally severed due to sin, rejecting our bodies and finitude, and ascending to communion with a spiritual world that will be our heavenly home after death. Rather, redemption is about reclaiming an original goodness that is still available as our true selves, although obscured by false ideologies and social structures that have justified domination of some and subordination of others. (Ruether 1998, 8)

The example of this original goodness feminists find in the life of Jesus, and not so much in his crucifixion. Jesus' life is paradigmatic because it shows ways to dissent from oppressive systems, to take the side of the oppressed, to follow a praxis of egalitarian relations and to provide care. Redemption is no longer regarded as one savior's sacrifice and a hope for salvation in a future world. Redemption becomes a responsibility here and now, because we can be the source of redemption for others and ourselves.

Changing Ourselves

Why do our moral standards often change when bad things happen to our loved ones, or to ourselves? One could call it hypocrisy, but it seems more appropriate to acknowledge that our moral opinions are better informed about the context when we consider cases that are near to us. It is not too difficult to form abstract principles and rules about moral questions that do not concern situations we know much about. An ethics of care tries to bring distant cases nearer to us by articulating the importance of particular contexts. A Christian notion of love can inspire us to open our eyes for the needs and sufferings of other persons, being aware that taking moral responsibility can create moments of redemption.

In the context of enhancement technologies an emphasis on suffering can lead to moral responsibilities that become ambiguous when we only focus on the boundaries between medical treatment and enhancement. An ethics of care focused on human suffering shows how particular situations determine whether people are in need of care. Attentiveness for those needs makes apparent that some people who are ill do not suffer, while others who are not ill do suffer. People who wish to enhance their bodies can suffer from social values that limit their well-being to a large extent. From the perspective of care ethics their suffering cannot evoke other responsibilities compared with equal suffering caused by illness.

A theology of love and redemption can remind us that attentiveness to human suffering can open us up to those we do not personally know, or whose suffering we do not understand. Through taking moral responsibilities, by creating good relationships of care, we can offer each other redemption.

By no means would I argue that enhancement technologies can relieve all human suffering caused by social values. If we look at the impact of some body-related values that cause suffering, we might rather consider whether we can remove the social pressure from those who do not conform to the average norm. But before we arrive at a society that can reach such an ideal, there is a moral responsibility to provide care for those who suffer from social practices. The use of enhancement technologies could be one way of providing this care.

References

Andolsen, B. Hilkert. 1981. Agape in feminist ethics. *The Journal of Religious Ethics* 9 (1), 69-83.

Becker, L.C. and C.B. Becker. 2001. *Encyclopedia of Ethics*, vol. 1. New York: Routledge.

Buchanan, A.E. 2000. *From Chance to Choice. Genetics and Justice.* Cambridge: Cambridge University Press.

Cahill, L. Sowle. 2005. *Theological Bioethics. Participation, Justice and Change.* Washington D.C.: Georgetown University Press.

Cassell, E.J. 2004. *The Nature of Suffering and the Goals of Medicine*, Oxford/New York: Oxford University Press.

Engster, D. 2005. Rethinking Care Theory: The Practice of Caring and the Obligation to Care. *Hypatia* 20 (3), 53-54.

Ensler, E. 2004. *The Good Body.* New York: Villard.

Farley, M.A. 2002. *Compassionate Respect. A Feminist Approach to Medical Ethics and Other Questions.* New York: Paulist Press.

Held, V. 2006. *The Ethics of Care: Personal, Political, and Global*, Oxford: Oxford University Press.

Juengst, E.T. 1998. What Does *Enhancement* Mean? In *Enhancing Human Traits*, ed. E. Parens. Washington D.C.: Georgetown University Press, 29-47.

Kittay, E. Feder. 1999. *Love's Labor. Essays on Women, Equality, and Dependency.* New York: Routledge.

Levine, C. 2004. *Always on Call. When Illness Turns Families into Caregivers.* Nashville: VanderBilt University Press.

Noddings, N. 1984. *Caring. A Feminine Approach to Ethics & Moral Education.* Berkeley: University of California Press.

Nussbaum, M.C. 2006. *Frontiers of Justice. Disability, Nationality, Species Membership*, Cambridge, MA: The Belknap Press of Harvard University Press.

Nygren, A. 1953. *Agape and Eros.* London: SPCK.

Parsons, S. Frank. 2002. *The Cambridge Companion to Feminist Theology.* Cambridge: Cambridge University Press.

Preamble to the Constitution of the World Health Organization. Adopted by the International Health Conference held in New York 19 June-22 July 1946, and signed on 22 July 1946. Official Record of World Health Organization 2, no. 100.

Reich, W.T. 1978. *Encyclopedia of Bioethics.* New York: The Free Press, vol. 1, 145-149.

Ruether, R. Radford. 1998. *Women and Redemption. A Theological History.* London: SCM.

Part Four

A MATTER OF ARGUMENT OR OF TRUST?

12   Religious Arguments in Political Decision Making

Patrick Loobuyck

Introduction

This contribution sketches the different political philosophical positions in the debate about the use of religious arguments in political decision making. We distinguish exclusionism from strong and weak versions of inclusions, and argue that from a deliberative democratic perspective, strong inclusionism gives us the most consistent approach to this subject. We will not only see that most arguments against inclusionism fail; it also seems that the critics of strong inclusionism work with an abstract notion of moral subjects and a problematic concept of autonomous morality.

The Political Philosophical Landscape: Exclusionism, Weak and Strong Inclusionism

Nowadays, it seems 'not done' in our secular Western European societies to use religious arguments in the political sphere. When Christians or Muslims publicly condemn the law permitting euthanasia or same-sex marriages for religious reasons, many people call it a threat to democracy and a violation of the principle of the separation of church and state. There is an increasing unwritten consensus that religious doctrines and institutions should play no role in political decision making. Many Christian democratic politicians also seem to accept this view. They acknowledge that religious beliefs can inspire their political engagement but in their political choices and in the public presentation of arguments that support these choices, they avoid appeals to their religious background.

We can call this standard understanding of public reason the 'exclusive view' (cf. Rawls 1993, 247; Perry 2003, x; Boettcher 2005, 499).

Versions of this exclusive view have been defended by liberal philosophers such as Charles Larmore, Bruce Ackerman, Richard Rorty, and Robert Audi. For Audi, religious people should be guided by a principle of secular rationale and of secular motivation in the political realm. In the attempt to justify political beliefs and actions, 'a commitment to a free and democratic society requires that one have, and be sufficiently motivated by, adequate secular reasons' (Audi 1989, 293; also 2000, 86ff.) Several authors defend a kind of 'conversational restraint' as a necessary condition to keep the political dialogue going. Larmore (1987, 53) argues that 'in the face of disagreement, those who wish to continue the conversation should retreat to *neutral ground*' and Ackerman (1989, 16) goes even further, when he writes that 'we should simply *say nothing at all* about this disagreement and put the moral ideals that divide us off the conversational agenda of the liberal state'.

However, most of the liberal political philosophers argue now for an approach that is more inclusive. The debate now mainly focuses on questions about the extent to which religious discourse and argument should be included in political decision making. (cf. Boettcher 2005, 497) It is interesting to see how some authors explicitly changed their mind about the subject over the years. Michael Perry for instance defended an exclusionist position in *Love and Power* (1991) and a more moderate exclusionist position in *Religion in Politics* (1997), but in *Under God?* (2003) he defends a form of inclusionism. Also Jürgen Habermas changed from a resolutely secular perspective (1962) to a post-secular perspective with a broad-minded acknowledgement of religion's special niche in the spectrum of public political debate (2006). Even Richard Rorty, one of the most famous exclusionist liberals, gives a restatement of his 'hasty and insufficiently thoughtful' ideas that he wrote in his article with the well-known title 'Religion as Conversation-stopper'. In that article Rorty (1999, 169) wrote approvingly of 'privatizing religion – keeping it out of [...] the public square', making it seem bad taste to bring religion into discussion of public policy. But in his 'reconsideration' he doubts if good citizenship requires us to have non-religious bases for our political view and he acknowledges that it is false that religion is 'essentially' a conversation-stopper. Rorty's view can now be summarized as: 'What should be discouraged is *mere* appeal to authority. [...] Citizens of democracy should try to put off invoking conversation-stoppers as long as possible' (Rorty 2003, 147-8; see also Stout 2004).

John Rawls also modified his position considerably. Unlike some of his critics suggest (cf. Quinn 1997; 2001), exclusionism was never defended in print by Rawls, but he acknowledges that at first he inclined to the more restrictive exclusive view (Rawls 1993, 247 n. 36). In the first edition of *Political Liberalism*, Rawls defends the idea of public reason based on reasons that can be agreed to by all reasonable people, irrespective of which comprehensive (religious or secular) doctrine they affirm. The ideal of citizenship imposes a moral 'duty of civility' to be able to explain to one another how their political choices and actions can be supported by the political values of public reason (Rawls 1993, 217). But Rawls makes a difference between the well-ordered society wherein the public reason must follow the exclusive view, and the nearly well-ordered societies and not well-ordered societies wherein the ideal of public reason allows the inclusive view. So in certain (unjust) situations it may be justified for citizens to appeal to comprehensive (religious) reasons 'provided they do this in ways that strengthen the ideal of public reason itself' (Rawls 1993, 247ff). Later Rawls revises his position. In the introduction of the paperback edition of *Political Liberalism* (1996) and in his article, 'The Idea of Public Reason Revisited' (2001), he more clearly stresses that the ideal of public reason should be applied only in the discourse of judges, government officials, and politicians when discussing constitutional essentials and matters of basic justice. The idea of public reason does not apply to the background culture (Habermas's public sphere, 1962) like civil society and media. (Rawls 2001, 134; 1996, I-Iii) Moreover, Rawls (2001, 152ff; 1996, Iii) introduces the 'wide view of public political culture'. Now comprehensive doctrines 'may be introduced in public reason at any time, provided that in due course public reasons [...] are presented sufficient to support whatever the comprehensive doctrines are introduced to support'. Rawls refers to this as *the proviso*. So religious discourse is only allowed as supplementary in public reason. The wide view of public reason is still a type of 'weak inclusionism' because it does suggest that on some occasions restraints on the appeal to religious and other comprehensive doctrines are warranted. (Boettcher 2005, 500) In fact the wide view of public reason cannot allow public justifications that rely *solely* on religious justification and cannot be translated in public political reasons.

The latter is defended by the so-called strong inclusionists like Christopher Eberle, Jeffrey Stout, Nicholas Wolterstorff, Paul Weithman, John Neuhaus, and Veit Bader. They argue that citizens are morally permitted to offer exclusively religious arguments in public debate. One of the most powerful statements of strong inclusionism is presented in Eberle's

Religious Convictions in Liberal Politics. He criticizes the authors who defend what he calls 'justificatory liberalism' (from Rawls and Gutmann to Ackerman and Audi) for their failure to present an adequate account of why religious believers should avoid relying solely on their religious convictions in their political choices and activities.

Also the defenders of deliberative democracy tend to be more inclusive than their colleagues who defend the standard liberal democracy. Since the early 1990s the so-called 'deliberative turn' has preoccupied the debates concerning democratic theory. Authors such as Jürgen Habermas, Seyla Benhabib, James Bohman, and Joshua Cohen had emphasized that democracy is much more than the aggregation of preferences into collective decisions through devices such as voting and representation. 'Under deliberative democracy, the essence of democratic legitimacy should be sought instead in the ability of all individuals subject to a collective decision to engage in authentic deliberation about that decision. These individuals should accept the decision only if it could be justified to them in convincing terms' (Dryzek 2000, v). Moreover, deliberative democratic theory works with another view on the 'moral self' that participates in public deliberations than other liberals. Rawls, for instance, does not view democratic citizens as 'socially situated or otherwise rooted, that is, as being in this or that social class, or as having this or that comprehensive doctrine' (cf. Rawls 2001, 171). In deliberative democratic theory citizens are not the Kantian, free-floating, abstract, generalized, equal, and reasonable subjects but concrete and unique individuals 'with a certain life history, disposition and endowment', and therefore 'there can be no coherent reversibility of perspectives and positions unless the identity of the other as distinct from the self, not merely in the sense of bodily otherness but as a concrete other, is retained' (Benhabib 1992, 10; 158ff). It is not surprising that deliberative democratic theorists reject the path of conversational restraint and argue for a more open, unrestricted deliberation. Shared political values (part of the overlapping consensus of comprehensive doctrines) are important, but the input in public and political deliberation cannot be restricted to those values. Contradicting Ackerman, Benhabib writes that citizens must feel free to introduce 'any and all moral arguments into the conversation field'. A deliberative model of democracy is therefore much more interested in 'background cultural conditions' and the contribution to public reason of comprehensive doctrines, because 'politics and political reasoning are always seen to emerge out of a cultural and social context' (cf. Benhabib 1992, 95; 1996, 74-77).

In sum, in the debate about the 'neutrality of public reason' there are many liberal perspectives and (sometimes changing) positions and the discussion is still going on. In our overview of the liberal landscape, we made a distinction between exclusionists and (strong and weak) inclusionists. Unfortunately, there is no standard terminology in the literature and it is not always clear for each author to which category he or she belongs. Some call Audi an exclusionist, while others (even Audi himself, cf. Audi 2000, 69-78) would like to be a weak inclusionist. Especially about the (changed) position of Rawls there was, and is, a lot of discussion (cf. Weithman 1994; 1997; 2002, ch. 7; Thiemann 1996; Habermas 1995).

However, we think that the distinction can be seen as follows: weak inclusionism not only acknowledges that religious arguments, motivation and justification are relevant for the person who defends a certain position (this personal relevance will not be denied by many exclusionists), the weak inclusionists are also convinced that (in some circumstances) religious arguments and reasons are relevant to the public and political deliberation itself. While weak inclusionists (in some circumstances) see the instrumental value of world views and comprehensive (religious) doctrines, strong inclusionists argue that citizens should not be discouraged from basing their political decisions and arguments solely on religious grounds because it is impossible and in essence undesirable that public reason makes no place for the contribution of comprehensive doctrines.

Arguments For and Against Strong Inclusionism

In the literature many arguments are given to reject (strong) inclusionism. Most of the arguments are focused on the exclusion of *religious* arguments: they would be conservative, unreasonable and uncritical, religious arguments would undermine the political stability of diversified societies, religious arguments would function as a conversation-stopper and would undermine the possibility of consensus. Religious arguments would be unintelligible for people who do not share that religion and as such the use of religious arguments would be a lack of respect for other participants in the public dialogue. Moreover nobody wishes that fundamentalism dominated public decision making. An extensive and detailed critical review of all these arguments is beyond the scope of this chapter, we only make some general remarks.

Religious arguments are not always uncritical and unreasonable. The religious life of people is much more than obedience to divine authorities. Let it suffice to mention the important Thomistic tradition that gives place to reason (*lumen naturalis rationis*) and individual conscience in Christian moral philosophy. This tradition wherein morality is accessible, at least in principle, to human reason, is until today an important part of the official Catholic doctrine. (cf. Riordan 2004, 191; Perry 2003, 67; Vatican I's *Dei Filius* (1870)) Here it is important to make a distinction between a political position that is inspired by religious commitments, beliefs, and ideas, and religious arguments for that position. People can take a position against abortion, torture, or capitalism because of their religious beliefs, but at the same time they can try to give us rational (secular or political) arguments to defend that position. (Gascoigne 2001, 188-211; Rawls 2001, 152ff.) Most people do not have problems with the idea that religious beliefs have an influence upon political positions as long as the justification can be given in neutral terms, independent of the religious beliefs itself. As such we must be aware that some religious positions are disavowed not because they are religious but because they are (sometimes indeed in a reactionary way) conservative. But there are many religious positions that are 'very human' and not conservative. (cf. Weithman 2002, 5, ch.2) We can think about the role of religious arguments in the Civil Rights Movement (Martin Luther King) and abolitionism, but also about the religious position toward irregular migrants, capitalism and ecology. With these 'politically correct positions', the religious contribution is much less controversial. (cf. Rawls 1993, 249-50) Sometimes church leaders are even praised when they take a stand that pleases political leaders, but in many other issues they are (hypocritically) rebuked. (cf. De Dijn 2003, 293)

What to do now with religious arguments? First it must be clear that not all religious arguments are conversation-stoppers, and not all religious arguments are used in a fundamentalist way. In many cases, the religious voice can be seen as a contribution to the ongoing conversation about moral, political issues. Moreover, nobody will disagree that there are also some secular arguments that can be used in an authoritative way. The secular use of Marx, Darwin, or the idea of absolute property rights can also put a brake on conversation. So why should we say that religion has to shape up without also saying that Marxism, Darwinism, and libertarianism has to shape up and ought to be privatized? 'Why isn't sauce for the goose, sauce for the gander?' (cf. Wolterstorff 2003, 136-7; Rorty 2003) Although religious contributions to the public discussion were, and are, sometimes dogmatic, there is no reason to believe that religious contributions are never deliberative. As Michael Perry (2003, 42) mentioned: 'at its best, religious discourse in public culture is not less dialogic – not less open-minded, not less deliberative – than is, at its best, secular discourse in public culture. (Nor, at its worst, is religious discourse more monologic – more closed-minded and dogmatic – than is, at its worst, secular discourse.)'

It can be true that it is easier to reach consensus when all people argue in neutral, political terms, independent of any comprehensive world view, but this is not a sufficient argument to keep different religious arguments out of political debate. First, reasonable deliberation cannot guarantee consensus, and our democratic political system is important because it gives us the best option so far to cope in a peaceful and civil way with these unavoidable moral and political disagreements (cf. Gutman and Thompson 1996, 26). Pluralism and (political and moral) disagreement are the very essence of our democracy's right to exist. With Wolterstorff we can ask: 'What's so bad about reaching an impasse in political discussions?' We can try to seek deliberative consensus, but democracy allows more than that. We can try to make some political deals or take a vote. As long as those who lose the democratic game think it's better to lose than to destroy the system, democracy survives. (cf. Wolterstorff 2003, 135-7)

Moreover, within one religious doctrine, there is often a degree of moral disagreement and some Christians may be more in agreement with a non-believer on a certain moral issue than they are with another believer (Kole 2002, 254). Religious plurality is, therefore, not the only cause of contemporary moral plurality, and the other way round, the use of different religious arguments does not necessarily prevent moral consensus with an atheist. People can argue from within their different comprehensive views and draw on the different religious, philosophical, and moral grounds those provide, but still an 'overlapping consensus' is possible. Maybe the justification for human rights or a conception of justice is incommensurable, but not the political position about human rights and justice itself (cf. Wong 1989; Taylor 1999; Rawls 2001, 147-8; Bader 1999, 617; Gascoigne 2001, 199).

Some authors suggest the idea that religious pluralism in the public debate could undermine the political stability. They then refer to the crusades, the Thirty Years War, the Bosnian or Palestinian conflict and terrorism. It is true that *in some (historical) circumstances* the intrusion of religion into the political sphere can be very inflammatory and can continue deep and problematic divisiveness, but this provides us – in contemporary Western Europe and the US – with no reason to exclude religion from the public and political debate (Eberle 2002, 158ff). Nowadays western people who use a religious argument are not necessarily dangerous people who want to eliminate the other. And of course secular (antidemocratic, illiberal) opinions and discussions can also undermine political stability and generate problematic division (cf. Chaplin 2000, 628, 641; Wolterstorff 1997b, 80; Perry 1997, 45; 2003, 40, 48-51). So the point is that democracy cannot allow antidemocratic commitments that lead to political chaos, war and destruction – therefore, laws against racism and hate speech can be justified – but this is not a sufficient argument to privatize religion in all circumstances.

One of the most important arguments in the debate about the place of religious arguments in the public sphere is the idea that people have to argue with each other in reasonable and neutral terms out of *respect* for others as free and dignified individuals. Respect for other people with other world views requires the use of arguments that everybody can share, understand and endorse (cf. Larmore 1987). With Gutmann and Thompson, Rawls defends 'the principle of reciprocity': it is reasonable to think that other citizens with other comprehensive ideas about the good life might also reasonably accept the reasons we offer for our political actions and choices (Rawls 2001, 136-7; Gutmann & Thompson 1996, chs. 1-2). However, the standard approach that respect needs a kind of 'neutral dialogue' is not unproblematic. Of course the norm of equal respect is essential for liberalism and indeed to treat an individual as a person is to offer him an explanation for our political and moral opinions, but it is not clear that this explanation has to be neutral. Galston (1991, 108-9) remarks that a respectful explanation does not necessarily appeal to beliefs already held by one's interlocutors. He suggests to show respect for others by offering them, by way of explanation, what we take to be our best reasons for acting and thinking as we do. Also Eberle and Weithman argue at length that an attitude of respect for one's fellow citizens as equal and free individuals does not require 'the exercise of restraint'. The use of religious convictions in political decision making does not necessarily exclude mutual respect in a democratic liberal framework (cf. Eberle 2002, 71, ch. 4&5; Weithman 1997; 2002).

Moreover, it seems not at all true that people with different world views cannot understand each other when they argue in terms specific for their world view. Socialists and libertarians use a radically opposite conception of freedom, but they can reasonably discuss with each other the themes wherein freedom is involved. The same is true for religious perspectives. It is not true that there is nothing to be done for secular atheists with what Christians or Jewish persons argue from their specific religious perspective. (cf. Habermas 2006; Chambers 2007) So why would Christians not offer a Christian perspective and atheists their secular perspective of, for instance, human life and ecology? As such, allowing people to use religious reasons is not a form of disrespect; it is rather a way in which one can show respect for another person in his or her particularity. 'Real respect for others takes seriously the distinctive point of view *each* other occupies. It is respect for individuality, for difference' (Stout 2004, 73; see also Wolterstorff 2003, 135; 1997b, 110ff). Also Rawls (2001, 154) wrote that 'it is wise, then, for all sides to introduce their comprehensive doctrines, whether religious or secular, so as to open a way for them to explain to one another how their views do indeed support those basic political values.'

So far, we have just given some negative arguments for strong inclusionism by showing how the arguments for exclusion fail. There are also some positive arguments for strong inclusionism in deliberative democracy. Some political issues cannot be discussed in a neutral way. Obvious examples are abortion, euthanasia, and the bioethical discussions about (human) cloning (cf. Roetz 2006). It is not difficult to show that the discussion for and against abortion rights cannot be neutral with respect to the underlying moral and religious controversy, and therefore must engage rather than avoid substantive moral and religious doctrines at stake. (Sandel 1996, 21; Hauerwas 1981, 196, 212) The political discourse on birth and death, fertilization, embryos and parenthood, but also on poverty, distributive and global justice and ecology is not (and cannot be) value-free. Political and democratic deliberation would be redundant if a neutral scientific discussion resolved all the tensions and antagonisms. As such, in some (important) issues it is undoubtedly an asset when the voices of different religions and world views are heard in public and political debate.

The most powerful argument has to do with the concept of the self that is used. Once we agree that citizens who participate in political deliberation are not the abstract, reasonable subjects as traditional liberalism proposes, it becomes clearer why we cannot keep religious arguments out of public reason. Religions and world views are constitutive elements for the moral identity and it is impossible to make abstraction of these elements when people enter the public space. With Sandel (1996, 18) we can ask if it is possible that 'however encumbered we may be in private, however claimed by moral or religious conventions, we should bracket our encumbrances in public and regard ourselves, *qua* public selves, as independent of any particular loyalties or conceptions of the good'. For believers who take their faith to be among the very most significant features of their being, how can we expect that they act and argue 'pretending' that they are not a Christian without violating their integrity? (cf. Weithman 1994, 8) Benjamin Berger (2002, 47) clarifies: 'From the perspective of the adherent, religion cannot be left in the home or on the steps of Parliament. The religious conscience ascribes to life a divine dimension that infuses all aspects of being. The authority of the divine extends to all decisions, actions, times, and places in the life of the devout.' Religion is not a 'hobby' – a private interest with no public policy implications. In other words, from the perspective of Christians it may be an 'existential necessity' to express religious moral beliefs in a public or political discussion (cf. Kole 2002, 251-3; Carter 1993, 54; Habermas 2006, 9; Wolterstorff 1997b, 105).

In fact the same is true for secular arguments, because it is a misunderstanding to think about *secular* reasons as *neutral* reasons. I agree with Rawls (2001, 143, 148) that secular reason is also 'reasoning in terms of comprehensive nonreligious doctrines'. Secular values, concepts and reasoning belong to a *particular* moral doctrine and are not independent of a *particular* comprehensive world view. As such, secular philosophical doctrines do not provide neutral public reasons. Quite often people seem to confuse secular and neutral reasons and believe that asking Christians to argue in neutral terms is asking them to argue in secular terms. This is not fair as it is possible that much of the Christian view will be lost in the translation, because much of the Christian view (e.g. about abortion) is not translatable in secular terms (cf. Hauerwas 1981, 212; Sandel 1996, 20-21; Greenawalt 1995, 83-84, 119-120). Moreover, the confusion between secular and neutral reasons conceals that *in fact* atheist humanists argue with their comprehensive terms and values while religious people may not do so. Again: 'Why isn't sauce for the goose, sauce for the gander?' The view often expressed 'that while religious reasons should not be invoked to justify legislation, sound secular arguments may be' (cf. Rawls's (2001, 148) formulation) is inconsistent and not tenable. Secularism is not the overarching neutral framework of public reason itself, but only one voice in political life, and it cannot be allowed to be the only one (Parekh 1997, 21).

The whole discussion goes back to the philosophical discussion about autonomous morality. The exclusive view presupposes that an autonomous freestanding morality – a morality that can be thought and justified independently of God, but also independently of any world view – is possible. Audi (2000, 139-41) is quite explicit on that matter: 'Liberal democracy, however, is committed, at least in its best-developed forms, to the *conceptual and epistemic autonomy of ethics.* [...] It is not too much to ask of conscientious religious citizens [...] that they abide by the principles of secular rationale and secular motivation.' The idea of an independent morality is not only endorsed by atheists, also many theologians (Audi is also a Christian) have advocated an autonomous conception of morality (cf. Auer 1971; Fuchs 1973).

However, this autonomous conception of morality is highly problematic because our moral considerations are not fully independent of our world view. Once the limits of platitudinous morality are passed, moral systems and moral theories, both secular and religious, will reflect what Iris Murdoch called 'a vision of life' (Murdoch 1956; Mitchell 1980, 97-105, 146; Brody 1981). What we believe 'is' (ontology and metaphysics) has consequences for what we believe to be 'good and bad' (ethics). This is true for religious believers *and* non-believers. Moral beliefs are not 'metaphysically neutral'; they are intertwined in a wide reflective equilibrium with particular (scientific, metaphysical and/or religious) background theories about human nature and the nature of the world (cf. Gascoigne 2001, 190; Daniels 1979, 258-9; Nielsen 1988, 21-2). So, we agree with Mitchell (1980, 97-8) that it cannot be made 'a reasonable ground of complaint against a religious ethic that it involves metaphysical assumptions, for this is true of any system of ethics. It is a mistake to identify secular morality with "morality" *tout court*.' The consequence for public reason is clear: the appeal to religious-moral reasons cannot be forbidden for their metaphysical presuppositions, because the permitted secular reasons also have (sometimes more implicitly) such presuppositions. When moral questions are discussed in the public forum, it is impossible for people not to argue from within their own comprehensive views and not to draw on the religious, philosophical, and moral grounds that those views provide. We have to acknowledge that religiously grounded moral beliefs inevitably play a role in political deliberation on fundamental matters, so 'it is important that such beliefs, no less than secular moral beliefs, be presented in public political argument *so that they can be tested there*' (Perry 2003, 39). There are too many issues that cannot be resolved or discussed solely on the basis of commonly accepted principles and scientific knowledge, because the disagreement goes back to a deep conflict of values. It seems, then, that the choice for exclusionism leaves a long list of important political questions unaddressed (cf. Greenawalt 1988, ch. 6-9; Galston 1991, 113; Stout 2004, 88-91).

Deliberative Democratic Restraints on Public Reason

In the light of the deliberative democratic perspective and our rejection of autonomous freestanding morality, strong inclusionism is the best theory when thinking about religious arguments in political decision making. However, strong inclusionism is not an 'anything goes' view. Insofar as strong inclusionism goes together with an ideal of democratic deliberation, it must also accept certain requirements and conditions associated with a deliberative approach to political decision making (cf. Boettcher 2005, 512; Habermas 2006). Citizens must incorporate deliberative-democratic attitudes and practices. One of them is the 'duty of civility': (religious) citizens ought to explain their reasons and present public justifications for supporting political choices and positions. Citizens can be asked to do this, as much as possible, with political or public (instead of moral or religious) reasons that can be agreed on by all reasonable persons, irrespective of which comprehensive doctrine they affirm (cf. Rawls's (1993) idea of the overlapping consensus). However, citizens are not discouraged from basing their political decisions or arguments on a religious rationale *alone*, and in some political discussions it seems impossible to maintain 'a wall of separation' between religiously grounded moral discourse and the discourse that takes place in public political argument (Perry 2003, 43; Eberle 2002, 10; Bader 1999).

The democratic attitude means, at the least, that citizens will not support any policy on the basis of a dehumanizing rationale (such as racism or Nazism) that denies the freedom and equal dignity of their compatriots. 'The important thing, given the priority of democracy, should not be whether arguments are religious or secular but whether arguments, attitudes, and practices are compatible with the principles, rights, culture, virtues, and good practices of social, democratic constitutionalism' (Bader 1999, 602; see also Thiemann 1996, 89ff., 173; Wolterstorff 1997a, 1997b, 1997c). Religious or other comprehensive positions that would like to force everybody to live according to that particular doctrine (e.g. the position that all women have to dress in a certain covered way) are problematic, and most of the time not welcome on the democratic forum because they are moving toward reducing the (religious) freedom of other citizens (cf. Audi 2000, 87).

In short, we can say that the deliberative democratic perspective requires respect for the other, involvement in search of the better argument, an engagement in dialogue with the other and the acceptance of democratic decisions (especially when you consider the decision to be immoral). One defining feature of deliberative democracy is that participants are ready for a rational transformation of their beliefs and preferences as a result of the reflection induced by political deliberation (Elster 1998, 1; Dryzek 2000, 31; Habermas 1992). An attitude of fallibility and mutual criticism is thus the basic requirement for every public and political engagement, also when it is based on strong religious commitments. The attitude of fallibility and mutual criticism is one of the most discussed conditions in the context of the use of religious arguments, because citizens who use their religion in the public dialogue are often characterized as people who 'regard themselves as bound to obey a set of overriding and totalizing obligations imposed upon them by their Creator' (cf. Eberle 2002, 183). Very often the critics of inclusionism think that all religious citizens are fundamentalists who are not open for the ideas of others and not willing to change their minds. However, this is not always what happens in reality. Religious people who participate as believers can also consider the arguments and criticism of other citizens with another mindset, and allow that other participants in the democratic deliberation make an evaluation of their reasons. Religiously committed citizens ought to be willing to learn from others and even change their commitments if given sufficient reason to do so (Eberle 2002, 102-8; Perry 2003, 39-44; 1988, 183; Waldron 1993, 817, 841-2).

This deliberative attitude also means that people should not uncritically rely on religiously grounded moral beliefs and must remain open to the criticism of other believers. For example, there is also widespread disagreement among Christians about many politically or morally contested subjects, like same-sex unions, the use of condoms, or abortion. Such disagreement should be an occasion for Christians to subject traditional beliefs to careful, critical scrutiny. This is especially true for the use of the Bible. The position that a citizen can use the Bible uncritically in a literal way, without any extra-Biblical information and in abstraction of human experience is 'obviously and straightforwardly indefensible' (Perry 2003, 55-97; Eberle 2002, 274).

Conclusion

From a deliberative democratic perspective, strong inclusionism is the best theory for thinking about the place of religious (and secular) comprehensive doctrines in public reason. Liberalism does not necessarily exclude the use of religiously grounded moral beliefs in public debate. With Michael Perry (2003, 44) we can conclude that it is not *that* religious convictions are brought to bear in public political argument that should worry us, but *how* they are sometimes brought to bear (e.g. dogmatically). But we should be no less worried about how fundamental secular convictions are sometimes brought to bear in public political debate.' It must be clear that strong inclusionism is not the same as the laissez-faire option. There are still the deliberative-democratic requirements, but these requirements are equally valid for religious as well as for secular participants in the political dialogue.

> All of them have to learn how to resolve the fundamentalist dilemma – namely, that in democratic deliberation and decision making, their 'truths' are no more than opinions among others. Instead of trying to limit the content of public reason by keeping all contested comprehensive doctrines and truth-claims out, one has to develop the duties of civility, such as the duty to explain positions in publicly understandable language, the willingness to listen to others, fair-mindedness, and readiness to accept reasonable accommodations or alterations in one's own view. (Bader 1999, 614; see also Wolterstorff 1997c, 145-7)

Political decisions should be neutral in their formulation of a proposition, but this does not exclude that there is some room for pluralism in the debate that precedes those decisions. From a democratic point of view there is no objection to religious political inputs, on the condition that citizens adopt a democratic attitude with regard to their own (comprehensive) views. Nobody can be excluded in virtue of the fact that he or she uses comprehensive doctrines to argue for his political choice. Only people who refuse dialogue and have no respect for other positions are a priori excluded from democratic decision making and put themselves outside the political community.

References

Ackerman, B. 1989. Why Dialogue? *Journal of Philosophy* 86 (1), 5-22.
Audi, R. 1989. The Separation of Church and State and the Obligations of Citizenship. *Philosophy and Public Affairs* 18, 259-296.
— 2000. *Religious Commitment and Secular Reason.* New York: Cambridge University Press.
Auer, A. 1971. *Autonome Moral und Christlicher Glaube.* Düsseldorf: Patmos-Verlag.

Bader, V. 1999. Religious Pluralism. Secularism or Priority for Democracy? *Political Theory* 27 (5), 597-633.

Benhabib, S. 1992. *Situating the Self.* Cambridge: Polity Press.

— 1996. Toward a Deliberative Model of Democratic Legitimacy. In *Democracy and Difference*, ed. S. Benhabib. Princeton, NJ: Princeton University Press, 67-94.

Berger, B. 2002. The Limits of Belief: Freedom of Religion, Secularism, and the Liberal State. *Canadian Journal of Law & Society* 17 (1), 39-68.

Boettcher, J.W. 2005. Strong Inclusionist Accounts of the Role of Religion in Political Decision Making. *Journal of Social Philosophy* 36 (4), 497-516.

Bohman, J. and W. Rehg. 1997. *Deliberative Democracy: Essays on Reason and Politics.* Cambridge, MA: MIT Press.

Brody, B. 1981. Morality and Religion Reconsidered. In *Divine Commands and Morality*, ed. P. Helm. Oxford: Oxford University Press, 141-153.

Carter, S. 1993. *The Culture of Disbelief. How American Law and Politics Trivialize Religious Devotion.* New York: Basic Books.

Chambers, S. 2007. How Religion speaks to the Agnostic: Habermas on the Persistent Value of Relgion. *Constellations* 14 (2), 210-223.

Chaplin, J. 2000. Beyond Liberal Restraint: Defending Religiously-based Arguments in Law and Public Policy. *University of British Columbia Law Review* (Special Issue on Law, Morality and Religion) 33 (2), 617-646.

Cohen, J. 1998. Democracy and Liberty. In *Deliberative Democracy*, ed. J. Elster. Cambridge: Cambridge University Press, 185-231.

Daniels, N. 1979. Wide Reflective Equilibrium and Theory Acceptance in Ethics. *The Journal of Philosophy* 76 (5), 256-282.

De Dijn, H. 2003. Cultural Identity, Religion, Moral Pluralism and the Law. *Bijdragen: International Journal in Philosophy and Theology* 64, 286-298.

Dryzek, J.S. 2000. *Deliberative Democracy and Beyond. Liberals, Critics, Contestations.* Oxford: Oxford University Press.

Eberle, C. 2002. *Religious Convictions in Liberal Politics.* Cambridge: Cambridge University Press.

Elster, J. 1998. Introduction. In *Deliberative Democracy*, ed. J. Elster. Cambridge: Cambridge University Press.

Fuchs, J. 1973. *Existe-t-il une moral chrétienne?* Gembloux: Duculot.

Galston, W.A. 1991. *Liberal Purposes. Goods, Virtues, and Diversity in the Liberal State.* Cambridge: Cambridge University Press.

Gascoigne, R. 2001. *The Public Forum and Christian Ethics.* Cambridge: Cambridge University Press.

Greenawalt, K. 1988. *Religious Convictions and Political Choice.* New York: Oxford University Press.

— 1995. *Private Consciences and Public Reasons.* New York: Oxford University Press.

Gutmann, A. and D. Thompson. 1996. *Democracy and Disagreement.* Cambridge, MA: Harvard University Press.

Habermas, J. 1962. *Strukturwandel der Öffentlichkeit. Untersuchungen zu einer Kategorie der bürgerlichen Gesellschaft,* Neuwied/Rhein: Leuchterhand.

— 1992. *Faktizität und Geltung. Beiträge zur Diskurstheorie des Rechts und des demokratischen Rechtsstaats,* Frankfurt am Main: Suhrkamp.

— 1995. Reconciliation through the Public Use of Reason: Remarks on John Rawls's Political Liberalism. *The Journal of Philosophy* 92 (3), 109-31.

— 2006. Religion in the Public Sphere. *European Journal of Philosophy* 14 (1), 1-25.

Hauerwas, S. 1981. *Community of Character: Towards a Constructive Christian Social Ethic.* Notre Dame: University of Notre Dame Press.

Kole, J. 2002. *Moral Autonomy and Christian Faith. A Discussion with William K. Frankena.* Delft: Eburon.

Larmore, C. 1987. Liberalism and the Neutrality of the State. In C. Larmore, *Patterns of Moral Complexity.* Cambridge: Cambridge University Press, 40-68.

Mitchell, B. 1980. *Morality: Religious and Secular. The Dilemma of the Traditional Conscience.* Oxford: Clarendon Press.

Murdoch, I. 1956-7. Vision and Choice in Morality. *Proceedings of the Aristotelian Society* Suppl. Vol. 30, 32-58.

Neuhaus, R.J. 1984. *The Naked Public Square: Religion and Democracy in America.* Grand Rapids: Eerdmans.

Nielsen, K. 1988. In Defense of Wide Reflective Equilibrium. In *Ethics and Justification,* ed. D. Odegard. Edmonton: Academic Printing & Publishing, 19-37.

Parekh, B. 1997. Religion and Public Life. In *Church, State and Religious Minorities,* ed. T. Modood. London: Policy Studies Institute, 16-22.

Perry, M.J. 1991. *Love and Power: The Role of Religion and Morality in American Politics.* Oxford: Oxford University Press.

— 1997. *Religion in Politics: Constitutional and Moral Perspectives.* Oxford: Oxford University Press.

— 2003. *Under God? Religious Faith and Liberal Democracy.,* Cambridge: Cambridge University Press.

Quinn, P.L. 1997. Political Liberalisms and their Exclusions of the Religious. In *Religion and Contemporary Liberalism*, ed. P. Weithman. Notre Dame: University of Notre Dame Press, 138-61.

— 2001. Religious Diversity and Religious Toleration. *International Journal for Philosophy of Religion* 50, 57-80.

Rawls, J. 1993 (1996). *Political Liberalism*. New York: Columbia University Press.

— 2001. The Idea of Public Reason Revisited. In *The Law of Peoples*, J. Rawls. Cambridge MA: Harvard University Press, 129-80.

Riordan, P. 2004. Permission to Speak: Religious Arguments in Public Reason. *The Heythrop Journal* 45, 178-196.

Roetz, H. 2006. *Cross-cultural Issues in Bioethics. The Example of Human Cloning.* Amsterdam: Rodopi.

Rorty, R. 1999. *Philosophy and Social Hope.* New York: Penguin Books.

— 2003. Religion in the Public Square. A Reconsideration. *Journal of Religious Ethics* 31 (1), 141-149.

Sandel, M. 1996. *Democracy's Discontent. America in Search of a Public Philosophy.* Cambridge MA: Harvard University Press.

Stout, J. 2004. *Democracy and Tradition*, Princeton NJ: Princeton University Press.

Taylor, C. 1999. Conditions of an Unforced Consensus on Human Rights. In *The East Asian Challenge for Human Rights*, eds. J.R. Bauer and D.A. Bell. Cambridge: Cambridge University Press, 124-144.

Thiemann, R.F. 1996. *Religion in Public Life.* Washington, D.C.: Georgetown University Press.

Waldron, J. 1993. Religious Contributions in Public Deliberation. *San Diego Law Review* 30, 817-48.

Weithman, P.J. 1994. Rawlsian Liberalism and the Privatisation of Religion. *Journal of Religious Ethics* 22 (1), 3-26.

— 1997. Introduction. In *Religion and Contemporary Liberalism*, ed. P.J Weithman. Notre Dame: University of Notre Dame Press, 1-37.

— 2002. *Religion and the Obligations of Citizenship.* Cambridge: Cambridge University Press.

Wolterstorff, N. 1997a. Why we Should Reject what Liberalism Tells us About Speaking and Acting for Religious Reasons. In *Religion and Contemporary Liberalism*, ed. P. Weithman. Notre Dame: University of Notre Dame Press, 162-181.

— 1997b. The Role of Religion in Decision and Discussion of Political Issues. In *Religion in the Public Square*, eds. R. Audi and N. Wolterstorff. London: Rowman and Littlefield, 67-120.

— 1997c. Audi on Religion, Politics, and Liberal Democracy. In *Religion in the Public Square*, eds. R. Audi and N. Wolterstorff. London: Rowman and Littlefield, 145-165.

— 2003. An Engagement with Rorty. *Journal of Religious Ethics* 31 (1), 129-139.

Wong, D. 1989. Three Kinds of Incommensurability. In *Relativism: Interpretation and Confrontation*, ed. M. Krausz. Notre Dame: University of Notre Dame Press, 140-158.

13   The Knowledge Deficit and Beyond: Sources of Controversy in Public Debates

Olga Crapels[1]

According to many biotechnological scientists, controversies over agricultural biotechnology (or any kind of biotechnology for that matter) are characterised by a knowledge gap between the lay public and the expert scientists (e.g. Yankelovich 1991; Irwin & Wynne 1996; Hornig Priest 2001). It is often claimed that the difference between adversaries and advocates is overlapping the distinction between public and experts. Hence, in biotechnology science communication research, the public/expert gap has often been said to be an important, if not the most important cause for biotechnology controversies. According to these scientists, what ought to be done to solve this controversy is to minimize this gap. They claim that the public's lack of information or a lack of understanding is the dominant reason for this gap. The gap can be minimized by educating the public into becoming semi-experts.

The central question of this essay is whether it really makes sense to locate this lack of information or knowledge as the central source of the biotechnology controversy. Can it not be the case that the difference between the public's and the scientists' perspective on biotechnology is caused by wholly different kind of problem? This article evaluates the claim that the public's lack of information or understanding is the main cause for the biotechnology controversy. Although it appears defensible to claim that there really is a lack of information and understanding among the public, I want to suggest that there are alternative and more plausible sources of controversy. Perhaps we should direct our attention away from the field of the public understanding of science by focusing on the scientists' understanding of the public.

Knowledge Deficit

Most scientific risk communication is still grounded in a *knowledge deficit approach*. This means that risk communicators think that many people don't have enough information about science and risks or that they don't understand this information. This is also referred to as the problem of science illiteracy. Risk communicators assume that this is the main reason why most people are reluctant to accept, for example, agricultural biotechnology. To them, this knowledge deficit is what characterizes the gap between experts and the lay public.

Although being a lay person does not automatically imply that you are not able to answer simple questions about science or biotechnology in particular, much empirical scientific research concludes that many people are in fact not able to do so. Important examples of such research are the EuroBarometer surveys (e.g. Gaskell et al. 2003), which always receive a fair amount of media and policy attention. Since the 1990s, these surveys have also been carried out to study how Europeans think about biotechnology. One of the striking and often-mentioned findings of the 1996 survey is that 25 to 35 per cent (and these numbers only increased in the 2005 survey) of the Europeans answer 'true' to statements such as the following:

- Ordinary tomatoes don't have genes, but genetically modified ones do.
- By eating a modified fruit, a person's genes could also become modified.
- Genetically modified animals are always bigger than ordinary ones.

None of these statements are correct. This seems to indicate a lack of information on biotechnology or a lack of accurately understanding this information among the public. As a result, these survey results are often taken as an important quantitative source for biotechnological risk-perception research. The aim of such research is to study why the public usually has such a different perception of biotechnological risk than experts do, and particularly, why they are so negative about biotechnology. A crucial point is that this research is often implicitly carried out in order to reduce this negativism to a minimum, to avoid controversy and to increase the level of acceptance of biotechnology.

Controversies are often characterized by uncertainties: cognitive uncertainties (due to a lack of information of lack of knowledge), socio-economic uncertainties, and moral uncertainties (due to a lack of commonly shared normative evaluatory guidelines) (cf. Hansen 2005, 10). Following survey results like those from the EuroBarometer, researchers studying risk perception (scientists or science-oriented scholars) argue that cognitive uncertainties must be the main reason behind people's negative attitude.

The EuroBarometer survey questioned Europeans about biotechnological controversies. It found out that most Europeans, in contrast to what the media state, are not very negative or technophobic about biotechnology. But they aren't very optimistic either. More specific findings show that most people are rather supportive of medical applications of biotechnology, while at the same time being much less supportive regarding agricultural use of biotechnology. This seems to correlate with people's uncertainty, measured in the same surveys, concerning the level of risk and benefits people think are linked to the application.

Because people are uncertain about the level of risk in the case of agricultural biotechnology, and because there is a controversy about GMOs (genetically modified organisms), the link is quickly made: it could be said that the public's uncertainty, according to some scientists only caused by blatant ignorance or stupidity, is the primary cause for this controversy. Science communicators see this risk perception research analysis as an important basis for their vision on science communication: science communication must aim at informing people about science and help them to understand this information better. The implicit assumption here is that knowledgeable, better informed people are more inclined to evaluate science positively. A positive evaluation of science means less opposition, a broader consensus, and thus less controversy. This is desirable in order to boost the public acceptance of science and to make further scientific development and progress easier.

However, while the results of EuroBarometer surveys show that there seems to be some relation between being negative or uncertain about biotechnology and knowing little about it, the EuroBarometer researchers do not conclude that a lack of knowledge tells the whole story. People can also object and feel uncertain about the introduction or development of a technology for other reasons, like moral or socio-economic ones. Factors such as trust, moral values, and religious beliefs play a very important role here. Thus, it is not only *cognitive* uncertainty that causes people's negative attitude. Informing people about the technical facts, so that they will not consider false statements to be true anymore, does, therefore, not automatically imply that they are more willing to accept the technology. Why then do risk perception researchers and science communicators still hold on to the belief that cognitive uncertainties are the ultimate cause of people's negative attitude and the source of the biotechnology controversy?

Science and Myths

Since the 1990s, many philosophers, sociologists, and others (e.g. Slovic 2000; Irwin & Wynne 1996) have looked closer into the issue of science communication, risk perception and public controversy. They also studied the knowledge deficit approach. Their conclusion has been that the public is not irrational, ignorant, or stupid. What is described by scientists as a lack of knowledge or information is in fact most of the time something completely different and, therefore, cannot be the main reason for a controversy or for the public to be negative about biotechnology. Marris et al. (2001) studied these findings and used the results of these studies to strengthen their own conclusion that scientists actually believe in 'myths'.

Marris and her co-authors have analysed literature and interviewed lay people about their ideas of biotechnology, as well as interviewing 'stakeholders':[2] 'those within governmental, regulatory, scientific (research and expertise) institutions, and commercial organizations (mostly biotechnology firms, less so food producers and food distributors)' (ibid. 2001, 75), and conclude that there are at least ten myths that these 'scientists' often believe in. For example:

> Myth 1: The primordial cause of the problem is that lay people are ignorant about scientific facts.
>
> Myth 2: People are either 'for' or 'against' GMOs.
>
> Myth 3: Consumers accept medical GMOs but refuse GMOs used in food and agriculture.
>
> Myth 5: Consumers want labelling in order to exercise their freedom of choice.
>
> Myth 6: The public thinks – wrongly – that GMOs are unnatural.
>
> Myth 7: The public demands 'zero risk' – and this is not reasonable.

Why are they called 'myths'? Humans have always created myths, in order to control, to give coherence and a sense of meaning to our experiences. Myths can inspire and guide us in our daily lives by helping us to deal with problems, fears or challenges. Like many other stories, myths make it possible for us to keep on living in a world that most of the times, seems uncontrollable and mysterious to us. But while myths can help us, they can also blind us by letting us believe in things that have no basis in reality. Marris et al. call scientist's perceptions 'myths' to stress the fact that these statements are not supported by empirical evidence, and in order to 'convey the fact that among certain circles of actors they are assumed to be obvious and *do not need to be* supported by empirical evidence. Thus they circulate, largely unchallenged, accompanied by a series of repeated anecdotes, which are accepted as confirmation of these views' (ibid. 2001, 75; italics added). One of these 'anecdotes' is that, historically speaking, the public has never been enthusiastic about new technologies (for example cars, planes, or vaccines) being introduced into their daily life, but once they found out the benefits of these technologies they were keen to accept them. In scientific circles, the main idea behind this 'anecdote' is that things will happen in the same way in the case of GMOs: lay people have groundless and even irrational opinions, but over time these will evaporate. Even so, what this 'anecdote' and other 'anecdotes' fail to recognize is that the technologies in question were modified, through regulatory and technological evolutions, before becoming accepted (e.g. extensive regulations concerning the driving and manufacture of motor vehicles). Moreover, they fail to acknowledge that many of the original risk concerns raised by the lay public have indeed been realized (e.g. pedestrian deaths from car driving, plane accidents, the Chernobyl accident, negative health impacts linked to vaccinations, and so on), and that some more or less unanticipated negative impacts have also occurred (e.g. harmful environmental impacts of motor vehicles) (ibid. 2001, 77).

The acceptance of new technologies thus may have followed the increasing familiarity with these technologies, but not without the modifications made that took into account some very real concerns people had. In the end, then, what these 'anecdotes' accomplish is a widening of a gap between what scientists consider to be real objective risks and rational opinions and what the public thinks.

This difference between what scientists claim as objective risks and what lay people perceive as risks (and what is later often acknowledged as real risk), and why this difference exists, has been extensively studied. One approach, of which Brian Wynne is a prominent proponent, concerns the quality of knowledge on which risk management and politics is built on, with an important theme being the apparent 'scientification of knowledge'. On the one hand, according to Wynne, policy makers and risk researchers put too much faith in scientific knowledge, even to the extent that it denies or excludes uncertainties inherent in all knowledge production and excludes other forms of knowledge. On the other hand, they are predisposed to misunderstand the concerns of the public which underlie a number of technological controversies. Wynne (1996) illustrates this by the case of the Cumbrian sheep farmers in the wake of the Chernobyl disaster. These farmers experienced radioactive fallout from this accident, which contaminated their flocks and upland pastures. The government restricted them from selling their sheep freely, although this was their primary form of income. Furthermore, scientists visited the farmers to inform them about the influence of radioactivity and to test whether it decreased to an acceptable level. These tests were a reason to extend the period in which sheep could not be sold. The relation between the scientists and the farmers did not develop very well, because the scientists had no ear for what the farmers said about, for instance, where their flocks grazed, so that the scientists could study that part of the land instead of a part that was never grazed upon. Thus, 'the farmers experienced the scientists as denying, and thus threatening, their social identity by ignoring the farmers' specialist knowledge and farming practices, including their adaptive decision making idiom' (ibid. 1996, 39). According to Wynne's analysis, the scientists failed to be credible in the eyes of the sheep farmers. From numerous interviews with the farmers concerned, he derives that there are several criteria that lay people have to judge to assess whether an authority is credible (cf. 1996, 38). For example: does the scientific knowledge work, are predictions accurate? Do scientists pay attention to other available knowledge; for example, when doing tests do they follow farmer's knowledge on sheep grazing instead of testing on a pasture where they never graze? Are scientists open to criticism? What are the institutional and social affiliations of scientists; are they trustworthy or is there a conspiracy with the government? In analysing the controversy between the sheep-farmers and the scientists, it becomes clear that it is not primarily a lack of technical information or a lack of knowledge that underpins the farmers' negativity about the scientists and scientific knowledge. This could pinpoint an alternative vision on what the most important source of biotechnological controversies is. Wynne's analysis suggests among other things that it is 'trust' and 'credibility' that are the key dimensions of the public's understanding and perception of risks. Perhaps the public's experience of not being taken seriously and their lack of trust and credibility in scientists and scientific institutions are better predictors for scientific controversy than a knowledge deficit.

Professional Responsibility

Although the knowledge deficit approach is still 'endemic' (cf. Hansen et al. 2003, 111) in some scientific circles, trust and credibility are nowadays also acknowledged by risk perception researchers as important factors in technological controversy. Even so, it remains unclear what they understand by 'trust', 'apart from the absence of controversy' (Hansen 2005, 72). In Marris et al. (2001, 87 ff.) the interviewed scientists were asked why they think the public does not trust them. Their answers suggested that it is actually the public itself that was to be distrusted, and there are several reasons for this, for example:

- the public's lack of *adequate* information;
- the public's failure to acknowledge their past errors in risk perception and to learn from past mistakes;
- the public's lack of sanctions for those responsible for mismanagement or fraud;
- the public's denial of inherent uncertainties, especially long-term or chronic impacts;
- the public's reliance on limited types of expertise.

In reading these reasons it becomes clear that 'scientists' mainly have no trust in the public or its abilities. In the few cases in which they think themselves involved they claim that better communication (to increase public understanding) could prevent a lack of trust (for a typical example of this type of reasoning see Marchant 2001). It may not come as a surprise, therefore, that Marris et al. firmly conclude that the knowledge-deficit approach still exists.

However, not all scientists blame the public, at least not directly. Some scientists acknowledge that it is not only information that is misunderstood or distrusted, but also institutions or people (e.g. the third bullet above). Sometimes they look in the mirror: among scientists it is pretty often thought that 'scientific excellence' is the manner in which a 'crisis of trust' and credibility can be dissolved. An excellent scientist is a credible scientist. Although not admissible as empirical evidence, this became really clear to me in a recent discussion with a friend who holds a Ph.D. in theoretical physics: he could not believe that the public could distrust an excellent scientist – what more can such a person do to be trustworthy than being very good at his job? Psychological and social scientific research studies suggest alternatives. In their 2003 article, Hansen et al. review some of these studies. One of the conclusions they derive from these studies is that the public makes a distinction between expertise or excellence, and trustworthiness. Although excellence might be something that can be objectively established, this is not the case with trustworthiness. People can perceive a scientist to be an excellent researcher, but at the same time not consider her to be a trustworthy person.

Annoying as that may be for hard working scientists, expertise is in the eyes of the public worth nothing without trustworthiness. And without trustworthiness there is no trust in science. Universities are acknowledging this by making it clear that researchers (scientists and scholars alike) and teachers at universities have a professional responsibility to do their work in such ways that it can be qualified as trustworthy. In its *Code of Conduct for Scientific Practice* (2004) the Association of Universities in the Netherlands (in Dutch: VSNU) provides a set of norms for teachers and researchers at universities that go beyond mere expertise; for example scrupulousness (being thorough and honest), reliability (being trustworthy), verifiability (that something can be checked and that results can be replicated), impartiality (not being led by personal or other interests), and independence (operating in academic liberty). These kinds of observations and codes can also be found in the business world. It is thus possible to draw a parallel between discussions on trust in science and trust in business organizations. In the business world the question of how to attain trust from the public is also a prominent topic. Public trust is necessary for the survival of companies. Without it, it would be impossible to develop and sell products. The public gives business its 'license to operate'. Businesses recognize that trust is not something one-dimensional; if it's not based solely on expertise, there must be other reasons that give the public reason to trust you. Koehn (1994, 11) confirms this: 'We do not base our decision to trust professionals upon cleverness or skilfulness. Since a given skill may be perfectly compatible with harmful service, our judgments of professionalism ultimately look beyond skill to some trust-engendering feature of professional practice.' Apparently then, there seem to be other forms of trust necessary than just professionals' expertise. However, the question remains as to what this 'trust-engendering feature' that Koehn refers to actually is.

In some literature (e.g. Nooteboom 2002; Hansen 2005) several forms of trust are distinguished, for example: trust in persons; trust in social roles or competences (doctors, judges, policemen); trust in procedures (that is not directly vested in actors; e.g. in the fairness and independence of courts); trust in materials (e.g. trust that machines will not fail).

What all these different forms of trust illustrate is that to overcome the public's distrust it is not enough for science communication researchers to provide information or to stress the credible source of their information, no matter how sound the scientific evidence or the scientist behind that source is. Scientists and scientific institutions are ever more almost 'pushed' in addressing the public's concerns and in showing that they take their professional responsibilities serious. Business organizations have already learned this lesson the hard way, something illustrated by the case of the dumping of the Brent Spar, a 'classic example of risk communication gone wrong' (cf Löfstedt & Renn 1997).

In May 1995, Shell and Exxon, two major oil companies, wanted to dispose of the oil storage buoy named Brent Spar. This decision received massive media attention. After this, everything went downhill for Shell. Although Shell communicated to the public that, environmentally speaking, dumping of the oil storage in deep water wasn't that bad, the public, especially in Germany, supported Greenpeace by boycotting Shell. Shell Germany received over 11,000 letters from lay people protesting against the dumping. Many of them complained that Shell was greedy: they had the money to dispose of the oil storage in a more responsible way, so why didn't they use it? Were they even thinking of the harm they could inflict on future generations (many people added photographs of their children)? Others stressed that, according to them, deep sea dumping was morally wrong, because it could hurt nature. Besides the boycott, Shell gas stations were threatened with bomb explosions. Shell was standing in the dark and had no idea how to counter the public's responses (cf Löfstedt and Renn 1997).

In the Dutch television documentary about the Brent Spar case, 'Een geschenk uit de hemel' ('A gift from heaven'; VPRO 2000), Shell officials acknowledged in retrospective that, at the time, they had a very weak risk communication strategy. What went wrong was that they:

> adopted a top-down approach rather than a dialogue approach...In so doing, they alienated the public immediately, and came across as arrogant and unmovable. Once the amplification process was at full speed, time was running out to launch such a dialogue approach. Second, Shell was not seen as trustworthy, while Greenpeace was (Löfstedt & Renn 1997, 134).

Shell learned from these events. In 1998, they published the report 'Profits & Principles – does there have to be a choice?' which marked their 'renewed' commitment to recognize the concerns of the public, and the need to listen, engage and respond, to the public. In the introduction to the 1999 brochure 'Listening and Responding', chairman Moody-Stuart states:

> We know that we will be judged by our actions, rather than by fine words...Of course, we don't expect you to see things just from our point of view. We know all real dialogue must be a two-way conversation, and so we've ended each advertisement with a request to our stakeholders to talk to us and let us know what they think (Shell 1999, 1-2).

What business organizations like Shell have learned from the public is that they really need a license to operate. The traditional business adagio has moved from 'trust us' via 'tell me' (information) to 'show me' (transparency) and 'involve me' (dialogue). Trustworthiness can be improved by being more socially responsive, by engaging in a real dialogue with the public, and by actively showing that you do something with the public's knowledge and concerns. This means that in order to enhance public trust in science, time (and money) need to be invested to study what really concerns people and what can be done to take these concerns seriously.

Taking Matters Seriously

'Was will das Weib?' is said to be one of the questions that haunted Sigmund Freud until the day he died. Maybe biotech scientists should experience that same haunted feeling considering the question 'Was will das Publikum?'. Of course, they could still choose *not* to think about possible answers to this question. Nelkin (1989) suggests that in the past, 'concerns about the effect of risk communication have spawned proposals to restrict public access of information' (1989, 110). 'From the perspective of industry, public discussion of potential risks could lead to the intrusion of burdensome regulations, fuel compensation claims, or require the installation of costly equipment to reduce risks' (ibid.). However, not informing people about what's happening in biotechnology is not a very realistic option. Clearly, there are costs and inconveniences for scientists and industries linked to the disclosure of information. But these costs and inconveniences must be weighed against what Nelkin calls the 'imperatives of open communication' (1989, 111 ff.):

- to engage knowledgeably as informed citizens in political choices, citizens must have access to information about the risks as well as the benefits of technology;
- informed consent must take precedence over efficiency;
- open communication may force public officials to be accountable to their constituents;
- open communication may help bring critical problems to the policy agenda.

So, as specified by Nelkin, 'there are sound political, ethical and pragmatic reasons for improving (...) access to risk information' (cf. Nelkin 1989, 111). However, what does Nelkins' plea for the imperative of open communication means concretely? According to many social studies (Hansen 2005; Irwin & Wynne 1996), the main thing the public wants is to be included in a dialogue with science and policy makers. In the case of the Cumbrian sheep-farmers, the scientists could have taken the farmers' practical knowledge seriously when they were applying their scientific knowledge to these people's flocks and pastures. In the case of the Brent Spar it means that Shell should have considered the public's ethical concerns before deciding on dumping the oil storage buoy.

Business organizations already learned from experience that the public wants to be included in a dialogue; slowly but surely words like ethics, integrity, values and responsibility became incorporated in management jargon. In the academic world, scholars acknowledge that the established sources of knowledge cannot always deliver solutions to problems that are satisfactory to all stakeholders involved (including the public). People's concerns have to be considered too. The question remains how this can be done sincerely, without letting it look like mere window-dressing (saying that you pay attention to the public's concerns or needs but actually doing nothing).

According to Karssing (2000, 19ff), some organizations might think that they don't have to take the people's concerns very seriously. However, he claims that there are very good reasons why organizations should do so; in the end it will only cost them if they think they can solve problems with 'window dressing'. Karssing distinguishes four motives for organizations to pay attention to people's concerns:
- because it limits their risks;
- because it is profitable;
- because it is the right thing to do;
- because they are forced to by law.

According to Karssing, these four motives do not exclude each other. Of course, organizations can have more than one reason to do something, just like individuals can have more than one motive to do something. Although it is never really clear what one's motives are, because they are invisible to other people, Karssing states that it would be very cynical to conclude that window-dressing is then always a possibility. Besides that, when it comes to business ethics: 'you can fool all of the people some of the time, you can fool some of the people all of the time, but you cannot fool all of the people all the time' (Abraham Lincoln, quoted by Karssing 2000, 22). Organizations or people (be it business organizations, scientists or scientific institutions) that fool people will have even more problems to be trusted in the future.

Conclusion

Most scientists experience the public/expert gap as the dominant reason for the biotechnology controversy on GMOs. According to many of them, what causes this gap is the lay public's lack of being technologically informed or the lack of having the knowledge to understand such information. In this paper I question whether this really is the primary source of the controversy. My conclusion is that it is not. I agree with Marris, et al., that there are certain 'myths' at the basis of this knowledge deficit approach. Risk science communicators should take more time to study what really lies beneath the controversy. This paper has argued that concepts like trust and credibility play a major role at the core of this controversy. It has argued that a more self-reflexive attitude on the scientists' side (having an eye for their own mistakes, weaknesses and responsibilities), and a more open attitude for the concerns of the public involved, could really help. Involving the public in a real dialogue might prove a better way to quench the heat of the biotechnology controversy. That this is an important subject for further study, becomes obvious when following the media attention for biotechnology. Not only is biotechnology still a very hot topic, controversies over biotechnology are only one example of the ever-recurring question of how we should think and act in situations when science and new technologies are involved.

Notes

1   I would like to thank Willem B. Drees and Edgar Karssing for their comments
    on a draft of this article. Research for this contribution was supported by the
    Netherlands Organization for Scientific Research, NWO.
2   Because 'stakeholder' is also a term that is often used in everyday life to in-
    clude the public as well, I will from now on say 'scientist' (between quotation
    marks) in cases when I also mean those within governmental, regulatory, and
    scientific institutions, and commercial biotechnology organizations.

References

Bauer, M. and G. Gaskell. 2002a. Researching the public sphere of biotech-
    nology. In *Biotechnology, the Making of a Global Controversy*, eds. M.
    Bauer and G. Gaskell. Cambridge: Cambridge University Press, 1-17.
—   2002b. The biotechnology movement. In *Biotechnology, the Making of
    Global Controversy*, eds. M. Bauer and G. Gaskell. Cambridge: Cam-
    bridge University Press, 379-404.
Gaskell, G., N. Allum, and S. Stares. 2003. *Europeans and Biotechnology
    in 2002 – EuroBarometer 58.02* (2nd edition). Brussels: EC Directorate
    General for Research.
Hansen, J., L. Holm, L. Frewer, P. Robinson, and P. Sandøe. 2003. Beyond
    the knowledge deficit: recent research into lay and expert attitudes to
    food risks. *Appetite* 41, 111-121.
Hansen, J. 2005. *Framing the Public. Three Cases in Public Participation in
    the Governance of Agricultural Technology* (thesis), downloaded from:
    http://www.iue.it/Personal/Researchers/Janus/Thesis_J_Hansen.pdf
Hornig Priest, S. 2001. Misplaced Faith. *Science Communication* 23 (2),
    97-110.
Irwin, A. and B. Wynne. 1996, *Misunderstanding Science? The Public Re-
    construction of Science and Technology*. Cambridge: Cambridge Uni-
    versity Press.
Karssing, E. 2000, *Morele competentie in organisaties*. Assen: Van Gorcum.
Koehn, D. 1994, *The Ground of Professional Ethics*. London: Routledge.
Löfstedt, R.E. and O. Renn. 1997, The Brent Spar Controversy: An Ex-
    ample of Risk Communication Gone Wrong. *Risk Analysis* 17 (2), 131-
    136.
Marchant R. 2001. From the test tube to the table. *EMBO Reports* 2, 354-
    357.

Marris, C., B. Wynne, P. Simmons, and S. Weldon. 2001. *Public Perceptions of Agricultural Biotechnologies in Europe. Final Report of the PABE research project*, downloaded from: http://www.lancs.ac.uk/depts/ieppp/pabe/docs/pabe_finalreport.pdf

Nelkin, D. 1989. Communicating technological risk: the social construction of risk perception. *Annual Review of Public Health* 10, 95-113.

Nooteboom, B. 2002. *Vertrouwen. Vormen, grondslagen, gebruik en gebreken van vetrouwen*, Schoonhoven: Academic Service.

Shell. 1998. *Profits & Principles – Does There Have to be a Choice?.* Shell Publicity Service.

— 1999. *Listening and Responding. The Profits & Principles Campaign.* Shell Publicity Service.

Slovic, P. 2000. *The Perception of Risk.* London: Earthscan.

VPRO. 2000. *Een geschenk uit de hemel.* Dutch television documentary.

VSNU. 2004. *The Netherlands Code of Conduct for Scientific Practice*, downloaded from: http://www.vsnu.nl/web/show/id=54033/lang-id=43

Wynne, B. 1996. Misunderstood misunderstandings: social identities and public uptake of science'. In *Misunderstanding Science? The Public Reconstruction of Science and Technology.* Cambridge: Cambridge University Press, 19-46.

— 1996b, May the Sheep Safely Graze? A Reflexive View of the Expert-Lay Knowledge Divide. In *Risk, Environment & Modernity. Towards a New Ecology*, eds. S. Lash, B. Szerszynski and B. Wynne. Thousands Oaks: Sage, 44-83.

Yankelovich, D. 1991, *Coming to Public Judgment. Making Democracy Work in a Complex World.* Syracuse: Syracuse University Press.

14 Public Trust and Nutrigenomics

Franck L.B. Meijboom

Introduction

> A trip to the diet doc, circa 2013. You prick your finger, draw a little blood and send it, along with a $100 fee, to a consumer genomics lab in California. There, it's passed through a mass spectrometer, where its proteins are analyzed. It is cross-referenced with your DNA profile. A few days later, you get an e-mail message with your recommended diet for the next four weeks. It doesn't look too bad: lots of salmon, spinach, selenium supplements, bread with olive oil. Unsure of just how lucky you ought to feel, you call up a few friends to see what their diets look like...(...) Nobody is eating exactly what you are. Your diet is uniquely tailored. (Grierson 2003)

This example is probably quite different from what we are used to as we do our daily shopping. What we put in our shopping trolley is often only to a marginal extent determined by our health status, let alone by our genotype. However, as the result of research in the field of nutrigenomics this scenario might become less like science fiction than it may appear now. Nutrigenomics is a generic term for a field of research that provides the opportunities to study the interactions between food, lifestyle, and genetic factors. This results in many new food and dietary products. Personalized dietary advices can be one of these products. The aim is to introduce dietary advices that fit the specific genetically induced risk profile of a person or of a sub-group within a population, while traditionally the aim is to develop advices that are beneficial for individuals in general (cf. Meijboom et al. 2003).

This is a useful example to use for an analysis of trust in new technologies, since it illustrates that nutrigenomics research does not only result in new opportunities of health promotion and preventive medicine, but also raises questions of trust. A personalized dietary advice that can reduce our individual risk of a certain ailment, for instance colon cancer, does not merely presuppose self-discipline, but also trust in numerous other agents. Our need to trust experts and (regulatory) institutions grows with the introduction of new technologies. On top of this issue of the increased need of trust, the combination of two sectors, the food and the health sectors, has as a result that existing routines that provide predictability are either unavailable or insufficiently clear, which complicates trust (Meijboom 2007).

This leads to the question of how we have to deal with public trust in nutrigenomics products. This question is especially relevant since public trust in food products has been subjected to a lot of discussion and academic attention during the last decade (cf. FAO 2003; Poppe & Kjaernes 2003). Especially the introduction of technologies such as biotechnology have raised various questions of trust.

The dominant (regulatory) approach to this problem aims at establishing trust by providing information on risks and increasing the predictability of the product. This is in line with some theories that claim that establishing trust is mainly an issue of risk calculation based on information. However, with all the efforts that have been made at the level of risk analysis and communication, we are still faced with a debate on the lack of public trust. This calls for an explanation and raises the question of how we have to deal with public trust when we are confronted with novel food products.

In this chapter I argue that the problems of trust can better be addressed as problems of trustworthiness. From this shift of focus, I analyse the tension between the improved risk analysis and information services and the problematic status of trust. First, I argue that trust is based on other considerations than risk calculation. Trusting and making risk calculations are two different, albeit sometimes complementary, mechanisms that help us deal with situations of uncertainty. Therefore, better risk assessment and more risk information do not necessarily lead to more trust. Second, information that enhances predictability is often proposed as a way to establishing public trust. However, enhancing predictability with respect to new food products is not an easy task. Moreover, showing that an institution is predictable does not necessarily entail that it is trustworthy. I also argue that a focus on trustworthiness illustrates the importance of taking the emotional aspect of trust seriously and claim that this calls for the introduction of two normative conditions for trustworthiness. The emotional aspect of trust explains why the same information and the same acts of the trustee are evaluated differently, depending on whether one trusts the other actor or not. The normative conditions illustrate why the vulnerable status of the individual should not be seen as an opportunity to take advantage of them, and that it is possible to formulate trustful expectations when we lack predictable actions.

Trustworthiness as the Key

Trust enables an individual to perform actions, such as buying and consuming food, despite the uncertainty and the lack of personal control he is confronted with. For instance, when I lack any kind of knowledge regarding the possible health effects of a nutrigenomics product, I am still able to buy and consume it. I would not buy it because I am indifferent to my own health, but because I trust certain agents in science, the food sector, or the government to take care of my health. In trusting, one acts 'as if' certain possible situations will not occur (Lewis & Weigert 1985). This acting 'as if' is not an escape into a make-believe world of certainty and control. When we adopt an attitude of trust we do not pretend, but we actually have a sincere belief that the other agent is trustworthy, that is, competent and adequately motivated to act in the expected way.

Since it is the attitude of the individual who is trusting that is decisive here, problems of trust are often addressed as a dilemma of the individual agent. Consequently, the problem is framed in terms of a failure of trust from the individual. Therefore, increasing trust is considered the most effective method to address the problem.

However, the definition of a decline in trust as a failure of individual agents has an incorrect starting point. To address problems of trust in a fruitful way, the question should not be 'How to increase trust?', but 'Why would an individual agent trust the other agent?' and 'Is this agent trustworthy?' To start with, he who wants to be trusted should be trustworthy. This shift has a practical reason, since institutional agents cannot change individuals so that they will adopt a trustful attitude. However, they can show themselves to be trustworthy. The shift in focus is important since defining a hesitance to trust in terms of the individual's problem only underscores and confirms the individual's vulnerable position.

The observed problems of trust can be interpreted as an important signal of the problems with respect to the trustworthiness of agents.

Therefore, the problems should better be addressed as problems of trust-worthiness (Meijboom et al. 2006; 2008) as opposed to problem of trust. Consequently, the aim is not just to build trust in novel food and dietary products, but to show oneself to be a trustworthy actor.

Public Trust as Different from Considerations of Risk

Most definitions of trust have one element in common: the idea that it enables agents to cope with situations of uncertainty and lack of control. The context of trust is always one of uncertainty and related to the inability to personally control the situation. This element can easily be recognized with respect to products of nutrigenomics. As a consumer you cannot but rely on experts in food safety, health claims, and dietary advices. We simply lack the knowledge and capacity to personally assess these issues. Trust, however, enables us to act in spite of this uncertainty and to make choices, even when we cannot fully control the situation.

As a result of this link between uncertainty and trust it is easy to argue that trust is a risky matter (Gambetta 1988) and that it is a venture (Luhmann 2000 [1968]). This close link between trust and risk leads some authors to the conclusion that trust is a bet about future actions of others and consequently 'copes with one type of risk by trading it for another type of risk' (Sztompka 1999, 32). In relying on others, we run a risk that we can never be sure whether the other party will act in the expected way. Consequently, the aspect of risk is considered as a central element in the understanding of public trust. In its most stringent form, trust is considered as just a subclass of those situations involving risk (Coleman 1990).

From this perspective, risk calculation is essential in the process of maintaining and building trust. When we consider trust in these terms, it is mainly a technical matter of calculation. It requires the assessment of the risks and benefits of trusting in the light of the aims and goals one pursues. This view of trust as a matter of risk calculation can easily be recognized in European policy measures that aim to build trust in new technologies that have an impact on the food sector, like biotechnology. The emphasis on risk assessment is particularly in line with the idea of trust as based upon risk calculation. It has been suggested that the results from improved risk analysis directly contribute to the individual's willingness to trust persons and institutions. Moreover, the risk analysis is assumed to be especially relevant for new technologies in food, such as nutrigenomics, that are surrounded by ongoing scientific and public discussions on the benefits, unknown societal consequences and long-term effects of the product.

Notwithstanding the relevance of an adequate food safety policy including attention to proper risk assessment, trust and risk are concepts on different levels. In empirical research evidence has been found that decisions to trust are not always thought of as risky gambles (Eckel & Wilson 2004). From another disciplinary background, Lagerspetz (1998) has drawn similar conclusions. In his philosophical analysis he underscores that trust is something fundamentally different from risk taking. He does not deny that trusting is important in cases of uncertainty and that entrusting certain objects to someone else may be related to risk. Yet he emphasizes that trusting is not the same as deliberately taking a risk. He states that 'considerations about risk taking can only motivate risk taking, not trusting' (56).

This confronts us with a dilemma. On the one hand, when a person trusts he is in a vulnerable position. Thus, trust appears to be a risky matter. On the other hand, Lagerspetz's view is also plausible. When a person trusts, it appears that he does not perceive the situation as risky or as a gamble, although he certainly will run a risk. This sounds like a contradiction, but it is not. The problem here is that the authors have a different focus, which illustrates the importance of a distinction between first-person and third-person perspectives. From a third-person perspective, trust is certainly a risky matter: A person who trusts takes a risk. In acting as if only one state of affairs were to be expected, one runs a risk and makes trust close to a gamble. Nevertheless, from a first-person perspective the picture is quite different. As a person who trusts one is not aware of taking this risk. If he were, he would be a risk taker and not a person who trusts. The person who trusts judges the trustee to be competent and properly motivated with regard to what is entrusted. He considers the trustee to be trustworthy. From the perspective of the individual who is trusting risks are not the main element of trust, only as an observer one may notice that this person runs a risk. An example to illustrate this point: in the case of faith, believers can sometimes take considerable risks – from a third-person perspective – without any sense of uncertainty. This is not the result of different views on risk management, but it is a result of the believers' consideration of God as ultimately trustworthy. The individual believer may not be able to assess the involved risks in relying on God, but that is not the point. Because he trusts he is certain about his acts. Only if he were to lack such trust, he will consider his way of acting as risky and uncertain.

This shift in focus has direct consequences for the idea of trust as the act of risk taking. In contrast to a risk taker, a trusting person is not calculating but coping with complexity. He is not calculating risks, but dealing with the uncertainty he is faced with. Trust is not something that you decide on with a personal computer. Hence I conclude that the act of taking risks and trusting are two complementary, yet different mechanisms to deal and cooperate with other agents in cases of uncertainty. A risk approach aims to clarify the uncertain aspects of the situation in which one has to rely on another agent. In this context a risk-benefit analysis provides tools to assess this probability and to evaluate the hazard, it helps to translate the problem of known uncertainty into one of risk. Consequently, I can make my personal assessment and decide whether it is worth to take the risk involved in relying on another agent or not. A risk-benefit analysis does not provide a direct reason to trust, but it can show that the risk, given our preferences, is worth it. Then I can choose to take 'the risk of cooperating with you on some matter even if I do not trust you' (Hardin 2002, 11).

A trust approach to uncertainty, on the other hand, has a different focus and starts where a risk focus ends. It focuses on those situations that remain uncertain even after all possible uncertain aspects have been turned into risk factors. The aim is not to try to make a risk-benefit analysis, but to personally assess the competence and motivation of the trusted agent. When I trust a company that offers novel foods I do not assess risks, but I make an assessment of the company's competence and motivation with respect to this new food product. In this process of assessing the competence and motivation, risk information may contribute to trust only as far as it serves as a signal or proof of the competence and motivation of the trustee. Suppose that the risk at stake is very low or the risk information is of a high quality, if I do not consider the other agent, on whom I have to rely, to be competent or to have any goodwill to me, I will not trust him. Maybe I consider it worth the risk and act nonetheless, in that case I am a risk taker, not a person who is trusting.

This explains why risk information or improved risk analysis does not directly influence the level of trust. It only has direct influence on a mechanism that helps us cope with uncertainty that is different from trust. In building trust, risk information only plays a secondary role, as far as it provides clarity about the trustworthiness of the other agent.

Communication to Enhance Predictability

I have concluded in the previous section that risk information is only of secondary relevance to trust. However, we should not jump to the conclusion that information in general about the trustee is irrelevant. On the contrary, information facilitates trust. To assess the competence and motivation of a company that offers novel food products an agent needs information. However, as improved risk analysis does not directly build or maintain trust, more information also turns out not to have a direct influence on trust. O'Neill shows that the availability of information is often not the real problem. She argues that although 'It seems no information about institutions and professions is too boring or too routine to remain unpublished' (2002, 66), we are still confronted with problems of trust. We do not need 'just' information, but the offered information has to be qualified; it should provide the truster with material that enables her to clarify what she can expect of the other party.

This additional criterion has been recognized in public policy on food. Consequently, a lot of attention has been paid to explicate routines and patterns in the food sector. Transparency has become a key concept. The argument that underlies this focus is that the real problem of trust is a lack of predictability and a need for structures that enable a truster to anticipate. At first hand, this seems a promising approach. Trust needs a certain level of predictability. This is what is meant by 'anticipatory trust' or 'predictive trust' (Sztompka 1999, 27-29; Hollis 1998, 10-11). In this type of trust one has the expectation that the other party will act according to normal patterns and routines. If patterns and routines are available, it is easier to predict how the trustee will react. Making a situation more predictable by providing information or by increasing transparency is a necessary, but not a sufficient condition in the aim to build public trust in new food technologies. I have two arguments that lead me to make this claim.

First, in the case of new food technologies or products that result from these innovations, trust based upon predictable patterns is complicated by (a) the lack of predictable patterns and (b) the capacity by which the available patterns are applicable. To start with (a): it is by definition that food technologies confront us with situations in which it is not easy to predict what we can expect. Concerning novel technologies, we often lack the predictability and familiarity that can serve as a first basis for trust; this is partly because we are confronted with new benefits, unknown carry-over and long-term effects of novel technologies, and partly because we lack a history in which trustees could have proven their reliability. There is no clear pattern or history that only has to be explicated or revealed in order to show the person who is trusting that his reliance is warranted. It takes time before trust based on routine is achievable. Until that moment, the problem of trust remains, because it is unclear what to expect of the other party. With respect to (b): issues of trust will arise as a result of conflicting patterns, but it is still difficult to predict how the trusted person will react and what to expect. Nutrigenomics combines different domains, such as food and health and the introduction of products, such as genotype-adjusted dietary advices, merges expectations and patterns of food production and consumption with those of preventive medicine and health promotion. We have clear patterns and traditions for both food and health care that provide a predictability that shows what we can expect regarding issues on for instance safety and justice. This helps the building of trust with regards to food and pharmaceutical products. However, dietary advices based upon nutrigenomics can be categorised in both groups. There is not one unambiguous pattern available upon which one can formulate trustful expectations. Trust is either based on patterns of the food sector, although the advice has a health-related claim, or it is based on patterns of the health domain, although it is a dietary product. Thus, the introduction of such dietary advices complicates pattern-based trust. In this situation more information or increased transparency contributes to the explication of patterns of behaviour and action, but it does not address the fundamental problem of which the conflicting patterns are the most applicable and serve as a warrant for one's reliance.

A second argument focuses on a conceptual problem of enhancing predictability to enhance trust. Trust is an attitude that enables agents to cope with situations of uncertainty by formulating a positive expectation towards another agent. Hence, clarity of what one may expect from another is essential. However, trust is more than mere expectations. It is a specific attitude that entails a positive expectation. Therefore, increasing predictability as such does not lead to trust. Suppose that I am regularly confronted with some criminals. After a while their doings become pretty predictable for me. Nevertheless, I would not say that I *trust* that they will burgle the university's new flat screens, although I *expect* that they will do so, based on my knowledge of their routines. Hence, 'If there were nothing other than expectations at issue, the current literature on trust would not exist' (Hardin 2006, 33). We do not merely rely on patterns. We rely on other agents since we have to consider them as being trustworthy or not.

Similarly to how I concluded the section concerning risks, I also conclude that the increase of predictability contributes to building trust only to the extent that it serves as a signal or is proof of the competence and motivation of the trustee.

Information As an Answer Rather Than a Matter of Knowledge

When we define problems of trust as problems of trustworthiness it is clear that merely increasing predictability is not a sufficient condition to build trust. Nevertheless, information is essential since we need evidence about the competence and motivations of the agent on whom we have to rely. Without any evidence on the other agent we can hope or gamble that he will act in the favourable way, but we cannot trust him. To trust we need information. The relation between trust and information, however, is complex. Some information can be conceived by person A as sufficient reason to entrust something to an institution, while person B considers the same evidence as neither sufficient nor an adequate reason to trust. Moreover, it is even possible to trust when we objectively lack sufficient evidence. To understand this we have to focus on the epistemology that is used in the case of trust and on the role emotions play in perceiving and evaluating information. In this section I analyse the relation between trust and evidence. The section thereafter deals with the emotional dimension of trust.

Trust, Knowledge, and Evidence

When we trust we have a sincere belief about the trustworthiness of the trustee. This, however, does not imply that we have knowledge. With respect to knowledge we must understand how reasons prove that the proposition *is* true, yet in a case of trust the focus is on the reasons that prove why you *think* it is true. It can be sufficient for the person who is trusting to *think* that the reason he has proves the belief to be true. For instance, as a consumer I trust science and industry to develop products based upon nutrigenomics that are beneficial to my health. This attitude is based upon what I know about the competence and motivation of agents in science and industry from my own experience and external sources, such as newspapers, the Internet, or hearsay. For my attitude it is important that I personally believe this to be true rather than that it *is* true, in the sense that my belief is justified by public criteria.

This illustrates that the epistemology that is needed in the case of trust does not and need not meet the standards of traditional epistemology that aims to find justified true beliefs. A person who is trusting does not primarily search for evidence that is justifiable on public criteria, but is after an answer to the question whether the other person on whom he has to rely is sufficiently competent and motivated to be trusted. To answer this question, he needs evidence. However, a truster wants to 'use' the evidence, 'not to verify or justify it' (Hardin 2003, 17). When the knowledge that leads to trust can be justified by universal criteria it may be an extra motivation for trust, but it is not a necessity. This pragmatic focus in the search for evidence demands a specific epistemology. In Hardin's terms, it asks for a subjective and pragmatic 'street-level epistemology' rather than an epistemology that focuses on justification, that seeks for knowledge and deals with truth claims (1993; 2003). A person who is trusting certainly will check the value of the information he has obtained, but this check does not need to meet external or public criteria of justification. Hardin stresses that the epistemic search is focused on usefulness rather than justification. If information provides an answer to the question whether the other agent is trustworthy it is relevant, even if it cannot be justified as true knowledge by any of the criteria of a standard epistemology. Obtaining knowledge with respect to trust is 'not simply a matter of analyzing the given information to get to some factual expectation on what will happen or has happened. It rather amounts to evaluating information in a certain way and asking certain questions' (Lahno 2001, 178).

Hearing this argument, it is evident that there are differences between the amount of knowledge a person needs and the extent to which they accept knowledge as evidence for the trustworthiness of another agent. It depends on their assessment of knowledge as a useful answer to the question of trustworthiness. There is no objective amount or quality of evidence that is both necessary and sufficient for someone to come to trust. This explains why the same information does not necessarily result in the same level of trust for all people who are trusting.

The Leap Element of Trust

As a person who is trusting, we not only use a pragmatic epistemology, it is even possible to trust when we objectively lack evidence, or to remain distrustful even though all evidence shows the trustee to be trustworthy.

This point illustrates that evidence is a necessary, but never a sufficient, condition for trust. Lewis and Weigert write: 'No matter how much additional knowledge of an object we may gain (...), such knowledge alone can never cause us to trust. (...) The cognitive element in trust is characterized by a cognitive 'leap' beyond the expectations that reason and experience alone would warrant – they simply serve as the platform from which the leap is made' (1985, 970).

There is a gap between the interpretation of the accessible information on the trustworthiness of the other agent and my trust in this person or institution. Evidence is essential with respect to trust, but there is 'something else' between the recognition of information as relevant for the assessment of trustworthiness and the actual trust in a person or institution. There is more than the evidence at stake. There is an element in the process of coming to trust that 'happens to us' rather than that we decide to adopt a stance of trust. Simmel defined the gap between the interpretation of the facts and the expectations that are the result of trust as a process of suspension (1950). It is a suspension of one's hesitation and doubt with regard to another person or institution. He identified in this gap between interpretation and expectation a 'mysterious further element, a kind of faith that is required to explain trust and to grasp its unique nature' (Möllering 2001, 404).

The reference to religious faith seems appropriate since coming to have faith in God equally entails a leap moment. Like trust, faith is not the logical conclusion from all possible situations. On the other hand, faith is not completely independent of the available information (cf. Berkhof 1993). Historical evidence, scientific research or formal rules of logic certainly influence one's faith in God, but do not fully determine whether or not one comes to have faith. This leads Kierkegaard, for instance, to claim that the reflection on the facts available can be halted only by a leap of faith. Otherwise, the subject 'is made infinitive in reflection, i.e., he does not arrive at a decision'.(1992, 105) This does not imply that one is no longer aware of the uncertainty or one's vulnerability, but that the commitment entailed with authentic religious faith is deeper than one's interest to justify one's attitude based upon identifiable reasons only.

The reference to commitment can also be recognized in the work of Giddens, who describes the additional element of trust as 'a leap to commitment, a quality of 'faith', which is irreducible' (1991, 19). He argues that the 'leap of faith' is a process of bracketing the lack of knowledge and ignorance (18-19; 224). This emphasizes that the need for trust remains unchanged: one still is ignorant or confronted with uncertainty; one still lacks control. However, the one who trusts brackets this problem and consequently trusts the other agent, since he has a commitment with respect to the trustee or the object of trust. Having a deep commitment, however, is not the only way to make a leap. Lewis and Weigert identify two other reasons. First, the particular psychological make-up of the individual can enable him to make the leap beyond evidence. If there is no balance of the basic trust over basic mistrust going beyond evidence becomes extremely difficult. Second, one is able to make a leap on the assumption that 'others in the social world join in the leap (...) Each trusts on the assumption that others trust' (1985, 970). This belief with respect to the participation of others illustrates that trust presumes trust, or in other words that we have to trust in trust (Gambetta 1988).

Explicating this leap element of trust illustrates that trusting is informed by, but not exclusively based on, evidence. Addressing problems of trust from the perspective of information easily ignores that the relationship between trust and evidence is more dynamic. Evidence is not only the input in the complex process of coming to trust. The direction is also the other way around: trust influences the way we perceive and evaluate information. The leap aspect of trust illustrates that at a certain point one can accept specific evidence and consider the provider as being trustful because of a certain commitment that does not have any further justification. This illustrates that trust has the ability to colour the value we attach to certain beliefs, make them resistant to change or exclude other beliefs from deliberation. This indicates that trust includes an emotional component.

Trust and Its Emotional Dimension

Trust cannot only go beyond the evidence, the evaluation of the available information also tends to confirm the pre-existing trust or distrust. The presence or absence of trust substantially influences the way we interpret information about the person who, or institution that, we have to rely on. This concerns the emotional dimension of trust. Adopting a stance of trust entails a positive belief on the subject or object of trust. These beliefs are informed by knowledge, however, we have seen that trust is not fully evidence-based. Emotions also play a role.

'A Lens of Trust'

Following Frijda (986; Frijda et al. 2000) emotions and beliefs are two mental states that are to be distinguished, yet mutually influence each other. Not only will our beliefs determine our emotions, this influence also works in the reverse direction: emotions can create and shape beliefs and can make them resistant to change. This influence of emotion on beliefs is possible because beliefs are more emotion-sensitive than knowledge (Frijda et al. 2000), but also because emotions 'permeate our experiences' (Solomon 1994, 296) and make us looking at the object 'through one's own window' (Nussbaum 2001, 28). Following this perspective, emotions are not merely unwanted disturbances of an otherwise completely rational calculation. As Nussbaum stresses, emotions are not just 'unthinking forces that have no connection with our thoughts, evaluations, or plan'. They are appraisals or value judgments that we ascribe to things and people that we regard as important for our own flourishing, yet are beyond our full control (2001, 26-27, 43, 90). This implies that our emotions modify action-readiness and define the way we perceive the world and our conception of the world (Frijda et al. 2000).

When we refer to emotions in these terms it is a small step to recognizing the emotional dimension of trust. In the literature on trust it has been regularly observed that 'trust is a way of seeing that guides our attention, colours our perceptions, and thus gives rise to certain beliefs' (Miller 2000). The presence of trust makes us interpret another's behaviour and the available information through a 'lens of trust' (Jones 1996, 13), which implies a way of evaluating information in a specific way (Lahno 2002). This view of trust explains why the available evidence can be sufficient reason for person A to entrust something to an institution, while person B does not consider the evidence as an adequate reason to trust. Information not only influences one's stance of trust, but the presence or absence of trust also colours the perception of the information and of beliefs as trustworthy. This influence can be so strong that we can hold an attitude of trust or distrust although we lack the evidence and even do not have the belief that it is justified. Suppose that the producer of a useful novel food product has been recommended by your local GP, who is a close friend. You believe that the producer is trustworthy. Nonetheless, you do not buy the product since you are unable to stop conceiving the company with suspicion because you look through a 'lens of distrust' at these kind of companies. Consequently, you see them as untrustworthy partners (cf. Jones 1996). If trust were to be a belief based upon justified knowledge your attitude would be unjustified, but your suspicion is sincere, even though it is hardly possible to articulate the reason for it. Ascribing this emotional dimension to trust can explain why we can remain hesitant to trust even when others or our own beliefs say otherwise, and it clarifies why we can remain trustful even if the evidence tells us not to trust.

Trust and Manipulation

The recognition of the emotional element of trust can lead to the conclusion that people who trusts are easily manipulated, since it is all about the individual's perception rather than about genuine trustworthiness. Thus, one can argue that when an institution wants to be trusted it only has to pretend that it is competent and motivated by the cares and concerns of individuals. Whether they are sincerely trustworthy or only motivated by strategic reasons does not really matter as long as the individual perceives the institution as trustworthy. This view, however, is problematic for two reasons. First, it disregards the reflective element in emotions. Emotions, as defined above, are more than mere feelings and not completely independent of rational reflection. Thus the inclusion of an affective element in trust does not make trust completely disconnected from any form of reflection and deliberation. A person who is trusting is still able to reflect on his emotions and the emphasis on the affective aspects of trust does not exclude the impact of critical reflection by other agents. Therefore, the assessment of competence and motivation does matter in the process of trust.

This leads to the second problem. Since trust is based upon someone's assessment of the trustworthiness of an agent it requires that the trusted person should be sincere in what he communicates concerning his competence and motivation. Pretending to be trustworthy for strategic reasons is not morally neutral. When the trustee does not respond to what is entrusted this can have serious moral implications, since the individual may suffer losses, for example, one's freedom to choose food products is limited or one's health is endangered. This has implications for the incentives of trust-responsiveness since the person who trusts is often not able to prevent this situation her/himself.

Two Normative Conditions for Trustworthiness

From the observation that harm can be done to individuals when they are not in the position to trust others, it would be too easy to conclude that there is an obligation for the trustee to respond to trust, however, it indicates two moral conditions for trustworthiness.

Trustworthiness ought to be motivated by a specific view of the *moral status of the person who is trusting*: the dependent and vulnerable position of the individual who is confronted with the products of a new technology is not to be taken advantage of, but it is an imperative for the trustee to act in a trust-responsive way, since one is faced with an individual with inherent worth. Thus Kant's second formulation of the categorical imperative: 'Always treat the humanity in a person as an end, and never as a means merely' also underlies trust. As for morality in general, trusting has to start from the assumption that human beings matter. The basic assumption that other agents should be treated as an end in themselves should underlie trusting as well. Trust and trustworthiness have to start from the fundamental moral requirement to 'acknowledge each human being aright' (Cordner 2007, 67). This is not to say that the trustee may not profit from trusting, but it implies that trust may not be used in a way that disrespects the inherent worth of the individual who will give the trust.

This shows that we have reasons to trust and to respond to trust. With respect to the latter, the vulnerable status of the person who is trusting is crucial. This vulnerability provides reason for reacting, since not responding to the vulnerable status of the trusting person implies a violation of his or her inherent worth. This requirement provides a direct reason to act in a trust-responsive manner and prevents an agent to only pretend trustworthiness.

Additionally, trustworthiness includes a second moral precondition with respect to motivation: the recognition of the trusting person as a *moral agent*. The issues concerning the case of nutrigenomics products are not merely technical or scientific themes, they also include moral issues. Products at the interface between food and health highlight questions concerning moral responsibility and the interpretation of well-known principles, such as justice and autonomy. In both the food and the health sectors it is relatively clear what we may expect of each other. However, at the interface of both sectors this is often less obvious. For instance, can we expect a company to live up to all the expectations we normally have regarding the medical sphere when they introduce a genetic test kit to provide genotype-adjusted dietary advice? To answer this question the use of ethical deliberation is inevitable.

An Additional Safeguard on an Institutional Level

The two conditions of trustworthiness raise a serious question: 'What incentive would an agent on an institutional level have to live up to the demand to take the moral value of the person trusting as primary and to reckon her as a moral agent?' This question also holds on an individual level. However, Niebuhr's idea of 'moral man and immoral society' (1934) shows why the issue is even more prominent on an institutional level. Moral problems that do not occur or are implicit on a personal level become problematic on a societal level.

This illustrates that the requirement to take the inherent worth of human beings as primary in trusting relationships needs an extra safeguard with respect to institutional trust. To take the inherent value of the person who is trusting as primary we do not only require rational agents who pursue their own interests and act strategically, but also *reasonable* agents. One is reasonable when one is 'ready to propose principles and standards as fair terms of cooperation and to abide by them willingly, given the assurance that others will likewise do so' (Rawls 1993, 49). As long as trust is just a strategy to promote one's self-interest, institutional *trust* will be highly problematic as it would not start from the recognition of the inherent value of the other, but from the aim to achieve one's goal. Therefore, the emphasis on reasonableness and the attached willingness to act on terms that others, as equals, might reasonably expect to approve is crucial for trust.

For this reason, we need to introduce a contractual element. This does not imply the replacement of trust by contracts, but entails the introduction of *moral* contractualism in order to safeguard the inherent worth of humans as being primary in a trusting relationship, even in an institutional context. Contractualist theories can provide this extra safeguard by insisting that rules of behaviour must be justifiable to each other. The moral value of each person entails that one must judge the actions and behaviour of trusted agents using the criterion of whether one can reasonably agree on the underlying principle, or more specifically, whether the trustee acts on principles they could not reasonably reject (Scanlon 1998). This implies that in trusting one does not only have a formal, but also a substantial reason to judge and even to veto the acts of the trustee. This can serve as an assurance that the individual is acknowledged as a moral subject that should be respected in his vulnerability even in an institutional context and can help to identify what one may reasonably expect of an institutional agent.

Public Trust in Products from Nutrigenomics Research

We can now formulate four concluding remarks on public trust in nutrigenomics products. First, there are good reasons to carry out strict safety studies before introducing novel products, such as personalized dietary advices, in order to assess the amounts of risk involved. However, to address problems of trust these studies and the underlying regulations are not sufficient, since trust and risk are on different levels and risk information is only relevant as far as it provides information on the trustworthiness of the agent on whom one has to rely. Trust requires an indication of the competence and motivation of the trustee, rather than a reduction of risk.

Second, the increase of predictability enables us to rely on others more easily, since we can better anticipate on their future actions. However, especially in the case of nutrigenomics, the explication of routines and patterns on which an individual can anticipate is highly difficult. Since nutrigenomics contributes to the interaction of the health and food sectors it is less clear what levels of competence and motivation can be expected of the agents to be trusted. Thus it is more difficult to asses the trustworthiness on the basis of routines and predictable patterns only.

Third, the explication of patterns and the increase of transparency in the sector show that the relation between providing information and establishing trust is complex. Information is highly relevant to address issues of trust since they provide the person who is trusting with knowledge about the competence and motivation of the trustee. However, when an institution aims to provide information in order to prove to be trustworthy it has to reckon with the fact that people who tend to trust use a subjective and pragmatic kind of epistemology, and that trust entails an emotional dimension that profoundly affects the perception and interpretation of the available information.

Finally, to act trustworthily implies that the trustee recognizes the person trusting as a moral subject with inherent worth and as a moral agent. The first condition prevents that the vulnerable status of the individual who is confronted with the products of nutrigenomics is seen as an opportunity to take advantage of. The second condition enables the trusting person to formulate trustful expectations when he lacks predictable actions. Only if it is clear what we can expect with respect to the competence and motivation of, for instance, a company that offers a genetic test to recommend a dietary product that reduces a consumer's risk of an ailment, is it possible to trust such a company. This is not a discussion about risks or predictability, but about moral responsibilities and the interpretation of moral values and norms that show us what we can reasonably expect of each other. The recognition of these moral questions is a necessary condition for being trustworthy and consequently for building public trust in new technologies.

References

Berkhof, H. 1993. *Christelijk geloof: een inleiding tot de geloofsleer,* 6th edition. Nijkerk: Callenbach.

Coleman, J.S. 1990. *Foundations of Social Theory.* Cambridge, MA: Belknap Press.

Cordner, C. 2007. Three contemporary perspectives on moral philosophy. *Philosophical Investigations* 31 (1), 65-84.

Eckel, C.C. and R.K. Wilson. 2004. Is trust a risky decision? *Journal of Economic Behavior & Organization* 55, 447–465.

FAO. 2003. *Expert Consultation on Food Safety: Science and Ethics.* Rome: FAO.

Frijda, N.H. 1986. *The Emotions.* Cambridge: Cambridge University Press.

Frijda, N.H., A.S.R. Manstead, and S. Bem, eds. 2000. *Emotions and Beliefs: How Feelings Influence Thoughts.* Cambridge: Cambridge University Press.

Gambetta, D. 1988. Can We Trust Trust? In *Trust: Making and Breaking Cooperative Relations,* ed. D. Gambetta. Oxford: Basil Blackwell.

Giddens, A. 1991. *Modernity and Self-Identity: Self and Society in the Late Modern Age.* Cambridge: Polity Press.

Grierson, B. 2003. What Your Genes Want You to Eat. *New York Times* 4 May 2003.

Hardin, R. 1993. The street-level epistemology of trust. *Politics & Society* 21, 505-529.

— 2002. *Trust and Trustworthiness.* New York: Russell Sage Foundation.

— 2003. If It Rained Knowledge. *Philosophy of the Social Sciences,* 33 (1), 3-24.

— 2006. *Trust.* Cambridge: Polity Press.

Hollis, M. 1998. *Trust Within Reason.* Cambridge: Cambridge University Press.

Jones, K. 1996. Trust as an affective attitude. *Ethics* 107, 13.

Kierkegaard, S. 1992. *Concluding Unscientific Postscript to Philosophical Fragments.* Princeton: Princeton University Press.

Lagerspetz, O. 1998. *Trust: The Tacit Demand.* Dordrecht: Kluwer Academic Publishers.

Lahno, B. 2001. On the emotional character of trust. *Ethical Theory and Moral Practice* 4, 171-189.

— 2002. *Der Begriff des Vetrauens.* Paderborn: Mentis.

Lewis, J.D. and A. Weigert. 1985. Trust as a Social Reality. *Social Force* 63 (4), 967-985.

Luhmann, N. 2000 [1968]. *Vertrauen, ein Mechanismus der Reduktion der sozialer Komplexität,* 4. Auflag. Stuttgart: Lucius & Lucius.

Meijboom, F.L.B. 2007. Trust, Food and Health, Questions of Trust at the Interface between Food and Health. *Journal of Agricultural and Environmental Ethics* 20 (3), 231-245.

— 2008. *Problems of Trust: A Question of Trustworthiness. An Ethical Inquiry of Trust and Trustworthiness in the Context of the Agricultural and Food Sector* (Dissertation, Utrecht University). Utrecht: Labor.

Meijboom, F.L.B., T. Visak, and F.W.A. Brom. 2006. From trust to trustworthiness: why information is not enough in the food sector. *Journal of Agricultural and Environmental Ethics* 19 (5), 427-442.

Meijboom, F.L.B., M.F. Verweij, and F.W.A. Brom 2003. You eat what you are. Moral dimensions of diets tailored to one's genes, *Journal of Agricultural and Environmental Ethics* 16 (6), 557-568.

Miller, J. 2000. Trust: The Moral Importance of an Emotional Attitude. *Practical Philosophy* 3 (3), 45-54.

Möllering, G. 2001. The Nature of Trust: From Georg Simmel to a Theory of Expectation, Interpretation and Suspension. *Sociology* 35 (2), 403-420.

Niebuhr, R. 1934. *Moral Man and Immoral Society: A Study in Ethics and Politics.* New York: Scribner.

Nussbaum, M.C. 2001. *Upheavals of Thought: The Intelligence of Emotions.* Cambridge: Cambridge University Press.

O'Neill, O. 2002. *A Question of Trust: BBC Reith lectures.* Cambridge: Cambridge University Press.

Poppe, C. and U. Kjaernes 2003. *Trust in Food in Europe: A Comparative Study* (Professional Report No. 5). Oslo: SIFO.

Rawls, J. 1993, *Political Liberalism.* New York: Columbia University Press.

Scanlon, T.M. 1998. *What We Owe to Each Other.* Cambridge: Belknap.

Simmel, G. 1950. *The Sociology of Georg Simmel.* New York: Free Press.

Solomon, R.C. 1994. Sympathy and vengeance: the role of the emotions in justice. In *Emotions, Essays on Emotion Theory*, eds. S. van Goozen, S. van de Poll, and J. Sergeant. Hilsdale: Lawrence Erlbaum.

Sztompka, P. 1999. *Trust: A Sociological Theory.* Cambridge: Cambridge University Press.

15   Deep Pluralism: Interfaith Alliances for Progressive Politics

Nancie Erhard

On the morning of 11 September 2001, I was in Manhattan. By noon, I was attending an improvised worship service, which included a Jew, a Christian, and a Muslim, each reading from his or her own scriptures. We prayed and sang together – in English, Spanish, and Portuguese. Many of us had friends and loved ones who worked in or near the World Trade Center. We prayed for their safety, of course. We prayed for the families and friends of the lost. We also prayed for peace and justice in the world. And we held onto each other.

Since that day, questions about pluralism that may once have been theoretical, even academic, have come to be widely discussed. Is there a set of values to which all citizens in the West, including immigrants, are expected to adhere? What if those values include freedom of religion, and yet the religious views of some contradict other values, such as tolerance? Is there a limit to tolerance? What is acceptable freedom of expression? Is it acceptable to criticize a minority religion? Does religion even have a role in a multicultural civil society? The implications of such questions need to be explored, and ways of engaging in conversations across different moral frameworks examined, in order for our deliberations on the intersections of science and religion with issues such as ecology and genomics to have any connection to our social realities.

In this context, the activities of multi-faith groups engaged in political action become an important location of discerning pluralist, as opposed to absolutist or relativist, approaches to ethics. I have closely examined the present activity in the United States, where it is at the moment intense, and surveyed it globally, where efforts have been building for over a decade. I have identified patterns of pluralist ethical discernment that, with further development, could be widely applied.

Origins and Contours of a Movement

For this study, I was interested in those groups that fit four criteria: multi-faith, multi-issue, politically active, and who sought membership beyond those who were professionally involved with religion, scholarship or politics. I looked at national and international organizations rather than local groups. There are thousands of local interfaith or multi-faith groups in North America, Europe, Asia, Pacifica, and Africa. Not only was it not possible to survey all of these, but I was looking for groups whose agendas included issues of broad relevance. Many local, as well as national and international, groups are focused on local issues or on interfaith relations per se, rather than specific political issues, as a primary focus. Many others have a single issue – often peace – as their driving objective. I was intent on those who saw issues such as peace or ecojustice in their widest context of social, economic, political, and ecological relations. I also want to acknowledge that there are groups within one faith – including ecumenical groups – that focus on multiple issues. (Kairos in Canada is a good example of this, where ecumenical Christian groups that dealt with distinct issues, such as poverty, health care, and ecology, were brought together under one organization after the 2000 Jubilee.) While they do important work, I was looking for groups with both diverse ethical sources and the widest sets of issues, which would necessitate discovery of links or demand prioritizing among issues. Many of the single-faith multi-issue groups and the single-issue multi-faith groups are included through overlapping connections to the groups on which I have concentrated. The other two criteria, political activism and participation beyond professional scholars or religious leaders, create a situation where theory is always in conversation with practical realities, and the discourse is widely accessible.

Globally, I am looking at groups such as the United Religions Initiative and the Council for a Parliament of World Religions. The latter, particularly, has worked to develop an explicit statement on a global ethic, an effort driven by Hans Küng. In the United States, there are two primary multi-faith groups that represent a resurgence of and a new level of co-ordination among progressive religious activism: Faithful America and the Network of Spiritual Progressives. Faithful America, a multi-faith initiative of the National Council of Churches, first came to my attention when they produced a television ad for Al-Jazeera featuring prominent members of different faiths apologizing for the abuses at Abu Ghraib and insisting that Bush and others did not represent them as people of faith in America. Presently, Faithful America functions chiefly as an Internet activist group, similar to MoveOn and TrueMajority, through which subscribers are informed about a variety of issues and are given an easy way to contact their political representatives. The Network of Spiritual Progressives (NSP), while also making extensive use of the Internet, has developed face-to-face activities, organizing chapters around the country and in Canada, and convening two national meetings to organize and launch the movement. Of the groups I have been studying, it is the most dynamic and the one most progressive in its positions. Their platform calls for action on global warming and global poverty, but goes further to demand new legislation governing corporations that would enforce social responsibility. Their vision of supporting families includes equal marriage for gay and lesbian couples, an extremely volatile subject in the United States.

Perhaps not surprisingly, people open to engagement with those of other faiths tend to have more politically progressive ideas, whereas those more exclusive about religion remain more religiously and politically conservative (Evans 2006). While the public and political religious voices in the United States have been overwhelmingly conservative over the last three decades, the involvement of religion in progressive causes draws on a long history. The language of the Reverend Dr Martin Luther King, Jr., was unapologetically biblical, and the core of his message about the goals and means of the Civil Rights movement – equality, love, redemption, and reconciliation through nonviolence – drew as much on Mahatma Gandhi and Jesus as it did the Enlightenment philosophies behind the Declaration of Independence and the US Constitution. This religious dimension of the Civil Rights movement of the 1960s is neither singular within nor confined to North America. Faith, and arguments from religion, contributed to the establishment of modern Western democracy, and were integral in the abolition of slavery and apartheid, in promoting temperance, women's suffrage, the anti-Vietnam War movement in the US, and – in Canada – establishment of universal public health care.

This history of religion in the service of progressive politics has been overtaken in more recent decades by another face of religion – absolutist groups within various faiths, not only Islam, but also Judaism, Christianity, and Hinduism. I refer to these groups as 'absolutist' rather than 'fundamentalist' because 'fundamentalism' has associations with a particular historical development of American Christianity. It is also somewhat misleading, since many people who share the same faith but not the same positions as those in extremist, absolutist groups would object that they are not reflecting what is actually 'fundamental' to the faith. 'Absolutism' is used here to indicate a religious and ethical position which claims singular and absolute truth for one's own beliefs and norms, a more fitting descriptor of these groups.

In the United States there arose the curious mix of televangelism, the 'prosperity gospel', and the political movement that began with the 'Moral Majority', aligning a particular form of conservative Christianity with American political neo-conservatism. This alliance of the political and religious right fused the agendas of free market capitalism and American militarism with a conservative view of sexual morality. Those Christians who originally forged that alignment were opposed to disarmament, racial desegregation of schools, court rulings that prohibited public prayer in government-operated schools, the equal rights amendment (for women – the ERA), and the legalization of abortion. They have lobbied, sometimes with temporary success, to have 'creationism' included in elementary school science curricula. Currently, their official opposition to racial desegregation has been buried, and the ERA is dead; they continue to oppose abortion and support US military power (including the 'war on terrorism'), but opposition to same-sex marriage and stem cell research have come to the fore. Through the efforts of organizations such as the Moral Majority and its successors – the Christian Coalition, the Family Research Council, Focus on the Family, and the American Family Association – extremely conservative Christians have been instrumental in the election of Presidents Reagan and Bush (both father and son), as well as the 1996-2006 Republican majorities in the Congress. The political campaigns of the religious right, which concentrated at first on leadership at higher levels, were later directed to every level, including state legislatures, city councils, and school boards.

They have more recently turned their efforts to the judiciary, and the Institute for Religion and Democracy represents yet another thrust – organizing 'renewal' groups within mainline Protestant denominations such as the Presbyterian, United Methodist, and Episcopal churches to reverse what they see as the 'liberal' swing of these churches. One of the most interesting facets of the religious right is that despite their evident political successes, the sense of fighting a losing cultural battle against the 'liberal' society is still pervasive.

Through the very effective public campaign that conservatives have conducted in the United States over the last thirty-odd years, the word 'liberal' itself has become a term of contempt, leading some to adopt the word 'progressive' as a self-descriptor instead. One of the difficulties is that some people use the two terms with identical meanings, whereas others want to maintain a distinction: 'liberal' carrying the worldview of the Enlightenment – a modern viewpoint that would stress such things as reason, tolerance, individual rights and liberties – and 'progressive' indicating a somewhat more radical position with a distinct critique of power and established systems, incorporation of group as well as individual rights and responsibilities, and more recognition of the postmodern. The political term 'left' is used, but widely identified as misleading and anachronistic. I use 'progressive' here primarily, and 'left' occasionally, to indicate those who maintain that the provision for those who are vulnerable in a society is foremost the responsibility of the state as the agent of the people, who work for ecological responsibility, who see racism and sexism in systemic terms, and who advocate for non-military responses to conflict and terrorism. Within these broad outlines, there is a wide variety of priorities, objectives, strategies and theories. Indeed, it has been the very diversity and plurality within the left that accounts for some of the inability to counter the conservative tide of the late twentieth and early twenty-first centuries in the United States.

The consequences of the rise of religious right in its US and global varieties have caused people to recoil in horror from the combination of religion and politics. But more recently, they have catalyzed a new impetus for cooperation among people of faith on the left domestically and internationally. The opposition to the Iraq War brought millions of people around the world into the streets in protest together with a sense of common purpose. Similarly, the campaign to 'make poverty history' has involved people of faith on the left in domestic and global politics around poverty. In the US, Hurricane Katrina has illustrated the consequences of governments whose policies have diverted public money from infrastructure and social welfare to militarism and private wealth, graphically connecting issues of imperialism, racism, poverty, and global climate instability. Further, actions of the US government that include eroding the domestic civil liberties on which the country was built, as well as abandoning multinational agreements (particularly the weakening the Geneva Convention by prolonged imprisonment, torture and degradation in the context of hostilities), have driven the progressive religious movement in the United States with a particular intensity and passion (Lerner 2005; 2006; Carter 2005).

I have called it a 'movement'. As such, its significance is not (yet) a matter of numbers, although Taylor Branch, biographer of Martin Luther King, Jr., and chronicler of the Civil Rights movement, told a gathering of members of the Network of Spiritual Progressives in a rundown church on Capitol Hill in May 2006, that they were more than enough to be a major movement. One aspect of its significance is that it brings complexity to the question of religion in politics. The extreme conservative religious voices of various faiths have been portraying themselves as battling a secular, 'godless', liberal modernity. When religion is relegated to the private sphere, it reinforces that world view. Conversely, when people who share their faith publicly use religious arguments for progressive causes, it gives the lie to this dichotomized view of the world. It may not convince the most adamantly conservative, but it demonstrates a wider set of positions than either/or: either an extreme version of a faith or 'godlessness'.

The history of religious conflict in Europe up to and including the religious wars of the Reformation has shaped the attitudes of that continent and North America toward the subject of the place of religion in the civil society. European countries devised a variety of formal solutions suited to their situations at the time. Those arrangements ranged from state-supported churches geographically determined to an intentionally secular state such as France. In practical rather than formal terms, recognized religious bodies may be supported by the state, but religious practice and belief tend to be regarded as a private concern, with an occasional nod to common Christian history and cultural influence (Germany may be a possible exception).

The United States, which was colonized in part by dissenting religious minorities, some intent on theocracy, devised its solution to conflictual religious plurality in the form of the first amendment to its constitution. This amendment is usually interpreted to prohibit the establishment of religion – the support of the state for one religious body. At the same time, though, it links free exercise of religion with free speech and assembly, as well as a free press and the right to petition the government for grievances. Placing religion in this context implies that religion is connected with political acts of public speech, assembly, and protest. What is prohibited is endorsement of one religious entity or point of view with the power of the state, not the public practice of religion (as long as it is not state-sponsored) or the use of religious ideas and language in public debate. This is an important distinction.

If religious points of view are seen as detrimental to the collective deliberation of civil society, something to be avoided in public debate, this in itself endorses and privileges a worldview that is anti-religious. In his essay in this volume, Patrick Loobuyck has concisely reviewed the history of this exclusionist argument and presents a fuller refutation of it from a philosophical basis than I will pursue here. As he points out, the idea that 'religion' can be banned from the public sphere erroneously presumes that sphere is or can be value-neutral. Although several philosophers who once overtly promoted an exclusivist position have recently moderated their stand, the idea of a secular ethos that represents a consensus of minimal, distilled, universal values that can enable all of us, 'religious' or not, to live together, is one of the legacies of modernity.

The problem with this position is not only its inaccuracy but what it prevents in terms of full democratic deliberation. By denying that certain operative values in much of the West, such as materialism, and those supported with particular fervor in American civil religion – individualism and market economics – are as much based on 'faith' as any values derived from our religious traditions, these values are entrenched as 'natural' or 'common sense', and the sources for opposing them are limited.

Without religious voices *as religious* in public debate, society as a whole loses the benefit of the wisdom of thousands of years. The distinct messages of religious traditions, their power to inspire us to breathe in the space of generosity and compassion, to suffer the pains of others, to dance with the imagination and the soul, to transcend our narrow interests, to struggle against entrenched power and ways of life that are destructive of humanity and the planet, and to find hope – these are lost to our common thought, and the whole of the society is diminished. Annika den Dikken's essay in this volume is an example of the contribution religious language and ideas can make. She demonstrates that the theological concepts of love and redemption enhance the approach of an ethic of care in a discussion of human enhancement technologies.

It would be a mistake to view this emerging movement in the United States as a mirror image of the religious right, which is one reason why the term 'religious left', while handy, is misleading. The progressive religious movement certainly opposes many of the positions of the religious right, but among what they oppose is the right's overt and covert perforation of the separation of church and state as provided in the first amendment, such as the inclusion of religious ideology in science education in public schools. In contrast with the religious right, which strategically moved to become a directing power within the Republican Party, the progressive religious movement is nonpartisan. They work within parties to get candidates nominated and elected, but it is not a concerted effort to ally with and direct a single party. Another difference is their sincere desire to find ways out of the polarization that has engulfed American public discourse, while at the same time remaining faithful to their religious insights and ethical convictions. This desire, along with the diversity within the movement itself, creates the necessity for pluralism in ethics.

Strategies of Ethical Pluralism

Ethical pluralism is related to, but quite distinct from, ethical relativism, the usual alternative to ethical absolutism. Ethical absolutism insists that the true and the good or right and wrong are wholly independent of differences in culture, philosophy, or religion (and identical with what the absolutist holds to be true, good, right or wrong, of course), a stand rejected by the relativist. The relativist views norms and values in the same category as custom and opinion, with no external standard by which those of others can be critiqued. Popular relativist expressions are 'when in Rome' and 'live and let live'.

The relativist position has much to be said for it. Its humility, recognition of the limits of human knowledge, and spirit of generosity and tolerance contrast with the rigidity and conceit of absolutism. The credibility of relativism is bolstered by the evidence of diverse norms and values. But does such descriptive relativism require prescriptive, or normative, relativism? Because it *is* this way does that mean that it *ought* to be? Ethical pluralism incorporates the strengths and insights of relativism – humility, recognition of the limits of knowledge, openness, and to a certain degree, tolerance. But it recognizes the limits and internal contradictions inherent in normative relativism: if tolerance is required, does one tolerate intolerance? If I cannot prescribe norms, can I require you not to prescribe them to me; isn't that itself a norm?

Pluralism is not merely a moderate version of relativism, any more than it is a moderate form of absolutism, because it is willing to declare that there are real evils to be resisted with all moral force, as well as universal goods to be promoted (Hinman 2003). The key distinction from both relativism and absolutism is its approaches to difference and contention, to building agreement and facing disagreement. My purpose is to examine the practices of people who are actively involved in pluralist ethical discourse for the purpose of achieving the common good. What I have found are patterns of pluralism that would serve beyond any particular context.

The strategies of pluralism that I have identified include three elementary moves and a cluster of practices I am calling 'deep pluralism'. The first three moves are elementary both because they each represent where people normally begin and because they are a prerequisite to deeper pluralism. They are (1) seeking a common moral vocabulary, (2) identifying moral equivalence across traditions, and (3) bracketing acknowledged difference in the service of a prioritized value or goal.

Common Moral Vocabulary

Seeking a common moral vocabulary is the most frequent approach, represented by the statement of the 1993 Council of the Parliament of World Religions 'Towards a Global Ethic'. I have seen two aspects within this strategy. The first is the attempt to translate particular religious values and ideas into 'universal' terms, claimed and comprehended by anyone, 'religious' or not: tolerance, justice, compassion, love, liberty. 'Towards a Global Ethic' claims to have identified a set of core values within religions, but the core values themselves are discussed in terms any humanist would use, without reference to any particular differences in conception. This translation into the 'universal' – meaning non-religious language – is often put to religious voices as an imperative, an expectation of them necessitated by the nature of civil society, since the only shared language is non-religious. Because of this, people within this movement sometimes advocate it as 'the best we can do'. While I would agree that there are circumstances that require it, I would not agree that this is the best or only option. As Jeffrey Stout has pointed out, the act of translation into non-religious terms can disguise authentic motivations, which does not foster relationships of integrity (2004, 72). It erodes the requirements of public trust. It also inhibits any distinctive contribution to the public conversation. The conversation can flatten, become generic and reductive rather than evocative. Religion employs music and the heart in its language. It moves the soul. My problem is not with the tactic itself but with it as a singular, superior, or coerced approach.

The second branch of this strategy does not aim at translation into a 'universal' secular vocabulary, but rather identifying 'widely-shared' terms and ideas that are still recognizably religious or spiritual. For example, Mary Elizabeth Moore says she now chooses the phrase 'transcendent possibilities' instead of 'grace' because the latter does not 'cross well' into multi-religious conversation (Network of Spiritual Progressives conference, July 2005). People choose many words and phrases for the divine (instead of 'God') out of consideration for non-theistic religious sensibilities, as 'Toward a Global Ethic' uses 'Ultimate Reality'. I think of the attempts to forge a common language, universal or widely shared, as the religious version of the kind of moral Esperanto that requires translation into 'neutral' or non-religious language. Such a move is useful, but limited.

Moral Equivalence

The attempt to find moral equivalence across traditions is less like Esperanto and more akin to simultaneous translation; it is the attempt to understand another's tradition on its own terms and function bilingually and even multilingually. At its simplest it is close to trying to find a common moral language, as in the claim that despite different expressions, the kernel of the 'Golden Rule' is present in many traditions, with different formulations. What makes this different from seeking a common moral language is that an original formulation stands and is linked. A clearer example of how this differs from the first strategy is the more complex performance of Ama Zenya when she links concepts of sacrifice across traditions – connecting submission to Allah in Islam with Esther's life-risking act for love of her people in Judaism, the self-emptying of Christ in his Incarnation, and the figure of the Bodhisattva in Buddhism – and contrasts this with the rhetoric of rights (NSP Conference 2005). Here, I think people are doing somewhat intuitively what Kupper et al. have done with their explicit methodology of analysis of focus group conversations about animals and biotechnology. They are retaining the integrity of particular language and looking for conceptual parallels.

Bracketing Difference

The third move, bracketing difference, also has two aspects. The simpler one is the recognition that different motivations for trying to accomplish the same end need not hinder action. As Patrick Loobuyck rightly observes in this volume, concepts of justice and justifications for human rights can be incommensurable, yet the goal of human rights is shared. This works easily when the goal is urgent or as compelling as human rights and actually may create the environment in which other strategies of pluralism, including those above, can take root.

The trickier aspect is when people share some convictions, but not others, and they decide that the shared convictions are of such priority that they can work together while they differ, even deeply, on other matters.

Where I see this strategy evolving is in the participation of some (not all) Evangelicals and Roman Catholics in this movement. I refer to those who may continue to oppose equal marriage and legal abortion, but have decided that poverty, war, materialism and the destruction of our environment are more pressing *moral* issues, more of a threat to families and the general society.

This aspect is tricky not only because it's more difficult, but because it can set up a situation of repressed difference, where those whose lives are more directly affected by issues that are deemed of less priority could feel ignored and demeaned, stoking resentment and fracturing alliances. An example would be the possibility that the willingness of Evangelicals and Roman Catholics to work within the movement on war, poverty, and ecological issues engenders a corresponding spirit of compromise so that advocacy for equal marriage, for instance, is marginalized. This is a potential outcome, not inevitable but certainly possible. The hopeful possibility is that relationships built by working side by side, discovering shared values, will be able to sustain work on the more difficult issues, and the question of what serves human dignity in sexuality is pursued in that spirit. But in order to do this, I think it takes moving into a deep form of pluralism.

Deep Pluralism

Deep pluralism is a more complex phenomenon than the elementary strategies outlined above. Its practice presumes at least the goodwill toward others that the elementary moves demonstrate and the level of knowledge that finding moral equivalence does. But pluralism must go beyond trying to find similarities and commonalities. It must deal with difference and conflict at times, not simply set them aside. Difference here means not only difference in sources, principles, values, practices or ideas. Dealing with difference means going to the meta-ethical level, paying attention to the contextual relationships, particularly differences in power and privilege, and what is probably the most challenging area, recognizing different *methods* of deliberation.

Working toward common statements of principle may be useful, but care is needed so as not to privilege the philosophical or cultural practices of some over others. Ethical deliberation is not limited to discerning, prioritizing, and applying principles, but occurs through various practices – narrative, poetry, art, ritual. These media have different standings and inflections in different religions and cultures. Deep pluralism would call

for attending to one another's stories, for example, without trying to reduce them to an abstract principle, and learning 'how they mean' in their
original context.

Recognizing power and privilege differences goes beyond even this to
discern how power relationships shape the meaning of events and practices. For example, take political cartoons, something that not long ago
caused passionate reactions, even violence. In common Western practice
this medium is normally used to ridicule a powerful person or group in
order to check that power in a democratic context. As such it is a treasured
form of liberty. But the dynamic is different when a cartoon characterizes
a minority race or religion as a threat to a majority group in a context of
fear, as the National Socialists did with cartoons in the 1920s and 1930s,
and, I would contend, as was happening in the recent Danish case. A radically different purpose is at work, one that is a danger of democracy. Deep
pluralism explores such differences in contexts and purposes; it does not
rest at abstract principles of 'tolerance' or press freedom.

Creating the space for deeply pluralist conversation takes time, personal interaction, attention to power and privilege, and the courage to
step outside one's own way of seeing the world. The organizations I have
named above, and many others whose agendas or constituencies may be
more limited, have been moving in this direction. The Network of Spiritual Progressives has observed that despite efforts to reach out to more
communities of colour, including providing free registration and transportation to the Washington conference and recruiting presenters from
racial minority groups, their constituency is still predominately white.
Further study would be needed to investigate whether this is a factor of
the substance of the Network's positions or is related more to process and
context. Several members of the Network who are members of minority
groups are undertaking an effort within their own communities to increase their representation. The Network also has less youth participation
than would be expected, given the activity of youth in anti-war and anti-
globalization movements. This may be related to a growing alienation of
many youth from religion in a country where conservative religious voices
have dominated the public consciousness.

Beyond attention to context and power, and a holistic approach to
communication and deliberation, a deeply pluralist conversation is one in
which disputes are handled in a radically different way than both absolutism and relativism, which both lead more often than not to impasse. Relativism recognizes the validity of multiple moral frameworks, but has very
few resources to deal with conflicts between frameworks beyond agreeing

to disagree. Absolutism recognizes only its own moral framework as legitimate and tries to persuade the other to conform to it. A deeply pluralist conversation does not try to persuade one who differs out of one's own framework, but enters into a conversation characterized by three things: a positive attitude toward conflict itself, willingness to 'think with' the other's moral language and reference, and openness to change. By a positive attitude toward conflict, I mean viewing conflict as an opportunity to see things from a different angle and so expand understanding, and to work to identify the good beneath positions and claims. 'Thinking with' the other involves what Jeffrey Stout terms 'immanent criticism', a Socratic conversation that takes the other side seriously enough to make an attempt to use another's convictions to give reasons for one's own conclusion (2004, 72). This is incomplete as a deeply pluralist conversation, however, unless the process operates in more than one direction, in other words, that all the partners of a conversation are as willing to be challenged as they are to challenge. In Lawrence M. Hinman's terms, this is the pluralist principle of fallibility. We must be willing and prepared to learn from others and 'to have some of our own moral shortcomings revealed to us by them' (2003, 58). This is a tall order, of course. Glimpses of the emergence of such conversations are rare, and they are tentative in nature.

One surprising area where I see this emerging is the discussion of abortion in the United States. Those who advocate that abortion should be 'legal, safe, and rare' are shifting from a rigid rhetoric about rights to employ the language of 'pro-life', in its fullest implications: the mother's life, access to health care, and the quality of the lives of children. They are conceding that some limits on abortion may be warranted. That this issue, which has starkly divided the conservative and progressive camps in the United States in bitter opposition, is an area where pluralist ethical discourse is being brought to bear is a hopeful sign that these patterns can be employed beyond a circle of fellow travelers.

In a world where religion can be used as a rationale for violence, or deemed irrelevant, it is crucial to attend to its potential to motivate us toward justice and compassion, the bases of ecological wholeness and peace. This may sound idealistic and unrealistic. The patterns identified above may seem feeble in the face of the hatred and violence erupting around us. But consider the alternative: Is it practical to devote ever increasing resources to vigilance and destruction, while thousands die daily of hunger and preventable disease, and the life of the planet is being sapped away? Hypervigilance regarding security will weary us, and the exercise of force is proving counterproductive. These can only be short-term measures, because they will fail in the long term. The strategies of pluralism are demanding, yes, and more demanding the deeper we go. Education of enough people in multiple world views to be capable of pluralist conversation is critical, as is the cultivation of the grace of humility and hospitality to the stranger that all of our religious traditions – at their best – foster.

References

Carter, J. 2005. *Our Endangered Values*: America's Moral Crisis. New York: Simon & Schuster.

Hinman, L.M. 2003. *Ethics: A Pluralistic Approach to Moral Theory*. Belmont, CA: Thomson Wadsworth.

Küng, H. and K-J. Kuschel, eds. 1993. *Declaration Toward a Global Ethic*. Tübingen: Foundation for a Global Ethic. http://www.cpwr.org/resource/ethic.pdf.

Lerner, M. 2005. After the Fall: Why America Needs a Spiritual Left. In *Tikkun* 20 (1), 34-39.

— 2006. *The Left Hand of God: Taking Back Our Country from the Religious Right*. San Francisco: HarperSanFrancisco.

Stout, J. 2004. *Democracy and Tradition*. Princeton: Princeton University Press.

Websites of organizations

Council for the Parliament of World Religions, http://www.cpwr.org
Faithful America, http://www.faithfulamerica.org
Institute on Religion and Democracy http://www.ird-renew.org
Network of Spiritual Progressives http://www.spiritualprogressives.org/
United Religions Initiative, http://www.uri.org

Index

Contributors

Forrest Clingerman, Ph.D., is assistant professor of religion at Ohio Northern University, where he teaches classes in theology, ethics, and the history of Christian thought. His research is devoted to the ways that philosophical theology interrogates both the natural world and human culture in the contemporary world.

Olga Crapels is a Ph.D. candidate, Leiden Institute for Religious Studies, Leiden University, working in the NWO-funded project *Misplaced Vocabularies? Scientific and Religious Notions in Public Discourse on Ecology and Genetics*. She studied philosophy (MA, Groningen 2001), and is specialized in ethics. With Edgar Karssing, she edited the book *Filosoof in de praktijk* [*Practicing Philosophy*] (2001), and has worked at the Dutch institute for technology assessment, the Rathenau Instituut.

Peter Derkx is professor of humanism and world views at the University for Humanistics in Utrecht, where he heads the research groups 'Towards a *lingua democratica* for the Public Debate on Genomics' and 'Ageing Well: Wellbeing, Meaning and Human Dignity'. Among his publications is 'Engineering Substantially Prolonged Human Life-spans: Biotechnological Enhancement and Ethics', in Ricca Edmondson and Hans-Joachim von Kondratowitz (eds.), *Valuing Older People: A Humanistic Approach to Ageing* (2009).

Annika den Dikken is a Ph.D. student at the Department of Theology and the Ethics Institute of Utrecht University. She writes about body images, vulnerability, and responsibility in ethical decision making concerning modern biotechnology. In 2003 and 2005 she was commissioned by the Dutch Ministry of Health to write two reports. The first of these was on intercultural ethics in the consulting room, and the second one was on enhancement of the human body. Den Dikken studied theology at Utrecht University.

Willem B. Drees is professor of philosophy of religion and ethics, Leiden Institute for Religious Studies, Leiden University. From 2002 until 2008 he served as the president of ESSSAT, the European Society for the Study of Science and Theology. As of 2009, he is editor-in-chief of *Zygon: Journal of Religion and Science.* Among his publications are *Religion, Science and Naturalism* (1996) and *Creation: From Nothing until Now* (1996).

Nancie Erhard is assistant professor of comparative religious ethics at Saint Mary's University in Halifax. Her research areas include religion and politics, religion and culture, and ecological ethics. Her most recent book is *Moral Habitat: Ethos and Agency for the Sake of Earth* (2007).

Francis Kadaplackal is lecturer on ethics, philosophy, religion, and world views at the Katholieke Hogeschool Sint-Lieven, an associate institution of the Catholic University of Leuven. He is also a doctoral researcher in moral theology at the Catholic University of Leuven. He holds a masters degree in religious studies (2003) and an advanced masters degree in theology (2005), both from the K.U. Leuven.

J.F.H. (Frank) Kupper is a researcher and lecturer at the Athena Institute, Vrije Universiteit, Amsterdam. His research project concentrates on the democratization of animal biotechnology ethics. He graduated in medical biology and in philosophy of the life sciences. His interests include philosophy and ethics of the life sciences and the development of interactive research methodologies in science, technology, and society studies.

Patrick Loobuyck is associate professor at the University of Antwerp and guest professor at Ghent University. His research is on multiculturalism, church-state relations, and secularization. His publications include articles in the journals *Ethnicities, Metaphilosophy* and the *Heythrop Journal.*

Franck L.B. Meijboom studied theology and ethics in Utrecht and Aberdeen (UK). His thesis was titled *Problems of Trust: A Question of Trustworthiness. An Ethical Inquiry of Trust and Trustworthiness in the Context* *of the Agricultural and Food Sector* (Utrecht, 2008). Since 1999, he has been affiliated with the Ethics Institute of Utrecht University. His fields of interest are agricultural, food, and animal ethics. He is secretary of the European Society for Agricultural and Food Ethics (EurSafe).

James Miller is associate professor of Chinese religions at Queen's University, Canada. His research investigates the intersection of religion, nature, technology, and modernity in China. He is the author of *The Way of Highest Clarity: Nature, Vision and Revelation in Medieval China* (2008), editor of *Chinese Religions in Contemporary Societies* (2006), author of *Daoism: A Short Introduction* (2003), and co-editor of *Daoism and Ecology* (2001).

Karen Pärna (1977) is a cultural studies scholar. She is a junior lecturer at the University College of the University of Maastricht. At the Leiden Institute for Religious Studies, Leiden University, she is completing her Ph.D.-thesis, entitled *Believe in the Net. Implicit Religion and the Internet Hype.*

Taede Smedes is a philosopher of religion and a theologian. He worked as a postdoctoral fellow at Leiden University and at the Catholic University of Leuven, and currently holds such a position at the Radboud University, Nijmegen. He is scientific programme officer of ESSSAT. He is the author of *Chaos, Complexity, and God: Divine Action and Scientism* (2004) and co-editor of *Creation's Diversity: Voices from Theology and Science* (2008). His website: http://www.tasmedes.nl.

Bronislaw Szerszynski is senior lecturer in the Department of Sociology, and director of the Centre for the Study of Environmental Change, at Lancaster University. He is the author of *Nature, Technology and the Sacred* (2005), and co-editor of *Risk, Environment and Modernity* (1996), *Re-Ordering Nature: Theology, Society and the New Genetics* (2003), and *Nature Performed: Environment, Culture and Performance* (2003).

Tony Watling is by training an anthropologist (University College London). Most recently he was at the Faculty of Religious Studies at Leiden University; his work there resulted in the book *Ecological Imaginations in the World Religions: An Ethnographic Analysis* (2009). Earlier research as a Wellcome Trust Research Fellow at UCL has been published as 'Singing the Lord's Song in a Strange Land: A Bio-Ethnography of Christianity and Genetic Engineering in Scotland' in the journal *Ecotheology*.

Michiel van Well, MSc, organized the project 'Dynamics between Technology and Religion' and edited *Deus et Machina: De verwevenheid van technologie en religie* (2008) for the Netherlands Study Centre for Technology Trends (STT). Previously Van Well worked at the Dutch institute for technology assessment, the Rathenau Institute. He was a lecturer in science dynamics at the University of Amsterdam and has studied biochemistry (Utrecht) and science dynamics (Amsterdam).